On the Road
around
Northern Italy

THOMAS COOK

On 5 July 1841 Thomas Cook, a 32-year-old printer from Market Harborough, in Leicestershire, England, led a party of some 500 temperance enthusiasts on a railway outing from Leicester to Loughborough which he had arranged down to the last detail. This proved to be the birth of the modern tourist industry. In the course of expanding his business, Thomas Cook and his son, John, invented many of the features of organised travel which we now take for granted. Over the next 150 years the name Thomas Cook became synonymous with world travel.

Today the Thomas Cook Group employs over 13,000 people across the globe and its Worldwide Network provides services to customers at more than 3000 locations in over 100 countries. Its activities include travel retailing, tour operating and financial services – Thomas Cook is a world leader in traveller's cheques and foreign money services.

Thomas Cook believed in the value of the printed word as an accompaniment to travel. His publication *The Excursionist* was the equivalent of both a holiday brochure and a travel magazine. Today Thomas Cook Publishing continues to issue one of the world's oldest travel books, the *Thomas Cook European Timetable,* which has been in existence since 1873. Updated every month, it remains the only definitive compendium of European railway schedules.

The *Thomas Cook Touring Handbook* series, to which this volume belongs, is a range of comprehensive guides for travellers touring regions of the world by train, car and ship. Other titles include:

Touring by train
On the Rails around France and Benelux (Published 1995)
On the Rails around the Alps (Published 1996)
On the Rails around Eastern Europe (Published 1996)
On the Rails around Europe (Third Edition Published 1998)
On the Rails around Britain and Ireland (Second Edition Published 1998)
Touring by car
On the Road around California (Second Edition Published 1996)
On the Road around Florida (Second Edition Published 1997)
On the Road around Normandy, Brittany and the Loire Valley (Published 1996)
On the Road around the Capital Region (Published 1997)
On the Road around the South of France (Published 1997)
On the Road around the Pacific Northwest (Published 1997)
On the Road around England and Wales (Published 1998)
Touring by car, train and bus
Touring Australia (Published 1997)
Touring Southern Africa (Published 1997)
Touring by ship
Greek Island Hopping (Published annually in February)

For more details of these and other Thomas Cook publications, write to Passport Books, at the address on the back of the title page.

ON THE ROAD AROUND

Northern Italy

Driving holidays and tours
in Tuscany, Umbria, the
Italian Lakes and Riviera,
Veneto and the South Tyrol

PASSPORT BOOKS
NTC/Contemporary Publishing Group

Edited by
Christopher Catling

A THOMAS COOK TOURING HANDBOOK

Published by Passport Books, a division of NTC/Contemporary Publishing Company 4255 West Touhy Avenue, Lincolnwood (Chicago), Illinois 60646-1975 USA.

Text:
© 1998 The Thomas Cook Group Ltd
Maps and diagrams:
© 1998 The Thomas Cook Group Ltd

ISBN 0-8442-9994-4
Library of Congress Catalog Card
  Number: 98-65239

Published by Passport Books in conjunction with The Thomas Cook Group Ltd.

Managing Editor: Stephen York
Project Editor: Deborah Parker
Map Editor: Bernard Horton
Route diagrams: Caroline Horton
Maps drawn by RJS Associates
Typesetting: Tina West

Cover illustration by Marianne Taylor
Picture research: Image Select International
Copy-editor: Robert Blackwell
Proof-reader: Pauline Smith
Text design by Darwell Holland
Text typeset in Bembo and Gill Sans using
  QuarkXPress for Windows
Maps and diagrams created using Macromedia
  Freehand and GSP Designworks
Printed in Great Britain by Fisherprint Ltd,
  Peterborough

Written and researched by
Lindsay Hunt
George McDonald
Paul Murphy
Tim Ware

Book Editor
Christopher Catling

ABOUT THE AUTHORS

Christopher Catling gained his first introduction to Italy as a student archaeologist, excavating a Roman villa in Tuscany in the mid 1970s. He returns to Italy at least once a year, and has written several guides to Italian cities and regions. Altogether Christopher has written some 35 guides books in a career spanning 12 years and many countries, and Italy remains his first love.

George McDonald is Scottish by birth and a journalist by inclination. Travel writing first became an obsession for him 12 years ago. He lives abroad and has contributed to a number of Thomas Cook Touring Handbooks. His hobbies include supporting Partick Thistle Football Club.

Paul Murphy's first 'solo' trip was to Northern Italy at the tender age of 12 and he has retained an affection for the region ever since. He is the author of 26 guidebooks, to holiday destinations all over the world, and has contributed to many more books and publications.

Lindsay Hunt turned to travel writing following a career in educational publishing and a year spent in Spain. After ten years with *Holiday Which?* magazine, she now works freelance, mostly on UK, European and US destination and hotel guides.

Tim Ware is a freelance travel writer who has been writing about Italy for more than 20 years. He has contributed to a wide range of publications, both in the UK and overseas, including *The Daily Telegraph, Sunday Times* and the *Guardian* For 13 years he was co-writer of the successful holiday programme *Wish You Were Here ...?* He is married and lives in London.

PHOTOGRAPHS

All the photographs in this book were supplied by Spectrum Picture Library with the exception of the following:

Back cover: Paul Murphy
Between pp. 32 and 33
(ii) Miramare; ice-cream seller: Paul Murphy. All photos on (iii) and (iv): Paul Murphy.
Between pp. 128 and 129
(i) Butcher: CFCL/ISI. (ii) Duomo: George McDonald. (iii) Sunrise: CFCL/ISI. (iv) Perugia: Christopher Catling
Between pp. 224 and 225
(i) All John Fisher. (ii) Trevi: Christopher Catling; Todi: John Fisher. (iii) Duomo: J Allan Cash/ISI; detail: Christopher Catling.
Between pp. 288 and 289
(i) Ostia: John Fisher. (ii) Elba: John Fisher; Palio: Trip. (iv) San Remo: Tim Ware; Pisa: CFCL/ISI.

ACKNOWLEDGEMENTS

5

The authors and Thomas Cook Publishing would like to thank the many individuals and organisations who provided help during the production of this book. Among them are:

Le Shuttle; Peter Mills and Christine Lagardère, Rail Europe; Dr Marco Panfilo and Alessandra Smith, Italian State Tourist Office (ENIT) London; Philip Frenguelli, Citalia; Piermichele Tafi, Italtourism, London; Grand Hotel Tremezzo Palace, Lake Como; Hotel Villa Madruzzo, Trento; Roberta Maraschin, Trento Tourist Board; Antonio Fazio, Genoa Tourist Board; Clara Tamayo, Transhire; Supersonic Travel. Heartfelt thanks are offered to the Tourist Offices in London and Italy who supplied information; museum curators and the staff of tourist sights; and all the hoteliers who provided accommodation and hospitality.

CONTENTS

ROUTES AND CITIES

In alphabetical order. For indexing purposes, routes are listed in both directions – the reverse direction to which it appears in the book is shown in italics.

See also the Route Map, p. 8, for a diagrammatic presentation of all the routes in the book. To look up towns and other places not listed here, see the Index, p. 347

6

7

REFERENCE SECTION

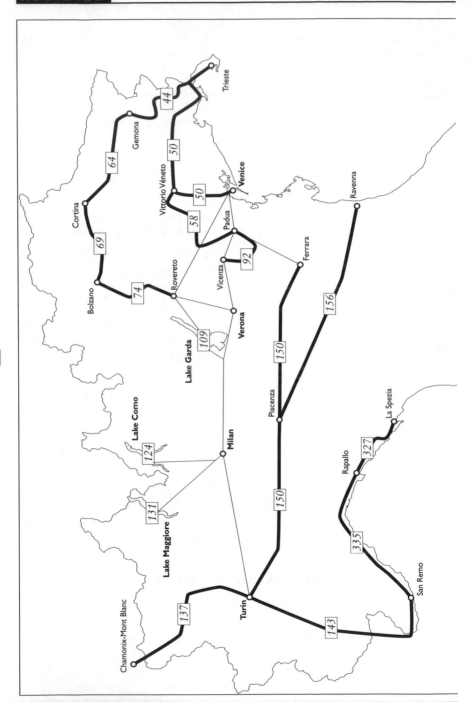

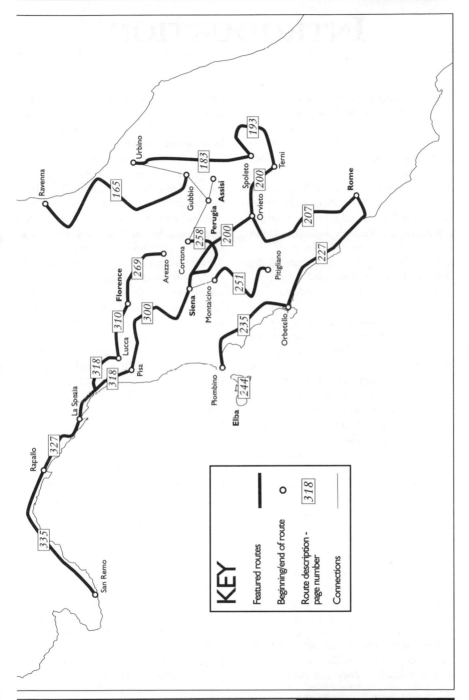

KEY

Featured routes

Beginning/end of route   o

Route description - page number   193

Connections

9

INTRODUCTION

'Italy is my magnet,' wrote Lord Byron, in a letter to Annabella Milbanke on 20 April 1814. Ever since the days of The Grand Tour, Italy – particularly northern Italy – has been popular with travellers. Whether it was enjoying boiled snails, fried frogs and garlic in Genoa, marvelling at the works of art in the Uffizi in Florence, gawping at Pisa's Leaning Tower, idling in a gondola on Venice's lagoon, or just enjoying the sheer splendour of the scenery, the peripatetic aristocrats of the 18th and 19th centuries found it a revelation after the desolation of the Alps.

Things have moved on since then, of course. Like everywhere else, cars clog the highways and unattractive apartment blocks scar the outskirts of towns and cities. But in many respects northern Italy's appeal is undiminished and, once you have penetrated the suburban spread, you will find medieval walled cities that have changed little in the last 500 years.

The air may not always be as 'sweet and temperate' as it was in the days when Byron, Shelley and others got to know it, but much of what impressed the great poets is still there to be enjoyed today. Italy begins with the lake region – Como, Garda, Maggiore and Lugano – lying at the foot of the Alps, with the mountains seeming to drop almost perpendicularly to the plain below. In summer, the highest Alpine peaks still wear their winter snow caps even if, down in the town square, the sun is hot enough for cappuccino lovers to seek shade under the bar awning.

Beyond the lakes, towns and cities fairly creak and groan under the full weight of their formidable history and culture, the hillsides are mantled with vines, orchards and gardens, and there are enough Utopian views to keep the most ardent landscape painter happy.

Parts of the north – such as the Alpe Adige and Trentino – enjoy a degree of independence from the rest of Italy, having the ability, for example, to raise taxes. The independence is a throwback to the days before World War I when the twin Dolomite provinces were part of Austria. Travel through this region today and you could be forgiven for thinking that you are still in Austria – the pristine towns and villages, as well as the cuisine (strudel as well as spaghetti on menus) and place names, giving the impression that you have strayed to the northern side of the Alps.

This region melts into Italy proper at the Veneto, which forms part of a highly developed region known as the powerhouse of the Italian economy – so much so that there are suggestions that the north should break away from the rest of the country. With Milan as its centre, Northern Italy derives its wealth from finance, industry and agriculture. Some of the world's leading fashion houses, such as Armani in Milan and Gucci in Florence, are to be found here, along with cultural landmarks, such as La Scala opera house.

To the east, the Lombardy plain merges into Veneto, where Venice offers the finest tribute to Italian architecture and art. Venice is impossibly beautiful and is at its best on a hazy spring or autumn day, without the crowds. Seeing Venice is, as Truman Capote once observed, rather like gorging a whole box of chocolates at one go. And what chocolates.

HOW TO USE THIS BOOK

ROUTES AND CITIES

On the Road around Northern Italy provides you with an expert selection of over 35 recommended routes between key cities and attractions in the northern part of Italy, each designed to offer a practical and flexible framework for making the most of a touring holiday. Smaller cities, towns, attractions and points of interest along each route are described in the order in which you will encounter them. Additional chapters are devoted to key cities, towns or regions, which begin and end these routes. These chapters form the core of the book, from p. 44 to p. 342.

The routes have been to chosen to take in as many place of interest as possible. However, where applicable, an alternative route which is more direct is also provided at the beginning of each route chapter. This will enable you to drive more quickly between the places at the beginning and end of the route, if you do not intend to stop at any of the intermediate towns. To save space, each route is described in only one direction, but you can follow it in the reverse direction, too.

The drives are organised as follows: starting from Trieste, in the north east of Italy, the routes head north up into the Alps, crossing the Dolomites from east to west, then down to the Véneto Plain and Venice. From here, the routes take you westwards, via the Italian Lakes and the great industrial cities of Turin and Milan, to Aosta and the French/Swiss border. We then head south east, in a straight line, following the great Po Valley, to Ravenna, on the Adriatic Coast. From here, the routes explore the glorious scenery and the historic hill town of Umbria, heading southwards to Rome. From the capital, the routes return northwards, up the west coast of Italy, via Tuscany and up to the Italian Riviera. These routes all follow on from each other, though there may be some driving in between, and provide a solid month's worth of touring options: faced with limited time, the most rewarding routes are probably those in Umbria and Tuscany.

To find the page number of any route or city chapter quickly, use either the alphabetical list on the **Contents** pages, pp. 6–7, or the master **Route Map** on pp. 8–9. The routes are designed to be used as a kind of menu from which you can plan an itinerary, combining a number of routes which take you to the places you most want to visit.

WITHIN EACH ROUTE

Each route chapter begins with a short introduction to the route, followed by driving directions from the beginning of the route to the end, and a sketch map of the route and the places along it described in the chapter. This map, not to scale, intended to be used in conjunction with the driving direction, summarises the route; for a key to the symbols used, see p. 13.

DIRECT ROUTE

This is the fastest, most direct and, sometimes, the least interesting drive, between the beginning and end of the route, usually along main roads or even motorways.

SCENIC ROUTE

 This is the itinerary which takes in the most places of interest, often using secondary and minor roads. Road directions are specific; always be prepared for detours due to road works, and so on. The driving directions are followed by sub-sections describing the main attractions and places of interest along the way. You can stop at all of them and miss out those that do not appeal to you.

SIDE TRACK

This heading is occasionally used to indicate departures from the main route, or out-of-town trips from a city or town, which detour to worthwhile sights, described in full or highlighted in a paragraph or two.

CITY DESCRIPTIONS

Whether a place is given a half-page description within a route chapter or merits an entire chapter to itself, we have concentrated on practical details: local sources of tourist information; arriving in the city by car; getting around in town and city centres (public transport options are included for those who want a break from driving, or want to leave the car at their accommodation and let someone else tackle the local one-way system); accommodation and dining; communications; entertainment and shopping opportunities; events and sightseeing. The largest cities have all this detail; in smaller places some categories of information are less relevant and have been omitted or summarised.

Although we mention good independently owned lodgings in many places, in the larger towns and cities we also list the hotel chains which have a property there, indicated by code letters. Many travellers prefer to stick to one or two chains with which they are familiar and which give a consistent standard of accommodation. The codes are explained in **Hotel Codes** on p.345, and central booking numbers are also given there.

MAPS

In addition to the sketch map which accompanies each route, we provide maps of major towns and cities (usually the central area). At the end of the book is a section of **colour road maps** covering the area described in this book, which is detailed enough to be used for trip planning.

THE REST OF THE BOOK

Travel Essentials is an alphabetically arranged chapter of general advice for the tourist new to Italy, covering a wide range subjects such as accommodation, opening hours and security. **Driving in Italy** concentrates on advice for drivers on the law, rules of the road and so on. **Background** provides a briefing on the history and geography of this fascinating area. **Touring Itineraries** provides ideas and suggestions and advice for putting together an itinerary of your own using the selection of routes in this book. **Getting to Italy** gives information on how to get there for visitors travelling from abroad. At the back of the book, **Driving Distances** is a tabulation of distances between main towns and cities, to help in trip planning. The **Conversion Tables** decode Italian sizes and measures. Finally, the **Index** is the quick way to look up any place or general subject. And please help us by completing and returning the **Reader Survey** at the very end of the text; we are grateful for both your views on the book and new information from your travels in Italy.

KEY TO MAP SYMBOLS

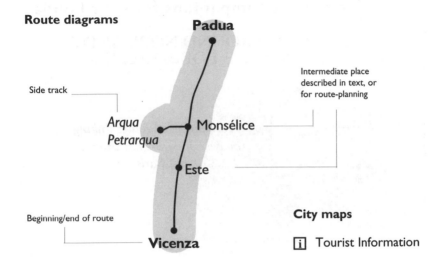

Route diagrams

Padua

Side track

Intermediate place described in text, or for route-planning

Arqua Petrarqua — **Monsélice**

Este

Beginning/end of route

Vicenza

City maps

[i] Tourist Information

ABBREVIATIONS USED IN THE BOOK

(For hotel chains, see p. 345)

A	autostrada e.g. A1	Pza	Piazza (square)
hr(s)	hour(s)	Pzle	Piazzale (square)
Jan, Feb	January, February, etc.	S	Strada eg S3 (road/street)
L	Lire	SS	Strada Statale (national road)
min(s)	minute(s)	V.	Via (street)
Mon, Tues	Monday, Tuesday, etc.	Vle	Viale (avenue)

KEY TO PRICE DESCRIPTIONS

It is impossible to keep up to date with specific tariffs for lodging and accommodation or restaurants. Instead we have rated establishments in broad price categories throughout the book, as follows:

Accommodation
(bed and breakfast, per person per night)

Budget	Under	£25
Moderate	Under	£50
Expensive	Under	£100

Meal
(for one person, excluding drinks or tip)

Cheap	Under	£10.00
Budget	Under	£15.00
Moderate	Under	£20.00
Pricey	£20.00 and above	

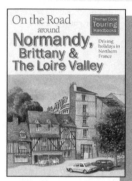
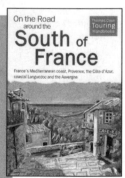

14

TRAVEL ESSENTIALS

Here, in alphabetical order, are a number of tips to help you plan your holiday in northern Italy and enjoy it to the full.

ACCOMMODATION

Italy has accommodation to suit most pockets and it is strictly regulated by the government. It can no longer be said that the country, particularly the north, is inexpensive when it comes to finding a place to stay, but it usually offers fair value and standards are consistent. Italians take pleasure in providing hospitality, particularly for foreigners, and will sometimes go out of their way to provide small, additional services for which no extra payment is demanded or even expected. But prices in the relatively wealthy north are higher than in the more poverty-stricken south. How much you pay for a night's accommodation depends where you are; a tent on a camping site in Florence or Venice could cost as much as a room at a simple hotel in an out-of-the-way mountain village.

Accommodation charges also vary not just with location and season, but with local demand. Expect charges to rise if your stay coincides with a special event — a festival, for example. One way of keeping down costs, assuming you know where you want to stay, is to book your accommodation before you leave through Thomas Cook or another reliable travel agent, who can usually negotiate a better deal with the hotel than the client who walks in off the street. In popular holiday areas, hotels also offer discounts for stays of three days or more and, of course,

inclusive fly-drive holidays with accommodation are also available through tour operators specialising in Italy. Again, details are available through Thomas Cook or your local travel agent.

Hotels

Hotels conform to the star system and are required by law to display their prices, including those for breakfast, lunch and dinner, in rooms. Many hotels are in historic buildings which have been converted from castles, convents, medieval palaces, abbeys and the like. The cheapest type of hotel is the *locanda*, of which there are not too many in the north. A *locanda* is a simple but usually clean guesthouse where you can expect to pay between L20,000 and L30,000 a night for a double room without bath or shower. The next category up covers *alberghi* or *pensioni*, rated on a system of one to five stars. Again, they are usually fairly simple but clean and reliable. Along the main highways groups such as Jolly and AGIP offer functional, if rather anonymous, accommodation. At the top end of the scale, Relais et Châteaux hotels are quiet and decidedly posh, while in Venice you could stay at the Cipriani, Gritti Palace or the Danieli — justly rated among the best in the world — but if you do it's possible you may be called in to see your bank manager on your return.

Villas and Agriturismo

Countless TV series are testament to the popularity of renting a villa or farmhouse for a week or two in northern Italy. This form of letting doesn't come cheap, but

15

invariably property is both well situated close to places of interest – such as Florence, Boulogna, and Pisa – and well furnished. *Agriturismo* is similar to the French gîte system where farmers let out unused buildings to tourists. Full details can be obtained from **Agriturist,** *Corso V. Emanuele 101, Rome; tel: (06) 6511 2342.* If you have plans to go walking or climbing in the mountains, there is a network of *rifugi* – mountain huts – some privately owned and some owned by the Club Alpino Italia, which offer spartan, but adequate, accommodation at low cost. The larger *rifugi* also offer meals. Further details from local tourist offices or **Club Alpino Italia,** *V. Fonseca Pimental 7, Milan; tel: (02) 2614 1788.*

Camping

Camping is popular in Italy. There are more than 2000 sites throughout the country, the great majority in the north. There is no shortage of well-equipped sites, some in stunning locations. The snag is that, when compared with some European countries, they're quite expensive and don't always work out that much cheaper than staying in serviced accommodation. This is particularly true of Venice where the sites can only be reached by an expensive and time-consuming boat ride to outlying islands, such as the Lido. Local tourist boards can provide information or, before you leave home, the **Centro Internationale Prentotazioni Federcampeggio,** *Casella Postale 23, 50041 Calenzano, Florence; tel: (055) 882 391.*

Youth hostels

There are around 50 youth hostels scattered throughout Italy but, as with the camping sites, they don't offer great savings on the cheapest hotel rooms. Some of the hostels in the north, such as Montagnanain in the Veneto, are beautifully situated. Most are members of the International Youth Hostel Federation and, although you should be a member of that organisation to use them, most hostels allow you to join on the spot. A full list of hostels in Italy is available from **Associazione Italiana Alberghi per la Gioventu,** *Quadrato della Cocordia, 00144 EUR, Rome; tel: (06) 462 342.*

AIRPORTS

The principal gateways for northern Italy are Milan, Venice and Rome, all of which are served daily by flights from Heathrow. Less frequent flights are operated to these cities from Gatwick, Birmingham and Manchester. There are also direct flights to smaller northern Italian cities such as

---

Architecture

Italy offers a remarkable legacy of buildings stretching back more than 2,500 years. The Greeks and the Etruscans, the Romans and the early Christians have all left their mark here. But, as with practically everything else in Italian life, there are regional variations. Nowhere is the Byzantine style more in evidence than in the basilica of San Marco in Venice, while the churches of the Lombardy plain are the most internationally influenced, resembling those of northern Europe. Romanesque, Gothic and Renaissance styles, with Baroque and Neo-classicism, go to make up the stunning towns and cities which bring visitors back year after year. And some of the buildings they cast an eye over took literally centuries to complete. The Gothic cathedral in Milan, for example, was begun in 1386 but the last stone wasn't in place until the beginning of the 19th century.

Art

I t is said that two-thirds of the art treasures of western Europe are to be found in Italy. Northern Italy, particularly, has made an outstanding contribution and you can scarcely stick your nose into a church or museum without coming across a pleasing work of art. Florence gave birth to the Renaissance – and the city's churches, galleries and museums are full of outstanding works by Michelangelo, Leonardo da Vinci, Botticelli and others. Correggio was influenced by the illusory ceiling of Mantegna in Mantua and went on to create one of his own – his *Vision of St. John on Patmos* in the dome of San Giovanni Evangelista in Parma. Venice, geographically well away from the influences of Rome and Florence, retained its own artistic integrity, seen today in the works of Titian, Tintoretto and Canaletto.

Genoa, Bologna, Florence, Pisa and Bergamo from London. Travellers heading for the northern part of Liguria, closest to the border with France, also have the option of flying to Nice. This is particularly beneficial if you are planning to hire a car, which can be done more cheaply in France than in Italy.

All the main airports in northern Italy have information desks and currency exchange bureaux – facilities which may be absent at those serving some of the smaller towns. Taxis are widely available and although rates vary from place to place, journeys have to be metered and the fares displayed.

BUSINESS HOURS

During the week, shops and offices in northern Italian cities generally follow the standard European habit of staying open throughout the day – that is, from 0800 or 0900 to 1700 or 1800. In smaller towns and villages, hours are more flexible. On Sunday, virtually everything apart from bars and restaurants closes down, although some food shops, such as the fishmonger and baker, do open until lunchtime. Bear in mind also that saints' days and national holidays, such as April 25 (Liberation Day) and May 1 (Labour Day), can make finding a hotel room difficult, although in holiday areas many shops remain open.

CAR HIRE

Car hire is expensive in Italy. Expect to pay at least £200 a week for a small car with unlimited mileage. All the leading international companies, such as Avis, Hertz and Europcar, are represented at the airports and in the leading towns and cities, and driving in Italy, except in the city centres, is not the nightmare it is made out to be.

17

CHILDREN

Children in Italy are greatly loved and attract a great deal of attention. You will find that you are given better and friendlier service in restaurants, and that shopkeepers will smile on you, rather than giving you their usual worried frown – provided that your children are well behaved, of course. Fair-haired children are especially regarded as lucky, and you may find strangers touching their heads as they pass in the street. Italy being the land of the pizza and of innumerable varieties of pasta, you will usually not have trouble in finding food that your children will eat. On the other hand, and despite their fondness for children, there are very few attractions designed especially for them. Gardaland, at the southern end of Lake Garda, is a theme park with lifesize models of dinosaurs and fairground attractions, and the Pinocchio theme park in Collodi, near Lucca, is designed for children, but both are rather pale and tame imitations of the kind of theme park that children may be used to from exposure to Disney and similar attractions. You will have to rely on the sheer magic of Italy's cities and the freedom of the beach to keep your children amused. Good destinations for children are Venice, which children love for its water, bridges and lack of traffic, Pisa, which scores highly for its Leaning Tower, and the beaches of southern Tuscany, around Orbetello, especially in the Maremma Nature Park.

CLIMATE

The main season runs from the middle of April to the end of September, but if the object of your visit is sightseeing you'd be well advised to travel in April, May, June, or September and October, when the weather is pleasantly warm but not too hot. If possible, don't travel in August, when the whole of Italy seems to be on the move. Spring and autumn are pleasant times to visit all parts of the north. In winter, the Ligurian coast can be quite warm, but inland the temperature drops sharply. Freezing temperatures are likely here in December and January, with fog being a problem on the plains, particularly around the large industrial conurbations of Milan and Turin. In the mountains, you are likely to need a sweater with you, even in summer.

CURRENCY

The lire is the Italian currency and in recent times it has been losing ground against many other units of exchange. Notes are of L500,000, 100,000, 10,000, 5000, 2000 and 1000 denomination. Coins are of L1000, 500, 100, 50, 20 and 10, although the last two are hardly ever used. The safest way of carrying money is through travellers' cheques, obtainable at a Thomas Cook exchange bureau before you leave, but increasingly credit cards can be used for buying major purchases, such as hotel accommodation, meals and car hire (many car hire companies insist you pay with a credit card).

Money can be exchanged at banks, but transactions can be slow. Banks are open Mon–Fri from 0800/0830 to 1330 and from 1430/1500 to 1600. Outside these hours money can be exchanged at foreign exchange bureaux and hotels, the latter usually giving less attractive rates.

The cost of living is similar to that in most other European countries, but higher than in North America. Joining a package tour remains the single most effective way of keeping down the basic cost of your holiday.

CUSTOMS

All items intended for your personal use (i.e. not for resale) can be imported duty free, and there is no limit to the amount of alcohol or cigarettes you can import for personal use – having said that, wine and tobacco in Italy is as cheap as anywhere in Europe, so there is no great point to bringing your own supplies. Customs checks are negligible as you drive in or out of Italy from neighbouring countries, or if you arrive by rail. Those who fly can claim the usual duty-free allowances, but these are due to be phased out in the near future.

To all intents and purposes, there are no restrictions between EU countries for goods bought in ordinary shops but, if you have excessive amounts, you might be questioned as to whether everything is for your personal use. Allowances are:
800 cigarettes, 200 cigars, 400 cigarillos and 1 kg tobacco.
+ 90 litres wine (max. 60 litres sparkling).

+ 10 litres alcohol over 22% volume
(e.g. most spirits).
+ 20 litres alcohol under 22% volume
(e.g. port and sherry).
+ 110 litres beer.

The allowances for goods bought outside
the EU and/or in EU duty-free shops are:
200 cigarettes, 50 cigars, 100 cigarillos and
250 g tobacco.
+ 2 litres still table wine.
+ 1 litre spirits or 2 litres
fortified/sparkling wine.
+ 50 g/60 ml perfume.
+ 0.5 l/250 ml toilet water.
+ other goods up to the value of £145.

CYCLING

The mountainous nature of much of the
terrain in the north means that cycling isn't
as popular here as elsewhere in Italy.
Having said that, the plains of Lombardy
and the Veneto are ideal for exploring on
two wheels. Bikes can be hired in the key
resorts and the more specialised mountain
biking is popular in, for example, the
mountain and lake regions of Trentino.
Mopeds and scooters are relatively easy to
hire – and you should expect to pay
around L50,000 a day for a machine – but
make sure you are well insured and always
wear a crash helmet.

DISABLED TRAVELLERS

Italy is not an easy destination for disabled
travellers, not for lack of will, but because
streets in Italy are typically steep and cobbled, and hotels, churches, museums and
attractions are often located in old buildings, approached by steep flights of stairs.
This should not deter anyone from enjoying Italy's delights. It just means that you
will need help from time to time – and the
Italian people will often give help cheer-
fully and ungrudgingly. Offices of the

Italian State Tourist Board have lists of
hotels suitable for disabled travellers, and
RADAR publishes guide books specifi-
cally for disabled travellers (*12 City Forum,
250 City Road, London EC1V 8AF; tel:
0171 250 3222*).

DISCOUNTS

Students are entitled to a range of discounts on admission prices and public
transport – you need evidence of your age
and status to claim. In theory, senior
citizens from other EU countries also
qualify for discounts, but in practice, these
are often restricted to Italian citizens.

DRINKING

Italians drink for pleasure, not pain.
Children are brought up to drink wine
from an early age and indiscriminate
drinking is a rarity and is frowned upon; it
is unusual to see a drunk in public. Just as
pasta is synonymous with Italy, so too is
wine (see separate section), but almost
every kind of drink is available in the bar,
with the emphasis on locally produced
tipples.

More functional than their British
counterparts, bars are available for everything from a simple morning *espresso* to
the Italian firewater *grappa*, made from the
leftovers from the wine-making process.
The drink, now available virtually everywhere, originally comes from the town
of Bassano di Grappa in the Veneto.
Wherever you happen to be, the pro-
cedure in the brightly lit Italian bar is
always the same, you either enjoy your
drink at the counter or sit at a table and
wait to be served. Sitting down virtually
doubles the cost of the drink – and more
than doubles it if you happen to be in a
tourist trap in, say, St Mark's Square in
Venice. But you need never pay too
much, since by law prices have to be

19

displayed behind the bar on the *listino prezzi*.

When it comes to choosing your coffee, the basic choice is between *espresso* (small and black) and *cappuccino* (white and frothy), with a number of variations like *caffè latte* (with milk) and *caffè lungo* (watered down espresso) in between. If you prefer tea, you can take it cold *(freddo)*, with lemon *(con limone)* or with milk *(con latte)*. In summer, you can cool down with a *cold tea (tè freddo)*.

EATING OUT

Italians frequently begin their day in a local bar with a simple breakfast of coffee and hot milk and a *cornetto* – a croissant filled with jam, custard or chocolate. In between, or maybe in place of, main meals, they can snack on pizza, spit-roast chicken in a *rosticceria* or enjoy *panani* – a breadstick roll with a generous filling of meat or salad. Lunch and dinner, whether taken in a restaurant, trattoria or *osteria* (an old-fashioned establishment specialising in home cooking) are serious rituals, often four-course affairs, although increasingly these days clients are prepared to miss out on the *antipasto* or *dolci* (sweet), but rarely on pasta or the main course. Expect to pay around L30,000 in a medium-priced restaurant at lunchtime, more for dinner. Service is usually included in the price, but as in bars the tradition is to leave small change for staff.

ELECTRICITY

The supply is 220volts and the plugs are the standard continental two-pin type. An adapter is needed to convert three-pin plugs and a transformer is needed for American-style 100-120 volt appliances.

ENTRY FORMALITIES

If you're a British, Irish or other EU citizen, you can enter Italy and stay as long as you like. American, Canadian, Australian and New Zealand citizens also only need a passport, but are restricted in the length of stay to three months. If you carry a passport to another country, you should consult the nearest Italian embassy or consulate to find out whether you need a visa and how long you can stay.

FESTIVALS

Italians love to party. Every self-respecting town and even village has its own local saint who is, annually, paraded through the streets amid much noise and celebration. There are many other occasions for a *festa*, perhaps to commemorate a local historical event or to show off local products or talent. Many of the events take place around Easter, in May or September and most have religious connotations. Good Friday is a favourite time for processions, when models of Christ are taken down from the cross and paraded through the streets. There are also a number of spectacular carnivals, such as the one at Viareggio in Tuscany, where the local residents spend a whole year preparing the floats. A number of arts festivals, such as the Venice film festival in August and September, have gained international recognition.

FOOD

Regional variations in food are as evident at the end of the 20th century as they ever were; Austrian influences in Alpe Adria for example, and French in Liguria. Apart from the ubiquitous burger bars which have sprung up in many large towns, northern Italy is free of non-indigenous eating. The exotic option here is to sample food from other Italian regions; Milan being arguably the greatest melting-pot for the nation's cuisine.

It's also true that food is deeply embedded in the nation's culture, celebrated in style not just in restaurants but in homes, too. Sunday lunch is still a tradition in many Italian families – an event rather than just a meal, in which participants wade through course after course. But even in entertaining there is little desire to venture away from the tried and trusty dishes offered by parents and grandparents. Vegetarian meals haven't caught on and a request for a wholemeal pizza is likely to be greeted with more than a raised eyebrow.

As one would expect, shopping for food is a serious business. The big difference is that most of the food shopping is done in markets and specialist shops rather than in supermarkets. Foodstores of every description abound in each town; butchers, bakers, delicatessans and small grocery shops, all competing to provide the freshest and tastiest produce. As a result, food shoppers in Italy are able to avoid the blandness of food prevalent in some countries.

In the production of certain foods, Italy – and particularly northern Italy – is in a league of its own. Parma ham and distinctive cheeses like *gorgonzola* and *parmesan*, not to mention the pasta, are sufficiently good to find their way onto the 'must buy' list of many visitors. Italian ice creams are equally renowned and who can resist *un cono* on a hot summer's afternoon?

Each northern province has its own distinctive cuisine – and often hallmark dish. In Liguria, it is *pesto* – the sauce made from pine nuts, basil, olive oil, *pecorino* and *parmesan* – which is usally served with pasta but can also be found in gnocchi and soups. *Polenta* (thick porridge) and rice dishes are widely eaten in Lombardy, while in the twin provinces of Trentino and Alto Adige you will find *polenta* and,

in Alto Adige, dishes of Germanic origin, such as *speck* (smoked pork), *knodel* (dumplings) and sauerkraut. In the Aosta Valley, beneath some of the highest peaks in the Alps – Mont Blanc, Monte Rosa and Monte Cervino – you'll find *fonduta* (the Italian version of fondue) and *vitello valdostana* (veal chops stuffed with soft cheese). Go to Tuscany and you'll find distinctive dishes such as *bistecca alla fiorentina* (rare grilled steak), while in the Veneto you'll be able to enjoy risotto and the delicious dessert *tiramisu.*

HEALTH

Today's travellers encounter few health hazards in northern Italy. Water supplies are sound and safe to drink and there are few of the tummy troubles encountered farther south. If you do fall ill and you are an EU national, you can benefit from treatment on exactly the same terms as a resident – providing you are carrying the E111 health form. In the unlikely event of falling ill and providing the problem is not serious, you can usually get help from the local *farmacia* (chemist.) If things are more serious, see a *médico* (doctor) or go to the casualty department of the nearest hospital.

INFORMATION

The Italian State Tourist Office (ENIT-Ente Nazionale Italiano per il Turismo) represents the country overseas, includin:g **UK**, *1 Princes St, London W1R 8AY; tel: 0171–408 1524.*
USA, *630 Fifth Ave, Suite 1565, New York 10111; tel: (212) 245 4822; 500 North Michigan Ave, Suite 1046, Chicago 60611; tel: (312) 644 0990; or 12400 Wiltshire Blvd, Suite 550, Los Angeles, 90025; tel: (310) 820 0098.*
Canada, *1 Placeville Marie, Suite 1914, Montreal, Quebec H38 2C3; tel: (514) 866 7667.*

Republic of Ireland, *47 Merrion Sq., Dublin 2; tel: (01) 766 397.*

In Italy, most towns and cities have an information point of some sort. Information offices come in a bewildering array of anonyms, such as EPT *(Ente Provinciale per il Turismo)*, APT *(Azienda Promozione Turistica)* and AAST *(Azienda Autonoma di Soggiorno e Turismo.)* They all usually have a good supply of pamphlets, leaflets, maps and the like, although often the literature is only in one language (Italian.) These offices are likely to open Mon–Sat 0900–1300 and 1600–1900 and sometimes, in larger towns and cities and at airports and rail stations, for a few hours on Sunday, too.

INSURANCE

Be sure to take out travel insurance to cover emergencies, such as medical care and flights home *in extremis*. If you are going skiing or mountaineering, or indulging in sports such as windsurfing or paragliding, be sure that your insurance covers you, and take out supplementary insurance, if necessary. Frequent travellers can save a great deal of money by taking out an annual insurance policy.

MAPS

Most tourist offices in northern Italy have a reasonable selection of maps covering the local town and area, frequently offered free of charge. For a good overview of the area, Michelin produces a 1:400,000 map of northern Italy, as does the Touring Club Italiano (TCI). For those planning to go walking, a 1:50000 map, such as the one of the northern Italian mountains produced by Studio FMB, is more useful. All these maps can be obtained before you leave home from stockists such as Stanfords, *12 Long Acre, London WC2E 9PL; tel: (0171) 836 1321.*

MUSEUMS

No country in the world offers such a staggering range of quality museums and art galleries as Italy. Museums and galleries are generally open daily from 0900 to 1300 and occasionally for a couple of hours in the afternoon, but are usually closed all day on Monday. For smaller establishments, opening hours are drastically curtailed in winter. Archaeological sites usually have longer hours, perhaps from 0900 until one hour before sunset. Admission charges vary enormously. You pay roughly between L2000 and L8000 for state-run museums, but the entrance fee can be as high as L13,000 at a popular site such as the Forum in Rome. Entrance is free in churches and monasteries, although it is usual to leave a donation. And if the custodian is required to open up the premises for you, it is customary to give a L1000 tip.

NATIONAL PARKS

Italy has five national parks, all in spectacularly beautiful scenery and well provided for with information centres, nature trails and *rifugi* (mountain huts). In the north, the Gran Paradiso National Park in the Aosta Valley, beneath some of the Alps' highest peaks, is one of most rugged and unspoilt in Europe. Though it's primarily a park for summer walkers, the 45 km Gran Paradiso cross-country ski trek is held in winter.

OPENING HOURS

Opening hours in Italy are a vexed subject – none are to be trusted (sadly, not even the ones published in this guide). Italy treats opening hours as something to be posted on the door, and then ignored in the greater interests of personal taste, whim or convenience.

Shops are fairly reliable, because they

22

depend upon trade to stay in business – so expect them to be open Monday to Saturday, 1000–1300 and 1600–1900 (2000 in summer). Shops in big cities and in popular tourist resorts may open later, for one night a week (as a quid pro quo they are closed Monday mornings), but Sunday opening is restricted to big out-of-town hypermarkets, flower shops, and traditional bakers selling bread and cakes. Your best bet late at night or on a Sunday is to look for convenience stores in the station area of larger cities.

About the only places open over lunch are bars and restaurants. Both must shut one day a week by law; a notice on the door will tell you which day it is. Many restaurants close for two weeks in August, the traditional holiday month, although this is less true for popular holiday areas, such as coastal resorts and the Lakes.

Banks are open Monday to Friday, 0820–13.20. Those in larger towns and cities may open again briefly in the afternoon, typically 1430–15.45.

Petrol stations are becoming more flexible – many open 0730–1300 and 1600–1900 daily except Sunday. Those that advertise 24-hour service in reality have a machine that you feed with notes in return for petrol – only to be used as a last resort, these are known to take your money and refuse to give out petrol.

Tourist offices follow local shop opening hours, except that many open on Sunday mornings in summer. Whether any tourist office is open at advertised hours depends upon a number of factors – in any event, the level of service provided by most is so low that you should not rely upon them for any kind of concrete help or assistance.

Museums are a law unto themselves, although stinging criticism from many quarters is at last beginning to have an effect. Strikes, so-called 'staff shortages' and general disgruntlement can mean that museums are often closed when they should be open. National Museums, controlled by the Ministry of Culture in Rome, have their opening hours set centrally – most are closed on Mondays and open Tuesday–Saturday, 0900–1300. Some open again in the afternoon, 1400–1700, including Sundays. Increasingly the most popular museums (including the Uffizi in Florence) are remaining open over the lunch period and for one late night a week. Local museums have much more variable opening hours.

Churches are usually open from 0800 to 1200 and 1600 to 1900 (or dusk in winter). Visitors are discouraged from walking round during services, which means that you may have limited time to tour on Sundays.

POST OFFICE

For small postal transactions – postcards and letters – you need never visit a post office, since tobacconists, newsagents and bars stock stamps and phone cards (look for a blue 'T' sign in the window) and this is where most Italians buy them. Post offices for other transactions, such as parcel post or poste restante, are open Monday to Saturday, 0800–13.30.

POSTAL SERVICES

The Italian postal service is one of the worst in Europe and don't be surprised if friends and relatives receive holiday greetings after you have returned home. Airmail rates for letters are L850 to Britain, L1250 to North America and L2000 to Australia and New Zealand. Postcard rates are about L100 lire less. Stamps can be bought in a *tabacchi* (tobacconist's shop), in your hotel or at gift shops in certain tourist resorts. Main post offices are usually open

Mon–Sat 0830–1930, but most post offices are only open Mon–Fri 0830–1350 and Sat 0830–1200.

PUBLIC HOLIDAYS

Public holidays are taken seriously in Italy – do not expect anything to be open, except for bars and restaurants. In addition, many businesses close for big local festivals, such as the Feast of St John (24 June) and for a period in August, the traditional holiday month.

1 January (New Year)
6 January (Epiphany)
Good Friday
Easter Monday
25 April (Liberation Day)
1 May (Labour Day)
15 August (Assumption)
1 November (All Saints)
8 December (Immaculate Conception)
25 December (Christmas)
26 December (St Stephen)

PUBLIC TRANSPORT

Private cars are a liability in big cities, such as Florence, Milan or Turin, so it is a good idea to park in a fringe car park, and use taxis or buses to get about. Taxis are plentiful and can be hailed in the street or from ranks. Like taxis all over the world, the drivers vary from honest to crooked, cheerful to belligerent; their cars range from immaculate Mercedes to battered bangers and their knowledge of their own city can be excellent or appalling. Bus systems vary from city to city, but most require you to buy tickets in advance from tobacconists or bars. You time-stamp them when you get on the bus, and they are valid for an hour's travel.

SAFETY

Everyone knows of the activities of the Mafia, but the biggest threat to personal safety in Italy comes not from organised crime, which has no interest in tourists, but from gangs of *scippaatori* (bag snatchers). These gangs operate on foot or on scooters and will snatch anything they can get their hands on – wallets, jewellery and watches, as well as bags. In the unlikely event of an incident, report the matter to the *polizia statale*, which has responsibility for thefts, or to your tour representative if you are travelling on a package arrangement. Emergency telephone numbers are 112 for the police, 113 for the ambulance, 115 for the fire brigade and 116 for assistance if you break down on the road.

SECURITY

Italians are very honest people, and crime is not a big problem in rural Italy – but big cities and crowded streets attract professional thieves, so sensible precautions need to be taken to ensure that you do not become the next victim. Never leave valuables in an unattended car, and never carry your valuables in a way that exposes you to the attentions of cutpurses, bag-snatchers and pickpockets.

SHOPPING

Whether you are interested in high fashion from Milan, Venetian glassware or an unusual gift to take home for a friend or relative, you'll find it here. Northern Italians have raised shopping almost to the realms of an art form; even the smallest country town has its celebrated fashion shop which would not look out of place in London's Burlington Arcade or New York's Fifth Avenue. 'Good buys' in northern Italy are normally denoted by such items as silk ties, scarves and dressing gowns, ceramics and exquisite handicrafts, but that is really only the beginning. Each region, each town even, has its own speciality; you can travel the length of northern Italy, devoting your time to just collecting ceramics, for example.

But it is a mistake to believe that bargaining is the rule. There are, of course, exceptions, but in the better shops prices are fixed. There may be occasions when you are given a discount. If you are that way inclined, it is always worth asking – but the final price will never be a third off. What is true is that shops in the home regions will offer the same goods for considerably less than the asking price in tourist 'traps' such as Florence and Venice. And, in the main, goods can be bought for less than they would cost at home. The wise shopper will find this applies especially to clothes and leather goods. Here is a breakdown of what you can expect to find in the main cities:

Florence

The very atmosphere of Florence lends itself to shopping and this is the second most important shopping centre in Italy after Milan. It is particularly good for high fashion and leather goods – and, of course, antiques. The most fashionable street is *V. Tournabuoni*, which runs from the Arno to the *V. Cerretani*. If the prices seem too high here, try the network of streets which runs down to the Ponte Vecchia. The Ponte Vecchia is a colourful bazaar of gold and silversmiths' shops. The city has been a centre for jewellery since the Middle Ages and Florence is also a great place for craftsmen. Here you can get almost anything made, mended, custom-carved or restored. There are even workshops specialising in marble. Most Florentine shops open 0900–1300 and 1530/1600 to 1930/2000. They close on Monday morning in winter and Saturday afternoon in summer.

Milan

It should scarcely come as a surprise to discover that the world's fashion capital is also a mecca for shopaholics. The fact is brought home not just in the array of glittering shops, but in the wrap-around fur and sparkling jewellery of the Milanese women – the *gran signora*. The centre of all this elegant activity is the *V. Monte Napoleone*, which has no fewer than ten top jewellers, as well as designer fashion boutiques and antique stores. Close by, in *V. Sant'Andrea*, are the premises of Giorgio Armani, Gianni Versace and Giafranco Ferre. More affordable outfits are available from Fiorucci, Benetton, Biff, Komlas or the department store La Rinascente, in *Pza Duomo*. Shrewd Milanese also make their way to the numerous factory outlets and discount stores, where designer label goods can often be found at 30–70% discount, while designer shoes can often be found at the Wednesday and Saturday markets at the outdoor market in the *Pzle Martini*. Other places worth visiting include the smart leather goods store Prada and the doll shop Lenci, both of which are in Galleria Vittorio Emanuele.

Rome

In the world of fashion, Rome plays second fiddle to Milan – but that isn't to say that Rome doesn't have appeal for clothes shoppers. Wander down *V. Condotti* and the famous names stand out from the shop fronts. Richard Ginori and Gucci, Bulgari and Beltrami, Barilla and Battistoni. But overall Rome can compare with any other centre – Bottega Veneta for leather goods, Al Sogno for children's toys (notably stuffed animals), Frette for linen and embroidery, and Spazio Sette for kitchen gadgetry. Stray just a few streets from *V. Condotti* and prices drop considerably. There are any number of good value shops and stores close to the Vatican, for example.

25

Venice

In Venice, the glassware is almost as famous as the gondolas – but the city is also good for shoes, jewellery, lace and carnival masks. Venice's carnival is a big event on the international, as well as the local, calendar and shops selling masks have mushroomed in almost every area of the city. Go to Venice, also, for the gorgeous textiles produced by Fortuny, and for notebooks bound in marbled paper.

SPORT

Sports – particularly spectator sports – are popular in Italy. Top of the nation's list is *calcio* (**football**) which is not so much a sport in Italy, more a religion. Milan is home to Inter Milan and AC Milan, who play on alternate Sundays during the season at the G. Meazza stadium, *V. Piccolimmina 5; tel: (02) 4870 7123*. Turin is home to Juventus and Torino, and Italian League games are played at many other towns and cities in the north. Expect to pay between L15,000 and L70,000 for tickets.

After football **basketball**, introduced by the Americans after World War II, is the most popular team sport. Italians also enjoy **tennis, motor racing** and, increasingly, **golf.** With the mountains and lakes on the doorstep, northern Italians are keen, too, on outdoor pursuits such as **skiing, climbing, walking,** and **mountain biking.** Water sports – **sailing, windsurfing** and **waterskiing**, as well as **swimming** are also popular on the lakes and along the Ligurian coast.

STORES

Italy has two main department stores, **Upim** and **Standa,** which can be found in many large towns. Neither is particularly expensive and they are good places to stock up with basic requirements, such as toiletries. Some of the stores have food halls attached.

TELEPHONES

Public telephones take L100, L200 and L500 coins as well as *carte telefoniche* (telephone card). Phone cards can be bought from newstands and *tobacchi*. The perforated corner of the cards has to be torn off before they can be used. Local calls can be made from phones in bars which take a *gettoni* (a L200 token). Call charges are highest on weekdays from 0800–1300 and cheapest from 2200–0800 on weekdays and all day on Sunday. Direct international telephone calls can be made by dialling 00 followed by 44 (UK), 353 (Eire), 1 (USA and Canada), 61 (Australia) and 64 (New Zealand).

TIME

Italy observes Central European Time, and is one hour ahead of Greenwich Mean Time from late September to late March, and two hours ahead in summer.

TOILETS

Railway stations, airports, bus stations and motorway (autostrada) rest areas have clean toilets, as do some museums, but elsewhere they scarcely exist. Bars have toilets, but they are for the use of customers – they are not a free public facility, and you should expect to buy a drink if you use them.

USEFUL ADDRESSES

Check out the literature available in your own country from the **Italian State Tourist Board (ENIT)**: *1 Princes Street, London W1R 8AY (tel: 0171-259 6322); 630 Fifth Avenue, Suite 1565, Rockefeller Center, New York, NY 10111, USA (tel: 212-245 4822).*

Also in the USA: *500 North Michegan*

Avenue, Chicago, IL60611 (tel: 312-644 0990); 12400 Wilshire Boulevard, Suite 4550, Los Angeles, CA90025 (tel: 310-820 0098). In Canada: Office National Italien de Tourisme, Italian Government Travel Office 1 Place Ville Marie, Montréal, Quebec H3B 2C3 (tel: 514-866 7667).

USEFUL READING

Italy is comprehensively covered in both guide books and travel literature. Most guide book series have volumes devoted to the north. They include the Thomas Cook Travellers series, which has editions covering *Florence and Tuscany*, *Rome* and **Venice**, and are published by Passport books in the USA and Canada. If you are planning to use trains or buses, another useful publication is the *Thomas Cook European Timetable*, which is published every two months, priced £8.40. *Tel: (01733) 503571/2* in the UK or *800 367 7984* in the US. For more details of Thomas Cook titles, see page 14.

Those considering booking their own accommodation will find *Michelin's Red Guide to Italy* indispensable for reliable restaurants as well as hotels. Other titles useful for background reading, with their UK publishers include: *Florence A Portrait*, by Michael Levey, Pimlico; *The Stones of Florence/Venice Observed*, by Mary McCarthy, Penguin; *Venice*, by Jan Morris, Faber; *A Traveller in Italy*, by H.V. Morton, Methuen; *Pictures from Italy*, by Charles Dickens, Granville; *Italian Hours*, by Henry James, Penguin; *A History of Venice*, by John Julius Norwich, Penguin; *Contemporary Italy*, by Donald Sassoon, Longman.

WHAT TO TAKE

Don't worry – anything you forget to pack, you can buy in Italy – in fact it is better to travel light and buy what you need as you go: prices in Italy can be cheaper than back home, and there is no lack of choice of all leading brands, from baby nappies to suntan lotions. You may have difficulty obtaining prescription medicines, so take an ample supply. Take spare spectacles if you depend upon them for driving, in case one pair gets damaged. Do not forget your passport (Italy may let you in without one, but will your home country let you back?) and your driving licence, without which you cannot hire a rental car.

WINE

One of the great joys of holidaying in Italy is sampling local wine. Italian wines have come a long way since the days when the market seemed to be dominated by cheap *soaves* and *chianti* in the straw-covered *fiaschi* bottles. These still exist, of course, but alongside them have come more distinctive wines. In the north-east – Trentino–Alto Adige, the Veneto and Friuli–Venezia Giulia – some of the best wines are made from grape varieties which have their origin in France, such as Chardonnay, Merlot, Cabernet, Riesling and Müller-Thurgau. Alto Adige, in particular, produces good quality wines at a reasonable price.

Tuscany is the home to some of Italy's best reds – wines such as *Brunello di Montalcino* and *Vino Nobile di Montepulciano* standing out beside the everyday *Soaves* and *Chianti*. In Trentino, dozens of DOC (*Denominazione di Origine Controllata*) wines – the equivalent of the French *Appellation Contrôlée* standard – are produced. Unlike elsewhere, some of the best Italian wines are produced for home consumption. So if you're travelling in your own vehicle and you come across a wine you like, it's well worth taking a case home with you in the boot of the car.

27

DRIVING IN ITALY

ACCIDENTS

The image of the Italian driver – aggressive, horn-tooting and inconsiderate – is, in most cases, undeserved. True, the letter of the highway code may not be observed quite so strictly as it is in some countries. But northern Italians are more inclined in temperament towards north Europeans than their southern counterparts.

In the (hopefully) unlikely event of being involved in an accident, stay calm. Place a warning triangle not less than 50m behind the car and get in touch with the police (telephone either 112 or 113). Avoid getting into arguments with other drivers – the chances are they will be just as upset and indignant as you are! Exchange names, addresses and insurance details, but do not, in any circumstances, make any statement which might incriminate you in the event of legal proceedings. If anyone is injured, telephone 118 for an ambulance and medical assistance. Some *autostrada* have emergency push-button call boxes as well as emergency telephones.

BREAKDOWNS

If you have a breakdown, put on your hazard warning lights and place the warning triangle at the obligatory, minimum 50m distance behind your vehicle. Dial 116 for the breakdown service offered by the **Automobile Club d'Italia (ACI)**, *V. Marsala 8, 00185 Rome; tel (06) 4998 21.* Emergency telephones are supposed to be found every two km along the *autostrada*, but there are some stretches of *autostrada* where the phones are spaced farther apart. ACI will then arrange for the vehicle to be towed to the nearest

ACI-affiliated garage. European motoring organisations such as the ACI and the British **Automobile Association** and **RAC** are affiliated to the **AIT** (International Tourist Alliance), whose members enjoy reciprocal breakdown arrangements in their respective countries. If you are unsure what the charges are, check with ACI before it instructs one of its garages to send a vehicle out to you.

Breaking down on the motorway is an expensive business. Expect to pay a starting charge of L150,000 to be towed off the motorway, plus L60,000 for the first 20 km and then L1350 for every km after that. If you are not a member of a motoring organisation, you can expect to pay L250,000 just for a garage to attend to your vehicle on the spot. Garages are allowed to charge their own rates to attend to a vehicle on the motorway. In theory they are supposed to publicise their charges, but of course there is no way a motorist who has the misfortune to break down can know what they are. If you are unhappy about the risks, take out a breakdown insurance policy such as those offered by the AA and RAC for peace of mind.

AUTOSTRADA

Italy has a comprehensive network of motorways amounting to more than 6000km of road. The north of the country is particularly well served. *Autostrada* radiate north, south, east and west from Milan, which means that it is possible to cross the north in four or five hours at the most.

Motorways are generally of a good

standard and are well signposted, with kilometre markings on the centre reservation making it easy for you to locate your position at a given time. Service areas are more frequent than in many countries and usually include café/bar, restaurant, mini market, bureau de change, information counter and, sometimes, a motel as well.

CARAVANS

If you are towing a caravan, check that the caravan braking mechanism is correctly set. You should also ensure that the cable linking the car with the caravan is firmly in position so that, if the two should happen to part company, the trailer brake becomes effective immediately.

CAR HIRE

The good news about car hire is that vehicles to rent in northern Italy are plentiful; the bad news is that choosing this option is expensive. Car hire rates in Italy are among the highest in Europe – reckon on at least £230 (around $385) for a week's hire with unlimited mileage for a small vehicle, such as a Ford Fiesta. You can hire everything from small family saloons to four-wheel drives, but unless you are a large group you might be better advised to go for a smaller vehicle with comfort. Summers in northern Italy can be extremely hot and hiring a vehicle with air conditioning makes sense as long as it doesn't present too great a strain on the budget.

The best deals to be had are usually through a tour operator who has negotiated low rates through car hire operators in Italy. For example, in the UK, **Citalia** *(tel: 0181 688 9989)* offers rates beginning at £196 ($329) – a rate comparable with the lowest off-the-shelf rate from a car hire company specialising in the holiday market, such as **Holiday Autos** *(tel: 0900*

300400.) Also, you must be over 21 and have held a valid licence for a year to drive a hire car in Italy.

It's easy enough to hire a car in Italy, but there are a number of things you should look out for. First, car hire companies often impose a ten per cent surcharge if you pick up the car from an airport (as opposed to a city centre depot) and a similar fee if you choose to drop it off in a different location from the point of collection. Moreover, as a refundable deposit, they will swipe your credit card for £150 ($250), which could affect the limit on your credit card.

Before you drive the car away, make sure you have all the car's documentation with you, including the road-tax disc, the registration papers and insurance details, which are usually kept in the glove compartment. Be sure to do this because you will need all these documents in the event of a random roadside check. Ensure, too, that you know how the vehicle's various controls work. It's little fun emerging from dinner on the first night and discovering that you don't know how to switch the car lights on! If necessary, get the car hire representative to give you a demonstration of all the vehicle's features before you set off.

All vehicles are hired with a full tank of petrol and should be returned full to avoid the car hire company charging for petrol at an unfavourable rate.

CAR THEFT

Theft of cars – as well as from cars – is increasing in Italy just as it is elsewhere. The police are attempting to combat the problem by making more spot checks, particularly on foreign-registered vehicles. Drivers have to be able to show proof of ownership, or have authorisation from owners to use the vehicle, or they will be

29

subject to on-the-spot fines. Cars can be conficated until the fine is paid.

DIFFICULT DRIVING

The most difficult driving conditions you are likely to encounter are in the **mountains.** The tortuous mountain roads are a test for the driver's patience as well as skill at any time of the year, particularly in summer when some of the roads, especially in the Dolomites, are clogged with holiday makers. Also, in summer, sudden thunderstorms can lead to flash floods, creating landslides on roads. Sometimes the rainfall is so great and the resulting force of water so powerful that rivers burst their banks, causing everything except concrete structures to be swept away. If the weather is doubtful, consult the local tourist or ACI office to discover if the road you want to use is passable and, if you are camping, which sites are liable to be flooded.

If you are planning to travel in **winter**, make sure that your car is able to handle the conditions. You should fit a high-temperature (winter) thermostat and ensure that the strength of the antifreeze mixture is sufficient to cope with the low temperatures you are likely to encounter. Winter in the Alps can be extremely cold and snowfalls great. The Alps and the Dolomites present a formidable challenge to motorists in winter, with visibility almost down to zero in blinding snowstorms. Tyres should have sufficient tread for all road conditions and, in really dangerous circumstances, be fitted with chains. It's not possible to hire chains in Italy, but they can be bought from garages and motor accessory shops. If you do fit chains or studded tyres, they must be fitted to all wheels and can only be used between Nov 15 and Mar 15. You are also advised to have mud flaps fitted behind the

rear wheels to prevent spray and slush from your wheels spraying any following cars.

If you do travel in difficult conditions, carry with you in the car everything you might need in the unlikely event of getting stranded. You should carry with you emergency food and water rations and plenty of warm clothing. In winter, take care also with the sun. The sun in the rarified air of high altitudes is extremely strong and it's easy to burn, so take with you plenty of sun block cream, lip-salve and a lotion for dry or cracked skin. A pair of sunglasses, designer or otherwise, will also be useful.

With the mountains acting as a barrier to weather systems, **fog** is extremely common during the winter months on the plains and multi-car pile-ups frequent on the *autostrada*. In foggy conditions, lower your speed and leave plenty of room between yourself and the vehicle in front. Never use full-beam headlights in fog, or you will blind oncoming drivers. Italian law dictates that, in these conditions, you should use dipped headlights.

DISTANCES

Distances in northern Italy are not great and, with motorways running both north-south and east-west, it is possible to drive across the country from, say, Genoa to Venice in three or four hours. On motorways you should reckon on averaging about 100 km an hour, but obviously much less on secondary roads. Delays can occur in the mountains at all times of the year and driving around the lakes in high summer (mid-July to late August) is sometimes a slow and arduous business.

DOCUMENTS

To drive in Italy, you need a new-style pink EU driving licence, or the even newer credit-card size photo licence. If you have the old-style green UK licence, it must be accompanied by an official Italian translation, which is available free of charge from the Italian Tourist Office or motoring organisations such as, in Britain, the AA and the RAC. In addition, although third-party insurance is included on policies carried by citizens of EU countries, an extension to domestic insurance is appropriate for those wanting full cover. Under Italian law, you are obliged to carry with you in the car documents relating to ownership and insurance.

DRINKING AND DRIVING

If you are driving, don't drink. The laws about driving are strict and the penalties if you are caught are severe.

DRIVING CONDITIONS

Traffic rules in Italy are along lines laid down in the Geneva convention. Driving is on the right and you should keep to the nearside kerb except when overtaking. This rule applies even if the road is empty. Give way at intersections to traffic joining the road from the right. Vehicles travelling in the opposite direction wishing to turn left must do so by passing *in front* of each other. Overtaking on the right is permitted when the driver ahead has signalled that he is turning left and has moved to the centre of the road. You can also overtake on the right when vehicles are travelling in parallel lines. In built-up areas, the use of the horn is prohibited except in emergencies – but, outside built-up areas, its use is compulsory when you need to give warning of approach. For warnings at night, flashing headlights should be used instead of the horn.

FUEL

Fuel prices in Italy are, unfortunately for visiting motorists, among the highest in Europe. Although, in principle, fuel stations can now compete with each other and therefore should be able to offer slightly lower prices, you must still expect to pay L1910 per litre for *benzina super* (four-star leaded), L1820 for *senza piombo* (unleaded petrol), and L1430 for diesel. The fuel is likely to cost you about L20 per litre more if you buy it at a motorway service station. Pumps dispensing unleaded petrol are often marked in English 'super unleaded'. Once it was extremely difficult to pay for petrol in Italy with a credit card, but it is estimated that about two thirds of the petrol stations now accept 'plastic'. On motorways, petrol stations are open 24 hours a day – but on other roads fuel is usually only available from 0700–1230 and from 1530–1930 (1530–1900 between October and April). Only about a quarter of these garages are open on Sunday and public holidays. Some garages close on Monday, too. The garage's opening time is displayed outside the premises, along with the address of the nearest garage which is open. It is prohibited to carry spare fuel in cans.

INFORMATION

To be forewarned is to be forearmed. Get as much information before you travel as you can. Good sources of information include the Italian Tourist Office – see Travel Essentials, p. 21. The respective Italian embassies in **South Africa, Australia** and **New Zealand** can also provide information on aspects of travelling in the country by car. The motoring organisations can also provide up-to-date information as well as comprehensive insurance packages in the event of breakdown.

The UK **Automobile Association's Five Star Standard Breakdown**

Assistance Plan costs £49 for 15 days (£54 for non-members). Details of this policy can be had from the **AA**, *Freepost, Erskine, Renfrewshire PA8 6BR; tel: (0345) 55 55 77.*

LIGHTS

The law permits full-beam headlights to be used only outside towns and cities. It is compulsory to use dipped headlights when passing through tunnels, even if the tunnel is well lit. Before leaving home, you should apply a sticker to each headlight to allow for the driving change from left- to right-hand side of the road, thus ensuring that you do not dazzle oncoming traffic. It is also recommended that you carry with you a spare set of vehicle bulbs. When visibility is restricted due to fog or snow, fog lights should be used, but only in pairs.

PARKING

Parking is allowed on the right-hand side of the road, the exceptions being in towns and, of course, on main roads and motorways. However, parking in many towns and cities is difficult and, in some, banned altogether. In town centres, drivers can park in blue zones between Mon and Sat (holidays excepted) between 0900–1430 and 1600–2000. Discs, obtainable from tourist and motoring organisations and from petrol stations, have to be displayed on the windscreen and can be used only for a maximum of one hour. There are green zones where parking is prohibited between 0800–0930 and 1430–1600 on weekdays. Cities which have particular parking problems include:

Florence: on weekdays, vehicles are banned from the centre between 0730–1830, although an exception is made for those making a delivery or staying in an hotel, guesthouse or on a camping site. If you are staying in the city, you can only stop to offload luggage and must then park outside a restricted area, such as in an hotel car-park.

Rome: The 'Eternal City' has eternal traffic problems. Parking is strictly prohibited, designated by a sign reading *zona tutelato*, in the central area on weekdays and illegal parking will result in a fine and, possibly, even a prison sentence.

Venice: Parking is extremely limited at the Venezia end of the causeway, in and around the *Pzle Roma*, so you are best advised to park at one of the special car-parks on the mainland, which are linked by ferry to the city. In the city itself, you are best advised to use the water buses – the *vaporetti* and the smaller *motoscafi* – both of which have a flat fare of L4000 for any one continuous journey.

POLICE

Italy has different police forces for different functions: as a driver, you need to be aware most of the *vigili urbani*, the traffic police, whose job it is to prevent infringements of the rules of the road. Their name is apt: they are vigilant, and transgressors are fined on the spot – being a visitor does not make you immune from traffic laws. Having said that, the traffic police are human and will distinguish between genuine errors and deliberate flouting of the law.

Colour section (i): The Dolomites (pp. 69–73).
(ii) Castello del Miramare (p. 51); Tyrolean-style architecture in the Dolomites (pp. 69–73); inset; Trieste (p. 45) ice-cream seller.
(iii) Cividale del Friuli from Devils Bridge (p. 48); inset (left) Tempietto Longobardo (p. 48); (right) the frescoed crypt of the Basilica, Aquileia (p. 52).
(iv) Venice (pp. 80–91); a view from the Campanile; the Basilica.

ROADS

Italian roads include some of the best, and some of the roughest, in Europe. Driving around Italy, you will find spectacular tunnels and viaducts, sweeping through and across stupendous mountainous countryside. Step off motorways and main roads, however, and you will encounter many hazards and obstacles: it is common Italian practice not to repair a potholed or frost-damaged road, but simply to put up a warning sign. You will also find so-called 'white roads' all over Italy – named because that is the colour they are on the map. You may have to drive along these unsurfaced farm tracks to reach an archaeological site: drive with care to avoid damage to tyres and rims.

ROAD SIGNS

Many road signs in Italy conform to the usual international pattern, but the glossary of words and terms which may not be familiar to foreign travellers include *entrata* (entrance), *incrocio* (crossroads), *lavori in corso* (roadworks ahead), *passaggio a livello* (level crossing), *rallentare* (slow down), *senso vietato* (no entry), *sosta autorizzata* (parking permitted – followed by an indication of the times), *sosta vietata* (no parking), *svolta* (bend), *uscita* (exit), *vietato ingresso veicoli* (no entry for vehicles) and *veitati transito autocarri* (closed to heavy vehicles).

SEAT BELTS

Seat belts have to be worn in all cars in which they are fitted, in both the front and back seats.

SPEED LIMITS

A speed limit of 50 kph is imposed on all vehicles travelling within a built-up area. Outside a built-up area, cars can travel at 90 kph on secondary roads, at 110 kph on main roads, and at 130 kph on motorways.

TOLLS

Pedaggi autostradali (motorway tolls) are levied on almost every stretch of the country's major trunk routes. A travel ticket is issued on entry and the toll is paid on leaving, with traffic divided into separate fast and slow tracks according to how you wish to pay. The method of calculation is based on the size of the vehicle and tolls are low compared with those in operation in some European countries. Here are some sample tolls covering smaller family saloon cars: Aosta Border to Genoa West (270 km), L29,000; Bologna Casalecchio to Parma (93 km), L7500; Florence North to Modena South (115 km), L10,500; Milan East to Venice Mestre (264 km), L22,000; Rome North to Florence North (281 km), L22,500. In addition motorists can buy a VIACARD for travel on the *autostrada*, operating in much the same way as a phone card, in other words, until the credit expires. The cards, which are available from motorway toll-booths, service areas, certain banks, tourist offices and tobacconists, are in three denominations – L150,000, L100,000 and L50,000.

33

TRAFFIC OFFENCES

Police are empowered to impose fines on drivers of foreign-registered vehicles. Drivers can be asked to pay up to a quarter of the fine on the spot. If the fine is contested, the driver is obliged to put up half the maximum amount of the fine, either in cash (which can be either in lire or foreign currency) or a surety, until the case is heard. If the guarantee is not deposited, the driver's licence may be withdrawn or, if the licence is not available, the car impounded until the money is put up.

BACKGROUND

GEOGRAPHY

The northern part of the Italian 'boot' contains the country's most spectacular scenery. Lakes, mountains and plains come together in a landscape of almost Utopian proportions. As the Irish author Sean O'Faolain once said: 'You travel Italy dazzled and you leave it in a daze'.

The most dominating feature of the region is the Alps. Created millions of years ago by volcanic action, the peaks of the Alps enjoy a general height of between 1500 and 2000 m but soar to more than 4800 m at Mont Blanc, straddling the border with France, Switzerland and Austria, and Monte Rosa in northern Piedmont (Piemonte). Running at right angles to the Alps is the limestone spur of the Dolomites, a relatively undiscovered range whose steep slopes test even the most ardent and talented skiers.

Italy's spine is created by the Apennines, an offshoot of the Alps, which in turn give way to minor ranges such as the Tuscan hills; green and softly contoured, their scenic beauty so quintessentially Italian – a fact not lost on poets and writers. East of the Apennines northern Italy's great plain extends across Lombardy into the Veneto, ending in Venice's wonderfully atmospheric marshy lagoons. South of Lombardy, the plain gives way to the rolling farmlands of Emilia-Romagna, the unspoilt hills and crumbling hill villages of Marche, and the tranquil lakes and silent valleys of Umbria.

Northern Italy is drained by the River Po and its tributaries the Ticino, Adda, Oglio, Enza and Panaro, and also by the Piave and Adige rivers, both of which empty into the Adriatic near Venice. Another feature of the region is the lake district. During the Ice Age, glaciers left in their wake great sheets of ice, which melted when the climate warmed. There are more than half a dozen lakes in the area north and east of Milan, the most famous, most beautiful and most visited of which are Como, Maggiore and Garda.

Climatically, northern Italy enjoys a Mediterranean climate with regional differences. Inland, the weather in the central plains is greatly influenced by the mountains. Summers can be hot and muggy, with afternoon thunderstorms frequent, particularly in July and August. In winter, the mountains block the warming effect of winds blowing in off the coast, bringing frequent frost and, particularly in autumn, fog. The Ligurian coast, an extension of the French Riviera, enjoys hot summers and pleasantly mild winters. Even in January, shirt sleeves can be the order of the day.

HISTORY

The Beginnings

Although the first modern human remains found in Italy can be traced back to around 20,000 BC during the Palaeolithic era, it was not until between 3000 and 1800 BC that the first advanced cultures settled in the country. The Ligurians arrived in what is now Liguria, on the border with France, and they were followed by migratory peoples such as the Picini and the Messapians, who arrived from the Balkans after crossing the Adriatic. About the same time were the Veneti, Umbrii and Latins,

34

who gradually moved down from the north to settle other parts of the peninsula.

Around 800 BC saw the rise of the Etruscan city-states. The Etruscans occupied much of what is now Lazio and Tuscany, between the Arno and Tiber rivers. History doesn't define where they came from; it's likely they were a mixture of indigenous and foreign peoples who became linked by a common language. Like the Greeks they were highly cultured – advanced in the fields of language, agriculture and technology – but militarily they proved no match for the Romans who, by around 350 BC, had all but defeated them.

The Romans

Legend has it that Rome was founded in 753 BC, although archaeological evidence seems to suggest that people could have been living in the city as long ago as 1200 BC. The Roman republic (res publica) was formed in 509 BC, after the ousting of the Etruscan kings. The idea was that the people ruled, but in practice there were constant disputes between the plebeians (lower classes) and the patricians (the military and political élite). In 494 BC the Tribune brokered peace and Rome expanded. As they became more powerful, the Romans came into conflict with Carthage, resulting in Hannibal's epic journey over the Alps to inflict defeats on Rome at Cannae and Trasimeno. But the Romans recovered their poise to win the third Punic War, and in so doing gained mastery of the Mediterranean and territories as far away as Jerusalem and Asia Minor.

For centuries, in the days of Julius Caesar and beyond, the Roman empire continued to dictate the politics not just of the Mediterranean, Asia Minor and North Africa, but also north-west Europe. Soon after the death of Augustus, the Romans invaded and occupied the southern part of Britain. Britons were ruled by Rome for almost 400 years, but this was virtually the Romans' last act of expansion. The empire fell into decay and ceased to exist after AD 455.

Barbarians and Byzantines

For 300 years after the Romans, the Italian peninsula was ruled by 'barbarians' – outsiders or foreigners – Goths, Franks and Lombards. When Rome was overrun in 410 by Alaric the Goth, the so-called civilised world was shaken to its foundations. It was another Goth, Odoacer, who displaced the last Western emperor, Romulus Augustus, in 476. After the barbarians, the Byzantines took over.

Soldiers and Saints

Northern Italy is both a land of saints and of important military figures. St Benedict was born in the Umbrian hilltown of Norcia in AD 480 and helped the Catholic church become a dominant force on European politics over the next 1,000 years by founding the first western monastic communities. He also established the Rule by which monks lived then and continue to live, even to this day. Some 700 years later, Frederick Hohenstaufen, also known as Frederick Barbarossa, was crowned Holy Roman Emperor by the Pope in 1152; this did not prevent him from conquering much of Northern Italy, and establishing the strong links with Germany that still characterise much of the region to this day. Best-known of all, St Francis of Assisi was the first saint to articulate ideas about the rights of animals, and of man's duty to respect the environment that are now part of mainstream conservationist philosophy.

Between 536 and 552, their emperor Justinian took over large parts of Italy, creating a Byzantine hegemony that lasted several centuries. Meanwhile, the Church took advantage of the uncertain times to increase its own influence in the affairs of Italy. In the north, power swayed between the emperor and the pope, but the struggle was becoming more complex. By 1307, the papacy had fallen so much under French domination that it moved to Avignon – and the maritime republics of Pisa, Genoa and Venice, having grown rich on trade and commerce, were also exerting influence.

The Middle Ages and the Renaissance

This was a period of great growth in northern Italy. The prosperous cities developed their own semi-autonomous form of government known as the *comune*, a sort of town council comprising merchants, guildsmen and minor nobility. But power struggles between and within cities led to power passing into the hands of a single family. In Florence, it was the Medicis; in Milan, the Viscontis; in Ferrara, the Estes; and in Urbino, the Montefeltros.

Wealth creation in the great northern cities, allied with the migration of scholars after the fall of Constantinople led to the revival of an interest in art, the *Rinascimento* – the Renaissance – which began in Florence and quickly spread to create the most awe-inspiring epoch in the development of Western art. For the first time, movement was brought into play in the visual arts. In 1429 Andrea Pazzi, the head of a Florentine family enriched by trade and banking, commissioned the architect Filippo Brunelleschi to design an addition (a chapterhouse and chapel) to the Monastery of S. Croce. In the Pazzi Chapel, Brunelleschi achieved what his contemporary Leon Battista Alberti described as the definition of beauty: 'a harmony and concord of all the parts achieved in such a manner that nothing could be added or taken away or altered except for the worse.'

Brunelleschi's contemporaries also credited him with another artistic achievement of far reaching effect – the invention of linear perspective. Various devices had been used by artists before to suggest distance in pictures and drawings. But Brunelleschi was the first to work out a system based on geometric principles, which could be used in a scientific way.

The Renaissance fired the imagination of all artists – painters, sculptors and inventors. In the wake of Brunelleschi came artists like Tommaso di Giovanni in his fresco of the Holy Trinity in Santa Maria Novella in Florence, and of course Lorenzo Ghiberti's beautifully carved east doors – 'The Gates of Paradise'– in the cathedral in Florence. Here Ghiberti expoited Old Testament subjects to display not only his own consummate skill as a craftsman, in the exquisitely refined modelling and finishing of every detail, but also as an artist in the representation of human figures.

The talents of Leonardo da Vinci, from the village of Vinci outside Florence, were considerable. Painter, philosopher, mathematician, scientist and engineer, he brought the same broad-brush approach to his life as to his canvas. Leonardo's image in *The Last Supper* of the beginning of Christ's agony makes hard viewing – Aldous Huxley called it 'the saddest painting in the world' – and the haunting beauty of his half-smile *Mona Lisa* is the most famous portrait ever painted. In physics, he was the first to understand inertia and, in physiology, he appears to have understood the circulation of blood a full 100 years before William Harvey.

The French, Spanish and Austrians

While the Renaissance brought new learning to northern Italy, foreign powers were eyeing with interest the dissent which was taking place at the same time among the city-states. Their territorial ambitions were too hard to surpress. A French king, Francis I, took Milan in 1515, having based his claim on a marriage between a Visconti and the French royal family. Spain later joined in when the troops of Charles V, Holy Roman Emperor and Habsburg heir to the Spanish and Austrian thrones, ransacked Rome in 1527 and then defeated the French in Pavia in 1526.

At the Treaty of Cateau-Cambrésis in 1559, Spain's hold over Milan and parts of Tuscany was ratified and, with France holding other areas, only the papal states and Venice were free of foreign dominance. In fact, the Spanish Habsburgs had a stranglehold in northern Italy until the Spanish War of Succession (1701–13), after which the Austrians took control. Napoleon, breaking the Austrians hold, briefly annexed large portions of Italy in his campaigns in 1796–1800. He was chiefly responsible for reducing papal power, reforming the feudal hierarchies and allowing Italy to move forward to become a modern state. Austrian control was restored in 1815 at the Congress of Vienna and during the next 50 years the unification movement gained momentum.

Unification and Unrest

Until the 19th century, Italy was merely a geographical expression – but the desire for a united country was growing. After Vienna, the years were filled with riots, protests and finally revolution. The chief

players in the move for unification were the political agitator Giuseppe Mazzini (1805–72) and the inspired military leader Giuseppe Garibaldi (1807–82). Both were of the view that unification could be achieved by linking the royal and republican causes, but the man who played the dominant role was Count Camillo Cavour (1810–61). A Piedmontese landowner, Cavour first worked for political, industrial and agricultural reform through his newspaper, *Il Risorgimento*. In 1852, he became Prime Minister of Piedmont and forced the great powers to recognise the country by sending troops to the Crimea to support Britain and France. In 1859, at Plombière, Louis Napoleon pledged France's support if Austria attacked Piedmont. War came and the Austrians were defeated at Magenta and Solferino and the Peace of Villafranca united northern Italy under the leadership of Piedmont. But Italian unification was only half complete; so in 1860, with 1000 men, Garibaldi overthrew the Bourbons. Naples and Sicily fell within four months, the papal states surrendered and Cavour lived to see Victor Emmanuel of Piedmont proclaimed King of Italy in February 1861. The addition of Venice in 1866 and Rome in 1871 completed Italian unity.

World War I

Italy was neutral at the beginning of the Great War, but by 1915, on vague promises of colonial rewards and the chance to gain the partly Italian-speaking regions around Trento and Trieste, it joined the Allied cause alongside Britain and France. It carried out campaigns against the Austrians and its ill-equipped army suffered several defeats, before achieving a last-ditch victory at Vittorio Veneto. At the subsequent peace conference it gained the present-day

37

Trentino-Alto Adige and Friuli-Venezia Giulia, but at terrible cost. During the war, 40 per cent of the 5.5 million Italians mobilised were either killed or wounded and the national assets fell by 26 per cent.

Fascism and the rise of Mussolini

After World War I, Italy entered a period of great economic and social unrest. The unrest was a fertile breeding ground for Fascism and a threatened general strike proved the excuse Mussolini needed for his 'March on Rome' in 1922. Fearing civil war, the king refused to back the incumbent government and Benito Mussolini, with an intimidating mob presence on the streets, was installed as prime minister. By 1925, Italy was ruled by a dictatorship and Mussolini decided to remodel the state on Fascist lines.

To begin with he achieved a measure of success at home and, bolstered by foreign success with a successful invasion of Abyssinia, intervention in the Spanish Civil War and the conquest of Albania, he made Italy a junior partner in the Axis Coalition in World War II, with disastrous results. Continuous defeats at the hands of the Allies resulted in a loss of prestige at home and he was forced to resign in July 1943. He later set up a 'Republican Fascist' government in northern Italy, but in 1945 he was captured by partisans while attempting to flee to Switzerland. In April 1945 he was shot and his body strung up in the *Pzle Loreto* in Milan.

The Mafia

Italy's most high-profile export, which began in the 19th century in Sicily, now prevails on the mainland, too, albeit not on quite such a grand scale. Ironically, it came into being originally as the result of the foreign powers who ruled Italy being unable to guarantee law and order and Sicilian landowners made their own provision for the defence of their property and that of their dependents. Most landowners spent time away and rented their estates out to entrepreneurial foremen – *gabelloti* – who were able to extort favourable terms from the peasantry by intimidation. Mafia functioned by the code of *omerta* – silence – summed up in a graffiti message once spotted on a prison wall: 'He who neither speaks, nor sees, nor hears, lives in peace for a hundred years'. The Mafia lives on today, although it is most unlikely if any visitor would be aware of the fact from personal dealings.

Post-war Italy

From the ruins of the Fascist dictatorship at the end of World War II, Italy is now a democratic republic. But democracy has been achieved at some cost – the government changes with unseemly frequency. There have been more than 50 changes since 1946. The government is overseen by a largely symbolic president who is based at the Palazzo Chigi in Rome and underpinned by a decision-making lower house with around 630 deputies and an upper house with 315 senators. Over the years the government has been beset by a series of scandals which has reached the highest echelons of power. (At the time of writing, the former Prime Minister, Giulio Andreotti, is awaiting trial on charges related to alleged Mafia activities).

The country's 21 regions enjoy a degree of self-government and some, including Trento-Alto Adige and Valle d'Aosta in the north, are semi-autonomous. The regions are divided into *provincia* (provinces) and *comune* (local councils). The largest political party is the centre-right Christian-Democrats, which shares power with the Socialists, Republicans, Liberals and Social Democrats.

Italy is still characterised by the enormous contribution it has made to fashion and the arts. Milan is still the fashion centre of the world and the nation's love of the feel-good factor can be seen just by wandering down any city centre street, or observing the evening *passeggiata* (stroll). In the cinema, Rome's Cinecittà, which was opened by Mussolini in 1938, has become one of the greatest studios in the world. Italy has produced any number of films now considered classics, like Guazzoni's silent masterpiece *Quo Vadis?*, Fellini's distinctive *La Dolce Vita* and Antonioni's 1966 classic *Blow Up*.

In music, too, there have been outstanding contributions. The Etruscans were inveterate music lovers, using the Phrygian double pipe and the syrinx and, of course, the Italian composer Monteverdi is looked upon as the father of opera. Throw in Bellini, Donizetti and the great Verdi and it is small wonder that Italy and opera have become synonymous. It is estimated that 70 per cent of opera worldwide is performed in the Italian language; nowhere more stylishly than at La Scala in Milan.

But in the 1990s, on the broader stage of life itself, more changes are apparent. The Roman Catholic Church no longer has the hold it once had. Latest statistics reveal that, although 97 per cent of Italians are baptised, only about ten per cent go to mass on a regular basis. Divorce, abortion and birth control are widely available and the birth-rate is one of the lowest in Europe.

On the horizon, other challenges loom, not least the question of the north–south divide. Northern Italians have for many years been somewhat critical of their less affluent southern brethren – and now the criticisms are becoming increasingly more open and strident. New political parties are springing up and none is more vocal than the Leghe, a coalition of political groups trading on the traditional belief that, economically, the north is subsidising the south. They are in favour of a more federal state. Some people even talk about the possibility of a breakaway state in the north of the country, although few people believe this is ever likely to come about. What it illustrates, though, is a divide in Italian society which is not evident to those visiting the country.

But, wherever you are in Italy, some things never change. Northern Italians, just as much as their southern counterparts, are passionately loyal to family and friends. *La Familia* still counts for much, acting as an insurance policy in difficult times. It works for the family – and it can even work outside the family.

A British holiday-maker recently had the experience of finding a scratch down the side of the hire car he had left in an hotel car-park at Alassio in Liguria. Discovering he would be required to pay a considerable sum to the rental company, he took the car into a garage for repair. He struck up a conversation with the owner of the garage who repaired the car, and was then told there would be nothing to pay for the work which had been carried out.

Needless to say, the holiday-maker was moved by the experience. And the garage owner? He had done a good turn for someone he saw as a friend – a member of his extended family. Unwittingly perhaps, he had achieved more for Italy's tourist industry at a stroke than a multi-million lire public-relations effort could have achieved in a year. The charm and friendliness of the Italians is just as powerful an inducement to visiting this wonderful country as the country's splendid art, history, scenery, food and wine.

TOURING ITINERARIES

The car is a sorcerer's apprentice. It can either be your servant or your master – and the choice is yours. Familiarity with Italy and things Italian – its history, culture, landscape and, not least, food – have given devotees of this wonderful country a taste for exploration. The problem is that there are so many different permutations and whether travelling in your own or a hired vehicle, it is wise to plan meticulously to avoid disappointments.

In this book we have divided northern Italy into a series of routes linking the country's main centres with areas of outstanding interest and scenic beauty. Everyone's holiday goal will be different, but by linking several of the routes outlined in these pages it is possible to create your own holiday itinerary, confident in the knowledge that you will be following a tried and tested path. But our suggestions are not set in stone; feel free to mix and match itineraries to meet your own needs.

PRACTICAL HINTS

Here are a few tips to help make your motoring holiday easier and more fun.

1. Perhaps most importantly of all, don't attempt to cram too much into your itinerary. Don't rush from place to place; allow yourself time to savour that mountain view, that museum visit or simply to sip a cup of *cappuccino*.

Italy, more than most countries, is a place for relaxation as well as exploration.

2 Travel armed with the most detailed and up-to-date maps you can lay your hands on. The maps found in these pages offer basic details about the routes and cities included. Michelin's 1:400,000 map of northern Italy offers a good overall view of the area covered by the book. But, particularly if you want to travel off the beaten track, you will find the **Touring Club Italiano**'s excellent 1:200,000 maps of specific regions invaluable, as are the 1:250,000 maps produced by the **Automobile Club d'Italia,** which are available free from offices of the Italian State Tourist Office (ENIT– see Travel Essentials, page 21). If you are planning to do any walking, you'll need at least a 1:100,000 map and preferably either a 1:50,000 or even a 1:25,000. Northern Italy's major mountain areas are covered by **Studio FMB** and **TCI** maps, which are widely available in the resorts.

3. If you are travelling in winter or in the mountains, always check local weather conditions before you set out on your journey. In the mountains, some of the alpine roads are only open at certain times of the year. For example, the SS46 mountain road from Rovereto to Vicenza, which climbs to a height of about 1159 metres, is usually open throughout the year. But the SS49 Merano to Vipiteno road, rising to 2094 metres, wonderfully scenic but with many hairpin bends, is closed

40

from November to May. Local tourist offices can advise which roads are open and which have been closed because of adverse weather conditions.

4. Unless you have booked accommodation, always arrive with plenty of time to find a hotel room. In summer, hotels in the resorts are usually fairly full. Conversely, it is usually much easier to find a room in a business city such as Milan or Turin – but not in Florence or Venice, which have huge numbers of tourists, particularly in July and August. If you know the area and where you want to stay, book the hotel before you leave home. Many Italian resort hotels offer discounts for stays of three days or more.

5. At the end of the trip, allow plenty of time to get to your departing airport/rail station. Passengers travelling on cheap tickets who miss their flights often face having to buy a full-price ticket home. If you are travelling home on a motorail service, make sure you know which station the train is departing from. In Milan, there are three different stations – all in different parts of the city – and driving across town, particularly at rush hour, can be a hair-raising experience.

THE BEST OF NORTHERN ITALY

The following three suggested tours cover some or parts of routes (and connections) featured in this book and, between them, provide a balanced overview of northern Italy. But the tours are purely an outline and are not meant to be followed slavishly. Take the best from each tour and do not be afraid to divert in order to follow your own instincts or preferences. Tours one and two can be combined, but you may want to cut out one or two places to avoid presenting yourself with too punishing a schedule.

TOUR ONE – 7 DAYS

For those with restricted time, a tour which combines the scenic grandeur of the Ligurian coast – one of the most spectacular in Europe – with the culturally rich cities of Genoa, Pisa and Florence.

Day 1: **Genoa**.

Day 2: Travel leisurely down the coast to **Rapallo**, side-track to **Santa Margherita Ligure** and **Portofino**. Continue on to overnight in the pretty seaside resort of **Lévanto**.

Day 3: Motor on to **Monterossa al Mare,** the most northerly of the five Cinque Terre villages. Abandon the car and explore the villages on foot – a footpath runs along the coast all the way to Portovénere.

Day 4: Spend a day relaxing at the halfway point in the tour in one of the Cinque Terre villages.

Day 5: Travel on to **La Spezia** and then down the coast, using the *autostrada* to save time, to **Pisa.** Overnight in Pisa.

Day 6: Head east to **Florence,** on the way making a small diversion to Leonardo da Vinci's birthplace at **Vinci.** On arriving in Florence, drive up to the *Pza Michelangelo* for an impressive panoramic view of the city.

Day 7: Before flying home, take a walking tour around the city to see the main sites, such as the cathedral, the Ponte Vecchio, and the Uffizi and Accademia galleries.

TOUR TWO – 7 DAYS

A tour linking two of Italy's greatest cities – Florence and Rome – with an opportunity to stop off *en route* in the wonderful hill country of Tuscany and Lazio.

Day 1: **Florence**.

Day 2: Time to explore the city.

Day 3: Head south to **Siena**, home of the annual Palio festival. Behind its formidable medieval walls, Siena is a self-contained and still quite rural city – a contrast to Florence.

Day 4: Drive on to **Montepulciano**, at more than 600 m the highest of the Tuscan hill towns. Throw in **Orvieto** and you have two noble wine towns in one day!

Day 5: Continue on to **Rome** – an easy drive of 121 km.

Day 6: Take a tour of the 'Eternal City' taking in some of the key attractions, such as the Forum, the Colosseum and the Vatican City; plus some good restaurants.

Day 7: Rome.

Tour Three – 14 days

This tour begins in Verona and passes along the western shore of Lake Garda to Trento. It then continues up through Trentino–Alpe Adige, taking you along the spectacularly scenic Great Dolomite Road and Cortina d'Ampezzo, and then south through the Veneto to Venice.

Day 1: **Verona**.

Day 2: Verona to **Lake Garda**, the largest and most popular of the Italian lakes. Head along the southern shore of the lake to the village of **Sirmione,** jutting out into the lake on a peninsula.

Day 3: Drive up the west side of the lake to **Gardone Riviera,** one of the most attractive resorts on Garda.

Day 4: Continue up the west side via **Limone sur Garda** to **Riva,** at the northern end of the lake beneath towering Dolomite peaks.

Day 5: Follow the **Valley of the Lakes** north of Riva to **Trento,** former home of

Tips and Hints for a successful tour

Italy's biggest cities – Florence, Venice, Verona, Milan, Turin or Rome - are best toured without a car. If you include them in your driving itinerary, you will spend too much precious time coping with the traffic and finding somewhere to park. Instead, concentrate on rural Italy – Tuscany, Umbria and the Italian Lakes are ideal destinations for a week to ten-day tour.

the powerful Prince-Bishops of Trento.

Day 6: Travel north through the Adige Valley to **Bolzano (Bözen)**, stopping off *en route* for a wine tasting. Overnight in Bolzano.

Day 7: Head off along the Great Dolomite Road to **Canazei** and **Arabba,** within sight of Marmolada, at 3342 m the highest peak in the Dolomites.

Day 8: Continue along the Great Dolomite Road through some of northern Italy's finest scenery to **Cortina d'Ampezzo**, the Olympic winter-sports centre.

Day 9: In Cortina – time to explore one of Italy's most chic, if expensive, resorts.

Day 10: Drive east through the mountains to Pocol and then, following the Boite Valley, south-east to **Vittorio Veneto**, before joining the A27 *autostrada* for Venice.

Days 11 and 12: In **Venice**, soaking up the atmosphere and sightseeing in one of the world's great cities.

Day 13: Take time out to relax at Venice Lido, even if it isn't quite so smart as it was when Thomas Mann (and Visconti, the film director) set *Death in Venice* here.

Day 14: Venice.

GETTING TO ITALY

BY AIR

Flying offers the most direct and, in some cases, the cheapest way of reaching northern Italy. With many smaller airlines, such as **Air UK, Meridiana** and **AzzuraAir**, now joining the national airlines, **Alitalia** and **British Airways**, in offering regular flights, lower, more competitive fares are available, particularly for those prepared to travel outside peak times. Shop around for the best fly-drive deals and keep an eye on the travel pages of the newspapers for special offers.

CROSS CHANNEL/RAIL

With the opening of the Channel Tunnel, crossing the sea to France is no longer the problem it once was. **Le Shuttle** through the Channel Tunnel (24hr service, departures every 15 mins at peak periods) now means that you can put your car on the train in Folkestone and be in France 35 minutes later. This in turn has spurred competition over the sea, with ferry and hovercraft operators, **Hoverspeed, P&O European Ferries, Holyman Sally Ferries, SeaFrance** and **Stena Line**, offering not just lower fares but improved facilities on the short, eastern Channel crossings from Folkestone, Dover and Ramsgate to Boulogne, Calais, Dunkirk and Ostend. Once in France, the most expeditious way of reaching northern Italy in your own car is to use **Rail Europe's** motorail service, which allows you to travel overnight with your car direct from Calais to Nice (if your destination is northern Liguria), Bologna, Livorno, Milan, Rimini and Rome. Motorail is not cheap, but it avoids the hassle and cost (accom-

modation, meals, petrol, motorway charges, etc.) of travelling across France, allowing you to arrive fresh and in a fit state to start your holiday. Motorway tolls alone can add as much as £30 in each direction to the cost of the holiday.

CROSS CHANNEL/ SELF-DRIVE

The shortest route from the Channel to Italy is probably the Alpine route via Germany and Switzerland, but many people prefer to drive to the south of France and enter Italy via the Riviera. In the UK, both the **AA** *(tel: 01256 20123)* and the **RAC** *(tel: 0800 500 055, toll-free)* provide comprehensive route-planning services. If you are driving all the way, go with sufficient insurance, not just for yourself but for the vehicle. Breakdown insurance typically works out at around £50 for basic cover for 14 days. A European motoring kit, which contains all the legally required accessories, such as advance warning triangle and spare bulbs, is also beneficial and is available from the motoring organisations from around £33.

By road, the main points of entry are, from France, via the **Riviera motorway** into Liguria, or the **Mont Blanc Tunnel** at Chamonix, which connects with the A5 for Turin and Milan. Alternatively, from Switzerland, you can take the **Great St Bernard Tunnel**, which also connects with the A5, or, from Austria, the **Brenner Pass**, which links with the A22 to Bologna. If you are travelling in winter, bear in mind that the mountain passes through the Alps are frequently closed because of bad weather.

43

TRIESTE-GEMONA

Gemona del Friúli

S13

Cividale del Friúli

S54

Udine

S356

S56 **Gorizia**

ROUTE: 132 KM

S55

Sistiana

Trieste

This route links three of Friúli's past and present key towns. Trieste is the grandest in every sense, a once-great Istrian port in a dramatic setting between sea and sky, but much diminished by 20th century events. Cividale del Friúli, once the ancient capital of the Lombards, is now a charming backwater but retains important historical treasures. Udine, on few tourist itineraries, is the new capital of Friúli, modern and confident but with an attractive old heart to show visitors.

ROUTE

From the Trieste waterfront turn inland onto *V. Milano* and go across *V. Carducci* into *V. del Coroneo* which leads up a steep hill to Opicina. Just before the town of Opicina (after about 11 km) look for the first sign (left) to the **Grotta Gigante**. Keep your eyes peeled and drive slowly as there are several more signs to follow for the next 3–4 km and they are not prominent. From the Grotta Gigante head back towards Opicina, and follow the signs to join the *autostrada*. After about 12 km take the turn off down to the N14 scenic coast road and to **Sistiana**, a popular seaside resort set in a picturesque bay. 3 km further on is the landmark Castle of Duino (closed to the public). Turn off the coast road onto the S55 to **Gorizia** (22 km). From Gorizia take the S56 towards Udine and turn off right after around 10.5 km on the S356 to **Cividale del Friúli** (19.5 km). Take the S54 17 km west to reach **Udine**. Take the S13 (signposted Tarvisio/ Austria) for 27 km, turn off right and drive for 3.5 km to **Gemona del Friúli**.

TRIESTE

Tourist Office: *rail station; tel: 420182,* open Mon–Fri 0900–1900, Sat 0830–1330.

GETTING AROUND

The main square of Trieste is the *Pza Unità d'Italia*. From here the Capitoline Hill is a short bus ride (or a strenuous walk) directly behind the Piazza and most other points of interest are within a 10-min walk. However, the two biggest attractions, the Castello di Miramare, (see p. 51) and the Grotta Gigante, (see p. 47), are outside the town.

Public Transport

Tram di Opicina (see feature on p. 49).

Ferries

There are regular sailings to the Adriatic lagoon resorts of Grado (1 hr) and Lignano Sabbiadoro (75 mins); to the Istrian peninsular resorts of Pirano (Slovenia), Parenzo, Rovigno and Brioni (all Croatia) and to Lussinpiccolo in the Gulf of Quarnero. Reservations, call **Trieste–Agemar**, *Pza Duca degli Abbruzi; tel: (040) 363737,* also office at *Pza Unità d'Italia 6; tel: (040) 631300.* **Anek Lines** run four weekly car ferries to Greece (Igoumenitsa, Patras and Corfu); *tel: 363242.*

Communications

The post office is at *Pza Vittorio Veneto 1.* Telephone code for Trieste is *040.*

EVENTS

The biggest event of the year is the **Coppa d'Autumno (Autumn Cup) Regatta**, also known as the *Barcolana*, held on the second Sunday in Oct. It is contested by over 1000 sailing vessels, ranging from small, lightweight craft to boats in excess of 20 m. With bright, billowing

sails set against the backdrop of the Trieste corniche and Miramare Castle, it is an extremely picturesque event. Several other sailing events also decorate the shoreline from the middle of Sept onwards.

An **International Operetta Festival** is held between June and Aug at the Teatro Verdi. See *Discovering Trieste* for listings.

ACCOMMODATION

There are plenty of cheap options: just ask at the tourist office. Chain hotels in Trieste include: Starhotels.

For old-fashioned luxury, the waterfront **Starhotel Savoia Excelsior Palace** (expensive) is hard to beat, *Riva del Mandracchio 4; tel: (040) 77941.*

HI: **Ostello Tegeste**, *Vle Miramare; tel: (040) 224102,* is by the Castello di Miramare, some 7 km from the city centre. It draws a young and lively crowd and occupies a superb position with sea views. The latter is also true for **Camping Obelisco**, *Strada Nuova Opicina; tel: (040) 211655 or 212744* . Take the tram to the Obelisco stop from where the campsite is a short (signposted) walk.

EATING AND DRINKING

The most famous café in town is the Viennese-style **Caffè degli Specchi** in *Pza Unità*, though the oldest is the **Tommaseo** on *Riva 3 Novembre*, established in 1830. James Joyce (who lived in Trieste for some 12 years) patronised the **Caffè Pasticceria Pirona** at Largo Barriera Vecchia and it is said that it was here he conceived *Ulysses*. For other dining (and nightlife) venues pick up *Discovering Trieste* from the tourist office. There is a branch of the ever-reliable **Brek** at *V. San Francesco 10.*

An Eastern European flavour is often imparted to the Trieste menu with meat

45

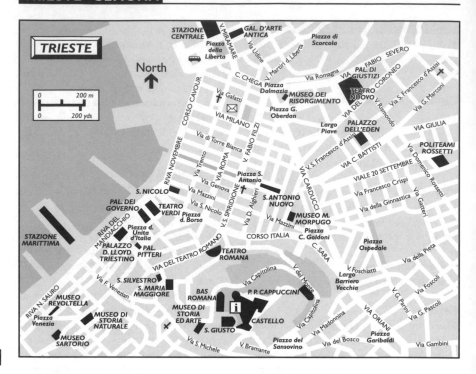

TRIESTE

North ↑

| 0 | 200 m |
| 0 | 200 yds |

dishes such as goulash and roast pork while the local fish speciality is grilled *sardoni in savor* (marinated sardines). Finish the meal off with strudel, a reminder of Trieste's Austro-Hungarian past.

SHOPPING

V. Carducci and **Corso Italia** are the two main shopping streets. The former hosts a general daily market (Tues–Sat). There is an **antique market** on the third Sun of each month at Cittavecchia.

SIGHTSEEING

The Capitoline Hill

The easy way to see the hill is to take bus 24 (from the seafront) up then walk down. If you are feeling energetic, however, the **Scala dei Giganti** is a monumental staircase which ascends the hill from the

western side (from *Pza Goldoni*), and the reward is some great views *en route*. The **Castello di San Giusto** occupies the very top of the hill and dates back to the 15th century. It now holds part of the **Civico Museo** collection of furnishings, weapons and armour, open Tues–Sun (Apr–Sept) Castle 0900–1900, Museum 0900–1300. Entrance fee L2000. Alongside is the 14th-century **Cattedrale**, a combination of two ancient churches, built in the 11th century and 5th century respectively. It features some excellent **mosaics** with the ones on the apses in the Venetian style, reminiscent of Torcello Cathedral. A few metres downhill is the **Museo di Storia de Arte e Orto Lapidario** (Museum of Art History and Stone Fragments Garden) *V. Cattedrale 5*; open 0900–1300 (Tues–Sun). Entrance fee L2000. This features Egyptian art and

Greek vases and examines the history of Trieste up to and including its Roman period. The best Roman remains are close by; alongside the castle is the **Basilica** (law court), with re-erected columns, and at the foot of the hill, on the seaward side, you can see into (but not visit) the **Teatro Romano**, a well-preserved amphitheatre.

Lower Town

The focus of attention (just below the Teatro Romano) is the monumental **Pza Unità d'Italia**, claimed to be the biggest *piazza* in Italy, but often derided for the heavy-handed, anonymous quality of its architecture. The piazza opens out onto the **seafront**, where large ocean liners and naval ships often lay at berth. Trieste was once the principal seaport of the Austro–Hungarian Empire and its scale at least is still impressive. On the Molo Pescheria (to the left facing the sea) you can see the sea's harvest both at the market place and in the **Aquario Marino** (Sea Aquarium), open 0900–1900 (Tues–Sun). Entrance fee L5000. Almost opposite, set back two blocks from the waterside, are the city's two principal art collections: the **Civico Museo Sartorio**, *Largo Papa Giovanni XXIII 1;* open 0900–1300 (Tues–Sun), entrance fee L3000; and the **Museo Revoltella e Galleria d'Arte Moderna**, *V. Diaz 27,* open (Tues–Sun) 1000–1300,1500–2000, closed Tues and Sun afternoons. Entrance fee L2000. Both encompass a wide range of works.

To the other side of the *Pza Unità d'Italia* is the **Canal Grande**, a pompously named short stretch of canal which stretches three blocks inland. Alongside, the impressive, blue-domed Greek church of **San Spiridone** is worth a visit. There are several other small, mostly specialist, museums around the town (see *Discovering Trieste* for details).

Grotta Gigante

The Grotta Gigante (Giant Cave) is well named, as its main chamber is 130 m long, 65 m wide and 107 m high, capable of swallowing up the Basilica of St Peter's in Rome. It is the largest cave in the world accessible to the general public and it is the sheer scale that will remain in the memory when its stalactites and stalagmites are forgotten. The cave is also used as a seismological research station. Two 105 m long steel cables, wrapped in plastic tubing for protection, are suspended from the ceiling and pick up the earth's most minute movements and tremors. Admission is by guided tour, which takes around 45 mins, and there is a pre-recorded commentary in English, which is activated at certain points along the tour.

The cave is open Tues–Sun and tours take place every 30 mins 0900–1200, 1400–1900 (Apr–Sept); last tour 1700 (Mar-Oct); and tours hourly 1000–1200, 1430–1630 (Nov–Feb). Entrance fee L9000.

GORIZIA

Tourist Office: *V. Diaz 16; tel: (0481) 533870,* open Mon–Fri 0900–1300 and 1600–1800; 1500–1700 (winter).

Gorizia has been in the frontline of border conflicts for centuries as you will learn by visiting its **castle**. All but destroyed in World War I, it was faithfully reconstructed to its medieval form in the 1930s complete with a beautiful courtyard, dark and pokey prisons, torture rooms, a graceful hall used as an art exhibition area, a frescoed chapel and a handsome airy granary room. Captions in English relate the castle's often violent history.

The patrol walk offers excellent views over the town, open Tues–Sun 0930–1300 and 1500–1930 (Apr–Sept); 0930–1230 and 1400–1700; weekends opens 1030 (Oct–Mar). Entrance fee L8000.

For more on the region's turbulent recent history visit the **Museu Provincial** which includes the excellent **Museo della Grande Guerra** (Museum of the Great War). Videos, photographs and life-size mock-ups of World War I trenches bring home the horrors (and heroism) of the terrible conflict. The museum is next door to the castle entrance, within its grounds, open Tues–Sun 1000–1800. Entrance fee L12,000.

CIVIDALE DEL FRIÚLI

Tourist Office: *Largo Boiani 4; tel: (0432) 731398*, open Mon–Fri 0900–1300 and 1500–1700/1800.

You enter Cividale across the high narrow 15th-century Ponte del Diavolo (Devil's Bridge). Turn right and park in the *Pza del Duomo* outside the **Museo Archeologico Nazionale**. As well as the usual Roman tablets there are interesting Lombard remains, some splendid 16th-century reliquary busts and the superb Roman bronze head of Zuglio, open Tues–Sat 0930–1230, Sun morning only. Entrance fee L4000.

The pride of the adjacent **Duomo** is its early 13th-century silver altarpiece. Attached is the **Museo Cristiano** which features two masterpieces from the 8th-century. The **Battistero di Callisto** is a beautifully carved and decorated large octagonal baptismal font, while the **Altar of Ratchis** contains fine carvings of scenes from the life of Christ. Museum open daily 0930–1200 and 1500–1900, entrance free. Opposite the Duomo is the charming medieval **Palazzo Communale** and a statue of Julius Caesar, who founded the town in 50 BC.

Turn left out of the Duomo and follow the sign, left, to the Tempietto

The Lombardic Style

Udine and Cividale del Friúli have many churches built in the style known as Lombardic, after the Lombards, Germanic tribesmen from the Danube valley, who invaded northern Italy in the 6th century, and established an important principality. Superb examples of their armour and jewellery can be seen in the museums in Cividale, and in Verona. They embraced Christianity in the 8th century, and founded many churches and abbeys in a style which owes something to Romanesque, but which has its own style: carvings of man-eating lions are commonly found at the entrance to Lombardic churches, and fonts and pulpits are boldly carved with mythical beasts.

Longobardo, through the narrow cobbled streets alongside the river. Note the tiny Casa Medioevale *en route*. The **Tempietto Longobardo** (Lombard Temple) is a gloriously decorated tiny atmospheric chapel with wonderfully rare carved stucco reliefs of virgin saints. It is the most precious work of the 8th century in all Italy. *Pza San Biagio*, open daily 0900–1300 and 1500–1830, entrance fee L2000.

Walk back to the main street and cross the **Ponte del Diavolo** to enjoy the classic picture-postcard view of the city.

Follow the main street Corso Mazzini (back past the *Pza del Duomo*) to the **Pza P Diacono**, the social centre of town and enjoy some local refreshments at the venerable **Caffè Langobardo**.

UDINE

Tourist Office: *Pza 1 Maggio 7; tel: (0432) 504743*, open Mon–Sat 0900–1300 and 1500–1800.

Exploring the Carso

The easiest way of seeing the Carso, the limestone plateau which sits above Trieste and extends into neighbouring Slovenia, is to ride the splendid Opicina Tramway route which dates from 1902. You sit in an old blue tram with wooden seats, which is hauled at a dizzying angle up the slopes of the Carso behind the city by a funicular traction engine (departs from *Pza Obidan* every 22 mins, tickets from the *tabacchi* (tobacconists) by the tram stop). The views of Trieste against the brilliant blue Adriatic, changing perspective at every twist and turn, are stunning. Most tourists ride to the terminus at Opicina then visit the Grotta Gigante cave (see page 47). As an alternative get off at the Obelisco stop and enjoy a straight, level walk along a peaceful cliff-top path known as the Napoleonica. The path continues north for 5 km to the village of Prosecco (above Miramare) so you will have to retrace your steps if you want to return to Obelisco. The pathway offers marvellous views along much of its length; far below is the landmark Faro della Vittoria (Victory Lighthouse), while high above is the brilliant white, ultra-modern triangular church of Santuario di Monte Grisa/Tempio Mariano, built in 1959.

Park at the *Pza 1 Maggio* and walk up the castle hill to enjoy the views over the town. The 16th-century castle is now home to the **Museo del Castello** and the **Galleria d'Art Antica** featuring works by Tiepolo, Pordenone, Caravaggio and Carpaccio, open Tues–Sun 0930–1230 and 1500–1800, Sun closed afternoon, entrance fee L4000. Walk down the other side of the castle hill to emerge onto the **Loggia di San Giovanni** facing the **Pza della Libertà**. This glorious architectural ensemble pays homage to Venice who conquered the city in 1420. The loggia features a **Torre dell'Orlogio** (clock tower), built in 1527, with two Moors who strike the hours (à la San Marco in Venice), plus fountains, statues of Hercules and Justice, and the obligatory Lion of St Mark. Opposite, the beautiful, pink-and-white striped brickwork of the **Loggia del Lionello**, built in 1448, echoes the Doge's Palace. Behind is the **Municipo** (town hall) housed in the handsome Palazzo d'Aronco. Turn right past here into **Pza Matteoti**, a delightful arcaded square graced by the church of San Giacomo, with its early 16th century facade in the Lombardic style.

Head back to the **Duomo**, which features paintings by Giambattista Tiepolo though it is his frescos in the **Oratorio della Purità** (on the opposite side of the road, ask in the cathedral for admission) and in the **Palazzo Arcivescoville** which are his masterworks in Udine. *Pza del Patriarcato*, open Wed–Sun 1000–1200 and 1530–1830, entrance fee L7000.

Of the town's other museums, the Museo delle Arti e Tradizione Populari, and the Cathedral Museum (in the campanile), are both closed at time of writing. Check at the tourist office.

Accommodation is relatively easy to find. A convenient drivers' option is **Hotel La'Di Moret**, (expensive) on the main road north, and less than a 5-min drive to the centre of town, *Vle Tricesmo 276; tel: (0432) 545096*. It also features a swimming pool and tennis court and is famous for the quality of its food (expensive), for which it has won numerous awards. There are many other good restaurants in the city centre.

49

TRIESTE–VENICE

The Venetian Gulf and its hinterland have something for almost everyone; the dramatic Trieste corniche and a romantic, melancholy castle; seaside fun at Grado; magnificent mosaics and Roman remains at Aquileia; the rolling wine hills of Prosecco around Conegliano; and the charm and style of Treviso, whose canals whet the appetite for Venice.

ROUTE: 237 KM

Vittorio Véneto–
Padua p. 58

Vittorio Veneto — Pordenone

P71   S13

S51   S252   Palmanova

Conegliano   S352

Susegana

S13   Aquileia

Treviso   Grado   Castello del Miramare

Mestre   Trieste

Venice

50

ROUTE

From the centre of Trieste take the coast road north-west for 7.5 km to **Castello del Miramare** (see box feature, opposite). In summer the whole of this stretch is lined with the parked cars of holiday-mak-ers who sunbathe on the roadside promenade; there is access to the sea at many points but there is no beach.

Continue on the coast road, admiring (with care) the wonderful sea views, particularly down to the marina of Sistiana. Skirt the industrial port of Monfalcone

Castello Del Miramare

Miramare is famous for its beautiful white castle, perched on the very edge of the Adriatic, commissioned by the Habsburg Emperor Maximilian in 1856. Despite its strategic position it was built purely as a family home and is devoid of any defensive capabilities. Although the castle was not to be completed in his lifetime, Maximilian lived here, on and off, until 1864 when political intrigues led to his appointment as Emperor of Mexico. From the peace and security of Miramare Maximilian entered a volatile and complex political cauldron. His agrarian reforms helped the peasants at the expense of landowners who rebelled against his rule and in June 1867 he was captured and executed. The castle was finally finished in 1870 and acquired the legend of putting a curse on anyone sleeping under its roof. The Archduke Franz Ferdinand slept here in 1914 *en route* to his assassination in Sarajevo (the incident which precipitated World War I), and premature death also came to the Duke of Aosta who owned the castle in the 1930s. When the Allies liberated the castle from the Germans (who were using it as a headquarters) in 1945, a New Zealand general took the legend seriously enough to camp out in the grounds.

A melancholy charm still attends the castle whose rooms, preserved in their original condition, reflect Maximilian's love of the sea – his bedroom is an intriguing panelled replica of a ship's cabin – and of exotic places, most notably the Japanese and Chinese salon. Each is well captioned in English. Around the castle the emperor also commissioned a beautiful park with flowers, water features, pavilions and views of the glorious riviera, open daily 0900–1800 (summer); 0900–1700 (Oct and Mar); 0900–1600 (winter), entrance fee L8000. For the full romantic treatment attend one of the summer Luci e Suoni (light and sound) shows where a narrator relates the tragic tale of Maximilian. On certain nights, music (classical, operetta or jazz) adds a further atmospheric dimension to the show, entrance fee L10,000; concert nights L15,000. Shows are in English on certain nights, ask for details at the Trieste tourist office (see page 45) or tel: (040) 638020.

51

(28km from Trieste) and turn left towards Grado, passing through cypress avenues and Grado Pineta (Grado Pinewoods), where there are campgrounds. Note in the lagoon to your right, the picturesque tiny island of Santa Maria di Barbana. From **Grado** a narrow causeway across the Adriatic Lagoon points due north for 6 of the 11km to **Aquileia**. Continue due north on the S352 for 28km to **Palmanova**. Leave Palmanova by the same gate through which you entered, heading back to Grado and after less than 1km turn right on the S252 and stay on here for some 50km to **Pordenone**. Take the S13 for 18km to Cordignano, then the

P71 13km west to **Vittorio Véneto**. Take the S51 south for 13km to **Conegliano**. Take the S13 south for 5km and to your right, perched on a hillside, are the dramatic fortifications of **Susegana**.

Return to the S13 and continue south for another 23km to **Treviso**. Keep on the S13 for a further 18km where the smokestacks and industrial skyline of **Mestre** and Marghera offers an inauspicious welcome to the Venetian lagoon. The S11 leads south 5km to **Venice**.

GRADO

Tourist Office: *Vle Dante 72; tel: (0431)*

8991, open Mon–Sat 0900–1300 and 1500–1800. Closed Sun pm.

Once a major Roman port serving Aquileia (see below) these days Grado is a popular seaside playground and thermal spa, attracting German, Austrian and local sun lovers. Fishing is also very important to the town (though pleasure boats are almost as numerous as working vessels) and Grado is known for its fish restaurants.

In appearance, Grado borrows a little from other Venetian islands. Its beaches and modern commercial areas resemble Lido, its older parts hint at Venice and Torcello, and as on Burano, fishing boats lie at anchor next to houses. There are two **beach** areas, both on the south of the island. The one by the hotels is narrow, congested and only the far end where it is backed by pines is appealing. The other beach is a broad expanse sitting in a man-made bay. Both stretches of sand are a rather murky grey, despite the resort's 'golden island' tag. Grado's most bizarre seaside activity is the thermal 'cure' of baking clients in the sand, so that only their head is above ground! The lure for non-sunbathing, non-spa visitors is the old centre where the atmospheric **Duomo** contains 6th-century mosaics. Note too its fine pulpit. Close by there are more mosaics of similar age to admire in the church of **Santa Maria delle Grazie**.

An enjoyable excursion is a boat trip on the lagoon to the **Isoli di Barbana**. *En route* you will spot rustic *casoni* (traditional thatched fishermen's cottages) and hopefully some of the lagoon wildlife, including herons.

AQUILEIA

Tourist Office: *Pza Capitolo* (next to the Basilica); *tel: (0431) 919491*, open Fri–Wed 0900–1300 and 1600–1800 (Apr–earlyNov); daily 1430–1800 (Nov– Mar).

Built by the Romans as a bulwark against the warring tribes to the east, Aquileia flourished as a major trading centre, thanks in large part to its outer port facility (now the town of Grado, see above). The Barbarian invasions put an end to its wealth and although the city recovered partially during the Middle Ages, the silting up of its river proved its death knell. Today it is little more than a village trading on its rich Roman heritage.

There are several sites to visit but the unmissable one is the **Basilica**. Built and rebuilt many times since the early 4th-century the present building is mainly of Romanesque and Gothic styles. It is a large and handsome structure with a 14th-century ship's bottom-style roof and great Gothic arcades, but what makes it outstanding is its **mosaic floor** – the largest early Christian example in Westen Europe, surpassing anything even Rome has to offer (see panel). It also features a magnificent **frescoed crypt** which was painted in the 12th century and depicts in glowing colours early Christian historical episodes. There is another crypt, **Cripta degli Scavi** ('The Crypt of the Excavated Finds'), where there are more superb floor mosaics.

The bell tower displays the most recently found mosaics, only discovered in the 1970s, and it's a good idea to climb to the top (armed with a free map of Aquileia, from the tourist office). From this 73 m high vantage point you can clearly see the remains below, and therefore get an idea of how the Roman town was arranged. In the distance is the Adriatic lagoon to the south and the pre-Alps to the north.

Basilica open daily 0830–1900. Entrance: Basilica free; single ticket to both crypts L3000; bell tower L2000.

Adjacent to the Basilica is the **Museo**

The Mosaics of Aquileia

The mosaic floor of the Basilica in Aquileia dates back to the original early 4th-century church and covers approximately 760sqm. To negotiate your way around pick up the excellent *Visitors Shortened Guide* pamphlet.

You will soon discover that many of the mosaics are symbols which were used secretly by early Christians to avoid persecution. The fish is perhaps the best known symbol, still widely used today to denote Christ or a Christian. Other symbols, however, are much less familiar; brightly plumaged birds, such as peacocks, symbolise eternal life in Heaven, whereas the 'Battle Scene between the Cock and the Turtle' represents the forces of good and evil.

Other scenes represent Biblical episodes and most visitors' favourite is Jonah and the Whale or, in this case, Jonah and a strange looking sea monster. This too has a hidden meaning with Jonah's escape symbolising the resurrection, while the adjacent scene, of Jonah resting beneath a pumpkin bower, refers to the ascent of Jesus into Heaven.

Don't be too anxious about finding meanings in every tile, however, the mosaics are enjoyable works of art in their own right. They have survived in such splendid condition because they were covered in clay, then by the medieval floor, and only rediscovered early this century.

Civico (Patriarch's Civic Museum). *Via Popone*. Open Tues–Fri 0900–1200. Sat, Sun 0900–1230 and 1430–1800. Entrance fee L5000. A few metres away (off the main road) is the **Museo**

Archeologico Nazionale. *V Roma 1*. Open daily 0900–1400 (winter); 0900–1700 (summer). Entrance fee L5000.

From the Basilica a walking trail leads to the main excavated sites including the large baths and the impressive 350m long *porto fluviale* (the old river docks). On the opposite side of the river the **Museo Paleocristiano** occupies another ancient basilica, *Località Monastero*. Open daily 0900–1400. Entrance free.

Most prominent of all the remains are the standing columns and fallen statuary which mark the site of the old **Forum**, now bisected by the Grado–Aquileia road. All sites open daily dawn–dusk, free entrance.

PALMANOVA

Tourist Office: *Civico Museo Storico* (**see below**)*; tel: (0432) 923535*. Open Mon–Fri 0900–1300 and 1600–1800, Sat 0900–1300.

53

Palmanova is a unique surviving example of a perfectly symmetrical, star-shaped, fortified town. It was built in the 16th century to fend off marauding Turks and Habsburgs with gun batteries at each of the nine points which make up its star shape, and alongside defensive ditches. It was besieged just once, in 1848. Monumental gates provide just three narrow entrances (from Grado you enter through the Porta Aquileia) which converge on the handsome and perfectly hexagonal **Pza Grande** with its **Duomo**, elegant *palazzi* and *loggias*. Without the benefit of an aerial view it's difficult to visualise the unique shape of Palmanova so a visit to the small **Civico Museo Storico** is essential. Corner of *Pza Grande* and Borgo Udine. Open daily 1000–1200 and 1500–1800. Entrance fee L3000. If you want to learn more about the town's fortifications the **Museo Storico**

Militare (Military Museum) occupies part of the Porta Cividale at the Cividale exit of the town. Open daily 0900–1200 and 1600–1800 (summer); 1400–1600 (winter). Entrance free.

> **↱ SIDE TRACK**
> **FROM PALMANOVA**

Around 23km west of Palmanova, just before Codroipo, you will see signs for **Villa Manin**, one of the largest of all the Venetian villas, built in 1738. It was the residence of the last doge of Venice, Lodovico Manin, and Napoleon stayed here for a while. There is a good collection of weapons though most of the rooms are now empty and used to stage exhibitions. Open Tues–Sun 0930–1230 and 1400–1700. Entrance fee L5000. Continue on through Codroipo, onto the S13, 32 km to Pordenone. ⬔

54

PORDENONE

Tourist Office: *Corso Vittorio Emanuele; tel: (0434) 521218.* Open Mon–Fri 1000–1250 and 1630–1800, Sat 1000–1250.

Although it is a busy provincial capital, for sightseeing purposes old Pordenone is basically one street, the handsome pedestrianised **Corso Vittorio Emanuele**. This is a long stretch of porticoed buildings (some dating back 500 years and retaining original frescos) which comes to a beautiful finale at the charming Gothic 13th-century **Palazzo Communale** (town hall). Admire its 16th-century clock while enjoying a coffee at the venerable Caffè Municipio. Opposite, housed in a 15th-century *palazzo*, is the **Museo Civico** which displays works by the town's most famous son, Il Pordenone. Open Tues–Sun 0930–1230 and 1530–1830. Entrance fee L5000. Just around the corner the **Duomo** features an altarpiece

by the same artist. Its 72m landmark campanile, reminiscent of St Mark's in Venice, is a superb piece of Romanesque brickwork.

There are some very elegant shops and good-looking eating establishments along the Corso Vittorio Emanuele. If you are on a budget try **City Self-Service**, *V. Borgo San Antonio* (running parallel to the Corso, off *V. Mazini*, at the *Pza Cavour* end of the street).

VITTORIO VÉNETO

Tourist Office: *Pza del Popolo 18; tel: (0438) 57243.* Open Mon–Sat 1000–1300 and 1600–1800.

In 1866 Vittorio Véneto was formed by the union of the two separate towns of Cèneda (below) and Serravalle (above). Each still has its own individual characteristics. Cèneda is the less interesting commercial part of the city, but still worth a visit for its elegant 16th-century Loggia del Sansovino which houses the **Museo della Battaglia** (Museum of the Battle). The conflict in question was the final battle of World War I on Italian soil, fought here in October 1918. *Pza Giovanni Paolo I.* Open Tues–Sun 1000–1200 and 1630–1830 (May–Sept); and 1000–1200 and 1400–1700 (Oct–Apr). Entrance fee L5000, includes entrance to Museo del Cenedese and San Lorenzo dei Battuti, (see below). The grounds of the **Castello di San Martino** which towers above the town and dates from the Longobard period are also open.

The upper walled town of Serravalle occupies a romantic picture-book location at the foot of a gorge and, with its cobbled porticoed streets and numerous *palazzi*, served as a backdrop for Zeffirelli's film version of Romeo and Juliet. The *Pza Flaminio* is the centre of town where the Palazzo della Communità (town hall) hosts the **Museo del Cenedese**. Open Wed–Mon 1000–1200 and 1630–1830 (May–Sept); 1000–1200 and 1500–1700 (Oct–Apr). Entrance fee, see above, (Museo della Battaglia). On the same square is also the **Duomo** featuring an altarpiece by Titian. Nearby, near the town's south gate, is the flagellant's church of **San Lorenzo dei Battuti**, entirely covered in a remarkable 15th-century fresco cycle. *Pza Vecellio*. Open daily: same hours and entrance ticket as Museo del Cenedese.

CONEGLIANO

Tourist Office: *Via Colombo 45; tel: (0438) 21230.* Open Mon–Sat 1000–1300.

Conegliano has two main claims to fame. It is the wine capital of the Veneto and the birthplace of the great painter, Cima de Conegliano. Its sights lie on and just above **V. XX Septembre**, the beautifully preserved, arcaded and cobbled historic main street. This is lined with *palazzi* dating from the 15th to the 17th centuries, including Conegliano's acclaimed wine school which is the oldest in Italy (no admission). The street's major landmark is its imposing 19th-century **Teatro Accademia**, set back on the large *Pza G. B. Cima* and guarded by bizarre half-woman, half-lion statues. Adjacent is the **Casa di Cima**, the house where the painter was born. Today it is devoted to a display of reproductions of his greatest works. *V. Cima 24*, open Thur 0900–1200 and 1530–1900, Sat 1530–1900, Sun 1000–1200 and 1530–1900 (summer); Thur 0900–1200 and 1500–1800, Sat 1530–1800, Sun 1000–1200 and 1530–1800 (winter). Note: hours may vary, *tel: (0438) 21660* Fondazione Cima, to confirm. Entrance fee L2000. To see one of Cima's originals visit the 14th-century **Duomo** next door, where his altarpiece

Virgin and Child with Saints is acclaimed as one of his finest works. Attached to the Duomo is the **Scuola di Sta Maria dei Battuti** which features some excellent frescos (open Sun 1500–1900, other days except Wed 0900–1200 but must *tel: (0438) 22606* in advance. Entrance fee L3000, includes Museo Civico, see below).

It's a 10–15mins walk up the hill behind the theatre, along the processional route of *V. Madonna delle Nevi*, to the **Castello di Conegliano**. The views from the castle terrace are magnificent, sweeping over the hilly winelands of Prosecco. There is also a very pleasant café-restaurant where you can sit down with a cool drink and take it all in. The castle keep now houses the **Museo Civico** and retains some medieval rooms complete with suits of armour, frescos by Il Pordenone and paintings of the Cima school. From its roof the 360-degree views are even better than down below. Open Tues–Sun 1000–1230 and 1530–1900 (Apr–Sept); 1000–1230 and 1500–1830 (Oct and Dec–Mar). Entrance fee L3000, includes admission to Scuola di Santa Maria dei Battuti (see above).

The best place to eat in Conegliano is the **Canon d'Oro** which specialises in regional cuisine (moderate–expensive). *V. XX Septembre 129; tel: (0438) 34246.* It is also a pleasant place to stay the night (moderate price). Its modern-style rooms are unremarkable but it boasts a lovely garden. Another recommended eating option is the **Casa del Re**, Chinese restaurant. Corner of *V. Carducci and Corso Vittorio Emanuele; tel: (0438) 22122.* Budget–moderate price.

⇄ SIDE TRACK
FROM CONEGLIANO
Oenophiles may like to note that the

55

Castello also marks the start of the picturesque **Strada del Vino Bianco** (White Wine Road) which heads west from here for 40km to Valdobbiadene (see page 60). Along the way vineyards offer sampling opportunities and at San Pietro di Feletto (after 7km) the parish church features beautiful 15th-century frescos. ⬛

SUSEGANA

This small hill town is dominated by the striking **Castello di San Salvatore**, one of the largest surviving medieval fortified complexes in Italy. Open daily 0930–1100. Entrance free.

Adjacent is the **Museo dell'Uomo** (Museum of Man), an interesting local ethnographical collection with features on wine and farming. *V. Barriera 35*. Open Tues–Sun 0900–1200 and 1400–1900. Entrance fee L3500.

TREVISO

Tourist Office: *Pza Monte de Pietà* (behind the *Pza dei Signori*); *tel: (0422) 547632*. Open Mon–Fri 0830–1230 and 1500–1800, Sat 0830–1200. Pick up the excellent free city map.

ACCOMMODATION AND FOOD

Treviso is a wealthy town, used to daytrippers but not so well geared to overnight tourism, and budget hotels are sparse. The best is **Beccherie**, small and friendly, and located right in the historic heart of town. *Pza Ancilotto 10; tel: (0422) 540871*.

For good cheap fish dishes and typical Venetian cooking, right by the fish market, visit the basic, friendly **Trattoria Al Calice d'Oro**. *V. Pescheria 5; tel: (0422) 544762*.

A branch of **Brek** can be found at *Corso del Popolo 25*.

SIGHTSEEING

The provincial capital of Treviso is full of charm, character and historical interest, and merits a leisurely full-day visit. The old centre is small and easily covered on foot.

Start at the *Pza dei Signori*, dominated by the landmark **Palazzo dei Trecento**, the 13th-century town hall, its lower arcade now home to a bustling café. Alongside is the **Palazzo del Podestà** with its huge tower. Both buildings have been part-reconstructed, following a devastating air raid in 1944 which destroyed around half of the old town in just a few minutes. Behind here a warren of alleyways leads through the colourful fruit, vegetable and flower markets to the **fish market** (*pescheria*, open Tues–Fri). It is situated on a small river island so that at the end of each day's trading it can be easily flushed clean.

Look across from the island to **Vicolo Molinetto** where an old mill wheel is still turning. Treviso was once the centre for milling wheat to supply Venice with its bread and retains a few other wheels around the town. Nowadays most of its rivers, lined with willows and poplars, are too languorous to turn wheels and are simply picturesque features of the town. However the main artery, the River Sile, is still navigable and evening excursions to the Venetian lagoon run from June–Aug (ask at the tourist office for details).

Close to *V. Pescheria* is the **Canale dei Buranelli**, one of the most photographed spots in Treviso. Artists can often be seen sketching at the end of the canal. It is worth wandering around this quarter at random, enjoying the old frescoed waterside houses and some Venice-like vignettes.Return to the *Pza dei Signori* and take the **V. Calmaggiore**, Treviso's elegant, arcaded main street, to the *Pza del*

Duomo (turn left). The **Duomo** is an imposing seven-domed building, founded in the 12th century but much rebuilt since. Its artistic highlight is the **Capella Malchiostro** which contains frescos by Il Pordenone and an *Assumption* by Titian. The two artists were in fact sworn enemies and it is written that Pordenone even carried a sword into the church in case Titian should turn up. Note too the 16th-century monument to Bishop Zanetti on the left-hand side of the altar (by Pietro Lombardo) and don't leave without paying a visit to the **crypt** or the **Museo Diocesano d'Arte Sacra** (open Mon–Thur 0900–1200, Sat 0900–1200 and 1500–1800. Entrance free).

Take *V. Jacopo Ricatti to Borgo di Cavour* and turn left to the **Museo Civico** which houses an archaeological section and a large collection of art which runs the gamut from medieval to 20th-century works, including acclaimed works by Lorenzo Lotto, Titian and Jacopo Bassano. *Borgo di Cavour 24.* Open Tues–Sat 0900–1230 and 1430–1700, Sun 0900–1200. Entrance fee L3000. Follow the town wall along the *V. Mura San Teonisto* to the *V. San Nicolò* and turn left to the large Dominican church of **San Nicolò**.

Built in the 14th century, this holds some superb tombs and features frescos by Tomaso da Modena, the star pupil of Giotto. Don't miss the **monks frescos** in the adjacent Seminario Vescovile (entrance on *Pza Benedetto XI*, open 0800–1230 and 1500–1730, admission free).

Tourist Information: *Rotatoria Villa Bona Sud, Marghera; tel: (041) 937764.* Open Mon–Fri 0900–1300 and 1600–1800.

Most of the Venetian workforce live on the mainland in Mestre where accommodation is affordable and there are more workaday facilities (such as supermarkets, schools and jobs outside tourism) than can be found on the historical island.

However Mestre is largely a dull place, devoid of any historical or cultural attractions and there is little to recommend to visitors, except perhaps as a cheap place to stay awhile or for its good restaurants. For budget travellers there is a branch of **Brek** at *V. Carducci*.

57

See Venice chapter, pages 80–91.

VITTORIO VÉNETO–PADUA

There is a lot more to the Véneto than the set piece cities of Venice, Verona, Vicenza and Padua. The cultured historical towns of Belluno and Bassano del Grappa both enjoy extremely picturesque natural settings while the romantic ancient hill settlements of Feltre and Asolo are almost time capsules. Also on this route is arguably the finest villa in the north and some of the region's best-preserved medieval fortifications.

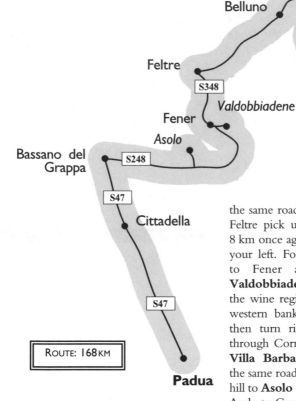

58

ROUTE: 168KM

ROUTE

From **Vittorio Véneto** head north on the picturesque S51 for 24 km and at Ponte nelle Alpi turn left to follow the River Piave for 8 km to **Belluno**. Continue on the same road for 31 km to **Feltre**. From Feltre pick up the S348 and after some 8 km once again you will see the Piave to your left. Follow this for around 10 km to Fener and cross the river to **Valdobbiadene** if you wish to explore the wine region. If not, continue on the western bank of the river for 10.5 km, then turn right, away from the river, through Cornuda towards Maser and the **Villa Barbaro** (5 km). Continue along the same road, then wind your way up the hill to **Asolo** (another 9 km). Return from Asolo to Casella (4 km) on the main S248 road and turn right to **Bassano del Grappa** (15 km). Head south on the S47 to **Cittadella** (14 km) and continue to **Padua** for a further 29 km. Route length 168 km.

BELLUNO

Tourist Office: *V. Rodolfo Psaro, 21* (corner of *Pza dei Martiri*); *tel: (0437) 940083,* open Mon–Sat 0800–1300.

Two good central hotel choices are **Centrale**, *V. Loreto 2,* behind *Pza dei Martiri*; *tel: (0437) 25192* (budget price range) and **Astor**, *Pza dei Martiri 26; tel: (0437) 942094* (budget–moderate).

Belluno enjoys a dramatic site, enclosed in a horseshoe-shaped peninsula formed by the rivers Piave and Ardo, and seated at the beginning of the Dolomites. The best place to appreciate this is from the **campanile** of the **Duomo** which gives one of the finest views in all the Véneto (of which Belluno is the northernmost part). The Duomo was built in the 16th century by Tullio Lombardo but reconstructed twice following earthquake damage. Directly opposite lies the city's most handsome building, the 15th-century **Palazzo dei Rettori**, former residence of the city's Venetian governors. The adjacent sturdy, square 12th-century **Torre Civica** is the only vestige of Belluno's medieval castle. Just off the square in *V. Duomo* is the **Museo Civico** which features the works of local hero Sebastiano Ricci, and (also born in the city), his nephew Marco Ricci and sculptor Andrea Brustolon, open Tues–Sat 1000–1200 and 1500–1800, Sun 1000–1200. Admission free. *V. Duomo* leads to the city's most charming square, the tiny **Pza del Mercato**, also known as the *Pza delle Erbe*, which is surrounded by porticoed Renaissance buildings. Take the old main street of *V. Mezzaterra* off here and on the left *V. San Croce* leads to the 14th-century **Porta Rugo**, a stately gateway which offers another wonderful view across to the mountains.

A popular short excursion from Belluno, and the easiest way to explore the Dolomites, is to drive 11 km south to **Nevegal** then take the chair lift to Rifugio Brigata Cadore at 1612 m. In summer there's a botanic garden and some lovely walking trails to enjoy, in winter the slopes are thick with skiiers.

FELTRE

Tourist Office: *Pzta Trento y Trieste 9; tel: (0439) 2540,* open Mon–Sat 0900–1300.

One of the most charming and best kept Renaissance towns in the Véneto, the old part of Feltre took on its present appearance in 1510 following its sacking by the troops of the Emperor Maximilian and rebuilding by its protector Venice. The steep cobbled streets of the old town start at the **Porta Imperiale** gate on *Largo Castaldi* and lead up past the tourist office, past several **frescoed buildings** – a feature of the town – eventually reaching the **Pza Maggiore**. This is as perfect an example of a Venetian square as you could wish to find. Framing the *piazza* is the portico of the Palazzo dei Retorri (Municipio) designed by Palladio, the medieval castle keep, the Church of San Rocco and the 19th-century Palazzo Guarnieri. In the centre, fountains, steps and statuary form a graceful ensemble. Above all towers the winged Lion of San Marco. The **Palazzo dei Retorri** holds a small wooden theatre, built in 1802, occasionally open (mornings) to the public. Continue up the main street to reach the **Museo Civico**. This has been closed for years for long-term repairs, but inside are works by Cima de Conegliano and Gentile Bellini plus Roman and Etruscan archaeological finds. The town's other collection is the **Museo Rizzarda**, dedicated to local artist Carlo Rizzarda (1883–1931) who specialised in beautiful wrought-iron artworks. There are plenty of other modern art exhibits here too.

59

V. Paradiso 8 (off *Pza Maggiore*), open Tues–Sun 1000–1300 and 1600–1900 (June–Sept). Entrance fee L3000.

Back through the Porta Imperiale arch in 'the lower town' is the **Duomo**, unremarkable except for a 6th-century Byzantine Cross with 52 scenes from the New Testament. The **Café Comercio** on *V. Roma* (between the Duomo and the Porta Imperiale) has a nice relaxed, almost 1940s, atmosphere and serves great *bruschettas*.

Take the S348 Treviso road from Feltre for 3 km and turn left up a steep slope to the **Santuario di Santi Vittore e Corona**. Described rather overenthusiastically by the Feltre tourist board as 'the most important artistic building of the Upper Véneto' it was built in 1100 and features some fine 13th-century frescos. (If you don't wish to drive it is a pleasant 30-min walk from Feltre.)

SIDE TRACKS FROM FENER

Valdobbiadene is the western end of the Strada del Vino Bianco, which runs for 34 km to Conegliano (see p. 55).

VILLA BARBARO (VILLA ER)

The Villa Barbaro, commissioned in 1555 by Daniele Barbaro, the patriarch of Aquileia, is one of Palladio's finest achievements (see feature p. 99) and also marks one of the artistic highlights of the career of Paolo Veronese. The brilliant interior **frescos** include some of the best *trompe l'œil* effects you are ever likely to see. People and animals peer from behind balustrades, realistic garden scenes open from imaginary windows and a huntsman (presumed to be a self-portrait of Veronese) steps into the room through a solid wall. There

are also fine stucco carvings, by Alessandro Vittoria, both in the villa and in the beautiful Nymphaeum behind the house, open Tues, Sat, Sun 1500–1800 (Mar–Oct); Sat, Sun 1430–1700 (Nov–Feb). Entrance by guided tour only, fee L8000. Just outside the gates on the main road is the **Tempietto di Villa Barbaro**, also designed by Palladio as a pantheon (note how the road has been diverted to accommodate the church).

ASOLO

Tourist Office: *V. Sta Caterina 258; tel: (0423) 524192*, open Mon–Sat 1000–1200 and 1600–1900.

The medieval walled 'Città dai

Paolo Veronese (1528–88)

Born in Verona (hence his name), Paolo Veronese was, along with Tintoretto, one of the two most prolific and popular Venetian school artists of his day. Unlike Tintoretto, who painted brooding and emotive religious pictures, full of dark forebodings, Veronese delighted in the worldly – his Last Supper painting (now in the Accademia in Venice), replete with jugglers, dwarfs, dogs, drunks, lovers and courtly costumes, got him into trouble with the Inquisition; asked to justify the secular tone of the painting, Veronese neatly side-stepped the issue by renaming the picture, the Feast at the House of Levi. Veronese's frescos at the Villa Barbaro are in the same celebratory spirit, perfectly complementing Palladio's light airy rooms with illusionistic paintings of false balconies and doors, non-existent windows with lovely rural views, and portraits of the owner's family with their pet birds and spaniels.

60

cento orizzonti' ('City of 100 horizons') is one of the most charming hilltop towns in northern Italy, even though it is much smaller than a city and only the most romantic would attribute so many horizons. But then Asolo has long drawn romantics including the late Freya Stark, traveller and writer, who settled here and helped to revive the local silk-weaving industry. In the 16th century Caterina Cornaro, former Queen of Cyprus, ruled here from 1489 to 1509 and attracted a cultured court, one of whom, Cardinal Bembo, coined the verb *asolare*, meaning to indulge oneself in aimless or random pleasures. Though in the case of the Queen this was a bitter-sweet experience since she had once been the ruler of all Cyprus. Born in Venice in 1454, she was later married to the King of Cyprus, James II, who died eight months after their wedding, leaving Caterina as sole ruler. The Venetian Council persuaded her that it was her 'patriotic duty' to abdicate and give the island to the Venetian Republic, in return for her palace in Asolo. Many writers and artists were subsequently attracted to Asolo, including Robert Browning who lived here and dedicated his last volume of poems, *Asolanda*, to the town in 1899. In the 1920s the American classical actress and siren Eleanor Duse, retreated from the glare of publicity to Asolo where she resided in the 16th-century Casa della Longobarde and chose to be buried here (in 1924), in the church of Sant'Anna. More recently the celebrated English travel writer Dame Freya Stark became an Asolo resident and on her 90th birthday in 1984 was presented with the keys to the town.

The **Loggia del Capitano** with a pretty 16th-century frescoed façade holds the **Museo Civico** which contains memorabilia of the town's famous residents and sculptures by Canova (see panel below). It is currently being restored but should reopen in 2000. The same is true of the **Castello**, where Queen Caterina lived. The **Duomo** features works by Lorenzo Lotto and Jacopo de Bassano.

All of these sights cluster around the picturesque small central **Pza Maggiore**. After that it's time to *asolare* around the narrow steep side streets. There is an inordinate amount of high-class food shops and galleries, all of which hope to tempt the rich trippers of Venice and Milan who come here at weekends. The most élite of these will be staying in the **Villa Cipriani**, one of the most renowned and expensive hotels in the Véneto; *V. Canova 298; tel: (0423) 952166.* Cheap accommodation is scarce and all but impossible to get on the second weekend of each month when an antiques fair (which is worth a visit) comes to town. At any time of the season however you should try to arrive early to avoid parking and queueing problems. ☒

POSSAGNO

Fans of the great neo-classical sculptor Antonio Canova (1757–1822) should divert 8 km north (on the minor road via Castelcucco) to **Possagno**. Here he was born and in the grandiose **Tempio Canoviano**, based on the Pantheon in Rome and designed by Canova, he now lies. At the bottom of the road leading from here is his birthplace, **Casa di Canova**, which now also accommodates a *gipsoteca* (plaster cast gallery) where you can study the casts and models for some of his greatest works, open Tues–Sun 0900–1300 and 1500–1800 (May–Sept); 0900–1200 and 1400–1700 (Oct–Apr). Entrance fee: L4000. ⬛

BASSANO DEL GRAPPA

Tourist Office: *Largo Corona d'Italia 35* (opposite train station); *tel: (0424) 524351*, open Mon–Sat 0900–1230 and 1500–1845.

The town is not well endowed with budget accommodation. The **Instituto Cremona** hostel offers the cheapest rooms, *V. Chini 6; tel: (0424) 522032*, while the 2-star **Albergo Nuovo Monde** is also central with more comfort, *V. Vittorelli 45*, off *Pza Garibaldi*; *tel: (0424) 522010* (budget price range). For the last word in luxury in a beautifully restored country house hotel, 5 mins from the centre, try the **Villa Palma**, *V. Chemin Palma, Mussolente* (very expensive price range); *tel: (0424) 577407*.

There are many good places to eat in Bassano and the town is famed for its white asparagus. One of the most popular budget choices with travellers and locals is *Birraria Ottone*; a beer-hall-cum-café-restaurant which serves a wide variety of dishes and is renowned for its goulash, *V. Matteoti 50; tel: (0424) 22206* (budget–moderate price range).

Bassano del Grappa is a delightful ancient walled town famous for its beautiful covered bridge, **Ponte di Bassano**, and *grappa* the after-dinner firewater which is produced in and around the town. You can sample both together at **Nardini's**, a small old-fashioned bar actually located at the beginning of the bridge, where you can taste *grappa* and other local drinks by the glass before buying by the bottle (closed Mon). Opposite Nardini's is a small **Museo del Grappa**, sponsored

by the distillers Poli, open Tues–Sun 1000–1300 and 1500–1900. Entrance free. The bridge itself was designed by Palladio in 1570 and was re-christened the **Ponte degli Alpini** this century in honour of the Alpine soldiers who died fighting against the Austrians and Germans in World War I. Cross the bridge and turn left onto the opposite bank for the magnificent picture-postcard **view** of the bridge, town, River Brenta and mountains.

Old Bassano is centred around three adjacent squares: **Pzta Monte Vecchio e Monte di Pietà** is the smallest, though it was the town's main medieval square, retaining the municipal coat of arms and numerous other inscriptions; **Pza Liberta** is graced by the 16th-century **Loggia del Commune**, with its handsome 18th-century clock and **Pza Garibaldi** is dominated by the 13th-century **Torre di Ezzelino/Torre Civica** and the campanile of San Francesco. On *Pza Garibaldi* you will also find the excellent **Museo Civico**, open Tues–Sat 0900–1230 and 1530–1830, Sun 1530–1830. Entrance fee L5000. The art gallery section is inevitably a showcase for the works of the Dal Ponte family, particularly Jacopo (better known as Jacopo di Bassano). One of its highlights is the 14th-century crucifix **Croce Dipinta** (Painted Cross) by Guariento (see p. 96 – Eremitani Museums, Padova). The museum also includes an archaeological section with Greek and Apulian ceramics and a large collection of 18th-century prints, including many by Canova. Your ticket also admits entrance to the **Museo della Ceramica**, *V. Schiavonetti* (off Pzta Monte à Vecchio e Monte di Pieta), open Tues–Sat 0900–1230 and 1530–1830, Sun 1530–1830 (Apr–Sept); Fri 0900–1230, Sat–Sun 1530–1830 (Oct–Mar). Located on the river bank, close to the bridge, in the grand rooms of the 18th-century

62

Palazzo Sturm, this is dedicated to the majolica ware for which Bassano is renowned.

CITTADELLA

Tourist Office: *Pza Scalco 13; tel: (049) 597 0627.*

Cittadella is remarkable for the state of preservation of its city **walls**. Constructed in the 13th century by the Paduans as a riposte to Castelfranco Véneto (see below), these are still almost completely intact and at several points in the small town you can view them, through the streets, to north, south, east and west. They are up to 13 m tall and punctuated by 16 towers and 16 turrets. The **Torre di Malta** (Malta Tower) is the most infamous of these, used as a prison and a torture chamber by the mid 13th century despot Ezzelino da Romano. He was nicknamed the 'Son of Satan' and his cruelty earned him a place in Dante's *Inferno*, condemned to boil eternally in a river of blood. The tower now hosts various cultural events and exhibitions. In the 18th-century **Duomo** are frescos by Jacopo da Ponte (Bassano), an altarpiece by Palma il Giovane and a small museum.

SIDE TRACK
FROM CITTADELLA

Castelfranco Véneto was completely encircled by high brick walls in 1199 by the Trevisans to protect themselves against the Paduans. The walls still mostly remain though they are not so impressive as those of Cittadella and what makes the town more worthwhile is that it was the birthplace of the great Venetian artist Giorgione (*c.* 1478–1510). The **Madonna and Child with Saints** altarpiece in the Duomo, is reckoned to be one of his finest works – though only a handful of paintings have ever been indisputeably attributed to him. The **Casa Giorgione** opposite the cathedral contains reproductions of the artist's great works, including *The Tempest* (see p. 88 Accademia, Venice) which assured him of his place in the annals of Venetian art history. The only original artwork in the house is an interesting *chiaroscuro* frieze attributed to Giorgione, open 0900–1230 and 1500–1800; closed winter mornings. Entrance fee L2000.

Connections from Padua

From Padua it is a short distance to **Venice:** simply follow the A4 for 20 km to Mestre, then follow signs to Venezia for 11 km, over the N11 lagoon causeway. To reach **Ferrara** from Padua, head south on the A13 autostrada for 60 km.

Grappa

The word *grappa* is not derived from the onamatopeaic sound that issues from your throat on tasting Italy's most blood-curdling drink, it comes from *graspa*, the Italian for the residue of pips, skins, stalks and other detritus of the grape which remain after wine is fermented. In fact it takes 100 kg of grapes to make just one 70 cl bottle of *grappa*. These are then distilled to make the colourless, liver-crippling liquid loved by some and loathed by many. It may come as no surprise to learn that it was originally made (in early medieval times, if not before) as a medicinal elixir. There are many differing degrees of quality and *grappa* is also often flavoured with various types of fruit.

You will find it on sale all over the north of Italy but its spiritual home, Bassano del Grappa, is the best place to buy, with shops on every other corner offering a bewildering variety of flavours.

GEMONA–CORTINA ALPINE PASSES

This route starts in the northern part of Friuli where, in 1976, a catastrophic earthquake laid waste the area and killed 1000 *Friulani*. The rebuilding of Gemona and particularly Venzone is a tribute to their spirit and energy. The road leads on through the sub-Alpine part of the Carnia region to the Cadore, the Dolomites mountain region where the scenery is breathtaking.

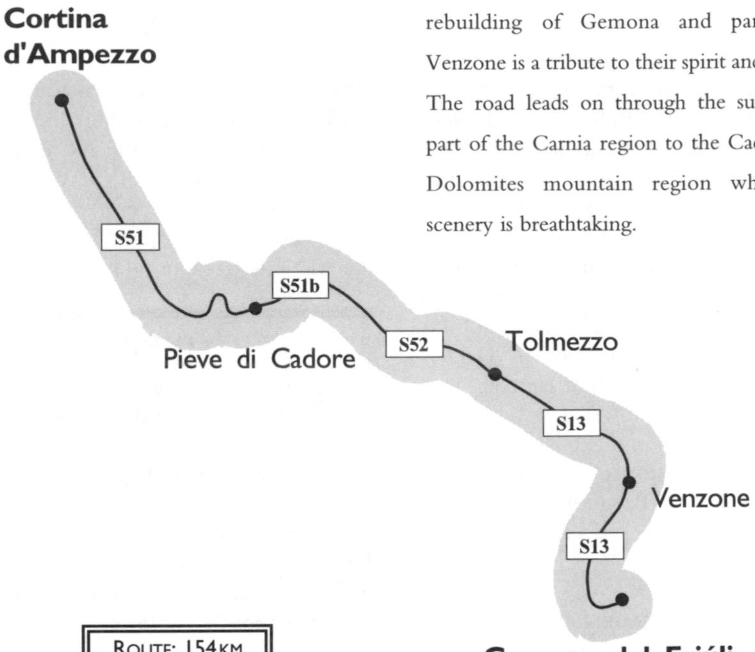

Cortina d'Ampezzo

S51

S51b

Pieve di Cadore

S52

Tolmezzo

S13

Venzone

S13

Gemona del Friúli

ROUTE: 154 KM

64

ROUTE

From **Gemona del Friúli** head north for 3.5 km, turn right onto the S13 and after 5km you reach the walls of **Venzone**. Continue on the S13 for 17 km to **Tolmezzo**. From Tolmezzo take the S52 for 64 km, passing through the villages of Ampezzo, Forni di Sopra (at which point the mountain views start to become spectacular) and Vigo di Cadore. Pass through the latter and turn left onto the S51bis for 12 km to **Pieve di Cadore**. Just beyond here turn right onto the S51 and skirt the villages of Borca di Cadore and San Vito di Cadore, both of which enjoy a beautiful setting and would make a worthwhile halt. 11 km beyond San Vito di Cadore is **Cortina d'Ampezzo**.

GEMONA DEL FRIÚLI

This small hill town, spectacularly located at the foot of the mountains, was at the epicentre of the earthquake, over 300 of the town's people lost their lives. Consequently much of the old centre looks quite new, though it has been rebuilt in the traditional style. There are photographs of the destruction in the fine, late 13th-century Romanesque–Gothic **Duomo** which itself was mostly turned to rubble and even now many of its pillars lean at an angle of around 70 degrees. On its façade a striking 14th-century statue of St Christopher looms some 6 m tall.

VENZONE

The beautiful small walled town of Venzone, listed as a national monument in 1965, also suffered terribly in the 1976 earthquake when 47 folk died and 90 per cent of the town's buildings were laid waste. The tragic story is told (in English) under the arches of the 15th-century **Palazzo Communale** in the town centre. This was the only building which survived the disaster, thanks to reinforcements that had been added in the 1950s. Don't miss the atmospheric Duomo, where in Sept 1964 Pope John Paul II celebrated mass. The extensive damage – great cracks and leaning pillars – is still very evident. The beautiful, poignant **wooden sculpture** inside, inscribed *Del Profondo Gride a te o Signore*, 'With great cries to you O Lord' was made from a single 135-year-old cedar tree in 1996 to mark the 20th anniversary of the disaster. Note next to this the marvellous brass font cover.

A good place to stay or eat in this area is the **Ristorante Hotel Carnia**, *4 km north of Venzone: on the S13; tel: (0432) 978106.* (Hotel moderate price range; restaurant: moderate–expensive price range).

TOLMEZZO

Tourist Office: *V. Umberto I 15; tel: (0433) 929290*, open Mon–Sat 0900–1200 and 1600–1800, Sun 0900–1200.

Although the capital of the Carnia region, Tolmezzo is a modest town. It too felt the effects of the 1976 tremor though today signs of damage are not apparent. It has a pleasant central *piazza* with the usual grand café and just off here, housed in a 19th-century *palazzo*, is the **Museo Carnico Arti Popolari** (Museum of Carnian Folk Art) where you can see examples of local arts, crafts and costumes, open Tues–Sun 1000–1200 and 1400–1600.

PIEVE DI CADORE

Tourist Office: *V. XX Septembre; tel: (0435) 31644*, open Mon–Sat 0900–1200 and 1500–1800, Sun 1000–1230.

The chief claim to fame of this small town is that it is the birthplace of the greatest of Venice's 16th-century masters, Titian. The building on the site of his old home, **Casa Tiziano**, is an atmospheric balconied 16th-century period piece with 15th-century furnishings, though it is not the actual house in which Titian (Tiziano Vecellio) was born *c.*1485. *V. Arsenale*, open 1000–1200 and 1600–1830 Entrance fee L2500. There is little inside that is linked directly to the artist though an altarpiece, **Madonna with Saints**, in the nearby parish church is thought to have been his work. Also in the centre of the town, in the *Pza Titiano*, is the pompously named **Palazzo della Magnifica Comunità Cadorina**. This handsome early 16th-century former town hall building now houses a small local archaeological and historical museum on its top floor while below is the town's best café-restaurant, the **Gran Tiziano**. Outside is a statue of the eponymous painter.

65

Titian aside, Pieve di Cadore is a popular summer and winter resort for walking, hiking and skiing and hanging above the town is the immense Marmarole peak of the Dolomite range.

If you are visiting just before Christmas you will probably also notice that this is the adopted home of the Italian Father Christmas, Babbo Natale, who 'lives' in the town park.

CORTINA D'AMPEZZO

Tourist Office: *Pzta S Francesco 8; tel: (0436) 3231*, open Mon–Fri 0900–1230 and 1500–1900, Sat 1000–1200 and 1600–1900, Sun 1000–1200.

It distributes pamphlets and leaflets on local attractions, but cannot book accommodation. Hotel bookings can be made through **Cortina Holidays**, *Corso Italia 81; tel: (0436) 860813.*

ACCOMMODATION

Cortina has grown, in 50 years, from a small Dolomite village to a major international resort, almost as familiar to the jet set as is St Moritz in Switzerland. Hardly surprising, the cost of staying here has risen accordingly; expect to pay a third more for accommodation in Cortina as you would in a less fashionable northern Italian resort. However, Cortina is very seasonal, with the peak running between Christmas and Easter and, to a lesser extent, in late July and August. Outside these periods, with hotels competing with each other for limited business, rates are much more competitive.

Cortina comprises predominantly private, family-owned hotels rather than those affiliated to large chains. Standards of comfort even the most demanding jet-set traveller could wish for can be found at the **Miramonti Majestic**, an imposing and luxurious hotel set in its own grounds about a mile from the centre at *Pezzie 103; tel: (0436) 4201.* City centre hotels include the **De La Poste**, *Pza Roma 14; tel: (0436) 4271.* The hotel has been run by the same family since 1836, when Gottardo Manaigo converted his already accommodating Post and Messages building for more demanding horse-drawn carriage visitors. Generations of the Cardazzi family have likewise honed another traditional hotel, the **Europa,** *Corso Italia 207; tel: (0436) 3221.* More modest, but clean and comfortable, are the **Fanes** at *V. Roma 136; tel: (0436) 3427,* and the **Impero** at *V. Cesare Battisti 66; tel: (0436) 4246.*

One of the best of the less–expensive hotels is the 2-star **Villa Nevada**, *V. Lungo Boite; tel: (0436) 4778* (budget–moderate price range). A more costly but very central option is the 3-star **Albergo Aquila**, *Corso Italia 168; tel: (0436) 2618* which has a basement swimming pool (moderate price). There are limited spaces in convent hostels for women but for most budget travellers camping in one of the four sites on the outskirts of town (summer only) or accommodation in private houses is the only choice.

EATING AND DRINKING

Like the hotels, the menus of Cortina restaurants seem to err towards more affluent customers though if, you can afford it, Cortina offers some of the best mountain restaurants in the country. The best restaurants are invariably attached to hotels – notably those of the previously-mentioned **Miramonti Majestic** at Pezzie, and the **De La Poste.** Also reliable, if rather less grand, is the **Astoria** at *Largo della Poste 11; tel: (0436) 2525* and the **Ancora**, *Corso Italia 62; tel: (0436) 3261.* If you prefer the intimacy of a restaurant outside an hotel, try **Da Beppe**

Sello, *V. Ronco 68; tel: (0436 3236.)* At lunchtime, the **Croda Café**, *Corso Italia 163; tel: (0436) 866589,* offers reliable pizza and pasta dishes at reasonable prices, but sometimes service here can be slow.

For skiers the views at the **Rifugio Averau** are world class and the service and food are also exemplary. At a lower altitude **El Camineto**, accessible to non-skiers by road, does wonderful pastas and grills. Other out-of-town choices are at Pocol where **El Toulà** is a shrine to *haute cuisine*. *V. Ronco 123; tel: (0436) 3339.* Slightly more affordable is the renowned **Al Lago Ghedina**, which specialises in local game and serves food on a terrace overlooking the eponymous lake: closed Tues; *tel: (0436) 860876.* All these restaurants are in the very expensive price range. If you are eating on a budget in Cortina your options are mostly limited to snacking at the small

Winter Sports Facts and Figures

The bare statistics of Cortina's winter sports make impressive reading: 387 km of downhill slopes, 438 km of cross-country ski runs, 163 lifts, 9 bobsleigh and toboggan tracks, 21 alpine skiing schools, 15 cross-country skiing schools and 7 snow-board schools. The good news for those not yet in the Olympic class is that 33 per cent of the ski runs are graded easy and 62 per cent are of medium difficulty. Perhaps surprisingly, it is estimated that only 30 per cent of Cortina's winter visitors actually ski!

cafés which line the main street. The cosiest of these is the **Caffè Sport** at the western end of the *Corso Italia*. For lunch

North-eastern Italy

One of the great surprises of north-eastern Italy is the sheer variety of landscapes to be found here, from the sweltering heat of the marshes fringing the Adriatic, to the snow-covered peaks of the Dolomites. Once all this territory was ruled by Venice, and huge numbers of trees were felled from the Cadore and Carnia regions of alpine north-eastern Italy. Made up into rafts, they were floated down the region's rivers when they were in full spring spate, eventually to arrive in Venice, where they were used as piles, underpinning the lagoon city's many palaces, churches and towers, and for structural timber.

Carpenters from the Cortina region found plenty of employment as builders in Venice, and as workers in the great shipyard, the Arsenale. They also dominated the gondola-construction trade, which explains why their workshops (of which several survive, such as the Squerro di San Trovaso, in Dorsoduro) look just like Tyrolean farms, complete with timber balconies, and hanging cascades of scarlet geraniums.

Later, this mountainous region of Italy came under the influence of the Austro-Hungarian empire, and the cultural impact of this relationship is evident in the distinctive Tyrolean style of the mountain chalets and farms, and in the occasional onion-dome, or Turk's cap, used to finish off a church tower, carrying with it echoes of the architecture of the great Hungarian Plain.

Visitors to the region will come away with different impressions depending on the time of the year. As the snows melt, skiers depart and their place is taken by walkers and nature lovers, attracted here by the marvellous carpets of alpine flowers that emerge in spring and continue through to the last of the autumn crocuses.

stock up from the range of delicious picnic provisions from the supermarket basement of the Cooperativa department store.

Those seeking an unusual drinking hole could point their feet in the direction of **Bar Arnika,** in the *Galleria Croce Bianca, tel: (0436) 3266.* The walls of the bar are lined with more than 400 bottles of malt Scotch, Irish, American, Canadian and even Japanese whisky, with about 40 brands on sale.

SIGHTSEEING

Cortina is the premier ski resort in Italy, pampering the monied classes of Turin and Milan and offering excellent **winter sports** facilities. Its status was confirmed in 1956 · when it was chosen to host the Winter Olympics and the most obvious sign of this is the giant ski run, which you will see, on your right, just before entering the town (which is actually little more than a large village). Despite all its man-made sports amenities Cortina's greatest attraction is its magnificent natural setting amid the snowy grandeur of the Dolomites and in the summer months (July–Sept) it is a wonderful base for **walking**, aided and abetted by an extensive cable-car and chair-lift system. The helpful tourist office supply an excellent free walking map with estimated times of routes and will also advise according to individual requirements on degree of difficulty, which cable cars to take, etc. The Cortina Group of Alpine Guides organise daily excursions for groups of adults and children and there are also a number of companies who organise more serious mountain walks (details can be obtained from the tourist office). Another option is to join one of the excursions (on foot, on skis or on horseback) offered by the outdoor activity company called **Cortina No Limits,** *Via dello Stadio 18; tel: (0436) 860808.*

Sports and walking aside there is little cultural interest in Cortina which is basically a one-street town, spread along the *Corso Italia.* Its modern architecture is of no interest (a fire in 1976 swept away what was left of the old town). As a place with a relatively short history, sightseeing is limited, unless you count the three smallish museums, covering modern art, fossils and anthropology, all housed *at V. del Parco 1; tel: (0436) 866222.* The museums are open 1600–1930 (Jan–Mar, July–Sept), 1030–1230 and 1600–1900 (Dec). In the season, however, the *Corso Italia* is an exuberant *aprés-piste* thoroughfare with packed bars, a lively nightlife, snow sculptures in winter and a *passegiata* of the highest fashion. Like most such resorts, however, out of season it is a very different sort of place.

CORTINA–BOLZANO THE GREAT DOLOMITE ROAD

La Grande Strada delle Dolomiti – a drive through the Dolomites – provides one of the great scenic pleasures of Europe. No other mountain range on the continent can approach the sight of the 30 or so jagged, limestone peaks which lie in an arc from Lake Garda to Italy's north-east border with Austria. The Great Dolomite Road is at the heart of the range, bringing together the best

of mountain, lake and valley scenery. Colour adds yet another dimension to the drive – the greens of meadows and forests contrasting with the white of the limestone peaks, turning pink in the final glow of sunset. Given an uncluttered road, it is possible to drive the route in two hours – but to enjoy it to the full you are well advised to take a couple of days, spending a night or two along the way.

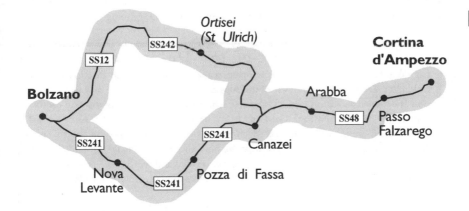

ROUTE

The Great Dolomite Road runs for 135 km from the Olympian winter sports resort of Cortina d'Ampezzo to the bilingual town of Bolzano (Bozen). From Cortina d'Ampezzo, the most direct route follows the SS48 to Canazei, the largest of the resort villages that dot the Dolomite

ROUTE: 135 KM

Road. Spectacular scenery continues all the way to Bolzano; equally picturesque is the sidetrack north to the Tyrolean town of Ortisei.

CORTINA TO BOLZANO

At the bottom of Cortina's main street, cross the bridge over the Boite and turn right on to the SS48 to Falzarego. You are now on The Great Dolomite Road, the splendidly named route that links some of the finest of the region's peaks and cliffs. The road, smooth-surfaced for the most part, twists and turns through the Cortina 'suburbs' of Ronco and Pocol, climbing all the time between stands of conifers and meadows dotted with attractive chalet houses and, above, vertical columns of rock. By the time you reach **Passo Falzarego,** 10 km away, you are already at 2117 m.

Falzarego is a stopover for motorists and walkers – half a dozen shops, souvenir stalls and bars, with a cable car running up to Monte Lagazuoi.

ARABBA

Tourist Office: *V. San Andrea 5, 32100*

Belluno; tel: (0437) 959111. There is also a helpful tourist information office in the middle of Arabba, *tel: (0436) 79130,* open Mon–Sat 0900-1230 and 1530–1830; and Sun 0900–1230 (Dec–mid Apr, June– Sept).

ACCOMMODATION AND FOOD

Some 3000 visitors can now be accommodated in Arabba at any one time, in hotels, apartments and chalets, with most coming during the winter months. There are definite seasons here; most hotels only open mid Dec to mid Apr and mid July to mid Oct.

The emphasis here is on family-run hotels, such as the 3-star **Sporthotel Arabba,** *tel: (0436) 79321,* the recently modernised, chalet-styled **Evaldo,** *tel: (0436) 79109;* and the **Portavescovo**, *tel: (0436) 79159.* The resort has a small selection of bars, restaurants and a pizzeria, but don't expect fine dining.

The Geology of the Dolomites

It is doubtful if there is any more dramatic scenery in Europe than that found in the Dolomites. Set apart from the rest of the Alps by their unique geology, they were named after the French geologist Déodat Dolomieu, who lived in the last half of the 18th century. Running in a wide arc from Lake Garda to Italy's border with Austria, the 30 or so self-contained massifs are ancient coral reefs which, millions of years ago during the earth's development, were thrust up from the bed of what we now know as the Mediterranean by violent volcanic activity. They have since been compressed, uplifted and weathered – the coral reefs explaining the incredible crags and pinnacles and the pinky-orange colour, the Dolomites' hallmark, seen to good effect at sunrise and sunset.

In one sense, the Dolomites are the most inaccessible of the alpine peaks, in that the limestone pinnacles and towers are so steep that they can only be negotiated by the most experienced rock climbers. In another sense, though, the peaks are accessible because literally hundreds of cableways have been built, providing access to the cols and plateaus and, because of the lack of glaciated snow fields, making high-level walking possible. Bolzano and Cortina d'Ampezzo are the best bases from which to study the Dolomites – Bolzano for the massifs of Sciliar and Puez-Odle, Cortina for Sesto, Cristallo and Tofana di Mezzo – but Marmolada, the highest peak, is most easily explored from Canazei. At the margins, the water run-off creates more spectacular scenery in the form of gorges and waterfalls.

SIGHTSEEING

Arabba is a substantial Alpine village which has grown into a resort.

The town has a modern feel to it, but there is little to do here unless you are looking for an outdoor holiday. The surrounding countryside is attractive enough; the jagged Dolomite peaks, including the massive Marmolada, at 3342 m the highest peak in the chain, ring the village, and lush meadows and lakes provide additional scenic appeal.

Continue along the Great Dolomite Road, through superb mountain scenery. Just beyond Passo Pordoi turn left to **Canazei**, which is about 20 km from Arabba.

CANAZEI

Tourist Office: *V. Roma 34; tel: (0462) 611113.*

ACCOMMODATION

As the largest and most popular holiday village on the Great Dolomite Road, Canazei has plenty of accommodation across the price range. Again, though, this is very much a seasonal resort, with many of the hotels only open between Dec–mid Apr and July–Sept. Centrally situated, the **Dolmiti**, *tel: (0462) 61106,* combines old-world charm with modern comforts and is just a short walk from the ski school. Other favourites include the 3-star **Hotel Tyrol**, *Vle Cascata 2; tel: (0462) 60115,* a member of the family-managed Logis d'Italia chain.

SIGHTSEEING

There is no better equipped resort for both winter and summer sport activity than Canazei, which is at the head of the Val di Fassa. The village is at the heart of the huge 'Dolomiti Superski' area, covering a network of 450 lifts, many of which are available during the summer as well as the winter season. It's from here that you reach the high passes – the Gruppo di Sella and the Viel del Pan, opposite Marmolada. This is great walking, as well as skiing, country. The Gruppo di Sella is like a lunar landscape – an arid plateau surrounded by the distinctive, pink Dolomite peaks. Less ambitious walking can be done from Passo Pordoi along the Viel del Pan – 'trail of bread' in the Venetian dialect – a grain-smuggling route in the 17th century.

Bolzano is 51 km from Canazei along the Great Dolomite Road. Continue on the SS48 east as the road winds its way through wild scenery to **Pozza di Fassa** and just outside the village turn right on the SS241 to **Nova Levante (Welschnofen)**. The road enters the Val d'Ega, a corridor of waterfalls and gorges, and there are splendid views of the Catinaccio and Latemar massifs before the road drops down into Bolzano.

⤵ SIDE TRACK FROM CANAZEI

The alternative route to Bolzano is via the SS242. This takes you past the teeth of the Sasso Lungo, one of the most dramatic peaks in the Dolomites, into Val Gardena. Here the Germanic influence of bilingual Alto Adige is all apparent – squeaky-clean guesthouses, pristine meadows and woodcarvers by the, literally, thousand.

Three thousand woodcarvers are employed in the valley, turning out religious sculptures and hand-carved toys. If you're buying, make sure it's the authentic item.

ORTISEI (ST ULRICH)

Tourist Office, *Pza Stetteneck; tel: (0471) 796328.*

Neolithic Fritz

Climbers walking in the Alps During September 1991 came across the desiccated remains of a man lying in the snow. The body was taken to Innsbruck for a post mortem, and it rapidly emerged that the remains were not those of a recently deceased human – Frozen Fritz, as he was then dubbed, had been lying in the ice of the Similaun Glacier for some 7000 years.

Careful archaeological examination established some remarkable facts. Fritz was a neolithic shepherd, dressed in animal skins and wearing leather boots, into which he had hay to keep himself warm. He was carrying a bow some six feet (1.8 metres) in length and 14 arrows in a quiver, as well as a copper hatchet blade and a stone knife. He was in his 50s and had recently eaten a meal of meat and ground wheat porridge or bread. His back and limbs bore remarkable tattoos.

Most controversially of all, scientists found wheat grains in his clothing of a type known only to have grown in the Italian plains during the neolithic era – perhaps Fritz was really Giovanni. The Italian authorities despatched surveyors to the site where he was found – it turned out to be within the Italian border by a matter of a few feet. In the face of much protest from the Austrian scientific community, Fritz was returned to Italy in 1998, and is now on display on Bolzano Museum.

ACCOMMODATION AND FOOD

As the largest village in the valley, Ortisei has plenty of accommodation, but because many hotel stays require half-board, there are fewer restaurants. There are traditional hotels such as the **Gardena-Grödnerhof**, *tel: (0471) 796315,* and the **Genziana-Enzian**, *tel: (0471) 796246,* and also **La Perla**, *tel: (0471) 796421,* which has its own indoor swimming pool.

Smaller hotels include the **Ronce**, *tel: (0471) 796383* and the **Villa Louise**, *tel: (0471) 796498.* Good local cuisine can be sampled at the **Concordia** restaurant at *V. Roma 41; tel: (0471) 796276.*

SIGHTSEEING

Ortisei is a pretty village which is not just bilingual but trilingual. The Ladin language, derived from a Latin dialect traceable to the Roman occupation, is spoken in these parts. A museum, the **Cesa di Ladins,** at *Reziastraasse 83,* celebrates the local culture. The museum is open daily 1500–1800 (Feb–Apr, June–Sept); 1000–1200 and 1500–1900 (July–Aug). Entrance is free.

From Ortisei, continue along the SS242 and then follow the signs along the SS12 for the 36 km journey to Bolzano.

BOLZANO (BOZEN)

Tourist Office: *Pza Walther 8; tel: (0471) 970660,* open Mon–Fri 0830–1800, Sat 0900–1230. For information about the region, there is the provincial tourist office at *Pza Parrochia 11/12; tel: (0471) 993808.*

For mountaineering information, the **Club Alpino Italiano (CAI)** is at *Pza dell'Erbe; tel: (0471) 971694.*

ACCOMMODATION AND FOOD

There is a fairly wide range of accommodation available from the expensive to the moderately affordable. **Park Hotel Laurin** at *V. Laurin 4; tel: (0471) 311000,* falls into the first category. It is both luxurious and centrally situated and has an elegant garden. More modest, but comfortable, accommodation is available at the **Asterix**, *Pza Mazzini 35; tel: (0471) 273301,* and the **Gurhof**, *at V.Rafenstein 17; tel: (0471) 975012.* For accommodation up in the nearby Colle/Kolhern, take the cableway from *V. Campiglio.*

Camping: the **Moosbauer** campsite is situated on the main Bolzano–Merano road, just outside the city; *tel: (0471) 918492.*

Bolzano is at the heart of the Alto Adige wine-growing industry, so both wine shops and restaurants are abundant. For a celebration, try the elegant **Da Abramo** at *Pza Gries 16; tel: (0471) 280141,* whose menu veers towards the nearby Veneto in influence. Good *cucina traditionale locale* (local cooking) is available at **Vögele**, *V. Goethe 3; tel: (0471) 973938.*

SIGHTSEEING

Is this Austria or Italy? A good question since, while the street names may be in Italian, dishes on restaurant menus are distinctly German, as is the architecture. But Bolzano's position at the junction of the rivers Talvera and Isarco, and only 3 km from where the larger Adige River joins, makes it ideal as a base for exploring the region. The focus of Bolzano's outdoor life is the **Pza Walther** where open-air cafés compete for custom in the shadow of a statue of the troubadour. Walther von der Vogelweide. To one side of the square is the **Duomo**, a 14th- and 15th-century building which became a cathedral only in 1964. Gothic in style, it has a colourful mosaic roof and an ornate spire.

Better than the Duomo, however, is the **Chiesa dei Francescani**, the Franciscan church on *V. dei Francescani.* Built in the 14th century, it has a wonderful Gothic cloister. Inside, the altarpiece by Hans Klocher is worth making an effort to see. The **Chiesa dei Domeniciani**, the Dominican monastery in *V. Capuccini,* is now the Conservatory of Music. Worth seeing, also, are the 15th-century frescos in its cloister and, in its chapel, frescos of the School of Giotti. To the north-west, in the suburb of Gries, are the baroque abbey of the Benedettini and the ancient parish church of Gries.

73

BOLZANO–ROVERETO

Along a stretch of not much more than 160 km of motorway beside the fast-flowing Adige River, you are whisked from German-influenced Alpe Adige – the Südtirol – to pure Italianate Trentino. The contrasts are vivid. In Bolzano, provincial capital of Alpe Adige, you feel you could have strayed over the border into Austria, so Teutonic is the

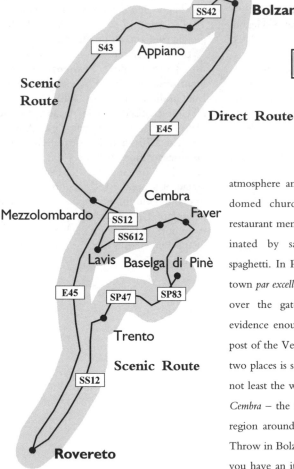

SS42 — Bolzano

S43 — Appiano

Scenic Route

DIRECT ROUTE: 85 KM

Direct Route

E45

74

Cembra

Mezzolombardo — SS12 — Faver

SS612

Lavis — Baselga di Pinè

E45 — SP47 — SP83

Trento

Scenic Route

SS12

Rovereto

atmosphere and way of life. Gothic onion-domed churches dot the landscape and restaurant menus are likely to be more dominated by sauerkraut and strudel than spaghetti. In Rovereto, an Italianate hill top town *par excellence*, the gilded lion of St Mark over the gateway into the old town is evidence enough that this was once an outpost of the Venetian Empire. In between the two places is some stunningly varied scenery, not least the wine growing area of the *Val di Cembra* – the Cembra Valley – and the lake region around the town of Baselga di Pinè. Throw in Bolzano, Trento and Rovereto and you have an itinerary which could keep you occupied for a full week.

ROUTES

DIRECT ROUTE

→ If you are in a hurry, the E45 Brenner–Verona *autostrada* allows you to complete the 85 km between Bolzano and Rovereto in 1¼ hrs.

SCENIC ROUTE

⇢ The scenic route more than doubles the distance – and the pleasure. Head south-west from **Bolzano** along the SS42 to Appiano and then continue along the wine route to **Mezzolombardo** and then cross under the motorway and continue on the SS12 to Lavis. From here take the SS612 through the Cembra Valley and then the SP83 to Baselga and eventually to **Trento**. Rejoin the SS12 to Rovereto.

TOURIST INFORMATION:

The route covers places in both the South Tyrol and Trentino. For **South Tyrol,** the provincial tourism information office is at *Pfarrplatz 11–12, Bolzano (Bozen); tel: (0471) 993808.* **Trentino Tourist Office** is at *V. Romagnosi 11, Trento; tel: (0461) 497353.* The Trentino office, which is open Mon–Fri 0830–1230, and 1430–1800, Sat 0900–1230, has helpful staff and a wide range of literature, including an excellent castles guide, and maps covering the whole province.

BOLZANO TO CEMBRA

South-west of Bolzano is some of South Tyrol's finest scenery. From the city centre, head south-west along the SS42, not just a road but a s*trada del vino* – wine route. The road loops past vineyards, past Renaissance churches and the ancient Bellavista Marklhof monastery. Nearby, **Termeno** is the home of the famous Traminer wine. About 6 km along the road is the village of the scattered community of **Appiano sulla Strada del Vino (Eppan)**.

APPIANO

Tourist Office: *Pza Municipio 1; tel: 0471-662206.*

ACCOMMODATION AND FOOD

Appiano is a scattered community, with a few hotels in San Michele, the main village, and others in the nearby villages like Pigeno, Cornaiano and Monte. In San Michele, the **Tschindlhof,** *tel: (0471) 662225,* has a pleasing garden and outdoor swimming pool. Others worth considering include the characterful **Schloss Englar** at Pigeno; *tel: (0471) 662628,* and the **Schloss Freudenstein** at Monte, *tel: (0471) 660638.* The **Bellavista Marklhof,** *V. Belvedere 7, Cornaiano; tel: (0471) 52407,* is a former Benedictine monastery, now specialising in venison dishes, and serving its own wines.

75

SIGHTSEEING

As well as vineyards, Appiano has a clutch of castles in varying states of repair – Aichberg, Angerburg, Englar, Freudenstein and Hocheppan – all evoking memories of chivalrous days gone by, even if one or two look quite tame, more like manor houses than the stirring, crenellated bastions found farther south. Some have been converted into hotels or restaurants. But one which has maintained its original status is Hocheppan, whose chapel beside the ruins of the main building is worth a visit for its unusual frescos. Hocheppan is open daily (Apr–Nov), closed Tues except in July.

From Appiano, the road climbs all the time as it ascends Mt Mendelwand (good views back to Bolzano) and then continues south through more vineyards to **Caldaro (Kaltern)**. The Lago di Caldaro brings another dimension to this most scenic of scenic drives and nearby the 14th-century **Castello di Monterotondo (Ringberg)** has a wine museum, open 0930–1200 and 1400–1800 (Apr–Oct); closed Mon and public holidays. From here, the wine runs due south again to **Termeno (Tramin)** and, after another 20 km, to **Mezzocorona**. From here, cross the Adige River and join the SS12 for the 5 km run down to **Lavis**.

Lavis is only 5 km from Trento, but with time on your side, rather than continuing along the SS12, take the SS612 east through the Cembra Valley. This relatively narrow road loops through impressively unspoilt scenery – vineyards clinging to steep, sometimes precipitous, slopes of porphyritic rock. Until a few years ago farmers had to carry the soil for the vines (Müller Thurgau and Schiava are the favoured varieties here) in baskets up the slopes from one terrace to another – a tedious task which had to be repeated every time a thunderstorm washed away the soil.

CEMBRA

Tourist Office: *V. 4 Novembre 3; tel: (0461) 683110.*

Cembra's accommodation is very much geared to the holiday market. **Albergo Europa**, *V. San Carlo 19; tel: (0461) 683032,* has pleasant, well-furnished rooms and a good restaurant, as does **Hotel el Caminetto,** *V. Cesare Battisti 2/a; tel: (0461) 683007.*

Both the above-named hotels have good restaurants, with the Hotel el Caminetto offering excellent *risotto al funghi* – risotto with mushrooms. With so much wine grown in the area, it's small wonder there are also plenty of wine (and *grappa*) tastings, a good example being the **Vinoteca** wine bar, *V. Carmine 7, Lavis,*

open Tues–Fri 0900–1200 and 1500–1900, Sat 0900–1200, Mon 1500–1900.

Continue east along the SS612 and about 2 km along the road, at Faver, turn right over the Aviso River to Segonzano (see accompanying section on 'Pyramids of Segonzano'). The scenery as you drop down into the floor of the valley is impressive: the vineyards rising up the steep slopes, with the villages, each crowned by its church, popping up like cardboard cutouts.

> ## SIDE TRACK
> ## TO PIAZZO
>
> About 2 km along this road, follow the sign to Piazzo, a village so old that there is only just room to squeeze the car between the walls of the buildings. The road peters out at a look-out point, shaded by a pine tree, from where there is a view to the crumbling walls of Segonzano Castle, jutting out on a spur on the opposite side the valley. The castle, built in the 13th century, was badly damaged during the French occupation between 1796–97.
>
> Retrace your steps and then continue past Segonzano to Sover and then take the SP83 to Baselga di Pinè. The road twists and turns, climbing all the time, until it reaches the *Altopiano di Pinè* – a tableland of forests and lakes which, at its height of about 1000 m, is tailor-made for both summer and winter tourism. Here the great outdoors takes on its full meaning. Although primarily a summer destination, the opening in 1986 of the Olympic Ice Stadium has promoted the winter cause.
>
> The road, well surfaced for the most part, takes you past the Piazze and di Serraia lakes to Baselga di Pinè.

BASELGA DI PINÈ

Tourist Office: *V. Cesare Battista 98; tel: (0461) 557028.*

ACCOMMODATION

There are more than 50 hotels in and around Baselga, with plenty of inexpensive, family-run establishments, and a handful offering more expensive rooms. In the centre of town, the 3-star **Hotel Krone**; *tel: (0461) 553160*, offers comfortable, well-furnished rooms and a good restaurant specialising in tagliatelle, tortellini and veal dishes. The hotel is open throughout the year, apart from November and March. Others worth considering are the **Villa Anita**, *tel: (0461) 557106;* and the **Edera**, *tel: (0461) 557221*. Noted restaurants, both of which have a small number of rooms, include the **2 Camino** at Vigo, *tel: (0461) 557200;* and **La Scadola** at Miola, *tel: (0461) 557647*.

From Baselga, it is a straightforward, 15km run down to **Trento** on the SP83 and then the SP47, which leads you straight into the centre of the city.

TRENTO

Tourist Office: *V. Alfiera 4; tel: (0461) 983880,* has a wealth of material on the city, including booklets, pamphlets and maps and copies of the city magazine *Viva Trento*. The office is open Mon–Fri 0900–1200 and 1500–1800, Sat 0900–1200. From mid June to mid Sept the office is also open Sun 1000–1200. Staff are helpful and there are English versions of most of the literature.

ACCOMMODATION

As a business centre and 'capital' of Trentino, the city is well endowed with luxury hotels and has a growing number of less expensive establishments to cater for the growing number of tourists. As a way of escaping the summer heat, **Villa Madruzzo**, *Ponte Alto 26, Cognoli; tel: (0461) 986220, fax (0461) 986361,* is a splendidly furnished centuries-old villa which has been transformed into a hotel. It stands in its own grounds and has commanding views of the city and the Adige Valley. It also has an excellent restaurant, particularly good for fish, veal and pasta dishes. In the city itself, the **Accademia,** *Viocolo Colico 4–6; tel: (0461) 233600,* is a friendly, characterful hotel a short stroll away from the main square, the *Pza del Duomo,* and **Hotel America**, *V. Torre Verdi 50; tel: (0461) 983010,* also benefits from a good position and comfortable rooms. Less expensive options include **Hotel Venezia**, *Pza del Duomo 45; tel: (0461) 234114* and **Al Cavallino Bianco** at *V. Cavour 29; tel: (0461) 231542.*

EATING AND DRINKING

Few cities of similar size can compare with Trento for the quality of its food and restaurants. This is where Italian and Germanic gastronomic influences collide head on so, on restaurant menus, expect to find these very different cuisines in tandem. In addition to the hotels, **Chiesa**, *V. San Marco 64; tel: (0461) 238766,* housed in a 14th-century building near Buonconsiglio (Castle of Good Counsel), offers *riostto alle mele* (risotto with apples) and actually has a special seven-course menu featuring apple with every dish. Other notable restaurants include **Alla Mora**, *V. Grande 8; tel: (0461) 984675,* which has been transformed from an unpretentious trattoria to a restaurant of some style and elegance, while the **Green Tower**, also near the castle at *V. Vanetti 31; tel: (0461) 233150,* is an inexpensive, all-purpose restaurant serving everything from pizzas to prime steaks. **Le Due**

Spade, *V. Don Arcangelo Rizzi 11; tel: (0461) 234343,* is an *osteria* serving good, traditional local food, while in and around the *Pza del Duomo* are several cafés with pavement views which are excellent for a quick lunch or for enjoying a coffee.

SIGHTSEEING

The Romans knew Trento as Tridentum; the modern city's main square occupies the site of the Roman forum, and the fine 18th-century statue of a trident-wielding Neptune in the square is an allusion to the ancient name.

In the 16th century the city was chosen as a neutral point, between Protestant Germany and Catholic Italy, in which to hold meetings of the so-called Council of Trent. This body was convened over 18 years (from 1545 to 1563) in order to institute reforms designed to encourage breakaway groups – in particular the Protestant churches of Germany, the Netherlands and England – to return to the Catholic fold. In as much as the reforms eventually ushered in the harsh and repressive Counter Reformation, the Council was not successful, but it left Trento with the legacy of some splendid buildings, where meetings of the Council were once held.

Meetings of the Council would begin and end in the splendid Duomo, which was begun in the 13th century and completed in the 16th, but is nevertheless all of a piece architecturally – the builders wisely decided to ignore the Gothic style and continue building in the solid and robust Romanesque style that prevailed when it was started, with the result that the building has unusual integrity and harmony. Alongside is the Palazzo Pretorio, with its massive campanile, housing the **Museo Diocesano Tridentino**, *Piazza del Duomo 18*; *tel: (0461) 234419),* with a dis-

play of paintings depicting the meetings of the Council, as well as some charming reliquaries carved in ivory and some Flemish wall tapestries.

Nearby streets are full of good shops and cafés, and link the main square to the huge and imposing palace of the prince-bishops, now the **Castello del Buonconsiglio** and its **Museo Principale d'Arte**, *V. Bernardo Clesio 5; tel: (0461) 230770,* open daily except Mon 1000–1800 (Apr–Sept); 0900–1200 and 1400–1700 (Oct–Mar). The museum is full of good furnishings and wood carvings, as well as some most unclerical frescos of virile satyrs chasing half-undressed nymphs. Best of all is the intimate Torre del'Aquila, decorated with charming 14th-century frescos of the Months of the Year. Trento also has a **Museum of Modern and Contemporary Art**, housed in *Palazzo delle Albere, V. R da Sanseverino 45; tel: (0461) 986588,* with 2000 paintings, drawings, engravings and sculptures dating from the 19th century to the present day. For outdoor enthusiasts, there are walking and mountaineering possibilities in the Brenta Dolomites – details from **Trento Alpine Guide Committee**; *tel: (0461) 981207,* or local tourist offices.

From Trento, follow the SS12 south again, past the airport to **Rovereto**. The road runs through the valley, parallel with the Adige, past vineyards and fruit orchards to Rovereto, 28 km away.

ROVERETO

Tourist Office: *V. Dante 63; tel: (0464) 430363.*

ACCOMMODATION AND FOOD

For a small town, Rovereto has a number of good hotels, notably the **Rovereto**, *Corso Rosmini 82; tel: (0464) 435222* and the **Leon d'Oro**, *V. Tacchi 2; tel: (0464)*

The Pyramids of Segonzano

Le Piramidi di Terra di Segonzano, to give the site its official name, lies in the Cembra Valley, north of Trento, and is one of the most remarkable geological phenomena in Italy. Geologists believe they were formed millions of years ago in the Quaternary period of the earth's development, when glaciers swept and deposited large amounts of material in the valley. The classic shape of a pyramid is a cone of limestone, some as high as 45 m tall, with a block of stone on top. The stone is important to the survival of the pyramid, because it deflects rain water and therefore delays erosion. Ideally the stone should be at an angle, so that the water runs straight off. Fragments of other material left by the glaciers also help preserve the life of a pyramid – as does the presence of vegetation, whose roots, mosses and leaves bind the earth and impede erosion.

The three groups of pyramids, which are about 6 km from Cembra, can be visited from Rio di Regnana. They are well signposted off the SS612 state provincial road. From the car-park at Rio di Regnana, follow the path which leads up beside the café through the picturesque valley in which the pyramids are situated. The climb is fairly steep and the first sighting of the pyramids is made after about 20 mins. You can either return straight away or take a longer, circular route back along the river bank. Entrance to the site is free.

437333, which, although it doesn't have a restaurant, has comfortable rooms. There are good restaurants, too – with **Al Borgo**, *V. Garibaldi 13; tel: (0464) 436300,* which specialises in fish and veal dishes, probably the pick. Also worth considering are Mozart **1769**, *V. Portici 36–38; tel: (0464) 430727,* and for a splendid setting, **La Terrazza sur Leno**, *V. Setaioli 2a; tel: (0464) 435151,* a spacious restaurant offering tables inside and out, overlooking the River Leno.

SIGHTSEEING

There are few more peaceful old towns for exploring than Rovereto, but it hasn't always been so. Savage battles were fought here over the centuries, not least in World War I. Fallen heroes are still remembered in the tolling of the bells each day at dusk and in the **Museo della Guerra** (War Museum) in the 12th-century castle, open 0900–1200 and 1400–1800 (Mar–Nov). Also worth seeing is the **Casa Museo Depero**, *V. della Terra 53; tel: (0464)*

434393, dedicated to the modern artist Fortunato Depero, open 1000–1230 and 1430–1900 (mid Jun–mid Sept); 0900–1230 and 1430–1800 (winter). The museum is closed on Mondays.

⟷ Connections: Rovereto to Lake Garda and Venice

Lake Garda is 17 km from Rovereto via Mori on the SS240 – but be prepared for delays on this road, particularly at weekends in summer, as traffic is heavy.

Venice can be reached by several different routes. The fastest way is to continue south for 90 km to **Verona**, using the A22 autostrada, joining the A4 autostrada just south of Verona and heading east for 120 km to Venice via Padova and Mestre. A slower, but more scenic, route is to take the A22 autostrada north for 24 km back to Trento, then head east on the N47, following the Sugana Valley for 90 km to Bassano del Grappa where you can pick up the Vittorio Veneto–Padua route, described on p 62.

VENICE AND ITS ISLANDS

With its familiar icons of gondoliers, St Mark's Sq and the Bridge of Sighs, Venice (Venezia) is so engrained in the popular psyche that you may think it will hold few surprises. You couldn't be more wrong; in the words of its famous dramatist Carlo Goldoni, 'Venice is so unreal that one cannot have any idea of what she is like unless one has actually beheld her'. Welcome to the world's most individual and perhaps most beautiful city.

TOURIST INFORMATION

The most central **Tourist Office** is at *Palazetta Selva, Giardinetti Reale, San Marco; tel: (041) 522 6356.* Offices are also located at the *Aeroporto Marco Polo; tel: 541 5887,* and the rail station, *Ferrovia S Lucia; tel: (041) 529 8727.* For drivers coming from Padova there is an office at *Dolio–Arino Sud* on the *autostrada; tel: (041) 966010,* and another on the mainland at Marghera on the *rotatoria autostradale; tel: (041) 937764,* open daily 0900–1300 and 1600–1900.

Youth and student information can be obtained at the **Commune di Venezia Assessorato alla Gioventù**, *Corte Catarina* (just off the Pza San Marco) *San Marco; tel: (041) 270 7650* open daily 0800–1300 and 1600–1900 and at the **Ufficio Informativo Rolling Venice** at the rail station; open daily 0800–2000 (July–Sept); *tel: (041) 524 2851.* **Rolling Venice** is an excellent scheme open to travellers aged 14 to 29 which, for a membership fee of L5000, offers discounts on restaurants, hotels, shops, the performing arts, in fact on just about everything in the city. The ACTV Rolling Venice card gives discounts on *vaporetti* tickets.

ARRIVING AND DEPARTING

Airport
Marco Polo International Airport is 10 km north-east of Venice. Facilities are limited. The cheapest and quickest way to Venice is by bus, either by the dedicated non-stop service which meets all scheduled flights (takes 15 mins), or the ordinary public service, no.5, which takes around 30 mins and departs every 30 mins. Both cost around L5000 and terminate at *Pzle Roma.*

The cheapest entry by boat is aboard the public **Cooperativa San Marco** launch which departs hourly, or every 2 hrs, depending on time of day. It takes around 50 mins and costs around L15,000 (one-way), landing conveniently close to the San Marco *vaporetto* stage. Tickets are bought from the office by the exit of the airport arrivals hall. Private water-taxis are also available but these are very expensive.

By Car
Venice is closed to all road traffic so park at either the *Isola del Tronchetto* or *Pzle Roma.* Parking charges are expensive. In summer, during Carnival and at Easter, cheaper parking lots are opened on the mainland at Fusina and San Giuliano in Mestre. If it fits in with your Veneto itinerary it may even be worthwhile parking at a neighbouring town with a direct rail link (e.g. Padua).

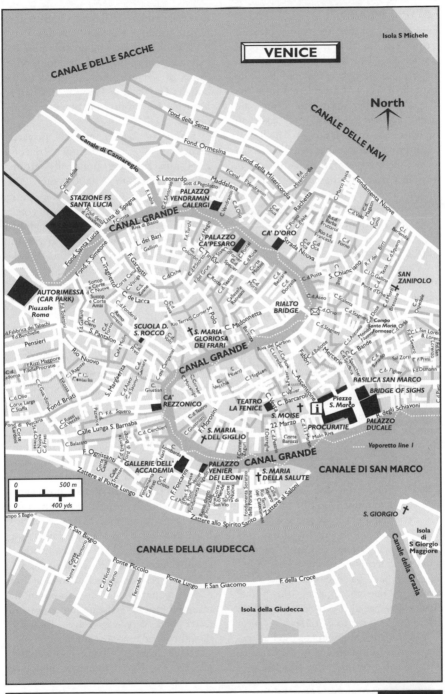

GETTING AROUND

Venice is probably the most pleasant tourist city in the world for getting around. The city is very compact and most major sights are only a few minutes walk from the *Pza San Marco*, referred to as 'the *Piazza*' (all other squares in Venice are *campi*). *Vaporetti* (see below) will take you anywhere else you want to go. The tourist office provide reasonable maps but these do not show the warren of narrow alleyways that make up the city so you may want to invest in a more detailed map. At first everyone gets lost, but as you will discover, it's all part of the city's magic.

Public Transport

In Venice this means *vaporetto* (plural, *vaporetti*) or water-bus. These are efficient, punctual, cheap and often very scenic. You can pay on board but it is cheaper to buy your ticket in advance, from the ticket offices on or close to the landing stages or at any shop displaying an **ACTV** sign. There is a flat charge for each line regardless of how far you travel. A 24hr or 72hr pass is well worthwhile if you intend doing a reasonable amount of sightseeing. You can also buy tickets in blocks of 10 or 20, which do not show a money saving but will save you time. Tickets are validated by punching them at the red and yellow machine on the landing stage before each journey. Don't be tempted to travel without a ticket, as you risk a steep fine. *Vaporetti* are also useful simply as a way of hopping across the Canal Grande – bridges and ferries (see below) are surprisingly few and far between. The main service is the no. 1, along the Canal Grande (see panel). Both nos. 52 and 82 go from *Pzle Roma* to *San Marco*.

Traghetti are old gondolas, used as ferries to cross from one side of the canal to the other. It's certainly the cheapest way to travel in this style and the etiquette is to remain standing, but do be careful!

Water-taxis (*motoscafi*) provide a fast but extremely expensive door-to-door service. Prices of certain routes are given in the booklet *Un Ospite di Venezia* ('A Guest of Venice'), free from your hotel or tourist offices.

Gondolas, which are all privately owned, are also very expensive. Prices for a 50-min ride are nominally around L70,000, rising to L90,000 after 2000 (prices also in *Un Ospite di Venezia*). In the low season you may be able to negotiate down, but conversely some gondoliers may try to charge you more, so confirm the price *before* you get in. A gondola holds a maximum of five passengers.

STAYING IN VENICE

Accommodation

Venice is one of the world's more expensive cities for accommodation. The costliest periods are at Christmas and in Feb during Carnival (see p. 85). In the sweltering heat of Aug and the chill of winter (defined as Nov onwards) it is much easier to find places. As a general rule the nearer you are to the *Pza San Marco*, the dearer the hotel. The most downbeat area is the *Lista di Spagna* near the rail station. One of the joys of staying in Venice however, is that most hotels are in historic and often characterful properties. There is a free hotel booking service at the rail station, but be warned that visitors without advance reservations are unlikely to find reasonably priced rooms in Venice at short notice – you may be offered rooms on the mainland instead. Self-catering options are scarce and very expensive. Enquiries should be made months ahead.

Hotel chains in Venice include: *BW, Ch, Ex, Pu, Ra*. If money is no object there are a number of famous 5-star hotels, of which the **Cipriani** is the most exclusive. It is the only hotel in Venice (excluding the Lido) with a swimming pool but is also somewhat isolated on the island of Giudecca. For more affordable luxury, albeit still at very expensive prices, try the **Metropole**, perfectly positioned on the *Riva degli Schiavoni; tel: (041) 520 5044*, or the popular **Flora**, off *C Larga XXII Marzo, San Marco* (book well in advance); *tel: (041) 520 5844*. Two other good expensive–moderate choices are **Sturion**, *C. del Storione, San Polo; tel: (041) 523 6243* and **Pensione Accademia Villa Maravegie**, *Fondamenta Bollani, Dorsoduro; tel: (041) 521 0578*. Also in Dorsoduro, in the moderate price bracket, is the charming **Agli Alboretti**, *Rio Terra Santa Agnese; tel: (041) 523 0058*. One of the best options in the budget category is the **Messner**, *Salute, Dorsoduro; tel: (041) 522 7443*.

HI: *Giudecca, Fond, Zitelle 86; tel: (041) 523 8211* enjoys a superb location. There are two other hostels: **Instituto Suore Canossiane** (women only), *Giudecca, Ponte Piccolo 428; tel: (041) 522 2157*; **Foresteria Valdese**, *C. Lunga Santa Maria Formosa, Castello; tel: (041) 528 6797*.

Campsites are located on the mainland or on the Lido. **Camping Fusina**, *V. Moranzani, Fusina; tel: (041) 547 0055*. **Camping Marco Polo**, *V. Triestina, Tessera; tel: (041) 541 6033*. **Camping Miramare Lungomare**, *Dante Alighieri 29, Punta Sabbioni; tel: (041) 966150*. **Camping San Nicolò**, Lido; *tel: (041) 726 74 15*.

Eating and Drinking

The price of just a coffee (never mind food!) at the famous *Piazza* cafés, **Quadri's** and **Florian's**, is astronomical.

Nevertheless, many people think it well worth paying for the privilege, particularly when their orchestras are playing. Wander just around the corner, however, take your drink at the bar with the locals and prices are back down to earth. In many places simply sitting down can double prices. If you want to eat economically and sample as many different kinds of local taste as possible look for the peculiarly. Venetian custom of *cicheti* (assorted snacks), which are displayed on the counter of *osterias* and wine bars. This is similar to the Spanish tradition of *tapas* and covers a range of tasty morsels from garlic meatballs (*polpette*) to cold slices of fried vegetables, seafoods and the ubiquitous *pizzetta* (mini-pizzas). A good place to look for such establishments is in the crowded narrow alleyways off the *Rialto*, particularly for **Do Mori** which is a Venetian institution. Wash down your *cichetti* with a glass of local wine, called (again peculiar to Venice) *una ombra*. *Ombra* means shade, from the old tradition of taking a glass of wine in the shade. Unless you specify *ombra rosso* you will be served white wine.

Venice has two other drinks to call its own. The *Bellini*, invented by Signor Cipriani of Harry's Bar (see below), is a delicious blend of *prosecco* and peach juice. A version of spritzer is also claimed by the Venetians, who add a bitter, such as Campari, to white wine and water. This not only gives an extra kick but makes a glorious sunset-coloured drink (just ask for *spritz*).

Typical Venetian starters include *sarde in saor* (sardines marinated in onions and a sweet-sour vinaigrette) and *carpaccio* (wafer-thin slices of beef). The *secondi piatti* is often dominated by seafood. Look for *granceola* (crab), *anguilla alla veneziana* (eel cooked in a lemon, oil and tuna sauce) and

83

seppie al nero (cuttlefish cooked in its own ink), traditionally served with *polenta*. The city's favourite meat dish is *fegato alla veneziana* (calf's liver with onions).

Avoid the obvious tourist traps and you will find excellent dining all over the city ranging from some of Italy's finest *ristoranti* to simple *trattorias, osterias* and *pizzerias*. Many are in atmospheric old buildings and eating out is often a very romantic occasion. The only deterrent is usually the affordability of an establishment.

To eat with the locals at budget–moderate prices try **Aciugheta**, *Campo Sti Filippo e Giacomo, Castello; tel: (041) 522 4292* (closed Wed); **Osteria Assassini**, *Rio Terra degli Assassini, San Marco* (closed Sun); *tel: (041) 528 7986*; **Rivetta**, *Ponte San Provolo, off Campo Sti Filippo e Giacomo, Castello; tel: (041) 528 7302* (closed Mon); **Taverna San Trovaso**, *Fondamente Priuli, Dorsoduro; tel: (041) 520 3703* (closed Mon).

For more style, but moderate–expensive prices, visit **Alla Madonna**, *C della Madonna, San Polo; tel: (041) 522 3824* (closed Wed); **Al Conte Pescaor**, *Piscina San Zulian, San Marco; tel: (041) 522 1483* (closed Sun); **Agli Alboreti**, *Rio Terra Sta Agnese, Dorsoduro; tel: (041) 523 0058*; **Al Graspo de Ua**, *C. dei Bombaseri, San Marco; tel: (041) 520 0150* (closed Mon).

Save up for a special (i.e. very expensive) occasion at: **La Caravella**, *C Larga XXII Marzo, San Marco; tel: (041) 520 8901* (closed Wed); **Antica Trattoria Poste Vecchia**, *Pescheria, San Polo; tel: (041) 721822* (closed Tues); **Do Forni**, *C. Specchieri, San Marco; tel: (041) 523 2148* (closed Thur).

Communications

The main **Post Office** is at *Fondaco dei Tedeschi, Rialto; tel: (041) 271 7111*, open daily 0815–1900, lobby open 24hrs for telegrams, faxes and express and registered letters. The main sub-office is at *C. dell'Ascensione, San Marco; tel: (041) 528 59 49*, open Mon–Fri 0810–1325, Sat 0810–1200.

Money

There is a **Thomas Cook bureau de change** at *Piazza San Marco, 142; tel: (041) 522 4751*.

Consulates

Belgium: *San Marco 1470; tel: (041) 522 4124*.
France: *Dorsoduro 1397; tel: (041) 522 4319*.
Germany: *Cannaregio 4201; tel: (041) 523 7675*.
Netherlands: *San Marco 423; tel: (041) 528 3416*.
South Africa: *San Croce 466/G; tel: (041) 524 1599*.
UK: *Campo Santa Maria della Carità, Dorsoduro 1051; tel: (041) 522 7207*.

ENTERTAINMENT

Outside of Carnival time (see below) Venice is not a city that generally lets its hair down. The most famous bar/nightspot in town is **Harry's Bar**, also recommended for its food (very expensive). Harry's Bar is famous for its *bellinis* (see above) and for the celebrities it attracts. The atmosphere is at best refined, at worst snooty. There are numerous other bars but none that are worth a major detour.

Thanks to an elderly resident population and a high proportion of day-trippers, nightlife is relatively muted. Get hold of a copy of *Rolling Venice Agenda* (see Tourist Information) for a list of nightspots. A long- established favourite is **Paradiso Perduto**, *Fondamente della Misericordia, Cannaregio* (closed Wed). **El Souk**, near the Accademia (closed Mon), is the city's only disco.

High rollers can visit the **casino** which resides at the Lido from Apr to Sept and at the Palazzo Vendramin Calergi on the Canal Grande (see panel) for the rest of the year.

Venice's **churches** frequently stage musical events and it can be a magical experience to hear the works of Italian composers, such as Vivaldi, on their home patch.

Sadly for theatre goers **La Fenice**, one of Europe's most beautiful small theatres burned down (once again) in 1996. It is planned to restore the theatre for the millennium. Meanwhile, the resident opera company performs in various locations around Venice.

See *Un Ospite di Venezia* for details of all nightlife and keep an eye open for fly posters.

Events

The most famous event of the year is **Carnevale**, which comprises music, comedy and drama, yet by Latin carnival standards celebrations are relatively tame. These occur in the ten days before Lent although costumes, masks and decorations are in the shops all year round. The rather sinister looking garb of mask, tricorn hat and cloak dates back to the *commedia dell'arte* characters of the 18th-century.

Equally colourful is the **Regata Storica**, a Renaissance costume pageant and regatta which takes place on the first Sun in Sept on the Canal Grande. Other historical celebrations well worth catching are **La Sensa**, (Sun after Ascension), the **Festa del Redentore** (third Sun in July) and the **Festa della Salute** (21 Nov).

The city is also famous for two modern arts events. The **Venice Film Festival**, second in importance only to Cannes, is held at the Lido, late Aug to early Sept, while the **Biennale** – one of the oldest and most important exhibitions of contemporary art in the world – is staged in odd years between June and Sept in the Biennale Gardens. Unfortunately it is very difficult for the public to get tickets to the film festival, while the majority of avant-garde exhibits displayed at the Biennale are (to the general public at least) simply absurd.

SHOPPING

Venice's main shopping street is the **Merceria**, running from the *Piazza* to the *Rialto*. There is a plethora of expensive **art and antiques** shops and galleries throughout Venice. Look out for beautiful hand-printed, marbled paper – an old Venetian craft. **Glassware** is the most famous tradition and although Murano (see Islands below) has the best selection its prices are not necessarily the lowest. Plastic gondolas aside, the ubiquitous **Carnival masks** make affordable and very typical Venetian presents.

85

SIGHTSEEING

There are guided walking tours of the city (enquire with your hotel or at any travel agent) but Venice is so easy to get around that you only need to be armed with a good guide book and a fistful of *vaporetti* tickets.

San Marco

This area is the heart of Venice and one from which most day-trippers never stray. Consequently it can become very crowded so do your sightseeing either early or late in the day.

Start with an overview by taking the lift to the top of the 99 m tall **Campanile di San Marco** (St Mark's Bell Tower). The views are stunning, open daily 0930–

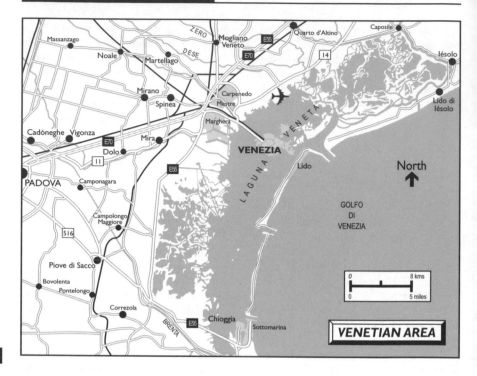

1900, closed Jan, entrance fee L6000. Below is the **Piazza**, fringed with magnificent architecture and often echoing to the strains of classical music from the café orchestras. The major attraction is the **Basilica di San Marco** (St Mark's Basilica), a magnificent blend of East and West encapsulating the old Venetian republic's ambition as the successor to Constantinople. It was built between 1063 and 1094 to house the body of St Mark. There are guided tours in English in July and Aug. The Basilica is packed with treasures, not least the fabric of the building, adorned with magnificent interior and exterior **mosaics**. Regarded as the most important pieces, however, are the gilded **Bronze Horses of San Marco** and the **Pala d'Oro**. Like so much in the Basilica both were looted from Constantinople. The horses now reside in the Basilica's

museum (those outside are copies) and were cast in Rome, or Greece, around AD 200. The Pala d'Oro (golden altar screen) is the Venetian equivalent of the crown jewels, with a dazzling display of precious stones set on gold. Basilica and museum opening hours Mon–Sat 1000–1700, Sun 1400–1700 (museum also open Sun morning), entrance fee to museum, Treasury and Pala d'Oro L8000. Other major points of interest on the square include the 500-year-old **Torre dell'Orologio** (clock tower) with one of Venice's most colourful Lions of St Mark (the ubiquitous symbol of the Republic) and a superb zodiacal clock. The tower is topped by two Moors who strike the hours on the great bell.

To find respite from the crowds slip into the **Museo Correr**, a first–class collection of 13th- to 16th-century paintings, sculptures and Venetian history, open Wed–Mon 1000–1700, entrance fee L10,000. Adjacent to the Basilica is the equally breathtaking **Palazzo Ducale** (Doges' Palace). For some nine centuries this was the seat of the republic, council chamber, law court, prison and residence of most of the doges. The present structure dates from the 15th century and a series of highly impressive gates and stairs lead to the magnificent chambers (now mostly empty) where visitors pick up portable recorders for a guided tour.

The highlights are the **Sala del Consiglio dei Deici**, the room where the feared 'Council of Ten' used to meet, the armoury and the **Sala del Maggior Consiglio** (Great Council Chamber) where Tintoretto's *Paradise* is the largest Old Master painting in the world. Finally you will pass across the **Bridge of Sighs** (Ponte dei Sospiri), only to learn, rather disappointingly, that only petty criminals were confined in the cells here, open daily 0900–1800 (Mar–Sept); 0900–1600 (Oct–Feb).

Castello

Continue around the waterfront along the bustling promenade of **Riva degli Schiavoni** ('Quay of the slaves'), past the exterior of the Bridge of Sighs and the church of **La Pietà**, where Vivaldi, in his function as concertmaster, wrote many of his finest works. By the time you reach the Arsenale **vaporetto** stop after a few hundred metres, the crowds, even in high season, will have disappeared. The **Arsenale** was once the greatest shipyard in the world, employing 16,000 men to building the warships of the Venetian empire. Napoleon destroyed the Arsenale in 1797 and today only the splendid entrance arch remains. The spirit of the age is evoked, however, at the excellent **Museo Storico**

Navale (Naval History Museum), which features models and full-size ships, open Mon–Sat 0900–1300, entrance fee L8000

The artistic highlight of the Castello *sestiere* (quarter) is the **Scuola di San Giorgio degli Schiavoni** (a *scuola* is a confraternity of laymen under the banner of a particular saint). This captivating and intimate building was founded in 1451 as the guildhall of the city's Dalmatian merchants. In 1500 they hired Vittore Carpaccio to completely decorate the hall which he did with nine exceptional pictures. His rendition of *St George and the Dragon* is particularly memorable. *C. Furlani*, **vaporetto stage:** *San Zaccaria*, open Tues–Sat 0930–1230 and 1500–1830, Sun 0930–1230 (Apr–Sept); daily 1000–1800 (Oct–Mar), entrance fee L8000.

There are three outstanding churches in Castello. The beautiful early 16th-century **San Zaccaria** has an eerie flooded 8th-century crypt where early doges occupy watery graves; **vaporetto stage** *San Zaccaria*. The cavernous church of **San Zanipolo (Santi Giovanni e Paolo)** was completed in 1430 and is known as the 'Pantheon of Venice'. Its many splendid monumental tombs include some 25 doges; **vaporetto stage**: *Fondamente Nuove* or *Ospedale Civile*.

Close by, to the north, lies one of the city's most charming churches, **Santa Maria dei Miracoli**, which the Venetians call their *scrigno d'oro* (golden jewel box). It is beautifully marbled within and without in delicate shades of pink and white and grey and has just been restored, though opening hours are dependent upon the whims of the custodian; **vaporetto stage**: *Rialto*.

Dorsoduro

The *sestiere* of Dorsoduro lies directly

87

opposite the Canal Grande from San Marco and features one of the city's most often-photographed landmarks, the great baroque church of **Santa Maria della Salute**. The Salute was erected in gratitude for the end of a plague in 1630, and ever since 1670 on 21 November each year Venetians have literally walked across the river (on pontoons of boats) to pay homage at the church. The interior features works by Tintoretto and Titian but, after the magnificent exterior, it is rather disappointing; **vaporetto stage**: *Salute*.

Dorsoduro's other claim to fame is the **Accademia**, reached on foot by a beautiful wooden bridge, built in 1932. This gallery houses the greatest collection of Venetian art assembled in one building. There are 24 rooms in total, spanning the 14th to 19th centuries and highlights include: *Crucifixion of the Ten Thousand Martyrs* by Carpaccio (room 2); *St George* by Mantegna (room 4); *The Tempest* by Georgione, *Pietà* by Titian (room 5); *Feast at the House of Levi* by Veronese, *Transport of the Body of St Mark* by Tintoretto (room 10); *Blessed Lorenzo Giustinian* by Gentile Bellini (room 23). Room 20 is the greatest of all with four huge masterpieces. Gentile Bellini's *Procession around the Piazza* shows how little San Marco has changed in 500 years, while Carpaccio's epic *The Miracle of the Holy Cross at the Rialto Bridge* depicts the former Rialto Bridge and familiar gondola scenes. Finally in room 21 is Carpaccio's much admired *St Ursula* cycle. Note, the Accademia restricts its admissions to just 180 people at a time so to avoid long queues, get there preferably early in the morning (as only natural light illuminates the works), or late in the evening; **vaporetto stage***: Accademia*, open (last admissions) Mon–Sat 0900–1830, Sun 0900–1330. Entrance fee L12,000.

Literally a few steps, but artistically centuries away from the Accademia is the **Collezione Guggenheim** (Peggy Guggenheim Collection), acclaimed as one of the finest collections of modern art in Europe. After a surfeit of the heavy religious art for which Venice is famed, the airy light–filled rooms and comparitively uncluttered works here are a breath of fresh air. It comprises some 200 works, including paintings and sculptures by Ernst, Miró, Picasso, Magritte, Kandinsky, Mondrian and Brancusi, which represent almost every modern movement; **vaporetto stage***: Accademia*, open Wed–Mon 1100–1800, entrance fee L10,000.

The third major Dorsoduro attraction is the **Ca'Rezzonico**, though it is the palatial 17th-century building which is the star attraction, as much as the exhibits within. It is one of the few *palazzi* on the Canal Grande open to the public and holds the **Museo del Settecento Veneziano** (Museum of 18th-century Venice). Ceilings by Tiepolo and Canal Grande paintings by Canaletto (ironically very rare in Venice) vie for attention with a stunning ballroom, an 18th-century apothecary's shop and a puppet theatre; **vaporetto stage**: *Ca'Rezzonico*, open Sat–Thur 1000–1700 (1600 winter). Entrance fee L8000.

Close by at the **Scuola Grande dei Carmini**, the former headquarters of the Carmelite confraternity, there are more splendid ceilings by Tiepolo to enjoy; *Campo Carmini,* **vaporetto stage**: *Ca'Rezzonico*, open Mon–Sat 0900–1200 and 1500–1800. Entrance fee L8000.

The Rialto
Straddling the *sestieres* (one of six Venetian districts) of San Marco and San Polo, the **Rialto Bridge** attracts a seemingly endless

chain of daily visitors. The present handsome structure was built between 1588 and 1591 and has become the most famous landmark on the Canal Grande. In fact not until 1854 was another crossing (at Accademia) built at all. Just across the bridge are the most colourful **markets** in Venice, the *erberia* (fruit and vegetables) and *pescheria* (fish) where Venetians have been shopping for over 900 years. Arrive early to see the best of the stock (open Mon–Sat) then mingle with the traders and shoppers in some of Venice's most atmospheric small bars and cafés.

Walk on through San Polo to the **Frari**, Venice's second most important church after the Basilica di San Marco. This huge lofty structure was built between 1340 and 1469 and is a treasure house of paintings and monuments. Pride of place goes to Titian's exuberant *Assumption* though works by Donatello and Giovanni Bellini are equally noteworthy. The monk's choir features superb bas-reliefs and there are several bombastic **monuments**, most notably to Titian (who is buried here), Canova (whose heart lies here) and to the doges, Pésaro and Foscari; **vaporetto stage**: *San Tomà*, open Mon–Sat 0900–1145 and 1430– 1730, Sun 1500–1730. Entrance free.

Close by is the greatest of all the Venetian *scuole* (see above), the **Scuola Grande di San Rocco**. Tintoretto was commissioned to decorate the entire building (which took him 23 years) and Henry James later described the result as one of the three most precious picture collections in all Italy. It is a work of epic proportions and *Crucifixion* was ranked by Tintoretto himself as his greatest painting; **vaporetto stage**: *San Tomà*, open daily 0900–1730 (Apr–Nov); 1000–1600 (Dec–Mar). Entrance fee L8000.

Also in San Polo are three worthwhile museums. Close to the Frari is the **Casa Museo di Goldoni**, the house in which the famous 18th-century dramatist Carlo Goldoni lived. Still very popular today, his well-preserved Gothic palace house repays a visit, even for non *aficionados*; **vaporetto stage**: *S. Tomà,* open Mon–Sat 0830–1330. Entrance fee L2000.

To the north, on the Canal Grande, is the **Museo d'Arte Moderna**, housed in the beautiful Ca'Pésaro and featuring excellent works by the likes of Klimt, Klee, Miró, Matisse, Bonnard and Kandinsky; **vaporetto stage**: *Santa Stae,* open Tues–Sun 1000–1700. Entrance fee L8000.

Upstairs is the **Museo Orientale** featuring lacquered pieces and samurai arms and armour, open Tue–Sun 0900–1330. Entrance fee L6000.

Close by, also on the Canal Grande, is the **Museo di Storia Naturale** (Natural History Museum), a good standby for children, featuring various bygone monster-sized creatures including dinosaurs and a crocodile over 11 m long; **vaporetto stage**: *Santa Stae,* open Tues–Sun 0900–1300. Entrance fee L8000.

Cannaregio

Aside from its cheap lodgings, on the *Lista di Spagna*, Cannaregio is one of the city's least visited quarters. However, it features some fine churches, the famous Ca'd'Oro and the world's original ghetto.

The latter is a small quarter, named **Ghetto**, which at its peak during the 17th century housed some 5000 Jews. They were heavily taxed, forced to wear different clothing, barred from many professions and restricted to living only within this tiny area. It was Napoleon who in 1797 ended this restriction. Today only a handful of Jewish families live in Ghetto, but there is a **Museo Ebraica** (Jewish

89

Museum) in *Campo Ghetto Nuovo;* **vaporetto stage**: *Ponte Guglie,* open Sat–Thur 1000–1900 (summer); 1000–1630 (winter). Entrance fee L5000. English-speaking guided tours of the area's synagogues depart from here 1030–1530 every 30 mins.

The **Ca'd'Oro** boasts probably the finest façade on the Canal Grande and is regarded as the pinnacle of Venetian Gothic architecture. Sadly the interior has been largely gutted over the centuries and it is now home to the **Giorgio Franchetti Collection** where the striking prize exhibit is *St Sebastian* by Mantegna; **vaporetto stage**: *Ca'd'Oro,* open daily 0900–1330. Entrance fee L8000.

The islands

San Giorgio Maggiore is the nearest island, a mere 5-min ride away (*vaporetto 82*) and photographed on countless occasions from San Marco as a backdrop for bobbing gondolas. Choose a clear sunny day for your journey for the joy of this island is a magnificent **panorama** of Venice from its church campanile. The church and monastery of San Giorgio Maggiore was built by Palladio and features works by Tintoretto. **Murano** (*vaporetto 52, 12, 13*) is the home of Venetian glassware.

Hotels and touts offer free *motoscafi* rides to the island where, following the obligatory glass factory tour, a degree of sales pressure is applied. To avoid this it's best to visit independently. All glass making was moved here in the 13th century to reduce the risks of fire in Venice. Murano prospered and by the early 16th century it was the top glass producer in Europe. By the 19th century, however, foreign competition had brought the industry to its knees and today it is a mere shadow of its former self.

Venetian Palaces

Unlike Florence, where every tiny town is called a *palazzo* (palace), Venice deprecatingly refers to the most splendid of palaces as a casa (house), often abbreviated in Venetain dialect to Ca'. Many Venetian families owned a whole string of such palaces, so you will encounter the same names – Vendramin, Callergi, Corner, Foscari and Contarini, for example – again and again. Noble Venetians did not walk – they used private gondolas to get about, so the watergate facades of palaces are always more ornate than the street façades - one more reason why you must take to the water if you want to see the best of Venice.

The **Museo Vetrario** (Glass Museum) on *Fondamenta Giustinian* (**vaporetto stage**: *Museo*), houses some beautiful old pieces in a 17th-century bishop's palace. There's also a **Modern and Contemporary Glass Museum** annexe on *Fondamente Manin* (**vaporetto stage**: *Colonna*). Both open Thur–Tues 1000–1700 (1600 winter). Entrance fee L5000. Murano is basically a miniature Venice, not so attractive, but worth at least half a day. By the Glass Museum is the atmospheric **Basilica dei Santi Maria e Donato** with superb floor mosaics and a glowing golden Madonna mosaic.

Burano, 'pearl of the lagoon', is most visitor's favourite island (*vaporetto: 12, 14, 52*). It is like a scaled-down version of Venice with tiny houses crowding narrow canals, but unlike the dull brick of the 'mainland', here the houses are painted in a bright and beautiful rainbow of pastel shades. Some of the world's finest lace once came from Burano but today the tradition has almost died out and real Burano lace (if you can find it at all) is very expensive. Visitors are welcome to look in at the island lace-making school, the **Museo/Scuola dei Merletti**, *Pza Baldassare Galuppi*, and to visit the small museum attached, open Tues–Sat 0900–1900, Sun 1000–1600. Entrance fee L5000.

Torcello *(vaporetto: 12, 14)* is the most atmospheric of the populated Venetian islands. Now almost deserted, it was until medieval times the focus of the lagoon with a population of around 20,000. However, as its canals silted up and malaria drove its people away, and with Venice's ascendancy, it became quite literally a backwater. Today it numbers a mere 60 inhabitants and is basically a one-canal settlement. The glorious 11th-century Byzantine cathedral of **Santa Maria dell'Assunta** is the only reminder of its past glory with magnificent glowing Byzantine mosaics. Close by is the charming, serene church of **S Fosca** and the interesting little **Museo dell'Estuario** (Museum of the Estuary) open Tues–Sun 1000–1230 and 1400–1730 (1600 in winter).

The name **Lido** *(vaporetto: 1, 6, 14, 17, 52, 82 or buses A, B, C and 11)* may conjure up images of Shelley, Byron, *belle-époque* glamour, sandy beaches, film stars and Venice's summer casino, but unless you have the money to join the 'in crowd' you may as well not turn up. Nowadays the island is largely an atmosphere-free zone and the only decent bits of beach have been grabbed by the big hotels and are rented out to non-residents at exorbitant rates. However, paid for, or free, the water quality here often leaves a lot to be desired. There are good sporting facilities on the Lido (notably golf) but no significant historical sights.

The Canal Grande

Vaporetto no. 1 is called the *accelerato*, but as it stops every few metres, it is the perfect sightseeing vehicle for the **Canal Grande**. The banks are lined with over 200 *palazzi*, mostly built between the 14th and 18th centuries. Once aristocratic homes, most are now offices, hotels, museums or galleries. Here are just a few of its highlights. Travelling from *Pzle Roma* to *San Marco* look on the left bank for the following: (after the San Marculoa stage) the **Vendramin–Calergi**, large and in classical-style, now home to the winter casino; next to the Ca'd'Oro stage, the magnificent **Ca'd'Oro** (see above) sadly no longer gilded. Between here and the Rialto Bridge (see above) is the 13th-century **Ca'da Mosto**, one of the oldest houses on the canal. After the Rialto and Sant'Anglo stage is the **Mocenigo**, four adjoining *palazzi*, marked by blue-and-white *pali* (mooring posts) and a plaque stating that this was the home of Lord Byron. The **Grassi**, by the San Samuele stage, is now a cultural centre. Next to the graceful Accademia Bridge is the splendid **Cavalli Franchetti** (note the red-and-white *pali*) and adjacent is the **Barbaro**, a former haunt of many famous artists and painters.

Heading back to *Pzle Roma* look on the left bank for the small but beautiful **Dario** with its subtle marble façade, the **Venier dei Leoni** (home to the Guggenheim Collection, see above) and the adjacent **Barbarigo**, with colourful mosaics. At the Ca'Rezonnico stage is the **Ca' Rezonnico**, now a museum (see above). Nearby is the **Giustinian**, where Wagner lived, adjacent is the **Ca'Foscari** and next to that the **Balbi**. Opposite the San Marcuola stage is the **Fondaco dei Turchi** (now the Natural History Museum, see above).

91

PADUA–VICENZA
CITIES OF THE PLAIN

Padua (Padova) and Vicenza are two of Northern Italy's great art cities, both beautifully preserved, full of sightseeing and entertainment possibilities, and also compact enough to forget about your car for a couple of days. South of Padua the green volcanic humps of the Colli Euganei (Euganean Hills) provide a welcome change from the flat Veneto plain and shelter such gems as Arquà Petrarca and Monsélice, both little changed in centuries.

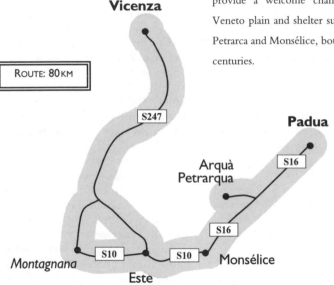

Vicenza

ROUTE: 80 KM

S247

Padua

Arquà
Petrarqua

S16

S16

S10

S10

Monsélice

Montagnana

Este

ROUTE

From Padua head south on the S16, following the signs to the Colli Euganei (Euganean Hills), for some 18 km. A small road on the right (signposted) leads, after 3 km, to **Arquà Petrarca**.

Return in the direction of the S16 for around 1 km and take the first turn right to **Monsélice** (7 km). Take the S10 9 km west to **Este**. From Este, continue on the S10 to **Montagnana**. Alternatively, take the S247 directly to **Vicenza** (46 km).

PADUA (PADOVA)

Tourist Office: rail station; *tel: (049) 875 2077*, open Mon–Sat 0900–1900, Sun 0900–1200. Pick up a free copy of *Padua Today*. Only the regional tourist office (APT) handles accommodation queries, *V. Riviera Mugnai 8; tel: (049) 875 0655*.

Thomas Cook Worldwide Network Licensee: CIT Viaggi; *Pza Madama 11; tle: (049) 663333*.

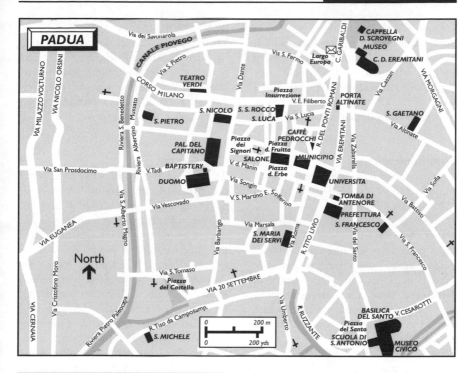

GETTING AROUND

The main sights are within walking distance of each other, clustered in the old city centre and stretching from the *Prato della Valle* (south) to the *Capello degli Scovegni* (north, towards the rail station). Buses 3, 8 and 12 run between Prato della Valle and the station, or it's around a 15 min walk. A 24 hr ticket, valid for all urban buses, costs L5000.

Padua is on the main Venice–Milan and Venice–Bologna rail lines and is the nearest major town to Venice, a 30-min ride away.

STAYING IN PADUA

Accommodation

The best place to seek out budget hotels is *Pza del Santo*.

Hotel chains in Padua include *GT*.

Beware that hotels are full around the Festa di Sant'Antonio, 13 June, when thousands of pilgrims fill Padua.

Recommended if you like ultra-modern style is the recently refurbished luxury hotel, **Grand'Italia**, *Corso del Popolo* (in front of the rail station); *tel: (049) 650877*. By contrast, at the bottom end of the moderate price scale is the **Albergo Leon Bianco**, small and friendly and bang in the centre of town next to the Caffè Pedrocchi, *Pzta Pedrocchi 12, tel: (049) 657225 or 875 0814*.

HI: *Ostello Città di Padua, V. Alcardi 30; tel: (049) 875 2219* (buses 3, 8 or 12 from station).

Eating and Drinking

There is a good range of high-class restaurants throughout Padua. For a list of approved eating places pick up a copy of

Ristorante e Trattorie from the tourist office. Cheap *trattorie* can be found around the university area. The most famous café in town is the **Caffè Pedrocchi** (see Sightseeing). Almost opposite here, in the corner of *Pza Cavour* is **Brek**, an excellent self-service establishment serving authentic local food.

Communications

The central post office is at *Corso Garibaldi 33*, open Mon–Fri 0815–1940, Sat 0815–1220, Sun 0830–1830.

Padua has a lively summer programme of classical music, and several concerts are staged outdoors in the **Giardini dell'Arena**, next to the Eremitani Museum. Another impressive venue which hosts the occasional concert is the **Palazzo della Ragione** (see Sightseeing). There is also an annual *I Solisti Veneti* festival from mid June to early July. The presence of the university attracts contemporary acts including rock, ethnic and jazz bands. Look in *Padova Today* for details and keep an eye open for posters around the university.

Events

The big event of the year is the **Festa di Sant'Antonio**, 13 June, when a statue and the actual jawbone of the patron saint is carried in a procession from the Basilica through the city centre.

The centre of Padua has a good range of fashionable Italian and international shops. There are food and general markets (Mon–Sat) around the *Palazzo della Ragione* and in the *Pza dei Signori* and an antiques market on the third Sun of each month in the *Prato della Valle*.

There are no regular guided tours of Padua by day but you can view the city's art and history after dark in summer (mid July to late Aug) by joining one of the free *Notturni d'Arte* (art nights) tours. Ask at the tourist office for details or *tel: (049) 820 4547*.

City Centre

The city centre is an attractive area, partly pedestrianised, and very well preserved. Start with a coffee at the Caffè Pedrocchi, an extraordinary building with one façade like a Classical temple. It has been a meeting place for students and intellectuals for over 160 years. The upstairs rooms are decorated in colourful styles representing many ancient civilisations including Etruscan, Greek, Roman, Moorish and Egyptian, open Tues and Thur–Sun 0930–1230 and 1530–1800; entrance fee L5000. The **University of Padua** occupies the 16th-century *Palazzo del Bo* which is diagonally opposite Caffè Pedrocchi (just along *V. VIII Febbraio*) and is referred to as **Il Bo**. Guided tours are conducted and highlights include the world's oldest galleried anatomy theatre and the pulpit from which Galileo lectured between 1592 and 1610. Entrance on *V. Marzolo*, daily 0900–1300 (Mar–Oct); tours on the hour, L5000.

Dominating the centre is the **Palazzo della Ragione**, also called the Salone (Great Hall). It was built as the law court and council chamber in 1218 and measures a staggering 80 m long by 27 m wide by 27 m high. Its spectacular roof is the largest keel-vaulted example in the world and the hall itself is the largest undivided medieval hall in Europe. Around its sides are a series of 333 frescos depicting astrological subjects. There are only two permanent exhibits in this vast space; one is a giant wooden horse, inspired by Donatello's *Gattamelatta* outside the Basilica (see below); the other is the *pietra del vituperio* (stone of shame) on which debtors or bankrupts were forced to sit bare-bottomed and be subject to public ridicule. The hall is frequently used for exhibitions, open Tues–Sun 0900–1900 (Feb–Oct); 0900–1800 (Nov–Jan). Entrance fee L7000.

Note: a *biglietto unico* (single ticket) allows entrance to the Palazzo della Ragione, Museo Civico Eremitani, Capella degli Scrovegni, Battistero del Duomo, Oratorio San Giorgio and Orto Botanico for L15,000 on sale at all participating places.

In front of the *palazzo's* beautiful 15th-century loggia (designed by Palladio) is the **Pza delle Erbe**, the city's vegetable and flower market while on the opposite side the *Pza dei Frutti* (currently being restored) sells fruit. Adjacent to the latter is the **Pza dei Signori**, a handsome square which is host for six mornings per week to a general market. At its head the 17th-century **Palazzo del Capitanio** features a superb astronomical clock made in 1344. Turn left in front of here to the **Duomo**. The main church is of only passing interest but its **Battistero** (Baptistery) is completely covered with one of Italy's most complete medieval fresco cycles. It was executed in 1378 by the largely unknown Giusto de' Menabuoi and has been splendidly restored to its original glowing colours, open daily 0930–1230 and 1500–1800; entrance fee L3000.

South of the City Centre

A 10-min walk along the *V. del Santo* looms the huge and exotic outline of the **Basilica di Sant'Antonio**. Its roof is a Byzantine-influenced jumble of eight domes interspersed with campaniles and minaret-like spires, while its handsome façade comprises Gothic and Romanesque elements. Begun in 1232 to house the body of Sant'Antonio, it remains an important place of pilgrimage – witness the many souvenir stands. The **tomb** of *Il Santo* is lined with superb 16th-century marble reliefs and is more or less permanently thronged with pilgrims who leave votive offerings to the saint. Of macabre interest is Antonio's jawbone and tongue/larynx (labelled *apparato vocal*) displayed in a glass case in the treasury at the back of the church. Visit the **Museo Antoniani** in the cloister to learn more about Sant'Antonio, open Tues–Sun 0900–1300 and 1430–1900 (summer); 1000–1300 and 1400–1700 (winter), entrance free. The **altarpiece**, by Donatello, features more magnificent reliefs, but unfortunately visitors are not allowed close enough to get a good look and his great **equestrian statue**, outside the basilica is likely to be more memorable. It commemorates the Venetian mercenary nicknamed *Gattamellata* ('Calico' or 'Honey Cat') and as well as being an aesthetic triumph it represented a technical landmark, being the first large-scale equestrian work cast since Roman times.

Next to the Basilica is the **Scoula del Santo** where four of the many paintings depicting the life of Sant'Antonio are the earliest known works of the young Titian. Adjacent the **Oratorio San Giorgio** features rather better quality Giotto-school frescos by Altichiero. Both open 0900–1230 and 1430–1900 (1700 winter), entrance fee (each) L3000.

A short walk along *V. Donatello* leads to the **Prato della Valle**. Once a malarial swamp where Sant'Antonio preached, this field (*prato*) was transformed in the late 18th century to an elliptical 'square' of heroic proportions and is claimed to be the largest public square in Italy. Around it flows a canal which is lined with 78 over-size statues of local luminaries, and crossed by four stone bridges, while the centre is laid to lawns with fountains. To the south is a triumphal arch and the Basilica of Santa Giustina, echoing the influence of Sant'Antonio.

Just off *V. Donatello* is the **Orto Botanico** (Botanic Garden), established in 1545 and claimed to be the oldest in Europe. It's a peaceful spot but there is little colour or visual interest and it is only notable in a botanical history context, open daily 0900–1300 and 1500–1800 (Apr–Oct); 0900–1300 (Nov–Mar). Entrance fee L5000.

North of the City Centre

A 5-min walk north leads to the **Eremitani** church which boasts some very impressive wall tombs and a fine roof. Sadly, only small fragments remain of the Mantegna frescos for which the church was once famous. They were all but destroyed, along with much of the church, in an air raid in 1944.

Adjacent is the **Museo Civico Eremitani**, a very rich and large collection comprising three separate museums (there is too much to see in one visit). The highlight of the **Archaeological Museum** is the Roman section while the **Museo Bottacin** features more than 50,000 coins, medals and seals and is one of the most important numismatic collections in the world. However, most visitors come for the **Medieval and Modern Art Museum** containing some 3000 paintings which present Venetian art from the early 14th century up to the 19th century. A special (permanent) exhibition entitled *From Paduanini to Tiepolo* highlights around 170 paintings from the 17th and 18th

centuries. There are contributions from Giorgione, Titian, Bassano, Veronese, Tintoretto and Giambattista Tiepolo, but perhaps the most striking works are the beautiful 14th-century series of panels painted by Guariento (his *Angels in Armour* series is a great favourite). In a similar striking golden vein is the museum's greatest treasure, *Crucifixion* by Giotto, designed for the Capella degli Scrovegni (see below). *Pza Eremitani*, open Tues–Sun 0900–1900 (Feb–Oct); 0900–1800 (Nov–Jan). Entrance fee L10,000 (includes Capella degli Scrovegni).

The **Capella degli Scrovegni** (Scrovegni Chapel) is generally regarded as the pearl of Padua and was built by Enrico Scrovegni in 1303, in the hope that this might save the soul of his father, an infamous usurer who had been damned by Dante in his *Inferno*. The chapel's decoration was painted by Giotto over three years, completely covering walls and ceiling in scenes which mainly depict episodes from the lives of Mary and Christ. It is a work of great beauty and was one of the principal influences of its time, breaking from the stiff linear design of the Byzantine tradition and developing a more naturalistic and dramatic style, characteristic of the Renaissance. A guide pamphlet is given to visitors. The chapel is extremely popular and, as only a limited number of visitors are allowed in at once, long queues can build up. Try to visit early in the morning or late in the evening to avoid these. Entrance through the Eremitani Museum foyer. Hours and entrance fee as above, also open Mon (Feb–Dec).

The Capella degli Scrovegni is also known as the Capella (or Madonna) dell'Arena after the adjacent Arena or Roman amphitheatre. Part of its shell remains and the site, known as the **Giardini dell'Arena**, is now a pleasant

The Euganean Hills

Rising from the flat Veneto Plain is the highly distinctive ridge of cone-shaped hills, known as the Colli Euganei, or Euganean Hills. Cloaked in a woodland mixture of oak, sweet chestnut, arbutus and laurel, these are the remains of volcanoes that have long been extinct, though hot sulphurous springs testify that subterranean activity has not entirely ceased. The area is a perfect rural retreat from the developed Padua region, and wealthy city dwellers like to spend the weekend here walking among the woods and indulging in the spa treatments available at thermal establishments in Abano Terme and Montegrotto Terme.

Picturesque Arquà Petraraca, retirement home of the medieval poet, Petrarch, gets most of the visitors, but any visit to the region should take in the beautiful cloister at the Benedictine Abbazia di Praglia, 6km west of Abano Terme, where the monks give guided tours of their Renaissance church (closed on Mondays; *tel: (049) 9900 010*) and sell herbs in the monastic shop.

Scores of fine villas dot the Euganean Hills, built by wealthy Paduans in the past, but only one is regularly open to the public,. This is the Villa Barbarigo, at Valsanzibio (to the north of Arquà Petrarca, open March–November, 1000–1300 and 1300–1700; *tel: (0444) 760310*). The villa itself is a relatively simple structure, reflecting the Renaissance classical ideal of simplicity and rationality. The garden by contrast, is a baroque creation of 1669, full of ebullient fountains, statues and reflective pools of water.

park which provides a summer venue for classical music productions.

Il Burchiello

The **Burchiello** is a luxury motor launch which runs along the Canale Brenta, between Padua and the Venetian Lagoon (terminating near Fusina). *En route* there are a number of fine Palladian villas to admire, three of which are open to Burchiello passengers: the Villa Fóscari, the Villa Widmann-Foscari and the Villa Pisani. The full trip takes around 8½ hrs and departs from Padua to Venice on Wed, Fri, Sun and vice-versa on Tues, Thur, Sat. Bookings must be made through a travel agent and included in the price is the bus transfer to the boat, and the return journey by train or bus (around 45 mins).

ARQUÀ PETRARCA

The prettiest of the Euganean settlements,

Arquà added its Petrarca suffix in 1868 in honour of the medieval poet Francesca Petrarca (known in English as Petrarch, 1303–74) who spent his final years here. At the bottom of the village his bombastic red marble sarcophagus dominates the front of the church; from here it is a steep winding climb to the top of the village and the Casa Petrarca. The poet lived in this charming house from 1370 to 1374 and both house and the views over the glorious countryside are little changed since, open Tues–Sun 0900–1230 and 1500–1730, entrance fee L5000.

MONSÉLICE

Tourist Office: *V. Roma; tel: (0429) 783026*, open Mon–Fri 1000–1300 and 1400–1700, Sat 1000–1300.

The pride of this pleasant small hill town is its castle, **Il Castello di Monsélice/Ca'Marcello**, which is a few metres walk just up the hill, along the

V. Del Santuario, behind the tourist office. It was built at various stages between the 11th and 16th centuries but by the 19th century had fallen into complete disrepair. It was rescued in 1935 by the famous industrialist Count Cini and has been superbly restored to its appearance during the medieval and Renaissance periods. Outstanding are its armoury and its medieval kitchen though all the rooms are atmospherically decorated with period furnishings including fine frescos and rich tapestries, open Tues–Sun, by guided tour (in English) on the hour 0900–1200 and 1400–1700 (Apr–Nov). Entrance fee L8000.

Continue on the *V. Del Santuario* past the Duomo Vecchio (old cathedral – rarely open) and bear left up along the pilgrim's way, the **V. Sette Chiese** (Way of the Seven Churches). Six small chapels lead to the seventh church, San Giorgio, built in 1592. It is normally only open for services but you may be able to get the key from the adjacent Villa Duodo (now used by the University of Padua) and admire its fine inlaid marble work. A monumental flight of steps offers panoramic views over the town and on a clear day you can see as far as Venice and the pre-Alps.

ESTE

Tourist Office: *Pza Maggiore 5; tel: (0429) 3635*, open Mon–Sat 1000–1300.

Drive through the town centre until you see the tall towers of the **castle**. Turn right to go past its front entrance and follow it around to the left where you can park conveniently inside the castle grounds. Built in the 14th century, only the impressive walls and a keep remain. The rest of the grounds have been turned into a pleasant park and also hold the 16th-century Palazzo Mocenigo, now home to the **Museo Nazionale Atestino**. The

museum takes its name from the local Ateste tribe who were the region's original prehistoric settlers and who left behind a very rich legacy of archaeological finds. They flourished from the 9th century BC up to the 4th century AD when they were subdued by the Romans, open daily 0900–1900, entrance fee L4000.

> ### ⬀ SIDE TRACK
> ### FROM ESTE
>
> If Este has whetted your appetite for more ancient walls, make a detour 15km west to **Montagnana** (along the S10) to see some of the best-preserved medieval fortifications in the country. They extend for almost 1900 m, are entered by four gateways and are punctuated by 24 towers. By the Padua Gate is one of Palladio's best works, the Villa Pisani (see box, page 99). Head north through Noventa Vicentina to pick up the S247 and rejoin the route to Vicenza. ⬔

VICENZA

Tourist Office: *Pza Matteoti* (next to Teatro Romano); *tel: (0444) 320854*, open summer: Mon–Fri 0900–1230 and 1430–1800, Sat opens 0830, Sun closed afternoon; winter closes 1730 and all day Sun. The free city map also covers outlying areas and is a good source of general information.

GETTING AROUND

The centre of Vicenza is very compact and easily covered on foot; most points of interest lie in the largely pedestrianised zone off *Corso Palladio* which runs between *Pza del Castello* and *Pza Matteoti*. Just south of town the main sights of Monte Berico, Villa Valmarana and Villa Rotonda are clustered conveniently close to each other.

Palladio

Andrea di Pietro della Gondola, born in Padua in 1508, acquired his classical nickname Palladio while working as a stonecutter in Vicenza. Inspired by the designs of ancient Rome, particularly the ideals of symmetrical planning and harmonic proportions, Palladio first made his name with the Basilica in Vicenza and then effectively made the city his own showcase with several gracious palazzi and other buildings including his epic swansong the Teatro Olimpico. Outside the city he designed the churches of San Giorgio Maggiore and the Redentore in Venice and dozens of villas for wealthy Venetians. His greatest works include; Villa La Rotonde (Villa Capra) near Vicenza (see p. 102); Villa Pisani, Montagnana (see p. 98); Villa Thiene, Quinto Vicentino; Villa Maser (Villa Barbaro), near Asolo (see p. 60). Long after his death, his books, particularly *I Quattro Libri dell'Architettura* (The Four Books of Architecture), continued to influence architects throughout Europe and ultimately led to the elegance of the English Georgian and American Colonial styles of the 18th century.

A word of warning on visiting villas in the Veneto; opening times are irregular and subject to change at short notice (due to staff shortages, etc.). Ask at the tourist office and telephone ahead to avoid disappointment.

Communications

The central post office is on *Pza Garibaldi*, open Mon–Fri 0800–1930, Sat 0800–1300.

STAYING IN VICENZA

Cheap accommodation in Vicenza is relatively scarce so book ahead if you want to stay in any of the city centre's four budget-price 2-star hotels. Recommended is the **Vicenza**, *Stradella dei Nodari 5–7; tel: (0444) 321512*. The best hotel in town is the (expensive) 4-star **Campo Marzio** in a quiet but central location, with charming rooms and excellent staff; *Campo Marzio, off Vile Roma; tel: (0444) 545700*.

Hotel chains in Vicenza include *Forte Agip*.

There are no hostels and the nearest camping is well outside town, though conveniently close to the Vicenza Est *autostrada* exit; **Campeggio Vicenza**, *Strada Pelosa; tel: (0444) 582311*.

EATING AND DRINKING

Surprisingly, given the wealth of the city, there are a number of good cheap and moderate eating and drinking places. There is a branch of the excellent **Brek** (see p. 94) located right at the *Pza Castello* end of *Corso Palladio*. Another cheap self-service option is **Righetti**, *Pza del Duomo*, where the food is good and the atmosphere is convivial (though the logistics are chaotic and a good command of Italian would be helpful). Nearby on *Contrà Fontana*, just off *Pza Duomo*, don't miss the atmospheric wine bar **L'Ombra al Campanile**. On the *V. Cavour* side of the *Pza Signori* there are two old-world *caffè-pasticceria* establishments which are tourist sights in their own right. The **Offelleria della Meneghina** dates back to 1791 and features beautiful mid-19th century fittings. Close by (next to the statue of Palladio) and of similar vintage is the **Pasticceria Soraru**. The best moderately priced restaurant in the centre is **Antica Casa della Malvasia**, where the atmosphere, service and food are top quality. *Contrà delle Morette* (off *Corso Palladio*); tel: *(0444) 543704*.

99

ENTERTAINMENT

Classical concerts, dance, theatre and jazz music are all staged at the Teatro Olimpico. In Sept, classical plays by Sophocles, Euripides, Shakespeare and Goldoni are performed (in Italian). There is also a summer season of *Concerti in Villa* (mostly classical concerts, but also some jazz) staged in the Palladian villas in the province of Vicenza. Ask the tourist office for programmes for both.

Youth entertainment is low key. There are a couple of incongruous disco-bars in the centre, otherwise follow the crowds who gather on Fri and Sat nights around the cafés of the *Pza Signori*.

SIGHTSEEING

Vicenza is known as the City of Palladio and it is hard to escape his presence in the beautiful central streets which could have almost been built for a film set. Since 1994 the city has been included in UNESCO's World Heritage List.

The most important sight is the **Teatro Olimpico**, Europe's oldest surviving indoor theatre, built between 1579 and 1585. Palladio began work on it, but died in 1580 and its completion was left to his pupil Vincenzo Scamozzi. It occupies a large walled complex which was formerly the castle, but only two rooms plus the stage are open to the public. The first room, the Odeon, was used for music recitals and features some notable frescos. The auditorium was designed by Palladio to replicate the experience of sitting in an ancient classical outdoor theatre, complete with a blue-sky ceiling and 'marble' (painted wood) steps. The highlight is Scamozzi's **stage set**, representing the Greek city of Thebes featuring more plaster and wood 'marble' pillars and clever *trompe l'œil* techniques to give added depth. *Pza Matteoti*, open Mon–Sat

0900–1215 and 1415–1645 (summer); Sun open until 1845; closed Sun afternoon (winter). Entrance fee L5000.

Note there are various *biglietti cumulativi* (single ticket) options; to the Teatro Olimpico and Museo Civico costs L9000; adding on the Museo Naturalistico Archaeologico costs L12,000; also adding on the Museo de Risorgimento e della Resistenza costs L14,000.

Opposite the Teatro Olimpico, the **Museo Civico** occupies Palladio's Palazzo Chiericati. Look up in the entrance hall for Carpione's striking ceiling fresco of a naked sun god charioteer. The collection features many fine pictures, open Tues–Sat 0900–1230 and 1415–1700, Sun 0900–1230 and 1400–1900. Entrance fee L5000.

A few metres along *Corso Palladio* on the right is the imposing church of **San Corona** which contains two acclaimed altarpieces: *The Baptism of Jesus* by Giovanni Bellini, and the *Adoration of the Magi* by Veronese. Note too the magnificent inlaid polychrome marble and mother-of-pearl high altar.

A little further along *Corso Palladio*, also on the right, is **Contrà Porti**, a small street remarkable for the number of handsome Palladian *palazzi* it holds. After exploring the street, retrace your steps back to the *Corso Palladio* and take either *Contrà dell Monte* or *Contrà Morette* to enter the **Pza Signori**. This splendid square is the heart of the city, dominated by the huge **Palazzo della Ragione** (also known as the **Basilica Palladiana**) and its slender 82 m tower which dates from the 12th century. The building was Palladio's first public commission and his brief was to save it from collapse and to enhance it in the style of a Roman basilica. This he did with two splendid tiers of colonnades which you are free to wander among,

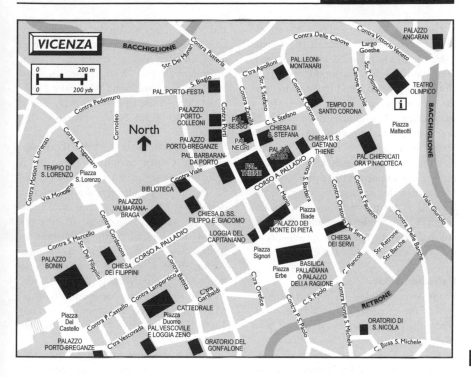

open Tues–Sat 0930–1230 and 1430–1700, Sun morning only. Entrance free. Beneath the great green copper roof, the huge hall (used for exhibitions) is generally open to view during the same hours. The *loggia* of the Basilica is also a good vantage point to look across to the beautiful **Loggia del Capitaniato** (another of Palladio's triumphs) and the adjacent huge Palazzo del Monte di Pietà range which is punctuated by the church of San Vincenzo, topped with statues of the saints. The upper rooms of the Capitaniato contain the Sala Bernada council chamber which may be visited via the **Palazzo Trissino** (entrance on *Corso Palladio*). The Trissino also features the breathtaking Sala Stucchi by Scamossi (of Teatro Romano fame), open Mon–Fri 1000–1200, also Tues and Thur 1700–1830. Entrance free.

On the opposite side of the Basilica is the **Pza dell'Erbe** where the city's fruit and vegetables and flower merchants set out their stalls. Note too the pensive **statue of Palladio** at the *V. Cavour* end of the Basilica. From the *Pza dell'Erbe* stroll down the *Contrà Pescaria* and turn right to see the exterior of the city's most beautiful house, the **Casa Pigafetta**, an eclectic Spanish-Gothic masterpiece built in 1481. It was the birthplace of Antonio Pigafetta, who in 1519 sailed around the world with Magellan. Continue on the *Contrà Pescaria* to the bridge across the lazy River Retrone. From here there is a good view to the **Ponte San Michele**, a charming stone bridge, built in 1621, with some colourful houses around it.

Monte Berico

Clearly visible from town, the **Basilica di Monte Berico** sits on top of the green hill just south of the centre. It's a 20- to 30-min walk in total – through the *Campo Marzio*, across the horribly busy main road, then into the *Vile X Giugno*. Here the road climbs sharply and *portici* (colonnades) run the whole way up to the church. It's a steep climb. The church is dedicated to the Virgin, who appeared here during a plague in 1426-28 to tell the Vicenzans that they would be spared. Ever since it has been an important place of pilgrimage. It's an attractive baroque building but the best reason for non-pilgrims to make the ascent is the **view** over the city, best enjoyed from the terrace of the self-service café-restaurant opposite the church.

Palladian villas

From Monte Berico it's a short walk to two of the province's most famous villas. (From the centre of town catch bus 8 from *Corso Palladio* to the *V. San Bastiano* stop, or take the Este road, if you are driving.) The closer is the **Villa Valmarana**, also known as the **ai Nani** ('of the Dwarfs'), after the bizarre statues of restricted growth which decorate the surrounding walls. Aside from this, the building is un-remarkable; it is the frescos inside which draw trippers by the coachload. They were executed in 1757 by Giambattista Tiepolo (with help from his son) and draw on themes as diverse as rustic peasant life, the Orient and the classical epics of Homer

and Virgil. They are bright, cheerful, very accessible and well explained by notes given to each visitor. *V. del Nani*, open mornings all year Wed, Thur, Sat, Sun 1000–1200. Afternoons Wed–Sun 1430–1730 (Mar–Apr); 1500–1800 (May–Sept); 1400–1700 (Oct–Nov). Entrance fee L8000.

A short walk away the **Villa Rotonda**, or **Villa Capra**, as it is also known, is Palladio's most famous villa, built 1550-52. Its simple yet effective dome-on-cube design has become an architectural icon, adopted, adapted and copied all over the world. By contrast to the Valmarana its beauty lays in its exterior appearance; within there is relatively little to see, so don't worry if only the gardens are open. *V. delle Rotonda*. Interior open Wed (mid Mar–mid Oct). Garden open Tues–Thur 1000–1200 and 1500–1800. Entrance fee to villa L8000.

Follow the signs for the A4 *autostrada* and head west (Brescia, Milan direction) to the Verona Sud exit (51 km, toll route).

←→ Connection: Vicenza to Rovereto

Vicenza and Rovereto are linked by the SS46 road which, for the first 50km from Rovereto to Schio, twists and turns through scenic foothills; at Schio, the road descends to the Veneto Plain, and the final 30km to Vicenza is very straightforward.

VERONA

Away from Venice, Verona is the most visited, best preserved and most attractive large town in the Veneto. Many day-trippers are attracted by the legend of Romeo e Giulietta (Romeo and Juliet) but of far more interest is its very real and rich historical heritage and in particular its splendid Roman remains.

TOURIST INFORMATION

There are two **Tourist Offices**: *V. Leoncini 61* (town hall); *tel: (045) 592828.* Open Mon–Sat 0900–1800 (winter); Mon–Sat 0830–1930 (summer) and Sun 0830–1430 during July and Aug. *Pza XXV Aprile* (rail station); *tel: (045) 800 0861.* Similar hours as above (closed Sun). The APT is at *Pza Erbe* (Mattei Palace); *tel: (045) 800 0865.* Open Mon–Fri 0800–1700, Sat 0800–1330. The *V. Leoncini* office will assist with finding accommodation. There is also the **CAV** hotel booking office at *V. Patuzzi 5; tel: (045) 800 9844.*

There is a **Youth Information Centre** at *Corso Porto Bosari, 17 tel: (045) 801 0795.* Open Mon 1500–1800, Tue 1000–1300, Wed, Fri 1000–1300 and 1500–1800.

ARRIVING AND DEPARTING

By Air

Verona Airport is 9km south-west of the city centre. Facilities are fairly basic by international standards though several major car hire companies are represented.

By Car

The A4 autostrada provides the fastest route from both Milan and Venice to Verona. The autostrada exit which serves the centre of town is marked Verona Sud. All major hotels and attractions are well signposted.

GETTING AROUND

Most of the main sights are within walking distance, conveniently located between two main squares: **Pza Brà** (the site of the Roman Arena) and **Pza dell Erbe**. Much of the town centre is pedestrianised or traffic restricted.

Pick up a free map from the tourist office. The *Passeggiando per Verona* (walking through Verona) map is particularly good.

Public Transport

Bus tickets are sold at *tabacchi* (tobacconists) look for the white on black T-sign). The ticket is validated by inserting it in the machine on the bus and is then good for one hour.

Communications

The main post office is *Pza Viviani*. Open Mon–Sat 0815–1930.

Money

There is a **Thomas Cook bureau de change**, *c/o CIT, at Pza Brà 2; tel (045) 592145.*

STAYING IN VERONA

There is a good choice of accommodation with moderately priced and more expensive hotels right in the centre and cheaper lodgings just across the river in the university quarter.

Accommodation is most sought after and most expensive during the opera season (July and Aug). Booking well in advance is essential during this period.

Hotel chains in Verona include *Forte Agip, Ib.*

Two recommended small, central, 3-star hotels in the moderate price category are: **Antica Porta Leona**, *Corticelli Leoni* (next to the Porta Leoni Roman gate); *tel: (045) 595499*, and the **Giulietta e Romeo**, *Vicolo Tre Marchetti* (just off *Pza Brà*); *tel: (045) 800 3554*. Both have friendly staff and small rooms with fans or air conditioning.

HI: *Ostella della Gioventù, Salita Fontana del Ferro 15; tel: (045) 590360*. Friendly staff, bright rooms and great views make this one of Europe's best hostels.

EATING AND DRINKING

The most expensive cafés and restaurants are inevitably on *Pza Brà* and *Pza delle Erbe* and the well-tramped route between them. However, you can dine very well and inexpensively at **Brek** on *Pza Brà* with a great view across to the Roman Arena. This is an excellent self-service establishment pleasantly furnished and serving good quality authentic local food; *tel: (045) 800 4561*.

The best area for cheap eats is across the river (take the Ponte Nuovo) in the university quarter.

ENTERTAINMENT

There are two major venues for the performing arts, both of Roman vintage. The **Arena** is world-famous for its opera productions (x-ref) though out of the opera season major pop and rock performers play here.

The much smaller **Teatro Romano** (Roman amphitheatre) just across the river, also provides an atmospheric stage for an annual Shakespeare Festival (in Italian) plus ballet, jazz and blues music. All these events are usually staged from mid-June to the end of Aug. Ticket sales are handled by the Arena (x-ref); for more information *tel: (045) 807 7111*.

A third impressive (indoor) venue is the **Teatro Filarmonico** which stages an anuual *Primavera Festival* (Spring Festival) of drama, music and opera from mid-Apr through early May; for information, *tel: (045) 590109*. Pick up a copy of the excellent *Passport Verona* (from the tourist office or your hotel reception) for a list of *dancing e discoteche* venues and for other what's on information.

SHOPPING

For fashion, **V. Mazzini**, linking *Pza Brà* and *Pza delle Erbe*, is the place.

There are outdoor **markets** Tues–Sat at various venues (see *Passport Verona* for details).

SIGHTSEEING

There is a **bus tour** of the city, departing from *Pza Brà* (in front of the Palazzo Gran Guardia), Tues–Sun 1000, 1140 and 1530 (July–7 Sept). It lasts 90 mins, offers a hilltop view of the city and costs L20,000; for information, *tel: (045) 887 1111*. Tickets are bought on board and allow unlimited free travel on city buses.

Pza Brà

Verona's main square is dominated by the Roman **Arena**. This is the third largest amphitheatre in the world (after Rome and Capua) and its interior has been kept virtually intact since the 16th century. Oval in shape, its external dimensions are 152m by 123m. Its mighty arches rise two storeys, though a third tier, of which just a

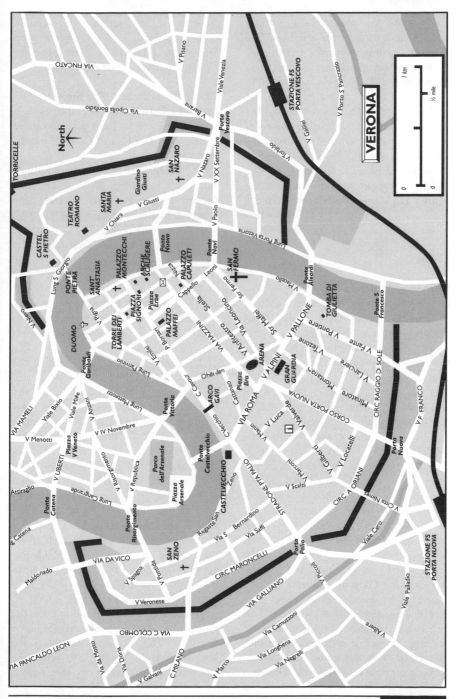

small portion (known as the *Alla* or Wing) survives, once took it over 30 m high. The Arena is certainly worth the entrance fee for its scale and atmosphere, though there is nothing to tell you of the days when, in the name of entertainment, gladiators and wild beasts spilled the blood of each other and of thousands of Christians, prisoners of war and criminals. Open Tues–Sun (outside opera season); 0800–1530 (during opera season) Entrance fee L6000.

On the opposite side of *Pza Brà* is the **Museo Lapidario Maffeiano** which is a collection of Roman and Greek monuments, tablets and stone fragments. Open Tues–Sun 0800–1300. Entrance fee L4000.

Romeo e Giulietta

In the Middle Ages, Verona was smitten by internal warfare between rival local families – such as the Capulets and the Montagues – and so became the setting for the world's most famous tragic love story. This was penned locally in the 1520s and later adapted by Shakespeare. There are two main sites which claim an historical link, though neither is proven.

The lesser site is the **Tomba di Giulietta** (Juliet's Tomb), a 5–10 min walk from *Pza Brà*. It's just an empty sarcophagus in a crumbling monastery, but judging from the love letters stacked up here it still attracts many young romantics. *V. del Pontiere 5*, open Tues–Sun 0800–1830, entrance fee L5000 (includes the Museum of Frescos on-site).

Of much greater fame and general interest is the **Casa di Giulietta** (Juliet's House), a handsome, restored 13th-century building which allows you to stand on *that* balcony. Below, in the courtyard, heaving crowds line up to have their picture taken with the statue of Giulietta, rubbing her right breast for luck! Note too

the extraordinary amount of 'love-graffiti' in the courtyard. *V. Capello*, house open Tues–Sun 0800–1830, entrance fee L5000. Courtyard open daily, free.

Pza delle Erbe and Pza Signori

Pza delle Erbe, named after the city's old herb market, is a handsome elongated square, with many fine buildings, monuments and frescos.

The **Lion of St Mark** atop a large column is a reminder of Venetian rule. Behind it the **Palazzo Maffei** how houses a luxury restaurant and the APT (see Tourist Information). The statue at the centre of the beautiful **fountain** in the middle of the square (almost hidden by the permanent jumble of market stalls and trinket stands) is actually Roman. Beside it, the marble arch known as the **Berlina** was once used as a kind of pillory, to which felons were tied and pelted with rotten fruit.

The **Arco della Costa** (Arch of the Rib) takes its name from the whale rib hung above (for what reason is unsure) and leads to the monumental **Pza dei Signori**. A powerful **statue of Dante** looks onto the **Palazzo del Capitano**, the former home of Verona's military commander, and the **Palazzo della Ragione** (the law court). The courtyard of the latter has a splendid 15th-century external stone staircase. Just off the courtyard is the entrance to the **Torre dei Lamberti** which looms 83 m high above the city and offers magnificent 360 degree views down onto the town and as far as the Alps. Open Tues–Sun 0930–1830 Entrance fee (lift) L4000 (stairs) L3000.

Just off the *Pza dei Signori* don't miss the spectacular **Arche Scaligeri** (Scaligeri Tombs). The Scaligeri family ruled Verona from 1277 until 1387 when the city was at the peak of its city-state powers

Opera at the Arena

Every summer since 1913 operas have been staged at the Roman arena. It is the largest open-air theatre of its kind in the world accommodating around 25,000 spectators. Typically, the festival, which runs through July and Aug, includes such favourites as *Carmen, Madame Butterfly, Rigoletto* and *Aida* and is graced by world-famous performers such as Placido Domingo. *Aida* is the most famous and most spectacular production.

The best seats are in the first section of the stalls and cost (in 1997) a whacking L230,000. A hefty advance booking fee is also charged until 24 hrs before any performance. The second sector stalls cost L165,000 while the best numbered seats on the stone steps cost L135,000. *Gradinata* (unreserved stone steps) cost a mere 35,000. You'll want to arrive well in advance for the latter to get a good seat; the best compromise of view, acoustics and fresh air (it can be stifling at the bottom) is achieved around half way down the 44 tiers. A cushion is a must for the stone steps, so bring your own or hire one (for around L12,000). Shortly before the performance begins at 2100, each member of the audience lights a small candle (on sale) which bathes the Arena in a magical flickering glow.

Serious opera buffs should take note that the acoustics are less than perfect, the crowd may be noisy and children may even be running around during the performance! Bring your own drinks and snacks (no glass containers) and beware, toilet facilities are poor.

The box office is in *V. Dietro Anfiteatro* (in front of the Arena wing), open year round Mon–Fri 0900–1200 and 1515–1745, Sat 0900–1200. From early July until the end of Aug open on performance days 1000–2100; on non-performance days 1000–1745. Reservations can also be made by post or *tel: (045) 800 5151, fax: (045) 801 3287.* Book as far ahead as possible.

and despite their violent and brutish nature were patrons of the arts, sponsoring Dante among others. Both these facets are combined in their elaborate militaristic Gothic funerary monuments. Note the tomb topped with an armoured horseman, belonging to the head of the family, nicknamed **Cangrande I** ('Big Dog' I).

Castelvecchio

The name means old castle and this was built by Cangrande II between 1355 and 1375. Today Castelvecchio is a fascinating museum, with walkways at varying levels offering views of the castle and the river alongside. Its exhibits range from late Roman remains through early Renaissance art, arms and armour and fine works by Bellini and Veronese. It is the setting, however, which remains memorable. *Corso Castelvecchio*, open Tues–Sun 0800–1830, entrance fee L5000. Adjacent is the handsome **Ponte Scaligero Bridge**, built at the same time as part of the castle defences. The views from here are excellent. On the other side of Castelvecchio is the Roman triumphal arch of **Arco dei Gavei**, moved aside a few metres from its original position on the *Corso Cavour*. Heading back towards *Pza delle Erbe* is another 1st-century gate, **Porta dei Borsari**, in its original position.

City Churches

Verona has a wealth of historic churches and eight of the most interesting have formed the *chiese vive* (living churches) association. A minimum admission fee of

L4000 is charged which allows admission to two or more churches (depending on which cluster you choose), but the best buy is the all-inclusive ticket which covers all churches for L9000 and also includes an excellent booklet (available from all participating churches).

Just along the *Corso Anastasia* from *Pza dei Signori* is **Sant'Anastasia**, a great Gothic barn of a church which is the largest in the city. Look for the unusual holy water stoups supported by superbly carved hunchback figures. In the aisle to the right of the main altar look up high to see the remains of a famous fresco of San Giorgio e la Principessa (St George and the Princess) by Pisanello.

A short walk along *V. Duomo* leads to the **Duomo** of Santa Maria Matricolare. It has a superb façade featuring a richly sculptured portal while the highlight of the interior is Titian's *Assumption* (1535–40). The Romanesque cloister of the Duomo actually contains two more earlier churches on this same site. The Baptistry is known as **San Giovanni in Fonte**, originally dating from the 8th century, but rebuilt in the 12th century. Its eponymous magnificent font also dates from this period. Adjacent is **Santa Elena**, built in the 9th century and restored in 1140. Its interior is sparse but atmospheric.

Close to Castelvecchio on *Corso Cavour* is the charming and very atmospheric church of **San Lorenzo**, with 13th-century frescos and unusual upper galleries

from which women (out-of-sight) could attend services.

The finest city church of all is **San Zeno Maggiore**, a 15min walk, or bus 31, 32 or 33 from Castelvecchio. It was completed in 1135 to house the shrine of Verona's patron saint, San Zeno, and is famous for its 48 superb bronze door panels, many of which depict scenes from the life of the saint and date from the 8th–9th centuries. Inside is a beautiful ship's keel ceiling and a renowned triptych altarpiece (1457–59) by Mantegna.

Across the river

The main reason to cross the River Adige is the **Teatro Romano** (Roman Theatre) which is reached appropriately by the 1st-century Roman **Ponte Pietra** (Stone Bridge, also known as the Ponte Romano). The amphitheatre's semi-circular seating area has survived well though most of the original stage has perished. At the back of the theatre a lift conveys visitors up through the cliff to the **Museo Archeologico** which occupies the site of an old monastery. There are some good mosaics here but the main attraction is the panoramic **view** across the river. *Rigaste Redentore*, open Tues–Sun 0800–1300, combined entrance fee L5000.

Note on entrance fees: there is free entrance on the first Sun of the month to the Arena, Roman Theatre, Castelvecchio and Juliet's Tomb.

LAKE GARDA

Lake Garda is the largest of the Italian lakes – and also the most popular. Its popularity is a blessing and, at the same time, a curse. The plus factor is that there is no shortage of good quality accommodation and food. The minus is that, because it is so popular, the resorts and roads can become very congested, particularly at weekends and in high summer. But there are compensations, not least some splendid scenery, especially at the northern end of the lake, where the southern extremity of the Dolomites provides a sheer wall of rock behind Riva del Garda. And winters are mild, making the lake a pleasant place to be outside the main holiday season.

LAKE GARDA

The best way to reach Lake Garda from the south and west is via the A4 autostrada. From Turin it is 228km along this busy motorway to the southern tip of the lake: from Lakes Como and Maggiore you first have to drive south to join the A4 north of Milan.

The lake's proximity to the junction of two main motorways – the E45 Brenner–Verona and the E70 Padua–Brescia – means that Garda can be circumnavigated in about two hours without stops. However, the best way – it could be argued, the only way – of seeing Lake Garda is to follow the road which runs at the water's edge, apart from a few kilometres in the south-west. The drawback is

that, in season, the road is extremely congested, making for slow progress. All the more reason to take two or three days over the trip, stopping off in one of the attractive lakeside resorts, perhaps Malcesine, Sirmione, Desenzano, the largest town at the southern end of the lake, or, on the western shore, Limone sur Garda.

Travelling along the SS240 from Rovereto, the first place, at the north-eastern end of the lake, is **Tòrbole**; popular with windsurfers from all over Europe.

TÒRBOLE

Tourist Office: *Lungolago Verona 19; tel: (0464) 505177.* The tourist office, which is conveniently situated on the lake front, between the town centre and the jetty, is open Mon–Sat 0900–1200 and 1500–1830, Sun 0900–1200. If it is closed, you can book accommodation through a freephone service which is available to a number of hotels.

ACCOMMODATION AND FOOD

There are plenty of good hotels across the price range. Among the most comfortable are the **Piccolo Monde**, a charming family-run establishment, full of character and with a good restaurant and swimming pool, *V. Matteorri 7; tel: (0464) 505271;* the **Lido Blu**, *tel: (0464) 505 1180;* and **Club Hotel la Vela,** *V. Strada Granda; tel: (0464) 505940,* which also has a pool and, with plenty of entertainment during the season, is popular with families.

As a family resort, much of the dining here is on a half board basis in hotels, but for a special occasion try **La Terrazza**, *V. Pasubio 15; tel: (0464) 506083,* which not

109

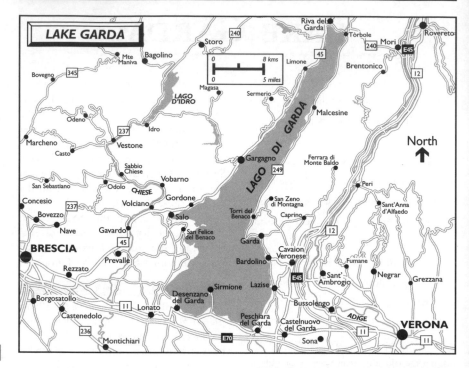

only has good food, but fine views over the lake. The restaurant is closed on Tues and in Feb, Mar and Nov.

SIGHTSEEING

The biggest sightseeing attraction here is people-watching. Tòrbole, which looks out on to a sickle-shaped bay, played a part in the war in 1439 between the Visconti and the Venetians. But it was the German writer Goethe who stayed here in 1786 and helped put the place on the map by describing it as 'a magnificent scene of nature'.

Today the magnificence is all about sun-tanned, lycra-clad tyros who come here to windsurf and sail. The consistent winds make this the windsurfing capital of the Lakes – a place to see and be seen, with excellent café life, even if it is a little short on tourist attractions.

TÒRBOLE TO DESENZANO

From Tòrbole, the SS249 hugs the eastern shore of the lake virtually all the way to Desenzano, as it does so it passes through some of Garda's prettiest villages. The first of any note is **Malcesine,** 9.5km from Tòrbole, which is distinguished by its 13th-century Scaligero Castle, rising on a slab of rock directly above the water. It was in this castle, in 1786, that Goethe was imprisoned briefly on suspicion of being a spy after he had been caught making sketches of the lake! The castle, and the small natural history museum housed in one of the towers, is open daily in summer from 0930–1900 and in winter from 1130–1700. If your interests are more active, there are marked trails up **Monte Baldo,** the 1752m ridge behind the resort which has a reputation as the 'Botanical Garden of Italy' for the rarity of its plant

life, protected by two nature reserves. A funicular (every half hour in summer, 0800–1745; 0800–1645 in winter) makes for an easier ascent, but be prepared for long queues at peak times in summer.
Tourist Office: *V. Capitanato del Porto 6–8; tel: (045) 740 0044.*

ACCOMMODATION

Malcesine has a good selection of hotels, some squeezed into the village's narrow streets, others on the outskirts. The difficulty is that many are used by package tour firms, which means finding a room can be difficult in high season. The **Vega,** *Viale Poa; tel: (045) 740 0151,* is a small, comfortable hotel with a swimming pool in the garden. Larger is the **Excelsior Bay,** only 200m from the centre of the village at *V. Madonnina Lungolago 13; tel: (045) 740 0380,* which has a health centre with gym, sauna and solarium as well as swimming pool. Also worth considering is the **Maximilian,** *V. Valdi Sogno 6; tel: (045) 740 0317,* which is 2km south of Malcesine at Val di Sogno.

From Malcesine, the SS249 continues along the lake, beneath the massive bulk of Monte Baldo, through other villages which make their living principally from tourism. **Torri del Benaco,** about 20km from Malcesine, is arguably the prettiest of the lakeside villages – its old centre comprising just a single street – the *Corso Dante* – with tunnelled alleyways running off it. At one end of the street is the 13th-century castle, which is illuminated at night and has a long glasshouse built along one side to protect the lemon trees inside from any bad weather.

Five kilometres farther on, the road swings round the Punta San Vigilio – another scenic vantage point – where there's an excellent pay beach, with sun loungers and picnic tables scattered on a grass bank planted with pines. Tucked inside the promontory is Garda itself.

GARDA

Tourist Office: *Lungolago Regina Adelaide; tel: (045) 725 5194.*

ACCOMMODATION AND FOOD

In Garda, the accommodation choice is wide. Just about the grandest is the **Regina Adelaide,** *V. San Francesco 23; tel: (045) 725 5977,* which has a good restaurant and pleasant garden. Also worth considering are the **Poiano,** *V. Poiano 59; tel: (045) 720 100,* the **Flora,** *V. Giorgione 27; tel: (045) 725 5348,* which has a garden and an outdoor swimming pool, and the **San Marco,** *largo Pisanello 3; tel: (045) 725 5008.* There are also any number of good restaurants in Garda, notably **Tobago,** *V. Bellini 1; tel: (045) 725 6340,* which is closed on Mon and in Oct and Mar and, just outside the town, **Stafolet,** *tel: (045) 725 5427.*

111

SIGHTSEEING

Garda is a lively resort which, as a place for a holiday, is as popular with Italians as foreigners. The fishermen's cottages in the narrow, winding alleys may now be given over to souvenir shops and the like, but the atmosphere of the old Garda remains during the nightly *passeggiata* – the ritual stroll along the promenade – which is still very much a feature of everyday life. The beach and the town dominate holiday activity, but for something different there is a pleasant walk up from the church of Santa Maria Maggiore to the *Eremo dei Camoldolesi,* a 17th-century hermitage. In 1810, the monks here were ousted by Napoleon. They bought the place back again later in the century, but only began living here again in 1972. The hermitage is open to visitors on Tues, Thur, Sat

0830–1130 and 1430–1630.

Back on the main road and in 3.5km you reach **Bardolino**, another attractive little place, with a jaunty promenade of palm and pine trees and ice cream parlours (try Cristallo, on the lake front near where the ferry docks). This, of course, is the place where the famous red wine comes from and Bardolino comes into its own in Sept and Oct during the *Festa di Uva*, when the new vintage is tasted. But needless to say you can taste wine throughout the year at Costarica, *V. Cesare Battisti*.

Another 3.5km down the road is **Lazise**, a walled village which was once a major Venetian port. Today its castle is now privately owned and linked in with the old customs house and makes for an attractive corner on the lake, even if most of the rest of the village seems to be given over to the needs of holidaymakers in search of pizzas and ice creams.

Some 9km farther on, at the lake's south-eastern extremity, **Peschiera del Garda** was once one of the four corners of the Austrian 'quadrilateral'. The town's impressive fortifications, begun in 1553 by the Venetians and later strengthened by Napoleon and the Austrians, can be seen on the right-hand side of the road, just after northern Italy's Disneyland – the Gardaland Amusement Park (worth a stop if you have children who need to let off steam). Try to reach Peschiera on the hour, when the town hall clock in the main square is struck by two bronze eagles.

On the western outskirts of Peschiera, join the road which loops around the southern shore of the lake to Desenzano. Some 9km along this road, at Colombare, take the road which leads up the peninsula to **Sirmione**. In summer and at weekends, progress on this road can be slow, but persevere. Sirmione is worth an hour or two of anyone's time.

SIRMIONE

Tourist Office: *V. Marconi 2; tel: (030) 916245.* The office can supply details on hotels, as well as the main sights, walking, horse riding and skiing.

ACCOMMODATION AND FOOD

Sirmione's total of 100 or so hotels and guesthouses is remarkable for a village with a population of only 5600. **Villa Cortine,** *V. Grotte 12; tel: (030) 990 5890,* is an elegant, if expensive, hotel. It's in an imposing position, high on a hill with impressive lake views, and is set in the private park of an 18th-century Palladian villa with marble public rooms, outdoor pool, beach restaurant and bar. **Hotel Sirmione,** *Pza Castello 19; tel: (030) 916331,* is in the centre of the village close to the castle and offers thermal health treatments using water from the village's thermal springs. Less expensive hotels include the **Golf e Suisse**, *V. Condominio 2; tel: (030) 990 4590,* and the **Speranza,** *6 V. Casello 6; tel: (030) 916116,* neither of which has a restaurant. This isn't a problem, since there are dozens of restaurants to choose from, including **Signori**, *V. Romagnoli 23, tel: (030) 916017,* where you can dine on a terrace overlooking the lake. Also reliable are **San Salvatore,** *V. San Salvatore 5; tel: (030) 916248,* and **Grifone,** *Vicolo delle Bisse 5, tel: (030) 916097.*

SIGHTSEEING

The Romans were the first to spot Sirmione's potential as a spa and on the way to the tip of the peninsula is the **Grotte di Catullo**, the ruins of their bathhouse. But most visitors head for the **Rocca Scaligera**, a 15th-century castle, almost completely surrounded by water and built by the Veronese Scaligera family, which is open, Tues–Sun 0900–1800 (Apr–

Sept); 0900–1300 (Oct–Mar), but there's not much to see inside. Otherwise, Sirmione is a well-kept village of picture postcard proportions, whose San Piero Church contains 13th-century frescos. There are good opportunities for picnicking and bathing in the lake, as well as 'taking the waters'.

From Desenzano, instead of continuing around the south-west corner of the lake, take the SS11 to **Brescia,** a distance of 31km.

BRESCIA

Tourist Office: *Corso Zanardelli 34; tel: (030) 43418.* The office, which is open Mon–Fri 0900–1230 and 1500–1800, Sat 0900–1230 has a good supply of pamphlets and maps.

SIGHTSEEING

Brescia is not one of Italy's most attractive cities, but it does have several attractive corners. **Pza della Logia** dates back to the 15th century when Venice was invited to rule the city to save it from the Viscontis of Milan. Palladio and Titian had a hand in the flowery *Loggia* and the *Torre dell'Orologio,* modelled on the campanile in Venice's St Mark's Square. Also worth seeing are the 12th-century **Duomo**, the **Rotonda,** and the **Capitolino**, a Roman temple built in AD 73 and later re-fashioned in red brick.

In the abbey of **San Salvatore Santa Giulia** can be found the Museo Cristiano (Museum of Christian Antiquities) and the Galleria d'Arte Modurna (Gallery of Modern Art). Open daily 1000–1230 and 1500–1800 (June–Sept); 0900–1230 and 1500–1700 (Oct–May). Admission free. Fine dining is available at **La Sosta,** *V. San Martino della Battaglia 20; tel: (030) 295603,* while **Osteria dell Elfo** at *Piazza del Vescovato 1b; tel: (030) 377*

4858, booking advisable, offers good value.

BRESCIA TO RIVA

From Brescia, retrace your steps on the SS11 and just beyond Rezzato fork left on to the 45bis. After 20km, at Volciano, the 45bis bears right and then hugs the western shore of Lake Garda all the way to Riva, 75km from Brescia.

The west side of the lake is less developed than the east – partly because there is little enough land to build on the mountainous western side, though to compensate there is a spectacular corniche road, and the west bank does have several resorts which offer possible stopping points, notably **Gardone Riviera, Limone** and **Riva,** all splendidly positioned to make the best of the sun, and with great views of the lake.

GARDONE RIVIERA

Gardone Tourist Office, *V. Repubblica 35; tel: (0365) 20347.*

Perhaps the most refined resort on the lake, Gardone has a number of suitably refined hotels, slumbering in lush gardens and along the promenade, notably the **Grand,** *corso Zanardelli 72, tel: (0365)* 20261 and **Villa Capri,** *Corso Zanardelli 148; tel: (0365) 21537.* For dining out, try **La Stalla,** *Strada per il Vittoriale, tel: (0365) 21038,* or the more expensive **Casino,** *Corso Zanardelli 142; tel: (0365) 20387 .*

LIMONE

Tourist Office: *V. Camboni 115; tel: (0365) 954070.*

Many of Limone's hotels are given over to visitors who arrive on package tours, so it can be difficult sometimes finding a room at the height of the season. **Park Hotel Imperial,** *V. Tamas 10b; tel: (0365) 954591,* has both indoor and out-

The Red Cross

In the village of Solferino, south of Lake Garda, is a memorial to the Red Cross – a chapel containing the bones of 7000 French and Austrian soldiers who died in 1859 at the Battle of Solferino. It was after witnessing the aftermath of the battle the following day that Henri Dumant, a businessman from Geneva who was holidaying at the time on Lake Garda, went home and later published a pamphlet, *A Souvenir of Solferino*, describing graphically what he had seen. The horror included a description of a man having his leg, which had turned gangrenous during the battle, sawn off without anaesthetic. In the pamphlet he concluded 'Would it not be possible to create societies in every European country whose aim would be to assure that prompt and devoted care is given to the wounded in battle'.

The pamphlet had an immediate impact and a conference was convened in Geneva on 26 October 1863. Sixteen countries attended and 12 signed the first Geneva convention on warfare, setting up an international committee to protect war wounded and prisoners. The symbol of the new committee was a version of the Swiss flag – a red cross. Today, the International Red Cross, together with associated organisations like the Red Crescent, is established in more than 100 countries. The Red Cross memorial at Solferino, which was erected in 1959 on the centenary of the battle, is built with stone quarried in each member country. As well as the memorial, there is also a museum containing details of the battle.

door swimming pools. Other smaller, comfortable hotels include the **Costa,** *V. Tomas 11; tel: (0365) 954042,* and the **Lido,** *V. IV Novembre 34; tel: (0365) 954574.*

From Limone, it is only a further 10km along the 45bis, through a series of interconnecting tunnels, to **Riva** in the northwest corner of Garda. Riva's position is stunning, squeezed in between the lake and sheer walls of rock.

RIVA

Tourist Office: *Giardini di Porta Orientale 8; tel: (0464) 554444.* The office is open Mon–Sat 0900–1200 and 1500–1830.

Riva has some of the best hotels on the lake, including the **Du Lac et du Parc,** *Vle Rovereto 44; tel: (0464) 551500,* a luxurious hotel set in spacious grounds. Also worth considering is **Villa Giuliana,** *V. Belluno 12; tel: (0464) 553338,* and the 30-room **Bellavista,** *Pza Cesare Battisti 4; tel: (0464) 554271.*

From Riva, you can drive the 3km back to Tòrbole or head north to Trento, along the 45bis, through the Valley of the Lakes. The scenery is quite superb; the road twists and turns through a landscape of mountains, valleys and castles like Toblino, perched at the water's edge.

MILAN (MILANO)

Milan is the commercial hub of Italy, a city packed with banks and financial institutions, which boasts a standard of living high even for the wealthy north. Its industrial and commercial acumen were chiefly responsible for the Italian post-war economic miracle. Be prepared for inflated prices.

Milan gained importance during the Middle Ages under the authority of a series of influential bishops. It was ruled by the Visconti and Sforza families during most of the 13th–16th centuries. The Viscontis started construction on the Duomo, while the Sforzas built the castle and brought to Milan many leading artists and thinkers of the time.

Modern Milan is one of Europe's great cities, although undervisited by tourists, partly because at first glance it is not as becoming as Florence, Rome or Venice. The city centre is filled with huge 19th- and 20th-century apartment blocks and quaint corners are hard to find. Nonetheless, they do exist: there are pretty Lombard Romanesque churches, tree-filled squares dominated by statues and a vast early Renaissance castle as the city's focus.

TOURIST INFORMATION

Main APT office: **Palazzo del Turismo**, *V. Marconi 1; tel: (02) 7252 4300*, to the right of the Duomo. Free maps and guides in English, open Mon–Sat 0800–2000, Sun 0900–1230 and 1330–1700. **Branch office**: *Stazione Centrale*; 1st Floor, near the Gran Bar. Same hours as main office; *tel: (02) 7252 4360*.

Thomas Cook Worldwide Network Licensee: CIT Viaggi, *Galleria Vittorio Emanuele; tel: (2) 863701*.

ARRIVING AND DEPARTING

By Air
Malpensa, about 50 km north-west of Milan, serves intercontinental and charter flights. **Linate**, 7 km east of Milan, handles domestic and European flights. Buses for both airports arrive at and depart from the **bus terminal**, *Pza Luigi di Savoia; tel: (02) 6698 4509*, beside Stazione Centrale (Malpensa by Airpullman every 30 mins between 0530 and 2030; Linate by STAM every 20 mins between 0540 and 2100).

By Car
Milan is one of Italy's best-connected cities, sitting at the hub of the northern Italian autostrada (motorway) network. The A4 provides a fast route to Milan from Venice, Padua, Verona, Brescia (for Lake Garda) and Bergamo, to the east, while Lakes Como and Maggiore are even closer, lying just to the north of the city. Coming from the west, the A4 links Milan to Turin, and the A5 from Aosta joins the A4 just south of Ivrea. From Genoa and the Italian Riviera, the A7 motorway provides a fast link, while the A1 brings visitors from Bologna, Parma and Piacenza.

Parking in Milan isn't easy: the city centre is closed to traffic between the hours of 7.30am and 6pm, except to those

115

with residency permits. Rush hour traffic is aggressive and heavy, and commuters soon snap up all the available space at central car parks. Your best chance of parking is to book into a hotel with its own garage, or to arrive after 6pm and use on of the signposted car parks, accepting that you will pay a heavy price for overnight parking; alternatively, leave your car behind and come to Milan by train.

By Train

The vast majority of trains serve the monumental and fully-equipped **Stazione Centrale,** *Pza Duca d'Aosta; tel: (02) 147 888 088* (metro line 2).

GETTING AROUND

Milan is big, busy and fast moving. Two vital accessories are a free city map from the tourist office, and a paid-for map of the public transport system from the metro stations at Stazione Centrale and Duomo. Most attractions are in the city centre, but even here walking can be a tiring option. The best way to get around is a mix of walking and public transport.

The public transport system is operated by **ATM**; *tel: (02) 669 7032*, and the same tickets are used on the metro, trams and buses. Single tickets (L1500) are good for one journey on the metro or 1 hr 15 mins travel on the buses. Books of ten tickets cost L14,000. Tickets are available from machines in metro stations or from tobacconists (*tabacchi*) and newspaper kiosks. A day pass (L6000) and two-day pass (L9000) are available from metro stations.

Metro

Metropolitana Milano (MM), is clean, efficient and easy to use. There are three colour-coded lines: M1 (red), M2 (green) and M3 (yellow). Cancel tickets in the gates at station entrances.

Trams and Buses

The **tram** and **bus** systems are more comprehensive and more complicated, but stops have details of each route serving them. Buy tickets in advance and validate them in the machines on board.

Taxis

Milan's taxis, coloured yellow or white, can be expensive. There's a substantial flat fare to start with and extra charges are applied for baggage and travel on holidays or late at night. There are large ranks at Stazione Centrale and *Pza Duomo*. To call a cab, telephone **Radiotaxi**, *tel: (02) 5353*; or **Arco**, *tel: (02) 6767*. Avoid touts offering unofficial taxis, as you are sure to be grossly overcharged.

STAYING IN MILAN

Accommodation

Accommodation does not escape the inflated prices endemic in the city, but there are plenty of pensions around the station and the town centre. Hotel chains include *Ch, Ex, Hd, Hn, Ib, Nv, Rd, Rm*. The tourist office will provide a full list of accommodation. Alternatively, **Milan Hotels Central Booking**, *V. Palestro 24; tel: (02) 805 4242, fax: (02) 805 4291*, can help find a room.

Milan has a wide range of hotels, from the super-luxury class to the budget. At the top end are such 5-star establishments as the **Principe di Savoia**, *Pza della Repubblica 17; tel: (02) 62 301*; **Grand Hotel Duomo**, *V. S. Raffaele 1; tel: (02) 88 33*; and **Duca di Milano**, *Pza della Repubblica 13; tel: (02) 62 841*; and the 4-star **Accademia**, *Vle Certosa 68; tel: (02) 39 21 11 22*; **Andreola**, *V. Scarlatti 24; tel: (02) 67 09 141*; **Rubens**, *V. Rubens 21, tel: (02) 40 302*; and **Washington**, *V. Washington 23; tel: (02) 48 13 216*. In the

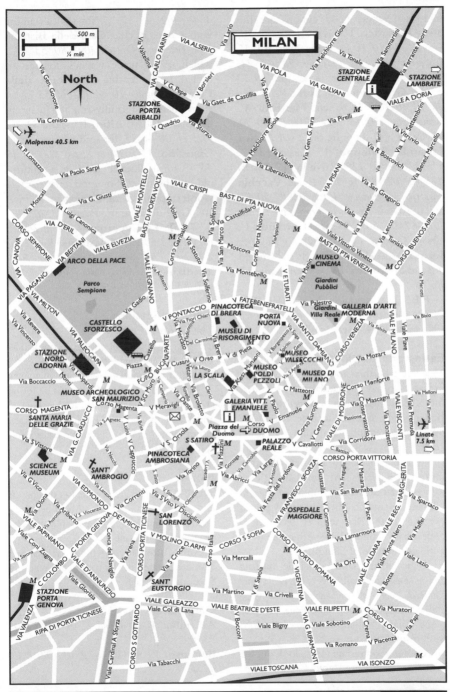

mid-price range, good options are the 3-star **Adriatico**, *V. Conca del Naviglio 20; tel: (02) 58 10 41 41*; **Delle Nazioni**, *V. Cappellini 18; tel: (02) 66 98 12 21*; **Fenice**, *C. Buenos Aires 2; tel: (02) 29 52 55 41*; **Gran Duca di York**, *V. Moneta 1a; tel: (02) 87 48 63*; and **Manzoni**, *V. Santo Spirito 20; tel: (02) 76 00 57 00*. At the lower end, there are the 2-star **Antica Locanda Solferino**, *V. Castelfidardo 2; tel: (02) 65 70 129*; **Rovello**, *V. Rovello 18; tel: (02) 86 46 46 54*; and **Vecchia Milano**, *V. Borromei 4; tel: (02) 87 50 42*; and the 1-star **Arno**, *V. Lazzaretto 17; tel: (02) 67 05 509*; **Cesare Correnti**, *V. Cesare Correnti 14; tel: (02) 80 57 609*; **Jolanda**, *C. Magenta 78; tel: (02) 46 33 17*; and **Speronari**, *V. Speronari 4; tel: (02) 86 46 11 25*.

HI: *Vle. Salmoraighi 1, tel: (02) 3926 7095*. **Camping:** *V. G Airaghi 61; tel: (02) 4820 0134*, open Apr–Sept.

Eating and Drinking

Milanese take their food seriously and are prepared to pay substantial sums for their meals. Restaurants can be very expensive. Better value eateries include reasonable self-service restaurants around the town centre. Away from the centre, there are family-run *trattorie* and a variety of other inexpensive places. At lunch-time, customers often eat standing up. Pizzerias and Chinese restaurants offer reasonably priced evening meals. Bars tend to serve more coffee than alcohol, along with *panini* (rolls with a multitude of fillings).

Regional specialities include *cotoletta alla milanese*, an Italian version of *Wiener schnitzel, risotto alla milanese* and the vegetable and pork soup *minestrone*. Despite being inland, Milan has excellent fish, fresh from the coast.

Among good restaurants to look out for in the city centre are **Peck**, *V. Victor Hugo 4; tel: (02) 87 67 74*, for typical cuisine with a touch of chic; **Casa della Bisteca**, *Pza Beccaria 14a; tel: (02) 80 53 732*, which, as its name implies, focuses on grilled beef; **Antica Trattoria della Pesa**, *Vle Pasubio 10; tel: (02) 65 55 74*, an atmospheric old family-run restaurant in the Brera district; **Alfio**, *V. Senato 31; tel: (02) 76 00 06 33*, for seafood specialities; **Giannino**, *V. A Sciesa 8; tel: (02) 55 19 55 82*, for traditional cuisine in a century-old establishment. Some pizzerias that are worth stopping at for an inexpensive meal are: **Grand'Italia**, *V. Palermo 5; tel: (02) 87 77 59*; **La Cucuma**, *V. Pacini 26; tel: (02) 29 52 60 98*; **Malastrana**, *Ripa Porta Ticinese 65; tel: (02) 83 78 984*; **Tradizionale**, *Ripa Porta Ticinese 7; tel: (02) 83 95 133*.

Communications

The **Central Post Office**, *V. Cordusio 4; tel: 869 2069*, is open Mon–Fri 0815–1900, Sat 0815–1740 (24 hrs daily for faxes and telegrams).

Public **telephone offices** can be found at *Galleria V Emanuele II, V. Cordusio 4*, and Stazione Centrale. Public phones take either coins or phonecards, the latter available from kiosks.

Money

There is no shortage of bureaux de change and banks in Milan. At weekends, exchange facilities are available in *Pza Duomo* and Stazione Centrale and at both airports. Automatic machines that convert cash are located in the town centre and in Stazione Centrale.

Consulates

Australia: *V. Borgogna 2; tel: (02) 7601 3330.*
Belgium: *V. A. Vespucci 2; tel: (02) 2900 4755.*

Canada: *V. Vittorio Pisani 19; tel: (02) 669 7451.*
France: *C. Venezia 42; tel: (02) 794341.*
The Netherlands: *V. S. Vittore 45; tel: (02) 4801 1723.*
UK: *V. S. Paolo 7; tel: (02) 869 3442.*
USA: *V. Principe Amadeo 2; tel: (02) 290351.*

ENTERTAINMENT

Milan's daily newspapers, *La Repubblica* and *Corriere della Sera* produce weekly supplements detailing Milan's entertainment and nightlife.

The city's most famous institution is the grand **La Scala** opera house. Donizetti, Puccini and Verdi all staged operas here. Tickets are extremely elusive, but you may be able to get them on Mondays, for a performance of classical music rather than opera. The **Conservatorio** also hosts concerts.

Nightclubs tend to close around 0200–0300. Le Scimmie (Monkeys) is one of the most famous. Two of the more trendy areas of town are **Porta Ticinese** and **Brera**, with a high concentration of bars and nightlife venues. The **Navigli** district also has many bars.

Cinemas cluster around *C. Vittorio Emanuele*, near *Pza Duomo*.

Events

The **Italian Grand Prix** in Formula One motor racing is held each year at the famed **Monza Circuit**, to the north of the city, which can be reached long *Vle Monza*.

SHOPPING

Milan is shopping heaven, but it's expensive, particularly for clothes, shoes, furs, modern furniture and jewellery. The variety is astonishing and usually of exceptionally good quality.

Milanese are serious dressers: you rarely see anybody badly dressed. Governing the façade they present to the outside world, regardless of wealth or poverty, is the concept of *bella figura* (looking good). The chic shops are in *V. della Spiga*, where Versace and Krizia have their shop windows, and neighbouring *V. Sant'Andrea* (Armani, Moschino), *V. Monte Napoleone* (Gucci, Ferragamo) and *V. Borgospesso*. Those with smaller bank accounts should visit the shops in *V. Torino* and the department stores **La Rinascente** and **Coin**.

The longest and busiest shopping street is *C. Buenos Aires* where it is possible to buy almost anything. Otherwise, the *Vle Papiano* **market** (Sat) in the Navigli district is good for cheap clothes and a variety of other bargains. The Brera district is worth visiting. There is a Mon market at the *Pza Mirabello*, while Naviglio Grande is the scene of a monthly **antiques fair** (last Sun of the month).

SIGHTSEEING

Piazza del Duomo

Milan's signature building is the **Duomo**, *Pza Duomo 14* (metro: *Duomo*). Adorned with pinnacles, tracery and buttresses, it is an oddity in a country not noted for the Gothic style of its cathedrals. Napoleon was crowned King of Italy here in 1805. Work started in 1386, at the behest of Gian Galeazzo Visconti. Wanting a son, and finding his prayers granted, he built this remarkable edifice as a tribute to the Virgin Mary. It was not until 1958 that the last pinnacles were finished in a pale marble from the Candoglia quarry.

The Duomo is a magical and extravagant Gothic structure. Artisans from the north were responsible for producing it, and although attempts were made to refashion it in prevailing Renaissance and baroque styles, it has survived as something

119

of a misnomer in the annals of Italian architecture. It overflows with belfries, statues and pinnacles in white marble. It shimmers in the sunlight and glows in the winter fog. The comparatively stark interior is lit by vast quantities of fine stained glass and there are works of art dating from the cathedral's late Roman and early medieval predecessors.

Stairs lead up to, over and around the extensive roof system, from which there are fine views over the city to the Alps. It also provides the opportunity to examine close up some of the adornments to the cathedral's exterior – not to mention the 15th-century dome whose spire is topped by a gilt statue of the Madonna. The **Museo del Duomo** is in the Royal Palace just by the Duomo, *Pza Duomo 14* (metro: *Duomo); tel: (02) 860358,* open Tues–Sun 0930–1230 and 1500–1800. Entrance fee L8000. Houses sculptures, carvings, stained glass, tapestries and other treasures removed for safekeeping from the cathedral.

On the north side of *Pza Duomo* is the **Galleria Vittorio Emanuele II**, a monumental 19th-century iron-and-glass shopping arcade known as the **Salon de Milan**. Here there are elegant cafés in which to shelter from the city's interminable winter drizzle. The Galleria leads through to *Pza della Scala*, home of **La Scala** (more properly the Teatro alla Scala), probably the most famous opera house in the world. For such a famous place, the scale and proportions of the theatre are remarkably sober – even though it can seat 2800 spectators. The **Museo Teatrale alla Scala**, *tel: (02) 805 3418,* open Mon–Sat 0930–1230 and 1400–1730, entrance fee L5000, in the building, exhibits a huge array of opera memorabilia – scores, costumes, portraits and set designs.

Pza di Brera

The **Pinacoteca di Brera**, *V. Brera 28; tel: (02) 722631,* open Tues–Sun 0900–1730, entrance fee L8000, is Milan's finest art gallery. Situated in a rare surviving quarter of old streets and alleys, it was founded by Napoleon and opened in 1809, housing many artefacts looted from northern Italy. The collection concentrates on Italian artists of the 14th–19th centuries, although foreign schools of the 17th–18th centuries are also represented. There are some outstanding works – notable among them Raphael's *Marriage of the Virgin* and Mantegna's *Dead Christ.* There are also works by Piero della Francesca, Bramante, Carpaccio, Bellini, Caravaggio, Veronese, Rembrandt, El Greco and Van Dyck. A wing houses the 20th-century collection which contains, among others, works by the Futurist painters Severini and Balla. The gallery is housed in part of the Palazzo di Brera; in the courtyard stands a statue of Napoleon I dating from 1809.

Pza Pio XI

More priceless artworks are displayed in the Pinacoteca Ambrosiana, *Pza Pio XI 2* (metro: *Duomo* or *Cordusio); tel: (02) 8645 1436,* open Tues–Sun 0900–1730. Entrance fee L8000. The collection was begun by Cardinal Federico Borromeo early in the 17th century, and over the centuries judicious additions have been made so that today it is one of Italy's finest collections of paintings. Works by Leonardo da Vinci include the portrait of the musician Caffurio. Here, too, is Caravaggio's *Basket of Fruit* and Raphael's cartoons for the School of Athens fresco in the Vatican. There are works by Pinturicchio, Jan Brueghel the Younger, Giorgione and Titian.

The gallery also houses the **Biblioteca**

Ambrosiana, a library founded by Cardinal Borromeo. One of the greatest libraries in 17th-century Italy, it still houses a Virgil manuscript, a 5th-century version of the *Iliad*, early editions of Danté's *Divine Comedy* and a host of drawings by Leonardo da Vinci. In all, there are over 30,000 manuscripts.

Churches and monasteries

Milan's most famous painting, Leonardo da Vinci's *The Last Supper* (1495–97), dominates the old Dominican monastery refectory next to **Santa Maria Delle Grazie** (metro: *Cadorna*), *Pza Santa Maria delle Grazie 2; tel: (02) 498 7588*, open Tues–Sun 0800–1345. Entrance fee L12,000. *The Last Supper*, depicting Jesus saying 'One of you will betray me', attracts large crowds and a hefty entrance fee. It is one of the great paintings of the Renaissance. The church itself, a Renaissance building designed by Solari, and worked on by Bramante, is also worth a look. Bramante was responsible for the tribune (1492), choir, sacristy and cloister. Its external appearance exemplifies the Lombard Romanesque brick-and-terracotta style of architecture.

Not far from **Santa Maria Maggiore** is the **Monastero Maggiore** in *V. Luini*, whose little 16th-century church of **San Maurizio** houses frescos by Bernardino Luini, an avid follower of Leonardo da Vinci. The monastery contains the **Museo Civico Archeologico**, *C. Magenta 15; tel: (02) 8645 0011*, open Tues–Sun 0930–1730. Entrance free. Milan's archaeological museum includes Greek and Roman ceramics, Roman glass, Etruscan objects and a collection of finds from the Holy Land.

The **Basilica of Sant'Ambrogio**, *Pza Sant'Ambrogio 15* (metro: *Sant'Ambrogio*) was built in the late 4th century by St Ambrose, patron saint of the city and former Bishop of Milan. Most of what is standing today dates from the 12th century, although the smaller *campanile*, 300 years older, is one of the most ancient in the region. You enter through a huge porticoed atrium dominated by two towers, the left-hand Canon's Campanile (built 1144) and the right-hand Monks Campanile (built in the 9th century). In the church itself is some particularly fine Romanesque sculpture, including the pulpit. There are 10th and 11th-century mosaics in the apse and even older ones (5th-century) in the little Sacello di San Vittore in Ciel d'Oro, at the end of the south aisle. In the crypt are the remains of St Ambrose.

Where *V. Spadari* meets *V. Torino*, is the church of **San Satiro**. Rebuilt by Bramante in 1476, it acquired a new façade in the 19th century. Don't be deterred by that however – or by the busy commercial surroundings. This is one of Milan's finest churches. Also by Bramante is the little Baptistery situated at the edge of the right aisle. Here too is the Cappella della Pietà, a rare surviving example of Carolingian architecture (9th-century).

The **Museo della Basilica di Sant'Ambrogio**, *tel: (02) 8645 0895*, open Mon, Wed–Fri 1000–1200, 1500–1700, Sat, Sun 1500–1700. Entrance fee L3000, has a similar history to Sant' Ambrogio, having been built around AD 500 and reconstructed some 700 years later. A notable portico of 16 columns from a Roman temple stands in front.

Museums and Galleries

The **Castello Sforzesco**, the castle of the Sforzas in *Pza Castello* at the end of *V. Dante* (metro: *Cairoli*); *tel: (02) 6208 3940*, open Tues–Sun 0930–1730, entrance free, is a distinctive, seemingly indestructible fortress whose walls are nearly 4 m thick in places. The present building was constructed by Francesco Sforza in the second half of the 15th century on top of an earlier Visconti fortress. It has been much knocked about throughout subsequent centuries, and during the last war it suffered extensive damage during air raids, following which parts of it were rebuilt – including its towers. Today the castle houses an encyclopaedic collection of galleries and museums, displaying everything from arms to furniture, from Egyptian art to musical instruments.

The pick of the bunch are probably the art gallery, the **Museo d'Arte Antica**, and the **Pinacoteca**. The first contains Renaissance sculpture (its most magnificent piece is Michelangelo's *Rondanini Pietà*), furnishings and decorative arts. The second displays the works of a variety of Italian painters including Bellini, Mantegna and Lippi.

The *Cortile della Rocchetta,* a courtyard designed by Bramante and Filarete, gives access to the **Museo di Strumenti Musicali** which contains a spinet on which Mozart played. Here too are the **Egyptian Collection** and the **Prehistoric Collection**. Behind the castle is **Sempione Park**, the largest green space in central Milan. At the far end is the **Arco Della Pace** (Arch of Peace), which has seen many wars in its 150-year lifetime.

The **Museo Poldi Pezzoli**, *V. Manzoni 12* (metro: *Montenapoleone*); *tel: (02) 794889* was originally assembled by Gian Giacomo Poldi-Pezzoli, a well-to-do Milanese collector, and donated to the city in 1879, open Tues–Sun 0930–1230, 1430–1800 (Sat 1930, closed Sun afternoon Apr–Sept). Entrance: L10,000. It includes an excellent collection of Renaissance paintings including works by Botticelli, Pollaiuolo, Bellini, Lotto, Raphael and Mantegna. There is also a collection of Renaissance armour and bronzes and a diverse and eclectic array of tapestries, glass and rugs.

20th-century Italian art is displayed at

Italian Fashion

Giorgio Armani, Gianni Versace, Mariuccia Mandeli (alias Krizia), Fiorucci, Gucci, Benetton, Ferragamo: the stars of the Italian fashion firmament are household names the world over, at least among those who can afford their sparkling, big-ticket items. Milan is proud of its fashionable status, as you can see from a casual glance at the style of most people in the street – here, the Italian desire to *fare bella figura*, to cut a fine figure, is deeply ingrained in the city's psyche. (Some of the best-known fashion houses are, however, mired in allegations of tax fraud and assassination has struck at two of them – Versace and Gucci – in recent times.)

Milan is the spiritual capital of Italian fashion, and a strong contender for the title of world fashion capital. A stroll through the 'Golden Quadrangle', the luxury shopping district flanking the cathedral of San Babila and enclosed by *V. Senato, C. Venezia, V. Montenapoleone* and *V. Manzoni* is evidence enough of this, while the high-priced real estate between the Golden Quadrangle and the Duomo (Cathedral) houses many of the world's biggest fashion names.

Visitors who do not want to spend all their time window shopping, but want to take back something with them, can do no better than visit the department store **La Rinascente** in *Pza del Duomo*. If your senses become overloaded on a tour through its many departments, you can take time out at its snack bar or La Terrazza gourmet restaurant.

the **Museo di Arte Contemporanea**, *Palazzo Reale, Pza Duomo 12 (*metro: *Duomo); tel: 6208 3219,* open Tues–Sun 0930–1730. Entrance free. It has an excellent collection of works by a range of Italian artists of this century including De Chirico and Modigliani. **The Civic Gallery of Modern Art**, on the edge of the Giardini Pubblici (Public Gardens), *Via Palestro 16 (*metro: *Palestro); tel: (02) 7600 2819,* contains works by a variety of French Impressionists and their Italian contemporaries, open Tues–Sun 0930–1730; entrance free,

The gardens themselves, the **Giardini Pubblici**, were laid out in 1782 and provide welcome respite from the unrelenting urban quality of this vast, busy metropolis. Children can play – there is a zoo and a playground – and here too is the **Natural History Museum**, *C. Venezia 55; tel: (02) 6208 5404,* open Tues–Fri 0930–1730, Sat–Sun 0930–1830. Entrance free.

The Leonardo da Vinci Gallery in the **Museo Nazionale della Scienza e Tecnica**, *V. San Vittore 21 (*metro: *Sant'Ambrogio); tel: (02) 485551;* open Tues–Fri 0930–1650, Sat–Sun 0930–1830, entrance free, is not just an attempt to capitalise on the great man's name. In addition to displays relating to Leonardo's own ideas, including a model of his famous air-screw (precursor of the helicopter), the museum houses exhibits relating the evolution of science, collections of musical instruments and radios, clocks and computers, and trains.

Other Sights

At the intersection of *V. della Spiga* and *V. Manzoni,* the **Archi di Porta Nuova**, the arches of one of the old city gates, the Porta Nuova, is a rare surviving feature of the city's 12th-century walls.

In the western suburbs stands a modern

The Edict of Milan

One of the most celebrated events in Milanese history was the issuing, in AD 313, of the Edict of Milan, by Constantine the Great. The effect of the edict was to end the policy of persecuting Christians because of their refusal to comply with the state religion. Their stress on one God, in place of the Roman panoply, and their refusal to treat the emperor as divine, resulted in many martyrdoms in the amphitheatres of the Roman Empire, but Constantine's greater tolerance rapidly led to Christianity becoming the official religion. Doubts exist whether Constantine himself ever became a Christian – the Church claims he was baptised on his death bed, and that he bequeathed the Roman Empire in its entirety to the Papacy.

---

structure as distinctive and monumental as either the Duomo or Sforza Castle. The **San Siro Stadium**, *Pza Meazza,* home on alternate weekends to the city's two crack soccer squads, Inter Milan and AC Milan, is a futuristic construction of steel lattices and huge concrete cylinders, visible for miles in all directions.

A different kind of Milan can be seen in the **Navigli** district (metro: *Porta Genova*). Once a district of workshops, warehouses and bars catering for the needs of sailors and focused on two navigable canals – the Naviglio Grande and the Naviglio Pavese – this part of the city still has the flavour of a seaport. It is Milan's answer to London's Covent Garden or New York's Greenwich Village. Trendy, full of art galleries and funky shops, bars, clubs and restaurants, it is a haven from the often oppressively bourgeois flavour of the rest of the city.

LAKE COMO

Wishbone-shaped Lake Como, created with its twin Lake Lecco, is the most romantic of all the lakes. 'This magnificent scene of nature', gushed Goethe. Wordsworth said it was 'a treasure that the earth keeps to itself'. But you could hardly say that today. As well as the most romantic of the Italian lakes, Como is also the most crowded, no doubt because it is the lake closest to Milan. But nothing detracts from its beauty – its picture-postcard pretty villages, stately villas built by rich merchants and bankers and gorgeous gardens. You can drive round Como in four hours. But to get the most out of the trip, to savour the stunning views and leave time to see the many attractions along the way, you are better advised to take two or three days over it, with at least one overnight stop in, perhaps, Tremezzo, Menággio or Bellagio, combined with a journey by lake steamer, in order to view the lakes from a different perspective.

124

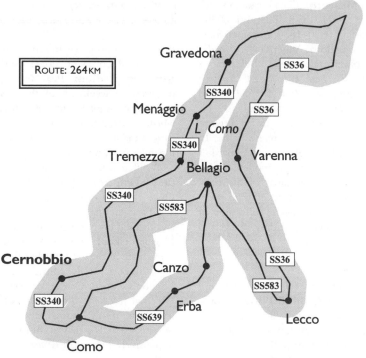

ROUTE: 264 KM

ROUTE

Come off the A9 motorway from Milan at the Como Sud exit. Take the road towards Monte Olimpino and then branch off on the SS340. Keep in the left lane as you approach a large roundabout, and then take the third exit signposted Cernobbio and Menággio. The road follows the shore of the lake (see map, p. 130) and Cernobbio is the first place of any size. This road continues up the western side of the lake to **Tremezzo, Menággio** and **Gravedona**. At the northern end of the lake, cut across the flat spit of land known as the Piano di Spagnato to the SS36, which runs down the east coast of the lake to **Varenna**, where you can take the car ferry to **Bellagio**, at the point where the lake takes a two-legged stride – one going to the town of Como (well worth visiting) and one going to Lecco (predominantly industrial).

From Bellagio (and for a bird's-eye view of the lake) take the mountain road to **Canzo** and **Erba**, before completing the circuit on the SS 639.

TOURIST INFORMATION

For general tourist information for the area contact the **Azienda di Promozione Turistica del Comasco,** *Pza Cavour 17, Como; tel: (031) 262090.*

CERNOBBIO

Tourist Office: *V. Regina 33b; tel: (031) 510198,* open Mon–Sat 0930–1230 and 1500–1800 and has a selection of local pamphlets and maps.

ACCOMMODATION AND FOOD

Cernobbio must be the only town in Italy whose main attraction is an hotel. The **Villa d'Este**, *V. Regina 40; tel: (031) 3481,* was built in 1568 as the summer residence for Cardinal Tolomeo Gallio and

remained in the family for more than two centuries. But it is more famously known as the 19th-century home of the forsaken and voluntarily exiled Caroline of Brunswick, Princess of Wales. It was converted into an hotel in 1873 and today, in its magnificent position at the water's edge, set amid flowers, fountains and gardens, it offers a discreet, luxurious and expensive retreat for those who want complete privacy (recent guests have incuded Donald and Marla Trump, Mel Gibson, Madonna and John F. Kennedy Jnr), with services to match.

More modestly, you can stay at the 42-room **Miralago**, an old-fashioned hotel of style and character, *Pza Risorgimeto; tel: (031) 510062,* or, 2km to the north-east, at the **Asnigo**, *V. Noseda 2; tel: (031) 519962.*

Cernobbio is also well served by restaurants. In addition to the three hotels mentioned here, the food at **Cernobbio**, *tel: (031) 512710,* is also reliable.

SIGHTSEEING

Cernobbio is a pleasing lakeside village, full of sturdy villas – in addition to the Villa d'Este, Villa Besana and Villa Erba are also attractive in their own right. Every Wed there's a large market in the centre of the village, the stalls leading off the main square to the waterfront. Cernobbio is also the starting point for the 130 km walk through the mountains on Como's western shore, known as the **V. dei Monte Lariani**. Details from the tourist office.

CERNOBBIO TO TREMEZZO

One of the most attractive stretches of the whole route. The lakeside road twists and turns, through a series of tunnels between, on one side, sheer slabs of rock and, on the other, the clear blue waters of the lake. The road bypasses most of the villages, but for a glimpse of the Comasco way of life drop down into little villages like Brienno, which see relatively few visitors and are content to remain trapped in their own time capsules.

TREMEZZO

Tourist Office: *V. Regina 3; tel: (0344) 40493*, open 0900–1200 and 1530–1830 (Apr–mid Oct), but hours seem variable. The office has a good supply of local pamphlets and maps, and helpful staff, but does not take accommodation bookings.

ACCOMMODATION

Tremezzo has plenty of accommodation to suit all budgets. The **Grand Hotel Tremezzo Palace**, *V. Regina 8; tel: (0344) 40446*, dates back to the turn of the century and is in the traditional Como mould – spacious and elegant rooms (those facing the lake have stunning views). It also has an attractive, terraced garden and good sports facilities – a tennis court and outdoor swimming pool – and a restaurant which is highly rated, particularly for the standard of its fish and pasta dishes. Other hotels worth considering include **Albergo Lenno**; *V. Lamazzi 23; tel: (0344) 57051*, overlooking the lake at Lenna; and the smaller **Albergo Russal**, *V. San Martino 2; tel: (0344) 40408*, 1 km or so from the centre, in the hills behind the resort.

EATING AND DRINKING

Fine dining in the hotels is backed up by a good selection of restaurants, many of which offer fine views over the lake to go with foods as only Italians can prepare. A good example is **La Darsena**, *V. Regina 3; tel: (0344) 40423*, where you dine in a tastefully furnished upstairs room, overlooking the water. The restaurant serves excellent fresh fish from the lake at reasonable prices.

Two other restaurants worth considering are 1.5 km away in the adjoining village of Rogaro: **Al Veluu**, *tel: (0344) 40510* and **La Figurida**, *tel: (0344) 40676*. There are any number of inexpensive lunch places in the centre of Tremezzo and, back towards Como at Argegno, the restaurant of **Hotel Argegno**, *V. Milano 14; tel: (031) 821455* has a wide range of pizzas.

SIGHTSEEING

The area immediately around Tremezzo, sheltered by a headland, has the gentlest climate in the whole of Como. Small wonder, then, that in the 19th century the aristocracy who decided to set up home on Como chose the Tremezzina, as the area is known, as the place where they should build. The setting is magical: Tremezzo is situated almost midway up the lake, looking out across to the evening lights of Bellagio. There is no more romantic spot on the lake.

Tremezzo has its fair share of *belle époque* palaces, villas and gardens, none more famous than **Villa Carlotta**, a couple of minutes walk north of the village, right next to the Grand Hotel Tremezzo Palace. The villa, which is open daily 0900–1600 (summer); 0900–1130 and 1400–1630 (Mar and Oct), is a pink and white neo–classical building constructed by a Prussian princess for her daughter, Carlotta. It houses a fine collection of 18th-century statues, including Canova's *Cupid and Psyche* and a frieze of Alexander entering Babylon, which was commissioned by Napoleon, though the French leader was exiled before he could pay for it. But it is the glorious gardens – 14 acres of azaleas, camelias and rhododendrons – which make Villa Carlotta the most visited place on the shores of Como.

The road from Tremezzo leads through

Cadenabbia, a somewhat uninspiring resort lacking Tremezzo's style, to **Menággio**, a pretty enough place in which to swim, sunbathe or simply watch the world go by.

MENÁGGIO

Tourist Office: *Pza Garibaldi 8; tel: (0344) 32924.* The office is open throughout the year Mon–Sat 0900–1200 and 1500–1800 and is well organised with accommodation lists, events and details of walks in the area.

ACCOMMODATION

As the second largest resort on Lake Como, Menággio's accommodation is predominantly summer seasonal. The two leading hotels are the **Grand Hotel Menággio**, *V. IV Novembre 69; tel: (0344) 30640,* and the **Grand Hotel Victoria**, *V. Castelli 11; tel: (0344) 32003.* Both have swimming pools and are good for families. On the outskirts of town, at Liveno, the smaller **Royal Hotel**; *tel: (0344) 31444,* and **Loveno**; *tel: (0344) 32110,* enjoy rural aspects and good views over the lake.

EATING AND DRINKING

Most visitors eat in hotels, but Menággio has a number of good, reasonably-priced restaurants, such as **Lario**, *V. IV Novembre; tel: (0344) 32368* and **Lugano**, *V. Como 26; tel: (0344) 31664.* At lunchtime, good pizzas are available at **Giara Pizzeria**, *V. Roma 22; tel: (0344) 32259,* while **Café del Pess**, *Pza Garibaldi 8,* serves good sandwiches and ice creams.

MENÁGGIO TO BELLAGIO

In the centre of Menággio, take the right fork (the left fork goes to Switzerland, Lugano is 30 km away). The scenery in the northern part of the lake is less

attractive than farther south and you can safely miss out most of the small towns and villages along the way, after you have paid tribute to **Dongo**, the place where Mussolino was captured, and believed executed, while attempting to flee to Switzerland in 1945. At the northern end of the lake, just after Sorico, turn right on the link road which runs for just over 3 km to join the SS36, the main road down the eastern side of the lake to Lecco. This is a busy, noisy road, with long stretches of tunnel. In a short gap in the tunnel, follow the signs to Bellano and then take the road to Varenna, from where you can catch the car ferry (roughly every hour in summer) to Bellagio. If you miss this turning, you will have to travel virtually all the way to Lecco without being able to turn round. The ferry trip takes ¼ hr.

BELLAGIO

Tourist Office: *Pza della Chiesa 14; tel: (031) 950204.*

ACCOMMODATION

Bellagio's most famous hotels are the stately lakeside mansions so beloved by the well-heeled travellers of yesteryear – notably, the **Grand Hotel Villa Serbelloni**, *Lungolago Bellagio, V. Roma 1; tel: (031) 951529,* which enjoys, like many hotels in the resort, stupendous views of lake and mountains. Other less ostentatious establishments worth considering include the **du Lac**, *Pza Mazzini 32; tel: (031) 950216,* one of three hotels sharing a privileged position on Bellagio's small arcaded promenade.

EATING AND DRINKING

Again, much of the fine dining tends to take place in the hotels. But if you have the time and inclination to try something

Lake Steamer Trips

Take a boat trip across Lake Como and it's easy to appreciate just how the romantic poets became so enthralled. As you zigzag from one side of the lake to the other, Como works its theatrical magic: the parade of gardens seems never ending and, floating among them, the villas, built by cardinals, merchants and princes, stand out amid blooms of hydrangeas, azaleas and rhododendrons.

Transport on the lake operates like a bus service and is both fairly regular and punctual. There are three main types of transport – *batelli* (boats), *traghetti* (car ferries) and *aliscafi* (hydrofoils). The boat service operates on a frequency of one every 2 hrs to any particular destination. A service operates from the extreme south-western point (Como) to the the extreme north-eastern point (Colico). There is also a less frequent service from the centre of the lake (Bellagio) to the south-eastern extremity (Lecco). Car ferries are the most frequent and serve predominantly the *Centro Lario* – the central part of the lake – that is, Cadenabbia, Bellagio, Varenna and Menaggio. Hydrofoils offer the quickest means of transport and cover the same areas as the boats, although they only stop at the main towns and they are the most expensive. To help visitors find their way around, timetables have been compiled in colour coding: blue for services operating from Mon to Sat, yellow for Sun and *festiva* (holidays), and white for daily services. A 20 per cent discount is available, on production of a passport, to EU citizens over the age of 60.

different, **La Pergola** at *Pescallo; tel: (031) 950263,* offers excellent freshly caught lake fish dishes, grilled or baked, served on the terrace. Pre-dinner drinks? Settle for any bar with a view of lake and mountains.

SIGHTSEEING

Bellagio is the pick of the lakeside resorts in terms of setting and atmosphere (apart, that is, from the odd tasteless souvenir shop). But sightseeing is limited after you have strolled round the village and seen the magnificent house and gardens of the 17th-century **Villa Serbelloni**, on a hill behind. There are guided tours morning (1100) and afternoon (1600), Easter–mid-Oct. The neo-classical **Villa Melzi**, at the Como end of the village, is also open to visitors in summer.

From Bellagio, rather than sampling more lakeside driving, take the road which leads over the top of the mountain behind, between the two legs of the lake. The scenery up here is spectacular and, as you climb up to 743 m at **Civenna**, passing the tiny church of the Madonna del Ghisallo, dedicated to cyclists, you get yet another mountain–lake perspective, before returning to Como via **Canzo** and **Erba**.

COMO

Tourist Board: *Piazza Cavour 16; tel: (031) 269712.* It has a wide range of pamphlets, maps and brochures, distributed by helpful staff. There is also a tourist

Colour section (i): Tremezzo (see p. 126) viewed from Lake Como; Verona and the Roman Arena (p. 104). Inset, a butcher slices parma ham (p. 157).

(ii) Milan (pp. 115–123): The Duomo; La Scala Opera House.

(iii) Lake Maggiore (pp. 131–136): Isola Bella Gardens; sunrise over Lake Maggiore.

(iv) The Hermitage, just east of Assisi (p. 182); inset, Palazzo dei Priori at Perugia (p. 179).

information office at the town's **San Giovanni rail station**; *tel: (031) 267214.*

ACCOMMODATION

Como has more accommodation than any other town on the lake because of its importance as a business and conference centre. In the town centre, **Hotel Metropole**, almost next door to the tourist office at *Pza Cavour 19; tel: (031) 269444,* is family owned and close to the shops. On the outskirts of town, **Il Grand**, *V. Antelami; tel: (031) 5161,* and **Villa Flora**, *V. Cernobbio 12; tel: (031) 573105,* are hotels in the traditional Como style. **Park Hotel**, next to the Stadio Sinigaglia at *Vle Rosselli 20; tel: (031) 572615,* offers comfortable, air-conditioned rooms. Inexpensive hotels in the old town include the 1-star **Hotel Piazzolo**, *V. Indipendenza 65; tel: (031) 272186.*

EATING AND DRINKING

Take your pick from a bar overlooking the water (expensive) to one in a side street, where the same drinks are available at half the price. Noted Como restaurants include, for views, the aptly named **Ristorante Bellevista**, at the top of the Brunate funicular, *tel: (031) 220012,* and, in town, **Sant'Anna 1907**, *V. Turati 1–3; tel: (031) 505266,* and **Lario**, *V. Coloniola 44; tel: (031) 303952.*

SIGHTSEEING

The magic of Como is its setting – at the head of the lake, with the stucco villas rising above the water's edge, and the pleasant gardens where you can go for a stroll, *gelato* in hand. But within the town there is plenty of interest – not least the **Duomo** generally reckoned to be the finest Gothic-Renaissance architecture, also rich in tapestries and paintings.

Silk from Como

In the 17th century, Milan was the European centre of silk production, but that situation rapidly changed when the overtaxed silk millers of Milan decided to head for Como, then under a more enlightened Austrian administration – enlightened at least as far as trade and taxation were concerned.

Soon Como was supplying the courts of Vienna and further afield with gorgeous silks for clothing and furnishings. In the 18th century it was a Como silk miller, one Cesare Bonanone, who invented the power loom that ushered in Northern Italy's Industrial Revolution.

Competition from the Far East threatened the local industry in the 19th century but in the end it was Chinese silk that rescued Como – an epidemic wiped out the local silkworm population, but Como's silk manufacturers survived by importing raw silk from the land where silk was first discovered, centuries previously. Today, Como silk factories continue to import raw silk, making it up into richly dyed and patterned fabrics, much sought after by the couturiers of Milan and Florence.

129

The second of the town's two great churches is the 11th-century **Basilica of Sant'Abbondio**, near the main rail station on *V. Regina*. Como is also the centre for the silk industry and the **Silk Museum** at *V. Vallegio 3;* is open Tues–Sat 0900–1200 and 1500–1800. Book in advance for Saturday visits. If you have the time take the **cable railway** up to the resort of Brunate which, as well as offering good views, is also a popular starting-point for walks in the mountains. The railway operates roughly every ½ hr in summer.

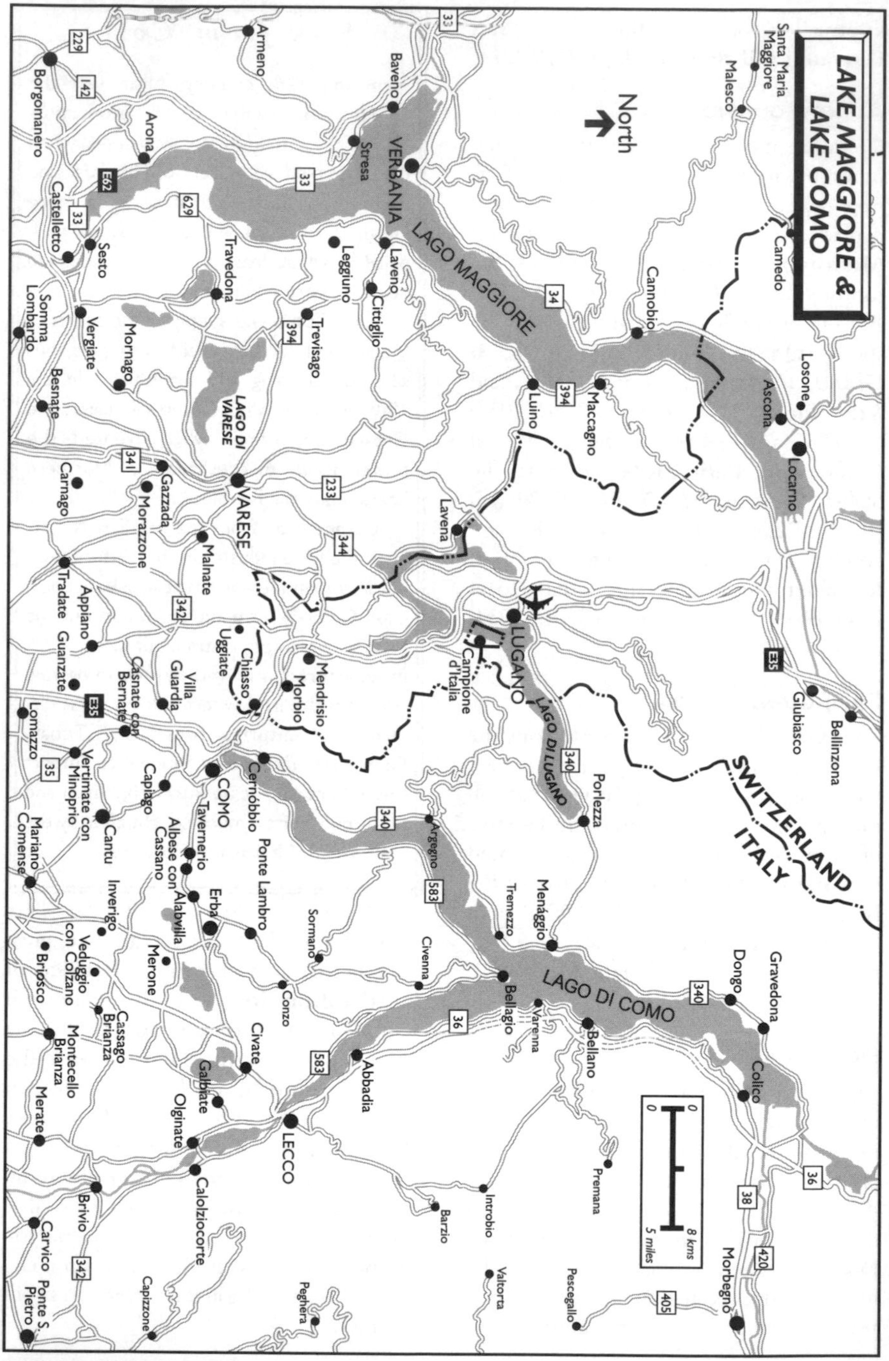
LAKE MAGGIORE & LAKE COMO
North
LAGO MAGGIORE
LAGO DI VARESE
LAGO DI LUGANO
LAGO DI COMO
SWITZERLAND
ITALY
VERBANIA
VARESE
LUGANO
COMO
LECCO
Santa Maria Maggiore
Malesco
Camedo
Cannobio
Losone
Ascona
Locarno
Maccagno
Luino
Lavena
Giubiasco
Bellinzona
Campione d'Italia
Porlezza
Armeno
Baveno
Stresa
Arona
Borgomanero
Castelletto
Sesto
Somma Lombardo
Vergiate
Mornago
Besnate
Travedona
Leggiuno
Laveno
Cittiglio
Trevisago
Carnago
Gazzada
Morazzone
Malnate
Tradate
Appiano
Guanzate
Uggiate
Chiasso
Mendrisio
Morbio
Villa Guardia
Casnate con Bernate
Lomazzo
Vertimate con Minoprio
Capiago
Cantu
Cernobbio
Tavernerio
Albese con Cassano
Mariano Comense
Inverigo
Erba
Alabvilla
Ponte Lambro
Sormano
Argegno
Tremezzo
Menággio
Civenna
Conzo
Merone
Veduggio con Colzano
Briosco
Cassago Brianza
Montecello Brianza
Merate
Civate
Galbiate
Oginate
Calolziocorte
Brivio
Carvico
Ponte S. Pietro
Capizzone
Peghera
Bellagio
Varenna
Bellano
Abbadia
Dongo
Gravedona
Colico
Premana
Introbio
Barzio
Valtorta
Pescegallo
Morbegno
0
0
8 kms
5 miles
33
229
142
E62
629
34
394
233
341
344
342
E35
35
340
583
36
38
420
405

130

LAKE MAGGIORE

Left behind by retreating glaciers at the end of the last ice age, Lake Maggiore (also known as Lake Verbano) lies at the foot of the Alps, separates Lombardy from Piemonte and extends into the Italian-speaking Swiss canton of Ticino. It is Italy's second largest lake, a fjord-like finger of blue water 64km long

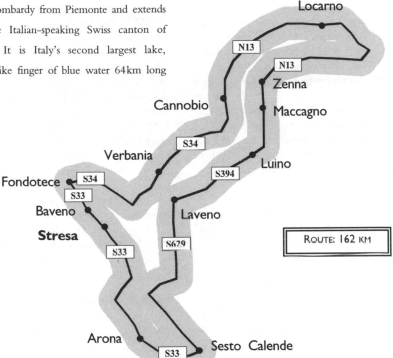

131

ROUTE: 162 KM

which varies in width from about 2–4km. Its deepest point is 372m below the surface and it covers an area of 212 square kilometres.

This is a splendidly scenic part of Italy, with a warm, mild climate. Its proximity to the heavily urbanised north Italian plain guarantees a heavy inflow of day-trippers, and summer visitors from northern Europe. The eastern shore is less heavily populated, and has fewer

big resorts, so it is generally far quieter than the western shore. Allow at least a day to drive the 162km around Lake Maggiore. You will find this to be the minimum if you want to stop occasionally along the way, to admire the view of the sail-studded lake and visit some of the lakeside resorts. An overnight stay will diminish the pressure and add to the pleasure.

ROUTE

This circuit begins at **Stresa**, a resort just off the A26 about 20 km north of the point where the A8 from Milan joins the A26 from Turin, but in fact it could start almost anywhere on the lake's circumference. In a left-hand drive car, a clockwise route is better from the front-seat passenger's point of view, and vice versa for right-hand drive cars (of course, most drivers go around clockwise, so you are liable to have less traffic hassles by going in the opposite direction). Drivers should resist the temptation to constantly switch their attention from the road to the lake, as the road is winding and often narrow, and traffic can be busy, with an ever-present menace of impatient drivers overtaking and suddenly appearing directly in front of you. It is better to change drivers after a time, if possible, and to stop frequently at appropriate places.

From Stresa, take the lakeside S33 to where it joins the S34 at **Fondotoce**, and follow this along the west side of the lake to the **Swiss border**, where it becomes the N13 to **Locarno**, around the northern tip of the lake, and back into Italy at **Zenna**, from where the S394 runs to **Laveno**. Keeping to the shore, take the S629 to **Sesto Calende**, then the S33 round the southern tip, back to Stresa.

Getting about on the water is easy: some 30 car ferries, tour boats and hydrofoils zigzag from shore to shore, stopping at all the main places, including the **Borromean Islands**, and the **Brissago Islands** in the Swiss section of the lake. Contact **Navigazione Lago Maggiore**, *Vle F. Baracca 1, Arona; tel: (0322) 46551; fax: (0322) 249530.*

STRESA

Tourist Office: *V. Principe Tomasa 70–72; tel: (0323) 30150, fax (0323)* 32561. Open Mon–Sat 0830–1230 and 1500–1815, Sun 0900–1200 (May–Sept); Mon–Fri 0830–1230 and 1500–1815, Sat 0830–1530 (Oct–Apr). Ask about programmes for the week-long international classical music festival held here at the **Palazzo dei Congressi**, *V. R. Bonghi 4; tel: (0323) 31095*, in late Aug/early Sept.

ACCOMMODATION

There is a wide range of accommodation in Stresa, most of it blessed with coveted lakeside views and much of it very expensive. At the top end is the 5-star **Des Iles Borromées**, *C. Umberto I 31; tel: (0323) 30431*, where doubles run to more than L700,000 a night. In the mid-price range, there is a reasonable choice, and although most hotels are busy in summer there is always the possibility of last-minute rooms.

Good options are the **La Fontana Meublé**, *V. Sempione Nord 1; tel: (0323) 32707*, and the **Da Cesare**, *V. Mazzini 14; tel: (0323) 31386*. In the lower price bracket, there are fewer options and what there is tends to be modern.

EATING AND DRINKING

Stresa is packed with restaurants, most of which seem to have exactly the same menu and prices. Try **La Sacca**, *V. Sempione 50; tel: (0323) 31165*, which has a tree-shaded terrace with a view of the lake, or the **Taverna del Papagallo**, *V. Principessa Margherita 46; tel: (0323) 30411*, a more authentically Italian restaurant than is common in this very touristic area.

The **Gelateria–Cremeria Fantasia**, *V. Principessa Margherita 38*, is a superior example of the Italian ice cream parlour.

SIGHTSEEING

One of the most charming towns on Lake

The Borromean Islands

These four handsome little islands float like graceful swans in the western arm of the lake, between Stresa and Verbania. Frequent ferry and excursion services operated by Navigazione Lago Maggiore link the islands to these two resorts, and others around the lake. Motor launches also sail to them from Stresa and Verbania.

Isola Bella is probably the most celebrated, having received favourable notices from Byron, Stendhal, Goethe and Wagner. In the 17th century, Count Carlo Borromeo III commissioned Angelo Crivelli to lay out a garden in a series of ten formal terraces; an extravagant gift designed to indicate his devotion to his wife Isabella. Exotic plants, statuary, fountains, peacocks and a sumptuously decorated villa, the **Palazzo Borromeo**; *tel: (0323) 30556*, completed the picture. Open daily 0900–1200 and 1330–1730 (Mar–Sept); 0900–1200 and 1330–1700 (Oct). Entrance fee L12,000. The palace's art collection includes works by Tiepolo and Van Dyck. Beautiful it might be, but it has succumbed to the ravages of tourism.

Isola Madre, the biggest island, is generally much quieter than Isola Bella. It too has a famous **ornamental garden** and a small **Palace**; *tel: (0323) 31261*, of the Borromeo family, which houses an exhibition of marionettes. Open daily 0900–1200 and 1330–1730 (Mar–Sept); 0900–1200 and 1330–1700 (Oct). Entrance fee L12,000

More peaceful than Isola Madre and Isola Bella, because it lacks the imposing villas and gardens of its neighbours, **Isola dei Pescatori** (also known as Isola Superiore) is no less picturesque. Once one of Toscanini's favourite hideaways, it has held onto much of its original fishing-village charm and is the focus of many afternoon outings.

Tiny **San Giovanni** island is private.

133

Maggiore, Stresa has been a much-visited holiday resort since the 19th century. It is an elegant, low-key place famous for its views and for its proximity to the magical **Borromean Islands** (Navigazione Lago Maggiore sails to the islands from here). It is very popular in summer and its facilities tend to get overloaded, partly because it makes an excellent base from which to explore the lake.

A **cable car** leaves from the lake shore at **Carciano** on the western edge of Stresa and climbs up **Monte Mottarone** (1491m), from where a magnificent view of the lake and the mountains can be had, as well as some scenic walks. Depending on the season, you may spot some of the region's alpine plants - look out for orchids and gentians, hiding shyly among the grass, and for the martagon or Turk's

cap lily. The cable car runs every half hour from 0930–1200 and 1330–1700; the ascent takes 18mins. South of Stresa at a distance of 1km is the **Villa Pallavicino**, a botanical garden and animal park, open daily 0900–1800 (Mar–Oct). Entrance fee L10,000. There is a street market in Stresa every Fri.

BAVENO

Tourist Office: *C. Garibaldi 16; tel/fax: (0323) 924632.*

Baveno, west of Stresa, is a popular resort, particularly in peak season. Queen Victoria holidayed here in 1879 and Baveno has been favoured by the British ever since. Navigazione Lago Maggiore sails to the Borromean Islands from here. There is a street market in Baveno every Mon.

VERBANIA, INTRA AND PALLANZA

Tourist Office: *C. Zanitello 8; tel/fax: (0323) 503249.*

Verbania, along with nearby **Intra** and **Pallanza**, form a kind of lakeside mini-conurbation, and the most heavily populated section of the shore – a fact that becomes even more pertinent when the summer crowds pile in. In compensation, there are plenty of accommodation and restaurant possibilities, most of them a shade less costly than those of Stresa.

Some 6 km inland from Verbania is the **Valle Grande National Park**, reachable from the village of **Cicogna**, and a good place to hike off some of the excess kilos you may have picked up in the restaurants hereabouts.

Pallanza's main attraction is the **Villa Taranto**, *V. Prossanò; tel: (0323) 44555.* Open 0830–sunset (Apr–Oct) (ticket office closes 1830), whose 50 acre gardens were planted in the 1930s with some 20,000 different kinds of plants – including giant Amazonian water-lilies – by a Scotsman, Neil McEacharn, who was keen to take advantage of the area's mild climate. He set out to create one of the best botanical gardens in the world, and he certainly made a brave effort to achieve this. Navigazione Lago Maggiore sails to the Borromean Islands from here.

Navigazione Lago Maggiore also operates a landing-craft car ferry service from **Intra** across the lake to Laveno. At peak times, there are two crossings an hour in each direction from early morning until late at night. There is a street market in Intra every Sat.

Moving up the lake beyond Intra, **Ghiffa** and **Cannero Riviera** are pretty stone-built villages with wonderful lake views, and the latter has steep streets leading down to the waterfront. Some fortified

islets in this area were the haunts of pirates who infested the area in medieval times.

CANNOBIO

Tourist Office: *Vle. V. Veneto 4 28052 Cannobio; tel/fax: (0322) 71212.* Ask here about the numerous camping and caravan sites in this area, some of which lie conveniently (if not exactly handsomely) beside the water.

Cannobio, the last major halt before entering the Swiss stretch of Lake Maggiore, is a pretty town with cobbled streets in the old centre, where you can stroll among arts and crafts market stalls. This makes a good place for dining at a lakeside terrace, and a quieter option than the Stresa-Verbania area. In addition to its general medieval atmosphere and good looks, Cannobio has at least one notable site: the Bramante-inspired **Santuario della Pietà** which San Carlo Borromeo had built at the location of a miracle. There is a market in Cannobio every Sun.

An interesting diversion to make at this point is westward into the narrow and scenic **Valle Cannobina**, following the course of the Cannobino stream.

LOCARNO

Tourist Office: *Largo Zorzi; tel: (091) 751 0333; fax: (091) 751 9070.* The country code for Switzerland is **41**.

Locarno belonged to Milan from 1342–1512, when it fell to the Swiss. The town is known for the Locarno Pact of 1925, which 'guaranteed' the post-World War I European frontiers – a treaty that went by the board when Adolf Hitler came to power in Germany eight years later. Nowadays, this holiday and health resort with a population of about 20,000 is better known for the **Locarno International Film Festival** held in the town every August. The lowest point in

134

Switzerland, 192m above sea level, is here, at the shore of Lake Maggiore.

One of the big attractions in Locarno is the **Casino di Locarno**, *Lago Zorzi 1; tel: (091) 751 1537*. Open Sun–Thur 1200–0200, Fri–Sat 1200–0400. Other points of interest are the church of **Madonna del Sasso** (1480), and the 14th-century **Castle of the Dukes of Milan**.

MACCAGNO

Tourist Office: *Vle Garibaldi 1; tel/fax: (0332) 561200*.

A twin town – 'Superiore' and 'Inferiori' – stands on the lake at the head of the scenic **Valle Veddasca**, and is notable for the 15th-century **Santuario della Madonnina** and a medieval fortification called the **Torre Imperiale** (Imperial Tower).

LUINO

Tourist Office: The **IAT** office in Luino is at *Vle Dante 6, 21016 Luino; tel/fax: (0332) 53 00 19*.

The 4-star **Camin Hotel Luino**, *Vle Dante 35; tel: (0332) 53 01 18*, is a characterful place with a location beside the lake, although it is on the high end of the price range for the eastern shore.

There are two interesting Renaissance churches in the town: the **Church of S. Pietro** and the **Church of S. Giuseppe**, as well as a **Monument to Garibaldi**. There is a street market in Luino every Wednesday.

LAVENO

Tourist Office: The provincial **APT** office covering the east shore of the lake is at **Varese**, 22km east of Laveno, *Vle Ippodromo 9, 21100 Varese; tel: (0332) 284624; fax: (0332) 238093*. The **IAT** office in Laveno is at the *Palazzo Municipale; tel/fax: (0332) 666100*.

ACCOMMODATION

Laveno (also known as Laveno Mombello) is reasonably well supplied with hotels and restaurants, making it a fairly popular resort for the east shore. Good options are the **Europa**, *V. Ceretti 5; tel: (0332) 667252*, and the moderately priced **Pensione l'Isola**, *V. Rebolgiane 68; tel: (0332) 666031*. The **Hotel Sasso Moro** at the hamlet Arolo di Leggiuno; *tel: (0332) 647 30*, 7 km south of Laveno, is one of the best-sited and charming mid-price hotels in the area, with a fine waterside location.

EATING AND DRINKING

Reasonably typical Italian dining possibilities in Laveno are the **Concordia**, *Pza Marchetti; tel: (0332) 667380*, and the **Trattoria Le Chicchere**, *V. Gramsci 11; tel: (0332) 626493*.

SIGHTSEEING

Navigazione Lago Maggiore operates a landing-craft car ferry service across the lake to Intra, a few km north of Verbania and Pallanza, and also sails to the Borromean Islands (see feature, p.133) from here. At peak times, there are two crossings an hour in each direction from early morning until late at night.

From Laveno a **cable car** climbs the **Sassa del Ferro** (1062m). There is a hotel, bar and restaurant at the cable car station on the mountain, and a magnificent view over the lake to the Alps beyond.

Laveno is a centre for high-quality pottery. The pottery-making tradition here dates back to 1856, when the Società Ceramica Italiana was founded in the town, and it has evolved both artistically and commercially since then, enjoying particular popularity with the art deco style of the 1920s and 1930s. You can see some of the best examples at the **Museo della Ceramica** in the **Palazzo Perabò** at **Cerro** just outside Laveno; *tel: (0332) 666530.* Open Tues–Thur 1430–1730, Fri–Sun 1000–1200 and 1430–1730 (all afternoons in Jul and Aug 1530–1830). Entrance fee L5000, with pieces from 1895–1935 on display. The *palazzo* itself, dating from the 16th century, is well worth seeing. You can also buy contemporary pieces at several shops in the town. Try, for example, **Ceramica Artistica DEAM**, *V. XXV Aprile 83; tel: (0332) 667479.*

At Christmas, Laveno divers set up an underwater crib in the lake close to the harbour – floodlit, the Nativity scene is clearly visible through the clear water.

Angera, 22km south of Laveno, is dominated by a dramatically sited hilltop castle, the **Rocca Borromeo**, *V. alla Rocca; tel: (0331) 931300.* Open daily 0930–1230 and 1400–1800 (Apr–Sept); 0930–1230 and 1400–1700 (Oct). Entrance fee L8000. Dating from the 14th century and built by the Visconti family, it passed to the Borromeo family in 1449. The castle's rooms are decorated with frescos in the Lombard style and it houses the magical **Museo della Bambola e della Moda Infantile** (Doll and Children's Fashion Museum), displaying more than a thousand antique dolls. There is a street market in Angera every Thur.

The more adventurous visitors might like to try their hand at hang-gliding and experience the beautiful lakeland scenery from a unique viewpoint. Contact **Club Icaro 2000**, *V. Verdi 19, Sangiano; tel: (0332) 648335.* Sangiano is 5km south of Laveno.

ARONA

Tourist Office: *Pzle Duca d'Aosta; tel/fax: (0322) 243601.*

Smaller Lakes

If you want to compare the experience of touring one of the big lakes with that of the smaller ones, Lake Maggiore has a retinue of diminutive satellites. Tiny **Lago di Mergozzo** lies just 1km west of Verbania, and is effectively an extension of the lake's western arm. **Lago d'Orta** lies to the south-west, across Monte Mottarone from Stresa, and is perhaps the best choice. Generally a lot more tranquil than Maggiore, Lago d'Orta is just 14km long and 2km wide, but it packs a lot of scenery into its wooded shoreline.

To the south-east of Lake Maggiore lie even smaller **Lago di Monate** and **Lago di Commabio**, and beyond them **Lago di Varese**, which is closer to the provincial capital **Varese**.

Arona, 16km south of Stresa, is a better option than the bigger resort for camping and for less expensive hotels. **Camping**: **Lido**, on the lake shore, very close to the station; *tel: (0322) 243383.*

Arona is chiefly known as the birthplace of San Carlo Borromeo (1538–84), a church reformer and an instigator of the Council of Trent who once claimed that he was far too ugly to be anything but a priest. A huge bronze statue of him towers above old Arona and the castle in which he was born. There is a street market in Arona every Tues.

◄► Connection: Lake Maggiore to Milan

From **Stresa**, on Lake Maggiore, the lakeside road (SS33) heads south to join the A8 autostrada, which heads straight for Milan. A new motorway link from Stresa to the A8 is under construction

TURIN–MONT BLANC

Bordering France and Switzerland and up to its ears in the Alps, this is one of the most scenic areas in Europe. A wonderland of mountains, forests and plunging rivers, you can breathe more fresh air here in five minutes than a city denizen gets in a year. The highest peaks in the Alps lie inside and along the borders of the Valle d'Aosta. In winter, skiing is the big draw around here and in summer it is an unrivalled location for hiking, mountain-biking and, yes, driving.

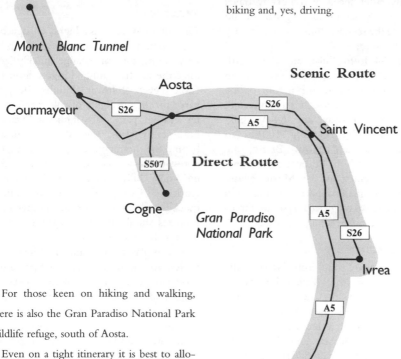

137

For those keen on hiking and walking, there is also the Gran Paradiso National Park wildlife refuge, south of Aosta.

Even on a tight itinerary it is best to allo-cate at least two days to this area: one for exploring the Valle d'Aosta by car, and another for walking in the national park (spending more time would be better, of course).

DIRECT ROUTE: 160 KM

ROUTES

DIRECT ROUTE

▶ There *is* a direct route into and through the valley, the A5 *autostrada*. It follows pretty much the same general course as the scenic route – there isn't much else it can do given the valley's constricted width – so it may make sense to use it for at least part of the way, particularly if you are pressed for time. The disadvantage is that it can be very busy, and carries a lot of heavy trucks, while the typically faster speed of motorway travel leaves less chance for looking around and admiring the scenery. Plus you have to pay tolls, of course.

The A4 from Milan and the North Italian Lakes joins the A5 from Turin some 20km south of the mouth of the Valle d'Aosta near **Ivrea**, via a connecting stretch of motorway, the A4-A5 link. From Ivrea the A5 runs 100km to **Courmayeur** and **Mont Blanc**, the highest mountain in Europe, on the border with France at the **Mont Blanc Tunnel**, the main connection to France in this area, bypassing **Aosta** some three-quarters of the way along the road.

SCENIC ROUTE

▶ The scenic route from **Ivrea** to the head of the Valle d'Aosta at **Courmayeur** is the S26. As indicated above, it parallels the A5 all the way through the valley, a distance on this road of 71km to **Aosta** and 125km to Courmayeur. The main differences – apart from the S26 being toll free – are the chance to drive more slowly and enjoy the scenery, experience the towns and villages along the way, and branch off easily on any side-road that takes your fancy. Likely restaurants and hotels are also more easily identified.

There are several possible permutations of how to do this route. One is to drive up through Aosta and Courmayeur to **Mont Blanc** on the scenic route and overnight in Courmayeur. Then go back partway down the valley to a point 6km short of Aosta and turn off south on the S507 to **Cogne**, 22km along the road, to spend the day hiking in the **Gran Paradiso National Park**. Overnight in Cogne, then return to the main Valle d'Aosta road and pick up the A5 for a fast descent to the North Italian Plain.

WEATHER

The Alpine weather is a highly changeable phenomenon. While in summer it can be very warm, this can change quickly, and once the sun has vanished it gets distinctly cooler, even at lower altitudes. Be prepared for the possibility of colder and wetter weather, particularly if hiking. Even on hot, sunny days, the sun goes down behind the mountains early, and sitting on a restaurant terrace in the evening can become a chilly experience without warm clothing. Conversely, the sun burns quickly at high altitudes and proper precautions should be taken against getting too much ultraviolet radiation.

If you plan to hike into the higher altitudes, you must be fit and well prepared: proper clothing and footwear, detailed maps, and food and water. It is dangerous and potentially fatal to do otherwise.

Once the winter snows begin, you won't drive far in the mountains, legally or physically, without winter tyres and chains. It can of course be very cold at this time, although there will still be sunny days when sunburn is a factor to watch for.

NORTHERN VALLEYS

Tourist Information: there are **APT** offices at *Villa Margherita 1, 11025*

Valle d'Aosta and Gran Paradiso National Park

Lying north of Turin and north-west of Milan, and within easy striking distance of both, the Valle d'Aosta winds up from the North Italian Plain through increasingly steep Alpine foothills until it bumps into Mont Blanc (4807m), usually considered to be Europe's highest mountain (Mount Elbrus on the border of Russia and Georgia is higher, at 5642m), near the chic ski resort of Courmayeur. The Valtournenche side valley leads to the Matterhorn.

Flanking the main valley to the south, the Gran Paradiso National Park is an awesomely scenic wilderness area and wildlife refuge. It can be reached via several narrow valleys branching off from the Valle d'Aosta, along which you can easily escape from the summer crowds who throng the main valley, while the park itself is great walking country – in good weather.

Gressoney-Saint-Jean; tel: (0125) 35 51 85; fax: (0125) 355895; at Champoluc, 11020 Ayas; tel: (0125) 307113; fax: (0125) 307785; at V. Varasc 16, V. Roma 45, 11028 Valtournenche; tel: (0166) 92029; fax: (0166) 92430; and at V. Carrel 29, 11021 Breuil-Cervinia; tel: (0166) 949136; fax: (0166) 949731.

From Valle d'Aosta's southern border to **Saint-Vincent**, three side valleys branch off to the north, all of which are well worth exploring, if you have enough time, before continuing up the valley. The easternmost, **Val di Gressone**, leads to **Monte Rosa** (4634m), Italy's highest mountain. From the vicinity of **Gressoney-la-Trinité**, cable cars and trails give access to its slopes.

The middle valley, the **Val d'Ayas**, follows a scenic route along the **Evançon** stream to **Champoluc** and **Gran Tournalin Mountain** (3379m). The westernmost valley, **Valtournenche**, leads to **Breuil Cervinia** at the Swiss border, and the slopes of the spectacularly rugged – and frequently deadly – **Matterhorn** (4480m), as well as those of neighbouring **Monte Cervino** (3491m).

SAINT-VINCENT

Tourist Office: *V. Roma 48; tel: (0166) 512239; fax: (0166) 513149.*

More worldly pursuits for the Valle d'Aosta are available at the **Casino de la Vallée** in Saint-Vincent; *tel: (0166) 5221.* Open Sun–Fri 1500–0300, L10,000; Sat 1500–0330, L20,000; Jun–Sept, various mornings 1030–1400, free. Otherwise there is not so much of interest in the town to justify stopping at Saint-Vincent.

AOSTA

Tourist Office: *Pza Chanoux 8; tel: (0165) 336627; fax: (0165) 34657.* Open daily 0900–1300 and 1500–2000.

Although attractive enough, Aosta is not a big enough draw by itself to keep most visitors away from the mountains. It does, however, have a wide range of accommodation and good transport links to the rest of the valley. Particularly at peak periods these may be important factors in deciding how long to spend there. Hotel chains in Aosta include *Hd*. The **Valle d'Aosta**, *C. Ivrea 146; tel: (0165) 41845*, has almost as good facilities for a significantly lower price. Further down the price ladder, the 3-star **Roma**, *V. Torino 7; tel: (0165) 40821*, and in the budget class **La Belle Epoque**, *V. d'Avise 18; tel: (0165) 262276*, are both good options.

Aosta (pop. 38,000) is capital of the

Valle d'Aosta region, Italy's smallest region, which has an area of 3260 square km and a population of some 120,000. The town was founded by the Romans around 25 BC at a strategic point on the road to the Alpine passes. Named Augusta Prætoria, it was laid out in the grid pattern typical of a Roman legionary base. Among the ruined monuments that survive from that time are the **city walls**; the **Porta Prætoria**, *V. Porta Pretoriane*, which was the city's main eastern gate; the **Arci di Augusto**, *Pza Arci di Augusto*, outside the gate to the east; the **Amphitheatre** and **Theatre**, both reached off the *V. Porta Pretoriane*; and the **Forum with Cryptoportico**, in the centre, off *V. Mgr. de Sales*. All of the Roman remains are permanently open and can be visited free.

The church of **Sant'Orso**, *V. Sant'Orso*, outside the walls to the east, is a mixture of Romanesque and Gothic styles, reflecting different stages in its construction and rebuilding between the 8th and 15th centuries. The cloister is particularly charming, and there are the faded remnants of 9th-century frescos in the church. The **Duomo**, *Pza Giovanni XXIII*, dates mostly from the Middle Ages, despite its neo-classical façade.

Should you find all the fresh air and wide open spaces of the Valle d'Aosta a bit agoraphobic, you could visit the **Spazio Cogne**, *V. Paravera 18; tel: (0165) 302683*. Open Tues–Sun 1000–1900 (mid-June and Sept–Dec); daily 1000–1900 (July–Aug), where in a closed steel-works converted to a museum, adjacent to the railway station, the history of the region's mining industry is on display. Tuesday is **street market** day in Aosta.

There are some 130 medieval castles and fortified towers in the Valle d'Aosta, many of which can be seen from the main road. One very good example which can be visited is the **Castello di Saint-Pierre**, atop a rocky outcrop 6 km west of Aosta; *tel: (0165) 903485*. Open Wed–Mon 0900–1200 and 1500–1900 (Apr–June and Sept). Entrance fee L2000. Inside is the **Museo Regionale di Scienza Naturale**, devoted to the natural history of the Valle d'Aosta, with exhibits on wildlife, environment, geology and mineralogy.

North of Aosta, the S27 runs 27 km to the **Colle del Gran San Bernardo**: the Great Saint Bernard Pass through the Alps to Switzerland. There is an **APT** office on the way, at *Str. Nazionale Gran San Bernardo 13, 11014 Etroubles; tel: (0165) 78559; fax: (0165) 78568*.

VALLE DI COGNE

Tourist Office: *Pza Chanoux 36; tel: (0165) 74040; fax: (0165) 749125*. Open daily 0900–1230 and 1500–1800.

There is no shortage of charming Alpine hotels in **Cogne**. Top of the range is the **Bellevue**, *rue Grand Paradis 22; tel: (0165) 74825*. Other good bets are the mid-range **La Madonnina del Gran Paradiso**, *Rue Laydetré; tel: (0165) 74087*, and the entirely rustic **Nôtre Maison**, *Fraz Crétaz; tel: (0165) 74104*, just outside town. There are seven camping sites in and around the village (the tourist office in Cogne has full details), with perhaps the best being those located at the neighbouring hamlets of **Valnontey** and **Lillaz**.

Wood-timbered restaurants are a speciality here. Try the **Brasserie du Bon Bec**, *V. Bourgeois; tel: (0165) 749288*, or the **Les Trompeurs**, *V. Dr. Grappein; tel: (0165) 74804*.

The **Valle di Cogne** is a lot quieter than the main Valle d'Aosta and makes a good place for walking. Cogne village at the end of the valley road is one of the main access points to the Gran Paradiso National Park, and it is embedded in the midst of mountains, forests and streams. It is also a good location for those who like their Alpine walks to be scenic but none too strenuous, as there is reasonably flat and easy country around the village before the slopes start to steepen towards Gran Paradiso Mountain.

Look out for the sign about one-third of the way along the road to Cogne for the **Ponte Romano**, an arched and covered Roman-era bridge 50m above the **Grand Eyvia** stream that is still in use today.

GRAN PARADISO NATIONAL PARK

Tourist Office: The **Gran Paradiso Mountain Community Tourist Office** *Località Champagne 18, 11018 Villeneuve; tel: (0165) 95055; fax: (0165) 95975.*

Gran Paradiso Mountain rises to 4061 m south of Aosta, and is embedded in the 200 km² of Italy's first national park, established in 1922 from just part of a former royal hunting reserve, once maintained exlusively for the use of members of the House of Savoy. With some 450 km of trails, there is no lack of hiking and plain ordinary walking possibilities in what is a spectacularly scenic place. Such activities may be enhanced by sightings of chamois, ibex and other species protected in the park or just by the lovely Alpine flowers (see box, p. 142). From east to west, four main valleys snake into the national park from the Valle d'Aosta: the **Valle di Cogne** (see above), **Valsavarenche, Val di Rhêmes**, and **Valgrisenche**. The last-named leads to the beautiful **Lago di Beauregard**, whose waters mirror sky and mountains.

COURMAYEUR-MONT BLANC (MONTE BIANCO)

Tourist Office: *Pzle Monte Bianco 13; tel: (0165) 842060; fax: (0165) 842072.*

Guided tour information is available from the tourist office and from the **Società delle Guide di Courmayeur**, *Pza Henry 2; tel: (0165) 842064; fax: (0165) 842357.*

ACCOMMODATION

With 67 hotels to choose from, there is no lack of choice in **Courmayeur**, but don't let sheer numbers fool you: these places fill up fast at peak times, particularly weekends, so it makes sense to reserve in advance. That doesn't mean to say you won't find a room at the last minute, just that it isn't wise to rely on it. The **Gallia Gran Baita**, *Str. Larzey; tel: (0165) 844040*, where a suite will set you back up to L600,000 a night, is the choice of those to whom money is no object (of whom there seem to be no shortage in Courmayeur). The **Cresta et Duc**, *V. Circonvallazione 7; tel: (0165) 842585* is a good mid-range choice, with a fine restaurant. Budget locations are thin on the ground, but the **Venezia**, *V. delle Villette 2; tel: (0165) 842461*, is a good value hotel. There are five camping sites in the vicinity of Courmayeur (information from the tourist office).

SIGHTSEEING

Courmayeur, at an altitude of 1224 m, is one of the fanciest resorts in the Italian Alps, noted for its wealth of chic shops. It is overlooked by 4607 m Mont Blanc. Skiing, climbing and hill-walking are among its most popular attractions, although soaking up the sun on a café terrace has its legions of adherents also. Adventurous spirits can take to the water with the **Courmayeur Kayak and Rafting School**, *Morgex; tel: (0163) 560957*, and run the risk of getting a cool Alpine ducking on the fast-flowing Sesia and Dora Baltea rivers. One of the most spectacularly sited golf clubs anywhere in

141

Wildlife in the Gran Paradiso National Park

Among the forests of larch and fir, the edelweiss, lilies and other Alpine flowers, from the valley meadows to the rocky, glacial slopes, the Gran Paradiso is, as its name implies, a grand paradise for wildlife. It was originally established in 1856 by King Victor Emmanuel II as a Royal Hunting Reserve – to save the mountain ibex from being driven to extinction by hunters with no blue blood in their veins. Today, it is a vital resource for many Alpine species whose habitat is threatened and whose range is increasingly constricted elsewhere by tourism-related developments.

The ibex is the star of the show, and a herd of these goat-like creatures (which are actually more closely related to the deer) can make quite a sight, pinned to the steep slopes. The male has long curved horns and the female has shorter ones; in November and December their head-butting is part of the mating ritual. There are some 5000 of them in the park, roaming free along with 8000 chamois (goat-antelopes). The marmot, a cute rodent with a distinctive whistle can also be seen – or at any rate heard.

In the sky, a recent returnee is the carrion-eating bearded vulture. An indigenous bird , it has not been seen in the park since 1912, but the species is being reintroduced from Savoy (Savoie) in France. Golden eagles are around in greater numbers and it is not so hard to spot them soaring on the air currents. Another avian species worth looking out for is the orange-red (in males) crossbill, whose crossed over beak is designed for extracting seeds from pine cones. At night you may hear the hooting of Tengmalm's owl. Closer to the ground birdlovers should look out for the ptarmigan, chough and black grouse, while wall creepers may be seen on rock faces, and nutcrackers on the woodland edge.

There are several varieties of frog in the Alpine lakes, the most distinctive of which is the reddish-brown coloured red frog.

Europe is just 6km away in the **Val Ferret**, *Località Val Ferret; tel: (0165) 89103*. Mountain bikes can be hired at **Lo Caraco**, *V. Roma 150; tel: (0165) 844152*.

If the thought of hiking in these mountains makes you weak at the knees, going by cable car is a lot easier. There are several cable car routes into the Mont Blanc massif from around Courmayeur, and it is possible to take an organised tour across the mountain on five different cable cars and one telecabine to **Chamonix** in France, returning to Courmayeur by coach through the 12km **Mont Blanc Tunnel**. The price per adult is L105,000 (full details from the tourist office).

An easy way to see the Alpine flowers all in a bunch is at the **Giardino Botanico Alpino Saussurea**, *Pavillon del Mont-Fréty; tel: (0165) 89925*. You get there by cable car to the first stop on the Punta Hellbronner cable car line. The garden is at 2187m, and displays many varieties of Alpine flowers.

For detailed information on Mont Blanc, the Alps and the flora, fauna, mineralogy and history of the mountains, visit the **Museo Alpino Duca degli Abruzzi di Courmayeur**, *Pza Henry 2; tel: (0165) 842064*.

About 5km south of Courmayeur, the S26 runs 26km south-west to the **Colle del Piccolo San Bernardo** (Little Saint Bernard Pass), through the mountains to France.

TURIN–SAN REMO

Turin is not high on the agenda of most visitors to Italy. Yet it has its attractions, some of which, dating from medieval times and the 19th century (the city was capital of Italy for three years in the 1860s), are the equal of those in better advertised places. The route passes through the fertile agricutural plain south of Turin, watered by tributaries of the River Po, then begins to climb into the Ligurian Alps before reaching the

Mediterranean not far from Nice, Monaco and Monte Carlo. The coast around San Remo is busy and popular, especially in summer, but it also has medieval towns and is backed by the mountains, which offer plenty of avenues of escape from the crowds.

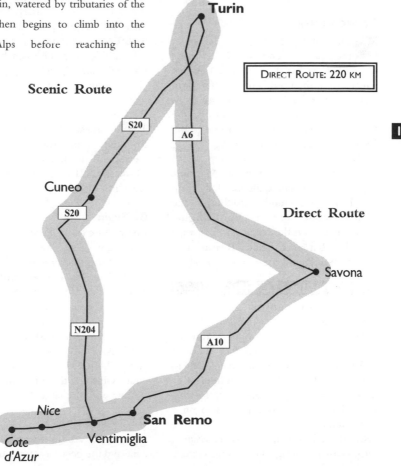

Turin

DIRECT ROUTE: 220 KM

Scenic Route

S20

A6

Cuneo

S20

Direct Route

Savona

N204

A10

Nice

San Remo

Cote d'Azur

Ventimiglia

ROUTES

DIRECT ROUTE

➡ There isn't really a direct route from Turin to San Remo because the Ligurian Alps get in the way, but if you want to take the *autostrada* you can get there on the A6 south-east to the coast at Savona, then south-west along the Riviera di Ponente on the A10, a distance of 220 km. You pick up the A6 in Turin by following *C. Massimo d'Azeglio* from its starting point downtown at *C. Vittorio Emanuele II*.

SCENIC ROUTE

➡ The 190 km scenic route begins at the eastern end of *C. Vittorio Emanuele II*, across the Umberto I Bridge over the Po, then south on *C. Moncalieri*. This becomes the S393 going south to Carmagnola, then continues south on the S20 through Savigliano and **Cuneo** to the French border at Colle di Tenda.

The stretch of road passing south through French territory in the Maritime Alps is the N204, emerging into Italy again at Fanghetto, and reaching the Mediterranean coast at **Ventimiglia**. Continue east on the scenic S1 coast road (the *V. Aurelia*) to **San Remo** (see Rapallo–San Remo route, pp. 335–342).

TURIN (TORINO)

Tourist Information: The main **Tourist Office** is at *V. Roma 226; tel: (011) 535901*, and is open Mon–Sat 0900–1930. Turin has another **Tourist Information Office** at *Porta Nuova Station; tel: (011) 531327*. Both offer a free 'room-finding' service. Ask here for listings information – concerts and so on – and remember to look in the national/local daily newspaper, *La Stampa*, for up-to-date listings. For young visitors, there is also **Informagiovani**, *V. Assarotti 2; tel: (011) 4424976*, open Mon, Wed–Sat 1030–1830.

Thomas Cook Worldwide Network Licensee: CIT Viaggi, *Piazza San Carlo 205; tel: (011) 562 5652*.

ARRIVING AND DEPARTING

By Air
Caselle Airport, 15 km north of the city, *tel: (011) 577 6361*, handles mainly domestic flights. There are services from several important European cities (London, Paris, Brussels, Amsterdam, Frankfurt). The airport bus is operated by **SADEM**, and runs every ½ hr from 0600–2230, from the main bus station at *C. Inghilterra 3; tel: (011) 433 2525* (journey time 35 mins).

By Car
The autostrada A4 links Turin with Milan. A6 heads south from the city, towards Genoa and the Ligurian Riviera. East of Turin, the A21 heads along the Po Valley: see Turin–Ferrara route, p. 150.

By Train
Porta Nuova is Turin's main rail hub. It is right in the city centre – on the *C. Vittorio Emanuele II; tel: (011) 561 3333*. There is another station at **Porta Susa** on the city's west side, and another, **Torino Ceres**, which is a regional line serving towns like Cirie, Lanzo and Ceres.

The main **bus station**; *tel: (011) 433 2525*, is on *C. Inghilterra*. From here, a comprehensive bus service links the countryside and the ski resorts of the Valle d'Aosta with the city.

GETTING AROUND

Most sights are in the compact central zone and the best way to see them all is on

144

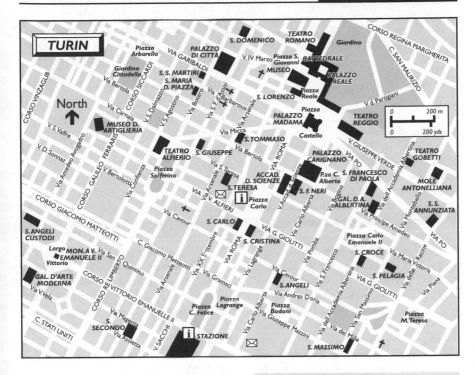

foot. It is a bracing walk, however; it might be better to use the trams or buses, or to take a taxi.

Buses and Trams

Before using either trams or buses, you must be in possession of a valid ticket – buy them at *tabacchi* (tobacconists), in bars, or at the city tourist office at Porta Nuova Station. Cancel them in the machine on boarding.

Taxis

Licensed taxis are not hard to find and not cheap. There are ranks by the train and bus stations and elsewhere – in the *piazze* and so on. Avoid unlicensed cabs, which are even more expensive. To call a cab, telephone **Central Taxi**, *tel: (02) 3399*; **Pronto Taxi**, *tel: (011) 5737*; or **Radio Taxi Torino**, *tel: (011) 5730*.

STAYING IN TURIN

Accommodation

Turin is not the busiest tourism city in Italy, though it is a major venue for trade fairs and for business travel. This is reflected in the range of accommodation – or rather, the lack of it – available. The **Turin Palace**, *V. Sacchi 8; tel: (011) 562 5511* is opulent, and the **Venezia**, *V. XX Settembre 70; tel (011) 562 3012* is characterful, while most others tend to cater for business travellers and are modern and rather featureless.

At the other end of the scale they tend to be very downmarket indeed. The cheapest accommodation, not always the most salubrious, is to be found near to Porta Nuova Station. There is very little in between, but you could try the **Bologna**, *C. V. Emmanuele II; tel: (011) 562 0191,* or the **Eden**, *V. Donizetti 22; tel: (011) 669 9545*. Hotel chains in Turin include *Hd, Md, Jolly*.

HI: *V. Alby 1; tel: (011) 660 2939*, open 0900–1800. Take bus 52 from the station.

Eating and drinking

Some of the richest food in Italy comes from Turin. Much of it has a heavy, almost Germanic tone which is quite unlike what you will find even just a few miles further south. Upmarket restaurants are generally very sophisticated – and expensive. However, there are many moderate or reasonably priced places serving a variety of Torinese specialities as well as more popular and traditional Italian dishes. As always, you can cut costs by opting for fixed-price (*prezzo fisso*) meals which give you a choice of first and main courses, fruit or cheese. Restaurants outside the main sightseeing semicircle are usually cheaper than those catering to visitors close to the main sights. The cafés in Turin are famous. The classics are **Baratti e Milano**, *Pza Castello*, and **Caffe Torino**, *Pza San Carlo 204*. For picnic ingredients try an *alimentari* (grocery shop) – but remember that they shut for lunch.

Communications

The main post office is at *V. Alfieri 10; tel: (011) 54 68 00*. You can buy stamps here or from a tobacconist. Attached is a telephone centre where you can make international calls.

Money

Banks which change money usually display the sign Cambio (Exchange). There are also exchange kiosks at Porta Nuova Station, the airport, and at numerous city centre locations. Eurocheques are also widely accepted, and credit cards are accepted in many shops and restaurants. There is an automatic cash dispenser at *V. Roma 224* (beside the tourist office).

ENTERTAINMENT

There is plenty to see and do in Turin. Not only is it a city burgeoning with museums and galleries – one or two of them of real international importance – but there is great architecture, theatre, ballet and music. The nightlife may not be as trendy as you might find in Milan or Bologna, but there are still plenty of clubs and other venues. A particular time to come is during Turin's St John's Day (24 June) folklore festival. *Torino Giovani* is a useful listings publication for young people, available from the tourist offices. Turin is home to two internationally famous football clubs, **Juventus** and **Torino**. Both play at the **Stadio Comunale**.

Nightlife

A fairly lively, local youth culture is given a boost in the student area around *V. Po* where there are plenty of pubs and clubs, and venues for jazz and African rhythms, rock and reggae. There is often an admission fee for the larger discos and drinks are usually very expensive. Some venues allow one free drink with the admission fee.

Theatres, Cinemas and Concerts

Many recent US and UK releases come to major city-centre cinemas undubbed. The main theatre venue is the **Teatro Carignano**, while the **Teatro Reggio** is used for opera and, from late autumn to late spring, ballet and symphony concerts. An arts festival, the Punti Verdi (plays, ballet, concerts) is held annually in July and August, while *Settembre Musica* is a Sept festival focusing on classical music. Venues for this include local churches and theatres.

SHOPPING

Turin is not noted as a particularly special shopping city any more than, say, Rome or Venice are. However, as it is situated in the wealthy northern region of Italy, there will be no shortage of opportunities for buying all the things that make Milan such an important shopping capital – clothes and accessories, designer equipment, luggage, stationery, textiles and so on. On Saturdays, an antique and flea market is held in *Pza della Repubblica*. To bring home, you might consider buying foodstuffs from the delicatessen – dried sausage, cheese, oils, chocolates and biscuits.

SIGHTSEEING

In the north, Turin is one of Italy's most opulent cities. A former royal capital, today it is famous for its associations with the car industry – in particular Fiat. There are gilded *fin-de-siècle* cafés and a lovely baroque centre of ordered, elegant streets.

It is very easy to find your way around Turin, the centre of which is laid out on a grid pattern. Across its core, streets are lined with arcades which, in the rainy north, are practical and useful. The most fashionable street is *V. Roma* which links the *Pza Carlo Felice*, in front of Porta Nuova Station, with the *Pza Castello*.

Highlights of any trip to Turin should include the important **Egyptian Museum**, *V. Accademia delle Scienze 6; tel: (011) 561 7776*, open Tues–Sun 0900–1900, L12,000, second only to the museum in Cairo for its wealth of ancient Egyptian exhibits, and the **Galleria Sabauda**, *V. Accademia delle Scienze 6; tel: (011) 547440*, open Tues, Wed, Fri, Sat 0900–1400, Thur 1000–1400, Sun (alternate weeks) 0900–1400, L8,000, which contains the magnificent art collections of the House of Savoy, with works by, among others, Mantegna, Titian,

Van Eyck, Rembrandt and Poussin. Both museums share the former Palazzo dell'Accademia delle Scienze just off *Pza San Carlo*. The Egyptian Museum, the world's first, was founded out of a royal collection formed in the 17th century.

The Palazzo Carignano, nearby, is an important baroque building designed by Guarini. It contains in part the **Museo Nazionale del Risorgimento** (National Museum of the Unification of Italy), *V. Accademia delle Scienze 6; tel: (011) 562 1147*, open Tues–Sat 0900–1830, Sun 0900–1230. L8000.

A major highlight in a city which made its fortune in the car industry is the **Museo dell'Automobile Carlo Biscaretti di Ruffia**, *C. Unita d'Italia 40; tel: (011) 677666*, open Tues–Sun 1000–1830, L10,000, which houses an important collection of classic Italian cars. The **Palazzo Reale**, just off *Pza Castello; tel: (011) 43 61 455*, open Tues–Sun 0900–1900, L8000, was the residence of the Princes of Savoy until 1865, and it is possible to go on a guided tour of its interior. One other very interesting museum is the **Museo Nazionale della Montagna Duca degli Abruzzi** (just by the Capuchin church on *Monte dei Cappuccini*), *V. G. Giardino 39; tel: (011) 660 4104*, open Tues–Fri 0800–1915, Sat–Mon 0900–1230 and 1445–1915. L8000. This houses a fascinating collection of artefacts illustrating life and folklore in, and the geography of, Italy's mountains. The **Galleria d'Arte Moderna**, *V. Magenta 31; tel: (011) 562 9911*, open Tues–Sun 0900–1900, L8000, houses an excellent collection, reputed to be one of Italy's best, of modern art – including works by Klee, Chagall and Picasso.

Of the city's churches, **San Lorenzo**, *Pza Castello*, the former royal chapel, is the one you shouldn't miss. Its interior is by

147

the baroque architect Guarini and it is characterised by an octagonal dome. The cathedral of **San Giovanni**, *Pza San Giovanni; tel: (011) 43 61 540* (at the time of writing it was closed for restoration), is famous for containing the Holy Shroud of Turin. Housed in a casket – under lock and key – on the altar of the Cappella della Sacra Sindone (designed by Guarini), this is one of the most controversial relics in Italy, if not the world. The controversy centres on whether or not the shroud, which appears to bear the imprint of a bearded man wearing a crown of thorns, could possibly be Christ's burial shroud, or whether it is merely an elaborate hoax.

OUT OF TOWN

Two sights lie outside the city. One, the baroque **Basilica di Superga** (to the north-east), *Str. della Basikica di Superga; tel: (011) 898 0083,* open daily 0830–1200 and 1500–1700, free, is the architect Juvarra's masterpiece. Quite apart from the architecture, the views from the summit of the hill on which it stands are stupendous. They stretch all the way to the Alps in the north.

The other major sight outside Turin is the magnificent rococo former royal hunting lodge, the **Palazzina Mauriziana di Caccia Stupinigi** – 9 km south-east of Turin at Stupinigi; *tel: (011) 358 1220,* open Tues–Sun 0900–1700. L10,000. This too is the work of Juvarra. In reality it is a huge and stately country palace, and today it is run by the Royal Mauritian Order as a museum of 17th- and 18th-century furniture and furnishings from the former royal residences in Piedmont (Piemonte).

CUNEO

Tourist Office: *C. Nizza 17; tel: (0171) 693258.*

Cuneo is the capital of Cuneo Province and lies on the River Stura di Demonte near the southern end of the wide and flat agricultural country south of Turin. It fulfils the role of road and rail hub for the area, and gateway to the mountain valleys of the southern Piedmont, without being notably important or attractive in itself, although the old centre does have a faded, small-town charm.

From here you can side-track into the scenic and fairly tranquil valleys of the **Stura**, **Grana**, **Maira** and **Varaite** rivers, pointing westwards from Cuneo towards France, and tour the narrow side valleys that branch off from the main ones.

If, however, you are looking for somewhere to stay overnight, or to lunch on the road from Turin to San Remo, you could do worse than stop some 20 km south of Cuneo at the **Hotel Al Torrente**, *V. Nazionale 14; tel: (0171) 920191,* in **Vernante**. This pleasant hotel beside the busy main road has a restaurant that serves a kind of Italian nouvelle cuisine and attracts diners from as far away as Milan, yet is moderately priced.

From here the road winds into the mountains to the French border. It is best not to attempt this stretch on Sunday mornings from spring to autumn, but especially in summer, when it is liable to be jammed nose to tail with day-trippers and holiday-makers from Turin heading for the coast.

VENTIMIGLIA

Tourist Office: *V. Cavour 61; tel: (0184) 351183.*

Considering it is the Italian town closest to chic Monte Carlo and Monaco, Ventimiglia lacks a certain something in the looks department, being more of a rail interchange point and border town than a resort, although at least here you don't

The Susa Valley

The winding, scenic Susa Valley is the main westward route from Turin to France, with the A32 *autostrada* reaching almost to the French border, and the adjacent S24 and S25 roads allowing for more leisurely touring. The valley is beautiful indeed, and a river runs through it, the **Dora Riparia**, which joins the Po at Turin. This route is a popular excursion for people from Turin to make, as it is on the city's doorstep and easier to reach than the Valle d'Aosta, the lakes of Lombardy, or the distant Mediterranean.

Just beyond the city's western outskirts is **Rivoli**, a town with several interesting churches, which is most notable for the baroque **Castello di Rivoli**, dating from 1718 and occupying the site of castles dating back to 1280. These unlikely surroundings are the setting for a **Museo d'Arte Moderna** (Museum of Modern Art).

About 10 km further along the road is **Avigliana**, a handsome walled town with many monuments dating from the medieval and Renaissance periods.

Susa itself is a further 33 km westwards, at a point where the valley splits, with the course of the Dora Riparia branching northwards. An important Alpine town during the Roman Empire, Susa has an **Arch of Augustus**, the remains of an **aqueduct**, and a recently excavated **amphitheatre**. Other important monuments from later periods include the 18th-century **Fortezza della Brunette**, and the 11th-century **Duomo di San Giusto**.

The main road continues through increasingly rugged and beautiful country, past the **Castello di Exilles**, through the mountain villages of **Salbertrand** and **Savoulx**, to **Bardoneschia**, and the mountain tunnel leading to France.

149

have to put up with the stuffy pretension of those famed international watering holes nearby. Ventimiglia does have some ancient **Roman ruins**, and a medieval centre with a 12th-century **Duomo**, while the coast is marvellously scenic.

Some 8 km west of Ventimiglia is **Balzi Rossi**, a complex of caves occupied during the Stone Age, open daily 0900–1900. L5000.

For the final leg of the journey, join the A8 autostrada just north of Ventimiglia and drive the 17 km east to San Remo (see p. 342).

 SIDE TRACK FROM VENTIMIGLIA

It would seem a waste to be in this area and not cross over into France to catch at least a quick glimpse of **Monte Carlo** and the **Principality of Monaco**, 20 km from Ventimiglia, and perhaps even **Nice** another 20 km further west along the **Côte d'Azur**. In summer, however, this is one of the busiest coasts in Europe, and even this relatively short stretch may take a lot longer to do than you had counted on.

TURIN TO FERRARA
THE PO VALLEY

From its source in the Cottian Alps south-west of Turin, the River Po flows some 652km to reach the Adriatic south of Venice. It is Italy's longest river, irrigating and draining the effluent of its richest and most heavily populated region, the Po Valley. This is the most fertile agricultural land in the country, a fact that becomes abundantly obvious as you pass through it.

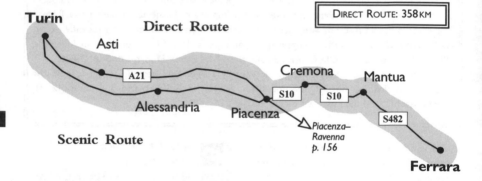

DIRECT ROUTE: 358KM

Turin

Direct Route

Asti

A21

Cremona

Mantua

Alessandria

Piacenza

S10

S10

S482

Piacenza–
Ravenna
p. 156

Ferrara

Scenic Route

ROUTES

DIRECT ROUTE

➡ The direct route if you're coming from **Turin** is out of town on the A6 *autostrada* for 4km to the junction with the A21 (you pick up the A6 in Turin by following *C. Massimo d'Azeglio* from its starting point downtown at *C. Vittorio Emanuele II*). Once on the A21 you can scoot easily down the motorway – pausing only to lighten your load by handing over money at the toll booths – to **Asti**, **Alessandria**, **Piacenza** and **Cremona**. Change to the SS10 at the north-eastern edge of Cremona for the cross-country run to **Mantua**. From Mantua, take the S482 for the final leg of the journey to Ferrara.

SCENIC ROUTE

⤏ The scenic route is the SS10, which more or less parallels the direct route, through **Asti**, **Alessandria**, **Piacenza**, **Cremona** and **Mantua**, for a total distance of 290 km. This gives the possibility of combining both approaches – driving on the *autostrada* whenever you need to press on quickly, and coming off onto the slower road to view the sights, save toll money, and get closer to the pace of the countryside. From Turin city centre, cross to the east bank of the Po and go north along the river on *C. Moncalieri* and *C. Casale* to *Pzle Marco Aurelio*, then turn right onto *C. Chieri*, which continues as the SS10.

ASTI

Tourist Information: The **APT** office is at *Pza Alfieri 34, 14100 Asti; tel: (0141) 53 03 57; fax: (0141) 53 82 00*. Mon–Fri 0900–1230 and 1500–1800. Sat 0900–1230. The office provides information on Asti's main festival the Palio (annually, mid Sept), and on the various regional wine festivals (Aug and Sept).

Famed as the home of sparkling wine, and in particular that breezy Champagne substitute, Asti Spumante, **Asti** stands on the banks of the River Tanaro and at the heart of scenic, hilly wine country and is one of the principal wine-growing centres of Italy. At some 650,000 hectolitres produced a year, Asti wines take second place only to Chianti. Come here also in search of seasonal delicacies like *tartufi* (truffles) and other culinary delights often associated with the many festivals that take place in the area.

ACCOMMODATION AND FOOD

Accommodation in Asti ranges from very expensive to moderately priced – all of it subject to great competition during the Palio. Book early if you want to be there. The 4-star **Aleramo**, *V. Emanuele Filiberto 13; tel: (0141) 59 56 61* and **Palio**, *V. Cavour 106; tel: (0141) 59 92 82*, are good bets, as is the 3-star **Rainero**, *V. Cavour 85; tel: (0141) 35 38 66*.

SIGHTSEEING

There is a good range of monuments to be seen in Asti. On the *C. Alfieri* is the 15th-century church of **San Pietro in**

Consavia. Its 12th-century Baptistery is now used as an exhibition space and, in a former hospice used by visiting pilgrims, is a little archaeological museum. Behind *Pza Alfieri* is the **Collegiata di San Secondo**, a late Romanesque–early Gothic church built on the site of the martyrdom of Asti's patron saint, whose relics are kept here. The banners used during the Palio are also housed here. See the polyptych by Gandolfino d'Asti, the town's one great Renaissance artist. There are further works by this master in the 14th-century **Duomo** (Cathedral) on *Pza Cattedrale*. Inside are some interesting holy water fonts made from converted Roman capitals in the 15th century.

At the heart of town, the arcaded **Piazza Alfieri** is named after a local poet, Vittorio Alfieri (1749–1803), who is famous chiefly for having absconded with the wife of Scotland's Bonnie Prince Charlie. You can see Alfieri's bust in the **Palazzo Alfieri**, *C. Alfieri 375*. Next to this is the 8th-century **Crypt of Sant'Anastasio** which has exceptionally fine capitals, and the **Museo Lapidario**, *V. Goltieri 3a; tel: (0141) 54 791*.

The **Palio** is held in the big *Campo del Palio*, near the *Pza Alfieri*. This event is a fairly recent revival of a medieval tradition dating back to 1275. Local town neighbourhoods compete in a bareback horse race against a backdrop of hearty eating and drinking. It coincides with Asti's other main festival, the annual wine fair, so the process of overindulgence continues unabated.

Elsewhere in Asti is a range of medieval towers and Renaissance palaces. Of the former, there is the 13th-century **Torre Comentina** (in the *Corso*) and the finer **Torre Troyana**. Of the palaces, **Palazzo Malabaya** in *V. Mazzini* is the finest.

An interesting side trip is to Asti's rival

151

as a wine centre, **Alba**, some 29 km south on the SS23 (it may be more convenient to pass through here on the road north from the coast at San Remo). In October Alba goes all hallucinatory, when everyone engages in mushroom picking and eating, and truffles are the *funghi* of choice, during the Fiera del Tartufo. For a side trip of a side trip, continue 9 km west on the SS231 to the village of **Cinzano** on the banks of the River Tenaro. At the next-door village of **Santa Vittoria d'Alba** you can visit the Cinzano cellars and sample the famous eponymous vermouth. Another 6 km brings you to **Bra**, which you might find worth it just for a snap of the destination board, but otherwise I suggest you go Bra-less on this trip.

ALESSANDRIA

Tourist Information: The **APT** office is at *V Savona 26, 15100 Alessandria; tel: (0131) 25 10 21; fax: (0131) 25 36 56.*

A good base for exploring the many castles in this area midway between Turin and Piacenza, **Alessandria** is also convenient for an overnight stay for those who are taking their time on the Po Valley route. Among its hotels are the 4-star **Alli Due Buoi Rossi**, *V. Cavour 32; tel: (0131) 44 52 52,* and **San Michele**, *V. Casale 2; tel: (0131) 23 62 26*; and the 3-star **Europa**, *V. Palestro 1; tel. (0131) 23 62 26.*

An important agricultural and wine market town, Alessandria was founded in 1168 as Civitas Nova, a name that was later nixed in honour of Pope Alexander III. The Dukes of Milan occupied the town in 1348. Remains of its **fortifications**, the **Duomo** (Cathedral), and the Romanesque-Gothic **Church of S. Maria di Castello** date from this period.

The **Sagra di San Baudolino**

(Festival of San Baudolino) agricultural and culinary fair is held each September in the gardens of *Vle della Repubblica.* Its big draw is the truffle display, with prizes for the finest specimens (as if finding one were not prize enough) plus a truffle-hunting competition with trained dogs, and enthusiastic eating of typical local dishes.

Several castles of Alessandria province are worth making a diversion to visit, and those that lie southwards along the S30 are easily reached. **Palazzo Zoppi**; *tel: (0144) 32 21 42,* open Sun 1000–1200 and 1530–1830; closed 25 Aug–8 Sept, L10,000, guided visit L5000, at **Cassine**, 22 km south of Alessandria, dates back to the 15th century and belonged to the Visconti family. It has a 14th-century Piedmontese-school *Madonna with Child* fresco and a series of 15th-century frescos of the Lombard school. The **Paleologi Castle**; *tel: (0144) 32 21 42,* open Sun 1000–1200 and 1530–1830; Wed-Sat 0930–1200 and 1530–1830, L4000, lies 13 km further south on the SS30, at **Acqui Terme**. It was owned by the Paleologi marquises, then by the Gonzagas and later by the House of Savoy. It now houses Acqui Terme's **Archaeological Museum**, and has a courtyard 'nature reserve'. **Melazzo Castle**; *tel: (0144) 32 21 42,* open Sun 1000–1200 and 1530–1830, L7000, 6 km south on the SS334, has imposing battlemented ramparts and is surrounded by a park. Saint Guido was born here in 1004, and the deposed King Edward II of England lived in the castle from 1330–1333.

More on the direct route to Piacenza is the **Palazzo Pretorio** at **Castelnuovo Scrivia**; *tel: (0131) 25 10 21,* open Sun 1000–1200 and 1530–1830, L3000, 12 km north of **Tortona**. The 14th-century castle in the medieval square has several large rooms with 15th-century decoration and a battlemented tower whose lower courses dates back to AD 400.

PIACENZA

Tourist Information: The **IAT** office is at *Piazzeta Mercanti 10, 29100 Piacenza; tel/fax: (0523) 32 93 24.*

Piacenza, on the River Po, was founded in 218 BC by the Romans, and ruled by the Visconti, Sforza and Farnese families, in addition to the Pope, during the medieval and Renaissance periods. Today it is a commercial centre.

It does, however, have a wide choice in hotels, including the 4-star **Grande Albergo Roma**, *V. Cittadella 14; tel: (0523) 23 201*, the 3-star **Florida**, *V. C. Colombo 29; tel: (0523) 59 26 00* and **Stella**, *V. Cipelli 41; tel: (0523) 71 20 80.*

Piacenza has several noteworthy churches and other monuments, including the 12th-century Romanesque **Duomo** (Cathedral) in *V. XX Settembre*, and the red-and-white 13th-century **Palazzo Publico** (Town Hall), known as **Il Gotico**, in *Pza Cavalli*, with its two Farnese equestrian statues. Still, it is not really worth losing time for, compared to Cremona and Mantua, if you have to choose between them.

CREMONA

Tourist Information: The **APT** office is at *Pza del Commune 5, 26100 Cremona; tel: (0372) 23 233; fax: (0372) 21 722.*

Founded by the Romans in the 3rd century BC, Cremona stands on the River Po and is a handsome market town and manufacturing centre – among the products it turns out are violins and pianos. It was an independent *commune* during the Middle Ages and later came under the sway of Milan, Spain and Austria. Cremona is perhaps best known for the outstanding violins and violas made here

from the 16th–18th centuries by the Amati and Guarneri families, and most notably by Antonio Stradivari. In another musical connection, the composer Monteverdi was born in Cremona in 1567.

Among hotels in Cremona is *Ib.* Its top-rated hotel is the 4-star **Impero**, *Pza Pace 23; tel: (0372) 46 03 37*. The town's mid-range hotels are generally good value for money, particularly the 3-star **Duomo**, *V. Gonfalonieri 13; tel: (0372) 35 242*, which has an animated restaurant and is just a few steps from the beautiful *Pza del Commune*. Other good options are the 2-star **Esperia**, *V. Novati 56; tel: (0372) 45 29 93* and the 1-star **Bologna**, *Pza del Risorgimento 7; tel: (0372) 24 258.*

For top-flight Cremonese cuisine, try **Ceresole**, *V. Ceresole 4; tel (0372) 30 990* and **Alla Borgata**, *V. Bergamo tel: 25 648; (0372) 25 648*. More moderately priced fare is available from **Vesuvio**, *Pza Libertà 10; (0372) 43 48 58* and **Cremonese**, *Pza Roma 39; tel: (0372) 20 636.*

The *Piazza del Commune* is the heart of Cremona, a medieval-Renaissance ensemble with a tranquil sense of history. Visit the **Palazzo Communale** (Town Hall), *Pza del Commune; tel: (0372) 40 72 06*, open Tues–Sat 0830–1800, Sun 0915–1215 and 1500–1800, L6000, which, like almost every other museum in Cremona, has historic violins on display.

A mixture of Romanesque and Gothic, the splendid **Duomo** (Cathedral), *Pza del Commune*, open Mon–Sat 0730–1200 and 1530–1900, Sun 0730–1300 and 1530–1900, has a spiritual quality that is often lacking in other such colossal edifices that are now more tourist attraction than church, and splendid timeworn medieval frescos glow on the walls.

If you still have an urge for violins, at the **Torrazzo** (Bell Tower), *Pza del*

153

Commune; tel: (0372) 27 057, open Apr–Oct Mon–Sat 1030–1230 and 1500–1900; Nov–Mar by arrangement, L5000, you can see violins being made, in a special workshop. The APT office has a list of violin workshops in the town that you can visit, and there is also the **Museo Stradivariano**, *V. Palestro 17; tel: (0372) 46 18 86,* open Tues–Sat 0830–1800, Sun 0915–1215 and 1500–1800, L6000. Finally, you can put a date in your diary for the year 2000, and the next triennial **Internazionale degli Strumenti ad Arco**, an exposition that celebrates anything and everything musical with strings attached.

An alternative to going the whole way from Cremona to Mantua on the direct route – the SS10 – is to go as far as **Piadena** (27 km) and turn south on the SS343 to **Casalmaggiore** on the banks of the Po, then north-east from there on the SS420. After 5 km you arrive at **Sabbioneta**, a place so serenely beautiful it would make any diversion worthwhile. Planned and built in 1558 by Vespasiano Gonzaga Colonna, the walled town was clearly an effort to build the ideal urban environment. There are dozens of architectural gems in Sabbioneta – palaces, villas, theatres, churches, galleries – but maybe its perfect late-Renaissance atmosphere is the biggest attraction.

MANTUA (MANTOVA)

Tourist Information: The **APT** office is at *Pza Mantegna 6, 46100 Mantua; tel: (0376) 32 82 53; fax: (0376) 36 32 92.*

Although founded by the Etruscans, **Mantua's** original claim to fame was as the birthplace of Virgil (Publius Vergilius Maro, 70–19 BC), the Roman writer who became a kind of poet laureate to the Emperor Augustus. Virgil's pastoral poems *The Eclogues* and *The Georgics* created an unforgettable image of Italy as a fertile paradise, while his great national epic *The Aenid* showed him to be the equal of Homer. In the Middle Ages and the Renaissance Mantua became extremely prosperous under the rule of the powerful Gonzaga family. The artist Andrea Mantegna (1431–1506), although born near Vicenza, settled in Mantua in 1460 and among other masterpieces painted the nine-work *Triumph of Caesar* series. The composer Monteverdi moved to Mantua from Cremona in his early twenties and was appointed director of music to the Gonzagas in 1601.

ACCOMMODATION AND FOOD

Mantua is well worth a visit, and you'll get the most out of it if you can afford to stay at the superbly-sited, 4-star **Albergo San Lorenzo**, *Pza Concordia 14; tel: (0376) 22 05 00.* By the station are a couple of reasonably priced hotels: the 3-star **Albergo Bianchi**, *Pza Don Leoni 4; tel: (0376) 32 64 65,* and the 2-star **Hotel ABC**, *Pza Don Leoni 25; tel: (0376) 32 23 29.*

There is no shortage of fine local restaurants in Mantua, a place that takes good care of its collective stomach. Among the best are the mid-priced **Abbadia**, *V. Conciliazione 33; tel: (0376) 32 53 07,* not far from the railway station, and the 193-year-old **Ai Garibaldini**, *V. S. Longino 7; tel: (0376) 32 82 63;* and the more expensive **Il Cigno Trattoria dei Martini**, *Pza d'Arco 1; tel: (0376) 32 71 01.*

SIGHTSEEING

Mantua has a graceful, walled centre dating from the medieval-Renaissance period, standing on a peninsula jutting into the River Mincio at a point where the river widens enough to be considered a lake – three lakes actually: Lago Superiore, Lago di Mezzo and Lago Inferiore. Its

Ferrara

No, not Ferrari – although you may see an occasional red Testosterone, or whatever they're called, coursing through the streets. Still, the near-miss in spelling is appropriate, because Ferrara long had a racy image. During the Renaissance, artists flocked to the proud and fiercely independent little city a hundred kilometres south of Venice on the banks of the River Po di Volano. At that time there was Venice and there was Milan, and lots of Italian *communes* had the life squeezed out of them by those two big and ruthless competitors.

Not so Ferrara. The Este family, who ruled it from 1264 to the end of the 16th century, did their capable best to avoid the squeeze. Victorious in the 14th century, they won themselves time and space to develop a brilliant court culture, a kind of Camelot-on-Po. They invited major painters and poets to Ferrara and firmed up their position by marrying their offspring into the royal houses of Italy and Europe.

One such alliance was between Lucrezia Borgia, the daughter of Pope Alexander VI, and Alfonso d'Este, who became Duke of Ferrara in 1505. Lucrezia enjoys one of those deliciously salacious female historical reputations, like those of Cleopatra, Messalina or Theodora. In fact she seems to have spent more time engaging in political intrigue and patronising the arts than painting the boudoir red. Of course, she might have been patronising the artists, including the painter Titian and the poets Ludovico Ariosto and Pietro Bembo.

In 1598, the party came to an end, when Pope Clement VIII took control of Ferrara. Among many surviving monuments are the 14th-century Este Castle, the Cathedral of San Giorgio (begun 1135), and the Renaissance Schifanoia and Diamanti palaces.

155

most prominent monument is the palace of the Gonzagas, the **Palazzo Ducale**, *Pza Sordello 40; tel: (0376) 32 02 83,* open Tues–Sat 0900–1400 and Sun–Mon 1430–1900, L 12,000, whose principal treasures are Mantegna's magnificent frescos in the Camera degli Sposi. **Mantegna's House** is open to the public, *Vle Acerbi 47; tel: (0376) 36 05 06,* open Tues–Sun 1000–1230 and 1500–1800.

Close by is the Gonzaga's alternate residence, the richly decorated **Palazzo Te**, **Vle** *Te; tel: (0376) 32 32 66,* open Tues–Sun 0900–1800, Mon 1300–1800, L 12,000, designed and decorated by Giulio Romano – as was the interior of the **Duomo** (Cathedral), *Pza Sordello,* open daily 0800–1200 and 1500–1900.

Piazza Mantegna is dominated by the façade of Alberti's late 15th-century **Basilica di Sant'Andrea** with its baroque **Campanile** (Tower), one of the seminal works of Renaissance architecture. Equally memorable is the adjacent **Rotonda di S. Lorenzo**, while **S. Sebastiano**, *V. Acerbi,* also by Alberti, was the first Renaissance church built on a central Greek cross plan.

Navigazione Negrini, *V. S. Giorgio 10; tel: (0376) 36 08 70,* operates small cruise boats on the River Mincio and its lakes, and as far as the River Po, while every third Sunday of the month sees the superb **Antiques and Curios Market** in *Pza Sordello.* Nature-lovers can enjoy the wetland nature reserves – the **Parco del Mincio** and the **Parco dell'Oglio Sud** – that lie along the Mincio and Po rivers around Mantua, enjoying the rich variety of birdlife to be seen here.

PIACENZA–RAVENNA

Considering the many and varied forms of Italian regional cuisine, you can easily make an argument that all routes in Italy are gourmet routes, but just as with equality some people are more equal than others, so with cuisine some routes are more gourmet than others. Anyway, you can eat and drink your way perfectly happily on this route through the Emilia-Romagna region, while visiting some outstanding places as you go.

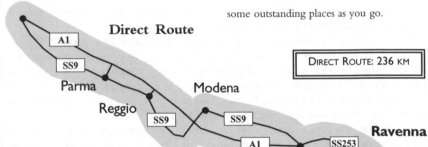

DIRECT ROUTE: 236 KM

ROUTES

DIRECT ROUTE

→ The direct route from **Piacenza** couldn't be simpler: you pick up the A1 *autostrada* at its junction with the A21, 4 km east of town, and from there you head southwards straight down the road, stopping at **Parma, Reggio, Modena** and **Bologna** to its junction with the A14. Continue south on the A14 beyond **Imola**, and turn west on the A14 to **Ravenna**, for a total distance of 236 km.

SCENIC ROUTE

⇢ The scenic route is the SS9, the *V. Emilia*, which more or less parallels the direct route, through **Parma**, **Reggio**, **Modena** and **Bologna**. Leave Bologna city centre by *V. G. Massarenti*, which runs into *V. Enrico Mattei* and becomes the SS253 as it leaves town. This road twists and turns through the flat countryside east of Bologna until it arrives at **Ravenna**, for a total distance of 234 km. There isn't a lot to choose between the two routes, except perhaps in the level of stress involved in driving them. The scenic route is calmer, but you'll get slowed down passing through some not especially interesting places on the way. Its main advantage lies in the ability to saunter easily off the main road for short diversions *en route*.

PIACENZA TO PARMA

On the road south from **Piacenza** (see page 153) to Parma, you can turn off at **Fidenza**, 9 km south on the SS359, for the thermal spa at **Salsomaggiore** in the Apennine foothills, which is a centre for mud therapy and hydromassage. See especially the extravagantly designed **Terme di Palazzo Berzieri**. A few km further along the road is **Tabiano Terme**, which specialises in treating respiratory complaints.

PARMA

Tourist Office: *Pzle Cesare Battisti 15; tel: (0521) 2109; fax: (0521) 238605*. The **IAT** office for Parma is at *Pza Duomo 5; tel/fax: (0521) 234725; fax: (0521) 238605*.

ACCOMMODATION AND FOOD

For de-luxe comfort, stay at the 4-star **Grand Hotel Baglioni**, *V. Piacenza 12c; tel: (0521) 292929*, or the **Park Hotel Stendhal**, *V. Bodoni 3; tel: (0521) 208057*. In the mid-price category, the 3-star **Farnese**, *V. Reggio 51a; tel: (0521) 994247*, and **Daniel**, *V. Gramsci 16; tel: (0521) 995147*, are good. In the 1-star category, the **Brozzi**, *V. Trento 11; tel: (0521) 272717* is near the rail station, and the **Lazzaro**, *V. XX Marzo 14; tel: (0521) 208944* in the centre.

Among many good restaurants in Parma are **La Pilotta**, *V. Bodoni 3; tel: (0521) 282865*, **La Greppia**, *V. Garibaldi 3; tel: (0521) 233686*, **San Barnaba**, *V. Trento 11; tel: (0521) 270365*, and **Antica Cereria**, *V. Tanzi 5; tel: (0521) 207387*.

SIGHTSEEING

Parma, the birthplace of Verdi and Toscanini, and the final resting place of Paganini, lies on the River Parma and is renowned for its Parmesan cheese and

Parma ham (see p. 158). Founded by the Romans in 183BC, it was a free commune during the 12th and 13th centuries, and part of the Duchy of Parma and Piacenza created by Pope Paul III in 1545. Spain picked up the duchy in 1749. In 1861, Parma joined united Italy.

Although heavily bombed by the Allies in World War II, the city is rich in artistic and architectural monuments. The Romanesque **Duomo**, *Pza Duomo; tel: (0521) 235886*, open daily 0900–1230 and 1500–1900, admission free, was restored in the 12th century following an earthquake that badly damaged the original 11th-century structure. Inside is Correggio's magnificent fresco *The Assumption of the Virgin*, dating from 1526–30. Beside the Duomo stands the 13th-century Gothic **Campanile** (Bell Tower), and the octagonal Romanesque-Gothic **Battistero** (Baptistery), *Pza Duomo; tel: (0521) 235886*, open daily 0900–1230 and 1500–1900, L3000, (1196–1260), begun in 1196 and built in pink Verona marble. The entire ensemble impressively evokes the medieval style.

The **Palazzo della Pilotta**, *Pza Pilotta;* one victim of the wartime bombing, still remains impressive. Its three vast quadrangles built by the Farnese family between 1580 and 1620 as a court palace today house a cluster of museums and other attractions. Among these are the **Galleria Nazionale** (National Gallery); *tel: (0521) 233309*, open daily 0900–1345, L12,000. This important gallery houses a major collection of works by Correggio, including the *Madonna of Saint Girolamo*, Leonardo da Vinci, Fra Angelico, Tiepolo, Canaletto, and foreign artists such as El Greco and Van Dyck; the **Museo Archeologico Nazionale** (National Archaeology Museum); *tel: (0521) 233718*, open Tues–Sun 0900–1830,

157

Parma Cheese and Ham

Two of Parma province's artisanal food products are famed throughout the world. One is the hard, dry Parmesan cheese (more properly called Parmigiano-Reggiano), which is generally grated and spread on macaroni, ravioli and other types of pasta dishes. The other is Parma ham (*prosciutto*).

The area around Parma and Reggio nell'Emilia where the cheese is produced is delimited by law, and the trademark Parmigiano-Reggiano is used exclusively for cheese produced in this zone. Tough legal standards also determine the methods used in production, and makers use milk only from cows from within the controlled production zone. It takes 14.5 litres of whole milk to produce 1 kg of Parmesan. Long, natural ageing is essential. With the slow passing of seasons and years the cheese develops its unique aroma, fragrance and flavour, natural nutritional values and high quality (Parmesan contains no preservatives, colouring or other additives). Its characteristics are guaranteed by the Consortium, the official society that protects the quality of the cheese.

Equal painstaking care is devoted to production of the cured Parma ham, widely considered to be Italy's best *prosciutto crudo* (raw, smoked ham), and once again legal requirements exist for what can be defined as *prosciutto di Parma*. Deep red in colour, it has a strong flavour and is generally bought in ultra-thin slices. It is expensive but only a little is used at a time, generally as a starter served with melon or figs.

L4000; the magnificent **Teatro Farnese**; and the **Museo Bodoniano** (Bodoni Museum); *tel: (0521) 28 22 17*, open by appointment only, admission free, recalling the life and work of Giambattista Bodoni (1740–1813), an Italian printer whose beautiful editions are among the best examples of Italian typography, and who has a typeface named after him still.

Behind the Duomo, the **Monastero e Chiesa di San Giovanni Evangelista**, *V. Dante; tel: (0521) 235992*, open daily 0630–1200 and 1530–2000, admission free, is a monastery with a Renaissance church built between 1498 and 1510, and with a baroque façade dating from 1607. The highlight here is the exceptional fresco by Correggio in the dome, *The Dormition of Saint John*, showing Christ descending in triumph among the apostles. While here, don't miss a stroll around the Benedictine monastery's tranquil cloisters and a visit to the old spicery.

If you're in need of a break from wall-to-wall monument visiting and fresco hopping in Parma, take in one of the magnificent gardens of the **Parco Ducale**. As a bonus here, you can easily go back to visiting famous monuments in the **Palazzo Ducale**, *Parco Ducale; tel: (0521) 230023*, open (park) daily 0600–2400 (May–Sept); 0630–1900 (Mar, Apr and Oct); 0700–1800 (Feb and Nov); 0700–1730 (Jan and Dec), admission free; (palace) Mon–Sat 0800–1200, admission free. The park dates back to the Farnese period in the 16th century with a small lake, and the palace dates mostly from this period too, with an extension built in the 18th century. The **Camera di S. Paulo**, *V. Melloni; tel: (0521) 233309*, open daily 0900–1345, is also known as the Camera del Correggio for its vault fresco of a bower by Correggio dating from 1519.

Several more Parma churches are worth visiting, including the 16th-century

Chiesa della SS Annunziata, *Strada Imbriani 4; tel: (0521) 234449*, open daily 1000–1200 and 1500–1700, and the sumptuous **Chiesa di Santa Maria della Steccata**, *V. Dante; tel: (0521) 234937*, open daily 0900–1200 and 1500–1800, admission free. The latter has a cycle of paintings by Parmigianino.

REGGIO

Tourist Office: *Pza Camillo Prampolini; tel: (0522) 451152*. It is open Mon–Fri 0830–1230, Sat 1430–1730.

Also called Reggio nell'Emilia to distinguish it from Reggio di Calabria in the far south, Reggio, like Parma though not so famously, is known for its cheese industry. In fact the cheese from these two cities is actually called Parmigiano-Reggiano, a fact that Reggio plaintively points out, to no great effect, at every possible opportunity. Founded by the Romans in the 2nd century BC, **Reggio** was ruled by the Este family from 1409–1796. The Holy Roman Emperor Henry IV did penance before Pope Gregory VII at **Canossa Castle** near Reggio in 1077 during one of the periodic struggles for supremacy between church and state.

Landmarks include the 13th-century **Duomo**, *Pza Prampolini*, and a 15th-century church, the **Chiesa di San Prospero**, *Pza Prampolini*.

MODENA

Tourist Office: *V. Scudari 8; tel: (059) 222482*, open daily 1030–1230 and 1600–1900.

An Etruscan settlement conquered by Rome in 183 BC, **Modena** lies on the River Panaro. It was a free commune in the 12th century but came under the rule of the Este family of Ferrara in 1288 and, apart from a time-out under the French from 1796–1814, was held by the Estes until 1859 when it became part of the Kingdom of Italy.

The **Duomo**, begun in 1099, stands in *Pza Grande*, and beside it is the **Torre Ghirlandina**, a bell tower completed in 1319. There are several museums, and also the **Biblioteca Estense** (Este Library), from 1598, which houses a superb illuminated Bible. The **University of Modena** dates from 1175. Other important buildings include the Este family's **Palazzo Ducale** (Ducal Palace), *Pza degli Estense*, begun in 1634, now a military academy.

If you haven't yet diverted south-west into the Apennine Mountains, leaving Modena is the ideal time to do it, as you can follow a long and winding road around **Monte Cimone** and briefly across the border into Tuscany. Take the SS12 to **La Lima** and switch there to the SS66, the SS632 at **Pontepetri**, then north on the SS64 to **Bologna**. It adds 209 km to the journey, so be sure you think a taste of mountain scenery and fresh air is worth it. (As an added bonus, 19 km outside of Modena the SS12 takes you within a whisker of the Ferrari plant at Maranello, where you can visit the **Galleria Ferrari**, *V. Dino Ferrari 43; tel: (0536) 943204*, open daily 0930–1230 and 1500–1800 (closed Mon in winter), L12,000.)

BOLOGNA

Tourist Office: *V. di Castagnoli 3; tel: (051) 218751; fax: (051) 218760*. There are **IAT** offices at *Pza Maggiore 6; tel: (051) 239660*, open Mon–Sat 0900–1900, Sun 0900–1300; at the **rail station**, *tel: (051) 246541*, open Mon–Sat 0900–1230 and 1430–1830, and at the **airport**, *tel: (051) 381732*, open Mon–Sat 0900–1300. All branches have free maps and guides in English (ask for *A Guest in Bologna*).

Central Bologna can be seen on foot.

159

The bus system covers the suburbs (the IAT office issues a route map). Tickets, available from tobacconists' kiosks, are good for 1 hr once validated on board. An 8-trip pass is available.

ACCOMMODATION AND FOOD

The tourist office has a wide ranging list of hotels and pensions in all categories. Among hotel chains in Bologna are *FE, HI, Jolly*.

Other hotel possibilities include the 4-star **Al Capello Rosso**, *V. Fusari 9; tel: (051) 261891* and **Grand Hotel Baglioni**, *V. Independenza 8; tel: (051) 225445*; the 3-star **Astoria**, *V. Fratelli Rossi 14; tel: (051) 521410* and **Donatello**, *V. Independenza 65; tel: (051) 248174*; 2-star **Berlino**, *V. San Mamolo 147; tel: (051) 581104* and **San Giorgio**, *V. Moline 17; tel: (051) 248659*; the 1-star **Minerva**, *V. de Monari 3; tel: (051) 239652* and **Panorama**, *V. Livraghi 1; tel: (051) 221802*. **Camping**: *Città di Bologna; tel: (051) 325016* (bus 25A or 30), open all year.

For local cuisine, try the **Cordon Bleu**, *V. Aurelio Saffin 36; tel: (051) 492230*; **Donatello**, *V. Augusto Righi 8; tel: (051) 235438*; and **Trattoria da Vito**, *V. Musolei 8; tel: (051) 349809*.

SIGHTSEEING

Bologna lies at the foot of the Apennine Mountains, at the southern edge of the Emilia-Romagna plain. The medieval town, although heavily bombed in World War II, is still a veritable living museum of the Middle Ages and the Renaissance, crammed with churches, towers, palaces and porticoes. It is altogether one of the best preserved towns in Italy and provides the visitor with a rich catalogue of architectural gems. Despite its antiquity, however, Bologna is not stuck in the past; interwoven with the array of monuments is a vibrant, commercial city. It is also reputed (at any rate by the Bolognese themselves) to have the best cuisine in Italy.

The central square, *Pza Maggiore*, is a good place from which to start absorbing Bologna's architectural treasures. On the four sides of the 13th-century square lie the **Palazzo Communale** (Town Hall), *Pza Maggiore 6*, which now houses Bologna's municipal and modern art collections, the **Collezioni Communale d'Arte**; *tel: (051) 203526*, open daily 1000–1800, L5000, and the **Museo Giorgio Morandi**; *tel: (051) 203646*, open daily 1000–1800, L5000, the 13th–15th-century **Palazzo del Podestà**, the **Palazzo dei Banchi** and the Gothic **Basilica di San Petronio** (with a 15th-century doorway by Jacopo della Quercia). The 16th-century **Fontana di Nettuno** (Fountain of Neptune), built in 1564, spouts in the north-west corner. At *Pza San Stefano*, the **Chiesi di San Stefano** (Churches of St Stephen) – **Crocifisso, Santo Sepolcro, Trinità, San Vitale** and **Sant'Agricola** – make up a complex, replete with cloisters and courtyards, that has retained its atmosphere through the centuries. The **Pinacoteca Nazionale** (National Picture Gallery), *V. delle Belle Arti 56; tel: (051) 243222*, open Tues–Sat 0900–1400, Sun 0900–1300, is filled with works by the Bolognese primitive, Renaissance and baroque schools.

The Bolognese architectural portfolio is also notable for its towers and porticoes. Towers, highly fashionable in the 13th century, were built as a sign of wealth, but also for defence in family feuds, and sometimes served as upward fire-escapes from the lower wooden buildings. The two most distinctive still standing are the 98 m **Torre degli Asinelli**, open daily

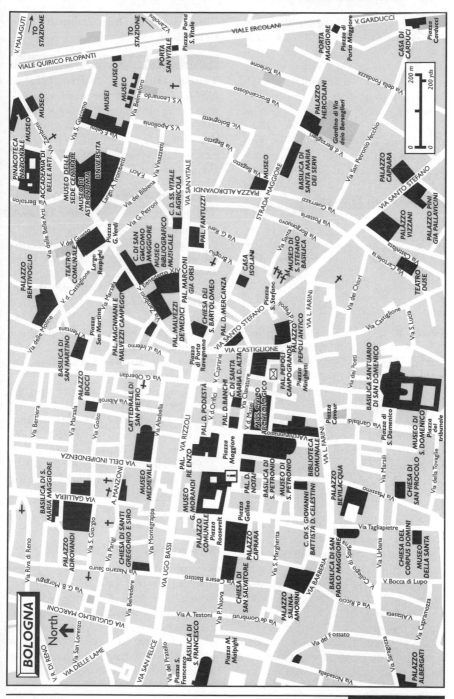

0900– 1800, L4000, and its smaller partner the **Garisenda**, both at *Pza di Porta Ravegnana*. Bologna's porticoes stretch throughout the city in a variety of styles, ranging from medieval through Renaissance to modern.

Among many other important churches worth a visit are the 13th–15th-century **Chiesa di San Giacomo Maggiore**, the early 13th-century **Basilica Santuario di San Domenico**, and the French Gothic-style, 13th-century **Basilica di San Francesco**.

Bologna's university, founded in the 11th century, is the oldest in Europe and its buildings are scattered through the city. The 16th-century **Palazzo dell' Archiginnasio**, *V. dell'Archiginnasio,* was the university's first permanent home and is today a library. The university maintains 21 museums created from work and research by its scholars, although many, such as the Museum of Domestic Animals' Anatomy, are of academic interest only. A booklet available from the tourist office locates and describes important university buildings and museums.

Instead of going direct to Ravenna on the SS253 from Bologna, you can divert south-east some 36km to **Imola**, site of the Formula One racing circuit. The Brazilian driver Ayrton Senna was killed here in a crash during the Italian Grand Prix in 1994. Another 16km along the SS253 is **Faenza**, one of the main centres of majolica production, and which gave its name to the term **faience**. This tin-oxide-glazed, painted earthenware pottery reached its summit of artistic quality during the late 15th and early 16th centuries. The true Faenza ware eschewed the polychrome style developed by other majolica centres in favour of plain white. Needless to say there are plenty of opportunities to buy faience in Faenza, and you can also

visit the **Museo Internazionale delle Ceramiche**.

RAVENNA

Tourist Office: *V. Maggiore 122; tel: (0544) 482961,* on the main approach road to the old centre; *V. Salara 8–12; tel: (0544) 35404,* in the centre of town; and at *V. delle Industrie 14; tel: (0544) 451539,* near the **Mausoleo di Teodorico** (Mausoleum of Theodoric).

ACCOMMODATION AND FOOD

Although there are only around 16 hotels in Ravenna itself, there are masses more in the nearby resorts along the coast. At the top end of the range in Ravenna is the 4-star **Bisanzio**, *V. Salara 30; tel: (0544) 217111.* The 3-star **Centrale Byron**, *V. IV Novembre 14; tel: (0544) 212225* and **Italia**, *Vle Pallavicini 4; tel: (0544) 212363* are also good options, as are the 2-star **Minerva**, *V. Maroncelli 1a; tel: (0544) 213711* and **Roma**, *V. Candiano 26; tel: (0544) 421515.*

Among many good restaurants in the town are **Cà Bruna**, *V. S. Vitale 84; tel: (0544) 461461;* **Il Brigantino**, *V. Marconi 57; tel: (0544) 402598;* **Bella Ravenna**, *Vle Pallavicini 2; tel: (0544) 32518;* **Chilò**, *V. Maggiore 62; tel: (0544) 36206;* **Enoteca dei Vini del Passatore**, *V. Corrado Ricci 24; tel: (0544) 30163;* **Osteria Quattro Gatti**, *V. Pier Traversari 35; tel: (0544) 219021.*

SIGHTSEEING

Ravenna is compact and with a pedestrianised centre, easy to get around, although the distance to some of its outlying points of interest can be disheartening on a hot summer's day – the only kind of summer's day you get here. Its quiet air today belies its former pre-eminence, both as a capital of the Roman Empire in the

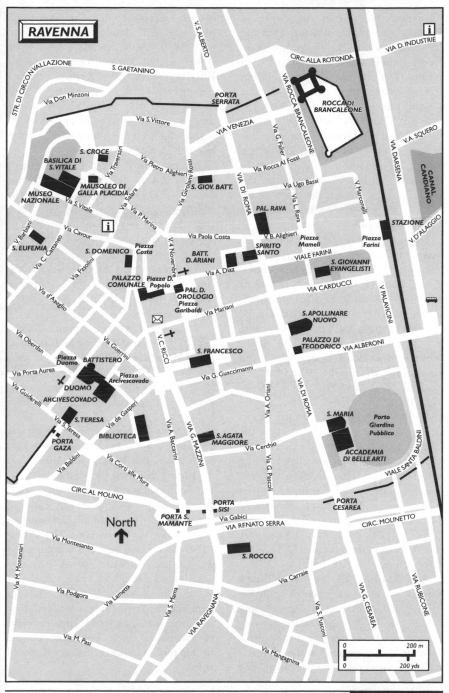

RAVENNA

STR. DI CIRCONVALLAZIONE
S. GAETANINO
Via Don Minzoni
Via S. Vittore
PORTA SERRATA
VIA VENEZIA
V. S. ALBERTO
CIRC. ALLA ROTONDA
VIA D. INDUSTRIE
VIA ROCCA BRANCALEONE
ROCCA DI BRANCALEONE
Via G. Falier
Via Rocca Al Fossi
VIA DARSENA
V. A. SQUERO
CANAL CANDIANO
V. D'ALAGGIO

S. CROCE
BASILICA DI S. VITALE
MAUSOLEO DI GALLA PLACIDIA
MUSEO NAZIONALE
Via S. Vitale
Via Traversari
Via Pietro Alighieri
Via Girolami Rossi
Via Salara
Via Via P. Marina
S. GIOV. BATT.
VIA DI ROMA
Via Ugo Bassi
PAL. RAVA
V. L. Rava
V. Marconelli
STAZIONE

Via Cavour
V. Barbiani
S. EUFEMIA
Via C. Catraneo
Via Fossolini
Via d'Azeglio
S. DOMENICO
Piazza Costa
Via Paola Costa
V. B. Alighieri
SPIRITO SANTO
Piazza Mameli
Piazza Farini
VIALE FARINI
S. GIOVANNI EVANGELISTI
V. A Novembre
BATT. D. ARIANI
Via A. Diaz
VIA CARDUCCI
V. PALAVICINI

PALAZZO COMUNALE
Piazza D. Popolo
PAL. D. OROLOGIO
Piazza Garibaldi
Via Mariani
S. APOLLINARE NUOVO
PALAZZO DI TEODORICO
VIA ALBERONI
Via Oberdan
Via Guerrini
V. C. RICCI
S. FRANCESCO
Via G. Guaccimanni
VIA DI ROMA

Via Porta Aurea
Piazza Duomo
BATTISTERO
Piazza Arcivescovado
DUOMO
ARCIVESCOVADO
Via Guidarelli
S. TERESA
Via de Gasperi
Via S. Teresa
BIBLIOTECA
PORTA GAZA
Via Baldini
Via Corti alle Mura
CIRC. AL MOLINO
Via A. Bacarini
VIA G. MAZZINI
S. AGATA MAGGIORE
Via Cerchio
Via A. Oriani
S. MARIA
Porto Giardino Pubblico
ACCADEMIA DI BELLE ARTI
VIA SANTA BALDINI

North

Via Montesanto
PORTA S. MAMANTE
PORTA SISI
Via Gabici
VIA RENATO SERRA
PORTA CESAREA
CIRC. MOLINETTO
Via M. Montanari
Via Podgora
Via Lametta
Via S. Maria
VIA RAVEGNANA
S. ROCCO
Via Carraie
Via G. Pascoli
Via S. Fusconi
VIA G. CESAREA
VIA RUBICONE
Via M. Pasi
Via Mangagnina

0   200 m
0   200 yds

163

5th century AD, and as the centre of Byzantine rule in Italy during the 6th and 7th centuries AD. Remnants of these periods include a fine collection of vivid mosaics. The city played an ignoble but perhaps sensible role in the last days of the Roman Empire in the west. Emperor Honorius skulked in safety behind the marshes that protected Ravenna while Alaric and his Goths rampaged through Italy, sacking Rome itself in AD 410. Honorius's main contribution to the struggle was to arrange the death of his only capable general, Stilicho, an act that sealed Rome's fate.

The major sights cluster in the north-west corner of the old town. The 6th-century octagonal **Basilica di San Vitale**, *V. San Vitale 17; tel: (0544) 34424*, open daily 0900-1900, L6000, features magnificent mosaics of the 6th-century Byzantine Emperor Justinian and Empress Theodora and their courtiers on the wall panels flanking the altar. Beside it is the **Mausoleo di Galla Placidia**, *V. Fiandrini*, open Mon–Fri 0930–1230 and 1500–1800, Sat 0930–1230 and 1500–1700, Sun 1200–1700, a cruciform chapel identified traditionally as the tomb of the sister of Honorius, who effectively ruled what little was left of the empire during the reign of her ineffective son, Valentinian III. It is lined with old mosaics in deep tones. The **Museo Nazionale** (National Museum), *V. Fiandrini; tel: (0544) 34424*, open daily 0830–1930, L8000, is also in the grounds of the Basilica di San Vitale.

The **Basilica di Sant'Apollinare Nuovo**, *V. di Roma*, open daily 0930–1830, L5000, dates from the same period; its walls are lined with mosaics showing processions of saints (on the men's side of the church) and virgins (on the women's side). In the south-west of town, the

Museo Arcivescovile (Archiepiscopal Museum), *Pza Arcivescovado*, open daily 0930–1830, L5000, has more relics from Ravenna's rich history. The 6th-century **Battistero degli Ariani** (Arian Baptistery), *V. degli Ariani; tel: (0544) 34424*, open daily 0830–1930, is one of the few original Arian buildings still standing, a relic from the 6th century and the reign of Theodoric the Great.

Among many other historic places worth a visit are the **Tomba di Dante** (Tomb of Dante), *V. Dante Alighieri 9; tel: (0544) 30252*, open daily 0900–1900 and the **Museo Dantesco** (Dante Museum), *V. Dante Alighieri 4; tel: (0544) 30252*, open 0900–1200 and 1530–1800, L3000 (free on Sun). As their names make clear, both are related to the poet Dante Alighieri (1265–1321), author of the *Divine Comedy*.

A short way out of the centre, on the road to the coast at **Marina di Ravenna**, is the **Mausoleo di Teodorico**, *V. delle Industrie 14; tel: (0544) 34424*, open daily 0830–1930, L4000, built for the Gothic king who united post-Roman Italy under his control.

If you've had about enough of ancient history by now, a breath of fresh air might be in order. The **Pineta San Vitale** and the **Pineta di Classe** pine forests lie north and south of Ravenna respectively. Of the great swamps that once lay around Ravenna, only the **Valle di Comacchio** (Comacchio Valley) remains. The **Punte Alberete** wetland between Ravenna and the Comacchio Valley is an extensive waterlogged forest, with many varieties of plants and flowers. Wildlife includes numerous birds (particularly waders, duck and other waterside birds), large numbers of amphibians (most important are the swamp turtle and the crested newt) as well as fish.

RAVENNA–GUBBIO

This lengthy route dips a toe in four different regions of Italy (Emilia-Romagna, Marche, Tuscany and Umbria), plus the tiny independent republic of San Marino. It traverses a wide span of scenery from the combed sands of the Adriatic Riviera through lonely uplands to the lush valley of the Upper Tiber. In terms of interest, it offers quite a mix, from seaside hedonism to quattrocento masterpieces. Allow at least a couple of days – longer if you want to sample Rimini's beaches at leisure.

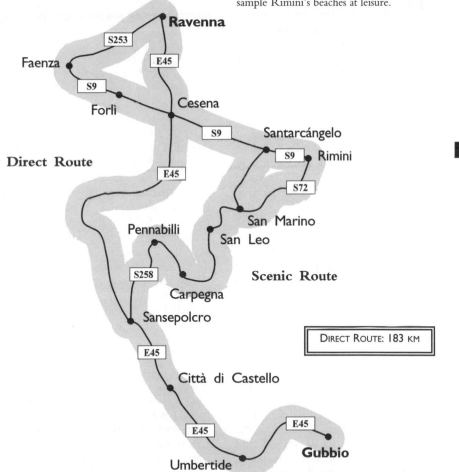

Ravenna
S253
Faenza
E45
S9
Forlì
Cesena
S9
Santarcángelo
S9 Rimini

Direct Route

E45
S72
San Marino
Pennabilli
San Leo

Scenic Route

S258
Carpegna
Sansepolcro

DIRECT ROUTE: 183 KM

E45
Città di Castello
E45
E45
Gubbio
Umbertide

ROUTES

DIRECT ROUTE

→ The most straightforward route from Ravenna to Gubbio follows the E45, mostly fast, toll-free dual carriageway. Looping tunnels burrow under the Appenines before the road carves southeast through the Tiber Valley. Turn north-east at **Umbertide** for **Gubbio**.

SCENIC ROUTE

····▶ The glittering mosaics of **Ravenna**'s San Vitale Basilica make a memorable springboard for this 280 km tour. Leave the city centre at Porta Adriana and continue north-west along *V. Maggiore* following signs for Ferrara/Bologna A14, then **Faenza** along the S253. After 10 km, just beyond Godo, the Faenza road forks left through Russi on the secondary S302. Faenza is reached after a further 18 km.

From Faenza, the *V. Emilia* (S9) continues its arrow-straight Roman course to the Adriatic through **Forlì** and **Cesena** to **Rimini**. You can avoid these built-up areas by slipping on to the parallel *autostrada* (A14), but it's a toll road and won't save you much time. All the routes around this section of the Adriatic coastal plain are straightforward and in reasonable condition. Scenically, though, they are dull, leading through scrappy, built-up countryside. Nor are the coastal roads a more enticing option, running through a string of amorphous seaside resorts around Rimini. Sea views are blocked by buildings and phalanxes of parasols; holidaymakers dodging between hotels and beaches a constant hazard.

Spare a thought as you whirl over an insignificant watercourse about 16 km west of Rimini (on the *V. Emilia* you will meet it at Savignano). This is the Rubicon, which Julius Caesar fatefully crossed with

his army in 49BC, challenging Pompey and the Senate for ultimate control of Rome.

From Rimini, the S72 leads inland to **San Marino**. This road is often choked with day-tripping holidaymakers and interrupted by countless traffic lights. Quieter secondary routes to San Marino include the S258 from Rimini or the road from medieval Santarcàngelo (10 km west of Rimini). Steadily, the scenery becomes more exciting as the roads clamber round hairpins; soon San Marino's toy-town fortress erupts on the horizon, improbably perched on its dizzy rockface against a postcard sky.

The mountain route between San Marino and **Sansepolcro** is the scenic highlight of this tour, jiggling through the Montefeltro Hills and the Alpe della Luna where wolves are said to roam. From San Marino, follow signs for **San Leo**, a delightful fortified town, then head south through striking, quarry-scarred limestone country to panoramic **Carpegna**. A picnic somewhere along this road makes an attractive proposition. From Carpegna, rejoin the S258 at **Pennabilli**, another castle-crowned hill town; follow this road over the Tuscan border to Sansepolcro. To the north the twin sources of the Tiber (**Vene del Tevere**) rise beneath Monte Fumaiolo (1407 m). From Sansepolcro, the straight, well-maintained E45 dual carriageway propels you swiftly into Umbria through the tobacco plantations of the Valtiberina (Upper Tiber Valley). Beyond the neat plots lie wild woods and pastureland teeming with rare species. Secondary roads and the railway line also follow the river, a slim and sprightly ribbon at this stage, through **Città di Castello** and **Umbertide.** Brief but worthwhile side trips can be made to **Anghiari** (7 km south-west of Sansepolcro), **Monterchi**

(10 km west of Città di Castello on the S221) and **Montone** (8 km north-east of Umbertide). At Umbertide, turn north-east along the S219 to **Gubbio**, a pleasant rural drive (28 km).

FAENZA

Tourist Office: *Pza del Popolo 1; tel: (0546) 25231.*

The town's name indicates its main industry. The decorated ceramics renowned throughout Europe as faience ware reached the height of their fame during the 15th and 16th centuries, and are still produced locally in about 60 small workshops, using traditional techniques. The characteristic lustre is produced by a complex tin-glazing process followed by a lead wash. The outstanding **Museo Internazionale delle Ceramiche**, *Vle Campidori 2; tel: (0546) 21240*, open Tues–Sat 0900–1900, Sun 0930–1300 and 1500–1900 (Apr–Oct); Tues–Fri 0930–1330, Sat 0930–1330 and 1500–1800, Sun 0930–1300 (Nov–Mar); L10,000, contains a huge collection of ceramics from near and far, including pieces by famous 20th-century artists. Modern versions of faience are on sale in the town.

Faenza's main historic sights can be seen around its interlinked central squares. Pza del Popolo contains the arcaded and crenellated **Palazzo del Podestà**, once home of the city magistate. The **Duomo** in Pza della Libertà is regarded as a fine example of the Tuscan Renaissance style. The reconstructed clock tower, ornate fountain and 18th-century **Teatro Masini** are also worth a look. Faenza's main festival is the **Palio del Niballo** (June), a medieval pageant.

FORLÌ

Tourist Office: *Corso della Repubblica 23; tel: (0543) 712434.*

This town doesn't have many reasons to tempt you into its one-way labyrinth, but a couple of hours' parking time in one of the outlying squares (the historic quarter is closed to traffic) are justifiable. Capital of the Romagna region, Forlì is an agricultural and administrative centre, dubiously distinguished by its associations with Benito Mussolini, born and buried in Predappio, 16km south-west of the town. Il Duce's political career began in Forlì's newspaper offices before he left for the brighter lights of Milan. Some of Forlì's grandiose civic architecture and monuments date from this interwar period, but its main sights are the **Museo del Risorgimento e del Teatro**, *Palazzo Gaddi, Corso Garibaldi 96; tel: (0543) 21109*, open Tues–Fri 0900–1400, Sat 0900–1330, Sun 0900–1300, L4000 and the **Pinacoteca** and **Museo Etnografico** (Ethnographic Museum) on *Corso della Repubblica 72*.

RIMINI

Tourist Office: Rimini has numerous municipal information centres scattered throughout the resort. The main ones (open all year) are in the historic quarter, *Corso d'Augusto 156; tel: (0541) 704110*, near the rail station at *Via Dante 86; tel: (0541) 51331* and by the waterfront at *Pzle Fellini 3; tel: (0541) 54319* or *54019*. Open Mon–Fri 0800–1300, 1400–1900, Sat 0800–1300, Sun 0930–1230, 1600–1900 (summer); 0800–1400 daily (winter).

ARRIVING AND DEPARTING

Airport: Aeroporto Civile Rimini–Miramare, *V. Flaminia, tel: (0541) 373132*, (4 km south-east), handles charter flights from all over Europe. Bus 9A/B connects the airport and the centre.

Station: *Pzle C. Battisti; tel: (0541) 53512.*

GETTING AROUND

An Orange Ticket (L5000 for 24hrs, L20,000 for eight days) gives unlimited travel on all public transport within the Rimini municipal zone and its satellite resorts. Single fares on local TRAM buses cost L1500. Tickets should be bought in advance and punched as you board. At night, Blue Line buses (L4000; high season only) serve the disco dancers. Bonelli Bus, *tel: (0541) 372432*, and the San Marino-based Fratelli Benedettini, *tel: (0549) 903854,* offer regular coach excursions to San Marino, San Leo, etc. Free car-parking is available along the seafront.

ACCOMMODATION AND FOOD

Hundreds of hotels and apartment blocks line the Adriatic Riviera in and around Rimini. It can still be difficult to find a room at short notice in high season. Some hotels insist on full board; out of season, many close. Rimini's tourist offices provide free accommodation lists. Specialist agencies (e.g. at the station) offer booking services. Most imposing of Rimini's hotels is the *belle-epoque* **Grand**, *V. Ramusio 1; tel: (0541) 56000* (expensive), immortalised in Fellini's *Amarcord*. A more affordable mid-range option is the modern, seafront **Club House**, *Vle Vespucci 52; tel: (0541) 391460.* **Verudella**, *Vle Tripoli 238; tel: (0541) 52316* and the **Hotel Pigalle**, *V. Ugo Foscolo 7; tel: (0541) 391054* are pleasant budget choices. *Vle Pola* is a good hunting ground for cheap rooms. Hostels and campsites lie outside the centre, but are easily reached by bus.

International fast food is the mainstay of the seafront eating places; snacks are better value than full meals. For something more interesting, try the old town. **Pic Nic**, *V. Tempio Malatestiano 30; tel: (0541) 21916* offers a lunchtime buffet, and evening piz-zas (cheap; closed Mon; garden). **Dallo Zio**, *Vicolo Santa Chiara 16; tel: (0541) 786160* (closed Wed) has good seafood. Tempting snacks and picnic provisions are sold in the daily covered market. Several supermarkets open all day near the main beaches; **Standa**, *V. Vespucci 133*. While in the region, sample some Romagna wines (Trebbiano and Sangiovese).

ENTERTAINMENT

Throughout the holiday season, Rimini provides a non-stop programme of exhibitions and events to amuse its four million cosmopolitan visitors. Major, annually staged happenings include several film festivals (appropriately for Fellini's home town), and the **Sagra Musicale Malatestiana**, a classical music festival held in the Tempio Malatestiano. There are dozens of daytime challenges to sunbed indolence, but Rimini's most distinctive form of entertainment blossoms along the seafront strip after the *passegiata*, when clubs, discos and bars burst into noisy neon. Some of the nightscene is unsavoury; kerb-crawling prostitution (gay and straight) is openly practised around the station. Elsewhere Rimini offers some of the most fashionable nightspots on the Mediterranean. Riccione's **Cocoricò**, *Vle Chieti 44; tel: (0541) 605183* (Sat, L50,000) is one of Italy's most dazzling discos. For the latest in-scene, check the listings magazine *Chiamami Città.*

SIGHTSEEING

Rimini is familiar to sun-seekers as one of Italy's liveliest seaside resorts. Quiet in the winter months, it explodes in a frenzy of tourist activity from June to Sept. More than 25 km of sandy beaches between Riccione and Cesenatico are divided by concessionaires into neat blocks of sunbeds and parasols, then rented by the hour to families smeared with suncream and ice cream in equal proportions.

Away from the seafront, Rimini is a more dignified place with a considerable past. Badly bombed in the last war, most of its present buildings are modern, but in Roman times it was a wealthy port at the junction of two great highways, the *V. Emilia* and *V. Flaminia*.

During the Renaissance, the powerful ruling Malatesta family kept the city buzzing with a lifestyle as lurid as the Borgias. Rimini's main sight, the **Tempio Malatestiano**, *V. IV Novembre* (open daily 0700–1200 and 1530–1900; free) dates from this period. Embellished by Sigismondo Malatesta in honour of his beautiful mistress, Isotta, in the 15th century, its exuberance reflects something of its sponsor's Jekyll and Hyde reputation for diabolical wickedness and artistic refinement.

Remains from Roman times include the **Arco d'Augusto**, **Anfiteatro**, and **Ponte di Tiberio**, all near the ramparts.

SAN MARINO

Tourist Office: *Contrada Omagnano 20; tel: (0549) 882400*, open Mon, Thur 0815–1415 and 1500–1800, Tues, Wed, Fri 0815–1415. **Branch office** at *Contrada del Collegio; tel: (0549) 882914,* open daily 0830–1730 (May–Sept); closed 1200–1430 (Oct–Apr). Both offices offer lavishly produced tourist literature and will stamp passports with San Marino visas on request (there are no border formalities). Tour guides can be booked from the Prenotazioni Ufficio Guide near Porta San Francesco; *tel: (0549) 882393.*

ACCOMMODATION AND FOOD

Most visitors choose to see San Marino on a day trip. Hotels are generally expensive.

Attractive choices include the central **Titano**, *Contrada del Collegio 21; tel: (0549) 991006*, with magnificent views and a terrace restaurant (closed mid Nov–mid Mar), or **La Rocca**, *Salita alla Rocca 37; tel: (0549) 991166*, with a swimming pool and a vantage point of the Rocca Guaita. Food is mostly geared to the tourist trade, with standardised results. **Righi la Taverna**, *Pza della Libertà; tel: (0549) 991196* offers regional cooking in a prime location; **Trattoria Panoramica**, *V. Lapicidi Marini; tel: (0549) 992305,* has appealing views.

GETTING AROUND

Sharp hairpins wind up to the town. Numbered car-parks are placed at intervals along the final ascent; tariffs increase as you approach the summit. Pressure on these limited spaces is intense in high season. An alternative is to park in **Borgomaggiore** at the foot of the hill (meters cost L1500/hr) and take the cable car (L3000 single; L5000 return; runs from 0800–2100 in July/Aug; closes earlier off-season) to the old town. A shuttle-bus service (L4000) runs from the *Vle Campo dei Guidei* car-park (no. 12) on the west side of town. Taxi tariffs are a basic L7000 plus L1500 per km; *tel: (0549) 991441.* Buses stop by the Porta San Francesco, leaving passengers with a stiff climb. There are regular bus services, and countless excursion coaches, from Rimini and Pesaro.

EVENTS

One of San Marino's most popular sights is the **Changing of the Guard** ceremony held in *Pza della Libertà* (hourly on the half-hour June–Sept 0830–1230 and 1430–1830; free). The republic hosts many events, including motorsports championships. Major festivals are the **Giornate Medioevali** (Medieval Days)

169

pageant with a crossbow tournament (July), and the **Investiture of the Captains Regent**, a colourful ritual held every Apr and Oct.

SIGHTSEEING

The minute landlocked state of San Marino occupies 60 sqkm of hilly territory bordering the Italian regions of Marche and Emilia-Romagna. It claims to be the world's smallest and oldest republic. Its curious history is said to date from the 4th century AD, when a Christian stonemason, St Marinus, fled to Monte Titano with a band of followers to escape persecution in the reign of the Emperor Diocletian. Despite many subsequent attempts to conquer it by force or cunning, San Marino retained its independence, which was formally recognized at the Congress of Vienna in 1815. Its constitution consists of two twice-yearly elected Captains Regent who chair a parliamentary council of 60 members. Today San Marino's economic mainstays of farming and small-scale manufacturing are outstripped by tourism; it is now a hugely popular and prosperous excursion destination. Summer visitors greatly outnumber the resident population of 50,000 or so, but few spend longer than a day here. The colourful postage stamps which adorn countless philatelists' albums are a major source of income. San Marino also mints its own currency, used interchangeably with Italian **lire**. Its much-vaunted low-tax status doesn't make much difference to prices; petrol and alcohol cost about the same as in Italy and apart from the stamps and coins there are few distinctive souvenirs. The thousand-strong army now performs picturesque ceremonial duties; in olden days skilled crossbowmen bravely defended the state's liberty. San Marino's brand of theme-park tourism is often derided, but the mini-republic is

justly proud of its honourable traditions of peaceful democracy and hospitality to political refugees.

The heart of San Marino is its capital (San Marino Città), a rocky citadel perched on the crags of Monte Titano, surveying a domain of eight scattered townships far below. Steep paths lined with souvenir stalls lead up to the fortifications. Three medieval towers linked by ramparts overlook truly startling views. Largest is the **Rocca Guaita**, *tel: (0549) 991369*, dating from the 11th century and containing a chapel dedicated to St Barbara, but more striking is the **Rocca Cesta**, spectacularly sited on a sheer rockface. It houses the **Museo delle Armi Antiche** (ancient historical weapons); *tel: (0549) 991295* . Below the walls the main attractions of the old town are the neo-Gothic **Palazzo Pubblico**, seat of San Marino's Parliament, in *Pza della Libertà; tel: (0549) 882708*. The cloister of **San Francesco** church in the lower town houses San Marino's **Museo Pinacoteca** (art gallery); *tel: (0549) 885132*. All these sights have the same opening times daily: 0800–1930 (Apr–Sept); 0830–1215 and 1400–1730 (Mar and mid Sept–Oct); 0900–1215 and 1400–1645 (Jan–Feb and Nov–Dec); closed Christmas week; and entrance charges for each cost L4000 (a combined ticket for the two main fortresses costs L6000). The rampart walks and **Montale** fortress (exterior only) are freely accessible. A clutch of lesser museums are devoted to waxworks, vintage cars, medical instruments, etc. Philatelists should head for the **Stamp and Coin Collections** in *Pza Garibaldi; tel: (0549) 882370*. The **Museo di Stato** (National Museum; archaeological, historical and art collections) is due to be rehoused in the renovated Palazzo Pergami in *Pzta del Titano*. Noteworthy churches are the

Basilica del Santo, where Marino's relics reside near the altar, and **San Pietro**, whose rock niches traditionally sheltered San Marino and San Leo. Giovanni Michelucci's undulating modernist **Chiesa della Beata Vergine della Consolazione** in Borgomaggiore, built in the 1960s, makes a striking landmark, located near to the cable-car station.

SANSEPOLCRO

Tourist Office: *Pza Garibaldi 2; tel: (0575) 740536* (open daily 0930–1230 and 1600–1830). Italy's curiously insular tourism fostered by rival regional interests makes life tricky in this area. Sansepolcro is (just!) in Tuscany; but Tuscan publications won't tell you anything about the Umbrian Tiber Valley only 2 km downstream, and vice versa. Look out for both sets of leaflets (Valtiberina/Arezzo and Alta Valle del Tevere/Umbria).

Sansepolcro is the largest town in the Upper Tiber Valley, a former lace-making centre now better known for spaghetti production (perhaps a related skill?). Its historic quarter within well-preserved walls (where there is useful parking space) makes a pleasant wander, but most visitors beat a determined path to the **Museo Civico**, *V. Aggiunti 65; tel: (0575) 732218*, open daily 0930–1300 and 1430–1800 (Oct–May); 0930–1300 and 1430–1930 (June–Sept); L10,000, where several masterpieces by the *quattrocentro* painter Piero della Francesca, a native of Sansepolcro, are on display. Most famous of these is *The Resurrection*, an enigmatic depiction of the central Christian mystery which has inspired reams of critical commentary. A martial-looking Christ steps purposefully from his tomb amid a surreal landscape of rocks and trees, some wintry, others with summer foliage. In the foreground, four guards slumber on,

oblivious of the miracle. The onlooker's temptation to shout 'Behind you!', is quelled by the Redeemer's steely gaze. Other works by Piero (as he is known locally) include a polyptych (multi-panelled altarpiece) called the *Madonna della Misericordia* where a regal, Wagnerian virgin shelters a saintly gathering beneath her outspread cloak. Other thought-provoking paintings in this collection make it essential viewing if you have any interest in early Renaissance art.

Other sights worth a glance are the 11th-century **Duomo** on *V. Matteotti* and the churches of **San Francesco** and **San Lorenzo**.

Sansepolcro fancies itself as something of a gourmet town and local restaurants are well promoted. **Il Fiorentino**, *V. L. Pacioli 60; tel: (0575) 740370* (closed Fri; also has attractive bedrooms), **Paolo e Marco Mercati**, *V. P. Togliatti 68; tel: (0575) 735051* (closed Sun), and **Da Ventura**, *V. Aggiunti 30; tel: (0575) 742569* (closed Sat) are praised for good regional cooking (all moderately priced).

On the second Sun in Sept, the town is the centre of attention for the **Palio della Balestra**, a time-honoured contest against the crossbowmen of Gubbio.

West of the town, a 7 km detour from the E45 takes you through tobacco plantations to the historic town of **Anghiari** with its **Museo Taglieschi**, *Pza Mameli 16; tel: (0575) 788001*, open Mon–Sat 0900– 1830, Sun 0900–1230, L4000, on the traditional crafts of the Upper Tiber. The 18th-century church of **Santa Maria delle Grazie** contains della Robbia terracotta work and a *Madonna and Child* by Matteo di Giovanni. Anghiari was the site of a famous battle between the Florentines and the Milanese in 1440. Leonardo da Vinci began working up some ideas for immortalising the

Florentine victory, but the project remained uncompleted to the chagrin of art historians.

From Anghiari, art lovers should head 8 km south-east to **Monterchi** just off the S221. This pretty hill town is the proud possessor of another Piero masterpiece, the *Madonna del Parto*, which can be seen in the cemetery chapel on *V. della Reglia; tel: (0575) 70713,* open Tues–Sun 0900–1300 and 1400–1900, L5000. This haunting painting is an unusual depiction of the Virgin in the final stages of pregnancy; a weary figure with mixed emotions about her momentous destiny. Critics speculate that much of the fresco's force stems from Piero's feelings for his mother, who came from Monterchi.

CITTÀ DI CASTELLO

Tourist Office: *Palazzo del Podestà, Pza Fanti; tel: (075) 855 4922* (open Mon–Sat 0900–1300 and 1530–1830, Sun 0930–1230). A well-stocked regional office with plenty of information about the Tiber Valley. For information on local walks, contact **CAI**, *V. della Tina 14; tel: (075) 855 6788.*

This ancient Umbrian settlement (**Tifernum** to the Romans) occupies a dominant place in the flat, green, trough of the Tiber basin. Destroyed by the Goths, the town regained its prestige in the 15th century under the ruling Vitelli family, great patrons of the arts. Vitellozzo Vitelli made the mistake of accepting a dinner invitation from the Borgias in 1502. From then on, control reverted to the papal states. The modern outskirts reveal some industry, based largely on the profitable tobacco fields all around. The historic walled centre has no very compelling buildings, but is pleasant to explore; the town hosts the **Umbrian Chamber Music Festival** in Aug–Sept.

There is a convenient pay-and-display car-park on *Vle Nazario,* outside the walls near the river. Earthquake damage is visible in the **Duomo**, an odd mix of Gothic and Baroque, with a circular campanile and fine portal carvings. Beside the **Duomo** stands the 14th-century **Palazzo Comunale**, most imposing of several grand mansions around the town. Opposite is the **Torre Comunale**, once the town's prison.

Best sights in town are its art collections. The **Pinacoteca Comunale**, *V. della Connoniera 22; tel: (075) 852 0656,* open 0930–1245 and 1500–1830 (end Mar–mid July); 0930–1245 and 1500–1915 (mid July–Sept); 1000–1245 and 1500–1700 (Oct–end Mar); Thurs 1300–2100 (Aug–Sept); closed Mon; L7000, has *graffito* decoration on its Vasari façade. Luca Signorelli's *Martyrdom of St Sebastian* (1498) and some damaged Raphaels are its prize exhibits. The **Museo del Duomo**, *Pza Gabriotti; tel: (075) 855 4705,* open Sat–Sun 1030–1230 and 1500–1700 (Oct–Mar); 1030–1300 and 1530–1800 (Apr–May); 1030–1300 and 1600–1830 (June–Sept); L5000, has a fine collection of palaeo-Christian liturgical silver and a Romanesque altarfront. The **Collezioni Burri**, *Palazzo Albizzini, V. F Pierucci; tel: (075) 855 4649* (open Tues–Sat 0900–1230 and 1430–1800, Sun 0900–1300; L8000) displays the colourful abstracts of contemporary artist Alberto Burri in a tobacco shed.

Six km north of Umbertide, detour east to the delightful village of **Montone**, where a spine from the Crown of Thorns is paraded through the streets at Easter.

UMBERTIDE

Tourist Office: *Pza Caduti del Lavoro; tel (075) 941 7099* (open Mon 1530–1800, Wed 1030–1330, Thur 1530–1800).

Besides the eyecatching **Rocca** in the central *Pza Fortebraccio* (modern art exhibitions; open Tues–Sun 1030–1230 and 1600–1900; free), Luca Signorelli's *Deposition* in the church of **Santa Croce** is worth seeing. Several local castles and churches are of passing interest. Umbertide is a gastronomic centre with specialities based on spit roasts, game, chestnuts and truffles. Wine, cheese, charcuterie and local ceramics are on sale in shops throughout the town.

GUBBIO

Tourist Office: *Pza Oderisi 6; tel: (075) 922 0693*, open Mon–Fri 0815–1345 and 1530–1830, Sat 0900–1300 and 1530–1830, Sun 0930–1230; off-season afternoons 1500–1800). This well-stocked office off *Corso Garibaldi* provides local and regional pamphlets. Another excellent English-speaking source of information is **Easy Gubbio** run by the local hoteliers' association GOTE, at *V. della Repubblica 11–13; tel: (075) 922 0066* (daily 0800–2200). It helps visitors to find accommodation, sells bus tickets, gives transport information, changes money, provides telephones, rents cars and organises the useful pay car-park in nearby *Pza Quaranta Martiri* (except Thur – market day).

GETTING AROUND

Free car-parking is available near the amphitheatre by San Domenico church and near the cable-car station at Porta Romana. Regular buses connect Gubbio with *Perugia* and *Assisi*, and with the main towns of the Tiber Valley. Frequent shuttle buses connect Gubbio with the nearest rail station at **Fossato di Vico** (19 km Rome–Ancona line).

ACCOMMODATION AND FOOD

This splendid Umbrian town makes an excellent touring base. Its well-heeled visitors demand a good range of restaurants, hotels and *agriturismo*. There are two attractive campsites just south of town off the Perugia road, one rated 4-star: **Villa Ortoguidone**; *tel: (075) 927 2037*. Old-town hotels include the **Bosone Palace**, *V. XX Settembre 22; tel: (075) 922 0688* (moderate), small and smart, in a frescoed *palazzo*.

Well placed for sightseeing with a garage and a good restaurant with an even better view (closed Wed). **Gattapone**, *V. Ansidei 6; tel: (075) 927 2489* and **Dei Consoli**, *V. dei Consoli; tel: (075) 927 3335* are pleasant, inexpensive and central hotels. Out of town, the **Villa Montegranelli**, 4 km south-west at *Monteluiano; tel: (075) 922 0185* (pricey) is handsomely set in peaceful grounds. Superb restaurant (closed Wed).

There are lots of good eating places in Gubbio, but dishes laced with the local black truffles don't come cheap. Well-established favourites include the **Taverna del Lupo**, *V. Ansidei 21a; tel: (075) 927 4368* (closed Mon), offering game and truffle pasta in a medieval setting, and **Alla Fornace di Mastro Giorgio**, *V. Mastro Giorgio; tel: (075) 922 1836* (closed Tues), set in the medieval workshop of a master potter. **Bargello**, *V dei Consoli 37; tel: (075) 927 3724* (closed Mon) offers excellent pizzas and a range of inexpensive regional dishes. For picnics try the stalls under the Weavers' Loggia. **Prodotti Tipici e Tartufati Eugabini** on *V. Piccardi 17* (0830–1300 and 1530–2000) sells cheeses and unusual charcuterie.

SHOPPING

Gubbio is a long-established ceramics centre. Graceful reproductions of black Etruscan vases are a modern variant on painted majolica. Try **Antichita A. M.**

173

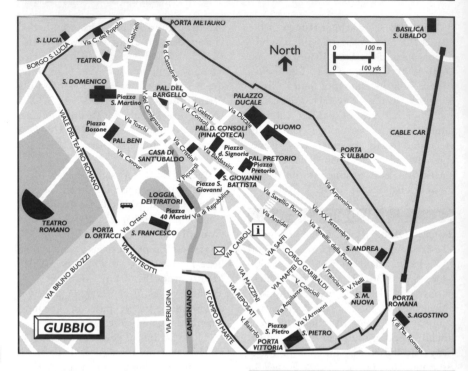

North

S. LUCIA
S. DOMENICO
TEATRO
BORGO S. LUCIA
PORTA METAURO
BASILICA S. UBALDO
PAL. DEL BARGELLO
Piazza S. Martino
PALAZZO DUCALE
Piazza Bosone
PAL. BENI
PAL. D. CONSOLI (PINACOTECA)
DUOMO
CABLE CAR
CASA DI SANT'UBALDO
Piazza d. Signoria
PAL. PRETORIO
PORTA S. ULBADO
Piazza Pretorio
S. GIOVANNI BATTISTA
Piazza S. Giovanni
LOGGIA DEI TIRATORI
Piazza 40 Martiri
TEATRO ROMANO
PORTA D. ORTACCI
S. FRANCESCO
S. ANDREA
S.M. NUOVA
PORTA ROMANA
S. AGOSTINO
GUBBIO
Piazza S. Pietro
S. PIETRO
PORTA VITTORIA

0 100 m
0 100 yds

Marcelli di Luigi Minelli at *V. del Popolo 23; tel: (075) 927 3687.*

Gourmet food products are another speciality: **Bartolini** at *V. XX Settembre 33; tel: (075) 927 4322* has beautifully packaged truffles, pâtés, oil and wine.

EVENTS

Gubbio's best-known festivity takes place on 15 May, when the **Corsa dei Ceri** rekindles a 900-year old tradition. Three huge 'candles' (enormous wooden frames, originally representing the various guilds of the town) are raced up the steep slopes of Monte Ingino – a feat of amazing stamina. On the last Sun in May, crossbow archers from Sansepolcro arrive to try their skills against their long-standing Gubbio rivals at the **Palio della Balestra** (there's a return match in Sansepolcro later in the year).

SIGHTSEEING

The whole of medieval Gubbio and its setting against the wooded backdrop of Monte Ingino is a feast for the eyes, with far too many fascinating corners to mention here. Down in the plain near the main car-parks is a 1st-century **amphitheatre**. Off *Pza Quaranta Martiri*, notice the unusual 14th-century **Loggia dei Tiratoi** (weavers' gallery), where cloth was stretched to dry. The nearby church of **San Francesco** contains lively frescos by Ottaviano Nelli. Climbing narrow alleys through the old town, visit the magnificent crenellated **Palazzo dei Consoli** on the grand *Pza della Signoria*. Gubbio's **Museo Civico** and **Pinacoteca** are inside the 16th-century rooms, *tel: (075) 927 42948,* open daily 1000–1330 and 1500–1800 (Apr–Sept); 1000–1300 and 1400–1700 (Oct–Mar); L4000. Prize

Olive Oil

All over Umbria and Tuscany, silvery olive groves testify to the importance of this basic ingredient of Italian cuisine. Increasing demand from foreign converts to olive oil (now believed to be a much healthier product than animal fats), has led to more industrialised methods of harvesting and manufacture, but there are still plenty of producers who pride themselves on traditional ways. You won't often see a donkey turning the grinding stones, but the end result is much the same. Harvest begins in about mid November and continues until Christmas, when the mills are in operation all day. The olives are washed and stripped of their leaves, then crushed to a pulp in the mill (including the stones). The paste is spread on discs and pressed to extrude a mixture of oil and water, which separates naturally into its components. The quality of olive oil depends on its acidity, which is largely a result of how fiercely the olives are squeezed. The best oil has a content of less than 1 per cent, and is known by that curious term 'Extra Virgin', which is suitable for salads and sauces. Less expensive grades are generally from successive pressings, and are used in more humdrum cookery. Be warned, not all oil bottled in Italy is grown there; large quantities are imported for processing.

Though olive trees look robust and live for many years, they take a long time to fruit and are very susceptible to frost. A single chilly night can ruin years of patient husbandry – hence the high prices on those gleaming bottles.

---

contents are the **Eugubine Tablets**, a series of bronze slabs inscribed with Etruscan and Latin characters. There are marvellous views from an upper loggia. Opposite stands the **Palazzo Pretorio.** Beyond the **Palazzo del Bargello**, a former prison, is the **Fontana dei Matti** (Fountain of the Mad) believed to send those who walk round it three times off their heads (if they aren't already).

In the *V. dei Consoli*, notice the blocked-up doorways, known as **Porte della Morte** (Doors of Death), whose purpose is debated. Higher up the town is the wagon-vaulted **Duomo**, and the imposing **Palazzo Ducale**, *V. Ducale; tel: (075) 927 5872 (Mon–Sat 0900–1330 and 1430–1900, Sun 0900–1330; L4000)* with a gracious Renaissance interior.

Near the Porta Romana lies an interesting cluster of churches, and a cable-car (*funivia*) takes passengers up the slopes of Monte Ingino to the **Basilica of Sant'Ubaldo**, housing the relics of Gubbio's patron saint and the huge *ceri* (see events). The cable-car runs from about 0900–1315 and 1430–1800 (precise times vary seasonally) and costs L5000 single; L6500 return. Journey time takes about 6 mins, and the open birdcage cabins (maximum 2 passengers) offer superb views of the town. Lift access is only for the spry, and not recommended for vertigo sufferers. Make sure your belongings are firmly attached before you set off! There's a panoramic bar/restaurant at the top, or take a picnic.

↔ Connections: Gubbio to Urbino and Perugia

Take the SS219 west for 2 km, then head north for 12km on the SS452 to join the N3; follow this main road north for 42 km to Fossombrone, then follow signposts west along the SS73bis to reach **Urbino** after 18 km. To reach **Perugia** from Gubbio, head south on the scenic SS298; Perugia is reached after 40km.

PERUGIA AND ASSISI

Less than 30 km apart, these two important Umbrian centres attract visitors for very different reasons. Perugia, Umbria's capital, combines historic interest and a splendid art collection with the multifaceted charms of a sophisticated modern city. The medieval hilltown of Assisi, birthplace of St Francis, has a more single-minded *raison d'être*, ranking second only to Rome as a pilgrimage site.

TOURIST INFORMATION

Perugia: *Pza IV Novembre; tel: (075) 572 3327* or *(075) 573 6458*, open Mon–Sat 0830–1330 and 1530–1830, Sun 0900–1300. The municipal office stands opposite the cathedral. **Head office** is at *V. Mazzini 21; tel: (075) 572 5341*, open Mon–Fri 0900–1300 and 1500–1900; a summer-only office is at the main railway station. Regional information is available at *Corso Vannucci 30*. Computerised *Digiplan* machines at the station and in Pza Italia give useful print-outs (when working). The monthly listings magazine *Perugia What, Where, When* (L 1000 from news-stands) is a helpful compendium of local information.

Assisi: *Pza del Comune 12; tel: (075) 812534*, open Mon–Sat 0800–1400 and 1530–1830, Sun 0900–1300. An overcrowded, poorly-stocked office where stone-faced staff grudgingly dispense a town map with scanty notes on the main sights. Accommodation lists, opening times and transport details may be prised from secret recesses by persistent visitors. Seasonal tourist offices can be found near *Largo Properzio (Porta Nuova); tel: (075) 816766*, and 4 km south down the hill in Santa Maria degli Angeli at *Pza Garibaldi; tel: (075) 812479*, and the railway station; *tel: (075) 813499*.

ARRIVING AND DEPARTING

By Air

Perugia's **Sant'Egidio airport** lies 15 km east of the centre; *tel: (075) 692 9447*. Most traffic is domestic; occasional *Alitalia* flights connect directly with London and other European cities. Taxis link the airport with the city centre.

By Car

Perugia's maniacal road systems make it a bewildering place for motorists. The city centre is inaccessible by car, and a steep uphill haul on foot. Less painful approaches are to follow signs to the centre as far as the car-parks (hourly tariff) in **Piazza dei Partigiani** (from the south), or **Viale Pellini** (from the west). Then take the escalators (*scala mobile*) up to the old town. The northern approach roads bring you in by the quieter university quarter, where there is parking at **Viale S. Antonio** and an easier walk to the centre. For a taxi, *tel: (075) 500 4888*.

Being a major tourist attraction, **Assisi** is very well signposted, and is easily reached from Perugia by following the N75 riad east from the city, then turning off on the SS147 after 10 km.

Assisi's historic quarter is also closed to tourist traffic and must be explored on foot or by the urban orange minibus service (buy tickets from news-stands, bars and tobacconists with ASP or Comune di Assisi sign). Pay car-parks can be found at intervals along the southern walls. The main ones are by *Porta Nuova* (south-east side) and *Pza Unità d'Italia* (near the Basilica). These get crammed with pilgrims and it's a steep climb to the town centre. A better choice is *Pza Matteotti* near the amphitheatre, which has another huge car-park with clean, free WCs. From here you can explore all the main sights without too much climbing, and enjoy the less thronged, more charming part of town before tackling Assisi's climactic Basilica. Free parking places can be found near the Rocca and Porta San Giacome on the north side of the walls.

By Bus

Perugia: Buses run to many Umbrian towns from *Pza dei Partigiani; tel: (075) 573 1707.* **Assisi:** The main bus terminal is in *Pza Matteotti;* buses also stop at Largo Properzio near the Basilica. There are regular services for Perugia Assisi is an immensely popular coach-tour destination.

By Train

Perugia: The main FS (state) railway station (Foligno–Terontola line) is on the south-west side of town in Fontevegge, *Pza V Veneto; tel: (147) 888088* a 15min bus ride from the centre. Services from Todi or the Tiber Valley towns use the private Ferrovia Centrale Umbra line and terminate at Sta Anna station; *tel: (075) 572 3947.* **Assisi:** rail station at Santa Maria degli Angeli, 4km south; *tel: (075) 804 0272* Regular services to Perugia. For Florence and Rome, change trains.

GETTING AROUND

Bus and train tickets can be purchased from **Agenzia Stoppini**, *Corso Mazzini 31; tel: (075) 812597.* Taxi ranks can be

found at the station and in several central squares. Assisi belongs to the Weekend in Umbria scheme: special tickets bought in conjunction with rail tickets entitle unlimited use of urban public transport at weekends and holidays for just L2000. Information from FS stations.

STAYING IN PERUGIA AND ASSISI

Accommodation and Food

Perugia: the regional capital is an important commercial centre with a wide range of hotels. Prices rise and vacancies evaporate during the popular July jazz festival. Motorists can obtain permission to drive to city centre hotels. Comfortable central hotels with garages include the luxury-bracket **Locanda della Posta**, *Corso Vannucci 97; tel: (075) 572 8925* (small and stylish), or the grand **Brufani**, *Pza Italia 12; tel: (075) 573 2541* and its slightly cheaper sister in the same *palazzo* , the **Palace Hotel Bellavista**, *Pza Italia 12; tel: (075) 572 0741.* Less pricey are the central **Fortuna**, *Vis Bonazzi 12; tel: (075) 22845*, or the cheerful **Rosalba**, *V. del Circo 7; tel: (075) 572 8285*, with easy access to parking and the old town. An excellent base outside Perugia (15km south-east) is the Lungarotti family's superb hotel **Le Tre Vaselle**, *V. Garibaldi 48, Torgiano; tel: (075) 982447*, with its outstanding restaurant (expensive) and wine museum (see also Out of Town). At the budget end, there are plenty of student rooms and *pensiones*. Youth hostel accommodation on *V. Bontempi 13; tel: (075) 572 2880* is a bit grim; the nearest campsite is 5km away in Colle della Trinità.

Eating in the city centre presents no problems, with lots of budget options catering for Perugia's student population. Elegant choices include **La Rosetta**, *Pza Italia 19; tel: (075) 572 0841* (closed

Mon); **Falchetto**, *V. Bartolo 20; tel: (075) 573 1775* (closed Mon); **La Taverna**, *V. delle Streghe 8; tel: (075) 572 4128* (closed Mon) or **Osteria del Bartolo**, *V. Bartolo 30; tel: (075) 573 1561* (closed Sun and part of Jan and Aug). For innovative but less expensive food, try **Aladino del Sole**, *V. delle Prome 11; tel: (075) 572 0938* (closed Mon and Aug). A Perugian speciality is chocolate, sold in beautifully packaged boxes throughout the town. Look for *Baci* (kisses) in silver paper. Sample a bottle of the famed Lungarotti wine from Torgiano while in the area – Rubesco and San Giorgio are among Umbria's best.

Assisi: About a hundred hotels, *pensiones* and hostels accommodate thousands of pilgrim visitors. Even so, they quickly get booked up in August and during major festivals such as Easter, Festa di St Francesco (3–4 Oct) and Calendimaggio in May. The tourist office has lists of lodgings in religious institutions and private rooms (some very cheap). Out of town there are *agriturismo* establishments, two campsites, and a couple of youth hostels.

Top-range hotels include **Subasio**, *V. Frate Elia 2; tel (075) 812206* and **Fontebella**, *V. Fontebella 25; tel: (075) 816456*. Less expensive but very charming is the **Albergo Umbra**, *V. degli Archi 6; tel: (075) 812240* (closed mid Jan–mid Mar), family-run with an excellent restaurant (closed Tues). Just outside the walls, the **Country House**, *San Pietro Campagna 178; tel: (075) 816363,* is a quiet, friendly place furnished with antiques. **Sant'Antonio's Guesthouse of the Suore dell'Atonement**, *V. G Alessi 10; tel: (075) 812542* is a peaceful and unascetic guesthouse run by American nuns (closed mid Nov–mid Mar).

Many of Assisi's restaurants cater indifferently for a captive tourist trade, with some notable exceptions. The **Buca di San Francesco**, *V. Brizi 1; tel: (075) 812204*, is one of the best, central, with a garden (pricey, closed Mon and July). **Medioevo**, *V. Arco dei Priori 4b; tel: (075) 813068* offers accomplished cooking in an elegant medieval setting (expensive, closed Wed, Jan and early July); **La Fortezza**, *Vicolo della Fortezza 2; tel: (075) 812418* is also recommendable (moderate, closed Thur and Feb). **La Bottega dei Sapori**, *Pza del Comune 34; tel: (075) 812294* has a lovely range of regional food products. **Pasticceria Santa Monica**, *V. Portica 4* sells Assisi's typical cakes and pastries made with fruit and nuts.

Communications

Post Office **Perugia:** *Pza Matteotti*, open Mon–Sat 0810–1930, Sun 0830–1730.

Assisi: *Pza del Comune; tel: (075 812355*, open Mon–Fri 0810–1825, Sat 0810–1300.

Money

Perugia: Currency can be exchanged at the main post office, the railway station, **CIT** on *Pza IV Novembre,* and most of the banks on *Corso Vannucci;* some in *Pza Italia* have automatic machines.

Assisi: Currency exchange at the main post office, the railway station, **Agenzia Stoppini**, *Corso Mazzini; tel: (075) 812597*, open Mon–Fri 0900–1230 and 1530–1900, Sat 0900–1230 and **Inter Change**, *V. San Francesco 20D; tel: (075) 816220*, open daily 0900–2000. There are autobank facilities at **Cassa di Risparmio**, *Pza del Comune* and *Pza Unità d'Italia*, **Banca Popolare**, *Pza Sta Chiara 19*, and **Banca Toscana**, *Pza Stan Pietro 6*.

Events

Perugia: Among a programme of cultural events, the **Umbria Jazz Festival** in mid

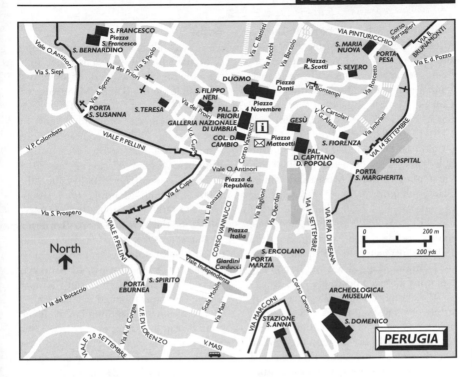

North ↑

PERUGIA

179

July is world-famous. Information: *tel: (075) 573 3363* or *573 2432*. Open-air theatre productions are held July–Aug; classical music concerts in Sept.

Assisi: Predictably, Assisi's calendar is geared to religious festivals. Easter Week stages mystery plays and processions. On Aug 1–2 sins are forgiven at the **Perdono**, and Oct 3–4 is the **Festa di San Francesco**, a pilgrimage celebrating the saint's birthday. On a more secular note, the **Festa di Calendimaggio** (first week in May) is a spring carnival, and the **Festa Pro Musica** a summer concert programme.

SIGHTSEEING

Perugia

Above busy industrial suburbs, the medieval city stands proudly intact on its hilly dais. The escalators from the Pza dei Partigiani car-park take you through an eerie subterranean labyrinth of the city's Etruscan, Roman and medieval foundations. Remains of defensive systems, and ancient water cisterns can be seen. From Piazza Italia and the Prefettura, the two broad thoroughfares of *Corso Vannucci* and *V. Baglioni* lead past smart shops and tidy squares to the city's heart. Major sights are clustered around *Piazza IV Novembre*, including the **Duomo**, open daily 0800–1200 and 1600–1930, free, housing the Virgin's agate wedding ring, and the splendid Gothic **Palazzo dei Priori** (now the town hall). The fourth floor houses the **Galleria Nazionale d'Umbria**; *tel: (075) 574 1247* (Mon–Sat 0900–1900, Sun and hols 0900–1300; L8000) with masterpieces by Perugino and Fra Angelico. Steps opposite the Duomo lead into the **Sala dei Notari** (lawyers meeting hall; daily June–Aug 0900–1300 and 1500–1900, closed Mon out of season; free). Separate entrances from Corso Vannucci give access to the **Collegio del Cambio** (exchange guild); *tel: (075) 572 8599*, open Mon–Sat 0900–1230 and 1430–1730, Sun and hols 0900–1230 (Mar–Oct); Tues–Sat 0800–1400, Sun and hols 0900–1230 (Nov–Feb); L5000 and the **Collegio della Mercanzia** (merchants guild); *tel: (075) 573 0366* (similar opening times; L2000; combined ticket for both costs L6000). These fine civic rooms are decorated with frescos and exquisite marquetry. In the square, notice the **Fontana Maggiore** with carved marble basins shrouded beneath a glass dome.

Wandering through Perugia's hilly streets past Etruscan arches and medieval towers and gateways is a delightful if tiring experience. Best bits lie around **Piazza Danti**, site of a fascinating Etruscan well (at No 18) dating from the 3rd century BC, and the church of **San Severo** on *V. Raffaello* containing damaged frescoes by Raphael, both open Mon–Fri 1030–1330 and 1430–1630, weekends and hols until 1730 (Oct–Mar); daily 1000– 1330 and 1430–1830 (Apr–Sept); joint ticket L3000. At the north-west end of town, the **Oratorio di San Bernardino** on *Pza di San Francesco* has a facade of wonderfully carved reliefs by Duccio. Notice the section depicting the Bonfire of the Vanities. Next to it stands the church of **San Francesco al Prato**, begun in 1253. Other churches to look out for include ancient **Sant'Angelo** on *Corso Garibaldi*, incorporating Roman masonry. **San Domenico**, Umbria's biggest church, containing the tomb of a poisoned pope and **San Pietro** with its magnificently decorated interior are at the south end of town, both on *Corso Cavour*.

Assisi

The town's hilltop setting below the slopes of Monte Subasio is best appreciated from the more rural northerly side of town. Best views are from the **Rocca Maggiore**, *tel: (075) 815292*, open daily 1000–dusk, L5000, a fortress originally built by Barbarossa in 1174. A combined ticket costing L10,000 also allows access to the **Pinoteca**, *Palazzo Comunale; tel: (075) 812579*, open daily 1000–1300 and 1500–1900 (mid Mar–mid Oct), 1000–1300 and 1400–1700 (mid Oct–mid Mar); L4000 and the **Museo e Foro Romano**, *V. Portica; tel: (075) 813053* (same opening times; L4000). On the central *Piazza del Comune* stands the **Tempio di Minerva**, the pediment and columns from a Roman temple (now incorporated in a church).

The commercialism found in many pilgrimage centres has not escaped Assisi, but all the churches are free of charge. In view of Assisi's indifferent tourist literature, it's worth investing in a decent guide to the basilica frescos. A handful of L500 coins is useful to light up the paintings, or for multilingual audio-guide machines in the churches. Visitors considered improperly clad may be refused admittance – sundresses, shorts, miniskirts and tank tops are unacceptable.

Assisi's dominant sight, unmissable at the west end of town from the S75 Perugia–Foligno bypass, is the colossal porticoed **Basilica di San Francesco**, *tel: (075) 813061*, open 0630–1930 (Mar–Oct), 0630–1700 (Oct–Mar), tourist visits not allowed on Sun am, feast days or during services. Tours take place in English Mon–Sat at 1000 and 1500. Pilgrims pay homage to Italy's patron saint; art lovers admire the amazing frescos that smother its walls. No visitor can fail to be struck by the contrast between the lavish grandeur of this church and the simple

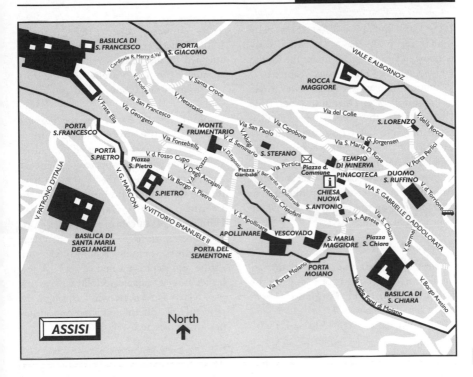

ASSISI

North
↑

asceticism of the founding Franciscan. The Basilica consists of two churches, a Gothic one superimposed on an older Romansque one. With characteristic humility, St Francis chose an anonymous burial site on 'Hell Hill', unconsecrated ground where criminals were executed. After his death in 1226, one of his most influential followers, Elias of Cortona, began masterminding a vast building project on the site of his grave, financed by the sale of indulgences. The saint's body now lies in a plain stone tomb in the crypt of the lower church, which contains bright medieval frescos by Martini, Lorenzetti, and Cimubue. The subjects include biblical and saintly episodes. The upper church (now sadly closed because of earthquake damage) contains a remarkable cycle of frescos by the school of Giotto (the extent of the master's involvement is debated), depict-

ing scenes from the life of St Francis. One of the most famous and charming panels shows the saint preaching to the birds. After leaving the Basilica di San Francesco, follow the city walls down to the Porta San Pietro to glance at the simple Benedictine church of **San Pietro**, and a wide panorama of the Vale of Spoleto.

For most pilgrims, the next priority on the Franciscan trail is the massively buttressed **Basilica di Santa Chiara**, *Pza Sta Chiara*, open daily 0700–1200 and 1400–dusk, last resting place of St Clare, the most devoted of St Francis's followers and the founder of the Poor Clares, the Franciscan order of nuns. Clare's gruesomely pickled body lies on view in the crypt. The Romanesque **Duomo**, *Pza San Rufino* (same opening times as Santa Chiara; crypt and museum, open daily 1000–1200 and 1430–1800 (Mar–Nov),

1000–1200 and 1400–1700 (Nov–Feb); L4000 for both) has a beautiful rose-windowed facade, and contains the font in which Clare and Francis were baptized.

Outside the walls among olive groves (1 km south), **San Damiano** (open daily 1000–1800) is the church where Francis heard the voice of Christ asking him to 'Repair my house', and where St Clare established her convent.

Further south, **Santa Maria degli Angeli** is a latter-day construction in baroque style on the site of the hut where Francis spent his final days.

OUT OF TOWN

While in **Perugia**, no wine enthusiast should miss the chance of a visit to the Lungarotti winery in **Torgiano** (15 km SE), *Corso V Emanuele 11; tel: (075) 988 0200*, open daily 0900–1300 and 1500–1900 (summer), closes 1800 (winter); L5000 where an excellent wine museum attached to the family's renowned hotel-restaurant (**Le Tre Vaselle**) tells the story of Umbrian viticulture. Local produce is sold.

North-east of **Assisi** lies the regional park of **Monte Subasio** (1290 m), a delightful expanse of dappled woodland and wildlife where visitors may experience a more vivid sense of the Franciscan spirit than in the town of his birth. Here, at the **Eremo delle Carceri** (Carceri Hermitage), 4 km east of Assisi from Porta Cappuccini, *tel: (075) 812301,* open daily dawn–dusk, Francis communed with nature and slept on a bed of rock. A few brown-robed Franciscans follow his example today. Tiny lanes wind through the peaceful hills, offering enticing opportunities for picnics and walks.

St Francis

St Francis of Assisi is probably the best-known of all Italian saints. His writings and teachings, underpinned by a life of exemplary humility and kindness, shook the worldly medieval Church to its foundations and endeared him to countless followers. Born in 1182 to a wealthy merchant, Francis had a privileged upbringing, and embarked on a predictably dissipated life of drinking and womanising. A long bout of illness concentrated his thoughts. After a damascene revelation during Mass in 1209, Francis renounced his former life by stripping publicly and dressing in sackcloth, to his father's furious amazement. He spent the rest of his days in poverty, preaching and travelling, but despite intense hardships, never lost his simple *joie de vivre*: 'Be not sad and gloomy like hypocrites, but be joyful in the Lord, merry and pleasant.' Gathering his own apostles, including St Clare, he eventually gained permission from the Pope to found a religious order dedicated to serving the poor. His writings, influenced by the troubadour traditions of southern France, include the *Fioretti* (Little Flowers) and the *Canticle of the Sun* (Brother Sun . . . Sister Moon). Many legends affirm his love of nature. He is said to have tamed a fierce wolf, and preached sermons to attentive birds. In 1224 Francis fell into a deep trance while praying at La Verna near Arezzo, and awoke to find the marks of the stigmata on his hands and feet. His health broken by tireless travelling and self-deprivation, he died aged only 45 near Assisi, leaving behind an influential but divided Order of zealots who rigidly upheld their founder's message of absolute poverty, and a more pragmatic group led by Elias of Cortona determined to achieve Franciscan aims by organised fund raising. Francis was canonised in 1228, just two years after his death.

URBINO–SPOLETO
THE VALE OF SPOLETO

Most of this tour follows an ancient Roman road, the *V. Flaminia* (now the S3), which starts on the Adriatic coast, slices through the Marches (Le Marche) and terminates, naturally enough, in Rome. It's a well-used primary route, easy to trace on a map, leading through green, hilly scenery for most of the way, and bypassing major towns. The final, low-lying stretch through the Vale of Spoleto passes beside an extinct lake bed and is drearily industrialised, but the hill towns just off the main road are real gems in classic Umbrian countryside, many with Franciscan associations. Highlights, however, lie at either end of the route, in Urbino and Spoleto. To explore them fully, allow several days.

Urbino

S3

Gualdo Tadino

S3

Spello

Foligno

S316

Bevagna

S3

Montefalco

Trevi

S3

Spoleto

ROUTE: 120 KM

ROUTE

The splendid town of **Urbino** makes a memorable starting-point for this tour. Spend a night or two there if you can. From Urbino, follow signs for Urbania from the town centre, then turn left on the minor Fermignano road just beyond the city walls. At **Fermignano**, take signs for **Acqualagna** along a minor road through a photogenic stretch of hills. Acqualagna is a renowned truffle centre. If you happen to be passing through this unremarkable little market town on a late autumn morning, a pungent scent may attract you to the stalls displaying the prized fungus. Detour briefly from Acqualagna north-east along the minor road to Furlo, pausing at the **Abbazia San Vincenzo al Furlo**, an 11th-century Lombardic church of frescoed limestone. Beyond lies a spectacular gorge (Gola di Furlo) cut by the River Candigliano, where you may spy eagles soaring on the thermals.

Heading south again on the S3 towards **Cagli**, you pass the scenic uplands of the **Parco di Monte Cucco** on your left hand before entering **Gualdo Tadino**. From here the well-engineered S3 continues south past the spa town of Nocera Umbra and through the wooded Topino Valley, where the hills of Monte Subasio rise towards Assisi in the west. The *V. Flaminia* joins the main Perugia road at the busy junction of **Foligno.** Detour 6km north-west to the magical town of **Spello**, then head 7.5 km south-west on the S316 from Foligno to **Bevagna** and then to **Montefalco**. Return through central Foligno (preferably avoiding rush hour!), then cross the S3 for a glance at the **Abbazia di Sassovivo**, 4 km east of the town. Returning to the main road, head southwards through the Vale of Spoleto, detouring through olive groves to **Trevi.** Pause 4 km south of Trevi at the tiny

Tempio di Clitunno (a tricky sign to spot) and the **Fonti del Clitunno** (1 km further on) before finishing the tour in **Spoleto**. This is another fascinating historic town worth at least one night's stay. Book well ahead during festival time (late June–July).

URBINO

Tourist Office: *Pza Rinascimento 1; el: (0722) 2613*, open Mon–Sat 0900–1300 and 1500–1800, Sun 0900–1300.

ACCOMMODATION AND FOOD

Smartest hotel in town is the 4-star **Bonconte**, *V. delle Mura 28; tel: (0722) 2463* in a fine position by the walls. Another attractive central hotel is the **Raffaello**, *V. Santa Margherita 40; tel: (0722) 4896* near Raphael's House. Lists of private rooms and student accommodation are available at the tourist office. Eight km up the Fano road, the **Locanda La Brombolona** in *Sant'Andrea* in *Primicillio 32, Canavaccio; tel: (0722) 53501* offers a peaceful country stay in a 16th-century church. Also outside the town, **Camping Pineta** has lovely views, *V. San Donato, Località Cesana; tel: (0722) 4710*, open Easter–Sept.

Urbino suits those on a tight budget, with a good cheap student cafeteria, **Mensa Universitaria**, *Colle dei Cappuccini; tel: (0722) 329251* and plenty of snack bars, self-service restaurants and takeaways. Despite Marche's penchant for meat, there are vegetarian places in town. Top-range restaurants include **Vecchia Urbino**, *V. dei Vasari 3; tel: (0722) 4447* (closed Tues) and **Cortegiano**, *V. Puccinotti 13; tel: (0722) 320307* (closed Mon and mid Dec–Jan). **Tre Pianti**, *V. Voltaccia della Vecchia 1; tel: (0722) 4863* (closed Mon) is a popular student trattoria with an attractive verandah. Grills and roasts, stuffed rabbit and pigeon and cured pork are specialities. Look out for *crescioni* (flaky pastry stuffed with savoury fillings) and *strozzapreti* (a solid kind of pasta).

SIGHTSEEING

Urbino would be a highlight anywhere in Italy; here in the unsung region of Marche it stands out like a beacon. Its monumental buildings rising from a steep hillside immediately instil the impression of grandeur and nobility which makes it in some eyes Italy's perfect surviving Renaissance city. Urbino is no aspic tourist town, however; its student population keeps life humming, especially during the June Jazz Festival. The old quarter is compact and, though hilly, can easily be explored on foot.

The most prominent sight is the **Palazzo Ducale**, distinguished by its fairy tale towers and interlinking loggias. This gorgeous Renaissance building now houses the **Galleria Nazionale delle Marche**, *Pza Duca Federico; tel: (0722) 2760*, open daily 0900–1400; L8000, a collection of paintings assembled by the Montefeltri family, 15th-century Dukes of Urbino. Best known among them are the *Città Ideale* (Ideal City), variously attributed to Luciano Laurana (the palace architect) and Piero della Francesca. Two other works by Piero also attract attention: a puzzling *Flagellation of Christ* and *La Madonna di Senigallia*, along with works by Raphael, Titian and Uccello and portraits of the one-eyed, hook-nosed warrior Duke Federico (the most famous likeness, by Piero, now hangs in Florence's Uffizi). The richly decorated palace interior makes a fine setting for the gallery. Don't miss the Duke's study (**Studiolo**) encrusted with magnificent intarsia panelling and the **library** with the family eagle painted on the ceiling.

Urbino's other sights are less blockbusting, but together the historic buildings form a harmonious ensemble linked on various levels by ramps and steps. On either side of the palace stand Urbino's prestigious **university** and the **Duomo**, an 18th-century refit after earthquake damage. The **Oratorio di San Giovanni**, and **San Giuseppe** next door, *V. Barocci* (Mon–Sat 1000–1200 and 1500–1700, Sun 1000–1230; joint admission L5000) are small chapels smothered with Gothic frescos. The **Casa di Raffaello**, *V. Raffaello 57; tel: (0722) 320105*, open Mon–Sat 0900–1300 and 1500–1900, Sun 0900–1300; L5000, where Urbino's famous native painter was born, is a museum. The elegant interior indicates something of Raphael's well-to-do background. The exhausting climb to the upper ramparts rewards you with astonishing views from the **Fortezza dell'Albernoz**.

GUALDO TADINO

Tourist Office: Pro Tadino, *V. Calai 39*.

Tadinum was a Roman staging post along the *V. Flaminia*, the scene of the battle where Totila the Goth was killed in 442 as he advanced destructively on Rome, and the birthplace of the painter Matteo da Gualdo in 1435. For all these historic footnotes, there isn't much to see today. The modern town prospers on its ceramics industry. In the old quarter the best buildings lie around its central *Pza Martiri della Libertà*: a Gothic **Duomo** with a wall fountain, a few churches and a couple of restored palaces. The town keeps some of Matteo's works on display at the **Pinoteca Comunale** *Pza Soprammuro; tel: (075) 916647*; the key is held at the main square's police station (*Vigili Urbani*).

For keen walkers, Gualdo Tadino's budget hotels make a convenient base for exploring the **Parco di Monti Cucco** to the north: a pleasant stretch of beechclad Appenines with a limestone cavern. A shorter excursion follows the minor road up to **Valsorda** 8 km north-east, climbing past verges splashed with wild flowers. The fact that this is a popular weekend walking spot explains the bar and *porchetta* van (serving rolls filled with roast pork carved off the bone), which provide simple sustenance at the end of the road. From here a broad track leads up Santa Serra (1421 m). Valsorda has basic camping facilities; *tel: (075) 913261.*

SPELLO

Tourist Office: **Pro Loco**, *Pza Matteotti 3; tel: (0742) 301009*, open Mon–Sat 0930–1230 and 1530–1830.

ACCOMMODATION AND FOOD

The increasing popularity of this charming medieval town has resulted in several smart new hotels – all pricey. Centrally placed are **Del Teatro**, *V. Giulia 24; tel: (075) 301140*, and the **Palazzo Bocci**, *V. Cavour 17; tel: (0742) 301021.* A pleasant choice on the west edge of town is **La Bastiglia**, *Pza Valle Gloria 7; tel: (0742) 651277*, a modernised mill overlooking woods and hills (moderate; closed Jan). **Camping Umbria** is the nearest campsite 2 km east at Chiona; *tel: (0742) 651772* (Apr–Oct). Smart restaurants include **Il Molino**, *Pza Matteotti 6; tel: (0742) 651305* (closed Tues) and **La Cantina**, *V. Cavour 2; tel: (0742) 651775* (closed Wed). **Pinturicchio**, *Largo Mazzini 8; tel: (0742) 301003* (closed Tues) is a good cheap trattoria. For informal eating, Spello offers panoramic picnic spots at the top of the town, mouthwatering displays of local *prodotti tipici*, and plenty of ice cream and cakes. Try the local speciality breads made with grape juice: *fregnaccia* or *rocci.*

SIGHTSEEING

Legionnaires pensioned off in the Roman town of Hispellum can't have grumbled about their retirement home. Set on the southern slopes of Monte Subasio, Spello is a gorgeous spot overlooking olive groves. Within a pilgrim's hike of Assisi, it has many Franciscan associations. St Clare set up her second convent here (the Monasterio di Vallegloria). Spello is easily accessible by public transport (bus and train) from Assisi and Perugia and often visited as a day-trip. The town comes alive during its Corpus Christi **Infiorate** festival when the streets are covered with flower carpets. In Feb the **Festa dell'Olivo** and **Sagra della Bruscetta** celebrate the local olive harvest.

Beyond the 14th-century **Porta Portanaccio** and the Roman **Porta Consolare** at the base of the town, *V. Consolare* and *V. Cavour* form a central spine leading past the main sights. Most striking of Spello's many churches is **Santa Maria Maggiore**, the walls of the Cappella Baglioni smothered with vivid biblical frescos by Pinturicchio (make use of the light machines to see them properly). The **Pinacoteca Civica**, open Mon–Sat 1000–1300 and 1530–1830; L5000, in the Palazzo dei Canonici contains another rich collection of Umbrian art.

Further up the hill lies **Sant'Andrea**, containing another Pinturicchio Madonna. At the top of the town, picturesque side alleys and belvederes offer bucolic views. From the **Rocca** a ruined amphitheatre is visible.

Lanes from Porta Montanara lead to the tumbledown 12th-century church of **San Claudio** and the **Villa Fidelia**, containing the private **Straka Coppa Collection** of Italian art and furniture, open Sat–Sun 1030–1300 and 1500–1800 (Oct–Mar); Thur–Sun 1030–1300 and 1600–1830 (Apr–June and Sept); 1030–1300 and 1600–1900 (July–Aug); L3000. Also accessible from this gateway are the monastery of **San Girolamo** (1 km); and the walled village of **Collepino** 6 km; (keen enthusiasts can continue up Monte Subasio to the Eremo di Carceri and Assisi from here).

FOLIGNO

Tourist Office: *Porta Romana 126; tel: (0742) 354459* or *Pza Garibaldi 12; tel: (0742) 350493.*

This sizeable town is a busy route hub now encased in industrial sprawl. In the middle ages it had an important paper industry, and it was here that the first copies of Dante's *Divine Comedy* were printed. A few bits of its medieval past survived wartime bombing, notably in the *Pza della Republica*, where the **Duomo** has a charmingly carved doorway showing signs of the zodiac and mysterious beasts. Close by, the frescoed **Palazzo Trinci**, former home of Foligno's ruling *signori*, contains the **Pinacoteca** with works from the Umbrian and Sienese schools.

East of the S3, a minor road winds 4 km up to the 11th-century **Abbazia di Sassovivo** on the wooded slopes of Monte Serrone. Still occupied by a Benedictine community, it has a Romanesque cloister of 128 marble columns.

BEVAGNA

Tourist Office: **Town Hall**, *Corso Matteotti; tel: (0742) 360123* or **Pro Loco**, *Pza F. Silvestri; tel: (0742) 361667*, open Mon–Sat 0930–1300 and 1500–1900.

Few visitors fail to be enchanted by this little town, which has preserved its medieval character almost perfectly. The original settlement is much older, pre-dating even the Roman municipium of Mevania which stood on a former routeing of the *V. Flaminia* (vestigial Roman tombs are still visible along the arrow-straight Bevagna–Foligno road). When the Romans jammed a new bypass through the Vale of Spoleto, Mevania became a backwater.

In June, Bevagna attracts many visitors for its lively medieval fair, the **Mercato delle Gaite**; for information; *tel: (0742) 361847.* Traditional crafts such as basket-making and hemp-spinning are demonstrated (rope-making was once a local trade). Hotels are scarce. Simple board and lodging is available at the **Monasterio di Santa Maria del Monte**, *Corso Metteotti 15; tel: (0742) 360133*, run by Benedictine nuns. *Agriturismo* places are listed nearby, and a 3-star campsite at **Pian di Boccio**; *tel: (0742) 360391.* Recommendable eating places include **Ottavius**, *V. del Gonfalone 4; tel: (0742) 360555* (closed Mon and early July) and **Da Nina**, *Pza Garibaldi; tel: (0742) 360161* (closed Tues). There's a regular bus service from Foligno.

Bevagna's main attractions focus on its lovely central square, **Piazza Silvestri**, where two fascinating Romanseque churches flank a graceful fountain. **San Silvestro** dates from 1195 and incorporates Roman masonry. Inside, once your eyes adjust to the gloom, notice the unusual Egyptian-style decorations on the columns, resembling papyrus fronds. **San Michele** opposite has wonderful gargoyles and portal carvings of angels and beastly demons battling for supremacy. A third church, dedicated to SS Domenico and Giacomo, has fresco fragments and 13th-century sculptures. Steps lead up to the

187

sturdy 12th-century **Palazzo dei Consoli**, which houses the tourist office and a delightful restored 19th-century theatre, the **Teatro Torti** (ask for the key at the tourist office and someone may let you peep inside). On *Corso Matteotti*, the **Palazzo Comunale** contains a small museum and art gallery, open Tues–Sun 1030–1300 and 1530–1800; L5000. There are more Roman remains near the well-preserved eastern walls including faint outlines of an **amphitheatre** and the pillars of a **temple** near *Pza Garibaldi*. Most memorable by far, though, is a marvellous black-and-white 2nd-century **mosaic** of writhing sea creatures in a bathhouse on *V. Porta Guelfa* (the key is held next door at no.2; free). In the nearby church of **San Francesco**, a plaque marks a stone from which St Francis allegedly preached his renowned 'Brother Birds' sermon at a spot on the Cannara road.

MONTEFALCO

Tourist Information: maps, walking leaflets and guides to the frescos are available from the **Museo Civico di San Francesco**,*V. Ringhiera Umbra; tel: (0742) 379598*, and also from the town hall (**Comune di Montefalco**), *Corso Mameli 68; tel: (0742) 378673*.

Known as the 'Balcony of Umbria', this little hill town enjoys panoramic views over olive groves and vineyards. The town itself is photogenic too, apart from its crass modern water-tower. Within the walls, its tidily swept streets lead past ancient churches to a wide horseshoe-shaped square. Just off it lies the 14th-century church of **San Francesco**, now the town's main museum and art gallery (see Tourist Information above), open daily 1030–1300 and 1400–1800 (Mar–May and Sept–Oct); 1030–1300 and 1500–1900 (June–July); 1030–1300 and

1500–1930 (Aug); Tues–Sun 1030–1300 and 1430–1700 (Nov–Feb); L6000. Its main interest is a cycle of clear and colourful frescos in the apse by Benozzo Gozzoli, a pupil of Fra Angelico. The subject is the life of St Francis. **Sant'Agostino**, on *V. Umberto I*, and **Santa Chiara** on *V. Verdi*, contain more frescos and some saintly mummies in glass cases. A 10-min walk south of town along *Vle Marconi* brings you to the monastery of **San Fortunato**, with more Gozzoli frescos.

Montefalco makes an attractive touring base for a night. The Bevagna bus route from Foligno passes through the town. Its best hotel is the **Villa Pambuffetti**, *V. Vittoria 3; tel: (0742) 378823* in lovely grounds (expensive). A more modest choice within the walls is the **Ringhiera Umbra**, *V. Umberto 1; tel: (0742) 79166*. Both these have good restaurants; another outstanding eating place is **Coccorone**, *Largo Tempestivi; tel: (0742) 379535* (it has a wine bar of the same name on *Pza del Comune*). While in Montefalco, be sure to sample some of the local **Sagrantino** wine, a powerful dry red made from a grape variety unique to the area. It's on sale in the town; try the *enotecas* on the main square for a taste.

TREVI

Tourist Office: *Pza Mazzini 6; tel: (0742) 781150*, open daily 0930–1300 and 1600–2000.

Three access roads (*tre vie* – hence the town's name) clamber from the *V. Flaminia* up the steep hillside on which Trevi perches, passing through a silver-green sea of olive groves. The town is famous for its high-quality oil, on sale locally. Some producers allow visits during pressing times (list available from the tourist office).

The walled centre, now spruced up for

visitors, is paved with patterned cobbles. Trevi is a lively place with an enterprising calendar of cultural events. On 27 Jan the **dell'Illuminata** procession honours St Emiliano by candlelight. **Trevi in Piazza** is a summer arts festival. The medieval **Palio dei Terzieri** takes place in Oct. A new museum complex, including the **Museo della Citta e del Territorio** and the **Museo dell'Olio**, along with the relocated **Pinacoteca**, now resides in the convent of **San Francesco**. The **Palazzo Lucarini**, next to the **Duomo**, open 1100–1300 and 1530–1900 holds the **Flash Art Museum** of modern art. The central cathedral church of **Sant'Emiliano** is ornate baroque within its quaint 12th-century shell. Further down the hillside, the **Madonna delle Lacrime** contains an *Epiphany* by Perugino, and frescos by Lo Spagna (if shut, ask for the keys at the orphanage next door). **San Martino** also has some worthy Umbrian art.

Trevi has few places to stay: **Il Terziere**, *V. Coste 1*; tel: (0742) 78359 and **Del Pescatore**, *V. Chiesa Tonda 5; tel: (0742) 780483* are probably the best bets. Both have excellent restaurants, especially the latter's **Taverna del Pescatore**; *tel: (0742) 780290* (closed Wed). Check menus for black celery, a local delicacy.

Regular trains run from Foligno and Spoleto to the station at the foot of the hill; from here, buses take you to *Pza Garibaldi*.

Back on the *V. Flaminia*, pause 4 km south of Trevi to look at the **Tempietto del Clitunno** on the west side of the road (the sign is small and easily missed). This intriguing little church was long thought to be a pagan temple, but is now (thanks to Goethe) recognised as a very early Christian building assembled from salvaged antiquities. Columns and pediments enhance an interior of faded frescos.

One km further south, pull off the road again at the **Fonti del Clitunno**, where the River Clitunno bubbles from scores of underground springs into a series of clear turquoise pools, romantically shaded by willows and poplars. Once sacred to the ancients and celebrated in classical and Romantic poetry, this idyllic spot is now a well-kept tourist enterprise with a restaurant and coach park, open daily 0900–1900; L1500.

SPOLETO

Tourist Office: *Pza della Libertà 7; tel: (0743) 220311,* open Mon–Fri 0900–1300 and 1400–1700, Sat–Sun 1000–1300 and 1630–1930; open daily until 2100 during Festival dei Due Mondi).

GETTING AROUND

Spoleto is well served by public transport. The **rail station**, *tel: (0743) 48516* (Rome–Ancona line, with local services to Foligno, Terni, Todi, etc.) lies 1 km north (ATAF bus connections to *Pza della Libertà* in the upper town; buy tickets from the newsagent). **Spolentina buses** serve the Nera Valley, Vale of Spoleto, Montefalco, etc., from various locations in town. Ask the tourist office for timetables. For motorists, Spoleto is less user friendly: driving and parking in the centre is very difficult. Best places to dump a car are around the Rocca or near the southern Porta San Matteo. The lower town carparks near *Pza Garibaldi* leave you with a lot of climbing unless you can find a bus.

ACCOMMODATION AND FOOD

Spoleto has over two dozen hotels, but during the popular Two Worlds Festival (June–July) demand outstrips supply.

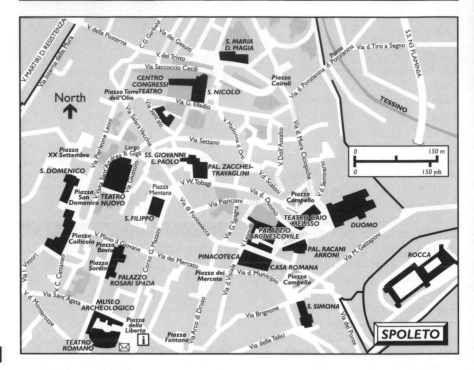

Book well ahead for a room, and expect high prices. By far the most attractively located of the central 4-stars is the stylish **Gattapone**, *V. del Ponte 6; tel: (0743) 223447* with a dazzling view of the Ponte delle Torri (parking; no restaurant). Most upper town hotels are tricky for motorists; the lower town is less appealing.

Just north of town, **La Macchia**, *Località Licina 11; tel: (0743) 49059,* is quiet and friendly, with good cooking (restaurant closed Tues) and easy parking. The tourist office has lists of private rooms and *agriturismo*. There's a nice little camp-site with super views, **Camping Monteluco**, *tel: (0743) 220358,* near San Pietro church 1km south-east (Apr–Sept).

Il Tartufo, *Pza Garibaldi 24; tel: (0743) 40236 (closed Wed and late July)* is one of Spoleto's top restaurants (pricey and truffle ridden). Book ahead. Less daunting

eating places include **Il Pentagramma**, *V. Martani 4; tel: (0743) 223141 (closed Mon)*; **Del Mercato,** *Pza Mercato 29; tel: (0743) 45325 (closed Mon)*; **Il Panciolle**, *V. del Duomo 3; tel: (0743) 45598 (closed Wed)* – all moderately priced and attractively set in the old town.

The wooded path towards Monteluco beyond the Ponte delle Torri is a good place for a picnic; buy provisions from the market stalls and mouthwatering deli-catessens around the *Pza del Mercato* (main market day is Fri). *Porchetta* (roast pork) is a speciality.

Events

The **Festival dei Due Mondi** (Two Worlds), mid June–mid July, has achieved international status since its debut in 1958 and is now Italy's leading arts festival (see box). Information and tickets available

The Festival of the Two Worlds

S poleto's annual Festival dei due Mondi is one of Italy's leading cultural events, attracting international audiences and performers of world renown. It was first held in 1958, when the composer Giancarlo Menotti selected Spoleto from a wide choice of possible venues. The aim was to fuse outstanding American and Italian artistic talent, hence the festival's name (the other 'world' is in Charleston, South Carolina).

The festival is held in late June/early July for a fortnight, but other associated events take place all summer. It encompasses all branches of the performing arts: music, opera, dance and theatre – including a healthy mixture of 'fringe' events. The opera star Luciano Pavarotti topped the bill in 1997. The festival's 40-year history has not been entirely harmonious; tensions between town authorities and the festival organisers (including Menotti's adopted son, Francis) have led to some discord in recent years. For all that, it continues to attract huge crowds, and tickets for major events can be extremely expensive and difficult to obtain.

Spoleto at festival time is a memorable place, but if the festival is not your main priority, the town is best enjoyed at a different time of year. If you want to experience the Due Mondi, book accommodation well ahead. Information is available from the tourist office in *Pza della Libertà* or the festival box office at the Teatro Nuovo; *tel: (0743) 40265* in Spoleto (tickets from mid May), or from booking agencies all over Italy. Programmes are published well in advance in Italian newspapers and through tourist offices. Special festival travel packages are available from tour operators overseas.

from **Teatro Nuovo**; *tel: (0743) 40265 or 224349*, open 1000–1300 and 1600–1900, (closed Mon) after mid May. Prepaid bookings can be made by mail (hefty commission), from **Biglietteria Festival dei Due Mondi**, *06049 Spoleto; fax: (0743) 224322*.

SIGHTSEEING

Spoleto's long history has left a tremendous legacy of monuments for a town of such a small size. Its most remarkable sight is the 14th-century **Ponte delle Torri** over the Tessino gorge. The name Ponte delle Torri means Bridge of Towers, but it was originally designed as an aqueduct rather than a bridge. Built by Gattapone on Roman foundations, its ten brick arches, like medieval arrow-slits, form an unforgettable silhouette 80m above a deep ravine. A walk across the bridge is highly recommended (take your camera). Above

the bridge stands the **Rocca**, Spoleto's fortress (also by Gattapone), currently being restored as a museum.

Back in the upper town, the other unmissable attraction is the **Duomo**, *Pza del Duomo*, open daily 0800–1300 and 1600–1800, free, which stands on a quiet sloping square in the upper town, its Romanesque façade pierced by eight elegant rose windows and flanked by a tall belltower. In the apse are the outstanding sweet-faced frescos of Fra Filippo Lippi immortalised in countless Christmas cards, depicting the Annunciation, Nativity, and the Death and Coronation of the Virgin. Have L500 coins ready for the light box.

Every nook of medieval Spoleto is a delight to investigate. Cobbled alleys and flights of steps wind darkly beneath buttress arches, emerging in seemly *piazzas* where fountains play. The central *Pza della Libertà* is a focal point, with Spoleto's main post office (foreign exchange) and tourist office. The main shopping streets descend to the adjoining squares of *Pza Garibaldi* and *Pza della Vittoria* in the lower town.

One of the town's best museums is the **Museo Diocesano**, *V. A. Saffi 13; tel: (0743) 223245*, open daily 1000–1230 and 1530–1900; 1000–1230 and 1400–1800 (winter); L4000, an above-average collection of religious art which includes a Lippi *Madonna*. A combined ticket of L5000 also gets you into the quaint 12th-century church of **Sant'Eufemia** in the same courtyard (1000–1230 and 1530–1900; L3000) now used for art exhibitions. Also on *V. Saffi* is the modest **Pinacoteca**, *Palazzo del Municipio, V. A. Saffi; tel: (0743) 218270*, open Tues–Sun 1000–1300 and 1500–1800; L5000 – also includes entrance to the **Casa Romana**, a small Roman building on *V. Visiale* and the **Galleria Comunale D'Arte Moderna**, *Corso Mazzini*). The **Museo Archeologico**, *V. Sant'Agata; tel: (0743) 223277*, open Mon–Sat 0900–1330 and 1430–1900, Sun 0900–1300; L4000 contains the Roman *Lex Spoletina* tablets, forbidding unlicensed woodcutting in the forests of Monteluco. The entrance ticket gives access to the adjacent **Teatro Romano**, used for festival performances in summer.

Other Roman ruins litter the old town: the **Arco di Druso** near the *Pza del*

Porchetta

If you want takeaway food in central Italy, nothing beats porchetta. Once a speciality of Umbria, it is now sold from wayside vans all over the region. Porchetta is made by boning a suckling pig, stuffing its interior with bundles of fennel, thyme, rosemary – plus handfuls of garlic – and roasting the result over a spit. The delicious slices of meat are then served in a rosetta, a large round bread roll.

Mercato, and a few vestigial arches of the **amphitheatre** on the eponymous *V. dell'Anfiteatro*. Spoleto's other main points of interest are churches. There are over a dozen worth seeing. Catch frescoed **San Gregorio**, *Pza Garibaldi* and pink-and-white **San Domenico**, *Pza Collicola*, before leaving the centre, but the most memorable ones lie outside the walls. North of town tucked among cypress trees on *V. del Cimitero* is the ancient **San Salvatore**, open daily 0700–1700 (winter), closes 1800 or 1900 (summer) with Palaeo-Christian features in classical style. Nearby stands 12th-century **San Ponziano**. South of town, the splendidly carved façade of **San Pietro** depicts amusing animal stories and terrifying scenes of eternal torment. **San Paolo inter Vineas** contains venerable frescos.

THE APENNINES: SPOLETO–TERNI

DIRECT ROUTE: 30 KM

Visso

Parco dei Monti Sibillini

S209

Castelluccio

Triponzo

Piano Grande

Norcia

S396

S320

Cascia

S209

Spoleto

S395

Monteleone di Spoleto

S209

193

S3

S471

Ferentillo

S521

Leonessa

Arrone

S209

Terni

Piediluco

Cascate della Mármore

West of Spoleto lie some of Umbria's most striking landscapes along the River Nera (a major tributary of the Tiber) and the wild, remote Monti Sibillini. The scenic route passes through border country, straying almost imperceptibly into the regions of Marche and Lazio at either end. Allow at least a day to enjoy this varied rural drive; the minor roads are slow and winding and the scenery well worth savouring. Norcia makes an attractive touring base; you can also stay (more simply) in a Valnerina village or one of the rugged Sibilline resorts. Almost any Italian journey promises art and architecture, but this tour rewards keen walkers and wildlife spotters too. Rugged sports such as rowing, canoeing, rock climbing, skiing and hanggliding can be pursued – at least vicariously. The region's gastronomic specialities make getting hungry a pleasure.

ROUTES

DIRECT ROUTE

➡ The S3 covers the 30 km between Spoleto and Terni.

SCENIC ROUTE

▪▪▪➡ Leave Spoleto by the S395, which branches east from the *V. Flaminia* (S3) just north of the town. This minor road wriggles 19 km through grand hills to the Valnerina (Nera Valley) at Piedipaterno. Turn north up the S209 through **Triponzo**, following the river upstream past willows and poplars to a steep-sided limestone gorge. Geologists will note some eye-catching tilted strata; others may be more struck by the alarmingly dented rockfall barriers which discourage any leisurely picnics on this stretch of road. Fortified settlements perch on crags to either side of the valley. Turn south-east at **Visso**, following the Nera through Castelsantangelo, a winter skiing area dotted with chalets. Take the **Castelluccio** road and continue across the extraordinary **Piano Grande**; one of Umbria's most unforgettable landscapes. At the T-junction near Forca Canapine, turn right and follow signs to **Norcia** via Santa Scolastica. Join the S396 in Norcia, heading west for 6.5 km, then south along the S320 to **Cascia**. Then take the S471 south through **Monteleone di Spoleto** to **Leonessa** over the Lazio border. From here, head west along the S521, a well-engineered road which crosses a spectacular viaduct near La Forca. Beyond Morro, follow signs to **Piediluco.** Several routes are possible; the most direct is a minor road past the dramatically sited medieval hill village of **Labro** (now full of Belgian holiday homes). Beyond the lake, follow the River Velino downstream to the **Cascate delle Mármore** waterfalls. A sharp elbow turn west of the falls (signed for the lower viewpoint) will lead you back to the S209 on the north bank of the Nera. Follow the river upstream again through the villages of **Arrone**, **Ferentillo**, **San Pietro in Valle** and **Scheggino.** Complete the tour by returning to Spoleto, or retrace your steps down the valley to **Terni**.

THE VALNERINA

Tourist Offices: small municipal offices can be found in the following villages: **Cerreto**, *tel: (0743) 91231*; **Monteleone**, *tel: (0743) 71421*; **Poggiodomo**, *tel: (0743) 79133*; **Preci**, *tel (0743) 99126*; **Sant'Anatolia di Narco**, *tel: (0743) 613148*; **Scheggino**, *tel: (0743) 613232*; **Vallo di Nera**, *tel: (0743) 61643.*

The Nera Valley can be explored by bus. Pick up detailed timetables from a local tourist office if you intend relying on public transport. The free walks pamphlet *20 Sentieri Ragionati in Valnerina,* produced by the Comunità Montana della Valnerina, is worth collecting if you want to explore on foot. There are several modest hotels scattered along the S209 and in the villages nearby.

The River Nera rises in the Monti Sibillini, a wild, high chunk of the Apennine ridge on the borders of the Marches. Celebrated in Virgil's poetry, it still forms one of Umbria's least spoilt valleys. Its clear waters race through steep gorges and wooded glens studded with fortified villages. Barren uplands and sheep pasture lie on either hand. Part of the valley is designated a Parco Naturale Regionale. Though peaceful today, the Valnerina (an obvious but easily defensible thoroughfare) witnessed many conflicts as passing armies clashed. Rural depopulation has affected some of the villages, but tourism and new enterprises such as fish-farming are steadily increasing local prosperity. There are no large or significantly industrialised towns north of Terni. If you're a keen walker, there's a spectacular day's hike through lovely coutryside along an old railway track between Sant'Anatolia di Narco and Spoleto. The route traverses dizzying viaducts (don't lean on the railings as they may be unsafe) and long tunnels (take a torch and a sweater). The stony track is hard going, so you need suitable footwear.

Many of the Valnerina villages make enjoyable pottering, with a church or castle worth inspecting. Some show signs of earthquake damage: a violent tremor shook the region in 1979. Downstream near Terni lie picturesque **Arrone** and **Ferentillo**, a rock-climbing centre with a bizarre collection of accidentally desiccated mummies in the crypt of San Stefano church. Arrone has accommodation and a good restaurant, **Grottino del Nera**; *tel: (0744) 389104* (closed Wed), in the nearby hamlet of Casteldilago.

San Pietro in Valle has a wonderful early church (notice the sculpted Lombard altar and Roman sarcophagus). Further north is the truffle town of **Scheggino**. A feature of the Nera Valley, especially around Scheggino's canals, is a number of high-tech fish-farming ventures, including crayfish and sturgeon as well as the humble trout. Needless to say, local menus are interesting. The riverside **Del Ponte** hotel, *V. Borgo 15; tel: (0743) 61131,* has pleasant rooms and an excellent restaurant offering local specialities (moderate; closed Mon). **Vallo di Nera** is a typical well-restored village with two frescoed churches (see the 'White Procession' in Santa Maria; those in San Giovanni are by Jacopo Santori who decorated part of Spoleto's Duomo). **Cerreto di Spoleto** has a wild setting among oakwoods (*cerreto*

means oak) and an ethnographic research centre in its San Giacomo monastery recounting valley traditions. Nestling in a confluence of several valleys, **Visso** is a popular modern resort and a gateway for the dramatic **Parco dei Monti Sibillini**. On the edge of the park, **Preci**'s large Benedictine **Abbazia di Sant'Eutizio** dates from the 12th century. Its monks were renowned for their knowledge of herbal remedies extracted from mountain plants. Preci was also famous for another branch of medicine. Its surgeons refined their skills from the local butchers who still practise around Norcia. They were much in demand in high places and had some celebrated clients, including England's Elizabeth I. One of their specialities was the castration of promising young singers destined for Italy's opera houses. Preci has accommodation, including *agriturismo*, a small hotel, **Agli Scacchi**; *tel: (0743) 99221* (inexpensive) and an attractive campsite, **Il Collaccio**, *Castelvecchio di Preci; tel: (0743) 939084* (Apr–Oct). Several side roads leading off the Nera Valley (S209) pass through beautiful scenery, notably those to **Monteleone di Spoleto** and **Norcia** (described later). You can set off along one route, and return to the main road via another.

195

PARCO DEI MONTI SIBILLINI

Tourist Information: there are park information centres (marked **Casa del Parco**) at **Norcia** (see below) and **Preci**; *V. Santa Caterina; tel: (0743) 99145.* Head office is at **Visso**; *V. C. Battisti; tel: (0737) 95262.* For information on skiing, contact the **Forca Canepine Skiing Centre**; *tel: (0743) 823005.* For walking maps and *rifugios*, contact the **CAI** (Club Alpino Italiano) in Perugia; *tel: (075) 5730334,* open Tues and Fri 1830–2000.

These wild, brooding hills were once

reputed to be the home of an ancient sibyl, hence the name. Despite their national park status, the region is relatively little known and underused; golden eagles and wolves hunt its fastnesses. In winter, some skiing is possible, particularly around Ussita and Arquata del Tronto. When the snow melts, rock climbers and potholers arrive. In late spring the upland meadows are full of flowers. It is exhilarating walking country, with marked trails and a few spartan mountain refuges, but conditions can be treacherous. Go properly equipped with a good map. Accommodation is limited and should be booked in advance. **Monte Vettore** is Italy's third-highest peak (2476m) from which, it is claimed, you can see both coasts of Italy on a clear day. Below it lies a curious lake, **Lago di Pilato**, habitat of a rare crustacean, and a repository of strange legends.

CASTELLUCCIO AND THE PIANO GRANDE

Castelluccio is one of the highest (1500m) and most isolated villages in Italy; a depopulated farming settlement with a back-of-beyond atmosphere. In winter, it is often cut off by snow or mist and its migrant shepherds head for the water meadows of Norcia with their flocks. In summer, it is no longer so deserted. Zefferelli aroused outsiders' curiosity by making it a backdrop to his film *Brother Sun, Sister Moon*. It is now one of the main hiking bases of the Monti Sibillini Park, and a great hanggliding centre. The church contains frescos of St Anthony Abbot, patron saint of shepherds. It has a single hotel, **Sibilla**; *tel: (0743) 870113* with good country cooking, including dishes made with Castelluccio's home-grown lentils. There are a few private rooms and a summer campsite, **Monte Prata**; *tel: (0743) 9828* in Schianceto to the north.

Most visitors head here, though, not to see the village, but the extraordinary karstic plateau of the **Piano Grande** (Great Plain) over which it presides. Far removed from conventional prettiness, it seems weirdly featureless except for a single road crossing it with relentless straightness, and a surface etched with dry watercourses like mysterious runes. Hills rise sharply all around. In unusual light or weather conditions, it seems even more peculiar. When mists shroud it completely, the bells of Castelluccio toll to guide disoriented villagers home. Close up, the plain reveals itself to be a dazzling carpet of rare Alpine flowers, best seen in May and June. There is another hotel at **Forca Canapine**; *tel: (0743) 823007*, south of the Piano Grande.

NORCIA

Tourist Office: Pro Nursia, *Pza San Benedetto; tel: (0743) 816701*. The **Casa del Parco**, *V. Solferino 22; tel: (0743) 817090*, gives information on the Parco dei Monti Sibillini (walks, wildlife, fungi posters, etc.). A couple of central bookshops and tobacconists sell walking maps and guides.

Norcia is one of the most attractive bases in the Valnerina/Sibillini area, with over a dozen hotels and alternative accommodation. Comfortable 3-star choices are the **Posta**, *V. C. Battisti 10; tel: (0743) 817434*, and the **Grotta Azzurra**, *V. Alfieri; tel: (0743) 816513*. Both have good restaurants. For a contemplative budget stay, try the **Monasterio Sant'Antonio**, *V. delle Vergini 13; tel: (0743) 828208*, a working convent on the edge of town with rabbits, pigs and bees. Try the nuns' home-made *pesto*. Eating is something Norcia takes seriously, using the hearty local produce you can see and smell in luscious food shops all around the town, and in many other regional centres. Hams, sausages, boars' heads and cheeses decorate window displays, competing for space with sacks of Castelluccio lentils and baskets of truffles. Fungoid concoctions such as truffle *grappa* and truffle chocolate may tempt the adventurous. The Sagra del Tartufo (Truffle Festival) takes place at the end of Feb. **Dal Francese**, *V. Riguardati 16; tel: (0743) 816290* is a popular trattoria (closed Fri).

Norcia's most famous resident was St Benedict, born here with his twin sister St Scholastica in 480. The town respects its religious connections and re-enacts its Easter rituals with genuine passion, but during the rest of the year gets on stolidly with its main preoccupation, which is making things to eat (mostly from pigs). The buildings clustered on the main square, **Pza San Benedetto**, are its principle monuments, guarded by charming lions apparently deep in conversation. **San Benedetto** church has a fine Gothic portal and some weathered stone basins formerly used as measures for wine and oil. Inside, the altar painting depicts Benedict's historic encounter with Totila the Goth. The crypt is covered in frescos, and bits of Roman masonry can be seen. Next to the church stands the elegant, multicoloured **Palazzo Comunale**. **La Castellina**, across the square, is a fortified palace containing the **Museo Civico Diocesano** (opening hours uncertain). The **Duomo** next to it was built in 1560. Its main feature is the Capella della Madonna della Misericordia, an ornate marble chapel.

Away from the main square, Norcia's old quarter makes interesting exploration. The squat, sturdy buildings are designed to withstand earthquakes (not all of them succeed and rebuilding is still continuing after the latest shockwaves). On *V. Umberto* to the north stands the small **Edicola** or little temple, carved with enigmatic symbols and reliefs. Beyond it lies an interesting old quarter once inhabited by shepherds. The **Oratorio di Sant'Agostinaccio** behind *Pza Palatina* has a fine wooden ceiling. There is some modern development on the outskirts, but all around the town, tantalising views of unspoilt hills can be glimpsed between the buildings.

CASCIA

Tourist Office: *Pza Garibaldi 1; tel: (0743) 71147*, open Mon–Sat 0900–1300 and 1600–1800, for information on the town, including hotels and pilgrim sights. The **Valnerina–Cascia Tourist Board** is based at *V. G. Da Chiavano 2; tel: (0743) 71401*, open Mon–Fri same hours, for east Umbrian regional information and maps.

Cascia is a great pilgrimage centre, drawing coachloads of pious visitors to the garishly painted modern **Basilica of St Rita**. This saint, little known outside Italy, attracts far more pilgrims than the much more important St Benedict from the neighbouring village of Norcia. Poor Rita (born Margherita Lotti in 1381) had an unfortunate life: married to a brutal alcoholic, her two sons proved equally disappointing. After their violent deaths Rita decided to renounce the world and fought a long battle to be accepted as a nun (a role normally restricted to virginal women). At last she succeeded and retreated to a convent, only to develop an ulcer on her forehead so hideous that her sister nuns avoided her. The sore was regarded as a sign of the stigmata, and after various miracles were attributed to her she was canonised in 1900. Today she is regarded as the patron saint of unhappily married women, and all hopeless causes. Many pilgrims (mostly women) confide their troubles to her uncorrupted body, displayed in a glittering casket. Candles, flowers and silver votive hearts bestrew her gilded shrine; the souvenirs on sale defy description. As an example of religious kitsch, Cascia is curiously compelling.

Beside its bizarre Basilica, Cascia has several more conventional older churches: **Sant'Antonio Abate** and **San Francesco** contain paintings and frescos; **Santa Maria** displays Rita's baptismal font.

Cascia has plenty of restaurants and large, charmless hotels to accommodate its pilgrims. Try **Cursula**, *V. Cavour 3; tel: (0743) 76206* if you need a meal. During religious festivals (Easter week and 21–22 May – St Rita's day) expect large crowds. Cascia has attractive surroundings: head west to **Roccaporena** (Rita's birthplace) or **Capanne** for walks and picnics in craggy, wooded scenery. South of Cascia, **Monteleone di Spoleto** retains its feudal appearance despite new development on the proceeds of truffles and tourism. The church of San Francesco is worth a look (carved portal and 15th-century frescos). Earlier this century some important archaeological finds were made near here; an Etruscan bronze chariot is now in New York's Metropolitan Museum (a copy can be seen in Monteleone).

Over the Lazio border, the small mountain resort of **Leonessa** has much character beyond its castellated gateway. The Corso leads past several churches and battered palaces to an attractive arcaded square dedicated to 51 victims of 'Nazifascism', and the Sanctuario di San Giuseppe, where a Capuchin missionary monk is buried. A cable lift operates up the neighbouring wooded mountainside.

PIEDILUCO

This village and its associated lake, the **Lago di Piediluco**, are instantly recognised among the rowing fraternity as a major venue for international regattas, and the Italian Rowing Federation's official training centre. Canoeing, fishing, and boat trips also take place, but the water is deep and cold, not very suitable for swimming despite the little beaches all around. It is Umbria's second-largest lake, irregular in shape with inlets running into wooded shores. Piediluco itself is a popular summer resort ringed by mountains, always crowded at weekends and during special events despite a fair range of accommodation, including several new hotels, a campsite and *agriturist* b&b. Best bet is the 3-star hotel, **Casalago**, *Voc Mazzelvetta 3; tel: (0744) 368421,* with a garden and lakeside views.

The **Festa delle Acque** (Water Festival) is a popular spectacle (late June–July). Piediluco is accessible by train from Terni or Rieti (the station is on the quieter south-west edge of the lake 1 km from the village), and by bus. Piediluco's main historic sight is the 13th-century **San Francesco** church, with frescos and Roman statuary. A ruined castle stands above the church.

CASCATE DELLE MÁRMORE

The **Marble Falls** 6km south-east of Terni are some of the highest in Europe (165m) and a great tourist attraction, no less amazing because they are largely artificial. The Romans first dreamt up the ambitious idea of diverting the River Velino into the Nera at this point to drain the surrounding marshy plains. The first channel was cut in 271 BC under the consulship of Curius Dentatus; later channels were cut in 1400 and 1785. The final touches were added to these grand falls during the 1930s, when the Lago di Piediluco was dammed to produce hydroelectric power. The Terni HEP scheme is Italy's largest; pylons trail high-voltage

---

Roman Umbria

The ancient Umbrian tribes who inhabited the territory east of the Tiber were no match for Roman might. Perugia fell in 309 BC, and the Umbrians, like their Etruscan neighbours to the west, soon threw their lot in with Rome. The Romans cannily allowed the conquered tribes some independence in their hilltop citadels, and extended them citizenship. They allowed them to practise their own religions. Thus they converted the tribes to useful allies instead of sullen enemies, and assimilated them by stealth and time rather than force.

The Romans put their energies into practical matters such as building the great road from Rome to the Adriatic, which is Umbria's most lasting Roman heritage. All along the V. *Flaminia*, they set up new towns, partly as retirement homes for their pensioned legionnaires, and partly as way stations along a vital artery between Rome and its northern territories. It brought great prosperity to the region, and was the route by which Christianity arrived in Umbria.

In 217 BC Hannibal appeared over the Alps and trounced the Romans in his audacious attack at the Battle of Trasimeno, fought at the spot called Sanguinea (literally 'bloody') on the northern rim of Lake Trasimeno. Even then, the Umbrians remained loyal to Rome, and repelled Hannibal from the gates of Spoleto and Todi. In the 1st century BC Perugia became embroiled in the struggles that followed the death of Julius Caesar, and the city was destroyed. After Octavius became Emperor Augustus, Umbria once again enjoyed peace and prosperity (Pax Romana), until northern invaders discovered the V. *Flaminia* was an unlocked back door through which to assail Rome.

---

cables in all directions from the plant below the cascades, and factories have sprung up along the valley floor. The flow of water is now manually controlled, with a well-publicised if complicated seasonal timetable available in local tourist offices, open daily for up to 3 hrs (mid-Mar–Sept); weekends only (Oct–mid-Mar) showing when it is 'switched on'. When the water is 'off', the falls dwindle to a mere trickle and are scarcely worth seeing. In summer there's a *son et lumière* show. Regular buses pass the falls from Terni and the Valnerina; a convenient station at Mármore serves trains on the Terni–Rieti line. There's a 2-star campsite in Mármore: **Loc i Campacci**, *Fraz Mármore; tel: (0744) 80824*, open June–Oct. One of Terni's finest restaurants can be found nearby: the **Villa Graziani**; *tel: (0744) 67138* (closed Sun eve, Mon and Aug) on the S209 at Villa Valle Papigno (4 km east of Terni).

There are two freely accessible viewpoints, one near the top of the falls in **Mármore** village (reached from the south side of the river on the Piediluco road). The other is along the S209 which leads to the Valnerina. A short, steep link road connects the two just west of the falls, so you can easily reach both vantage points if you have a car, but you need a detailed map to see the road junctions clearly. A steep muddy path also connects the upper and lower falls.

The falls feed swimming pools at the base of the cascade which can be used when the water is 'off'; insistent blasts from a siren warn swimmers to get out in good time. Expectant little crowds gather when the sluice gates are about to be opened, then the water crashes down the wooded cliffs in three foaming sections, tumbling over weedy rocks in thunderous rainbows of spray.

TERNI–SIENA

The most straightforward way to get from Terni to Siena is via Perugia, which takes you along fast motorways or quasi-motorways (some are toll routes), bypassing all major towns. Though not much longer in terms of distance, the more interesting route described below deviates past Roman antiquities along the old *V. Flaminia* and through two of Umbria's most enjoyable historic towns (Todi and Orvieto). Either would make an enjoyable touring base for a day or two.

Siena

S326

A1

ROUTE: 226 KM

A1

Colonnetta

Cerreto

S79

Todi

Orvieto

S448

S3bis

Orvieto–Rome p. 207

Acquasparta

Carsulae

Terni

200

ROUTE

Leave **Terni** at the north-west exit road (signed Todi), but instead of taking the main arterial routes, follow the minor road which winds up towards the village of **Cesi**. This is a pretty climb through olive groves, with some excellent views over the Nera Valley. The hillside church of **Sant'Erasmo**, dating from the 12th century, makes a pleasant detour on the slopes of Monte Torre Maggiore. From Cesi, continue north on the same minor road to the extensive Roman ruins of **Carsulae**, then cross beneath the main S3bis, still

heading north, to **Acquasparta** on the west side of the Naia Valley. From here, rejoin the main road, 53bis and continue a further 25km north to **Todi**. From Todi, a straighforward run along the S448 past the shores of Lago di Corbara takes you swiftly to **Orvieto**. If you fancy some serious eating, and don't mind the cost, one of Italy's most expensive gastronomic temples lies *en route*: the restaurant **Vissani**; *tel: (0744) 950396 (closed Sun eve, Wed and Thur lunch; book ahead)*. If you are in no hurry, the jiggling S79 to the north of the reservoir lake (via Cerreto and Colonnetta) makes a pretty rural drive through bare rock faces, ravines and woodland with plenty of chances for picnics. From Orvieto, the fast A1 *autostrada* takes you up to the Betolle intersection, where signs direct you west for Siena. More enticing alternatives to this dull if painless drive take you across the dramatic clay hills of the Crete, or the cool green slopes of Monte Amiata.

TERNI

Tourist Office: *Vle C. Battisti 7a; tel: (0744) 423047,* open Mon–Sat 0930–1230 and 1600–1900; closed Sun and public holidays. The regional tourist office is conveniently located next door at *Vle C. Battisti 5* (same tel and opening times).

Terni is Umbria's second-largest city and a provincial capital. A glance at its bleak post-war buildings indicates why it gets short shrift in most tourist guides. The city has been an important route hub for many centuries; roads, rivers and railways converge in its fertile plains, offering abundant supplies of water and, since the 1930s, hydro-electric power. Its industrial significance (steel, armaments, chemicals and plastics) made it a strategic target for Allied bombers during World War II, and by 1945, most of its fine historic centre had been pounded to smithereens. A few scraps remain, mostly around its large, rambling central *piazzas*. The striking **Palazzo Spada** (town hall) dominates *Pza Europa*. Near *Pza Europa*, **San Salvatore** is an early church with a domed rotonda and some damaged frescos. Nearby in Palazzo Fabrizi stands the **Pinacoteca**, *V. Fratini,* open Tues–Sun 1000–1300 and 1600–1900; L3000), with *The Marriage of St Catherine* by Benozzo Gozzoli and a notable 20th-century collection. Look out particularly for the naïve paintings of local artist Orneore Metelli (1872–1938).

The most attractive part of Terni lies around the public gardens near the **Roman amphitheatre**, which could hold over 10,000 spectators. Now its grassy confines witness nothing more combative than bowls matches. In this area west of the Corso, **San Francesco** and **Sant'Alo** are worth a passing glance: the former contains unusual Last Judgement frescos in its Paradisi Chapel; the exterior of Sant'Alo incorporates Roman and medieval carvings. The **Duomo** on *V. del'Arringo* has been much altered since its construction, but retains two fine carved portals. Opposite the Duomo, the 16th-century **Palazzo Bianchini-Riccadi** has beautifully decorated eaves. Two km south of the centre, the **Basilica di San Valentino** proudly displays the relics of St Valentine, patron saint of lovers (a claim challenged by both Rome and Dublin). They may all be right; at least three martyred Valentines are recorded in Italian hagiography.

Terni isn't a popular choice as a touring base, which means it is generally easy to find a room. With swift road and rail connections in several directions, it can be a convenient fall-back – if you can't stay in Spoleto at festival time, for instance. Try the top-range **Garden Hotel**, *V. Bramante 6; tel: (0744) 300041,* a pretty hotel with a swimming pool (moderate–pricey) or the cheaper **Brenta II**, *V. Montegrappa 51; tel: (0744) 273957* with well-equipped modern rooms. If you don't want to stay in Terni, you can certainly eat well at one of its excellent restaurants. Top billing goes to the **La Fontanella**, *Hotel Valentino, V. Plinio Il Giovane 3; tel: (0744) 402550.* Other good

201

choices include **Da Carlino**, *V. Peimonte 1; tel: (0744) 40163* (closed Mon) outside the city centre with a garden (inexpensive, closed Mon and Aug), and **Gulliver**, *V. Sant'Alo; tel: (0744) 425225* (eves only; closed Wed). The well-known **Caffè Pazzaglia** on *Corso Tacito* is a fine old pastry shop first opened in 1913.

CARSULAE

These extensive unfenced ruins form an evocative scene amid sheep pasture and brambles on a quiet road 15km north of Terni. The pale masonry emerges patchily from its grassy shrouds; a ghostly reminder of the Roman legions who once tramped along the *V. Flaminia*. The town was founded in about 220BC, and in its heyday was an important way station praised for its beauty by Tacitus and Pliny the Younger. Carsulae's downfall occurred at the end of the 1st century AD, not by warfare, but in a destructive earthquake. During the centuries that followed, its dressed stone and marble cladding were plundered for building materials. Some went to construct the 11th-century chapel of **San Damiano**, the site's most prominent building. Off the *V. Flaminia*, where chariot-ruts can still be seen, lie temples, fora, baths, funerary monuments, law courts, an archway, a theatre and an amphitheatre. The ruins are freely accessible, with display board plans.

ACQUASPARTA

This spa town is mildly interesting for its remaining walls and a few old buildings in the centre, most striking of which is the **Palazzo Cesi** (now an outpost of the University of Perugia). Galileo spent a month here in 1624. It has an fine courtyard and some grand rooms, which staff may be willing to show you on request. Ask at the town hall if there's no one

about at the palace. Some of the mineral baths are derelict, but the **Terme di Amerino** still reckons to cure your kidney stones and arthritis; *tel: (0744) 943921*, open (May–Oct). The town has a couple of modest hotels.

TODI

Tourist Office: **Pro Loco**: *Pza del Popolo 38; tel: (075) 894 2686*, is a municipal office under the arcades of the main square with telephones and transport information (Mon–Sat 0900–1300 and 1600–1900, Sun and public holidays 0930–1230). **Azienda di Promozione Turistica del Tuderte**, *Pza Umberto I 6; tel: (075) 894 3395* (Mon–Sat 1000–1300 and 1500–1800, Sun 1100–1300 and 1600–1800), by the steps up to San Fortunato church, supplies regional information. There's another small tourist office nearby, **Todi-promotion**, at *V. Ciuffelli 8; tel: (075) 894 3867*, open Mon–Fri 0900–1300 and 1500–1900; also Sat in summer 1100–1300 and 1600–1800. The main post office and exchange facilities can be found in the interlinked central squares, *Pza del Popolo* and *Pza Garibaldi*.

If you arrive by car, it's best to park outside the walls; space in the centre is hard to find in summer. If you find a place in the *Pza del Mercato Vecchio*, notice the four arched **Niccioni** (niches) in the high walls, which date from Roman times. Todi is served by the private FCU railway line (Terni–Perugia), but its two stations lie in the valley 5km and 6km from town with erratic connections on City Bus B. Out-of-town buses (to Perugia, etc.) stop near the church of **Santa Maria della Consolazione** (a steep 1km walk from the centre), and connect with local orange minibuses.

Todi hosts numerous events, including a prestigious summer arts festival, a national crafts exhibition (woodwork is a local speciality) and **Mongolferistico**, a hot-air balloon show (July).

ACCOMMODATION AND FOOD

Most of Todi's hotel accommodation lies (rather sadly) outside the walls, though motorists may find it hard to park closer to the centre. The 4-star **Fonte Cesia**, *V. L. Leoni 3; tel: (075) 894 3737* (expensive) is central with garage facilities. A budget choice is the **Zodiaco**, *V. del Crocefisso 23; tel: (075) 894 2625* near Porta Romana (where you can park). Outside the town, choices range from the luxurious country house villa, **Convento San Valentino**, at Frazione Fiore on the Perugia road; *tel: (075) 894 4103* to the more central **Villa Luisa**, *V. A. Cortesi 147; tel: (075) 894 8571*. The tourist board lists some private rooms in the town centre, and a good range of *aziende agrituristichi* in nearby villages (**La Palazzetta**, *Fraz Asproli; tel: (075) 885 3219* has exceptional facilities and location); inexpensive accommodation is also available in several local monasteries and convents.

Todi's popularity as a holiday centre means it has a good range of eating places. One of the best is **Umbria**, *V. San Bonaventura 13; tel: (075) 894 2390* (closed Tues) which has a panoramic terrace. The less expensive **Cavour**, *Corso Cavour 21/23; tel: (075) 894 3730* (closed Wed) serves black truffle tortellini in a cool dungeon. **Jacopone**, *Pza Jacopone 3; tel: (075) 894 2366* is a well-known trattoria. With wide views in all directions, Todi's shadier edges make good places for picnics; try the hilly park around the ruined 14th-century Rocca.

SIGHTSEEING

Todi's main monuments are churches and palaces, though the town as a whole is a delight to explore. Dating back probably to Iron Age times, it is a layer cake of history, with remains of three sets of defensive walls (Etruscan, Roman and medieval). With these substantial fortifications, this borderland town between Etruscan and Umbrian territory (the Tiber was the frontier) managed to hold at bay invaders as awesome as Hannibal and Totila the Goth. Today it is a peaceful place, the centre of a prosperous agricultural region, increasingly gentrified for weekending Romans and wealthy foreigners. Surveyors view the second homes of these incomers with some concern, as Todi's precarious hold on its triangular hilltop is steadily slipping. Hefty buttresses shore up many of its buildings.

Todi's most striking complex of landmarks lies in the medieval *Pza del Populo*. On the north side stands the **Duomo**, open daily 0830–1230 and 1400–1730 or 1500–1900 in summer, elegantly plain outside and reached by a flight of steps. Inside it has a number of interesting features: Corinthian capitals, 19th-century stained glass, a fine font (1507), a 14th-century *Madonna and Child*, a vaulted crypt and an incongruous Last Judgement fresco on the west wall. Two adjoining 13th-century palaces line the east side of the square. The **Palazzo del Capitano** (open daily 1000–1230 and 1600–2000), contains frescos and houses the Pinacoteca Civica and Museo Etrusco-Romano (closed for repairs). The **Palazzo del Populo** has swallowtail crenellations and an imposing exterior staircase much in demand for cinematic swordfights. The **Palazzo dei Priori**, opposite the Duomo, is now Todi's town hall. The coat of arms refers to a legend that the town was founded on the spot where an eagle dropped a tablecloth it had seized from a grand house.

203

Within the walls, **San Fortunato** above *Pza Umberto I* (0930–1230 and 1500–1700) is the other major church to see. It stands above a long flight of steps; the upper section of its Gothic/Romanesque façade pierced with holes which local swifts find useful nesting boxes. Inside its light, barn-like interior are scraps of fresco, a well-carved choir and the crypt where the mystic Jacopone di Todi is buried. The Cappella del Sacramento on the rear-right aisle is covered with graffitti.

Outside the walls stands the domed church of **Santa Maria della Consolazione** (open daily except 1300–1500), widely regarded as one of the best Renaissance churches in Italy. Certainly it is a most elegantly proportioned and beautifully set building from a distance. Two km further out of town, the **Convento di Montesanto** dates from the 13th century, and has marvellous views. Many villages with interesting churches and castles lie around the Tiber and Naia valleys. Collelungo, Colvalenza, Monte Castello di Vibio, and Fratta Todina lie within easy reach of Todi.

204

ORVIETO

Tourist Office: *Pza Duomo 24; tel: (0763) 341772* or *341911* (Mon–Fri 0800–1400 and 1600–1900; Sat 1000–1300 and 1600–1900, Sun 1000–1200 and 1600–1800). A good range of well-produced practical information and accommodation bookings; local bus tickets and the combined sightseeing ticket, **Orvieto Unica**, can be purchased here. Pick up the current version of *Welcome to Orvieto* for useful listings. Orvieto Tourist Board has Internet and e-mail addresses. The **Tourist Information Point** on *V. Duomo* is privately run and charges for most of its services.

The main post office is in *V. C. Nebbia;*

tel: (0763) 344528, open Mon–Fri 0815–1715, Sat 0815–1245 and has exchange facilities. **Multiservice**, *V. Largo Barzini 7; tel: (0763) 342297,* open 0900–1300 and 1430–1900 (summer); 1000–1300 and 1600–1900 (winter) also offers currency exchange.

GETTING AROUND

Like Perugia, Orvieto has tackled the challenge of its difficult site and parking problems with imagination, leaving its historic quarter pleasantly traffic free. The bus terminal (weekday ATC services to Bolsena, Narni, Terni, Amerlia and Todi) and rail station (Rome–Florence line, but not all services stop here) lies in Orvieto Scalo at the foot of the cliffs on the northeast side of town. If you arrive by car, park here (free) and take a bus or funicular up to the old town. A 2-min funicular ride (every 15 mins weekdays 0715–1230, Sun and public holidays 0800–2030; L1100 single or L1400 including a bus ride) takes you up to *Pza Cahen*; you can then walk or take any of the frequent buses (Line A or B) to the centre. There is another car-park on the south-west side of town in Campo della Fiera, linked by escalators and lifts to the old quarter. A day ticket costing L4000 allows unlimited use of all urban transport. Hold on to your ticket and you can get a reduction at the Museo Claudio Faina.

ACCOMMODATION AND FOOD

Motorists may find it more convenient to stay outside the centre and visit Orvieto on a day-trip. Cars are not completely banned from the old town, but you will have to pay for parking. If you want to experience the atmosphere of Orvieto at night, best-located central hotels (both inexpensive) are **Virgilio**, *Pza del Duomo 5; tel: (0763) 341882* (only a few rooms have views), or

Duomo, *V. Maurizio 7; tel: (0763) 341887*. The **Maitani**, *V. Maitani 5; tel: (0763) 342011* offers more luxury in a 17th-century palace with a garden and garage facilities. There are several attractive country-house choices within easy driving distance, all comfortably furnished with good restaurants and wine lists. Nearest is **Villa Ciconia**, *V. dei Tigli 69, Loc. Ciconia; tel: (0763) 92982* in park-like grounds (moderate; beware of the friendly kid goat which may munch your luggage). **La Badia** is about 5 km south of Orvieto; *tel: (0763) 90359* in a former Benedictine abbey with a distinctive 12-sided bell-tower (expensive). Not far from Canale (5 km south) is the **Fattoria La Cacciata**, *tel: (0763) 300892*, offering *agriturismo* on an estate producing wine and oil (inexpensive). The **Villa Bellago** is attractively located on Lago di Corbara about 12 km south of Orvieto (moderate). There are two campsites on the lakeshore too; the 3-star **Orvieto**, *tel: (0763) 950240*, is open all year.

Orvieto is famous for its wines: best-known are the crisp fruity whites made from Trebbiano grapes, but reds and sweet wines are also produced. Orvieto Classico wines come from a specific area immediately around the city. They are fermented and stored in the underground passages and caves which honeycomb the soft local tufa, and are widely on sale throughout the region; many under the Cardeto label (the largest Umbrian wine cooperative). Bars and *enotecas* offer a chance to taste before you buy. **La Bottega del Buon Vino**, *V. della Vaca 26; tel: (0763) 42373*, is an atmospheric place with good prices. Orvieto is full of good eating places, though prices are on the high side. **Le Grotte del Funaro**, *V. Ripa Serancia 41; tel: (0763) 343276* (closed Mon), **Il Giglio d'Oro**, *Pza Duomo 8; tel: (0763)* 341903 (closed Wed), **Trattoria Etrusca**, *V. L Maitani 10; tel: (0763) 344016* (closed Mon) and **Maurizio**, *V. del Duomo 78; tel: (0763) 341114* (closed Tues and Jan) are highly rated and fairly expensive. **Al San Francesco**, *V. Cerretti 10; tel: (0763) 43302* is a popular self-service cafeteria and evening pizzeria (cheap). There are picnic facilities in the Parco delle Grotte near the *Pza Duomo* (entrance L2000); the public gardens of the Rocca near the funicular terminal, can be enjoyed for free, and have fine views over the Paglia Valley.

EVENTS AND ENTERTAINMENT

It was in Orvieto in 1264 that Pope Urban IV first proclaimed the feast of Corpus Christi (known as Corpus Domini in Italy) to the Catholic world after the Miracle of Bolsena (see p. 208), when the communion host turned to blood and stained the altar cloth. Today Corpus Christi (June) is celebrated with costumed processions throughout the old town. At Pentecost, Orvieto marks the **Festa della Palombella** with fireworks. Summer sees a round of concerts, opera and open-air cinema, while Dec–Jan are enlivened by the **Umbria Jazz Winter**.

SHOPPING

Orvieto's smart shops sell many attractive specialities. Most prominent is the local dry white wine, packaged for carrying home easily. Craft products are much in evidence too, including ceramics, woodwork, lace, precious metalwork and wrought iron and leather goods.

SIGHTSEEING

Orvieto's setting on a raised plateau of volcanic tufa makes a striking impact amid a valley of vines. Dominating the town is the vividly striped **Duomo**, *Pza Duomo; tel: (0763) 41167*, open daily 0700–1300

205

and 1430–1730 (Nov–Feb), later in summer; one of Umbria's most exciting buildings, built in honour of a 13th-century miracle. If the triple-gabled exterior façade of gilded mosaics, bronze doors and magnificently carved reliefs were not dazzling enough, the interior frescos by Luca Signorelli are outstanding masterpieces depicting the Last Judgement in graphic detail. They can be seen in the **Cappella di San Brizio** in the right transept, open 1000–1245 and 1430–1715 (Nov–Mar); until 1915 in summer; L3000). The golden altar tabernacle in the adjacent **Cappella del Corporale** contains the miraculous bloodstained cloth which dispelled a Bohemian priest's doubts about Transubstantiation. Several grand buildings near the Duomo now contain museums. The **Palazzo Faina**, opposite the Duomo; *tel: (0763) 341216* or *341511,* houses the **Musei Archeologici Claudio Faina e Civico,** a marvellous collection of Etruscan and Attic vases, open Tues–Sun 1000–1300 and 1500–1900 (Apr–Sept); 1000–1300 and 1430–1700 (Oct–Mar); L7000 or L4000 if you can produce a funicular or local bus ticket). The **Museo Archeologico Nazionale** is in the Palazzo Papale by the cathedral's east end; *tel: (0763) 341039,* open (Mon–Sat 0900–1330 and 1430–1900, Sun and public holidays 0900–1300; L4000), a state collection containing Etruscan funerary artefacts and necropolis frescos. In the **Palazzo Soliano** or Palazzo dei Papi to the right of the Duomo are the **Museo Civico e dell'Opera del Duomo** with liturgical objects, and the **Museo Emilio Greco**, a collection of bronzes by the sculptor of the cathedral's modern doors, open Tues–Sun 1030–1300 and 1500–1900 (Apr–Sept); 1030–1300 and 1400–1800 (Oct–Mar); L5000). The **Pozzo di San Patrizio**,

Pza Cahen near the funicular terminal; *tel: (0763) 43768,* open daily 0900–1900 (Apr–Sept), 1000–1800 (Oct–Mar); L6000, is an astonishing cylindrical well with a diameter of 13m and a depth of 62m. A double-helix mule-ramp runs around the interior. It was completed in 1537 to provide an emergency water supply for the city in times of siege. There were once many similar wells in the city.

If you develop a taste for 'Underground Orvieto', ask the tourist office about guided tours around the **Grotte delle Rupe**, a vast maze of tufa caves beneath the city, excavated during many different periods as wells or cisterns, storage chambers, wine cellars, rubbish pits, etc. One well-publicised tour company is **Speleotecnica**, *V. della Pace 1; tel: (0763) 375084* . Tours in several languages depart from *Pza Duomo* daily at 1100 and 1600, lasting about an hour; L10,000. The **Crocifisso del Tufo** is a complex of Etruscan tombs from the 6th century BC on the west side of the town (follow signs from *Pza Cahen* 1km along the S71); open daily 0900–sunset; L4000.

A combined ticket costing L18,000, the **Carta Orvieto Unica**, allows access to four sights: the Cappella di San Brizio, the Museo Claudio Faina, Orvieto Underground and the Torre del Moro (a clock tower on *Corso Cavour*). It can be bought at any of the sights, or at the tourist office. Another cumulative ticket costing L10,000 includes entrance to the Pozzo di San Patrizio and the Museo Greco.

If you have only limited time, or if you want to avoid the stresses of driving in Rome, you may now choose to continue by driving up to Siena, by-passing coastal Tuscany. This is easily enough achieved by joining the A1 *Autosrada* at Orvieto and heading north to Sinalunga, then west on the S326.

ORVIETO–ROME

This route follows lengthy stretches of the Roman *Via Cassia* past a daisy-chain of volcanic lakes. The main roads are mostly uninspiring and increasingly busy as Rome's magnetic influence grows stronger, but brief diversions take in many points of interest: 13th-century miracles, Etruscan burial sites, wine towns, Mannerist villas, as well as palaces, churches, castles and the surprisingly rural scenery of the lakes. The provincial capital of Viterbo is one of the highlights of this tour, and makes an excellent touring base with lots to explore in all directions.

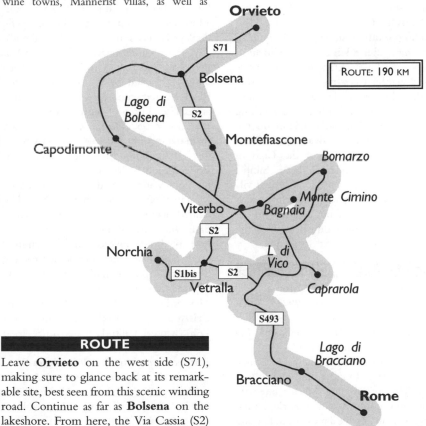

ROUTE: 190 KM

207

ROUTE

Leave **Orvieto** on the west side (S71), making sure to glance back at its remarkable site, best seen from this scenic winding road. Continue as far as **Bolsena** on the lakeshore. From here, the Via Cassia (S2) hugs the eastern lakeshore down to **Montefiascone**, then leads directly on to

Viterbo, but it is possible to drive right around the quieter western shore via Capodimonte and take a prettier, secondary route to Viterbo via Marta. There are good lake views especially from the northern side, where the roads climb high through the chestnut woods of the Monti Volsini. From Viterbo, several routes are possible, depending which excursions appeal. The peaceful minor roads pottering south-east through the Monti Cimini hills around the Lago di Vico are particularly attractive. Alternatively, take the section of fast but uncompleted dual carriageway leading south-west, turning off after 9 km for **Vetralla**. From Vetralla, take the S1bis (heading south-west, signed Tarquinia). Turn right after 8 km at Casale Cinelli to explore the lonely Etruscan necropolis of **Norchia** (the access track is partly unsurfaced, and entails a 1 km walk). Return to Vetralla, and head south-east again along the S2. Turn right after 8.5 km on the S493 via Veiano to **Bracciano**. From here, a complete tour of the Lago di Bracciano takes under an hour. Simple accommodation is available in several villages if you want a rural waterfront stay. Bracciano lies only about 30 km from the GRA (Rome's outer orbital road), if the capital is to be your next destination.

LAGO DI BOLSENA

Tourist Information: Bolsena: *Pza Matteotti 25; tel: (0761) 799923*, open Mon–Sat 0900–1200 and 1600–1800 (summer only); **Montelfiascone**: *Via Cassia Vecchia; tel: (0761) 826041.*

This is Lazio's largest lake, set in a huge volcanic crater 43 km round and 146 m deep. The surrounding soils are intensely fertile and, coupled with the lake's mild micro-climate, create a prosperous farming region. The wooded shores are intensively cultivated and lake fishing is an important

activity, using huge nets to catch eels. Campsites, restaurants and modest hotels are scattered all around the shoreline, as well as in the main towns of Bolsena and Montefiascone.

Bolsena itself is the main town, set on the north-east shore. Originally an Etruscan city (*Volsinii*) its well-preserved medieval core is stacked in picturesque tiers above the lake, culminating in a 13th-century castle containing the **Museo Territoriale del Lago di Bolsena**; *tel: (0761) 798630*, open Tues–Sun 0930–1330 and 1600–2000 (summer), Tues–Fri 0930–1300, Sat–Sun 0930–1330 and 1430–1830 (winter); L4000, a well-displayed collection of archaeological finds. Two early churches are dedicated to San Francesco and Santa Cristina, who miraculously survived being thrown into the lake weighted with stones for her Christian faith. The church of **Santa Cristina**; *tel: (0761) 799067, Corso della Repubblica*, open 0700–1230 and 1500–1730 (winter), until 1930 (summer) is more famous for Bolsena's other Miracle, when a communion wafer turned to blood during Mass in 1263 (see Orvieto, page 204). The stained altarcloth is now in Orvieto cathedral, but the stones on which the host bled are revered in this church. Predictably, Bolsena commemorates the feasts of Corpus Domini (June) and Santa Cristina (23–24 July) with special fervour. The 3rd-century **Catacombs of Sant Cristina**, open 0900–1200 and 1500–1730 (winter); 0900–1230 and 1600–1800 (summer); L5000 can be entered near the altar. For a meal, try **La Conchiglia**; *Viale Colesanti 27; tel: (0761) 799009* or **Angela e Piero**; *Via della Rena 98/d; tel: (0761) 799264* (closed Tues) with lakeshore views. **Gradoli**, further west, is the centre of a wine-producing area. **Capodimonte** on the southern shore is a quiet resort on

208

a wooded promontory guarded by the octagonal 16th-century Castello Farnese. It has small beaches of black sand, pedaloes and a good fish restaurant, **Riva Blu**; *Via Regina Margherita 7; tel: (0761) 870255* (closed Thur). Boat trips visit the two lake islets of Martana and Bisentina. Set back from the south-eastern edge, **Montefiascone** perches on the dead rim of the volcano beneath its ponderous baroque Duomo. Wine-lovers may like to visit the smaller but more interesting Romanesque church of San Flavinio; *tel: (0761) 826198*, open daily 0800–1200 and 1500–1700 (summer), 0800–1200 and 1500–1630 (winter); free on the Orvieto road, where Bishop Giovanni Fugger lies in bibulous ecstasy after discovering the tipple of his dreams, *Est! Est!! Est!!!* The Latin inscription on his tomb says 'On account of too much 'Est' here my Lord Bishop Fugger died'. The bishop's servant was instructed to write the word 'Est' ('Here it is') on inn doors where good wine could be found for his master. At Montefiascone, he wrote it three times, and the bishop died of a surfeit. The thinnish white wine with the exclamatory name is widely promoted in local restaurants and *enotecas*, and is worth trying, but not dying for. Two places where you try it are **La Commenda**; on *Strada Commenda 5km W; tel: (0761) 826161* (closed Tues) and **Rondinella**; *Via Cassia; tel: (0761) 824995* (closed Tues). Both have fixed price menus.

VITERBO

Tourist Information: PromoTuscia: *c/o ex-Chiesa Almadiani, Pza dei Caduti; tel: (0761) 304643* (Mon–Fri 0900–1400 and 1500–1900, Sat 0900–1330 and 1500–1830, Sun 1000–1330 and 1500–1830). There are other regional and seasonal offices elsewhere in town: *Pza San Carluccio 5; tel: (0761) 304795; Pza Verdi 4/A; tel: (0761) 226666* or *Pza della Morte; tel: (0761) 345229*. A useful booklet (*Annuario d'Informazione Turistica*) lists annually updated information for the whole province in English and Italian.

GETTING THERE AND AROUND

Viterbo has good transport links (bus and train) with Rome. There are two main railway stations, **Porta Fiorentina** to the north, and **Porta Romana** south. **COTRAL** buses serve local towns. Driving in the narrow streets of the old quarter is embarrassingly difficult; leave cars in *Piazza della Rocca* to see the north side of town, or one of the large car parks near *Piazza del Plebiscito* to explore the centre and San Pellegrino.

EVENTS

Viterbo's main festival of **Santa Rosa** (3 Sept) involves a procession with a huge 'macchina' (a 30 m gilded spire). Several ghastly accidents befel this event in the 19th century.

ACCOMMODATION AND FOOD

There are over a dozen hotels in or very close to the town. Avoid staying in the ugly suburbs. Comfortable central hotels include: **Leon d'Oro**; *Via della Cava 36; tel: (0761) 344444* or **Tuscia**; *Via Cairoli 41; tel: (0761) 344400* (both moderate). **Roma**; *Via della Cava 26; tel: (0761) 226474* is slightly cheaper. There are plenty of good restaurants too. Try **Il Grottino**; *Via della Cava 7; tel: (0761) 308188* (closed Tues) or **Enoteca La Torre**; *Via della Torre 5; tel: (0761) 226467* (closed Sun) for good local fare. **Porta Romana**; *Via della Bontà 12; tel: (0761) 307118* (closed Sun) and **Taverna Etrusca**; *Via Annio 8/10; tel: (0761) 226694* (closed Sun) have inexpensive fixed-price menus.

209

SIGHTSEEING

Viterbo's outskirts aren't much to look at, but the historic zone is extensive and full of interest. The local volcanic stone (called *peperino*) is dark grey and can look austere, but the monumental squares are enlivened by eyecatching fountains and jolly carved lions. Viterbo was Tuscia to the Romans; its present name derives from the Latin *vetus urbs* ('the old city'). In medieval times Viterbo was a favourite retreat for popes fleeing the violence and intrigues of the Vatican (some perished in mysterious circumstances once they arrived). Today, Viterbo is a big university town which extends far beyond its intact walls.

There are several sectors to explore. Oldest and quaintest is **San Pellegrino**, with narrow hilly streets branching crookedly off the spinal *Via San Pellegrino*, its towers and mullioned palaces gentrified with art galleries and antique shops. *Piazza San Pellegrino* has a splendid range of medieval buildings. *Via San Lorenzo* leads to the grand *Piazza San Lorenzo* with the 13th-century **Papal Palace** and the Romanesque Duomo. Other churches worth a look are **Santa Maria Nuova**, **Santo Sisto**, **Santa Maria della Verita** and **San Francesco**, containing the tombs of two popes. Viterbo's best fountain is the **Fontana Grande**, dating from the 13th century. The **Piazza del Plebiscito** bridges Viterbo's medieval and modern quarters with another handsome assembly of medieval buildings. The **Palazzo dei Priori** is now the town hall (you can glance inside free of charge).

There are several small museums in town. The **Museo Civico** is in the convent next to Santa Maria della Verita by the eastern walls; *Pza F Crispi; tel: (0761) 348275*, open Tues–Sun 0900–1900 (May–Oct), 0900–1800 (Nov–Apr); L6000 and contains archaeological finds and

pharmacy jars. The **Museo Nazionale** is in the Rocca Albernoz at the top of the town; *tel: (0761) 325929*, open Tues–Sun 0900–1800; L4000; and has a collection of historic material from Neolithic, Etruscan and medieval times. Just west of town off *Strada Faul-Bagni* are the **Orto Botanico dell'Universita della Tuscia** (University Botanic Gardens) with 6 ha of newly planted themed habitats (African oases, Northern Mexico's deserts, etc); *tel: (0761) 357097*, open Mon–Sat 0800–1300; L3000 – at other times the gardens are open by appointment).

> ↗ **SIDE TRACKS**
> **FROM VITERBO**
>
> Head north-east from *Piazza Gramsci* on *Viale Trieste* for 3 km, pausing at the lovely Renaissance church of **Santa Maria della Quercia**; *tel: (0761) 3069484* (if closed, ask for the key in the adjacent house). Continue along the S204 to the small town of **Bagnaia**, just 5 km east of Viterbo, which is dominated by a masterpiece of Renaissance landscape gardening. The **Villa Lante**; *tel: (0761) 288008* is considered one of the finest examples of the 16th-century style known as Italian Mannerism, an idealised interpretation of nature. Designed by Vignola, the gardens occupy the grounds of two late 16th-century pavilions built for cardinals (obligatory guided tours every half hour daily 0900–sunset; L4000). Amid the steep terraced slopes and classical statuary, watery jokes (spouting fountains and hidden sprays) lie in wait to soak unwary visitors. Family emblems (prawns, lions and stars) feature prominently in the decorative scheme. The adjacent parkland can be explored free of charge during daylight hours.
>
> Twelve km north-east of Bagnaia,

210

Bomarzo (signed off the S204) boasts another *outre* Mannerist sight, the **Parco dei Mostri** (Monster Park); *tel: (0761) 924029* (daily during daylight hours; L10,000), a fantasy land of grotesque sculptures and surreal inscriptions. Created by the Duke of Orsini in 1552, it seems to have more in common with 20th-century anxieties than the orderly Renaissance.

Bagnaia and Bomarzo are both on regular bus and train routes from Viterbo (buses are quicker and more convenient). 🔼

MONTE CIMINO AND THE LAGO DI VICO

Tourist Information: ENTE Provinciale per Il Turismo di Viterbo *Pza dell'Oratorio 1, S Martino al Cimino; tel: (0761) 291000*. For information about the nature reserve, contact Caprarola's *Centro Visite*; *tel: (0761) 646956*.

South-west of Viterbo, a green, hilly nature reserve surrounds another rounded crater lake. Though smaller than either of the lakes of Bolsena or Bracciano, the Lago di Vico is possibly the prettiest. Monte Fogliano and Monte Venere rise on either shore, but a higher mountain gives its name to the area: Monte Cimino (1053m). All are extinct volcanoes covered in beech and chestnut woods. The Via Cimina (signed from Viterbo's Porta Romana) makes a fine scenic drive with plenty of restaurants en route. Camping is possible around the lake, and there are recreational sports (canoeing, riding, cycling etc). Two interesting villages are **Caprarola**, which has a fascinating if dilapidated Mannerist villa, **Palazzo Farnese**; *tel: (0761) 646052*, open daily 0900–1900 (May–Aug), closes earlier off-season; guided tours of gardens 1000–1100 and 1500–1700; L4000. and **Sutri**, with

Etruscan remains and an amphitheatre, open 0800–1400; free.

VETRALLA

A cluster of mildly interesting churches makes Vetralla worth a brief stop (see Romanesque San Francesco and the cathedral). The Palazzo Comunale is in the Mannerist style. Intrepid visitors head west of town to the Etruscan necropolis of **Norchia** (turn right at Casale Cinelli down a 2 km track through farmland and mysteriously blighted eucalyptus trees). Park and take a 500 m footpath through fields buzzing with wildlife to a valley of cave-like tombs (2nd–4th century BC) cut from soft tufa. It's an atmospheric place, but access involves a tricky scramble down steep paths. It is not advisable to explore this isolated site alone. Self-appointed 'guides' from local houses may pester visitors, but the site is freely accessible at all times. A torch may be useful, though there's not much to see inside the tombs. Another Etruscan site can be found between Viterbo and Vetralla, at **Castel d'Asso**, with earlier tombs topped by a ruined 15th-century fortress (freely accessible). To reach it, take the south-west exit road from Viterbo towards the thermal baths (Bagni di Viterbo) once used by Etruscans and Romans.

LAGO DI BRACCIANO

This circular volcanic lake (9.5 km across) in the Monti Sabatini provides a popular weekend breathing space for modern Romans, but rarely gets overrun. The scenery is not especially spectacular, but the lanes which hug the lakeshore make an agreeable drive. Camping, *agriturismo* and modest hotels lie scattered around the waterfront.

The main town is **Bracciano** on the south-west edge of the lake, which is

211

Earthquakes, Volcanoes and Spas

Central Italy is geologically unstable. As the tectonic plates of Africa and Europe shift in relation to each other, the Apennine region is subject to great stresses, which manisfest themselves in periodic upheavals. Earthquakes and tremors occur quite frequently, though, fortunately, few cause major damage. Those that do can be very destructive. The Roman town of Carsulae was devastated at the end of the 1st century, and the city was so badly damaged that it was abandoned. Bad luck must have been associated with the site, because the buildings were not robbed of masonry, as was usually the case with fallen structures, and those buildings that the earthquake spared, including temples, theatres and baths, still stand to an impressive height.

The hill town of Norcia, located high in the Apennines, was badly damaged in 1979. For years, buildings on the edge of the town were left in a tumbledown state. During the 1990s, many were restored to create bijou residences for Roman weekenders and to cater for the nascent ski industry. Just as Norcians thought that their future prosperity from this source was assured, another major series of earthquakes struck the whole of Umbria. The earthquakes of autumn 1997 were devastating, and their scars will be visible for years to come, not least in Assisi, where famous frescos by Giotto and Cimabue fell off the walls. Northern Italy has no large active volcanoes like Vesuvius or Etna north of Naples, but low-level volcanic activity near Viterbo produces the hot springs responsible for many mineral spas.

The circular lakes of northern Lazio (Bolsena, Vico and Bracciano, plus several smaller pools) lie in ancient volcano craters, surrounded by the cooling embers of once-smoking hills. North-west of Lake Bolsena, the strange sulphurous waters of Saturnia gush into natural pools, creating hot baths that have been used for hundreds of years. Umbria is especially rich in mineral waters. The best-known thermal baths are at Città di Castello, Sangemini and Acquasparta, and are still in use for a variety of complaints. Other, more palatable springs are bottled for table use.

dominated by the imposing 13th-century **Castello Orsini–Odelscalchi**; *tel: (06) 648 1114.* (privately owned; hourly guided tours Tues–Sun 1000–1230 and 1500–1800, timings vary seasonally; L11,000); there are fine views from the ramparts. Small beaches in Bracciano provide swimming and boat trips. From Bracciano, the settlements (heading clockwise) include **Vicarello** amid olive groves, **Trevignano Romano**, one of the prettiest resorts with an old church and a ruined castle adding to a fine lakeshore setting, and **Anguillara Sabazia** high above the lake. There are places to swim and sunbathe, and several good fish restaurants (the lake is well-stocked with tench, trout and eels). Try Trevignano's **La Grotta Azzurra**; *Pza V Emanuele 4; tel: (06) 999 9420* (closed Tues). Some holiday development has taken place, but mostly the shores consist of unspoiled farmland. There are a couple of small museums: Trevignano's **Museo Archeologico** has finds from local Etruscan-Roman sites; Vigna di Valle's **Museo Storico dell'Aeronautica Militare** has a collection of World War I aircraft. The lake was once used as a test-site for dirigibles and sea-planes.

ROME (ROMA)

Founded, according to legend, by Romulus and Remus in 753 BC, Rome is a fascinating and contradictory place. Ancient and modern, stylish – yet racked by urban headaches – Italy's capital is a hugely likeable city with an infectious *joie de vivre*. Twentieth-century living goes on hedonistically amid its astonishing monumental heritage, which present-day Romans treat with little reverence. The rise and fall of the Roman Empire is a lifetime's study, but plenty has happened since. In post-war years, Rome has expanded into a city approaching four million inhabitants, with serious traffic and pollution problems. Poised between the two very different characters and aspirations of northern and southern Italians, the Eternal City looks set for some changes, as it did in the 5th century AD, when barbarians beat at its gates.

TOURIST INFORMATION

Rome's main **EPT** tourist office is at *V. Parigi 5; tel: (06) 4889 9253* (Tues–Sat 1000–1800, Sun 1000–1300). There are small information desks at **Leonardo da Vinci Airport**, *tel: (06) 6595 6074* and **Termini Station**, *tel: (06) 487 1270* (inconspicuously situated at Platform 4, often crowded).

Municipal information booths can be found in the city at *Largo Goldoni; tel: (06) 689 5027; Largo Corrado Ricci* (near the Colosseum); *tel: (06) 678 0992; V. Nazionale; tel: (06) 474 6262* (all open Mon–Sat 1000–1800; Sun 1000–1300).

For a city of such importance, the quality of Rome's official tourist information service is lamentable. Underfunded, disillusioned staff (with a few praiseworthy exceptions) and a lack of published material (much of what is available is out of date) are sadly prevalent. You may do better heading for a privately run agency, such as the helpful **Enjoy Rome**, an English-speaking office at *V. Varese 39; tel: (06) 445 1843* (Mon–Fri 0830–1300 and 1530–1800, Sat 0830–1300), which offers a free hotel booking service and left-luggage facilities, plus information about guided city tours. The provincial office is now closed to the public; so very little information is available on Lazio province if you are planning to tour from the capital. The **Vatican City** has its own efficient information office at *Pza San Pietro; tel: (06) 6988 4466* (Mon–Sat 0830–1900) for sights within the Papal See. Look out for the free listings magazine *Un Ospite a Roma,* a bilingual, fortnightly publication with some useful contents.

ARRIVING AND DEPARTING

By Air
Leonardo da Vinci, generally known as Fiumicino Airport; *tel: (06) 6595 3640* or *(06) 65951* lies 30 km west of the city, and handles all scheduled flights. Open 24hrs, with left-luggage and exchange facilities, accommodation agencies and car rental desks. Free shuttle buses connect international and domestic terminals, car-parks, etc. The airport is connected to the city by regular trains daily from about 0700–1000 (less frequent on Sun). The hourly express

213

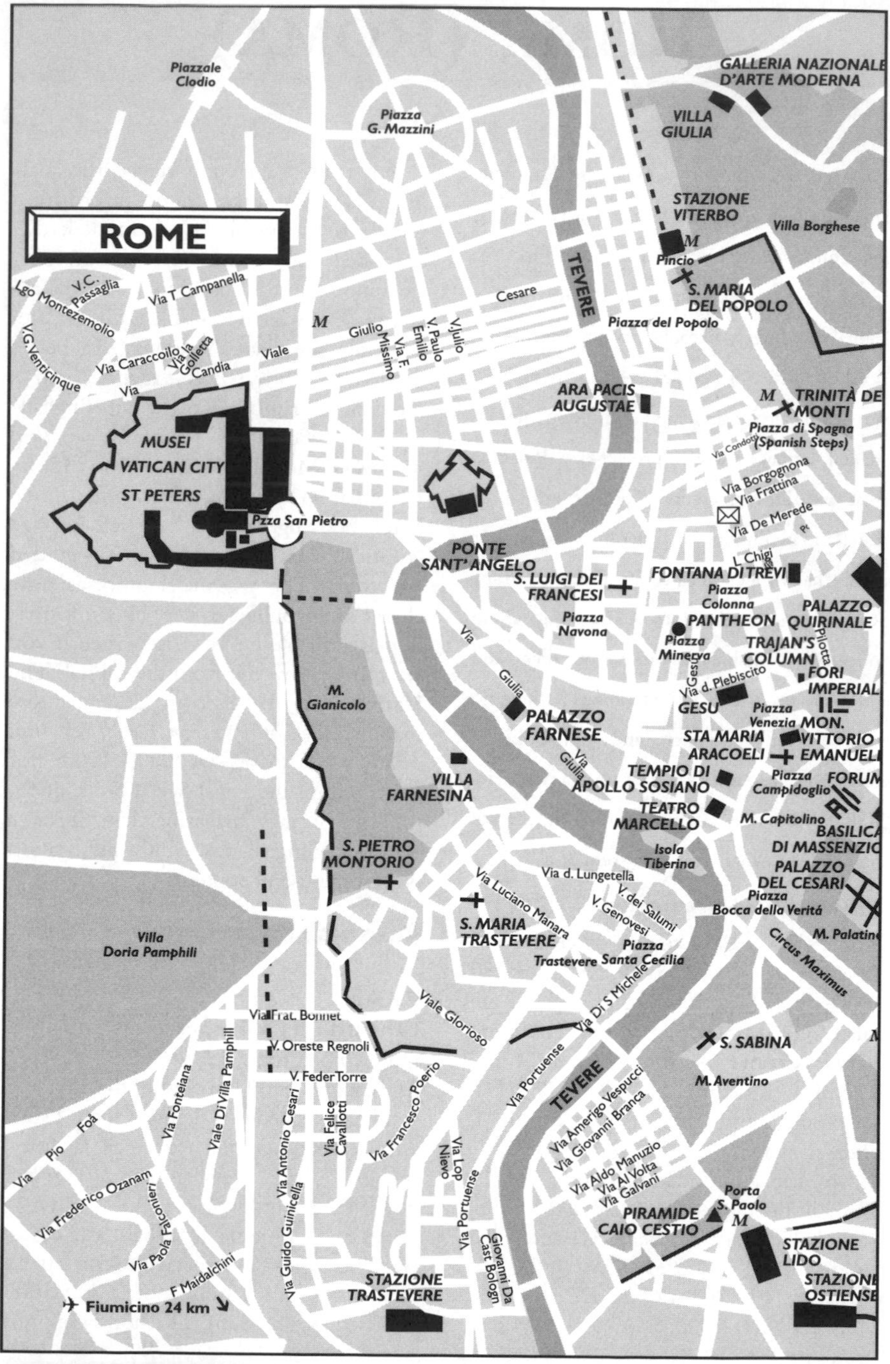
ROME
Piazzale Clodio
Piazza G. Mazzini
GALLERIA NAZIONALE D'ARTE MODERNA
VILLA GIULIA
STAZIONE VITERBO
Villa Borghese
M
Pincio
S. MARIA DEL POPOLO
Piazza del Popolo
TEVERE
V.C. Passaglia
Lgo Montezemolio
V.G.Venticinque
Via T Campanella
Via Caraccoilo
Via la Golletta
Candia
Via
Viale
M
Giulio
Cesare
V. F. Missimo
V. Paulo Emilio
V. Julio
ARA PACIS AUGUSTAE
M
TRINITÀ DEI MONTI
Piazza di Spagna (Spanish Steps)
Via Condotti
Via Borgognona
Via Frattina
Via De Merede
MUSEI
VATICAN CITY
ST PETERS
Pzza San Pietro
PONTE SANT' ANGELO
S. LUIGI DEI FRANCESI
L Chigi
FONTANA DI TREVI
Piazza Colonna
PANTHEON
PALAZZO QUIRINALE
Piazza Navona
Piazza Minerva
TRAJAN'S COLUMN
Pilotta
Via Giulia
Via d. Plebiscito
FORI IMPERIALI
M. Gianicolo
GESU
Piazza Venezia
MON. VITTORIO EMANUELE
PALAZZO FARNESE
STA MARIA ARACOELI
Via Giulia
TEMPIO DI APOLLO SOSIANO
Piazza Campidoglio
FORUM
VILLA FARNESINA
TEATRO MARCELLO
M. Capitolino
BASILICA DI MASSENZIO
S. PIETRO MONTORIO
Isola Tiberina
PALAZZO DEL CESARI
Via d. Lungetella
Via Luciano Manara
V. dei Salumi
V. Genovesi
Piazza Bocca della Verità
S. MARIA TRASTEVERE
M. Palatino
Villa Doria Pamphili
Piazza Santa Cecilia
Trastevere
Circus Maximus
Via Di S Michele
Viale Glorioso
Via Frat. Bonnet
V. Oreste Regnoli
V. Feder Torre
S. SABINA
Via Portuense
TEVERE
M. Aventino
Viale Di Villa Pamphill
Via Fonteiana
Via Pio Foà
Via Antonio Cesari
Via Felice Cavallotti
Via Francesco Poerio
Via Lop Nievo
Via Amerigo Vespucci
Via Giovanni Branca
Via Aldo Manuzio
Via Al Volta
Via Galvani
Via Frederico Ozanam
Porta S. Paolo
PIRAMIDE CAIO CESTIO
M
STAZIONE LIDO
Via Paola Falconieri
Via Portuense
F Maidalchini
Via Guido Guinicella
Giovanni Da Cast Bologn
STAZIONE TRASTEVERE
STAZIONE OSTIENSE
Fiumicino 24 km

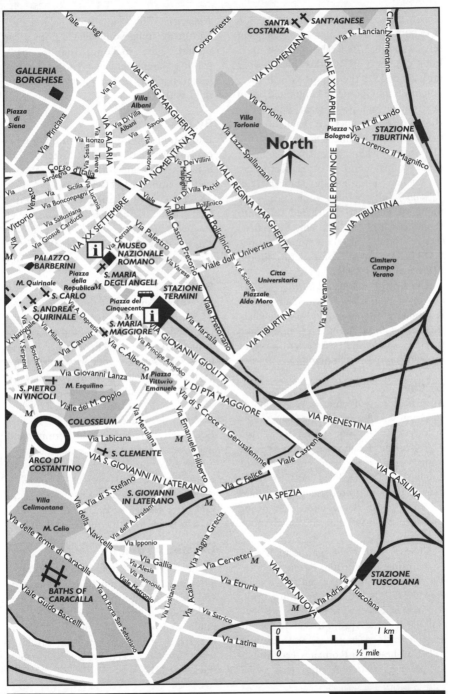

service takes 30mins to Termini Station (L15,000). A slower but more frequent service costing L7000 takes about 40mins. Look out for a **BIRG day pass** from a separate desk at the airport, which gives you travel into Rome and unlimited use of city public transport when you arrive (L8500). Remember to validate your ticket in the machine before you board. Depending where you are staying in Rome, it may be more convenient to get off at an intermediate station (e.g. *Tiburtina*) and continue your journey by metro or bus. Flat-rate shared taxis into Rome cost L11,500 (use only the official service; other cabs cost much more). **COTRAL** night buses to Rome (*Tiburtina*) cost L8000.

Ciampino Airport, *tel: (06) 794941* also open 24 hrs, lies 15 km south-east. It is a military base, also used by some charter flights. COTRAL buses ply into Rome (metro: *Anagnina*). Airport services (exchange, etc.) are limited.

By Car

All roads lead to Rome, as every school-child knows. As car drivers may subsequently discover, not always with ease. The **Grande Raccordo Anulare** is an orbital ring road (the equivalent of London's M25) enabling you to select your access point into the city. From then on, things may deteriorate; even major arterial routes may be in surprisingly poor condition.

Choose your hotel with care if you intend bringing a car into Rome. Parking is a problem, and driving centrally can be very stressful. If *Ben Hur* gave you a thrill, you may actually enjoy it. There are several large underground car-parks in Trastevere: *V. Marescotti 6*, and near the Villa Borghese. On Roman streets, watch for parking restriction signs (e.g. *Zona*

Rimozione – tow-away area) or you may end up rescuing your vehicle from a car pound. Blue markings indicate pay-parking zones – find an attendant. Do not leave anything of the remotest value in sight within the car.

By Bus

International and out-of-town buses generally terminate in the forecourt of Stazione Termini or near Repubblica metro station. COTRAL buses, *tel: (06) 581 5551,* serving Lazio province may run from other key metro stations, e.g. *Anagnina* (Frascati), *Rebibbia* (Tivoli), *Lepanto* (Cerveteri, Tarquinia, Bracciano, Civitavecchia).

By Train

Stazione Termini: *Pza dei Cinquecento; tel: (06) 4775* is the main station, always crowded and bewildering, and unsavoury at night. Beware of pickpockets and avoid touts. Check where your arrival train stops in Rome; an alternative station may be more convenient, e.g. Ostiense, Tiburtina, Trastavere. *Pzle Flaminio* (Roma Nord) is used for local services north of Rome. Both metro lines intersect at Termini, and many bus services terminate outside.

For rail or bus transport information and reservations, it may be easier to consult a good travel agency in the city centre (e.g. **CIT**, *Pza della Repubblica; tel: (06) 47941*) than to tangle with the queues at Termini.

GETTING AROUND

The best way to see Old Rome is on foot. The *centro storico* is not hugely extensive, and many of the smaller, more enticing, pedestrianised streets are inaccessible by public transport. Choose the shady side of the street, take advantage of drinking water fountains, and wear comfortable, thick-soled shoes.

Public Transport

The extensive bus and tram system is complicated, and one-way systems mean return routes may be quite different from outward journeys. A basic map and metro plan is available at the tourist office, but if you intend spending more than a day or two in the city, invest in the Roma Metro-Bus Map (L9000) from a newsstand, which plots all the bus and tram routes and Metro lines against the city streets. Trams serve outlying suburban areas. Orange **ATAC** buses serve the city centre between 0530–2400. Some services run at night. The main ATAC office is at *Pza dei Cinquecento, tel: (06) 4695 4444* near Termini Station. Useful routes include no. 64 (Termini–Vatican) and 218 (Colisseum, San Giovanni in Laterano, Appia Antica). Taking some of the longer bus routes is a relaxing, inexpensive and enjoyable way to explore the city, but choose off-peak travelling times. Etiquette dictates that you board at the rear and alight from the centre of the bus.

Two **Metro** lines (A and B) cross the city in a rough X-shape, intersecting at Termini Station. Many parts of the city are nowhere near a station, so though fast and efficient, the Metro is of limited use for sightseeing. Trains run about every 10 mins from 0530–2330. Useful stops on Line A include: *Spagna* (Spanish Steps); *Ottaviano* (Vatican Museums). On Line B: **Colosseo** (Colosseum); *Circo Massimo* (Baths of Caracalla).

Rome's ticketing system is now sensibly integrated for bus, tram and Metro use. The most convenient deal available is a **BIG**, stands for Billetti Interiore Generale, ticket costing L6000, which gives unlimited access for 24 hours to all inner-city and suburban transport (not Fiumicino Airport). Buy these from ATAC or metro ticket booths. A weekly CIS pass costs L24,000. BIRG, stands for Interiore e Regionale – Rome plus Lazio, one-day regional passes cover travel in Rome and Lazio (prices vary according to zone). Individual BIT tickets for single metro rides or any metropolitan bus services cost L1500 and are valid for 75 mins after punching. Buy them in advance from bars, tobacconists or newsagents displaying the appropriate logo. Automatic ticket-vending machines can be found throughout the city. Remember to validate your ticket as you board, or you may be liable for a fine of up to L100,000. Staff or other passengers are generally very helpful to tourists who look lost.

Bicycles and Mopeds

Cycling can be a pleasant way of getting round some parts of Rome, e.g. the banks of the Tiber or the Villa Borghese (remember Rome was built on seven hills). Scooters (*vespas*) or bikes can be hired (with safety helmets) from various outlets, e.g. around *Spagna* metro station. Rome's busy traffic makes it an unsuitable training ground for novice riders. Try **I Bike Rome**, *V. Veneto 156; tel: (06) 322 5240* or **Rent a Scooter**, *V. Filippo Turati 50; tel: (06) 446 9222.*

Taxis

Cabs can be obtained from ranks on the main squares, or by phone. They are not cheap. Supplements are charged for baggage, night journeys, airport trips and on Sun or holidays. Use only the official yellow or white metered cabs. For **Radio Taxi**; *tel: 3875.*

City Tours

Walking tours are arranged by several companies. Check **Enjoy Rome**, *V. Varese 39; tel: (06) 445 1843* or **American Express,** *Pza di Spagna 38;*

217

tel: (06) 67641, **Walk Thru the Centuries**, tel: (06) 323 1733 or **Secret Walks in Rome**; tel: (06) 3872 8728. Bus tours within and around Rome are advertised widely in tourist offices, listings magazines, hotels and travel agencies. Major companies include **Carrani Tours**; tel: (06) 474 2501, **Appian Line**, tel: (06) 488 4151 or **Green Line Tours**, tel: (06) 482 7480. An excellent and inexpensive way to see the main sights is to catch the Tourist Bus 110, a 3hr multilingual tour costng L15,000 operated by **ATAC** daily Apr–Oct (weekends only off-season). Buy tickets from the Pza dei Cinquecento ATAC office. Similar but pricier hop-on, hop-off sightseeing bus tours are operated by **Ciao Roma**, Pza del Esquilino 6; tel: (06) 474 3795 or **Trolley Tour**, V. Marghera 32; tel: (06) 446 3481 (this company also operates motorboat cruises on the Tiber).

Horse-drawn carriage trips can be hired from several points, e.g. Pza di Spagna, Pza Navona, Villa Borghese, St Peter's Sq, for a truly touristy ride round Rome. Prices from around L80,000 per hour (expect to haggle for rates).

STAYING IN ROME

Accommodation

Rome has some very charming hotels, and many charmless ones. Typical top-range hotels are grand, formal and expensive, and are not listed below. Try to book ahead if you have somewhere specific in mind. The tourist offices or specialist agencies will make accommodation bookings on arrival, but you must take pot luck at short notice.

Two excellent choices if you want to bring a car into Rome lie quite close together along V. Nomentana, one of the north-eastern arterial roads. This is quite a walk from the centre, but served by good bus routes. The **Villa del Parco**, V. Nomentana 110; tel: (06) 4434 7773, is a charming early 20th-century villa in walled gardens. Elegantly decorated and furnished inside, breakfast is served alfresco in summer. A little nearer the city centre, the **Villa Florence**, V. Nomentana 28; tel: (06) 440 3036 is another charming, family-run villa with pleasant terrace gardens. Neither has a restaurant, but both have parking facilities and are moderately priced.

If you want to be closer to the old town, two expensive but very attractive options are the **Valadier**, V. della Fontanella 15; tel: (06) 361 1998, a chic and well-equipped place just off the corso (garage 100m), or the gorgeous **Sole al Pantheon**, Pza della Rotonda 63; tel: (06) 6478 0441 with marvellous views of the Pantheon, a historic, ultra-stylish experience of Rome. More moderately priced boutique hotels near the Spanish Steps include the **Condotti**, V. Mario de' Fiori 37; tel: (06) 679 4661, or the **Carriage**, V. delle Carrozze 36; tel: (06) 679 3312. Cheaper still are the charming **Gregoriana**, V. Gregoriana 18; tel: (06) 679 4269, near the top of the steps, or the **Mozart**, V. dei Greci 23b; tel: (06) 3600 1915, in a quiet side-street. Down in medieval Rome are the quaint **Teatro di Pompeo**, Largo del Pallaro 8; tel: (06) 687 2812, in the vaults of Pompey's Theatre where Caesar was allegedly assassinated, or the simple **Campo dei Fiori**, V. del Biscione 6; tel: (06) 6880 6865, with many quaint features. Termini Station is a prime area for cheap accommodation, but most (not all) is rather grim. An attractive choice in this area is the **Villa delle Rose,** V. Vicenza 5; tel: (06) 445 1788, a civilised, family-run hotel with original features. If your budget is seriously tight, ask the tourist office about private rooms and pensioni.

Rome has several youth hostels and religious institutions which offer accommodation. Self-catering apartments or rooms in residential hotels may be a relatively inexpensive option if you plan to stay more than a week.

Eating and Drinking

It's easy to find inexpensive snacks in Rome. Stand-up bars and stalls serve rolls, sandwiches, pastries, fruit and slices of pizza everywhere from as little as L2000. But there aren't many picnic spots in the medieval centre, and at some point while you're exploring, you will definitely need a rest. Treat yourself at the English-style **Babington's Tearooms** near the Spanish Steps, **La Tazza d'Oro**, *V. degli Orfani* near the Pantheon or the **Caffè Greco** on *V. dei Condotti*. The *V. Veneto* is no longer what it was, but visitors searching for glimmers of Fellini's *La Dolce Vita* still head for **Harry's Bar**, **Doney's** or the **Café de Paris**. In the old town, try **Giolitti**, *V. dei Uffici del Vicario 40* or the **Tre Scalini** on *Pza Navona* for ice-cream. You may even be tempted by Rome's stylish branches of the burger chain **McDonalds**, *Pza di Spagna 46* or *Pza della Repubblica* which have excellent salad bars and surprisingly classical decor.

'Foreign' restaurants are still comparatively unusual in Rome, but you can try any variety of Italian regional cooking, and there are lots of fish restaurants. Roman specialities include *saltimbocca* (veal fillet rolled in ham), *gnocchi* (small potato dumplings) and *spaghetti alla carbonara*, besides types of offal you don't usually meet at the dinner table. Typical wines come from the local Castelli hills, notably Frascati. Popular tourist areas, such as the Vatican, tend to have fewer good-value restaurants, but a short step down to Trastevere will offer many lively pizzerias.

For an authentic Roman experience, avoid tourist menus in several languages. Many restaurants close for all or part of Aug.

In the *centro storico*, there's a fantastic choice at all prices. Top of the range eating may take you to **El Toulà**, *V. della Lupa 29/*; tel: (06) 687 3498 (closed Sat lunch & Sun), with antique furniture and Venetian specialities, or **Trattoria del Pantheon-da Fortunato**, *V. del Pantheon 58*; tel: (06) 6479 2788 (closed Sun), a sober institution near the House of Representatives offering classic, but reasonably priced dishes. Less expensively, try the **Pizzeria Baffetto**, *V. del Coverno Vecchio*; tel: (06) 686 1237 (closed Sun), or the **Orso 80**, *V. dell'Orso 33*; tel: (06) 686 4904 (closed Mon), a cheerful trattoria amid artisans' workshops.

Near the Spanish Steps, **Otello alla Concordia**, *V. della Croce 81*; tel: (06) 678 1454 (closed Sun), is especially popular at lunchtime for its shady courtyard setting and pleasant service, while **Il Piccolo Arancio**, *Vicolo Scanderbeg 112*; tel: (06) 678 6139, (closed Mon) one of three 'spider' (*arancio*) restaurants in Rome, serves specialities like *carciofi alla giudia* (stuffed artichoke). **Tavernetta**, *V. del Nazareno 3*; tel: (06) 679 3124 (closed Mon), near the Trevi Fountain features Sicilian and Abruzzese cooking. None of these will break the bank.

The Villa Borghese/*V. Veneto* area is exclusive and sophisticated, with **Sans Souci**, *V. Sicilia 20/24*; tel: (06) 482 1814 (closed lunchtimes and Mon), keeping the style of 1950s glamour afloat. Service is courteous, but dress for the occasion. **Coriolano**, *V. Ancona*; tel: (06) 4424 9863 (closed Sun, and Sat in July), near Porta Pia is expensive too, but presentation is immaculate.

Termini Station is not an area to cruise

at night, but if you need a meal here try **Fagianetto**, *V. F Turati 21; tel: (06) 446 7306* (closed Mon), an inexpensive family-run trattoria with reliable hearty cooking. Towards the Colosseum, the **Osteria da Nerone**, *V. delle Terme di Tito 96; tel: (06) 474 5207* (closed Sun), gives you good home-made pasta and a monumental view. Further south, try **Charly's Sauciere**, *V. di San Giovanni in Laterano 270; tel: (06) 7049 5666* (closed Sun and lunch Sat–Mon), for elegant French-Swiss cuisine.

Over the river, neighbourhood *trattorie* can still be found not far from St Peter's. Try the **Tre Pupazzi**, *V. dei Tre Pupazzi at Borgo Pio; tel: (06) 686 8371* (closed Sun), an ancient building with classic Abruzzese dishes, or the **Pizzeria Ivo**, *V. di San Francesca a Ripa 158; tel: (06) 581 7082,* a popular favourite worth a wait for a table (closed Tues). If you want to reach for the stars, **Les Etoiles**, *V. dei Bastioni 1; tel: (06) 689 3434* has a breathtaking view of the Vatican in the roof garden of the Atlante Star hotel. Just off Trastevere's famous *Santa Maria Sq*, **Paris**, *Pza San Calliso 7a; tel: (06) 581 5378* (closed Sun eve, Mon), has honest Roman cuisine and outside tables on a less-visited *piazza*.

Communications

24 hour fax, telex and telephone services are available at the main post office; *Pza San Silvestro*; *tel: (06) 679 5530* (postal services and currency exchange Mon–Fri 0900–1800, Sat 0700–1400). The Italian postal service does not have a good reputation (though it is better than it used to be) and letters can easily take two weeks, or more, to get home. It's worth noting that the Vatican City post office is much more efficient in this respect. Vatican City stamps can be bought locally and cost the same as Italian ones, so speed your postcards on celestial wings from St Peter's.

Money

Major banks can be found throughout the city, including automatic teller machines, e.g. on *Largo Tritone* and *V. Arenula*. Commissions vary between L6000–10,000. There are exchange offices at Termini Station and near many major sights (some have poor rates). **Thomas Cook** has several bureaux in Rome (most open Sun mornings): *V. della Conciliazione 23/25; tel: (06) 68300435/36; V. del Corso 23; tel: (06) 3230067, and Pza della Republica 0185; tel: (06) 486495.* Many post offices offer exchange facilities.

Embassies

US; *V. Veneto 121; tel: (06) 464741.*
UK; *V. XX Settembre 80a; tel: (06) 482 5441.*
Canada; *V. Zara 30; tel: (06) 445981.* (**New Zealand** is next door at no. 28).
Australia: *V. Alessandria 215; tel: (06) 852721.*

Several listings magazines keep you in touch with Rome's varied and rapidly changing cultural scene, *Trova Roma, Roma C'è, Wanted in Rome,* etc. A wide range of concerts is on offer at numerous locations, including free ones at many churches. Rock, jazz and pop concerts are held in summer. The main opera season runs from Nov–May at the **Teatro dell'Opera**, *Pza B. Gigli; tel: (06) 481 7003*, with a summer season in the Villa Borghese. **Cinema Pasquino**, *Vicolo del Piede; tel: (06) 580 3622*, shows English-language films. Rome no longer has quite the reputation of its *Dolce Vita* days for nightlife, but there is no shortage of bars, clubs and discos for night owls. If you prefer a drink without

220

music, try one of the atmospheric wine bars in the old city.

Events

Easter is the peak of Rome's religious calendar, when the Pope's message to the city and the world (*Urbi et Orbi*) is relayed from St Peter's Sq. Epiphany (6 Jan) is another big day, celebrated with a huge toy fair in *Pza Navona*. St John's Day (23–24 June) sees much feasting and dancing around the church of San Giovanni. On 8 December (Immaculate Conception) a garland of flowers is placed on the statue of the Virgin in the *Pza di Spagna* by the city's firemen (the only ones who can reach the statue on top of a column). In spring, huge vases of azaleas are arranged on the Spanish Steps (end Mar–early Apr).

SHOPPING

Rome has few very distinctive souvenirs that you cannot find elsewhere in Italy, unless you are a devotee of Vatican kitsch. But you will find dozens of small shops selling high-quality silk, leather, jewellery and accessories for that essential but elusive Roman asset – *bella figura*. The elegant streets between the Villa Borghese and the *V. del Corso* are mostly for window-shopping. Designer labels (Gucci, Versace, Valentino, Armani) command breathtaking prices, which in most cases are not even displayed (if you have to ask, you probably can't afford them). In some boutiques, you may need an appointment. There are one or two interesting second-hand shops, e.g. on *V. del Governo Vecchio*. During the afternoon siesta, metal shutters obscure the tempting displays. But things start humming again in the early evening, when it can be most interesting and cool enough to go shopping. The big stores include **Rinascente**, *Pza del Corso; tel: (06) 6479 7691*; **COIN**, *Pzle Appio 15;*

tel: (06) 708 0020 ; **Standa**, *Vle Trastevere 62–64; tel: (06) 589 5342* and **UPIM**, *V. del Tritone 172; tel: (06) 6478 3336.*

The maze of tiny streets in medieval Rome (either side of the *Corso Vittorio Emanuele II*) are full of tantalising workshops and studios, where restorers are hard at work on antiques with resin and polish. *V. dei Giubbonari* is lined with inexpensive clothes shops. *Campo dei Fiori* has an atmospheric fruit and flower market. In Trastevere, you will still find old-fashioned ironmongers or knife grinders. Porta Portese, located south of the Vatican City, holds a colourful flea market every Sun.

SIGHTSEEING

Suddenly, those long-forgotten school history and Latin lessons snap into focus. Rome is where many of the events that shaped Western civilisation actually happened. But you don't have to be mesmerised by history to enjoy the city – a vibrant, stylish and entertaining place by any 20th-century yardstick. Nor can you hope to see everything on a single visit. If you spend a week there, you may have a fairly good overview of its principle monuments and museums. But you should also allow time to absorb modern Roman life in its picturesque neighbourhoods, watch the fountains play in the *piazzas*, and enjoy an excursion outside the city. Some of the most interesting sites in northern Lazio are covered in Routes 21 and 23, but east and south of Rome lie other worthwhile touring destinations, especially Tivoli and the Castelli Hills.

The main sights are concentrated within the original walls, built in Julius Caesar's time. Before deciding what you want to see, collect an up-to-date list of opening times and entrance charges (these can be found in the listings magazines, such as *Un Ospite a Roma*), and spend a little time planning your sightseeing itineraries. This will save much fruitless trekking on hard, hot, hilly cobblestones. In the short space available here, only highlights are mentioned.

Ancient Rome

You can scarcely step a hundred paces in Rome without barking your shins on some antiquity, and it is tantalising to consider how many unearthed remains lie concealed beneath modern paving stones. Building projects in the city are constantly delayed by new archaeological discoveries. Many monuments are in a sad state of disrepair, their steady disintegration massively accelerated by modern traffic and pollution. At the same time, spurred by external pressure from visitors less blasé about Rome's heritage, and welcome injections of financial help from the European Union, there is a greater sense of urgency to rescue what is left than ever before.

There are several Roman forums (*fora* if you prefer). The main one is the **Roman Forum**, *V. dei Fori Imperiali 9; tel: (06) 699 0110* (Mon–Sat 0900–dusk, Sun 0900–1300; L12,000), the focus of political, religious and commercial life in the ancient city. It is an extensive site to explore, and can be bewildering. See it first from above (there's a good viewpoint on the *V. del Campidoglio*). Within it lie a huge range of temples, arches, basilicas and columns spanning 900 years. The nearby **Palatine Hill** (same ticket as Forum) is the site of Rome's earliest settlement, the legendary place where Romulus founded the city. It makes a good picnic spot. The 16th-century Farnese Gardens and Livia's House are worth seeing. Opposite the main Forum lie the Imperial Fora built by later emperors, including Caesar, Vespasian and Augustus. The most interesting are **Trajan's Market and Forum**, *V. IV*

Novembre 94; tel: (06) 679 0048 (Tues–Sat 0900–1900, Sun 0900–1300; L3750), dating from AD 113, whose main feature is the spectacularly carved pillar known as **Trajan's Column**, celebrating the emperor's military triumphs. The similar **Column of Marcus Aurelius**, *Pza Colonna*, adorns a square off the corso.

The **Colosseum**, *Pza del Colosseo; tel: (06) 700 4261* (Mon–Tues, Thur–Sat 0900–sunset, Wed and Sun 0900–1300; free to ground floor, L8000 to upper levels) is an unmistakable landmark, now hemmed in by busy road systems. Built by Vespasian in AD 72, it housed over 50,000 spectators and witnessed countless blood-thirsty struggles. Moth-eaten by time and post-classical vandalism, its dangerous condition is causing serious concern and it is undergoing massive restoration. Between the Colosseum and the Palatine Hill is the **Arch of Constantine**, built in AD 315 to celebrate the emperor's conversion to Christianity.

In the heart of Old Rome, the **Pantheon**: *Pza della Rotonda; tel: (06) 6830 0230* (Mon–Sat 0900–1730, Sun 0900–1300; free) is the best preserved of Rome's classical monuments, a domed brick building rebuilt by Hadrian in about AD 120 as a temple. The original bronze doors are still in place. Later it was used as a church and a market.

On the banks of the Tiber, a modern glass pavilion houses a reconstruction of the **Ara Pacis Augustae** (Altar of Augustan Peace), *V. di Ripetta; tel: (06) 671 0271* (Tues–Sat 0900–1900, Sun 0900–1345; L3750), dating from 13 BC, which commemorated the peaceful years of Augustus' reign. South of the city, the **Baths of Caracalla**, *Vle delle Terme di Caracalla 52; tel: (06) 575 8626* (Tues–Sat 0900–sunset, Sun–Mon 0900–1300; L8000), dating from the 3rd century AD, functioned as a Roman leisure and social centre.

Religious Rome

Rome is the most important Christian place of pilgrimage after Jerusalem, and for many visitors, St Peter's Basilica and a chance to see the Pope are the main reasons to visit the city. The Vatican City, of course, is not technically Rome at all, but an independent sovereign state set up in 1929, after the Church lost its temporal power in a unified and secularised Italy. Its Byzantine politics, inconceivable wealth and a wave of scandals have aroused lurid fascination ever since.

Besides the massive crowd puller of St Peter's, Rome itself has over 400 churches, spanning the period since the earliest *anni domini*. When visiting churches, remember to take some change to light up paintings. A strict dress code is upheld in some, particularly St Peter's. Most can be visited free of charge from about 0700–1900, with a 3–4 hr break at lunchtime. It is permissible to visit churches during services as long as no disturbance is caused to worshippers. Concerts are held in many Roman churches.

St Peter's Basilica, the world's largest Christian church, is open daily from 0700–1900. The present building dates from the early 16th century, and stands on the site of Constantine's original church built in 324–329. Its great dome, designed by Michelangelo, dominates the Tiber's right bank, and the huge square on which the Basilica stands. The interior can be seen free of charge, but the museum costs L5000 (0900–1830), and access to the dome costs L6000 by lift, L5000 by staircase (0800–1800). The main features inside are Bernini's huge **baldacchino**, a bronze canopy over the altar, and the baroque **Chair of St Peter** behind it.

Michelangelo's *Pietà* is protected behind glass in a side chapel.

No other church approaches St Peter's in importance, but try to catch at least some of the following. Near the Pantheon in Old Rome, **Il Gesù**, *Pza del Gesù*, is a Counter-Reformation church dating from about 1650. Its main interest is its lavish interior of gold, marble and lapis lazuli. The French national church of **San Luigi dei Francesi**, *Pza San Luigi dei Francesi*, contains several masterpieces by Caravaggio. Borromini's **Sant'Ivo alla Sapienza**, *Corso Rinascimento 40,* is notable for its spiral dome. **Santa Maria sopra Minerva**, *Pza della Minerva*, is an unusual example of Roman Gothic. It contains the tomb of Fra Angelico, Michelangelo's *Risen Christ* and 15th-century frescos by Filippino Lippi. On an impressive Rococo square, **Sant'Ignazio**, *Pza Sant'Ignazio*, has a sumptuous 17th-century interior with a *trompe l'œil* dome and a lavish altar.

Further afield south-east of the old city, don't miss Rome's **Duomo** near the *V. Appia Antica*, which is not St Peter's but the ornate church of **San Giovanni in Laterano**; *Pza San Giovanni in Laterano*. The huge, much-rebuilt church has a baroque interior and tranquil cloisters studded with mosaics. The Pope presides here as Bishop of Rome, and the adjacent Lateran Palace houses the Vatican Historical Museum. Nearby, the ancient basilica of **San Clemente**, *V. San Giovanni in Laternano*, is built over a 4th-century church. The upper church contains fine mosaics and frescos. Off V. Cavour, **San Pietro in Vincoli**, *Pza San Pietro in Vincoli*, houses the chains of St Peter beneath the altar, and Michelangelo's *Moses*. Heading north of San Giovanni, **Santa Maria Maggiore**, *Pza Sta Maria Maggiore,* is a splendid basilica church with Byzantine mosaics and baroque chapels.

223

Santa Maria della Vittoria, *V. XX Settembre,* is a High baroque church containing a well-known Bernini masterpiece, *The Ecstasy of St Teresa.*

Across the river, 12th-century **Santa Maria in Trastevere** has more superb Byzantine mosaics. On *V. Garibaldi Gianicolo,* **San Pietro in Montorio**'s Renaissance *tempietto* (1502) is one of Bramante's finest works. **San Francesco a Ripa** holds another Bernini spectacular, this time of the Blessed Ludovica Albertoni.

Outside the walls, **Sant'Agnese** and **Santa Costanza** stand next to each other on *V. Nomentana.* These very early structures contain palaeo-Christian catacombs and Byzantine mosaics. On *V. Ostiense* (easily reached by metro), track down **San Paolo**, site of St Paul's tomb, martyred under Nero. This famous pilgrimage church was destroyed in a fire in 1923 and is now grandly oppressive or impressive, but redeemed by its lovely cloister.

Museum Rome

Rome's museums are awesome places requiring much stamina. They are expensive to visit (no combined sightseeing tickets are available). State galleries and museums are usually closed on Mon. Recently, the magnificent Villa Borghese Gallery reopened, a long-awaited event after years of restoration.

The most heavyweight collection is in the Vatican City. The **Vatican Museums,** *Vle Vaticano, tel: (06) 698 3333* (Mon–Fri 0845–1700, Sat 0845–1400 (Easter and Jul–Sept); Mon–Sat and public holidays 0900–1400 (Oct–June); normally closed Sun, except last Sun of month when entrance is free (long queues build); otherwise L15,000) contain an astonishing assembly of art. It is impossible to see it all,

but you can get a good idea of the contents of this vast palace by following one of the suggested colour-coded itineraries, which last from 90 mins to 4 hrs 30 mins. A shuttle bus (L2000), takes you from the Vatican's information office in *St Peter's Sq,* passing through the lovely Vatican Gardens, otherwise accessible only on an expensive, prebooked guided tour; *Pza San Pietro; tel: (06) 6988 4466* (Sat 1000; L16,000). Highlight for most visitors is the **Sistine Chapel,** painted by Michelangelo over four agonising years. The *Creation of Adam* fresco has iconic status the world over; if you have never seen the original before, you will recognise it when you do. The other collections contain fabulous quantities of classical and Renaissance art. The Egyptian Museum, the Pinacoteca and the Raphael Rooms shouldn't be missed.

Another blockbusting assembly of museums is in the **Villa Borghese**, a huge open park towards the northern edge of the city. The major sights here are the restored **Galleria Borghese**, *Villa Borghese, V. Raimondi; tel: (06) 854 8577* (Tues–Sat 0900–1900, Sun 0900–1300; L4000), a palace of extravagant salons filled with sculpture (notice Canova's bewitching Pauline Bonaparte, undressed to kill), and the **Museo Nazionale di Villa Giulia,** *Pza di Villa Giulia 9; tel: (06) 320 1951* (Tues–Sat 0900–1900, Sun 0900–1300; L8000); Italy's foremost collection of Etruscan art housed in a charming

---

Colour section (i): On the Road: a view of Spoleto (p. 189); a viaduct en route to Cascia (p. 197); parked up in Orvieto.
(ii) A view of Trevi (p. 188); Brassware on sale in Todi (p. 202).
(iii) The Duomo in Orvieto (p. 205); inset, a detail from the façade.
(iv) Rome: the Spanish Steps (p. 225).

Early Christian Churches

Not surprisingly, Rome has some of the world's oldest surviving Christian churches, many containing relics of Apostles and saints. The earliest places of worship are the catacombs that are to be found on the fringes of Rome. The Catacombs of San Sebastiano *(V. Appia Antica 136)* and the Catacombs of Domitilla *(V. delle Sette Chiese 282)* consist of maze-like underground passages, with niches where the faithful were buried.

Once Christians were allowed to worship openly, they began to build fine structures, modelled on the basilicas, the law courts, of Rome. Many survive, albeit in the form of underground crypts, as in such magnificent churches as Santa Maria Maggiore – in fact, one of the pleasures of exploring Roman churches is to find that an apparently late 18th-century church actually has remains in the crypt dating back to the origins of Christian worship.

Best of all are the handful of tiny jewel-like churches whose walls were entirely covered with rich mosaics, made in the 5th to 9th centuries from glass incorporating gold, scarlet, green and deep azure minerals. Among the best are Santa Passede *(V. Santa Prassede 9A)*, San Clemente *(V. de San Giovanni in Laterano)*, and Santa Pudenziana *(V. a Urbana 160)*.

Renaissance villa. The **Galleria Nazionale d'Arte Moderna**, *Vle delle Belle Arti; tel: (06) 3229481* (Tues–Sat 0900–1830, Sun 0900–1300; L8000), is less compelling.

The **Musei Capitolini e Pinacoteca**, *Pza del Campidoglio 1; tel: (06) 671 0271* (Tues–Sat 0900–1900, Sun 0900–1300;

L10,000 but free last Sun of month) in twin palaces overlooking the *piazza*, offer another opportunity to blow a cultural gasket, this time with sculpture and Renaissance paintings assembled by the art-loving Pope Sixtus V. Prize exhibits include the unpleasant 'she-wolf' statue which is Rome's logo, the exquisite *Boy with a Thorn in his Foot* plus any number of Roman emperors.

Monumental Rome

The **Castel Sant'Angelo**, *Lungotevere Castello 50; tel: (06) 6880 5148* (daily 0900–1300; L8000) is a fortress on the Tiber, originally built as a tomb for the Emperor Hadrian. The museum inside contains weaponry and Renaissance furnishings. Notice the lovely **Ponte Sant'Angelo** spanning the Tiber alongside, adorned with Bernini angels.

Among Rome's many fine squares, one not to miss is the 17th-century **Pza Navona**, an oval square on the site of Domitian's stadium. A prime tourist location (partly for its ice-cream cafés), it is surrounded by beautiful old houses and the church of Sant'Agnese in Agone. It plays host to a lively *passegiata*, and an Epiphany toy-fair. Its centrepiece is a magnificent fountain (see box, p. 226).

Another place of pilgrimage for any visitor to Rome is the **Spanish Steps**, rising from the *Pza di Spagna* to the church of Trinità dei Monti at the top of the hill. In spring the steps are bright with azaleas; at other times of year cluttered with backpacking tourists. A familiar landmark dominating the southern end of the *corso* is the enormous white marble **Vittorio Emanuele monument** dedicated to the first king to preside over a unified Italy. Crowned by a vast bronze sculpture group, it houses the Tomb of the Unknown Soldier and an eternal flame.

The Fountains of Rome

One of Rome's most spectacular tourist attractions is Salvi's exuberant masterpiece, the Trevi Fountain, scene of Anita Ekberg's famous frolic in *La Dolce Vita*. Every day, hundreds of sightseers follow the time-honoured practice of tossing a coin into the melée of writhing figures to ensure their safe return to Rome. Altogether, Rome has more than 200 fountains, a legacy of the ingenuity of ancient Roman water engineers, who developed an amazingly complex system of aqueducts to feed dozens of public baths, *nymphaei* (sacred fountains), latrines and drinking basins. Turning a basic commodity into an art form and a source of entertainment, the Romans even invented grand water war-games (*naumachiae* – ship battles) enacted in special flooded amphitheatres. Today's visitors to Rome may find themselves developing an unexpected passion for fountain spotting. Grand set pieces can be found in most of the larger squares, but all over the city, quiet niches and shady parks reveal water gushing, spouting or trickling over a huge variety of sculpted forms. Besides the Trevi's baroque extravaganza of marble sea-gods exploding from a palace wall, Rome's grander fountains include the Fontana dei Quattro Fiumi in *Pza Navona* (1651), sculpted by Bernini with allegorical figures representing the Nile, Ganges, Danube and Plate (sadly recently damaged by boisterous revellers). Water nymphs disport themselves in the Fontana delle Naiadi (the Naiad Fountain) on *Pza dei Repubblica*. In *Pza Mattei*, look out for a gentle but imaginative masterpiece, the Fontana delle Tartarughe (Turtle Fountain), in which four boys hold tortoises up to the fountain basin. The *Pza di Spagna* contains another famous Bernini fountain, the Fontana della Barcaccia whose centrepiece is a leaking boat. Bernini's hand is visible again in *Pza Barbarini*'s Fontana del Tritone.

OUT OF TOWN

Within easy reach of the city centre, don't miss a chance to explore the **Via Appia Antica**, stretching south-east from Porta San Sebastiano. This road was completed in 312BC by Appius Claudius. Along it can be seen several catacombs, the ruined Circus of Maxentius and the Tomb of Cecilia Metella, the mausoleum of a Roman noblewoman who lived at the time of Julius Caesar. For more information about these antiquities, collect the informative leaflet from the tourist office. Bus 218 takes you there.

About 6 km south-west of central Rome lies the curious satellite suburb known as **EUR**, which you may see signposted from the outer ring-road. The initials stand for *Espozione Universale di Roma*, a project dreamt up by Mussolini as a monument to the glory of Rome (and Fascism). It is characterised by wide avenues and lifelessly grandiose architecture, but has several worthy museums, and is frequented by posses of wealthy, sun-tanned Roman youths in search of the good life. Easily accessible on Metro Line B.

More rewarding excursions can be made to the hill towns west of Rome, notably **Tivoli**, where **Hadrian's Villa** (daily 0900–dusk; L8000) and the **Villa d'Este** (daily 0900–dusk; L5000) can be visited. **Palestrina** on the slopes of Monte Ginestro is renowned for the **Palazzo Barberini**, now an archaeological museum. **Subiaco**'s main attraction is the 6th-century **monastery of St Benedict** built over a grotto where the saint lived. **Frascati**, famed for its white wine, has an **Aldobrandini villa** in splendid formal gardens.

ROME-ORBETELLO

This route covers several of the most important archaeological sites in north-west Lazio (Latium). You needn't be a classical historian to enjoy the tour; these sights are enjoyable in their own terms without much background knowledge. The excavated seaport of Ostia Antica gives a vividly authentic experience of a Roman town, and makes a fascinating day-trip from the capital. The other sites shed light on the mysterious Etruscan civilisation which predated the Romans in this part of Italy.

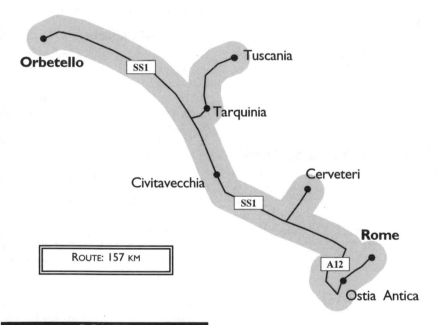

ROUTE: 157 KM

ROUTE

You can easily visit Ostia Antica by public transport from central Rome, but if you drive there, you can continue the tour northwards on the S296, crossing the Tiber without returning to Rome. This road skirts the airport zone and joins the A12 *autostrada*. The scenery of the Etruscan coast near Rome is drab, and there is little point in taking the old coast road (S1 – *V. Aurelia*), which churns through a series of charmless little resorts clogged with holiday traffic in summer. The motorway (toll) whisks you rapidly through the truck fumes, allowing easy access to **Cervéteri** and **Civitavécchia** from clearly signed junctions. North of Civitavécchia, the routes merge into the dual carriageway *V. Aurelia*, which continues up the Tuscan coast towards Livorno. Turn off at **Tarquínia,** and visit the Etruscan necropolis a couple of km southeast of the town. From Tarquínia, take the secondary road 25 km north-east to Tuscánia. Don't miss the church of San Pietro on the outskirts. Retrace steps to the *V. Aurelia* at Montalto di Castro, and almost immediately, take another right turn to the scattered necropolis of **Vulci.** The best places to stay lie further north, on the Maremma coast at Orbetello or Porto Ercolle. Pressure on coastal accommodation is intense in high season, so book ahead. Alternatively, head north across country on minor roads, where there are several pleasant small hotels across the Tuscan border (e.g. at Montemerano, Saturnia or Scansano).

OSTIA ANTICA

Tourist Information: pick up an English version of the guide and map to Ostia Antica at the tourist offices in central Rome, or at the ticket office by the entrance to the ruins. The nearest tourist office to the site is at *Pza delle Stazione del Lido 34; tel: (06) 562 7892* at Lido di Ostia.

ARRIVING AND DEPARTING

By Metro/train
From central Rome, take Metro Line B as far as the *Magliana* stop and transfer to the Lido railway line. There is a regular service to Ostia Antica and Lido di Ostia (the next and final stop) every ½hr. From Ostia Antica Station, cross the overpass and turn left, following signs for the excavations.

By Car
The *V. del Mare* leads directly from central Rome to Ostia Antica (30–40 mins' drive), a modern road running parallel to the old consular *V. Ostiensis* built by the Romans. You can also reach the remains fairly easily from the *superstrada Vle C Colombo* which runs through EUR (Mussolini's satellite suburb south of Rome) to Lido di Ostia, Rome's seaside resort. Ostia Antica may be approached conveniently from Rome's Fiumicino Airport (10 km north on the other side of the Tiber) by taxi or hired car, so could be treated as a first or last port of call by visitors flying into or out of Rome.

EATING AND DRINKING

There is no food or drink available on site, so take your own, or at least a bottle of water in hot weather. The ruins take several hours to explore properly, and it is a lovely place to enjoy a picnic. You can buy basic provisions at a shop on the castle road in the nearby village of Ostia Antica. Alternatively, there is a simple restaurant in the village: **Monumento**, *Pza Umberto 18; tel: (06) 565 0021* (closed Mon and late Aug–mid Sept).

SIGHTSEEING

Ostia Antica was the main port of ancient Rome, and its first colony. Founded in the 4th century BC at what was then the mouth of the Tiber, it became a bustling naval base and provisioning centre with a population (in its heyday) of over 80,000. Its inhabitants consisted of merchants, sailors, salt workers and slaves. Huge warehouses were built to handle shipments of grain from Africa, and commercial guilds representing all branches of trade and industry were established in the port. Gradually it outgrew its harbour and a rival seaport was constructed north of the

228

Tiber (Portus). Ostia's decline set in from the reign of Constantine, who favoured Portus, and eventually besieging barbarians and malarial mosquitoes made Ostia a ghost town. Pope Gregory IV attempted to revive Ostia Antica in the 9th century with the construction of the fortified *borgo* (suburb) nearby, but only a handful of people ever lived there. Adding insult to injury, even the Tiber deserted Ostia, silting up the harbour and stranding the former seaport uselessly inland; in 1575 a great flood shifted the river's course permanently northwards and smothered the decaying city in a thick blanket of alluvial mud. Saved from further pillaging and the ravages of the elements, Ostia remained peacefully submerged until excavations began in the 19th century. These have continued until the present day, steadily unearthing the city's fascinating outlines.

Today, a wander through the excavated remains of Ostia Antica gives a vivid flavour of a complete working Roman town. The site is smaller than Pompeii, and lacks the physical drama of an active volcano on its doorstep, but is in a much prettier setting and far less besieged by visitors and tour groups, open daily 0930–1700, until 1800 or 1900 (summer); L8000 including museum entrance – remarkable value compared with some sights.) Free tours are offered on Sun mornings in summer, but only in Italian. Follow signs for **Scavi di Ostia Antica** (excavations) up the entrance drive (part of the old *V. Ostiense*) to the car-park. The ticket office and entrance to the site lie by the Porta Romana, one of Ostia's three gates. Ahead lies the main street, **Decumanus Maximus**, which leads through the centre of the city. On either hand, walls of thin horizontal or lozenge-shaped bricks capped with protective cement outline the shells of the former

An Apartment in Ostia

Typically we think of the Romans as living in decorous villas with oodles of space for mosaic-floored dining rooms, and spacious bath suites, with cold plunges, saunas and warm rooms. In Ostia, life was nothing like as comfortable: many people lived in flats in multi-storey blocks, not greatly different from those of modern Rome – even the building method was similar, using lightweight bricks for the basic structure, covered with a coat of stucco-like plaster. Shops, wine bars, workshops, offices and warehouses occupied the ground floor, with apartments above, some with balconies, all built around an open inner courtyard.

buildings, now softened by poppies, oleander and tall pines, and alive with insects and scuttling lizards. An interesting group of buildings lies on the right-hand side about 200m from the entrance gate. The **Terme di Nettuno** (Neptune's Baths) were built by Hadrian and paved with marine mosaics; nearby are the barracks for the emergency services – firemen and police (Caserma dei Vigili). Next to the baths is a **theatre**, still used in summer for classical productions. Behind the theatre is the **Pzle delle Corporazioni**, surrounded by the offices, shops and insignia of Ostia's seafaring trade guilds. The **Forum,** further down the street, contains the **Capitol**, baths and a basilica. Wandering among houses, temples, warehouses and tombs, you will encounter a bakery and a laundry, mills and a roadside café (Thermopilium). The **Museo Ostiense** (daily 0930–1400; *tel: (06) 565 0022;* entrance included in site ticket) contains some of the sculptures and sarcophagi unearthed from the town. Near the museum are some **insulae** (Roman 'apartment blocks'); as space in the city grew scarcer, the houses were built on top of each other in an early high-density housing scheme with communal latrines. Needless to say, the well-off merchants and business community lived in more spacious and desirable accommodation. Sharp-eyed observers may spot a few graphic erotica among the murals and mosaics hidden away in the buildings, particularly if the bordello is unlocked.

In the medieval village near the excavations, the 15th-century **Castello di Giulio II** (Mon–Sat 0900–1300); *tel: (06) 565 0022* has circular towers and a pentagonal keep. A series of 16th-century frescos by Peruzzi can be seen in the adjacent **Palazzo Episcopale**. There are some pretty cottages once used by salt-pan workers.

Rome's seaside, **Lido di Ostia**, dates from the inter-war years. The grander villas from this more stylish era are now swamped by a rash of dreary apartment blocks, and though it is still used by thousands of locals in summer, it is not an enticing resort. The watchtower at the mouth of the river was designed by Michelangelo. Head southwards for cleaner water. There are extensive pine forests inland, now a nature reserve and public park.

On the north bank of the Tiber, more remains have been discovered on the site of Portus, the port which supplanted Ostia Antica, including a necropolis. Near the airport, the **Museo delle Navi Romane**, *tel: (06) 501 0089*, open daily 0900–1300, and Tues, Thur 1400–1700; L4000, displays the remains of several Roman boats. To visit the archaeological site of the Port of Trajan nearby, *tel: (06) 501 0089*.

CERVÉTERI

Tourist Office: *V. delle Mura Castellane 2; tel: (06) 994 2348* or *V. della Necropoli 2; tel: (06) 995 2304*, open Tues–Sun 0930–1230 and 1800–1930; or *Pza Moro 17; tel: (06) 994 2860*, open Mon–Fri 0900–1300 and 1630–1930. English-language guide books are on sale by the necropolis; look out for *Let's Meet the Etruscans: Cervéteri*.

Cervéteri is on a regular ACOTRAL bus route from central Rome (Lepanto stop), but the nearest station is 6km from town.

Modern Cervéteri seems little more than a village, and it is hard to imagine how significant it was in classical times. Its wealth was boosted by the rich mineral deposits of the Tolfa Hills to the north, and its influence spread far beyond its present boundaries. A thousand years before Christ, the Greeks knew it as Agylla, an important trading centre. During Etruscan times (when it was called Kysry) it had three ports and became one of the most brilliant cities of the Etruscan League. Gradually, Roman domination undermined its power, and after an ill-considered rebellion, ancient Caere (as the Romans called it) forfeited its rights to Roman citizenship and dwindled through the succeeding centuries. Malaria and Saracen marauders eventually drove its citizens away.

The present town has an attractive fortified medieval quarter set on a tufa outcrop. The 16th-century fortress houses the well-organised **Museo Nazionale di Cervéteri**; *Pza Santa Maria Maggiore; tel: (06) 922 1354*, open Tues–Sun 0900–1500, later in summer; L4000, containing some of the lesser artefacts excavated from the nearby necropolis. The most significant finds are now in major world museums. The square on which it stands is sometimes used for antique fairs. If you want to stay in town, try **El Paso**, *V. San Palo 175; tel: (06) 994 3033*, just off the main *piazza* (inexpensive). There are plenty of trattorias in the old town; look out for artichokes (Cervéteri's specialist crop) on the menu, especially in May and June.

Cervéteri's main interest for visitors is the huge and well-preserved **Etruscan Banditaccia Necropolis**, *tel: (06) 994 0011*, open Tues–Sun 0900–sundown; L8000, 2km north of town, reached by a rough but well-signed road lined with cypress trees (served by bus from the main square in summer). Rambling over more than 270ha in a wooded setting, this city of the dead has provided archaeologists with one of their most complete pictures of Etruscan civilisation. The burial chambers vary in style, depending on their age. The most characteristic look like African mud huts capped with mounds of grassy earth; inside they are complex house-like structures carved from the tufa rock, often beautifully decorated. Originally they were furnished with vases and sculptures to provide comfortable homes for the hereafter. Men and women were placed in separately marked 'rooms', alongside urns containing the ashes of their slaves.

Try to see the **Tomba dei Rilievi** (Tomb of the Low Reliefs) with stucco bas-reliefs of household utensils and weapons, the **Tomba dei Capitelli** and the **Tomba degli Scudi e delle Sedie** (Tomb of the Shields and Chairs). You can wander round freely; some marked routes are suggested. Access to individual tombs varies periodically; restoration is constantly taking place, and at certain times of year some chambers are flooded. Ask at the ticket office if you want to see any locked tombs; a guide may be able to show you round. Bring a flashlight if you have one, and a picnic lunch perhaps

washed down with a bottle of Cervéteri wine.

CIVITAVÉCCHIA

Tourist Office: *Vle Garibaldi 40–42; tel: (0766) 25348*, open Mon–Fri 0900–1300 and 1600–1900, Sat 0900–1230. There's an information kiosk by the ferry port.

There is no particular reason for a special journey to this busy industrial port unless you are catching one of the smart Sardinian ferries which terminate here, but if you are driving up the coastal highway, a brief stop rewards you with a handful of antiquities. Civitavécchia has good train and bus connections with central Rome. **Tirrenia Lines:** *tel: (0766) 500580* and **FS**, *tel: (0766) 23273*, serve the Sardinian ports of Olbia and Cagliari, charging similar fares (evening sailings). Adequate hotels and restaurants lie near the port area. The town is lively enough during the evening *passegiata* (which Civitavécchian youth enacts by motorscooter), but has few attractions as a touring base. Local beaches are badly polluted.

Civitavécchia was founded by the Emperor Trajan 107, and named Centumcellae. Destroyed by the Saracens in 828, it became a Mediterranean port of great strategic significance belonging to the Papal States during the Renaissance (Pope Gregory XII based his fleet in its sheltered, deep-water harbour). World War II did not improve its appearance. The main sights are the eight-sided fortress (guided tours) designed by Michelangelo, and the **Museo Nazionale Archeologico**, *Largo Plebiscito; tel: (0766) 235604*, open Tues–Sun 0900–1300; reduced hours in winter; free, which boasts a small collection of Etruscan and Roman artefacts. Near the motorway exit east of town are the remains of Trajan's extensive villa, including the **Terme Taurine** (baths). If you decide to track these ruins down, the scenic road leading past them towards **Allumiere** takes you through the ore-bearing Tolfa Hills, where there are more archaeological sites and the remains of ancient mines.

TARQUÍNIA

Tourist Office: *Pza Cavour 1; tel: (0766) 856384* (Mon–Sat 0800–1400); or *Pza Matteotti 14; tel: (0766) 842164.*

The Tarquin dynasty ruled Rome for over a hundred years (616–510 BC) from this powerful ancient city, leaving behind the huge **Monterozzi Necropolis**, *tel:*

(0766) 856308, open Tues–Sun 0900–1900 (mid June–mid Sept); Tues–Sat 0900–1400, Sun 0900–1300 (winter); L 8000), of subterranean tombs, some beautifully frescoed. Thousands of tombs have been uncovered, many of which have been vandalised or unscrupulously pillaged by amateur archaeologists. Most of the tombs on display in an enclosed site 2 km east of the town date from the 6th and 5th centuries BC. If you are driving, follow directions for Viterbo from the centre; the necropolis is signed from *V. Ripagretta.* City buses marked 'Cimitero' serve the site. Steps lead down to the tombs from unprepossessing concrete huts like public conveniences scattered around a rough field. Most of the painted chambers are protected from the atmosphere and sticky hands by glass screens and railings, and only a few can be seen on any single day. Try to catch the **Tomba dell'Orco** and the **Tomba dei Leopardi.** Souvenir reproductions of Etruscan artefacts are on sale outside the site, and some useful guidebooks. No useful information is provided at the officious ticket booth, but there are some display boards around the site.

The medieval town of Tarquínia stands on a hilltop, its massive fortifications and tall towers of volcanic stone intact and unsullied by modern development. The main sights in town include a 12th-century church, Santa Maria di Castello, with decorative mosaic work around the main portal, and the **Museo Nazionale,** *Pza Cavour; tel: (0766) 856036,* open Tues–Sun 0900–1900 and 0900–1400 (winter); L 8000 – sadly, separate entrance charges are now made for the museum and the necropolis), housed in a handsome Renaissance palace, and containing one of the finest assemblies of Etruscan art in Lazio. Terracotta winged horses from the

---

Etruscan Frescos

Much of what we know about the life of the ancient Etruscans comes from the remarkable sequence of frescos gracing the walls of tombs in Tarquínia. These gloriously colourful frescos include scenes of sport, music, dancing, feasting and hunting. Some are explicitly erotic, and the overall impression they give is of a people at ease with itself, with time to pursue the arts and enjoy a leisured existence, in which women and men play an equal part, and in which there is a full appreciation of the beauty of nature – trees, flowers and songbirds fill the backgrounds to these frescos. On the basis of this, D H Lawrence celebrated the ancient Etruscans as an example of the perfect community. Writing in *Etruscan Places,* he railed against the Romans for destroying Etruscan culture, asking: 'Because a fool kills a nightingale with a stone, is he therefore greater than the nightingale? Not he! Rome fell, and the Roman phenomenon with it. Italy today is far more Etruscan in its bones than Roman, and always will be.'

4th century BC take pride of place. Some startling activities occur on the painted vases in Room 6, should you wish to avert any delicate eyes.

Tarquínia makes an interesting night's stay, giving a chance to explore the intricate old quarter in more detail. Try the moderately priced **Hotel Tarconte**, *V. Tuscia 19; tel: (0766) 856141*. A good seafood restaurant is **Il Bersagliere**, *V. Benedetto Croce 2; tel: (0766) 856047* (closed Sun eve, Mon). The overdeveloped seaside resort of **Lido di Tarquínia** (6km south-west) is unexceptional but has more accommodation, with massive campgrounds and holiday hotels. The remains of the Roman port can be seen to the south; neighbouring salt-flats have been declared a bird sanctuary.

Tarquínia has good public transport links (bus and train): buses connect with Rome, Viterbo and Civitavécchia. The rail station (Rome–Grosseto line) lies 3km south of the old town near the coast; *tel: (0766) 856084* with regular local bus connections to the centre and the beaches.

TUSCÁNIA

Tourist Information: *Palazzo Comunale, Pza Basile.*

Many roads converge in this little town, but all around for miles is lonely sheep country, some of which makes attractive touring or walking territory. Tuscánia was a prominent Etruscan city during the 4th century BC, and continued to prosper even after the Roman conquest in the following century. Its location on the *V. Clodia* reduced its isolation until the 6th century AD, when the Longobards ushered in Tuscánia's Dark Age. The town shifted westwards to the adjoining hill in the 13th century and reconfigured its walls, leaving Etruscan remains and thermal baths stranded on the eastern edge

of town. Finds from these sites (notably sarcophagi) are on display at the **Museo Nazionale Etrusco,** in the convent of **Santa Maria del Riposo**, *V. XX Settembre; tel: (0761) 436209,* open Tues–Sun 0900–1330 and 1430–1800 (summer); 0900–1330 and 1400–1700 (winter); free.

Tuscánia's principal sights are two splendid Romanesque churches, both outside the walls to the south-east. **San Pietro** contains elements as early as the 8th century, but is mostly 13th century with swirling grotesque reliefs on its rose-windowed façade and oddly notched pillars inside. The nave is paved with mosaics, the crypt mosque-like. **Santa Maria Maggiore** which stands nearby is a mix of Gothic and Romanesque features with an octagonal font designed for baptism by total immersion.

The quiet medieval town is worth a wander, if only for the fine open views from its ramparts, best seen near the **Torre di Lavello**, where old timers gather for a gossip over drinks. If some of the walls look suspiciously latter day – they are. The town was hit by a devastating earthquake in 1971 (30 people died) and is still recovering. Tuscánia's central monuments (churches, palaces and fountains) cluster around **Pza Basile** and **Pza Bastiani.** Infrequent bus services connect Tuscánia with Viterbo and Tarquínia; there are no trains. Hospitality can be provided at **Al Gallo**, *V. del Gallo 22; tel: (0761) 443388,* a restaurant with rooms and a Michelin rosette (restaurant closed Mon).

VULCI

Little remains of this disparate, plundered site 11 km from the Montalto coast. Vulci was once a proud member of the dodecapolis (the 12 great cities of the Etruscan League). Scattered amid windswept moorland, thousands of tombs

233

The Etruscan Way of Death

E truscan civilisation flourished around the Tiber and Arno valleys from about the 8th century BC until the Romans (former Etruscan vassals) overthrew the Tarquínian dynasty in the 6th century BC. Popular imagination attributes the fatal spark to the tyrannical Tarquinius Superbus, whose nephew raped Lucretia the Roman governor's wife in 509 BC. In reality the fall of Etruria was much more complex and piecemeal. Gradually the 12 city states of the Etruscan League succumbed to the might of Rome, and over centuries, their distinctive culture vanished by dilution rather than extermination.

The influential people who ruled west central Italy before the Romans were obviously highly sophisticated, yet surprisingly little is known about them. No one is quite sure where they originally came from (though most experts believe it was somewhere in Asia Minor), and their language is still a mystery. Most current knowledge of their lifestyle has been deduced from the writings of contemporary Greek and Roman historians, or, like that of the ancient Egyptians, from their beautiful rock-cut tombs.

These elaborate necropoli have been unearthed in many places west of the Tiber and north of Rome, and though plundered through the ages, perversely disclose much more about Etruscan life than death. Adorned with frescos, graceful ceramics and a unique style of funerary statuary, they reveal a refined and hedonistic people capable of creating truly exquisite art. Colourful frescos depict Etruscan visions of the hereafter, which were largely re-runs of the more pleasurable aspects of life on earth – feasting, dancing, hunting, gardening and making love. The more portable tomb furnishings are now dispersed in archaeological museums worldwide, but wonderful examples can be seen in Tuscany, Umbria and Lazio. One of the best collections of Etruscan art is in Rome's recently reopened Villa Giulia, but there are also fine displays in Tuscánia and the Tuscan city of Voltessa, where you can see the extraordinary bronze figure known as the '*Ombre della Serra*' (Shadow of the Evening), a tall elongated figure of a man dating from the 3rd century BC.

unearthed here have been steadily ransacked since 1828, when a plough tore open one of the graves by chance and steered the region's grasping landlord **Lucien Bonaparte** (Napoleon's brother) towards a new career of dodgy antique dealing. Vulci's Etruscan treasures are now dispersed throughout the museums of the world, and even more are hidden away in private hands. Prince Bonaparte was only one of Vulci's grave robbers; many are still in action today. A few pleasing artefacts have been salvaged to place in a small archaeological museum: graceful black bucchero bowls and jars, bronzes, terracotta statues and funeral urns. The museum, open daily 0900–1300 and 1600–1900 (summer); 0900–1600 (winter), closed Mon morning; L4000, is housed in a 9th-century fortified abbey near the strikingly arched medieval Ponte d'Abbadia which spans the River Fiora. Amiable staff can show you a short film about the area, and indicate walks around the necropolis and the excavated city ruins, though there is little to see.

COASTAL TUSCANY: ORBETELLO–PIOMBINO

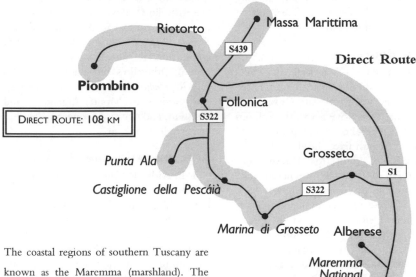

Riotorto

Massa Marittima

S439

Direct Route

Piombino

Follonica

DIRECT ROUTE: 108 KM

S322

Punta Ala

Grosseto

S1

Castiglione della Pescáiá

S322

Marina di Grosseto

Alberese

Maremma
National
Park

Scenic
Route

Talamone

Porto S Stefano

Orbetello

Monte Argentário

Port'Ercole

Ansedónia

Orbetello
Scalo

235

The coastal regions of southern Tuscany are known as the Maremma (marshland). The scenery here is very different from the typical Tuscan landscapes of vine and olive-clad hills that captivate most visitors further north. Yet the long sandy beaches and forests of luxuriant umbrella pines have their attractions, especially for lovers of quiet seaside and wildlife. The Parco Naturale della Maremma is a scenic highlight near Grosseto, offering fascinating walks through the varied habitats of Monti dell'Uccellina. The region is rich in archaeological sites, its food distinctively flavoursome, and its islands (Giglio and Elba – see p. 244) or virtual islands (Monte Argentario) tantalising. If the coast road gets busy in high season, few travellers venture far inland, where the countryside is emptily beautiful apart from an occasional picturesque hilltop settlement. Massa Maritima in the Colline Metallifere (Metal Hills) is a highspot in more senses than one.

ROUTES

DIRECT ROUTE

→ The *V. Aurelia* (S1), a busy, fast highway (signed Livorno) leads all the way up the Tuscan coast, ducking inland through Grosseto. Turn off at Riotorto for Piombino.

SCENIC ROUTE

⋯▸ Turn off the *V. Aurelia* (coastal highway) south of Orbetello Scalo to see the Roman remains of **Cosa** near Ansedónia, then drive across the isthmus through **Orbetello** to the peninsula of **Monte Argentario**, heading left for **Port'Ercole**, right for **Porto San Stefano**. From Monte Argentario, take the Tombolo di Gianella causeway back to the *V. Aurelia* and continue northwards for 8 km. Detour briefly to the pretty promontory resort of **Talamone**.

Back on the main road, pause at **Alberese** if you want to explore the **Parco Naturale della Maremma**. Follow the S1 inland to Grosseto, then take the S322 back to the coast and drive through the pinewoods to **Castiglione della Pescáià**. Access is restricted by private land around the exclusive headland of **Punta Ala**, so follow the S322 to **Follonic**a and turn north-east on the S439 for 13 km to **Massa Maritima**. Don't be tempted by the enticing secondary road through Montebamboli north-west of Massa; it is in frightful condition.

Return by the same road towards Follonica, rejoin the *V. Aurelia*, and make tracks to **Piombino**. Northwards lie some interesting Etruscan sites near **Populonia**, but the most popular destination from Piombino is the island of **Elba**, described in the following route.

ORBETELLO

Tourist Office: *Pza della Repubblica; tel: (0564) 868010*, open daily 1000–1230 and 1600–2000 (July–Aug); 1000–1230 and 1700–2100 (Sept–June). **Pro Loco Orbetello** is at *Corso Italia 121* (same tel).

Orbetello's railway station is on the mainland 4 km east at Orbetello Scalo; *tel: (0564) 862105* (Rome–Pisa line with connections to Siena); local buses run to central Orbetello's bus station near *Pza della Repubblica*, from where there are regular services to Monte Argentário and Grosseto, and occasional ones to Capálbio and Pitigliano inland.

ACCOMMODATION AND FOOD

I Presidi; *V. Mura di Levante 34; tel: (0564) 867601,* is a comfortable 3-star hotel with parking. **Piccolo Parig**i; *Corso Italia 169; tel: (0564) 867233* is charming, friendly and central. There are lots of campsites on the sandy outer causeways and more accommodation in mainland Orbetello Scalo, but there is little merit in staying on the busy *V. Aurelia*. Reliable restaurants include the **Osteria del Lupacante**; *Corso Italia 103; tel: (0564) 867618* (closed Wed); **Egisto**; *Corso Italia 190; tel: (0564) 867469* (closed Mon); or **Pizzaria Gennaro**; *Corso Italia; tel: (0564) 860210*. There is no shortage of bars and cafés in town.

SIGHTSEEING

Much of Orbetello's popularity derives from its unusual location, guarding the central causeway to the peninsula of Monte Argentario between two shallow tidal lagoons. Orbetello was artificially linked to the mainland in 1842, whereas the narrow necks of land on the outer edges of the lagoons are natural sandspits *(tomboli)*. A pleasant, low-key resort of palm trees and colourwashed buildings,

Orbetello has much life and character, especially at *passegiata* time or during its bustling Saturday market. In summer it is a crowded traffic bottleneck and accommodation is hard to obtain, but even then it never quite loses the self-possessed dignity of a Spanish citadel. In 1557 Philip II of Spain was granted this readily defensible toehold in Italy as part of an alliance deal, and made Orbetello the headquarters of a military presidio, fortifying its Etruscan foundations with ramparts and monumental gateways. In 1808 it was absorbed into the Grand Duchy of Tuscany.

The **Polveriera Guzman**: *Viale Mura di Levante; tel: (0564) 861242* was the former arsenal, now containing an archaeological museum (under restoration). The **Duomo** of Santa Maria Assunta in *Pza della Repubblica* has a Gothic facade and a Spanish baroque interior. A pre-Romanesque altar can be seen in a side-chapel. Also on the main square, the **Frontone di Talamone** is part of a reconstructed Etruscan temple on view at the town hall; *tel: (0564) 861242*, open daily 1000–1230 and 1600–2000 (summer), Fri 1600–2000, Sat and hols 1000–1230 and 1600–2000, Sun 1000–1230 (winter); L4000.

The **lagoon**s flanking Orbetello attract thousands of birds, including many rare migrants. Bird-watchers have noted over 200 species. The World Wide Fund for Nature has a nature reserve near Albinia with a visitor centre, *tel: (0564) 82097*; guided tours Sept–Apr; closed during the breeding season; L8000. The **Tombolo di Feniglia**, or southerly isthmus, is another good place to spot wildlife (car access is banned, but you can walk along it through dunes and pinewoods). There is a good beach on the southern side, and an attractive campsite, **Feniglia**; *tel: (0564) 831090*, open Apr–Sept.

⭲ **SIDE TRACKS
FROM ORBETELLO**

On the mainland side of the Feniglia isthmus lie the ruins of a Roman town just outside **Ansedónia**. Founded in 273 BC, **Cosa** was a thriving commercial community until the population was terrorised, according to the historian Rutilius, by mice! This may be hard to believe of the Romans, but the Visigoths completed the sacking process in the 4th century. Today, the hilltop ruins are reached by a quiet residential road. Walls, a forum, temples and an acropolis can be discerned in a grassy olive grove with lovely views towards the sea. On the site of the **Domus Domini** (governor's house) stands a surprisingly illuminating little museum; *tel: (0564) 881421* containing coins, figurines, pots, lamps and other domestic items unearthed from the ruins, with clear display boards (in English and Italian) explaining the history of the town, open daily 0900–1900; L4000 included in site entrance ticket). Inland, about 20 km east of Ansedónia, the hill village of **Capálbio** is one of the prettiest in the area and now a celebrity retreat with smart hotels and restaurants. A short distance south of Ansedónia, the cigar-shaped **Lago di Burano** attracts many birds, and has another WWF sanctuary; *tel: (0564) 820297*; guided visits twice daily; L8000. ⭹

MONTE ARGENTÁRIO

Tourist Office: *Corso Umberto 55, Porto San Stefano; tel: (0564) 814208*, open daily 0800–1400 and 1600–1830 (summer), 0800–1400 (winter) or *Port'Ercole; tel: (0564) 831019*.

The sandspits which link Monte Argentário to the mainland were formed in the early 18th century; until then it was a separate island. Its wild, rugged terrain of scrub and woodland makes an enticing contrast with the lowlying coastal Maremma. Much of the interior is inaccessible except on foot (forest fires are a risk in dry weather). The peninsula is a popular playground for wealthy Romans who stay in exclusive villas and berth glamorous yachts in the two fortified harbour towns of **Porto Santo Stefano** and **Port'Ercole** (both once part of Philip II's Spanish *Presidio*). In summer accommodation is scarce. Maps and roadsigns may encourage you to attempt the 39 km Strada Panoramica (peninsula tour). It is very beautiful, past cliffs and bays, vineyards, olive and citrus groves, but be warned, about 4 km of the stretch south of Port Ercole is exceedingly rough and could damage a conventional vehicle. Porto Santo Stefano is the larger and more developed of the resorts, now mainly modern despite its 15th-century origins. Ferries leave here for the island of **Giglio**, an hour's sail away. Two companies operate up to eight ferries a day in summer: **Toremar**; *tel: (0564 818506* and **Maregiglio**; *tel: (0564) 812920.* Buses connect Porto Santo Stefano with Orbetello train station.

Monte Argentário's other main village, Port'Ercole, is more charming and intimate, with fishing village appeal and two Spanish fortresses guarding the harbour. A plaque on the town gateway commemorates the artist Caravaggio, who died here in 1610, probably of malaria. There are good walks from the village: **Il Telegrafo** is a popular target, the peninsula's highest point, 635 m. The rough section of road beyond Port'Ercole is steep, but well worth exploring on foot.

Accommodation and restaurants are generally expensive, though there are

cheaper options; ask the tourist office for a list of private rooms. For a supremely luxurious stay, treat yourself to **Il Pellicano**, *Cala dei Santi, Port'Ercole; tel: (0564) 833801.* This charming, tastefully furnished villa complex in an idyllic rocky setting is the ultimate in Italian style (very expensive). **Belvedere** is a somewhat less expensive choice in Porto Santo Stefano; V. Fortino 51; tel: (0564) 812634. Porto S Stefano's pricey restaurants include **La Bussola**; *Pza Fucchinetti 11, Porto S Stefano; tel: (0564) 814225* (closed Wed; good fish); and **La Formica**; *Loc. Pozzarello; tel: (0564) 814205* (closed Mon); **Da Orlando**; *V. Breschi; tel: (0564) 812788* (closed Thurs) is more moderate. In Port'Ercole, try **La Lampara**; *Lungomare A Doria; tel: (0564) 833024* a Neapolitan restaurant.

MAREMMA NATIONAL PARK

Tourist Office: *V. del Fante; tel: (0564) 407098,* open Wed, Sat, Sun 0630–1800; Mon, Tues, Thur, Fri 0730–1800 (mid June–Sept); Wed, Sat, Sun only 0900–dusk (Oct–mid June). Useful maps, guides and leaflets in several languages are provided.

The Uccelina hills jut suddenly from the coastal plain north of Orbetello in a green whaleback, encapsulating a great variety of ecological habitats within an area less than 25 km from end to end, including dunes, cliffs, saltmarshes, forests, mudflats, pastureland, beaches and the aromatic Mediterranean underbrush known as *macchia*. Its dominant physical features are magnificent belts of pines and the swampy delta of the Ombrone river which debouches at the north end of the park. Several medieval watchtowers and a ruinous abbey comprise its few manmade landmarks.

Protected since 1975 by its enlightened

owners from indiscriminate development, and the Italian reflex to shoot anything that blinks, this small oasis shelters one of very few remaining sections of unspoilt Italian coastline and a host of wildlife. Most visible are the native long-horned white cattle and semi-wild Maremma horses; wild boar, roe deer and porcupines are shyer creatures; naturalists will spot rare plants, migrant birds, insects and snakes. The Maremma's most rampant species – the *Anopheles* mosquito, infected the area with malaria for centuries until the 1930s. The fertile fringes of the park are cultivated with many different crops. Local farms offer *agriturismo* holiday accommodation in converted farm buildings.

Motorists can reach the southern village of **Talamone**, a popular but still pretty fortified fishing port with a 16th-century Spanish castle and several smart hotels and restaurants. You can also drive to the northerly beach of **Marina di Albarese**. Apart from a shady carpark (L2000) and picnic area, the only facilities offered are clean sand, shallow sparkling sea and beautiful scenery. It's a popular spot on summer weekends, and numbers of cars allowed through the barrier at Spergolaia are limited.

To explore the rest of the park, you must be prepared to walk. Permits are sold at the Park Visitor Centre in the village of **Albarese**, where you can leave your car.

Malarial Marshes

Italians are notorious among conservationists for their indiscriminate destruction of wildlife, particularly migrant songbirds which are still slaughtered in thousands for the simple reason that they provide a moving target. Things are improving slightly; protected habitats are making a difference to some species, and the conspicuous presence of organisations like the World Wide Fund for Nature in the Tuscan Maremma is steadily making converts. Few people, however, lament the decline of one species, a scourge of the Tuscan coast for many centuries. The Anopheles mosquito, which transmits malaria, is much less prevalent than it used to be, but it is certainly still alive and biting, and recently on the upswing, due to the increased protection of wetland regions and the reduced used of pesticides. You can recognise it by its upturned behind in many a hotel bedroom. A light plastic fly swat is no bad thing to slip in your suitcase.

239

Malaria was finally eradicated from the Maremma in the 1930s, hence the region's noticeable gratitude to Mussolini. The word 'finally' must be treated with some caution, since drug-resistant strains of the disease are making a terrifying comeback in many tropical parts of the world. There is a real danger that malaria could become endemic once again in Italy.

The Romans, sometimes overpraised for their good government and engineering sense, were partly responsible for the appearance of the disease. They neglected some of the Etruscans' fine drainage systems and allowed the marshlands to encroach. By the end of the empire, when their control of the region was slipping, malaria had already established a foothold. It steadily gained ground during the chaotic Dark Ages that followed, and by medieval times, many coastal towns had simply been abandoned for healthier hill towns further inland. As political feuding diminished, more energy was put into sanitation. One of the region's great benefactors was the 19th-century Grand Duke Leopold II, who did much to drain the marshlands around Grosseto.

There are guided tours in summer (Wed, Sat and Sun, at 0700 and 1600). Guided visits cost L9500; unguided visits L6500. Hourly buses (L1500) take visitors to **Pratini** in the heart of the park; from there you can explore various marked trails, or head for the beaches. The terrain is tough going in places and you should be adequately equipped, with a supply of water. If wildlife is your main interest, avoid high summer. Visitor numbers are limited, and in busy holiday periods the park sometimes gets full. Albarese is accessible by bus from Grosseto, but services are infrequent (Mon–Sat only). Ring the RAMA bus company for information: *tel: (0564) 404169.*

GROSSETO

Tourist Office: *Vle Monterosa 206; tel: (0564) 454510,* open Mon–Sat 0800–1400, is the main provincial office. It is tricky to find, in Grosseto's bewildering northerly outskirts. Other more central sources of tourist information (some seasonal) include *Corso Carducci 1; tel: (0564) 488207; V. Cavour 5; tel: (0564) 484111; Pza del Popolo 3; tel: (0564) 25213.* Take your pick! Local tourist literature is well produced and generously distributed, with good pamphlets on the Maremma. The free listings magazine *Ouest di Paperino* covers the Livorno/Grosseto region (local events, restaurants etc).

Wartime bombing certainly made a mess of the place, but Grosseto is worth a look, if not a stay. It presides over a large, mainly agricultural province and is an important regional administrative centre. Some of its civic architecture dates from Mussolini's time, including its grandiose post office, endearing inside with a quaint display of old-fashioned postal equipment. The *centro storico* lies within star-shaped, red-brick walls. Park outside them and explore on foot. Walkways lead round the hexagonal defences, built by the Medicis on earlier Sienese foundations. Inside the walls, the **Duomo** presents a candy-striped neo-Gothic façade to *Pza Dante,* the main square. It contains some elaborate craftsmanship, particularly on the altar and 16th-century stoup. On the same square are the stage-set **Aldobrandeschi Palace** (county hall) in spanking 20th-century Sienese Gothic, and a monument to Leopold II (1846), showing the Maremma's chief marsh-drainer crushing the malarial serpent beneath his feet (Mussolini should be given some of the credit for this achievement, a significant factor in Grosseto's pre-war prosperity).

Grosseto has a couple of interesting museums. The **Museo Archeologico e d'Arte della Maremma**; *Pza Baccarini; tel: (0564) 455132,* open 0900–1300 and 1600–1930, Sun 0900–1300, closed Wed; L3000, contains material from regional excavations and some lovely Sienese Madonnas. The **Museo Civico di Storia Naturale**; *V. Mazzini 61; tel: (0564) 414701,* open Tues–Sat 0900–1230 and 1500–1930, Sun 0900–1300, outlines the social and natural history of the Maremma. The church of **San Francesco** contains a Duccio crucifix (1285).

One thing you can do well here is eat. Grosseto is a hearty gastronomic centre with excellent restaurants at all prices. Look out for *acqua cotta* (egg broth), artichoke risotto, wild boar stews and fry-ups of unmentionable offal. Try **Buca di San Lorenzo**; *Vle Manetti 1; tel: (0564) 25142* or the **Enoteca Ombrone**; *Vle Matteotti 71; tel: (0564) 414360* for interesting Maremma cuisine (not cheap). **Ximenes**; *Vle Ximenes 43; tel: (0564) 29310* is less pricey (closed Sun). There are plenty of pubs and pizzerias in town.

Grosseto is on main transport routes.

The station is about 15 mins' walk north-west of the old town (Rome–Genoa line) with regular connections to Siena, Livorno, and Rome. RAMA buses run to Siena and all local centres, including Orbetello, Pitigliano and Follónica.

⇄ SIDE TRACKS FROM GROSSETO

Archaeology buffs may like to track down the Etrusco-Roman ruins of **Roselle**, signed from the S223 10 km north-east; *tel: (0564) 402403,* open daily 0800–2030 (summer), 0830–1900 (winter); L4000. Outlines of walls, baths, amphitheatre and the forum can be seen. Nearby at Istia d'Ombrone lies one of the region's best restaurants, **Terzo Cerchio**; *tel: (0564) 409235* (closed Mon and Nov), with regional specialities. Further afield is another antiquity, **Vetulonia**, 17 km north-west of Grosseto, mainly Roman and medieval with some outlying Etruscan tombs; *tel: (0564) 919587,* open 0900–2000 (summer), 0900–sunset, Sun and hols 0900–1300 (winter); L4000. The village contains an enjoyable restaurant-with-rooms: **Taverna Etrusca**; *Pza Stefani 12; tel: (0564) 9494807* (closed Thur).

Grosseto's seaside, **Marina di Grosseto**, is a forgettable place of grid-like modern development. Northwards stretches a splendid belt of umbrella pines; tracks through the trees lead to an endless sandy beach, with regulations and safety advice posted in four languages. Camping is popular in this area. Beyond it lies **Castiglione della Pescara**, perhaps the most attractive resort in the northern Maremma. It's a lively place with a pretty old quarter and a good choice of places to stay. There's a helpful, well-stocked tourist

office at *Pza Garibaldi 6; tel: (0564) 933678,* open Mon–Sat 0900–1300 and 1530–2030, Sun 0930–1230 and 1730–1930. The wildly exclusive and entirely synthetic resort of **Punta Ala**, further west, shields its gilt-edged clientele and their posh yachts behind security barriers and Alsatian guard-dogs. It has good sports facilities (including golf and polo) and a quiet headland setting amid pinewoods, but if you can't get near the place, you haven't missed much. The workaday coastal mining town of **Follónica** is popular with locals but has few attractions for visitors. ⬩

MASSA MARITTIMA

Tourist Office: *V. N. Parenti 22; tel: (0566) 902756,* open Mon–Sat 0930–1230 and 1600–1800, Sun 0930–1230. Some information is also available at the museum ticket office in Palazzo del Podestà.

Despite the name, this town lies over 20 km from the sea, on a high ridge of the Colle Metallifere, or Metal-bearing Hills. A good straight road links it with the *V. Aurelia* and Follónica on the coast. In Etruscan times, local iron ore was exploited, supplemented by large deposits of copper and silver discovered by the Romans. Medieval glory under Sienese rule was followed by a long period of decline as malaria ravaged the town; in 1737 it had just 537 inhabitants. Mining restarted in the 19th century, and its magnificent monuments have survived to provide the town with much of its present prosperity. The main buildings cluster around *Pza Garibaldi,* and irregular square with the **Duomo** set at an angle above stone steps. This masterpiece of Gothic-Romanesque was begun in the 11th century in Pisan style, and enlarged over the next century. Inside and out it is a handsome structure, containing fine carvings and paintings, a splendid font and the tomb of St Cerbone. The carvings on the cathedral façade show scenes from the life of this 6th century saint who seems to have had an eventful life: the scene in which St Cerbone appears to be dancing with lions relates to his capture by Totila the Goth who, for his own amusement, decided to throw Cerbone into a pit of bears. Instead of being torn limb from limb and suffering intant martyrdom, Cerbone tamed the savage beasts and lived to tell the tale. Another scene shows him travelling to the Holy Land in a boat.

Cerbone seems to have had a winning way with animals. On his marble sarcophagus, the work of Sienese sculptor Gotro di Gregorio, the bears are shown again, licking the saint's feet, and another charming scene shows him taming wild does in order to milk them and supply food for his thirsty and starving companions. Opposite the cathedral is the **Palazzo Pretorio**, a group of tower houses containing civic offices. The smaller **Palazzo del Podestà** was built around 1230, and now houses the **Musei Civici,** an archaeological museum and picture gallery; *tel: (0566) 902289*, open Tues–Sat 1000–1230 and 1530–1700 (Oct–Mar), 1000–1200 and 1530–1900 (Apr–Sept), until 2300 (July–Aug); L5000. Highlight of the Pinacoteca is a *Maestà* by Ambroglio Lorenzetti, painted in 1330. This gorgeous painting shows Faith, Hope and Charity seated at the feet of the Virgin, the whole scene surrounded by musical angels.

Wandering uphill from the main square takes you past more palaces and churches to the *Città Nuova* (new town) and *Pza Matteotti*, graced by an archway, **Arco dei Senesi**. There is a small mining museum up here (Museo di Arte e Storia delle

Miniere), but much better is the one outside the town, the **Museo della Miniera**; *V. Corridoni; tel: (0566) 902289* (closed for repairs), with 700 m of galleries displayed in an old mine shaft once used as an air-raid shelter. Together these two museums cover the remarkable history of mining in Massa, which was governed by democratic laws and procedures, enshrined in the Codice Minerario Massetano, claimed to be Europe's oldest code of laws relating to the mineral and mining rights. Unfortunately, Massa's medieval wealth attracted the predatory Sienese, who conquered the town in 1337. Natural justice prevailed when, shortly afterwards, the mines turned out to be exhausted, so the Sienese gained little by their conquest, and the town became a little backwater.

Massa makes a delightful base for a night, especially during the **Balestro del Girifalco**, a colourful cross-bow festival, which takes place twice a year (end May and mid Aug). Book ahead if you want to stay.

Central hotels are tricky for motorists and may be a bit noisy; try **Il Sole**, *Corso delle Libertà 43; tel: (0566) 901971* or the cheaper **Cris**; *V. degli Alizzeschi; tel: (0566) 903830* if you want a bit of old-town atmosphere. Otherwise, two hotels on the western side of the walls provide a comfortable stay, with easy parking and good sunset views over an enticing slab of Tuscan countryside. **Il Girifalco**; *V. Massetana; tel: (0566) 902177* or **Duca del Mare**; *V. D Alighieri 1.2; tel: (0566) 902284* are both moderately priced. Several restaurants in the main square take advantage of the location with terrace tables; the streets nearby may be better value. Try the much-praised **Taverna del Vecchio Borgo**; *V. Parenti 12; tel: (0566) 903950* (closed Mon and Sun eve in winter), or **Osteria da Tronca**; *Vicolo Porte*

5; *tel: (0566) 901991* (eves only, closed Wed). Just out of town, **Bracali**; *V. P. Sarcoli, Loc. Ghirlanda; tel: (0566) 902318* has interesting Maremman cooking (closed Tues).

Several daily services connect Massa with Volterra, Grosseto, Florence and Siena. The nearest railway station (Rome–Pisa line) is in Follónica, on the coast (shuttle bus service to the town centre). There are parking places outside the walls; most convenient is the one near the Porta dell'Abbondanza.

PIOMBINO

Tourist Office: *V. Cellini 102; tel: (0565) 49121.* If you don't want to go into the town centre, look out for signs on the road to the ferry port, where there is a helpful tourist kiosk (summer only) in a huge car-park with lots of information about ferry services to Elba and lavish marketing of the Livorno coast (enticingly called the Etruscan Riviera); *tel: (0565) 224432.* Local brochures manage to disguise Piombino's less appealing aspects with consummate skill.

The main feature of the town is the rusting steelworks which make its ferry terminal perhaps the ugliest in Italy. The main reason to come here is to catch a ferry to Elba (see following route). If you need to stay overnight, there are comfortable central hotels, eg **Centrale**, *Pza Verdi 2; tel: (0565) 220188* (good restaurant) or **Esperia**, *Lungomare Marconi 27; tel: (0565) 42284*; the town has a few scraps of historic interest. There are several large campsites on the Follónica road. Piombino can be reached easily by bus and train; from the coastal railway line (Rome–Genoa), change at Campiglia Marittima and take the shuttle train down the branch line to the station by the port (don't get off in the town centre if you're after a ferry).

North of Piombino lie the important Etruscan remains of **Populonia**. A necropolis with several large tumulus graves dating from the 7th–5th centuries BC lies scattered around a grassy meadow by the sea on the approach road to the town, open daily 0900–1930; Oct–Mar 0900–dusk (Apr–Sept); L4000. The picturesque medieval *borgo* on the hilltop still has some of its Etruscan walls. From the 14th-century castle, open 0900–1230 and 1400–1900; L.2500, there is a marvellous view of the Bay of Baratti below. The unnaturally tidy main street is lined with souvenir shops. The small private **Museo Collezio Gasparri**; *tel: (0565) 29512,* open daily 0900–1900; L.2500, shows some Etruscan finds excavated from the ruins.

243

ELBA

Italy's third–largest island measures less than 30km at its widest, but has a ragged 150km coastline of capes and bays. Its sandy beaches, mild climate, and pleasant scenery are its main attractions. Elba forms part of the Tuscan archipelago which includes Giglio and Capraia, and is now immensely popular for brief excursions and package holidays, especially with German visitors, who have bought up significant holdings of land. German (rather than English) is the second language on Elba.

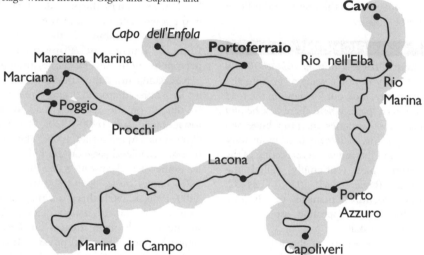

ROUTE

The tour is described anticlockwise, which gives motorists better coastal views. Drivers are advised not to spend too much time gaping at the scenery, however. Great care is needed on these narrow roads, especially in the busy high season. Many variations and detours are possible, and there are obliging pull-ins at photogenic intervals. When planning your route, try to drive with the sun *behind* you to avoid being temporarily blinded on hilly bends.

From **Portoferraio**, take the coastal road west to Capo d'Enfola, then retrace steps and head inland to San Martino and Napoleon's villa. Back on the main peripheral road, follow the north coast through **Procchio** and **Marciana Marina**, then duck inland again to the pretty villages of **Poggio** and **Marciana**. Continue round the west coast, stopping off at some of the beaches and resorts, as far as **Marina di Campo**. More inland detours are possible from here. Alternatively, continue eastwards, swooping through grand hills to **Lacona**. Before reaching Porto Azzurro, take the southerly road to **Capoliveri**. The southern cape of Monte Calamita is largely inaccessible to vehicles, but you can walk

Elba

In summer, its 30,000 native inhabitants are swamped by over a million visitors. Inevitably, parts of the island have become built up, but holiday development has been sympathetic compared with much of Italy's coastline. The resorts still look recognisably like fishing villages, and construction styles are in keeping with older buildings. Resort facilities are unpretentious but generally of high quality; it is possible to stay comfortably and eat well in most parts of the island, and participate in many activities from free climbing to hang gliding, plus golf and a host of watersports. Out of season it is enjoyably quiet.

It is easy to take a car to Elba (or hire one when you arrive) and tour the island at leisure. If you have more time, you can see much of it on local buses, or foot! Few people wish to stay as long as Napoleon did during his first exile (nine and a half months), but galloping round in a single day is a tiring prospect. There is plenty to occupy visitors for longer, including time on some of its attractive beaches, and in its mountainous interior. It has a large and varied range of flora and fauna, particularly marine life which can be observed in its clear waters.

Besides its Napoleonic connections, the island has long been known for its mineral wealth, and was first colonised in about 3000 BC, first for granite, then for copper and tin, components of the Bronze Age. Iron ore subsequently became its principal resource, exploited from Roman times until 1984 when its last mine closed. Wrecked Roman cargo ships have been discovered near Elba's shores. Elba has hundreds of different minerals; samples are displayed in several museums on the eastern side of the island, where the rocks and beaches glitter with pieces of fool's gold (iron pyrite).

245

here. Retrace the route to **Porto Azzurro**, **Rio nell'Elba** and **Rio Marina**. Dedicated explorers can drive around the northern cape via **Cavo**, though the scenery here is less appealing. Alternatively, take the scenic minor road from Rio nell'Elba back to Portoferraio to complete the island tour. You can, if pressed for time, catch a ferry to Piombino direct from Rio Marina or Cavo (fares are cheaper, but services less frequent).

TOURIST INFORMATION

Tourist Office: Calata Italia 26, Portoferraio; tel: (0565) 914671, open Mon–Sat 0800–2000 (Sept–June); daily 0800–2000 (July–Aug). The friendly main tourist office is easily tracked down on the first floor of the dilapidated ten-storey skyscraper by the waterfront in Portoferraio's ferry port (perhaps Elba's ugliest building).

Maps, ferry timetables, accommodation lists (including private rooms, holiday apartments, agriturismo and campsites) and a host of publicity leaflets on trips, transport, restaurants and island attractions can be collected. The tourist office will try to find accommodation, as will the Associazione Albergatori, also on Calata Italia; tel: (0565) 914754, though this can be tricky in July–Aug. There are other information points and helpful travel agents in all the main tourist centres, e.g. Procchio, Marciana Marina, Marina di Campo and Porto Azzurro. Much information is available only in Italian or German.

ARRIVING AND DEPARTING

By Ferry

Three ferry companies serve Elba from the mainland port of Piombino: **Toremar**, *tel:*

(0565) 31100, **Navarma**; *tel: (0565) 225211* (now marketed as **Moby Lines**, with a winsome blue whale logo) run conventional car ferries; and **Elba Ferries**; *tel: (0565) 220956*, which is a faster but pricier summer-only catamaran operation, which can also carry cars. Toremar also runs a fast hydrofoil (*aliscafi*) service in summer, for foot passengers only. Competition keeps tariffs and schedules of the large car ferries fairly similar (from about L9000 per passenger and L40,000 for a small car), but it is always worth checking which company offers the most advantageous fare on any particular day. The tourist offices in Piombino will tell you, or check at the ticket booths by the quayside.

The hydrofoil and catamaran services typically cost between 30% and 100% more than the large ferries, but are twice as fast, taking about 30 mins instead of an hour. You may feel the extra cost is worth the saving in time. Most services operate to the main Elban port of Portoferraio, but there are some Toremar services to the east coast resorts of Cavo, Rio Marina and Porto Azzurro too (which cost less).

Fares vary seasonally, and are always quoted one way, though there are sometimes special inclusive deals available for cars and passengers. Predictably, there are more sailings in summer. You would be unlucky to have to wait more than a couple of hours, but in high season (July–Aug), try to book in advance, especially if you plan to travel at a weekend or take a car. Any Tuscan travel agency displaying Elban ferry operator signs can organise a reservation.

By Air

Direct flights to Elba are available with **International Flying Services**; *tel: (035) 311255* (Bergamo) or *(0565) 976306* (Elba) from several Italian airports (Milan,

Bologna and Pisa) and various German cities. Elba's small airport lies north of Marina di Campo (the only flat bit of the island). For **airport information**, *tel: (0565) 976011*. Shuttle buses or taxis take passengers to local hotels; *tel: (0565) 977150*.

GETTING AROUND

There are several **car** hire offices in Portoferraio and at the airport, but on popular summer weekends, obtaining a car can be a scrum. Try **Maggiore**, *Calata Italia 8, Portoferraio; tel: (0565) 930212* or **Taglione Rent**, *tel: (0565) 977150*. Motorbike or moped hire is possible in most Elban resorts (L25,000–50,000 per day). Care is needed at all times on Elba's congested roads, and parking can be a problem near popular beaches. Taxis can be summoned in all the main resorts.

ATL buses, *tel: (0565) 914392,* serve virtually all the island villages reasonably regularly (seasonal variation), but there are no late evening services; one-day or six-day Elbacard passes are available for unlimited travel; L9000 or L30,000. Minibus services link the port and the old town in Portoferraio. Buy tickets in advance.

Boat trips are advertised in all the main resorts, and can be used to reach isolated beaches. Toremar ferries can also be used to travel between Portoferraio and the east coast resorts. Longer excursions ply to or around the neighbouring islands of the Tuscan archipelago: Capraia, Pianosa, Montecristo, Giannutri and Giglio. Contact **Elba Navigazione**; *tel: (0565) 914754*.

PORTOFERRAIO

Most visitors first spy Elba's largest and liveliest town from the decks of a ferry. It's an attractive sight after the rusting scrapyard of Piombino. The bustling port area of transport agencies and maritime commerce is guarded by 16th-century Medici fortifications designed to fend off Saracen sea raiders. The **Torre del Martello** and the **Porta a Mare** protect the harbour area, and the upper fortresses guard the city from their grandstand balcony over the sea: **Forte Falcone**, open daily 0900–2400 (July–Aug); 0900–1900 (Sept–June); L3000 and **Forte Stella**, open 0930–1300 and 1430–1700 (Easter–June), 0900–1300 and 1430–1900 (Apr–Oct); L2000. The **Villa dei Mulini**; *tel: (0565) 915846*, open Mon–Sat 0900–1900, Sun 0900–1300 (Apr–Oct); L8000 – entrance to the Villa di San Martino is included if you visit on the same day) at the top of the town was Napoleon's main home on Elba. A faded, modestly furnished house flanked by windmills (*mulini*), the interior displays his library and study, a couple of hankies into which he may have sobbed in desperate moments (he had many on Elba), and letters from exile. The subtropical gardens enjoy a superb bay view, though not, alas, towards the Emperor's beloved Corsica. Napoleon was, of course, not entirely a stranger in these parts. He had already spent some considerable time in Italy, and is remembered for his rapacity in ransacking the best of the art treasures to be found in the museums of Venice, Florence and Rome to furnish the endless rooms of the Louvre (many looted objects, including Etruscan tombs, remain in the Louvre, though international outcry persuaded the French to return certain treasures – including the four great bronze horses of St Mark's in Venice – ironically themselves looted by the Venetians from Constantinople in 1204). Having conquered Tuscany, Napoleon installed his sister, Elisa Baciocchi, as ruler of northern Tuscany, based in Lucca – amongst her many titles

she styled herself Princess of Piombino and she scandalised the Elbans by bathing naked in the local hot springs. The old town makes an agreeable wander, centering on *Pza della Repubblica* with its bars and cafés and a low-key, 18th-century Duomo. The **Museo Archeological della Linguella**, *Loc Linguella; tel: (0565) 937370*, open Mon–Sat 0930–1230 and 1600–1900 (Easter–June); 0930–1230 and 1800–2400 (July–Aug); L4000 is housed in a salt warehouse, with finds from all over the island.

Most of Portoferraio's accommodation lies outside town by little stony beaches, but there are plenty of places to have a (somewhat overpriced) snack or quick meal in the old town and around the port. It isn't the best long-term choice as a touring base, and most visitors see it *en passant*. If you need a night here, try **L'Ape Elbana**, *Salita Cosimo de Medici; tel: (05665) 914245*, Elba's oldest hotel in the heart of the old town, with Napoleonic connections. On the opposite side of the bay, **Villa Ottone**, *Loc Ottone; tel: (0565) 933042*, is a more luxurious choice in a 19th-century beachside villa. **Villa Ombrosa**, *Vle de Gasperi 3; tel: (0565) 914363*, is quiet with sea views west of town. **La Ferigna**, *Pza Repubblica 22; tel: (0565) 914129* (closed mid Nov–Jan and Tues off season), is one of the best restaurants in town. **La Barca**, *V. Guerrazzi; tel: (0565) 918036* (closed Wed off season) is a reliable trattoria above the port.

247

SIDE TRACKS FROM PORTOFERRAIO

The scenic northerly headland of Capo dell'Enfola makes an attractive cul-de-sac drive before leaving Portoferraio. *En route* round the island, be sure to visit Napoleon's country residence, the Villa di San Martino; *tel: (0565)*

914688 (same times and entrance ticket as the Villa dei Mulini), just 5 km south-west of the port. The neo-classical façade decorated with 'N' motifs and honey bees (Napoleon's heraldic emblem – to sting his enemies) was added in 1851 as a memorial to him. There isn't a great deal to see inside the simple, almost austere villa behind it except the Egyptian decorations of the Sala Egizia. Neither of the Napoleonic villas is well labelled, and there is no explanatory leaflet for the contents. ⛴

THE WEST

A tour around the western part of the island leads past the best beaches and the prettiest scenery. For most of the route, the corniche road hugs the coast, offering glimpses of sparkling sea below citrus groves and vineyards and *macchia*-covered cliffs. In places the vegetation is surprisingly exotic; agaves and prickly pears testifying to the island's low rainfall. The coastal headlands and the hilly interior are thickly wooded with chestnut, ilex and pine.

The north-west coast is characterised by several small but exclusive resorts, with pretty cove beaches tucked down hilly access roads. Most accommodation in the area is expensive, and there are some luxurious private villas. **Procchio** is one of the largest, at a busy road junction. It has about a dozen hotels and prominent watersports facilities. The sardine port of **Marciana Marina** has a pretty waterfront setting and a medieval Pisan watchtower. There are plenty of places to eat; **Rendez-Vous da Marcello**, *Pza della Vittoria 1; tel: (0565) 99251* (closed Nov and Wed off season) is a good bet. From here, the road leaves the coast and winds inland to the hill villages of **Poggio**, famed for its

spring water, and **Marciana**, the island's oldest and perhaps prettiest village with a charming old quarter of flower-decked cottages and flights of steps. There are one or two good restaurants up here. Try **Publius**, *Pza XX Settembre, Poggio; tel: (0565) 99208* (closed mid Nov–Mar and Mon off season) or **Da Luigi**, *Loc. Lavacchio; tel: (0565) 99413* (closed Nov–Mar and Mon midday in July–Aug). A small **Museo Archeologico** can be seen in *V. del Pretorio tel: (0565) 901215*, open 1000–1200 (Apr–June), 1000–1200 and 1600–1930 (July–Sept); L3000. Several small churches nearby are worth tracking down, including 12th-century San Lorenzo, and the sanctuaries of the Madonna del Monte and San Cerbone. A summer cable car runs to the summit of Monte Capanne (1018 m) the island's highest point, just outside Marciana; *tel: (0565) 901020* (1000–1215 and 1430–1800 (Apr–Sept), 1830 in June–Aug; L12,000 single, L18,000 return), rewarding passengers with magnificent views as far as Corsica and mainland Tuscany. It's a good starting-point for walks (the upper slopes are fairly flat and you may see mouflons or buzzards, and orchids in spring. Many people choose to walk down the wooded hillside rather than take the return journey by cable car. Napoleon is said to have been consoled by his Polish mistress, Maria Walewska, in this lovely part of the island, having failed to persuade his wife to join him in exile.

Returning towards the north-west coast again, **Zanca** and **Sant'Andrea** are quietly chic, almost hidden in lush vegetation. They are popular with divers for the clarity of the water. Several peaceful hotels with lovely gardens can be recommended in Sant'Andrea: **Cernia**, *tel: (0565) 98194*, **Piccolo Hotel Barsalini**, *tel: (0565) 908013*; **Gallo Nero**, *tel: (0565) 908017* and **Da Giacomino**, *tel: (0565) 98010* (fairly expensive).

A rugged fringe of cliffs drops to the west coast, but there are a few tiny villages and beaches tucked into rocky coves. **Fetovaia** returns to sea-level with a lovely beach sheltered by a rocky headland, and some smart accommodation. The road continues through more villages in low-lying terrain to the largest of Elba's resorts, **Marina di Campo**. It has a large and attractive crescent of beach and lots of holiday facilities, including sports, boat trips, guided walks, bike and car hire and accommodation of all types. North of the resort lies Elba's airport, and a couple of attractive villages with unusual churches (Sant'Ilario in Campo and San Piero in Campo). Eastwards, at Segagnana, is an **Aquarium**, *tel: (0565) 977881*, open daily 0900–1300 and 1430–1900 (Mar–Oct); 0900–2330 (July–Aug); L8000) with over 150 Mediterranean marine species.

EASTERN ELBA

The capes east of Marina di Campo are accessible only by footpath, or private tracks to hotels. The main road cuts above them, swooping through grand empty hills to **Lacona**, where there are more lovely beaches and some good hotels. Glass-bottomed boats take advantage of the clear water. The hotel **Capo Sud**, on the sheltered bay east of the long Capo della Stella peninsula, is a friendly family villa complex in a lovely peaceful position by the sea; *tel: (0565) 964021*. All along the coast, campsites and holiday villas are tucked discreetly into tiny bays. **Capoliveri**, on Elba's south-eastern cape, is a hilltop mining town of exceptional charm. Tourism has made it prosper anew, and it is much visited. It is one of the liveliest places on the island with discos and jazz bars (**Sugar**

Reef is one of the most promoted jazz venues, with music from midnight on the Porto Azzurro road). Attractive shops, art galleries and pavement cafés line its quaint old streets, their fortunes (past and future) largely dependent on the strength of the Deutschmark. On Thur a street market attracts locals as well as tourists. There's a tourist office at *V. Melina 9*. Capoliveri has some excellent restaurants and wine bars. **Il Chiasso**, *Vicolo N Sauro 13; tel: (05665) 968709* (closed Nov–Mar and Tues lunch off season), is one of the best places to eat on the island. Try **La Buca dei Vini**, *V. Roma 34* for local wine, or **Patelli Gelateria** on the same street for ice-cream. Accommodation (mostly apartments) is expensive, and in great demand. The **Madonna delle Grazie** church is much visited south of the village. Several quiet beaches (Morcone, Pareti, etc.) are accessible by road on the west side of the Capoliveri peninsula, and development is gradually encroaching, but much of the land still belongs to local mining companies and is out of bounds.

Porto Azzurro lies on the east coast. Again it is conspicuously pretty and upmarket, with smart pleasure craft and shops obviously designed for visitors rather than locals. Like Capoliveri, it has a fair bit of nightlife. The old quarter behind the harbour, closed to cars, is worth exploring. Boat trips ply along the coast from here, and there are some indirect ferry services to Piombino. The 17th-century fortress is now Elba's prison. **La Piccola Miniera**; *Loc. Pianetto; tel: (0565) 95250* (daily 0900–1300 and 1430–1900 (Apr–Oct); also 2100–2330 (July–Aug); L6000) is a reconstructed mine-working reached by a little train (tours every 30 mins, lasting 15 mins).

Further north, **Rio Marina** is a more workaday port with ferry connections to

Napoleon on Elba

'Able was I 'ere I saw Elba', runs the well-known palindrome. After his enforced abdication, Napoleon renounced the thrones of France and Italy, and was packed off to Elba in May 1814. The allied signatories of the Treaty of Fontainbleau granted him Elba as a 'separate principality for his lifetime, held by him in complete sovereignty'. Not a bad offer for a defeated emperor. He spent just over nine months on the island, but Elba's tiny confines proved insufficiently challenging for his prodigious ego. On February 1815 he slipped his leash and returned to France for another shot at ruling the western world. Napoleon recognised the limitations of his chosen place of exile on arrival: 'Ah, mon île est bien petite'. Nonetheless, he displayed the phenomenal energy of a man who liked to get things done. He got up at 4am on his first day and took a six-hour tour of inspection of his new domain before breakfast. Then he set about some improvements. He cranked the flagging iron-ore mines into full production, built roads, cleared land and (finding Portoferraio a bit smelly) dug some new drains. As many reforming governors have discovered, public works are not always gratefully received, especially when accompanied by swingeing taxation. Napoleon's unpopularity grew, and his coffers waned. Before leaving Elba, he told the people: 'I leave you peace. I leave you prosperity. I leave you a clean, fair city. I leave you my roads and trees, for which your children at least will thank me'. Tangible evidence of Napoleon's brief sojourn can be seen at the two houses he built near Portoferraio: the Villa dei Mulini and the Villa San Martino, which are now among Elba's principle tourist sights.

Piombino, Portoferraio and Porto Azzurro. Its beaches and even its road surfaces adazzle with pyrites, it capitalises on its defunct mining days, inviting visitors to explore its small **Museo dei Minerali Elbani** near the town hall, with over 200 Elban rock samples: *tel: (0565) 962747,* open Mon–Sat 0900–1200 and 1500–1800, Sun 0900–1200 (Easter–mid Oct); L3000.

Scrambling behind the village, keen geologists can glimpse something of Elba's mineral wealth still *in situ* at the **Parco Minerario**; *Cantiere Bacino; tel: (0565) 962088,* open daily 0900–1300 and 1600–2000; L7000 or L9000 including access to the mineral museums of Rio nell'Elba and Rio Marina). An old mining zone has been fenced off for visitors, where, for a rather excessive entrance charge, you can wander through a strange quarry littered with defunct machinery, identifying multi-coloured ores and sparkling crystals.

Inland, **Rio nell'Elba** has a pretty old quarter round a typical village church and yet another rock collection at the **Museo di Minerali**, *Passo dell Pieta; tel: (0565) 939294,* open 1030–1240 and 1800–2000 and 2100–2300 (June–mid July); 1000–1300 and 1630–2000 (July–mid Sept); L5000). The surrounding steep forested hills of pine and eucalyptus have suffered badly from forest fires, but there are several good walking routes nearby. Monte Capanello (496 m) and fortified Volterraio are popular destinations. Travelling northwards past the scarred red rocks of iron-ore country, **Cavo** at the tip of the peninsula has a downbeat and rather neglected air, offering a small beach and a ruinous Roman villa, but little more. There are few places to stay or eat in these north-eastern resorts.

SOUTHERN TUSCANY: PITIGLIANO–MONTALCINO

Montalcino

Monte Amiata

Abbazia di Sant'Antimo

Monte Amiata
Nature Reserve

ROUTE: 170 KM

S323

Abbadia San
Salvatore

S323

Scansano

Saturnia

Sovana

Soran‹

S322

Montemerano

Pitigliano

This mountain tour follows only minor roads, and must be taken at a leisurely pace, preferably with a picnic in the car. It passes through some lovely scenery, and several of Tuscany's most idiosyncratic and charming small towns. Additional attractions include natural hot tubs, gorgeous walking country, two ancient abbeys and some luscious local wine and food.

ROUTE

Most of the roads suggested are in reasonable condition, but you will need an accurate detailed map (such as the Touring Club Italiano Toscana map 1:200,000) and, if possible, a good navigator! Compared with many parts of Tuscany, this area is little visited and pleasantly quiet, and lonely out of season. The woodlands of Monte Amiata are a popular hiking destination in the heat of summer, but may be snowbound in winter. Only Montalcino, an easy excursion from Siena, is overrun with visitors at popular times. Allow a couple of days for the tour; longer if you want to explore Monte Amiata in detail and do some walking.

Start in **Pitigliano**, a fascinating and memorable town well worth a night's stay. Take the north-easterly exit route to the hill village of **Sorano**, then turn back west again to **Sovana** and the hot spas of **Saturnia**. Rejoin the S322 south of Saturnia at **Montemerano** and head west for **Scansano**. Turn along the S323 northeast towards the **Monte Amiata** nature reserve. A number of routes are possible through this area, the yellow roads being more predictably navigable than the white ones. Energetic vistors may like to tackle the well-marked **Anello della Montagna** circular walking route. In any case, pause at the region's main sight, the **Abbadia San Salvatore** in the village of the same name. From Monte Amiata, head northwest to **Montalcino**, another excellent touring base out of high season. **Siena** is an easy 28 km jaunt up the S2 from **Buonconvento** to the north; a more interesting route takes you through the Crete Hills (see Siena–Cortona, p. 258).

PITIGLIANO

Tourist Office: *V. Roma 6; tel: (0564) 614433*, open summer only.

This spectacular town looms above the wooded Lente Valley, its tall grey houses teetering on steep tufa cliffs riddled with Etruscan tombs. Some of these are now used as storehouses or garages. There are striking views along the approach roads from Sovana and Manciano, so have your camera ready. The foundations are Etruscan, and finds from this period can be seen in the imposing Orsini fortress which dominates one of the main squares near the entrance to the town. The castle was begun in the 13th century, and completed with the addition of the restored Renaissance **Palazzo Orsini**, *Pza della Fortezza Orsini; tel: (0564) 615606*, open Tues–Sun 1000–1300 and 1500–1800 and 1600–1900 in summer; L5000, which contains some fine ceilings and works of art. The **Museo Civico Archeologico di Arte Etrusco** (same opening times but a separate entrance charge: L5000) contains impressive *bucchero* vases. In the same square is a large aqueduct dating from 1543 and two modern fountains.

The medieval *centro storico* is a maze of flower-filled alleyways and steps leading to panoramic belvederes at the edges of the town. From the 15th century, Pitigliano provided a safe haven for Tuscany's Jewish community. Many fled here in the 17th century to escape papal persecution. The tall, rather forbidding stone houses of the old quarter are typical of the Jewish ghetto which thrived here until the end of World War II. A damaged **Synagoga Ebraica**; *tel: (0564) 616396*, open Wed, Fri and Sun (Apr–Oct) can be seen on *V. Zuccarelli*. The **Duomo** has a massive belltower, and two altarpieces by a notable local artist, Francesco Zuccarelli. The trapezoidal **Santa Maria** church in *V. Orsini* displays the crest of the Orsini family (a lion and a bear – Latin *orso*, a play on the name) and winged dragons. Nearby outside the Porto Capisotto is a stretch of Etruscan wall.

Pitigliano's main central hotel is the modest **Albergo Guastini**, *Pza Petruccioli; tel: (0564) 616065*, which has a reliable restaurant serving the local wine, Bianco di Pitigliano. There are several hotel possibilities outside the town: **Corano**, *SS Maremmana, Loc. Corano; tel: (0564) 616112* (south) or **Valle Orientina**, *Loc Valle Orientina; tel: (0564) 616611,* and some *agriturismo*. **Del Corso**, *V. Roma*, is a pleasant trattoria. Pitigliano is served by bus from Grosseto, Orbetello and San Quirico. A wine festival livens up the town in Sept.

SORANO

Tourist Office: *Pza della Chiesa; tel: (0564) 633277.*

This slightly grim hill village 9km north-east of Pitigliano is subject to landslides and has been largely abandoned for a more safely located modern suburb. Several sectors can still be distinguished in the old town: an uppercrust zone of plastered and decorated houses around *V. Roma*, a *borgo* of smaller dwellings and workshops for the merchant classes, and a Jewish ghetto to the north. Two **castles** guard the medieval quarter, dating from Orsini rule in the 15th and 16th centuries. The larger of these is the **Fortezza Orsini**, *V. San Marco; tel: (0564) 633023*, open daily 1000–1300 and 1500–1900 (June–Sept); Sat, Sun only 1000–1300 and 1500–1800 an impressive example of medieval military architecture built over an earlier fort belonging to the Orsinis' predecessors, the Aldobrandeschi family. It houses a small history exhibition. The smaller fortress, **Masso Leopoldino**, *V. del Poggetto; tel: (0564) 633023*, open daily 1000–1230 and 1600–1930 (June–Sept); off season open by appointment only,

offers good views of the surrounding countryside. The area is famous for its white wine, and has a wealth of Etruscan antiquities. The approach roads from Sovana and Pitigliano are spectacular, past walls of tufa burrowed with caves and tombs. The town contains a number of ceramics workshops and craft galleries which have revitalised its prosperity. Accommodation is simple and scattered.

SOVANA

Tourist Office: *Palazzetto dell'Archivo; tel: (0564) 614074.*

A perfectly preserved medieval fiefdom on a low ridge in beautiful surroundings, Sovana is no longer undiscovered, but in this lonely part of Grosseto province you are most unlikely to find it unpleasantly crowded. Discerning Romans seek it out at weekends. The Etruscans made Sovana a major base, and important ruins can be seen on the outskirts, including one of the finest and largest pre-Christian tombs in Tuscany. The **Tomba Ildebranda**; *tel: (0564) 633023*, open daily 1000–1230 and 1600–1930 (summer), Mon–Fri 1500–1700, Sat–Sun 1000–1230 and 1500–1700 (winter); L3000), lies on the west side of town near Poggio di Sopra Ripa, and consists of a temple-like structure with steps and pillars carved from the living rock (early 3rd century BC). The tomb is named after Hildebrand, an enlightened 11th-century pope (Gregory VII) of the Aldobrandeschi family who is thought to have been born at Sovana. Numerous other tombs of various types can be visited free of charge, including the Poggio Pesca and Pola graves; ask for a plan of the necropolis at the tourist information office.

The town itself, village-like in size and best enjoyed on foot (cars are not banned, but seem quite out of place in the centre), was the seat of the influential

253

Aldobrandeschi family in the 11th century. They held sway over much of southern Tuscany and Latium, dabbling in European *realpolitik* and building fortresses to great effect. Only ruins remain of the **Rocca** in their home town. A single neatly swept street of herring-boned brickwork, the *V. di Mezzo*, runs spine-like past low, balconied houses and a few shops and cafés from the castle to the **Duomo** at the top of the town, open daily 0900–1300 and 1500–1900 (June–Sept); weekends only off season; free. A very early church, its façade is decorated with delightful strapwork carvings and strange birds in Lombard style. In the small square at the lower end of the town stands the escutcheoned **Palazzo Pretorio** (containing a small local museum; *tel: (0564) 614074;* (same times as cathedral; L2000) and **Palazzo del Comune**, adorned with a clock and bells. The lovely old church of **Santa Maria** (same times as cathedral) is one of the most atmospheric churches in the region, cool and dim with romanesque arches and frescos. Its most interesting feature is a beautifully carved tabernacle called a *ciborium* over the altar, dating from the 9th century.

Sovana has two attractive little hotels: **Taverna Etrusca**; *Pza del Pretorio 16; tel: (0564) 616183,* and the cheaper **Scilla**; *V. del Duomo 5; tel: (0564) 616531.* Both have charming restaurants; Scilla closed Tues and Nov. Book ahead in high season. **La Tavernetta** is a good pizzeria on the main street.

SATURNIA

Tourist Office: *V. degli Aldobrandeschi, tel. (0564) 601273,* open 1000–1300 and 1500–1700.

Saturnia has legendary associations with Saturn, though Vulcan might be more appropriate. Mild volcanic activity in the area produces hot sulphurous springs which form natural jacuzzis in the rocks. One section, the **Cascata del Gorello** on the Montemerano road, is freely accessible and always popular with Italian families. The turquoise water cascading steamily over beds of pale tufa is a most peculiar sight. Unfortunately the area surrounding this natural curiosity is poorly kept and litter-strewn. Part of the stream has been diverted to an exclusive thermal spa in the grounds of a luxury hotel. Expensive cosmetic and therapeutic treatments are offered for just about any imaginable body part. For information, contact the **Terme di Saturnia**; *Strada Provinciale della Follonato; tel: (0564) 601061.*

Saturnia also has Etruscan remains: a small necropolis of stone chambers lies half concealed among wild flowers. Besides the spa, the village has cheaper accommodation, e.g. **Villa Clodia**, *V. Italia 43; tel: (0564) 601212* or **Saturnia**, *V. Mazzini 4, tel: (0564) 601007,* which has a good restaurant; and **Bacco e Cerere** (closed Tues). **I Due Cippi–da Michele**, *Pza Veneto 26/a; tel: (0564) 601074,* is another good eating place (closed Tues off season).

South of Saturnia, the pretty village of **Montemerano** makes an appealing stay, with a rustic hotel, **Villa Acquaviva** (1 km north), *Strada Scansanese; tel: (0564) 602890,* an excellent restaurant with rooms, **Locanda Laudomia** (2.5 km south-east), *Loc. Poderi di Montemerano; tel: (0564) 620062,* and a highly acclaimed but unassuming restaurant, **Da Caino**, *V. della Chiesa 4; tel: (0564) 602817* (closed Wed and Thur lunch). The church of **San Giorgio** has several intriguing works of art, including the anonymous *Madonna della Gattaiola* (the Catflap Virgin). Six km further south, **Manciano** is worth a passing glance, a market town grouped in geometrical blocks around a 15th-century

254

castle, with a good range of accommodation and regular bus links to Grosseto, Saturnia, Scansano and Pitigliano. The tourist office is at *V. Roma 2; tel: (0564) 629218*. West from Montemerano, **Scansano** is a sizeable hill village over a wooded gorge. It has a well-preserved medieval quarter and a fine parish church. Its summer tourist office stands at *V. XX Settembre*. There's a most attractive place to stay about 3 km east of the town: **Antico Casale**, *Loc. Castagneta; tel: (0564) 507219,* is a friendly, rustic, modernised farmhouse with a plant-filled terrace restaurant overlooking a glorious bowl of hills and woods, good country cooking and excellent home-produced wine called Morellino di Scansano. Horse-riding holidays are organised by the hotel.

MONTE AMIATA

Tourist Office: *V. Mentana 97, Abbadia San Salvatore; tel: (0577) 778608*. This is the regional headquarters, tricky to find in an upstairs office but with plenty of helpful information on local walking and tours. There's a **Pro Loco** and hotel association at *Pza Fratelli Cervi; tel: (0577) 778324*. Also in Abbadia San Salvatore, **Amiata Trekking**, *Pza Fratelli Cervi 21; tel: (0577) 777751* is another useful address. In Castel del Piano, there's a **Pro Loco** at *V. Marconi 9; tel: (0577) 955284* and a hotel and travel association based at the Hotel Impero: **Albergatori e Operatori Turistici Amiata Ouest**, *V. Roma 7; (0577) 955337*. Santa Fiora has a tourist office in *Pza Garibaldi; tel: (0577) 971124*.

The mountain after which this popular touring region is named is an extinct volcano, the highest point in southern Tuscany at 1738 m. Local soils are extremely fertile, consisting of decomposed trachite; a porous and mineral-rich volcanic rock used as a building material in many of the surrounding villages. Huge deposits of mercuric sulphide (from which quicksilver is extracted) were until recently a great source of wealth. The lush vegetation of Monte Amiata is still an important resource, providing the area with timber for fuel, construction and furniture. In autumn, the chestnut harvest adds variety to local cuisine, although it is no longer a vital part of the staple diet as it once was.

Small rural towns fringe the foothills, the main centre being **Abbadia San Salvatore** to the east. The medieval quarter is preserved from modern intrusions behind an *enceinte* of walls. The principal sight is a romanesque abbey dating from 743. Consecrated in 1036, the abbey was altered in the next couple of centuries as it passed from Benedictine to Cistercian hands. The **crypt** and its carved pillars is one of its most interesting features.

The other main Amiata communities are **Piancastagnaio**, **Santa Fiora**, **Arcidossa**, **Castel del Piano**, **Seggiano** and **Pescina.** Several of these have interesting churches and castles. Piancastagnaio has a weighty fortress built by the Aldobrandeschi – medieval *signori* of Amiata. The chapel of Santa Fiora and Lucilla, just outside Santa Fiora village, houses an impressive array of della Robbia terracotta. Most of the towns and villages have accommodation, including private rooms and *agriturismo*. Pescina has a popular restaurant with rooms: **Le Silene**; *tel: (0564) 950805* (book ahead for a table in summer). An attractive 3-star campsite, **Camping Amiata,** is in Castel del Piano; *V. Roma 15; tel: (0564) 955107*. The village is a good place to buy provisions.

The main attraction of Monte Amiata is the great outdoors. Much of it is a nature reserve inaccessible to vehicles. A cool green lung during summer heat, the luxuriant beech and chestnut woods, loud with rushing streams, are even prettier decked in spring and autumn colours. Hot springs, a legacy of the volcano, rise in many parts of the Amiata region, most spectacularly at Bagni di San Filippo to the north-east, where a calcite 'waterfall' makes a dramatic backdrop for a swim. Abbadia San Salvatore makes a good starting point for the ascent to the summit. It isn't an arduous climb, but you can cheat with a ski lift or a bus. A waymarked walking route, the 29 km **Anello della Montagna**, encircles the mountain at an altitude of around 1000 m. It can be joined from many points by car or on foot. The route is conveniently segmented into ten sections. If you don't want to do the whole walk you can catch a bus back to Abbadia from Santa Fiora or Arcidosso.

MONTALCINO

Tourist Office: *Costa del Municipio 8; tel: (0577) 849331*, open Tues–Sun 1000–1300 and 1530–1900 (May–Sept); Tues–Sun 1000–1300 and 1500–1700 (Oct–Apr). Accommodation lists, information about wine-producers and vineyard tours, and foreign exchange facilities are offered. There is a good bookshop for guides and maps at *V. Matteotti 22* (closed Mon).

All around the town, Montalcino's economic mainstay is on show, in the thriving vineyards that cloak the hillsides and in the smart retail outlets and *enotecas* offering the finished wares for sale. Montalcino is one of Tuscany's premier wine-producing regions. Its most celebrated product, Brunello di Montalcino, is regarded by many oenophiles as the king of Chianti, and by some as the finest wine in Italy. Even without this magnificently subtle red wine, however, Montalcino would deserve a visit. Strung out beneath its 14th-century hill top fortress, the town is a classic model of Tuscan architecture, scarcely altered since the 16th century. It looks magnificent on approach from the plain below, and unlike some towns, is no less enticing at close range. The historic quarter is effectively closed to tourist traffic, and a walk around the town is nothing but pleasure, with innumerable excuses for a rest in shops and restaurants. If possible, spend a night or two here; it is a marvellous base for several excellent tours. Book ahead at any time of year. You will rarely have the place to yourself. Bus services from Siena are more regular in the afternoons.

Montalcino fell to Siena in 1260, and remained loyal to its governing city, defying Florentine control for several years after the Medicis defeated Siena in 1555. In recognition of this brave but ultimately futile gesture, the town's medieval banner proclaiming 'The Republic of Siena in Montalcino' proudly heads the parade at Siena's Palio. The present affluence brought by wine and tourism is quite recent; until the 1960s, Montalcino was the poorest town in the province. Now the cafés and restaurants buzz with trade, and shops groan with beautifully packaged gastronomic produce at high prices: olive oil, honey and biscuits called 'dead bones' are typical of the region. For less alarming wine prices, try the **Coop** supermarket on *V. Sant'Agostino*. Rosso di Montalcino is a less exalted (and cheaper) wine than Brunello; Moscadello is a sweet wine. The market is held on Fri, in *Vle della Libertà*. There isn't much regular nightlife in Montalcino, but it holds summer music and theatre festivals. Its archery **Palio** (8 May and midAug) is a great draw; so is the costumed **Sagra di Tordo** (the Feast of the Thrush) at the end of Oct.

The **Rocca** or fortress lies at the

southern end of the town on *Pzle della Fortezza; tel: (0577) 849211*, open Tues–Sun 0900– 1300 and 1400–1800 (winter); Tues–Sun 0900–1300 and 1430–2000 (summer); daily (mid July–mid Sept) free. Construction started in 1361 and ramparts were added in 1571. Inside the walls lie a public park and a popular *enoteca* where you can sample Brunello. Access to the rampart walks overlooking luscious slabs of Tuscan countryside costs L3500. The **Museo Civico**, *V. Ricasoli*, in the old seminary of Sant'Agostino now combines the contents of several museums including a worthy collection of Sienese art, notably a very early *Crucifixion* and Benvenuto's *Madonna della Cintola*, which depicts a popular legend about Doubting Thomas. Nearby, **Sant'Agostino** church has patchy frescos. Beyond the **Palazzo Vescovile** (Bishop's Palace) on *V. Spagni* stands the **Duomo** of San Salvatore, a largely 19th-century creation. Montalcino's main square is the triangular **Pza del Popolo**, on which stands the **Palazzo Comunale** (town hall) in Sienese style, where wine fairs are sometimes held, faced by a lovely Renaissance **loggia**. Look out for a splendid 19th-century café, the **Fiaschetteria Italiana**, a focus of local life. At the north end of town are the 17th-century **Sanctuario della Madonna del Soccorso**, the 13th-century ex-hospital of **Santa Maria della Croce** and the large deconsecrated church of **San Francesco**, with an ancient washhouse nearby.

There isn't a vast range of hotel accommodation in Montalcino, and what there is tends to be in great demand, so book ahead. Good central choices include: **Il Giglio**, *V. Soccorso Saloni 5; tel: (0577) 848167* and **Dei Capitani**, *V. Lapini 6; tel: (0577) 847227*. Private rooms are an option if hotels are full. Restaurants are in better supply: poshest in town is **La Cucina di Edgardo**, *V. San Saloni 21; tel: (0577) 848232* (closed Wed and mid Jan–Feb). Four km south-west is another hallowed eating haunt in a fine setting: **Il Poggio Antico**, *Loc. Poggio Antico; tel: (0577) 849200* (closed Mon). Cheaper options include the **Pizzeria San Giogio**, *V. San Saloni,* (closed Mon) and **Il Moro** *V. Mazzini 44; tel: (0577) 849384* (closed Thur).

↗ SIDE TRACKS FROM MONTALCINO

Nine km south-east, the **Abbazia di Sant'Antimo**, *tel: (0577) 838269*, open Mon–Sat 1000–1230 and 1500–1800, Sun 0900–1030 and 1500–1800; free, is one of Tuscany's most glorious Romanesque churches, dating from the 12th century and allegedly founded by Charlemagne. Gregorian chant is sung at mass. On the way, stop off at the wine-producing estate **Fattoria dei Barbi**, *Loc. Podernovi; tel: (0577) 849357* (closed Jan, early July, Tues eve and Wed except Aug; book ahead) to see and perhaps taste or buy some of the local wine. A pleasant rustic tavern serves local cooking, making an ideal lunch stop. The **Azienda Agricola Greppo** just up the road produced the very first Brunello in 1888. Tours of the cellars can be arranged; *tel: (0577) 848087*. Sant'Antimo lies on the Monte Amiata bus route from Montalcino (not Sun), but services are not very regular. ⬕

⟷ Connection to Siena

To reach Siena from Montalcino, take the scenic road east via Lama for 9km to join the N2 road at Torrenier. From here, the N2 provides a fast and direct route to Siena via Buonconvento.

257

SIENA–CORTONA

South-east of Siena lies a strange landscape of eroded clay hills known as the Crete. Sunbaked, windswept and rainwashed in turn, these unprotected hills are gradually disintegrating. When the sun is low, bringing out the shadows and contours, they are a photographer's dream.

Beyond the Crete, the route passes through a string of small historic towns, mostly on secondary but well-used roads. Crossing the Umbrian border briefly near Chiusi, the journey takes in a waterfront drive past one of Italy's largest lakes, and ends in the austere Tuscan art town of Cortona. Highlights include a frescoed Benedictine abbey, and one of Tuscany's most appealing wine towns. Allow at least a couple of days to see the places mentioned on this route. Chances are they will whet your appetite for a longer stay. The

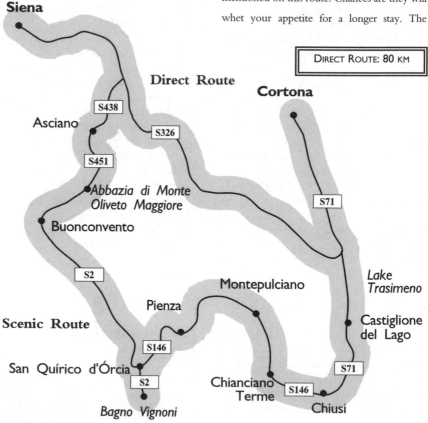

Siena

Direct Route

Cortona

DIRECT ROUTE: 80 KM

Asciano

S438

S326

S451

Abbazia di Monte Oliveto Maggiore

Buonconvento

S71

S2

Montepulciano

Lake Trasimeno

Pienza

Scenic Route

Castiglione del Lago

San Quírico d'Órcia

S146

S2

Chianciano Terme

S146

S71

Chiusi

Bagno Vignoni

countryside around is enchanting – less crowded and touristy than Chianti but full of unspoilt medieval villages, hilltop fortresses, river valleys, and marvellous opportunities for walking or riding. The area can be most agreeably explored from one of many rural *agriturismo* bases; ask for lists at the tourist offices.

ROUTES

DIRECT ROUTE

➡ The fastest way to reach Cortona from Siena is on the S326 Perugia road, which continues in motorway mode (75bis) beyond the Betolle/Val di Chiana intersection with the A1. Turn off after 12 km at the Cortona exit onto S71 northbound.

If you want to continue to Perugia, it's a very straightforward journey on highway now upgraded to *autostrada* status running along the northern shore of Lake Trasimeno, with some fine views in the Perugia vicinity.

SCENIC ROUTE

Take the S326 (signed Perugia) south-east of Siena, and fork right after 6 km along the S438 for **Asciano**. From Asciano, head south on the S451, diverting to the **Abbazia di Monte Oliveto Maggiore** after 9 km. Continue to **Buonconvento**, then take the V. Cassia (S2) 16 km as far as **San Quirico d'Orcia**. Turn left on the S146 to **Pienza** and **Montepulciano**, then continue east on the same road through **Chianciano Terme**, an important but uninspiring spa town, to **Chiusi**. Across the Umbrian border, take the S71 northwards along the shores of **Lake Trasimeno** through **Castiglione del Lago** to **Cortona**.

ASCIANO

Tourist Office: *Corso Matteotti 18; tel: (0577) 719510*, open May–Oct. Off season, try the **Comune**, also in *Corso Matteotti; tel: (0577) 718745* or **Pro Loco**: *V. Amos Cassioli 3. (no tel)*.

Sturdy walls built by the Sienese in 1351 still surround most of this medieval *borgo* nestling in the Ombrone valley at the heart of the Crete. Within them lies a rewarding handful of sights. Beyond the main street of palaces and smart shops stands the Romanesque **Basilica di Sant'Agata** with its striking façade of blind-arched travertine, and next to it the **Museo d'Arte Sacra**; *Pza Fratelli Bandiera; tel: (0577) 718207* (ask about admission at the basilica) containing late Sienese art. Ambrogio Lorenzetti's *St Michael* and Duccio's *Madonna and Child* take pride of place. The **Museo Etrusco**; *Corso Matteotti 46*, open Tues–Sun 1000–1230 (mid June–mid Sept) also 1630–1830; L3000, contains finds from Etruscan tombs in the **Necropolis di Poggio Pinci**, 5km east of Asciano. A combined ticket costing L5000 also gains access to the **Museo Amos Cassioli**; *V. Mameli* (same opening times), a display of works by a local 19th-century portraitist. Keen historians may like to track down the Roman **mosaics** unearthed in a cellar at *V. del Canto 11* (ask about admission in the lovely old chemist's shop called the **Antica Farmacia Francini Naldi**; *Corso Matteotti*). The Romanesque church of **San Francesco** and the 15th-century **fountain** on *Pza del Grano* are also worth a look. The **Palazzo del Podestà** is covered with heraldic crests.

Asciano can be reached by a single daily bus from Siena, but if you have a chance, try out the **Ferrovia Turistica** (Tourist Railway), an uneconomic branch line saved from closure in 1994 by keen

259

volunteers and enlightened Sienese authorities who have financed its resurrection. The scenic Val D'Orcia railway crosses the spectacular Crete hills to Asciano, then weaves back to Siena via Monte Antico to the south. Dubbed the **Trenonatura** (Nature Train) project, it runs on certain Sundays between Apr and Oct, using restored diesel rolling stock, and is linked with waymarked footpaths from the stations. Look out for leaflets in the tourist office, or *tel: (0577) 207413* or *(0577) 241254* or *(0577) 280551* for information. Tickets (L18,000 for a round trip from Siena; L12,000 Asciano–Monte Antico return; bikes L5000) are available on board. With your ticket, you can get cheap lunches in several restaurants, but you need to book ahead.

If you want to stay in Asciano, try **Il Bersagliere**: *V. Roma 39–41; tel: (0577) 718629*. **La Mencia**; *Corso Matteotti 77; tel: (0577) 718227* (closed Mon) can do a reasonable meal.

MONTE OLIVETO MAGGIORE

The lush grove of olives and stately cypresses surrounding this isolated monastery makes a striking contrast with the austere landscapes of Asciano. The **Abbazia di Monte Oliveto Maggiore**; *tel: (0577) 707017*, open daily 0915–1200 and 1515–1745 (summer), until 1700 (winter); free, was founded in 1313 by a former Sienese nobleman, Bernardo Tolomei, who renounced the world after going suddenly blind. Retreating to the lonely Crete hills with two companions, his fundamentalist Benedictine Order was soon recognised by the Pope, and its adherants became known as the Olivetans. The monks fearlessly tended sufferers of the Black Death which devastated Siena in 1348, and many of them died, including Bernardo. The survivors doggedly built the monastery into a powerful institution under papal patronage. After a Napoleonic interruption which lasted until the end of the last war, an Olivetan community was re-established in this amazing clifftop setting. Today the monks support themselves by restoring antiquarian books and producing olive oil, wine, honey and a herb liqueur called Flora di Monte Oliveto for sale in their shop.

As a working monastery, only certain parts of the extensive brick buildings are open to the public. Notice the Della Robbia ceramics at the grand gatehouse. A pleasant café-restaurant called **La Torre**; *tel: (0577) 707022* (closed Tues) serves snacks most of the day. Simple accommodation is sometimes available at the monastery, though a stay of more than one night may be expected. There is an *agriturismo* base at Chiusure: **Agricola Mocine**; *tel: (0577) 707105* (1km east). The monastery can be reached by bus, but the nearest stop is a 15-min walk.

The outstanding feature of the monastery is the **Chiostro Grande** (Grand Cloister) containing a massive and important fresco cycle depicting the life of St Benedict. Nine of the panels were painted by **Luca Signorelli**, the Cortona master who trained under Piero della Francesca. Giovanni Antonio Bazzi, otherwise known as **Il Sodoma**, completed the remaining 27 scenes some years later. They were not painted in chronological order; Signorelli's work is in the middle of the cycle, showing Benedict's monastic world and his meeting with Totila the Goth. Differences between the two artists' work are obvious, and Il Sodoma's paintings are also uneven (apparently he complained about his wages, and when they increased the quality improved). They are full of architectural and anatomical detail, and (some claim) homoerotic interest. Sodoma immortalised himself in one of the last scenes he painted; look out for him in panel 3 with his pet badgers (see box, below).

The 15th-century abbey **church** is in baroque style, and has fine stained glass and masterly intarsia work in its **choir stalls** by Giovanni da Verona. The library, pharmacy, refectory and chapterhouse can also be visited. The Blessed Bernardo's Grotto is a chapel on the site of the founder's hermit cell, reached by a path from the gatehouse.

BUONCONVENTO

Tourist Office: *V. Soccini 32; tel: (0577) 806012* .

Unlovely suburbs now encase this bustling little agricultural town on the V. Cassia, but the distinctive castellated brick gateways at the ends of the main street clearly mark the original medieval village. The evil reputation Buonconvento had for dishonesty and squalour among Grand Tourists of yesteryear seems heartily unjustified in its charming and well-kept old quarter today, and there are worse billets than its old-fashioned **Albergo Roma**; *V. Soccini 14; tel: (0577) 806021* which has a restaurant. If you prefer a rural base, try the attractive, good-value *agriturismo* complex of **Pieve a Salti**; *tel: (0577) 807244* (4 km east). Alternatively, head west for **Murlo**, another medieval *borgo* with an Etruscan museum and a good range of accommodation, including a well-equipped campsite. Look out for the local Val d'Arbia DOC white wine. Buonconvento has regular public transport links with Siena. Information: (bus) *tel: (0577) 204111* ; (train) *tel: (0577) 806104*.

Buonconvento's main sight is the **Museo d'Arte Sacra**: *V. Soccini 17*, open Tues–Sun 1000–1200 and 1500–1700 (Oct–Mar), 1000–1200 and 1600–1900 (Apr–Sept); L2500, containing fine

261

Il Sodoma

What a fate for an artist, to be known for all time as Il Sodoma (the Sodomite). At least his nickname is more memorable than his real name – who would remember an artist called Giovanni Antonio Bazzi? Born in 1477, Il Sodoma was an accomplished artists, but he was disliked by Vasari, who wrote the first (and deeply influential) history of Renaissance art, so he tends to have a bad press (Vasari says of him: 'his manner of life was licentious and dishonourable, and , as he always had boys and beardless youths around him, of whom he was inordinately fond, this earned him the nickname of Sodomite. Instead of feeling shame, he gloried in the name, writing stanzas and verses on it, and singing them to the accompaniment of his lute').

Like Michelangelo with the Sistine Chapel, Il Sodoma originally painted many of the male characters in the frescos at Monte Oliveto Maggiore as nudes. The scandalised monks ordered the naked bodies to be clothed – Il Sodoma mostly did as he was told, but he did leave one or two provocatively posed male nudes, and he occasionally manages to reveal more than he hides by the way that flimsy garments model the bodies' outlines.

The most charming scene in this fresco cycle shows the artist himself with his pets. Again Vasari thought it somehow reprehensible that Il Sodoma was so fond of animals (he kept squirrels, ravens and a pet badger, which followed the artist around like a dog; 'his house', Vasari says disapprovingly, 'was so full of strange animals that it resembled a Noah's ark').

devotional works by Matteo di Giovanni and Sano di Pietro, and some unusual sculptures. The church of **SS Pietro and Paolo** has a Matteo altarpiece. There are several Liberty-style mansions in the town, dating from the turn of the century, and a town hall encrusted with mayoral escutcheons.

SAN QUIRICO D'ORCIA

Tourist Office: *V. Dante Alighieri 31–33; tel: (0577) 897211* (June–Oct, Christmas and Easter 1030–1300 and 1530–1900). Off-season try the **Comune**: *V. Dante Alighieri 65; tel: (0577) 897506* or **Pro Loco**: *Pza della Libertà 2*. San Quirico is a main centre for the promotion of the Val d'Orcia region, now rather grandly termed a *Parco Artistico, Naturale e Culturale* ; *tel: (0577) 898303* . It is surprisingly well-documented, in English as well as Italian, and even has a Web site.

Standing at a major junction on the *V. Cassia* (S2), San Quirico has the advantage of good communications and transport links, but quite a bit of passing traffic. In medieval times another important route passed the town through the Orcia valley, the *V. Francigena*, a pilgrim way to Rome. Today San Quirico is a modest agricultural centre. Despite bomb damage in the last war, the 15th-century turretted walls are still mostly intact, and the Romanesque **Collegiata** church luckily retained its unusual façade and three doors sculpted with lions and strange figures. Inside is a triptych by Sano di Pietro, and some fine inlaid choir stalls.

While in the town, track down the 16th-century **Horti Leonini,** an Italianate Renaissance park of formal box hedges near the town walls, open daily dawn–sunset; free. There is some comfortable resort accommodation in the town, including the **Palazzuolo**, *V. Sta Caterina*

da Siena 43; tel: (05757) 897080 and the **Casanova**, *Loc. Casanova 6/c; tel: (0577) 898177* with a good restaurant, the **Taverna del Barbarossa**; *tel: (0577) 898299*. Both hotels have attractive views and extensive leisure facilities. **Il Poggio** is a well-promoted *agriturismo* farm southwest of San Quirico: *Loc. Ripa d'Orcia; tel: (0577) 897175*. In the same village the **Castello Ripa d'Orcia** is easy to spot; *tel: (0577) 897376*, a lovely hotel-restaurant set in a hilltop castle with stunning views.

BAGNO VIGNONI

This tiny sprinkling of houses 6km south of San Quirico is barely visible on the map, yet it boasts a most startling sight, a huge arcaded stone cistern of warm, gently bubbling water. These sulphurous hot springs have attracted attention since Roman times, and in summer you will find many visitors. Lorenzo the Magnificent came here to ease his rheumatism, and you may remember them as a backdrop in Tarkovsky's film *Nostalgia*. You can no longer splash around in the public pool, but it is possible to bathe where the waters emerge from the cliff below the village.

A spa hotel also takes advantage of the geothermals: **Posta–Marcucci**, *V. Ara Urcea 43; tel: (0577) 887112,* originally a 15th-century summer house built by Pius II. Overlooking the pool is the hotel **Le Terme**; *tel: (0577) 887150*. Both have restaurants; another excellent restaurant in the village is the **Osteria del Leone**, *V. dei Mulini 3; tel: (0577) 887300* (closed Mon). There is a bus service to Bagno Vignoni from San Quirico.

To the south of the village are the ruins of the **Rocca d'Orcia** near the memorable borgo of **Castiglione d'Orcia**, perching on an outer spur of the Monte Amiata volcano.

PIENZA

Tourist Office: *Pza Pio II; tel: (0578) 749071,* open Mon–Sat 1000–1300 and 1500–1900. **Pro Loco**, *V. Case Nuove 22; tel: (0578) 748072.* Either office can provide information on the Orcia valley and Monte Amiata regions, and occasional guided tours of the town.

The distinctive Renaissance core of this little town is all that remains of Pope Pius II's grand ambition to turn his modest birthplace, originally called Corsignano, into a *città ideale,* or model city (see box).

The main sights are all within a stone's throw of each other on the main *piazza.* The **Duomo** has an elegant façade emblazoned with the papal crests. The interior is light and spacious, modelled on the German hall churches which had impressed the Pope on his travels. Several outstanding Sienese altarpieces are displayed inside. Visitors may note with some trepidation the stress cracks appearing in the walls, especially at the apse end. If you look at it from outside you will see how perilously it hovers over the subsiding cliffside. Near the cathedral is the **Palazzo Vescovile** (Archbishop's Palace) in Gothic style, which Pius II gave to an aspiring young cardinal whose name – Roderigo Borgia – meant mercifully little to him. The **Museo della Cattedrale** (Diocesan Museum) has been rehoused in this building; its prize possessions being a magnificent cope, lavishly embroidered in England, and the Newton Collection of archaeological finds; *tel: (0578) 748072* (opening times are uncertain). The **Palazzo Piccolomini**, *Pza Pio II; tel: (0578) 748503,* open Tues–Sun 1000–1230 and 1600–1900 (June–Sept), 1000–1230 and 1500–1800 (Oct–May); L5000, designed as a residence for the Pope, was modelled on Alberti's Palazzo Rucellai in Florence. Its outstanding feature is a triple loggia at the rear, classical in design but innovative in purpose – to maximise vistas of the hanging gardens outside, and vast sweeps of Tuscan countryside. Be sure to see these views, which entranced Pius. The courtyard and gardens are freely accessible. Guided tours of the papal apartments (Tues–Sun 1000–1230 and 1600–1900, 1500–1700 in winter; L5000) inhabited until recently by the Piccolimini family, reveal an amazing bed and the civilised trappings of an ideal Renaissance life. In front of the palace is an elegant well, all part of Rossollini's grand scheme. A number of lesser palaces can be seen around the town, and a church predating the papal refit, **San Francesco,** which retains a few frescos. Little beyond the main square was completed after Pius II's untimely demise in 1464, but the little medieval lanes make an enjoyable wander. Just outside the town stands the lovely 12th-century church, **Pieve di Santi Vito e Modesto,** where Pius was christened (1 km beyond the Porta al Ciglio). Its unusual cylindrical tower was used as a shelter from raiders. The exterior displays carvings of mermaids and dragons.

Pienza's other delights include its famed *pecorino* cheese (also called *cacio* locally, and sometimes matured in a coating of ashes), from the neighbouring sheep-filled countryside. It can be bought in the town's many *alimentari* and *fattorie*, along with other regional produce to make gourmet picnics. An annual festival, the **Fiera del Cacio** (early Sept) is held in its honour, when the hard round cheeses are used in a ball game. Other edible specialities include *pici*, a local pasta, bread-based soups and salads and cakes called *ricciarelli di Pienza*. Pienza's craft shops sell ceramics and leather.

Try **Il Prato**, *Viale S Caterina 1/3; tel: (0578) 748601* (closed Wed) for a pleasant

263

meal. Also worth investigating are the **Latte di Luna**, *V. San Carlo; tel: (0578) 748606* (closed Tues) and **Dal Falco**, *Pza Dante Alighieri 7; tel: (0578) 748551* (closed Fri; rooms available). **Lo Sperone Nudo**, *V. G Marconi 3; tel: (0578) 748641* is a characterful tavern for drinks and snacks (closed Mon). If you want to stay, there are a couple of comfortable hotels: **Corsignano**, *V. della Madonnina 11; tel: (0578) 748501* and **Il Chiostro di Pienza Relais**, *Corso II Rossellino 26; tel: (0578) 748400.* As elsewhere in this region, there is a wide choice of *agriturismo* and furnished rooms to rent. Pienza has no railway connections, but regular TRA-IN buses call at Pienza between Siena and Montepulciano.

MONTEPULCIANO

Tourist Office: *V. Ricci 9; tel: (0578) 758787* or *757442* (Tues–Sun 0900–1200 and 1500–1800). A small seasonal office stands outside the Porta al Prato.

Strung out along a ridge of tufa, Montepulciano is one of the most picturesque of Tuscan towns, and also, at 605 m above sea level, one of the highest. At close quarters, though, it can be a tiring place to explore. Allow plenty of time for rests on the way. It deserves a leisurely stroll. The centre is closed to traffic, and the main street winds up and up from the main car-park north-east of the walls. There is some space near the fortress at the top of the town, but you can't avoid a climb one way or the other. Orange ATAF buses run through the town centre, but it is better to explore on foot. Out of town buses stop at two gates at opposite ends of the town (Porta al Prato and Porta di Farine). The railway station (Siena–Chiusi line) is 10 km away. The fortifications were built in 1511 for Cosimo I. Inside these sturdy wrappings is a jewel of a town, stuffed with palaces and churches at every turn. Its chief *palazzi* stand on the main square, or **Piazza Grande**, forming a blockbusting assembly of Gothic architecture. The **Palazzo Comunale**; *tel: (0578) 757034* is the 15th-century town hall, modelled on Florence's Palazzo Vecchio. The tower rewards the energetic with an exceptional view, open Mon–Sat; free. The **Palazzo Tarugi** and **Palazzo Cantucci** were designed by Sangallo: the latter offers a chance to taste Vino Nobile. The **Duomo** stands on the square too, plain outside, but elegant within, with a magnificent altarpiece in glowing colours by Taddeo di Bartolo (1401). Notice also Andrea Della Robbia's Altare dei Gigli (Altar of the Lilies) and the tomb of Bartolomeo Aragazzi. Close by the Piazza Grande are the **Palazzo Ricci**, housing the tourist office, and the **Palazzo Neri-Orselli** which contains the **Museo Civico**, open Tues–Sun 1030–1230 and 1630–1900 (Apr–Sept), by request in winter; L5000, a collection of Gothic and Renaissance art. There are several more palaces on the Corso (main street). Notice the Roman and Etruscan reliefs (collected by an antiquarian owner) on the façade of **Palazzo Bucelli**, *Corso 73.* Noteworthy churches include **Santa Lucia** (1633), containing a Signorelli *Madonna,* **San Francesco** with a damaged exterior pulpit, **Sant'Agostino** by the famous architect Michelozzo (1427), **Sant'Agnese** harbouring two famous *Madonnas* and **Santa Maria dei Servi**, a Gothic church with a baroque interior. West of the town walls, the **Madonna di San Biagio** is a masterpiece of Renaissance design by Sangallo, best seen as the setting sun warms up the creamy travertine.

Like Montalcino, with which Montepulciano is often compared (and

---

Pius II's Model Town

Aeneas Silvius Piccolomini, who became Pope Pius II in 1458, was born in Pienza (then called Corsignano) in 1405. He was an extraordinary figure: a scholar, poet, diplomat, historian, geographer, voluminous diarist and keen patron of the arts. In short, a neat embodiment of Renaissance Man. He even found a few spare moments for the Sisyphean task of reforming the church of Rome. His final years, however, were largely devoted to his home town, which he named Pienza in honour of his papal name. In 1458 he commissioned the Florentine architect Bernardo Rossellini to transform the town along classic Renaissance lines. Work proceeded at a cracking pace, but Rossellini, like many a builder before and since, over-shot his budget disastrously (rumours circulated that he had misappropriated some of it). Quaking with alarm, Rossellini was summoned to the holy presence to explain himself. But the Pope was so delighted with his work that he happily paid all the bills and showered Rossellini with presents, saying: 'You did well in lying to me about the cost. If you had told me the truth you could never have induced me to spend so much, and this great palace and church would never have been built.' Rossellini, however, does seem to have neglected a few basics in his search for proportional perfection. The Pope's palace was constructed without a kitchen, and the cathedral, projecting above an unstable cliff with inadequate foundations, could collapse at any minute. Pius died in 1464, and his dream of extending the new town across the hillside never materialised. Opinions still differ about his motives. Was rebuilt Pienza a generous gift to his home town, or a vainglorious monument to himself?

confused!), the town's prosperity revolves around the wine trade. The local nectar is called **Vino Nobile**, stocked by a host of *cantine, enotecas* and gourmet food shops all over the town. It isn't as exalted as Brunello, but certainly holds its head high among Tuscan wines. Versions of Chianti, white Valdichiana and sweet Vinsanto are also produced locally, while basic Montepulciano table wines are hard to beat for value. Besides wine, Montepulciano sells many other tempting goodies. Antique shops abound; local crafts include wood-carving and mosaic-making. There is a School of Mosaics on Piazza Grande with a permanent exhibition (free).

Montepulciano is larger and livelier than Montalcino, hosting a major per-forming arts festival in July–Aug. The **Cantiere Internazionale d'Arte** was founded by the composer Hans Werner Hence in the 1970s. Jazz and contemporary music is a major element. In mid August **Bruscello** celebrates the Feast of the Assumption with a historical pageant of masked plays and operetta; in late Aug the **Bravio delle Botti** is a jolly barrel race through the hilly streets. The delightful art nouveau **Caffè Poliziano**, just off the Piazza Grande at *V. di Voltaia nel Corso 27–29; tel: (0578) 758615* is a great centre of local life, especially during festival time. It serves cakes and snacks all day, full meals some evenings, has a base-ment art gallery and offers live music on Sat. Its card claims boldly it is *sempre aperto!*

For a full meal, Montepulciano has plenty of choice. **Il Marcozzo**; *Pza Savonarola 18; tel: (0578) 757262* is a pleasant family restaurant in an attractive historic hotel (closed Wed). Down in San Biagio, **La Grotta**, *Loc. S Biagio 16; tel: (0578) 757607* (closed Wed) is an attrac-tive 16th-century building with a garden.

The **Trattoria Diva**, *V. Gracciano nel Corso 92; tel: (0578) 716951* (closed Tues) has very good home-made pasta. The **Rosticceria di Voltaia**, *V. di Voltaia nel Corso 86* (closed Fri) does inexpensive meals and takeaways for picnics. The market is held on Thur near the Porta al Prato.

Accommodation is limited, so it is advisable to book if you want to stay. Apart from the Marcozzo (see above) best hotel choices in town are **Il Borghetto**, *V. Borgo Buio 7; tel: (0578) 757535* or the **Duomo**, *V. San Donato 14; tel: (0578) 757473*.

SIDE TRACKS
FROM MONTEPULCIANO

The walled village of **Montichiello** lies 5 km south west. A crooked watch tower is visible for miles around. In the **Pieve di SS Leonardo e Christoforo** is a *Madonna and Child* by the great Sienese artist Pietro Lorenzetti (ask for the key next door if it's locked). An understated delight is a little shop near the church selling gorgeous textiles, all hand–made locally and exported to *cognoscenti* worldwide. In July–Aug an open-air theatre festival is staged in the main square by the village's **Teatro Povero** (Poor Theatre). The **Taverna di Moranda**, *V. de Mezzo 17; tel: (0578) 755050* (closed Mon) is a good bet for lunch. At the beautiful village of **Montifollonico** (8 km north west) there is a very famous and expensive restaurant-with-rooms called **La Chiusa**, *V. della Madonnina 88; tel: (0577) 669668* (closed Tues). It has an amazing wine list and some of the best food in Tuscany. ◪

CHIUSI

Tourist Office: *V. Porsenna 67; tel: (0578) 227667*.

Chiusi was the ancient *Clusium* where Lars Porsena came from (immortalised in Macaulay's *Horatius*), a powerful city of the Etruscan League. A large necropolis lies outside the town. The **Museo Nazionale Etrusco**, *V. Porsenna 2; tel: (0578) 20177*, open Tues–Thur 0900–1400, Sat–Sun 0900–1300; L5000, contains lesser finds from the tombs (the best are in major national museums). Apply to museum staff if you want to visit the necropolis. Chiusi's **Duomo** consists of Etruscan and Roman masonry. The **Museo della Cattedrale**; *Pza del Duomo; tel: (0578) 226490*, open 0930–1245 and 1630–1730, (June–mid Oct), Mon–Fri 0930–1245 (mid Oct–May); L1500, gives access to Etruscan galleries beneath the city used as palaeochristian catacombs in the 3rd–5th centuries. Five km north is the Lago di Chiusi, offering a chance for a swim, a boat trip or a fish lunch.

LAGO TRASIMENO

Tourist Information: Castiglione del Lago; *Pza Mazzini 10; tel: (075) 965 2484*, open Mon–Sat 0830–1330 and 1530–1900, Sun 0900–1300.

Italy's fourth-largest lake has a perimeter of 45 km, but is barely 6 m at its deepest, its reedy, swampy margins once a prime breeding ground for the dreaded mosquito. Today the lake is a popular inland resort, its blue-green waters dotted with hundreds of pleasure boats and skimming windsurfers. It cannot be described as spectacular with its lowlying surroundings of olive groves and farmland, but an hour or two by its shores is no bad way to relax, possibly trying out some of the lake fish in its restaurants, or visiting its scattered islands. You can drive quite close to the waterline all around the lake, though frankly, it looks much the same from any angle. Beaches are stony or muddy.

266

The most attractive resort lies on the western shore. **Castiglione del Lago** is an unassuming little town with crenellated fortifications on an olive-clad headland jutting into the lake. A 16th-century **palace** with a few frescos, and a 13th-century **Castello** are not obligatory viewing, but try to see the *Madonna and Child* in the church of **Santa Maria Maddalena**, *Corso Matteotti*, painted in about 1500 by a disciple of Perugino. Several agreeable bars and a choice of hotels and campsites make it an overnight prospect. Try the modest *albergo* **Miralago**, *Pza Mazzini; tel: (075) 951157*, which overlooks the lake from the pleasing main square. The best-equipped campsite is **La Badiaccia**, *V. Trasimeno 1, Voc. Badiaccia; tel: (075) 965 9097*. From the promontory jetty, ferries (L10,000 return) run to the **Isola Maggiore**, which has a single delightful hotel-restaurant, **Da Sauro**, *V. G Guglielmi 1; tel: (075) 826168* (book ahead). There are boat trips from the northern resorts of **Passignano** and **Tuoro** as well, but these are slightly spoilt by indiscriminate holiday development, and traffic lashing along the Perugia *autostrada*. Passignano has an interesting early frescoed church, **S Cristoforo**. In late July it lets its hair down with the **Palio delle Barche**, an amphibious boat race, partly on the lake, partly through the town. Near Tuoro, historians can track down the site of the **Battle of Trasimeno**, one of the most wounding defeats ever suffered by the Romans. It took place in 217 BC, when Hannibal skilfully lured Flaminius (builder of the V. Flaminia) and his troops into an ambush. The subsequent massacre was so frightful that local rivers ran red for days, as the name of the nearest village, Sanguineto, indicates. A map of the site (*'un immenso*

sepolcreto' – a vast graveyard) is available in the tourist office by Tuoro's ferry terminal (summer only).

CORTONA

Tourist Office: *V. Nazionale 42; tel: (0575) 630352* (Mon–Fri 0800–1300 and 1500–1800, Sat 0800–1300). Bus and train tickets are available at this helpful office.

The astonishing views of Lago Trasimeno and the patchwork plain of Valdichiana far below would alone justify the 5 km climb from the main road to this historic hill town, but there is much else to see and enjoy. Cortona is proud of its ancient lineage (said to predate Troy). A few traces of cyclopean walls are visible from its days as a member of the Etruscan League, and several tombs can be visited in the surrounding countryside of vines and olives. Despite its strategic connections with the principal Tuscan and Umbrian cities, Cortona seems remote and aloof. It is easily reached by public transport, especially from Arezzo. Buses run hourly, and trains call at two stations in the valley: Camucia, 6 km, for local services; and Terontola, 10 km, for fast Florence–Rome trains. Both stations are connected by bus to the old town (but not always conveniently). Bus services stop at panoramic Piazza Garibaldi, from where it's a fairly level walk to the centre. The medieval heart is delightful, steep, ladder-like alleys spurting up the hillside from arterial *V. Nazionale* towards landmark churches and fortifications. The main sights are clustered around a series of stately piazzas. First is *Piazza Repubblica*, a popular gathering place at *passegiata* time with bars and restaurants, and a convenient grandstand provided by the exterior staircase of the clocktowered **Palazzo del Comune**. The adjacent square is Piazza Signorelli, graced by the **Palazzo**

267

Pretorio which houses the **Museo dell'Accademia Etrusca**; *tel: (0575) 630415*, open Tues–Sun 1000–1300 and 1600–1900 (Apr–Sept), 0900–1300 and 1500–1700 (Oct–Mar); L5000. This excellent collection includes a splendid bronze chandelier which held 16 oil lamps (4th century BC), a wooden funerary boat, and some exquisite jewellery. Local artists are represented, such as Luca Signorelli and the modernist Gino Severini. Opposite the 16th-century **Duomo**, all grey and white strapwork inside, stands the **Museo Diocesano**; *Pza del Duomo; tel: (0575) 62830*, open Tues–Sun 0900–1300 and 1500–1830 (Apr–Sept), 0900–1300 and 1500–1700 (Oct–Mar); L5000, a small but high-quality collection of devotional works, including some by Cortona native Luca Signorelli, Pietro Lorenzetti and Fra Angelico, who spent a decade in the city. Look for his etherial *Annunciation* and the *Madonna, Child and Saints*.

After this, Cortona is your oyster. Wander through the hilly streets to explore *V. Janelli's* quaint jettied houses, and the plain church of **San Francesco**, built by Brother Elias, who led the Franciscan Order after St Francis's death. Elias and Luca Signorelli are both buried here. Inside the church is an *Annunciation* by another celebrated Cortona painter, Pietro Berretini (known as Pietro da Cortona, 1596–1669), and a reliquary brought from Constantinople by Brother Elias. More of Signorelli's disturbingly muscular work can be seen in the little church of **San Nicolo**. At the top of the town, past *V. Crucis*, now a poignant war memorial decorated with Severini's mosaic work, is the church of **Santa Margherita**, dedicated to Cortona's mystic patron saint. Behind it is the Medicean **fortezza**, with yet more splendid views (a good place for a picnic). Below the southern walls, the church of

Santa Maria del Calcinaio is a masterly Renaissance work. Beyond it is the **Tanella di Pitagore**, the best of Cortona's Estruscan tombs.

Cortona has good cafés and restaurants. **La Loggetta** is one of the best central restaurants: *Pza Pescheria 3; tel: (0575) 630575* (closed Mon). **Tonino**, *Pza Garibaldi 1; tel: (0575) 630500* (closed Mon eve and Tues) has good *antipasti*. Try the **Caffè degli Artisti's** ice cream, *V. Nazionale,* or the piano bar at the **Teatro Signorelli**, *Pza Signorelli*. If you need to stay, the **Italia**, *V. 1 Maggio; tel: (0575) 630254* or the **Sabrina**, *V. Roma 37; tel: (0575) 630397* are comfortable central choices. There is also a pleasant **youth hostel** on *V. Maffei 57; tel: (0575) 601392* in an old monastery. **Il Falconiere**, *Loc. S. Martino; tel: (0575) 6126769* is a highly acclaimed and expensive hotel-restaurant in a superb location 3 km N (excellent restaurant; closed Wed off season). In the evenings, there is more going on than in some towns: an open-air cinema in the public gardens below Piazza Garibaldi, a 19th-century theatre, and a disco, **Tuchulcha** near Piazza Garibaldi. Bars and cafés stay open late. Best nightlife, perhaps, is watching the lights twinkling in the plain far below from the peace of the ramparts.

Connections from Cortona

To reach **Assisi** from Cortona, head south for 13km to join the A1 autostrada, then head east in the direction of Perugia: the lake skirts the northern shore of Lake Trasimeno, then passes Perugia, via a series of tunnels, with some fine views of the hilltop city. South of Perugia, you are greeted by a maze of interchanges; follow signs for Assisi and Spoleto and you will join the N75, from where it is another 16km to Assisi.

AREZZO–FLORENCE

This tour begins in one of Tuscany's wealthiest and most important cities, rich not only from its goldsmithing trade, but also in its artistic and architectural heritage. After Arezzo, the route is almost entirely rural, pottering quietly through the Casentino (upper Arno Valley) along some of the prettiest woodland roads in Tuscany. Be sure to have a picnic with you. Flower-lovers will be in their element. This is a celebrated gastronomic region, especially for smoked ham and salami, and for a profusion of *porcini* mushrooms. Art and history enthusiasts will appreciate a chance to visit the birthplaces of Michelangelo and Uccello, the fortresses of the Guidi counts, and tread in Dante's footsteps. The Casentino is best known, however, for its great religious houses, one of which is the hallowed Franciscan shrine of La Verna, containing brilliant ceramics by members of the artistic Della Robbia family.

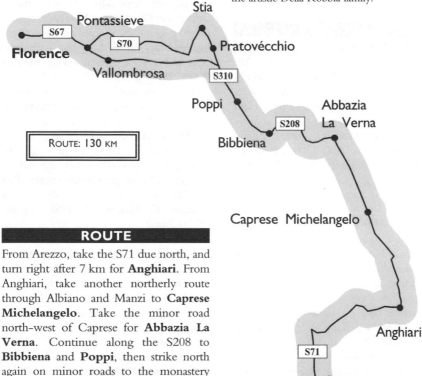

ROUTE: 130 KM

269

ROUTE

From Arezzo, take the S71 due north, and turn right after 7 km for **Anghiari**. From Anghiari, take another northerly route through Albiano and Manzi to **Caprese Michelangelo**. Take the minor road north-west of Caprese for **Abbazia La Verna**. Continue along the S208 to **Bibbiena** and **Poppi**, then strike north again on minor roads to the monastery (Eremo) at **Camaldoli**. Some of the forest roads are rather confusing here, so follow your map carefully. From the Eremo, take the track marked **Pratovécchio** and return to the S70 via **Stia**. Continue through the woods turning left towards **Vallombrosa** near Consuma. From Vallombrosa, glorious views of forest mark the route north via Tossi and Pelago, which descends for 30 twisting kilometres to join the N67 Arno Valley road at Pontassieve; from here it is an 18km journey into the eastern suburbs of Florence.

Near Vallombrosa there are several pleasant places to stay, but it's an easy run to Florence if this is your next port of call. Take care on the roads, however quiet they seem; there may be a surprising amount of holiday traffic, and some of the lanes are very narrow and winding.

AREZZO

Tourist Office: *Pza Risorgimento 116; tel: (0575) 23952* and *Pza della Repubblica 28; tel: (0575) 377678.* The little office in the rail station forecourt is very helpful, with lots of pamphlets about Arezzo (town and province), but does not book accommodation, open Mon–Sat 0900–1300 and 1500–1900, Sun 0900–1300 (summer); shorter hours (winter). For rail or bus information, go to the station ticket offices, not the tourist office.

ARRIVING AND DEPARTING

Arezzo is a spiderweb of radial exit routes connected by several concentric orbital road systems. The centre is pretty well signed from the motorway and main highways (and vice versa). Stop when you get somewhere near the station in the lower town and find a parking place. The tourist office is down here, so pick up a map and any other information you need while you can. Then walk up the pleasantly traffic-free *Corso Italia* (main shopping street)

which takes you straight to the main sights. The gradient is not too steep. You can take cars into the old quarter, but will be lucky to find somewhere legal to park.

Train and bus stations lie next to each other on *Pza Repubblica*. There are good connections to Rome, Florence, Perugia, Assisi, and many other centres; rail is better for long-distance journeys; buses for local hops in the Casentino or Valtiberina.

ACCOMMODATION AND FOOD

Arezzo's agreeable old town is sadly lacking in characterful hotels; accommodation caters mainly for the business community and is rather bland and expensive. It can also be hard to find, especially on the first weekend of each month (an antiques fair) and in early Sept when Arezzo's major festival, the **Giostra del Saraceno** (a costumed pageant with jousting), takes place. June and July can be busy too, with concerts and a rock festival called **Arezzo Wave**. Book ahead.

Two comfortable choices not too far from the centre with parking facilities are **Minerva**, *V. Fiorentina 4; tel: (0575) 370390* and **Etrusco**, *V. Fleming 39; tel: (0575) 984067.* There are a couple of more central places between the station and the old quarter: **Continentale**, *Pza G. Monaco 7; tel: (0575) 20251* and **Milano**, *V. Madonna del Prato 83; tel: (0575) 26836.*

Restaurants are easier to find in the old town at all price ranges, and there's no shortage of bars and cafés. The **Antica Osteria l'Agania**, *V. Mazzini 10; tel: (0575) 25381* (closed Mon and mid June), is favoured by antique dealers who recognise a bargain when they eat one. **Le Tastevin**, *V. de'Cenci 9; tel: (0575) 28304* (closed Mon and mid-Aug) and **Il Saraceno**, *V. Mazzini 6a; tel: (0575) 27644,* are reliable choices. Conveniently located near Piero's frescos is the **Buca di San Francesco**, *Pza San Francesco 1; tel: (0575) 23271* (closed Mon eve, Tues and July), a popular olde-worlde place with competent cooking. The lovely art nouveau **Caffè dei Constanti** on the same square is another enjoyable place to digest frescos, with cakes or ice-cream; *tel: (0575) 21660.*

SIGHTSEEING

The expensive-looking shops on the *Corso Italia* give some idea of Arezzo's Midas touch. One of its most lucrative trades is the production and export of gold jewellery. It has the largest gold manufacturing plant in the world. Antiques are another prosperous sideline; every month there is a major **Fiera Antiquaria** (antiques fair) in the *Pza Grande*. Wartime damage resulted in some remodelling of the oyster-shaped old quarter, and wider, straighter boulevards, but rebuilding has been mostly sensitive to its historic character.

Most of the main sights lie towards the top end of the town. Left off the *corso* on *V. Cavour* is Arezzo's priceless treasure: **San Francesco** church, a plain 13th-century shell housing in its choir chapel one of Europe's greatest fresco cycles. *The Legend of the Cross*, painted in the mid 15th century by Piero della Francesca, has been shrouded from view for some years, undergoing a painstaking conservation process to halt the damage inflicted by earthquakes, lightning, fires, military vandalism, damp and the misguided efforts of early restorers. Soon, we are promised, not too long now, 1996, 1997, 1998 . . . all these beauties will be on show again. Catch them if you can. The frescos, tackled with Piero's obsessive attention to perspective, are geometrical compositions relating a complicated quasi-biblical story which is explained in display panels in the church. You need to read this carefully, or buy a detailed guide, to understand the narrative. Other frescos in the church pale into insignificance beside Piero's work.

Arezzo has several other first-class sights. The **Pieve di Santa Maria** further up the *corso* would grace any city with its cleverly arcaded façade and elegant *campanile* of dashing double mullions – the tower of 100 holes (actually nearer 40) – dating from 1330. Notice the carvings over the main door, the *Reliefs of the Twelve Months*. Inside is a polytych by Pietro Lorenzetti, and an ancient crypt. The apse end of the church faces the **Pza Grande**, a fine sloping square surrounded by a harmonious assembly of palaces. Its main features are the **Palazzo della Fraternità dei Laici**, to the west side, and **Loggia del Vasari**, an arcade designed by the famous architect and painter, a native of Arezzo. The **Casa del Vasari**, *V. XX Settembre 55; tel: (0575) 300301*, was built and decorated in 1540 by Giorgio Vasari. It contains many portraits of contemporaries, some already immortalised in Vasari's entertainingly gossipy biographies, *Lives of the Most Excellent Italian Architects, Painters and Sculptors*. More palaces and churches stud odd corners of the old town, the most imposing being the **Duomo** on a large square. The Gothic interior is illuminated by lovely stained glass. A small fresco by Piero della Francesca and a terracotta *Assumption* by Andrea Della Robbia are just a couple of its interesting features. Notice also the tomb of Bishop Tarlati, ruler of Arezzo in the early 14th century. Across quiet public gardens, the ramparts of the Fortezza Medicea suggest a picnic with a view. Of Arezzo's several museums, the most worthwhile is the **Museo Archeologico**, *V. Margaritone 10; tel: (0575) 20882*, open Mon–Sat 0900–1400,

271

Sun 0900–1300; L8000. This is in the lower town, south-east of the rail station. Built on the site of the Roman amphitheatre, the museum's best exhibits are some wonderfully delicate red **coralline vases** dating from the 1st century BC. Labelling is in Italian only. In the southern suburbs, the graceful Renaissance church of **Santa Maria delle Grazie** (1444), *V. di Santa Maria,* contains more Della Robbia work around a fine fresco of the Virgin by Parri di Spinello.

CAPRESE MICHELANGELO

The stone mountain village that boasts such a famous citizen looks a modest enough place, perched on a cliff amid beech and chestnut woods. The name (formerly simply Caprese) was lengthened only in 1875, when Michelangelo Buonarotti's birth certificate was discovered four centuries after the event. This conclusive verification of his origins dashed the spirits of rival villages which also claimed the honour. His father was the local *podestà* (a sort of headman role combining mayor and magistrate), so the family was of some standing. The **Casa del Podestà** and the adjacent castle are now a **Museo Michelangelo**, *V. Capolugo 1; tel: (0575) 793912,* open 0930–1830 (Apr–Oct); 0930–1400 and 1500–1730 (Nov–Mar); L3000, which also dispenses tourist information. It contains a few not-very-riveting documents and photographs, along with reproductions of the artist's work. The walled grounds hold a collection of modern sculpture of rather less masterly quality. Michelangelo didn't spend much time in his native village, but he never forgot the area. 'If my brains are any good,' he told the architect and biographer Vasari, 'it is because I was born in the pure air of your Arezzo countryside.' When he needed some trustworthy timber for the perilous scaffolding in the Sistine Chapel, he selected it personally from the tall pines of the Valtiberina, which were floated down the river Tiber into Rome.

Many of the travellers through Caprese come not to pay homage to the Renaissance genius, but in search of mushrooms in the local woods. If you head about 5 km up the steep cul-de-sac road south-west of Caprese you will reach a rugged alpine restaurant with rooms which specialises in *funghi porcini* cookery. The **Fonte della Galletta**, *Alpe Faggetta, Caprese Michelangelo; tel: (0575) 793925,* makes a simple but delightful walking base for a night or two (inexpensive; closed Jan–Mar). Your length of stay will be dictated by your fondness for fungi (there isn't much else to eat). North-west of Caprese, the minor road to La Verna is exceptionally pretty, an excellent place for a picnic beside a dazzling show of wild flowers or a herd of white cattle.

ABBAZIA LA VERNA

A sharp ridge divides the upper valleys of the Arno and the Tiber. At La Verna the wooded terrain is extremely rugged, with tumbling precipices and rocky chasms. It was here, in 1213, that Count Orlando donated a piece of land to St Francis of Assisi. A small community of Franciscans settled here to pray and meditate, inspired by the beauty of their natural surroundings. Francis himself made six journeys here, and had many visions. In one revelation he saw the rocks of La Verna split apart at the moment of Christ's death (the damp cave in a cleft where Francis slept is reverently noted by all pilgrims). On his final visit, Francis became the first recorded recipient of the signs of the stigmata (Christ's wounds), a mark of sanctity which thereafter caused him immense suffering. The **monastery** of simple mud huts gradually expanded into the present extensive complex of churches, chapels, cloisters and a convent. Their plain, rustic look seems more appropriate to the Franciscan style than the florid ostentation of Assisi. The monastery receives many visitors, and is a popular coach tour from many local towns. Pilgrims arrive by the score for fervent religious reasons, and many stay in the monastery's guesthouse accommodation; *tel: (0575) 599356.*

Other visitors make shorter tours of the 15th-century basilica, the **Chiesa delle Stimmate** and the **Cappella di Santa Maria degli Angeli**, whose prized possessions are a series of 15 delicate glazed terracotta reliefs in blue, green and white. These exquisite creations from the workshops of the talented Della Robbia family are among the great glories of Tuscan art. Friezes of lemons make them especially charming. A walkway near the Oratory of St Antony leads out to a fenced ledge teetering over a sheer rockface. Here, legend says, Satan pushed Francis over, but the rocks below instantly softened like melted wax and he landed unharmed. A number of walks lead through the surrounding woods to panoramic vantage points. La Penna is one of the highest. Little chapels and hermitages mark the spots where the saintly monks used to pray.

BIBBIENA

Tourist Office: *V. Berni 25; tel: (0575) 593098.*

This sizeable town is now one of the main commercial centres of the Casentino, much expanded beyond its attractive old quarter in a rash of factories and modern housing. Tobacco production is a local activity. Its attractions for visitors are mostly confined to a palace or two and a couple of modest churches. **San Lorenzo**

contains examples of the Della Robbia ware you will find all over the region; **SS Ippolito e Donato** has some Sienese art and an altarpiece by Bicci di Lorenzo (1373–1452).

POPPI

Poppi's grand 13th-century **Castello**, *tel: (0575) 520294*, open daily 0930–1230 and 1500–1800 Apr–Sept, weekends only (Oct–Mar); L5000, makes an unmistakable statement on the skyline. Built by the powerful Guidi family, this is one of the best examples in the area, and bears a strong resemblance to the Palazzo Vecchio in Florence. It has a splendid courtyard and a frescoed hall. The tower can be climbed for magnificent views. A monumental bust of Dante, a local celebrity, surveys the town from the public gardens near the castle.

Poppi's ancient porticoed lanes and cobbled squares are delightful to explore. At one end of the main street is the **Badia di San Fedele**, a 12th-century Vallombrosan church with a fine *Madonna and Child*. Just outside the town, the **Primo Parco Zoo**, open daily 0800–2000 (summer), 0800–1700 (winter); L6000, L4500 child, may amuse younger visitors. It contains only European fauna, with a bent towards conservation of endangered species.

PRATOVÉCCHIO

This small village deserves a nod as the birthplace of Paolo Uccello (1397). Two km south-west, the church of **Piero di Romena** is one of the purest examples of Romanesque in the region. The Guidi fortress nearby was mentioned in Dante's *Inferno*. Dante took part in the battle of **Campaldino** in 1289 just south of the village, a crucial victory for Florentine ascendancy in Tuscany.

273

STIA

Tourist Office: *Pza Tanucci 65; tel: (0575) 504106.*

This is a lively little wool-producing town on the Arno. It has no very compelling sights but its authentic atmosphere is somehow immensely cheering after a binge of tourist towns. Catch it on market day, when stalls of sunglasses glint in the long main *piazza*, groups of locals sit and chat in the shade, and old ladies rinse their apricots at the bizarre fountain of spouting serpents. The plain Romanesque church of **Santa Maria Assunta** has a battered *Madonna and Child* by Andrea Della Robbia, and there are two Guidi **castles** on the outskirts. One houses an agricultural museum. The River Arno rises in the hills behind Stia, and the town has a mountain feel, with steep roofs.

ABBAZIA CAMÁLDOLI

Lovely sylvan trails lead north from Poppi and Bibbiena to the isolated hermitage and monastery of Camaldoli, founded in 1012 by St Romualdo, a Benedictine monk, who was granted a tract of forest by a noble landowner. Romualdo and his followers sought to emulate their hermit predecessors by a life of solitude, but then, as now, they were constantly badgered by visitors and pilgrims who distracted them from their contemplations. Two separate communities were set up: a **Convento** (monastery) with a more relaxed rule where visitors could be entertained, and an **Eremo** (hermitage) hidden 300 m deeper in the woods with a strict code of silence and non-fraternisation. In the monastery, the 11th-century cloisters, library and a lovely old pharmacy can be seen. The monks are self-sufficent vegetarians and great tree planters. They make herbal products for sale. Visitors may stay at the monastery in summer; *tel: (0575) 556013.*

There is other simple accommodation nearby. In the Eremo, the monks still live in separate cottage-like cells, but now work together and meet in church and at meals. Visitors may see the church, decorated by Vasari, but are unwelcome near the living quarters, open Mon–Sat 0830–1115 and 1500–1800, Sun 0830–1045, 1200–1230 and 1500–1800; free.

The surrounding woodlands contain a great variety of trees and wildlife which now constitute part of the vast **Parco Nazionale delle Casentinesi**; a protected area of about 11,000 ha and one of Italy's largest remaining forests. Waymarked paths lead through the woods. Badia Prataglia, east of Camaldoli, is a good starting-point. A leaflet outlining the walks is available from local tourist offices. In autumn, the area is a favourite haunt for mushroom gatherers.

VALLOMBROSA

Tourist Offices: Vallombrosa; *tel: (055) 862024*; **Saltino**; *tel: (055) 862003*, open summer only.

The name means 'shady valley'. As you approach through the dappled glades where coniferous species gradually outnumber the deciduous trees you will see how appropriate it is. The Vallombrosan order (like the Camaldolians, an offshoot of the Benedictine rule) was founded here in 1038 by a Florentine nobleman, Giovanni Gualberto Visdomini, who gathered a group of followers anxious to exchange a life of privilege and comfort for a regime of extreme austerity and self-discipline. The abbey became very influential in the centuries after Giovanni's canonisation in 1193, and controlled large amounts of land. Wealthy converts and benefactors donated their worldly goods to the order, as the grandeur of Vallombrosa indicates.

Magic Mushrooms

Central Italy is renowned for its edible fungi, a staple ingredient in much Tuscan and Umbrian cooking. Two species predominate: the *porcini* mushroom (which the French and British know as the *cep*) is particularly popular in Tuscany, while the costly truffle (black and white) is found more widely in Umbria. Rather than being used whole, these strongly flavoured fungi are often chopped, grated or mashed with other ingredients. The truffle is sometimes simply placed with other foods to impart its unique scent and flavour and then extracted before being cooked. Weight for weight, truffles are the most expensive foodstuff in the world, currently trading at around £150–£2000 per kilo, depending on species. They lurk underground, require very precise but unpredictable growing conditions, and resist all attempts at commercial cultivation, remaining in prime condition unpicked for only a matter of days. The musky scent is often alleged to be aphrodisiac, especially to female pigs (hence the former use of sows to find them; their ecstatic behaviour when successful was a drawback).

Porcini obligingly grow all year-round, but other species, including truffles, are much more seasonal and confine their elusive appearances to late autumn and winter, with scant regard for the tourist market. Frozen, dried or preserved in oil, they are but faint imitations of the freshly picked product. Such droves of mushroom-gatherers are out in force in autumn that it is hard to understand how there can be any wild varieties left, but it is a rare Tuscan or Umbrian menu without a few mushrooms in its repertoire. Some adventurous chefs experiment with other types of fungi such as morels, blewits and chanterelles.

275

The present abbey buildings are mostly 17th century in appearance after repeated remodellings, and look rather forbidding. Since 1866, when the monastery was suppressed, the surrounding woodlands have been owned by the state. A forestry school uses part of the premises. Reinstated in 1963, a small community of about 20 Vallombrosans still lives here, making herbal potions and lotions for sale in their shop. Guided tours are available by appointment; *tel: (055) 862029.*

Inside, it is glumly impressive, with a fresco-covered church, open daily 0630–1200 and 1500–1800; free, and numerous minor works of art. The poet John Milton visited Vallombrosa in 1638, and mentions it in *Paradise Lost*, though cynics may wonder whether the mellifluous name and the setting attracted him more than the abbey itself.

There are some good woodland walks and drives nearby, especially from Saltino (1 km west), and Monte Secchieta (1449 m), a winter skiing area with grandiose resort accommodation. In summer, walks with a Club Alpino Italiano guide can be arranged.

The village of Vallombrosa has restaurants, but there are better bases to stay down the road in **Regello** (**Villa Rigacci**, *Vaggio 76; tel: (055) 865 6718;* supremely comfortable and peaceful country house with excellent food), **San Donato** (**Fattoria degli Usignoli**; *tel: (055) 865 2018;* a large complex of farmhouse apartments overlooking the Arno Valley, with good leisure facilities) or **Incisa Valdarno** (**Il Burchio**, *V. Poggio al Burchio 4; tel: (055) 833 0124;* sociable house-party atmosphere with horse-riding and country cooking).

FLORENCE (FIRENZE)

Seen on a clear day from one of its surrounding hills, Florence's 15th- and 16th-century buildings mirrored in the Arno and dwarfed by the vast tawny dome of the cathedral make a romantic picture. At closer quarters, Florence reveals itself as a noisy modern city with traffic smog and far too many tourists. In some ways, Tuscany's capital is harder to love than Venice or Rome, or even its great ancestral rival Siena. Yet its credentials are irreproachable. Under Medici rule, the city-state of Florence became the driving force of the Renaissance, not just in art and architecture, but in science and mathematics, astronomy and geography, literature and economics. The fruits of that extraordinary cultural paroxysm between 1400 and 1550 demand to be seen, at least once in a lifetime.

TOURIST INFORMATION

Florence has several tourist offices, each of which modestly disclaims responsibility for being the fountainhead of knowledge. A central one lies near the **Duomo** at *V. Cavour 7; tel: (055) 23320 or 290932* (try this office if you need touring itineraries or information on the province of Florence). The others are more city oriented: there's a helpful one outside the **main rail station** by the bus stops: *Pza della Stazione; tel: (055) 230 2124,* and a third at *Chiasso dei Baroncelli 17r, off Pza della Signoria; tel: (055) 230 2033,* all should be open Mon–Sat 0815–1915, Sun 0815–1345 (summer); Mon–Sat 0900–1400 (winter). Try your luck at any of them. They are nearly always crowded, but can provide a fair map and some useful, glossily produced handouts (in English) on museums and galleries, accommodation, restaurants, events, etc. No accommodation bookings can be made; for this you must go to one of the specialist agencies. Be sure to pick up current editions of the invaluable booklets *Welcome to Florence* and *Concierge Information,* which list up-to-date details on just about everything, e.g. how to find petrol in the middle of the night, what a postcard stamp to Albania costs, and where to get your fountain pen mended. The **APT** headquarters is at *V. A. Manzoni 16, off Pza C. Beccaria; tel: (055) 23320,* some way east of the central sights, but this is mostly for administrative and official purposes.

ARRIVING AND DEPARTING

By Air
Amerigo Vespucci, *V. del Termine 11, Petètola; tel: (055) 306 1700.* This small business airport 5 km north-west of the city centre (off the A11 *Autostrada Firenze Mare* heading towards Prato) is currently used by a few international airlines, e.g. Air UK, Meridiana, Air France, Sabena and Lufthansa (daily flights from Gatwick). Bus 62 (ATAF) serves the airport every 20 mins (0600–2220); L1500; SITA buses ply every 50 mins from the bus station at *V. Santa Caterina da Siena 17; tel: (055) 214721;* L6000; journey time about 30 mins. Expect to pay around L25,000 for a

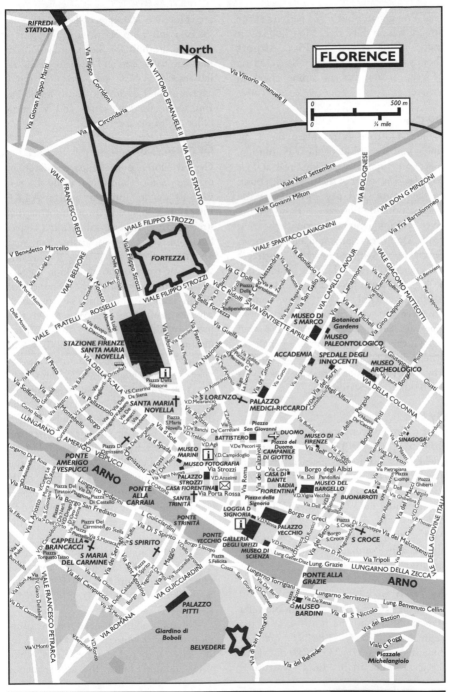

taxi. You get an hour's free parking at the airport, but no duty-free. Most holiday air traffic is still served by **Pisa Airport** (hourly trains to Florence; Santa Maria Novella Station has an airline check-in service).

By Car

Central Florence is no place for a car unless you are a resident. Leave it outside. There are large free parking areas at *Pzle Michelangiolo*, south of the river, with buses to the centre, and pay car-parks at the main station, the Fortezza da Basso, on the river embankments and around the ring roads. Don't leave any valuables on view. Several hotels with easy parking or garages are suggested below. Driving in Florence is 'big-city' stuff; he or she who hesitates is almost certainly a lost fellow tourist. Southern and western exits to the motorways are fairly straightforward and well signed; the northern suburbs are hell on wheels. If you're heading east, you can follow the Arno, but you can't do this if you are heading westwards.

By Bus

Half a dozen companies serve Florence from all parts of Tuscany and further afield. The main out-of-town operators are **SITA**, *V. Santa Caterina da Siena; tel: (055) 214721* (Siena, Volterra, San Gimignano, etc.) and **LAZZI**, *Pza Stazione 4; tel: (055) 215154* (Viareggio, Montecatini, Abetone, Lucca). Innumerable coach companies offer organised excursions to Florence.

By Train

The main station is **Santa Maria Novella** (Firenze SMN), to the north-west of the centre; *tel: (055) 288785* (general enquiries) or *(055) 235 2320* for local services. The main lines westwards

are Florence–Viareggio (Prato, Pistoia, Lucca), and Florence–Pisa (Empoli is a major route-hub for Siena, etc.). Eastern lines run to Arezzo and Perugia. Facilities: left-luggage, lost property, currency exchange and accommodation bookings. Bus terminals, taxi ranks and a tourist office are in the forecourt.

GETTING AROUND

Central Florence is compact enough to explore on foot, and this is really the best way to do it. Intrepid orange **ATAF buses** barge their way through the narrow streets with scant regard for parked vespas, litter bins or stray pedestrians. You may find buses useful for getting to outlying sights, car-parks or hotels, taking luggage to the station, exploring the Oltrano, etc. If you want to catch one, buy tickets in advance from shops with the ATAF sign (news-stands, *tabacchi*, etc.) or automatic machines. Single fares cost L1500; *biglietto multiplo* tickets cost L5800 (four 60-min tickets); timed tickets e.g. L2500 for 3hrs' use. You can also buy a day ticket, L6500, or a weekly *Carta Arancio*, L45,000, valid throughout the province. Validate tickets as you board, or risk a hefty fine. The main ATAF office is by the rail station; *tel: (055) 565 0222*, open 0700–2000. ATAF's bus map is well worth picking up, clearly showing all the numbered routes colour-coded. The electric microbuses marked B, C and D operate useful routes around the city.

Taxi ranks are at the station and *Piazza Repubblica*. Rides should be metered; expect to pay about L12,000–L20,000 for central journeys; *tel: (055) 4390 or (055) 4242*.

Florentine addresses need some explanation: business addresses are followed by the letter r (a red number on a white plate), and don't follow the same sequence as the domestic premises with the same number. Visitors should be aware that Florence has some urban problems, including petty street crime (beware pickpockets and gypsy thieves), and a drug scene (especially around *Pza Santa Maria Novella* and the Cascine park at night).

STAYING IN FLORENCE

Accommodation
Florence has a great many hotels, including grand and awesome ones, but not enough good (and affordable) ones to supply summer demand. Book ahead, or be prepared to stay somewhere outside the city. Prices are inevitably high, and many places are rather dreary, but budget options are bolstered by a significant amount of student-style accommodation in private rooms (available out of termtime). Some of Florence's central areas can be noisy, dusty, hot and unsavoury at night. Avoid touts offering cheap rooms at the airport or station. If you haven't any prebooked accommodation, try one of the reservation agencies at service stations on the exit motorways, or at the rail station: **Informazioni Turistichi Alberghiere**, open daily 0830–2100. A small commission is charged.

A memorable way to enjoy Florence, if you can afford it, is to stay at the beautiful and stylish **Torre di Bellosguardo**, *V. Roti Michelozzi 2; tel: (055) 229 8145*, on a peaceful hill south of the Arno. You needn't struggle with the city centre to find it, and there are no parking problems. This grand, 16th-century fortified villa has been imaginatively and tastefully converted into hotel accommodation, though anything less hotel-like is hard to imagine. No two rooms are alike; the spacious, frescoed interiors and antiques are gracious without being stuffy. Gorgeous gardens,

fine views and a charming owner add to its attractions. The centre is walkable, but buses run into town from the foot of the hill, or it's an easy taxi ride. Another agreeable place for motorists is the **Villa Belvedere**, *V. B. Castelli 3; tel: (055) 222501*, on another southern hillside with a convenient bus route to town. This friendly, family-run hotel is in a pleasant residential district, with excellent views and gardens. The well-equipped bedrooms are smart and comfortable; a limited range of snacks and pastas is served in the evenings, as there are few local restaurants.

Charmingly idiosyncratic central choices include the **Morandi alla Crocetta**, *V. Laura 50; tel: (055) 234 4747*, a former convent; the **Tornabuoni Beacci**, *V. Tornabuoni 3; tel: (055) 212645*, a Renaissance building on the most fashionable shopping street; the **Aprile**, *V. della Scala 6; tel: (055) 216237*, a Medici palace, or the **Hermitage**, *Vicolo Marzio 1, Pza del Pesce; tel: (055) 287216*, a stone's throw from the Ponte Vecchio. The **J and J**, *V. di Mezzo 20; tel: (055) 234 5005*, or the **Loggiato dei Serviti**, *Pza Santissima Annunziata 3; tel: (055) 289592*, are more stylishly urbane. Expect to pay for overnight parking. Florence has three youth hostels, including a lovely one west of the centre in a park: **Ostello Villa Camerata**, *V. le Righi 2; tel: (055) 601451*.

Fiesole is a popular base from which to explore Florence. It has several attractive hotels, and a campsite (see side tracks below).

Eating and Drinking
Needless to say, Florence has lots of restaurants at all price ranges (though generally higher than average). Some care is needed to avoid tourist traps, e.g. around the Duomo and on *Pza della Signoria* or

Pza della Repubblica. Florentine waiters can be haughty and brusque; some restaurants actually pride themselves on their rudeness to customers. Menus nearly always include the local speciality, *bistecca alla fiorentina* (grilled steak). Top gastronomic billing goes to **Enoteca Pinchiorri**, *V. Ghibellina 87; tel: (055) 242777* (closed Aug, Sun, Mon lunch and Wed), in a lovely garden setting (mind-boggling wine list). Less expensively, try the **Cantinetta Antinori**, *Pza Antinori 3; tel: (055) 292234* in an elegant Renaissance palace (closed weekends), or **Coco Lezzone**, *V. del Parioncino 26r; tel: (055) 287178*, a stylishly austere but accomplished trattoria (closed Sat–Sun in summer). For unusual Florentine specialities, head for **Cibreo**, *V. dei Macci 118; tel: (055) 234 1100*. The station and market areas are generally cheaper. In Oltrarno, try **Alla Vecchia Bettola**, *V. le L Ariosto 32r; tel: (055) 224158* (closed Sun, Mon and Aug). In Santa Croce, **La Maremmana**, *V. dei Macci 77r; tel: (055) 241226* has good set menus. One place no one should leave untried is **Vivoli**, *V. Isola delle Stinche 7; tel: (055) 292334*, a legendary ice-cream café near Santa Croce church (closed Mon). **Rivoire** is a famous (and pricey) outdoor café on the *Pza della Signoria* (try the chocolate). For some local colour, don't miss Florence's splendid food markets, the **Mercato Centrale** near San Lorenzo church, open Mon–Sat 0700–1400, Sat 1600–2000 or the **Mercato Sant'Ambrogio**, *Pza Ghiberti*, open Mon–Fri 0700–1300.

Communications

Post Office: *V. Pellicceria 8*, open Mon–Fri 0815–1800, Sat 0815–1230.

Money

The major banks can be found in the *Pza della Repubblica* area. Exchange counters at the station and airport give lower rates, but there are automatic machines throughout the city. **Thomas Cook** has an office at *Lungarno Acciaioli 6r; tel: (055) 289781*, near the Ponte Vecchio.

Consulates

UK: *Lungarno Corsini 2; tel: (055) 284133.*
US: *Lungarno Vespucci 38; tel: (055) 239 8276.*

ENTERTAINMENT AND EVENTS

Plenty goes on all year-round, and it isn't difficult to find out about it from local listings magazines such as *Time Off, Events, Firenze Spettacolo, Concierge Information*, etc. **Box Office**, *V. Faenza 139r; tel: (055) 242361* can give you up-to-date information and tickets. Piano bars, pubs and cafés lengthen *passegiata* time. Late-night entertainment, however, is less widely available than you might expect in a city of Florence's size. Concerts are held all year, especially during the **Maggio Musicale Fiorentina** (Apr–June) in the Teatro Comunale. Opera and church concerts are held in winter. English-language films are shown at the Cinema Astro, *Pza San Simone*. A summer music festival called **Estate Fiesolana** is held in Fiesole (June–Aug).

Soccer fans may like to watch the Florentines play their internecine matches of deadly rivalry in medieval costume: **Calcio Storico** (late June). Around Easter, the **Scoppio del Carro** takes place, involving a ox-drawn cartload of fireworks and a mechanical 'dove', which carries a spark that ignites the bangers. On Ascension Day the **Festa del Grillo** (Festival of the Cricket) is held in Cascine park, and caged crickets are released. The **Festa delle Rificolone** takes place on 7 September, when children process to

Pza Santissima Annunziata with paper lanterns. There's a **Festa dei Porcini** (mushroom festival) in August, and the **Florence Film Festival** in December. Florence is always packed for its **Fashion Show** (November).

SHOPPING

Jewellery glitters on the Ponte Vecchio, and top fashion designers line *V. dei Tornabuomi* (including the original Gucci store); sadly, window-shopping is all most of us can afford. Try **Antico Setificio Fiorentino**, *V. della Vigna Nuova 97r* for luscious hand made textiles. Leatherware is Florence's best-known speciality; the pungent scent of freshly tanned bags, belts and shoes permeates whole streets. Try the **Leather Guild**, *Pza Santa Croce 20r*. Another typical Florentine product is beautiful stationery, made into irresistible notebooks, boxes, etc. Much is mass-produced now, but you may be lucky enough to find a traditional workshop which can show you the original process. The ancient craft of paper-marbling was introduced to Venice from the Ottoman Empire, but the Florentines developed their own style of combed peacock patterns. Try **Giannini**, *Pza Pitti 37r; tel: (055) 212621*, **Scriptorium**, *Pza Pitti 6,b; tel: (055) 238 2272*, or **Et Cetera**, *V. della Vigna Nuova 82r*, for unusual stationery. *V. dei Fossi* is a good area to look for stationery and antiques.

A wander round the street markets is sure to produce a few bargains. Best of the markets is in Cascine park (Tues), but there are several central ones, e.g. around San Lorenzo church and near the Sant'Ambrogio food market. The **Mercato Nuovo** is a short distance north of the Ponte Vecchio. It once specialised in straw hats, but now has general souvenirs. Rub the nose of the bronze boar in the 'Piglet' fountain, and drop a coin in the basin for luck.

SIGHTSEEING

Tailor your sightseeing ambitions to the amount of time you plan to spend in Florence if you want to leave with good impressions of it. If you have no interest at all in Renaissance art, you may as well leave the city alone; a crash course of Florentine museums is not the most relaxing way to spend a Tuscan holiday. If this is a first visit, pick out a few highlights, intersperse them with plenty of fresh air and ice-cream, and promise yourself another trip. The sections below are arranged in approximate order of sightseeing priority, though this, of course, is a personal choice. In three days, you can scrape the surface of the main sights; with a week to spare, you can (and should) include an excursion or two to avoid cultural overload.

Despite the size of greater Florence, which now sprawls unattractively along the Arno and into the neighbouring hills, the area most visitors want to see is very compact. The surrounding province offers some enticing expeditions, especially the Chianti and Mugello regions. Fiesole, now a northern suburb, still preserves its historic character. Scattered in the countryside are a number of Medici villas, used by the Florentine rulers for much the same reasons as their present visitors – to escape from city bustle and summer heat.

Several quarters can be distinguished in the old city, though these blend into each other with little delineation. The great divide is the River Arno, carving east–west through the centre. It isn't an especially beautiful waterway, and its bridges, repeatedly swept away by floods and destroyed in wartime, are mostly forgettable latter-day structures. A single medieval landmark stands out: the **Ponte Vecchio**, built in 1345 and still surmounted by 16th-century goldsmiths' shops. Above the shops runs the **Vasari Corridor**, an elevated walkway which allowed the Medici rulers to travel between the Palazzo Vecchio and the Palazzo Pitti without having to mingle with the *hoi polloi* at street level, or get wet in the rain. If custodians are available, you can have a look at this on your Uffizi gallery ticket; *tel: (055) 23885*, open Tues–Sat 0930; L12,000.

North of the Uffizi is the statue-filled **Piazza della Signoria**, a glorious medieval square, dominated by the **Palazzo Vecchio** to the east, now part museum, part town hall, fronted by a copy of Michelangelo's *David* (the original is in the Accademia gallery – see below).

Most of the sights lie close to this square on the northern bank, but the **Oltrarno**, or southern side, deserves a visit for its less pressured atmosphere and artisan shops. It also has some fine monuments, notably the great museum complex of the **Palazzo Pitti**.

Churches

Most Florentine churches can generally be visited free of charge whenever there are no services in progress, from about 0730–1200 and 1530–1830. Take some change to illuminate interiors. Dress codes are less strict in Florence than in some places, but it is courteous to observe them (no bare shoulders or knees).

The **Duomo**, open Mon–Fri 0900–1800, Sat 0830–1700, Sun 1300–1700; free, is a 'must', even on a short visit. Florence's most conspicuous landmark in the centre of the city is visible for miles around by its huge russet **cupola**. As a piece of engineering, Brunelleschi's dome is sheer wizardry, the largest structure of its type ever attempted, and built without scaffolding. It can be climbed, Mon–Sat 0930–1730; L8000 – 463 steps. Apart from the dome, the Duomo's most memorable feature is its fantastically ornate façade of variegated marble, a 19th-century neo-Gothic addition matching the style of the much older 85 m **Campanile**, open daily 0900–1850, (summer); 0900–1620 (winter); L8000, designed by Giotto and Pisano, and decorated with bas-relief carvings. Inside, the Duomo is surprisingly austere apart from its maze-like mosaic floor, several funerary monuments and the Last Judgement frescos around the dome. The octagonal **Baptistery** is much older than the Duomo, dating from the 7th century. Both the exterior, clad in striking green and white marble with magnificent bronze **doors** by Pisano and Ghiberti, and the interior smothered in sumptuous **mosaics** are a *tour-de-force*. The cathedral complex stands on a cramped, constantly crowded square and is difficult to admire or photograph well at close quarters. Don't miss the attached **Museo dell' Opera del Duomo** (Cathedral Museum), *Pza del Duomo 9; tel: (055) 230 2885*, open Mon–Sat 0900–1850 (Mar–Oct); 0900–1720 (winter); L8000, an important repository of Florentine sculpture, notably Michelangelo's modified *Pietà* and works by Donatello, Pisano and Luca Della Robbia.

The church of **Santa Maria Novella**, open 0700–1130 and 1530–1800; free, is a Dominican church, built between 1279 and 1357. It has one of the richest church interiors in Florence. The Gothic **façade** of multicoloured marble is the first thing to hit you across a spacious *pza* near the station. Inside, its main features are marvellous frescos by Masaccio, Ghirlandaio, and Filippino Lippi, among others. The attached **museum**; *tel: (055) 282187,* is in

282

The Medici Tombs

The Medici mausoleum, at the rear of San Lorenzo church, is one of the most poignant memorials in the city to several generations of the family that ruled Florence, and later Tuscany, for some 400 years. The upper part of the mausoleum contains the huge marble sarcophagi of the later princes and dukes of Tuscany, and for all the bombast of this chapel, it contains some charming examples of the Florentine art of *pietro dure*, the creation of pictures in coloured marble – most especially in the coats of arms that adorn the floor and tombs.

Downstairs in the New Sacristy, by complete contrast, are two cool white marble tombs that stand amongst Michelangelo's most magnificent works. The Medici members so honoured are minor players in the history of the city, but the allegorical figures draped across the tombs are strikingly memorable, depicting, in opposed pairs, Night and Day and Dawn and Dusk.

Ironically, Michelangelo was in hiding from the Medici at the time he was working on these tombs. In the long and complicated politics of the time, Michelangelo had sided with his fellow citizens against the Medici, who had been expelled from the city. They returned and held the city to siege. Michelangelo helped plan reinforcements for the city defences, but then ran away when the battle got going (Vasaria, telling the story, forgives this apparent cowardice, putting it down to Michelangelo's artistic temperament). Michelangelo sought refuge in the New Sacristy and, in the small room to the left of the altar, you can see pencil graffiti on the walls, including architectural mouldings sketched by Michelangelo, amongst other sketches drawn by his pupils.

the cloisters, open Mon–Thur, Sat 0900–1400, Sun 0800–1300; L5000, and contains more remarkable frescos by Paolo Uccello.

San Lorenzo was the Medici family's parish church, a lavish but austere building. The cool grey-and-white interior was redesigned by Brunelleschi, and its great prizes are two magnificent bronze pulpits by Donatello. Attached to the church are the **Biblioteca Laurenziana**, housing the Medici manuscript collection (notice Michelangelo's astonishing staircase), and the **Medici Chapels** complex, *Pza Madonna; tel: (055) 23885*, open Tues–Sat 0900–1400, Sun 0900–1300; L10,000. The **Cappella dei Principi** and the **New Sacristy** together form the Medici mausoleum; an impressively chilly sepulchre.

Santa Croce church, open 0800–1230 and 1500–1830; free, is a Gothic edifice (1294) on a large square near the river. It contains Giotto frescos and some celebrated tombs and commemorative monuments (Michelangelo, Galileo and Machiavelli). Tombstones pave the floor of the nave. Brunelleschi's **Cappella dei Pazzi** (Pazzi Chapel) in the cloister is a Renaissance masterpiece containing Della Robbia works. In the attached **museum**, both open Thur–Tues 1000–1230 and 1430–1830 (Mar–Sept); 1000–1230 and 1500–1700 (Oct–Feb); L3000, notice Cimabue's *Crucifixion,* showing damage caused by the disastrous floods of November 1966. The high-water mark is still visible on the walls.

Many lesser churches are worth exploring if you have time. Track down the extraordinary **Orsanmichele** on *V. dei Calzaiuoli*, originally a 14th-century corn-market. Sculptures in the exterior niches (now copies) include works by Ghiberti, Donatello and Giambologna. Inside is a richly decorated tabernacle (1359).

Santissima Annunziata, on the square bearing the same name, contains ethereal frescos by Andrea del Sarto and Pontormo in a heavy baroque setting. Nearby, the convent of **San Marco** is now deconsecrated and contains a museum of Fra Angelico's work. **Ognissanti** near Ponte A. Vespucci is a 13th-century church with paintings by Ghirlandaio and Botticelli, one including a likeness of Amerigo Vespucci, the Florentine navigator who gave his name to a continent. **Badia**

Masaccio (1401-28)

Masaccio died at the tender age of 27, yet in his short life he transformed the course of Western art, and established all the themes and ideas that were to characterise the Florentine Renaissance. Few enough of his works survive, but these few have been enormously influential. The Trinity fresco, in Santa Trinita church, shows his pioneering use of geometrically precise perspective in painting, using architecture as a framework for his subject, and to create a three-dimensional effect.

His figures have all the grandeur and weight of those he so much admired in the work of Giotto, but unlike his predecessors, Masaccio paints real people of flesh and blood, rather than idealized figures. Nowhere is this more true than in the great cycle of paintings on the life of St Peter, in the Brancacci Chapel of Santa Maria del Carmine church. Here, the realistic depiction of cripples and beggars, cured of their illnesses by the passing shadow of St Peter, was revolutionary for its time. Even more powerful is the psychological expressiveness of the figures of Adam and Eve, burdened with despair, guilt and shame, as they are expelled from the Garden of Eden.

Fiorentina, *V. del Proconsolo*, is one of Florence's oldest abbeys opposite the Bargello. Inside is one of Filippino Lippi's finest works, an altarpiece entitled *The Virgin Appealing to St Bernard*. Across the river, **Santo Spirito** is a fine example of Brunelleschi's work with another Lippi altarpiece. Two blocks west, **Santa Maria del Carmine** has a wonderful fresco cycle on *The Life of St Peter* by Masaccio and Masolino (later completed by Filippino Lippi) in the Bracacci Chapel. A short walk uphill from *Pzle Michelangiolo* (take a no.13 bus from the centre) stands **San Miniato al Monte**, a lovely and very early Romanesque church. The marble façade contains a 13th-century mosaic.

Museums and Galleries

As elsewhere in Italy, opening hours are sometimes unpredictable, and the unexpected closure of a gallery or room for some unfathomable reason can be disappointing. Be philosophical. Whatever treasures happen to be off-limits in Florence when you visit, there will be plenty left. Combined entrance tickets are available for some of the city museums, though only a couple of these (Santa Maria Novella Cloisters and the Palazzo Vecchio) are ones to prioritise. Remember that many museums close on Mon in Italy (some on Sun too). *Concierge Information* lists places to visit on Sun, and during the long siesta.

The **Galleria degli Uffizi**, *Loggiato degli Uffizi 6; tel: (055) 23885*, open Tues–Sat 0900–1900, Sun 0900–1400; L12,000 – ticket also valid for the Vasari Corridor, see above, is Italy's finest picture gallery. Though not very extensive by world standards, the contents are of extremely high quality. Housed in the 16th-century *palazzo* which served as the offices (*uffizi*) of the Medici governors, it was bequeathed to the people of Florence by the last Medici, Anna Maria Lodovica, in 1737. It has to be somewhere near the top of your visiting list. Queueing is a serious problem. Try to time your visit carefully in high season. It's often better to go late in the day; crowds build well before opening time. Last admission is 45 mins before closing. The Uffizi is still recovering from a terrorist bomb, possibly Mafia inspired, which killed five people in May 1993 and caused serious damage to many paintings. Much renovation work has still to be done. Mercifully, the Uffizi's location on upper floors saved most pictures from the floods of 1966. Highlights are too numerous to list, but don't miss Uccello's *Battle of San Romano* (1456), Botticelli's *Primavera* (1480), Leonardo's *Adoration of the Magi* (c. 1475), Raphael's *Madonna of the Goldfinch* (1506) and Michelangelo's *Holy Family* (1506–8). Titian's sensuous *Venus*

of *Urbino* (1538) and Botticelli's *Birth of Venus* (1485) are two of the greatest celebrations of female beauty in Western art. Giotto's *Ognissanti Madonna* (1310) was a turning point in the understanding of perspective. Another great master of perspective, Piero della Francesca, is represented by two superb portraits, *The Duke and Duchess of Urbino* (1460). If you need a sit-down at some point, head for the coffee bar and enjoy the views of the Palazzo Vecchio.

The **Accademia**, *V. Ricasoli 60; tel: (055) 238 8609*, open Tues–Sat 0900–1900, Sun 0900–1400; L12,000. The notable collection of Renaissance paintings are dwarfed by the gallery's most famous work, Michelangelo's *David* (1504). If you want an idea of what David looks like you can see him for nothing in a thousand copies and reproductions all over the city, lifesize if badly streaked by

285

Piero della Francesca (c. 1415–1492)

However little you know about Tuscan or Umbrian art, one name is impossible to avoid as you tour Northern Italy. After centuries in relative obscurity, Piero della Francesca is now recognised as one of the greatest artists of the Renaissance. Twentieth-century art critics have lavished superlatives on him; during World War II, an Allied commander even shelved attack plans to save a Piero masterpiece.

Born in Sansepolcro in about 1415 (the precise date is unknown), Piero was technically a Tuscan, though his work can be seen in Umbria too. He was much in demand by the discerning patrons of the day (notably Duke Federico of Urbino), despite taking an agonisingly long time to complete his work. He was a theoretician, an intellectual painter of great mathematical genius, retreating for weeks at a time to wrestle with precise linear perspective. In the process he drove himself almost insane, and as his eyesight failed, he had to give up painting. He spent his last years working on treatises on perspective.

His greatest work can be seen in Arezzo cathedral (the frescos of the *Legend of the Cross*), the Uffizi in Florence (portraits of *Federico da Montefeltro* and *Battista Sforza*), Urbino (*The Flagellation of Christ*), Monterchi (*Madonna del Parto*) and Perugia (the *Madonna & Child* polyptych). Best and most mysterious, however, are the works on display in his home town (*Resurrection* and the *Madonna della Misericordia*). These geometrical puzzles with their powerful use of light and colour are completely lacking in sentimentality and oddly detached, yet remain among the most haunting and surreal works of the *quattrocento*.

The Bargello

Less well-known than the world famous Uffizi, the grim Bargello, once the city prison, place of execution and home of the city's head of police, now houses the world's greatest collection of Renaissance sculpture. Just as you can trace the development of the Renaissance through the paintings in the Uffizi, so here you can se the masterworks in stone and bronze that mark key stages in the development of a classically inspired realism in art, the defining characteristic of the Florentine Renaissance.

Unfortunately, the sculptures here are not presented in chronological order, so many early pioneering works are not to be seen until you are halfway round the museum. They include the two panels, made by Ghiberti and Brunelleschi, for the competition to choose an artist to make the doors of the Baptistery. The artists were asked to depict the story of Abraham and Isaac, and both did so in a way that marks a new desire for both realism and psychological drama. Ponder both panels and ask who you would have adjudged the winner if you had been a judge – stuck to choose between them? So were the judges in 1401, so they awarded the prize to Ghiberti on the laudable grounds that he was more economical in his use of bronze and that his doors would be cheaper.

Such petty considerations did not apply to the sculptures commissioned by the city's guilds to adorn niches around the walls of Orsanmichele church. Donatello's *St George*, now moved to Bargello, is a masterly psychological study of a man both nervous in anticipation of the battle to come and inspired by his faith. Other great works not to be missed here are Michelangelo's gloriously drunken *Bacchus*, Donatello's seductive *David*, the first nude in western art since classical times, Cellini's flighty *Mercury* and Giambologna's wonderful *Turkey*, part of a series of bird sculptures made for a Medici villa garden.

pollution in *Pza le Michelangiolo* and *Pza della Signoria*. Opinions differ; many carp at the disproportionately sized hands and the inappropriate gallery setting; one critic even describes it as the ugliest masterpiece of Western sculpture. Others (this writer included) find the original sculpture dazzlingly graceful and could gawp at it for hours.

The **Bargello**, *V. del Proconsolo 4; tel: (055) 238 8606* (Tues–Sun 0900–1400; L8000) occupies an ancient building: the original town hall and a former prison. Today it houses a magnificent assembly of Renaissance sculpture, including Michelangelo, Donatello, Cellini and Ghiberti; in its way, as important as the Uffizi.

Across the Arno, another vast treasure-house awaits discovery in the huge Medici **Palazzo Pitti**, *Pza Pitti; tel: (055) 210323* (Tues–Sun 0900–1400). The grandiose building dates from 1457, and was originally commissioned by a rich banker, Luca Pitti. Several museums are housed inside, and it is an exhausting and expensive task to see them all (separate entrance fees are charged for each section). The paintings in the **Galleria Palatina** (L12,000) are a patchy lot (catch Pietro da Cortona, Raphael and Titian). The **Argentaria** (L8000) is a rich collection of decorative artefacts; many in precious metals. The palace apartments, a modern art gallery, porcelain and costume museums can also be seen. Don't miss the palace's landscaped **Boboli Gardens**, open daily 0900–sunset; L4000, one of

Florence's most charming open spaces. The Bacchus Fountain (1560), an image much copied by postcard sellers, shows Cosimo I's court dwarf riding a tortoise. For a marvellously panoramic picnic, head for the grounds of the **Belvedere Fortress** next to the gardens, open daily 0900–sunset; free.

In a minor key, two private collections are worth seeing. The **Museo Horne**, *V. dei Benci 6; tel: (055) 244661* (Mon–Sat 0900–1300; L6000) has an interesting collection of art and domestic artefacts assembled by a 19th-century English antiquarian and left to the Italian state. The **Museo Bardini**, *Pza de'Mozzi 1; tel: (055) 234 2427*, open Mon–Tues, Thur–Sat 0900–1400, Sun 0800–1300; L6000, displays the salvages of an acquisitive antique dealer.

Piazzas and Palazzi

Florence's main square is the **Pza della Signoria**, an oddly asymmetrical jumble of architecture and sculpture. Besides a copy of *David*, the *Pza* displays Cellini's *Perseus*, Giambologna's *Rape of the Sabine Women* and an equestrian statue of the grand old Medici himself, Duke Cosimo I. The Neptune Fountain by Ammannati (1575) is an eye-catching if not very appealing monument. A focal point for Florentine political rallies, The *Pza* was the site of Savanarola's *Bonfire of the Vanities* (and his own funeral pyre). Recently it was the scene of a huge and very Italianate corruption rumpus when its ancient paving stones were replaced by hideous concrete blocks.

The main building is the **Palazzo Vecchio**, *tel: (055) 276 8465*, open Mon–Wed, Fri–Sat 0900–1900, Sun 0800–1300; L10,000, in castellated Gothic topped with a tall campanile. Inside, the ornate state rooms include the first-floor council chamber, **Salone dei Cinquecento** (1495), decorated with frescos by Vasari. More charmingly, the little **Studiolo** is smothered with small paintings. Several outdoor restaurants and cafés offer a ringside seat. The elegant **Loggia dei Lanzi** dates from 1382.

In north central Florence, the **Pza della Santissima Annunziata** is graced by the nine-bay arcade of Brunelleschi's **Spedale degli Innocenti** (1419), a foundling hospital and one of the very first buildings of the Renaissance. The ceramic roundels on the façade showing swaddled infants are the work of Andrea Della Robbia.

As you wander round old Florence, look out for the **Palazzo Rucellai**, *V. della Vigna Nuova*, the **Palazzo Davanzati**, *V. Porta Rossa 13*, the **Palazzo di Parte Guelfa**, *Pza di Parte Guelfa*, and the **Palazzo Strozzi**, *V. Tornabuoni* – all in classic Renaissance style. The **Pzle le Michelangiolo**, south of the river, has a marvellous view of Florence and the hills, and yet another copy of *David* to admire. The Iris Garden, just off the *piazza*, has a wonderful display of the city's emblematic flowers (best seen in May), followed by the Rose Garden in May and June.

> ### ⇄ SIDE TRACKS
> ### FROM FLORENCE

The historic hill town of **Fiesole** makes one of the most popular excursions from Florence. The town predates Florence, and retains some archaeological remains from Roman and Etruscan times. Finds from the excavation sites are on display in a small **museum**, *V. Portigiani 1; tel: (055) 59477*, open Wed–Mon 0900–1800 (winter), daily except 1st Tues of month 0900–1900 (summer); L6000. Easily reached by bus (no. 7) from the station or Duomo,

Michelangelo (1475–1564)

Of all the dozens of Italian artists who lived during the Renaissance, two towering figures, Michelangelo Buonarroti and Leonardo da Vinci, have achieved truly 'household name' status. Michelangelo was born in the upper Tiber village of Caprese, where his father was the local magistrate, but his family soon moved to Florence, and Michelangelo began his artistic training under Ghirlandaio. Ghirlandaio was well connected with the ruling patrons of Florence, and soon the young Michelangelo was making his mark on Medici marble. In 1496, Michelangelo left for Rome, where his *Bacchus* (now in the Bargello) and *Pietà* (in St Peter's) established his reputation as the foremost sculptor of his day. For the rest of his life, Michelangelo split his time between Florence and Rome. During another period of work in Florence, *David* emerged to great acclaim from a shallow, flawed block of Carrara marble which presented enormous technical difficulties, which Michelangelo characteristically accepted as a challenge.

Besides being a sculptor of genius, Michelangelo was also an accomplished architect and a highly proficient fresco and easel painter. In 1508, the vast labour of decorating the Vatican's Sistine Chapel began. Michelangelo didn't want the commission, and his relationship with Pope Julius II gradually deteriorated to the point of fisticuffs on the scaffolding. The ceiling's exuberant nudity vexed some papal opinions, and one of Michelangelo's pupils was given the ignominious task of adding loincloths to the more conspicuous figures. These have since been removed.

Michelangelo's legacy in sheer aesthetic terms is unmatched, but his technical mastery sometimes disguises how far he revolutionised Renaissance art. His passionate representation of the human body was developed by his followers into an exaggerated, sometimes distorted style known as Mannerism, quite at odds with the serenity and spirituality of earlier schools.

288

it makes a pleasant place to stay or have lunch, but don't expect to have it to yourself in summer. Its luxury hotel, the **Villa San Michele**, *V. di Doccia 4; tel: (055) 595451,* is a converted monastery and a place for a very special treat. Less dauntingly expensive are the pleasant old **Bencista**, *V. B. da Maiano 4; tel: (055) 59163* or **Il Trebbiolo**, *V. del Trebbiolo 8, Molin del Piano; tel: (055) 830 0098* just north of Fiesole on a quiet hillside. Try **I'Polpa**, *Pza Mino da Fiesole 21/22; tel: (055) 59485* (closed Wed and Aug), for a pleasant meal.

Settignano (bus no.10 from the station or *Pza San Marco*) is less crowded than Fiesole, with lovely views of Florence and several nearby villas. At the abbey of San Salvi, Christ passes Judas the bread in Andrea del Sarto's fresco of the *Last Supper* (1522). ⬛

Colour section (i): The landscape of The Crete (see Siena– Cortona route, pp 258–268); Ostia Antica (p. 228).
(ii) Marina Di Campo on Elba (pp. 244–250)
(iii) A view of Florence over the cathedral and city (pp. 276–278).
(iv) A street in San Remo (p. 342); inset, Pisa's Leaning Tower (p. 321).

CHIANTI AND SIENA

The province of Siena is arguably the most rewarding in Italy for the sightseer. It encompasses dozens of gorgeous towns and villages, and much of Tuscany's best-loved countryside. For the British, that section of central Tuscany journalistic wits dub *Chiantishire* has long been an obsession, as familiar (even to those who have never been there) as Provence or the Dordogne. Sadly, it is now equally fashionable to deplore its overcrowded roads, overbooked villas and overpriced restaurants. Out of high season, it is easy to see why its rolling landscapes and cheering wines are so appealing, but if you want to avoid your compatriots (especially your local MP), it is best not to go to Chianti in the summer. If you find Chianti too gentrified for your taste, head south-west from Siena to the little-known Montagnola, a beautiful wooded region of hidden monasteries and churches (see side tracks from Siena).

The provincial capital doesn't rank with the 'Big Three' (Florence, Venice and Rome) in terms of heavyweight sightseeing, but many visitors find the city of Siena just as captivating, and more enjoyable to explore. It has its share of tourists, but rarely suffers the zoo-like pressures of the larger cities in summer. Steep, dark alleys lined with Gothic mansions splay from the scallop-shaped *Pza del Campo* in a masterly earth-toned composition of terracotta, umber, ochre and that classic *burnt sienna* (a pigment extracted from the local hills), as though straight from some quattrocento painting. Its homogeneous architecture and beautiful setting on three converging ridges give it a unique charm.

CHIANTI

Sandwiched between the two magnificent cities of Siena and Florence is an archetypal Tuscan stretch of hill towns, cypresses, vineyards and gentle woodland known as Chianti. The provincial boundary divides it roughly through the middle, but Siena has the better section of it. Hazily recalled through ruby-tinted glasses of its most famous product, Chianti spells Italian perfection for many holiday makers. Viewed through a less seductive smog of August heat haze and traffic fumes, it may not seem quite so idyllic. A jaded eye may see roads jammed with foreign number plates, ancient farmhouses relegated to holiday homes, brash billboards scarring the countryside, and pretty villages depressingly dedicated to pleasing tourists for money. This commercialisation was not caused entirely by tourism. Italian land laws changed during the 1960s, and affluent foreigners simply filled the vacuum produced by a rapid exodus of rural dwellers to the towns. If you can, try to enjoy Chianti out of high season, when there is less pressure on local facilities. Then, by stepping just a short distance off the beaten tracks, paradise is quickly regained.

289

CHIANTI

290

Barberino di Mugello
San Piero a Sieve
Borgo San Lorenzo
Vicchio
Váglia
302
65
325
E35
SIEVE
551
Dicamano
Sesto Fiorentino
65
Rúfina
67
Campi Bicenzio
Fiésoli
FIRENZE
Pontassieve
Scandicci
Bagno a Ripoli
Galluzzo
222
ARNO
69
San Casciano in Val di Pesa
Impruneta
Figline Valdarno
Reggello
TOSCANA
E35
Tavarnelle Val di Pesa
Greve in Chianti
Panzano
MONTI DEL CHIANTI
San Giovanni Valdarno
Barbarino Val d'Elsa
2
Volpaia
408
Montevarchi
69
429
429
Poggibonsi
Castellina in Chianti
Radda in Chianti
Gaiole in Chianti
Búcine
Pérgine Valdarno
69
Colle di Val d'Elsa
222
540
Castelnuovo Berardenga
San Dalmazo
SIENA
73
Sovicille
438
Rapolano Teme
Rosia
Monte San Savino
Torri
223
Monteroni d'Arbia
Asciano
438
73
North
451
Vescovado
2
San Giovanni d'Asso
Buonconvento
RISERVA NATURALE TOCCHI
Torrenieri

Alpe di San Benedetto
67
310
Premilcuore
Santa Sofia
San Godenzo
EMILIA ROMAGNA
MT FALTERONA (1654m)
Campigna
310
PARCO NAZIONALE DELLE FORESTE CASENTINESI MONTE FALTERONA CAMPIGNA
Stia
Badia Prataglia
Consuma
70
Pratovécchio
71
RISERVA NATURALE VALLOMBROSA
Poppi
208
Bibbiena
ARNO
Santa Mama
71
Loro Ciuffenna
Talla
Subbiano
71
Terranuova Bracciolini
Laterina
AREZZO
73
327
CANALE M.D. CHIANA
71
Castiglion Fiorentino
326
Lucignano
Foiano d. Chiana
Sinalunga
326
Torrita di Siena
E35
326
Montepulciano

0   20 kms
0   12 miles

To explore the region in any detail, you really need a car, though occasional buses serve the main centres. There is no obligatory sightseeing; Chianti is a place for relaxed pottering, walking, eating and drinking. After forced route-marches through Florence or Siena, this is one of Chianti's primary charms. The S222, known as the *V. Chiantigiana*, runs through the heart of Chianti, connecting Strada, Greve, Panzano and Castellina, past a string of small castles and churches. This well-used route gives a flavour of the region, but the real joy of Chianti is its hidden byways with hamlets and tracks so small that they appear only on the largest-scale maps. East of the S222, towards the slopes of Monti del Chianti, the landscape is wilder and less frequented.

TOURIST INFORMATION

Greve in Chianti has one of the main regional offices: *La Torre, V. Luca Cini; tel: (055) 854 5243*, open Mon–Sat 1000–1300 and 1600–1900. Other offices can be found in: **Castellina in Chianti**, *V. della Rocca 12; tel: (0577) 740620*; **Gaiole in Chianti**; *tel: (0577) 749411*; **Radda in Chianti**; *tel: (0577) 738494*; **Barberino Val d'Elsa**, *V. Cassia*, open Mon–Fri 0930–1300 and 1600–1830, Sat 0930–1300. Information about wine producers, guided tours, *agriturismo*, restaurants, villas and apartments is readily available all over the region. Many specialist English-speaking agencies promote local facilities. Look out for the free monthly magazine *Chianti News*.

ACCOMMODATION AND FOOD

All over Chianti, you will find estate farms called *fattorie* producing wine and olive oil, sometimes linked with restaurants or *agriturismo* businesses. Many offer *degustazioni* (wine tastings) and *vendita diretta*

(wines for sale). The cuisine of Chianti is much the same as classic Tuscan cooking elsewhere, a hearty, flavoursome diet containing game, olive oil, pork products, and beans. In this much-touristed area, some restaurants are over-elaborate, and prices are generally high. The countryside of Chianti is liberally sprinkled with lovely places to stay; some are converted *casas colonicas* (manor farms). In high season (which extends from June–Sept in Chianti), it is best to book accommodation well ahead. Castellina has several possibilities. One of the most famous is **Tenuta di Rivavo** (3 km north-west), *Loc. Ricavo 4; tel: (0577) 740221*, a hamlet of small stone houses, extremely well kept (top-class restaurant). **Salvipolpi** (500 m north-west), *V. Fiorentina; tel: (0577) 740484*, is a simpler country guesthouse with rustic furnishings (no restaurant). **Villa Casalecchi** (1 km south), *Loc. Casalecchi; tel: (0577) 740240*; **Le Piazze** (6 km west), *Loc. Le Piazze; tel: (0577) 743190*; **Il Colombaio** (1 km north), *V. Chiantigiana 29; tel: (0577) 740444* or **Belvedere di San Leonino** (9 km south), *Loc. San Leonino; tel: (0577) 740887* are other agreeable choices. In the centre of town, the **Antica Trattoria La Torre**, *Pza del Comune 1; tel: (0577) 740236* (closed Fri) or the **Albergaccio di Castellina**, *V. Fiorentina 35; tel: (0577) 741042* (closed Sun) are two of the best bets for a meal.

Panzano's well-promoted hotel is the **Villa Le Barone**, family seat of descendants of the Della Robbia family. It is a pleasant and relaxing place in attractive grounds. In central Radda, the **Relais Fattoria Vignale**, *V. Pianigiani 15; tel: (0577) 738300* is one of the most celebrated hotels of Chianti, where the famous black rooster symbol was created for the Consorzio Vino Chianti Classico.

Its restaurant, **Vignale**, is in a separate building at *V. XX Settembre 23; tel: (0577) 738094* (closed Thur). Other pleasant bases include **Vescine** (6.5 km west), *Loc. Vescine; tel: (0577) 741144* (expensive; no restaurant) and the friendly **Podere Terreno** (5 km north), *V. Terreno 21, Volpaia; tel: (0577) 738312.* Several of Gaiole's many castles have been converted into attractive accommodation: **Castello di Tornano**, *Loc Lecchi; tel: (0577) 746067* or *(055) 746067* (bookings) offers simple self-catering apartments; just outside the town, **Castello di Spaltenna**, *tel: (0577) 749483*, is an expensive but ultra-refined experience.

SIGHTSEEING

From Siena, the first major centre along the Chiantigiana is **Castellina in Chianti**, medieval head of the Chianti League. A peaceful and charming place, now prosperous from wine and tourism, it was once a war zone caught between the feuding Florentine and Sienese armies. The fortress and ramparts make prominent landmarks, now dwarfed by the massive modern wine co-operative on the main road. Local products are on sale throughout the town, especially at the **Bottega del Vino Chianti Classico**, *V. della Rocca 10; tel: (0577) 740247.* Just outside the town is the **Ipogeo Etrusco di Montecalvario**, a 6th-century Etruscan tomb.

Panzano, 14 km up the road, is now quite built up, in a prime wine-producing zone. The Romanesque **Pieve di San Leolino** (3 km south) is one of Chianti's oldest churches. **Greve**, the main centre of the Gallo Nello region (see wine box), stages a large wine fair in Sept and has a multitude of wine shops. The **Enoteca del Chianti Classico**, *Pzta Santa Croce 3; tel: (055) 853297*, is one of many such outlets. Several villas can be visited near

the town, including **Uzzano** (formal gardens) and **Vignamaggio** (a backdrop for Kenneth Branagh's Tuscan idyll, the film of *Much Ado About Nothing* , and the birth-place of Lisa del Giocondo, the lady with the enigmatic smile).

East of the S222, **Radda in Chianti** shouldn't be missed. This charming village was another principal base of the Chianti League, and retains a grandeur far beyond its present size. Its medieval streets radiate from the main *piazza* and a Palazzo Comunale embellished with coats of arms. Nearby, visit the similarly ancient villages of **Volpaia** and **Ama**, and the **Badia a Coltibuono**, a fine Romanesque abbey surrounded by a monastic wine estate with an excellent restaurant; *tel: (0577) 749424* (closed Mon, Nov–Mar). **Gaiole in Chianti** is an important wine town in an area sprinkled with castles.

SIENA

Tourist Office: *Pza del Campo 56; tel: (0577) 280551*, open Mon–Sat 0830–1930 (summer); Mon–Fri 0830–1300 and 1530–1830, Sat 0830–1300 (winter). Despite the pressure of visitors, this office is helpful and its tourist literature much better produced than in many towns, with good maps and informative, multilingual text. Pick up the useful booklet *Tourist Information* which lists opening times and entrance charges for the main sights of Siena province, and the separate fold-out leaflets about individual towns. Accommodation lists are available, including rooms in private houses. The tourist office will help find accommodation, or try the specialist agencies: **Cooperative Siena Hotels Promotion**, *V. le Curtatone; tel: (0577) 288084*, open Mon–Sat 0900–2000 (summer); 0900–1900 (winter) or **Protur**, *Fontanella 4; tel: (0577) 45900*, open Mon–Sat 0900–1400 and 1500–

1930 (summer); Mon–Fri 0900–1300 and 1500–1900, Sat 0900–1300 (winter).

ARRIVING AND DEPARTING

If you are simply driving *through* Siena, it is easily negotiated on the S2 (*V. Cassia*) which merges into toll-free *autostrada* at Siena on its way north to Florence. Access to the motorway system is straightforward from the S73, S222 or S223 approach roads. If you're stopping to explore (as indeed you should), Siena's old quarter is much harder to reach by car. The orbital road systems are confusing and the centre is virtually inaccessible to tourist traffic, especially in the summer months. You are strongly advised to leave your car on the outskirts and walk or take a bus to the centre. It is very difficult to find parking space anywhere near the major sights. There are some public pay-parks inside the walls near *Pza Gramsci* and the stadium, but you are more likely to be lucky outside the eastern walls, e.g. near Porta Romana or V. le Minzoni. Market day (Wed) adds increased pressure on parking space.

If you arrive by bus, you will probably be dropped towards the western side of the old town. Local TRA-IN buses stop on *Pza Matteotti*; there is a ticket and information office on nearby *Pza Gramsci*; *tel: (0577) 204246*. Out-of-town buses stop near San Domenico church, which also has a ticket and information booth; *tel: (0577) 204245*. It's an easy stroll into the centre from either. There are good TRA-IN (bus!) connections with Poggibonsi, San Gimignano, Montalcino and Montepulciano. SITA or LAZZI buses serve other destinations, including Florence, Volterra, Massa Marittima and Rome.

By rail, you arrive quite a way from the centre, in *Pza Fratelli Rosselli* (2km northeast); *tel: (0577) 280115* and must get a connecting bus (no.5 is useful) or taxi, *tel: (0577) 44504,* to the centre. Siena connects with the Florence–Pisa line at Empoli, with services to Rome and Umbria at Chiusi, and with Grosseto and Orbetello to the south. The useful SETI travel agency in the tourist office premises, *Pza del Campo 56,* saves a long trek to the station for tickets or information.

ACCOMMODATION AND FOOD

The main hotels are obligingly well signed on the approach roads, but you have to be quick to scan multiple lists in fast-moving traffic. Alert your passengers to keep their eyes peeled. It is not usually quite so difficult to find a room in Siena as in Florence, the great exception being during the Palio weeks (early July and mid Aug), when you **must** book ahead.

An excellent choice for motorists is the **Villa Scacciapensieri**, *V. di Scacciapensieri 10; tel: (0577) 41441* (moderate) just 2km north-east of the centre, a 19th-century villa in pleasant suburbs with lovely shady gardens and a swimming pool. Here you can park easily, enjoy city views from a peaceful distance, and best of all, catch a regular bus right outside the hotel gates to the heart of the old town. On the same street, also on a bus route, there is a well-equipped campsite, **Siena Colleverde**; *tel: (0577) 280044,* open late Mar–mid Nov.

For more luxury, the **Certosa di Maggiano**, *V. Certosa 82; tel: (0577) 288180* (expensive; romantic restaurant), is a very elegant Carthusian monastery 1km south-east of Porta Romana, a nice walk for the energetic, but most who stay here can afford a taxi ride. Just outside Porta Romana is the pleasant old **Santa Caterina**, *V. Piccolomini 7; tel: (0577) 221105* (no restaurant; good value). Within the city walls, try the **Antica**

293

Torre, *V. Fieravecchia 7; tel: (0577) 222255* (no restaurant) or the **Palazzo Ravissa**, *Pian dei Mantellini 34; tel: (0577) 280462*. Both are inexpensive, and have lots of character. They are popular, so book ahead.

No one need starve in Siena, as the gorgeous edible shop-window displays along *Banchi di Sopra* indicate. Some care should be taken to avoid tourist traps. There are good central restaurants, e.g. **Osteria Le Logge**, *V. del Porrione 33; tel: (0577) 48013* (closed Sun), **La Torre**, *V. Salicotto 7; tel: (0577) 287548* (closed Thur) or **Nello**, *V. del Porrione 28; tel: (0577) 289043* (closed Sun eve, Mon), but by leaving the popular Campo area and straying into the outlying *contrade* you can generally find quaint old bars and family *trattorie* offering better value. No one, however, should pass up the chance to investigate one of Siena's great institutions, **Nannini**, *V. Banchi di Sopra 22–24*, and several other branches, which does the last word in cakes and ice-creams. Siena's famous speciality is *panforte*, a rich, dense slab of fruit, nuts and honey. *Ricciarelli* are soft almond cakes with vanilla. *Cavallucci* are aniseed and spice biscuits.

The **Enoteca Italia** in the Medicean fortress off *V. C. Maccari* is an excellent place to sample regional wines, open daily 1500–2400 such as Chianti, Brunello di Montalcino and Vino Nobile di Montepulciano. The sweet Vinsanto, traditionally served with crisp macaroon-like biscuits, is found all over the town. Siena is also renowned for its salami products.

EVENTS AND ENTERTAINMENT

Siena is a cultivated place, kept lively by its student population, many of whom are foreigners studying the city's exceptionally pure spoken Italian. The city cannot be described as raucous, but there is some

nightlife of bars and *enotecas*, including live music or screened football. There are several clubs and discos, e.g. **Al Cambio**, *V. di Pantaneto 48*. Concerts, films and exhibitions take place all through the summer (information from the tourist office). A prestigious classical music festival takes place in late Aug: **Settimana Musicale Senese**. **Siena Jazz** precedes it in late July–August. Eclipsing any of these events, however, is Siena's great twice-yearly horse-race, the **Palio** (see box).

SIGHTSEEING

Siena's medieval history was bound up with a bitter and convoluted war of attrition against its arch-rival Florence, which repeatedly attacked it, meanspiritedly lobbing sewage over the walls in an attempt to spark off plague. Siena's finest hour came in 1260, when it defeated Florence at the Battle of Monteperti. The Republic of Siena then controlled most of southern Tuscany. Under a strong Guelph Government during almost a century of peace, Siena grew immensely rich on the wool trade, and the merchant classes financed an ambitious programme of urban development. Most of present-day Siena dates from this golden age.

As the building works rose to their zenith in the bell-tower of the Palazzo Pubblico, disaster struck. In 1348 the Black Death annihilated over a third of Siena's citizens, and its social fabric crumbled in internal strife between the quarrelsome *contrade* (districts) which still play an important role in city life. Florence took advantage of its weakened enemy and after a lengthy and catastrophic siege in 1554–5, Siena capitulated to Cosimo I – Florence's Medici overlord. By this stage the population had plummeted from its medieval 100,000 to less than 8000. Even today, it is only about 60,000. A straggling band of diehards carried Siena's tattered banner to Montalcino, but the Republic of Siena was effectively dead and its surroundings laid waste. Fossilised by history, its beautiful Gothic buildings remained untouched. In the 18th century the crushed Sienese economy gradually began to revive, though Henry James found it a 'cracking, peeling, fading, crumbling, rotting city' only a century ago. Today, sympathetically restored and prosperous again, it is a ravishing place.

Like its speciality *panforte* cake, Siena is compact, rich and potentially indigestible. It would be exhausting, if not impossible, to see everything on a single visit. The blockbusting monuments lie conveniently close to the **Pza del Campo**, but sprinkled through the outlying districts are dozens of fascinating minor sights, far too numerous to mention below. Siena, of all Italian cities, deserves a second glance. Try to catch at least one good bird's-eye view of its russet pantiled roofscape from an upper loggia or belfry.

The deceptively small walled city is built on three ridges, each a separate district or *terzo* ('thirds' rather than quarters). These are divided by swooping valleys of olive groves and market gardens which take some time to negotiate. The *terzi* are further split into 17 smaller neighbourhoods or wards known as *contrade*. Dating from medieval times and symbolised by animals (snail, porcupine, eagle, etc.) they still play a major role in local activities. Visitors generally become aware of the *contrade* during the intense tribal rivalry of the Palio season (see box), but during the rest of the year they are an important source of social cohesion. *Contrada* membership is an automatic birthright bestowing lifelong community loyalties, which may explain the city's remarkably low incidence of urban problems. Each

contrada has a museum which explains more about its activities, besides providing a display case for Palio trophies. These open erratically by appointment, but if you are interested, the tourist office may be able to organise a visit. Tel nos are listed in the tourist information booklet.

The heart of the city is the magnificent sloping **Pza del Campo**, a theatrical public space of rosy herring-boned bricks, divided into nine fan-shaped sections representing the Council of Nine (Siena's medieval governors). Surrounded by elegant *palazzi*, it is the focus of tourist attention, the scene of the evening *passegiata* and the setting for Siena's famous bareback horse-race, the **Palio.** Its main landmark (apart from the tourist office tucked into a shady side arcade) is the **Palazzo Pubblico**, *Pza del Campo 1; tel: (0577) 292263,* and its vaunting *campanile*, known as the **Torre del Mangia**, open daily 1000–1530 (winter); 1000–1930 (summer); L5000, the second highest in Italy at 102 m (505 steps), ranged along the south flank. The administrative offices of Siena's town hall are not open to the public. The **Museo Civico**, open Mon–Sat 0930–1800 (Mar–Oct); hours extend slightly towards high season, Sun 0930–1330; daily 0930–1330 (Nov–Feb); L6000, is in several ornate state rooms on the upper floors. The main council chamber is the **Sala del Mappamondo**, frescoed with a map of the world by Ambrogio Lorenzetti and some tantalising works by Simone Martini: a wonderful *Maestà* and *Portrait of Guidoriccio da Fogliano* – an eyecatching equestrian scene of debated authenticity. The **Sala della Pace** contains more frescos: Lorenzetti's *Allegory of Good and Bad Government.* The **Sala del Risorgimento** is decorated with later 19th-century frescos relating to the unification of Italy. Climb the stairs

SIENA

nearby to see the view from the rear **loggia.** In the centre of the **campo** is a copy of the **Fonte Gaia**, a rectangular marble basin carved by Jacopo della Quercia in 1419 (the original is in the Museo Civico).

Just off the **campo** stands the **Palazzo Piccolomini**, *Banchi di Sotto 52; tel: (0577) 41271, open Mon–Sat 0900–1300; free.* This fine Renaissance palace, another commission by the great scholar – Pope Pius II (Aeneas Sylvius Piccolomini), houses the **Archivo di Stato** (State Archives). Staff show visitors round the huge bundles of leather-bound documents and city account books – many very ancient. Notice the painted wooden panels used as book jackets. The elegant **Logge del Papa** next to it was also built for Pius II.

Siena's imposing **Duomo** may seem impressive enough, but if the Black Death had not intervened it was planned to be even larger. The present structure is one of the most spectacular in Italy: a vividly striped affair of black and white marble, with a dazzling sculpted **façade** and a mullioned **bell tower**. The Latin cross interior has three massive aisles and an amazing inlaid marble **floor** (sadly partially covered with unaesthetic protective mats – why on earth couldn't they make them transparent? – but briefly unveiled for two weeks in August). Outstanding among many features of interest are its **pulpit**, carved by Nicola Pisano (1268), stained glass, 14th-century wooden choir and a number of tombs. Midway along the left side of the nave is the entrance to the **Libreria Piccolomini**, open 1000–1300 and 1430– 1700 (Nov–mid Mar); 0900– 1930 (mid Mar–Oct); L2000, containing frescos by Pinturicchio and illuminated medieval hymnals. Notice the **Piccolomini altar** on the same aisle, and the **Cappella del Voto** with a revered Bernini *Madonna* surrounded by supplicatory hearts and crash helmets.

Next to the Duomo is the **Museo dell'Opera Metropolitana**, *Pza del Duomo 8; tel: (0577) 283048*, open 0900–1330 (Nov–mid Mar); 0900–1930 (mid Mar–Sept); 0900–1800 (Oct); L6000, in part of the unfinished cathedral's nave. Its collection of Sienese art is outshone by a single masterpiece, Duccio's *Maestà*, painted around 1310 and displayed separ-

ately in an upper room. Marvellous views are visible from a loggia. Approached by steps between the Duomo and the museum is the Gothic **Battistero** (baptistery) containing a large bronze font embellished by various artists including Donatello, and some 15th-century frescos, 1000–1300 and 1430–1700 (Jan–mid Mar); 0900–1930 (mid Mar–Sept); 0900–1800 (Oct); 1000–1300 and 1430–1700 (Nov–Dec); L3000. Before leaving the cathedral complex, one sight definitely worth seeing is the fascinating **Spedale di Santa Maria della Scala**, *Pza del Duomo*, open daily 1030–1730, slight variations

---

The Wines of Chianti

Chianti is Italy's best-known wine, an enormous money-spinner for Tuscany. About 90 million litres are currently produced annually. It is often thought of as a lightweight product for informal quaffing. Quality varies widely. Those bulbous raffia-covered bottles called *fiascos* (the name tells you all you need to know about these) are spurned by *aficionados*. It is better to buy decent ordinary Chianti from a supermarket shelf and not pay for the fancy packaging. Superior Chianti is sold in claret-shaped bottles, and should improve over several years. More rigorous quality control in recent years has resulted in much finer and more carefully produced wines. Chianti has an ancient pedigree; it was the world's first officially defined wine-producing area in 1716, when Cosimo III established fixed boundaries within which the name could legally be used. The wine-loving Prime Minister Bettino Ricasoli established the formula for modern Chianti in the 1860s. In 1924 a consortium for the protection of Chianti Classico was founded. In 1984 Chianti became a DOCG (*Denominazione di Origine Controllata e Garantita*) region (unfortunately in one of the most disastrous vintages it had ever had). DOCG status implies Chianti is selected and approved by a government panel of experts, but it is not always a stamp of infallible quality. Overproduction has resulted in wine lakes, bankrupt producers and a loss of confidence.

Chianti is made primarily from a Sangiovese grape (75–90%, though pure Sangiovese Chianti is also produced), with small blends of other grapes such as Trebbiano and Canaiolo and Malvasia. Riserva wines are aged in wood for three years. There are seven classified regions, the best being Chianti Classico, made in the Chianti heartland and marked by the famous black cockerel symbol, the Gallo Nero, which was once the emblem of the Lega di Chianti. One of the great houses is Antinori, which is widely exported, but there are dozens of good producers who are not necessarily the big names. Good recent vintages include 1993, 1994 and 1995. One of the great pleasures of exploring the Chianti region is sampling – you can squabble about who drives and forgoes this pleasure in your own time.

297

The Palio

This spectacular event is a great tourist draw, but unlike many of the colourful pageants of Italy, it is still firmly rooted in local traditions. The bareback horse race has taken place almost without interruption since the 13th century – in theory in honour of the Virgin – but more particularly for the glory of the winning *contrada*. Siena's 17 districts (*contrade*) compete furiously for the prized Palio (a silken banner, these days designed by well-known contemporary artists).

In its present form it consists of a hectic three-lap circuit of the Pza del Campo. Attempts are now made to minimise injury with sand and mattress padding, but it remains a potentially dangerous event for horse and rider. The race is notorious for malpractices – bribery and all manner of schemes take place to rig results, nobble horses, and corrupt jockeys. Interfering with another rider's reins is forbidden; otherwise, no holds are barred before or during the race. Whipping, obstructing, or deliberately unbalancing another rider are commonplace tactics. The jockeys are often not Sienese at all, but hardbitten Sicilians or Maremma cowboys. Animal lovers may find the Palio upsetting; the horses are often frightened by the crowds and riding techniques are savage.

The actual race lasts less than 2 mins, but the preparations for it start just as soon as one Palio is over, and the actual day is full of spectacular pageantry with costumed processions, flag-hurling and drumming. On the day of the Palio each *contrada* drags its horse unwillingly into church to be blessed (the poor creatures are not keen on the entrance steps).

The race is held twice a year, on 2 July and 16 August, but there are practice races and qualifying heats which are easier to get into. You can watch it free of charge in the centre of the campo, but it is a long, hot, crowded wait. For a grandstand seat, you must book months ahead and pay high prices: *Palio Viaggi, Pza Gramsci 7; tel: (0577) 280828*, can organise it for you. If you aren't in Siena during Palio time, you can get a rather sanitised idea of it from a film presentation in several languages at the Odeon cinema, *Banchi di Sopra 31; tel: (0577) 42976*, open Mon–Sat 0930–1700; English performances hourly from 1130–1530; L10,000.

298

according to season; L5000; a medieval hospital containing wonderful frescos of its history and charitable work, which has only just relinquished its 800-year role of tending Siena's sick. A **Museo Archeologico** (Mon–Sat 0900–1400, Sun 0900–1300, closed 2nd and 4th Sun of month; L4000) occupies part of the hospital premises (Etruscan and Roman finds).

For more helpings of Sienese art, head for the **Pinacoteca Nazionale**, *V. San Pietro 29; tel: (0577) 281161*, open Tues–Sat 0900–1900, Sun–Mon 0800–1300; L8000, housed in the splendid 14th-century Palazzo Buonsignori. Outstanding works include Lorenzetti's *Two Views* (a break from the seamless tradition of devotional art) and Pietro da Domenico's *Adoration of the Shepherds*.

Further afield, Siena's delights are too numerous to list. Look out for the headquarters of one of the world's most venerable banks on *Pza Salimbeni*, the **Monte dei Paschi di Siena**. Banking was a principal source of Sienese medieval wealth. The Monte dei Paschi was set up by the Republic in the 15th century as an antidote to usurious excesses. Now it is one of Italy's major financial institutions. Its palatial Gothic and Renaissance premises house a fine art collection, which can be viewed with prior notice; *tel: (0577) 234595.*

Two saints are venerated in Siena. Siena's patron, Catherine Benincasa (1347–80), was a stigmatised mystic whose relics lie in the huge Gothic church of **San Domenico**. The **Casa di Santa Caterina**, *Costa di Sant'Antonio; tel: (0577) 44177*, open daily 0900–1230 and 1530–1800 (summer); 0900–1230 and 1420–1800 (winter); free, reveals much about her varied life, which incorporated both practical and contemplative roles in the ideal Domenican manner. Besides meditating and having visions, she tended the sick and played a considerable part in papal politics. Together with St Francis, she is Italy's patron saint.

St Bernardino was born in the year that Catherine died. Also a Dominican, he became one of the most famous Italian preachers and is commemorated in the **Oratorio di San Bernardino**, open daily 1030–1330 and 1500–1730 (Apr–Oct); L2000. Bernardino was a formidable lawyer who used his skills in peacemaking. He attempted, with little success, to persuade the quarrelsome *contrade* to settle their differences and adopt a single emblem, the sun symbol of the risen Christ that appears on the cathedral façade. A combined ticket costing L9500 is available for the Libreria Piccolomini, the Museo dell'Opera Metropolitana, the Battistero and the Oratorio di San Bernardino.

⇄ SIDE TRACKS FROM SIENA

The hilly Montagnola region lies due west of Siena, rarely visited by tourists. Pilgrims traversed it on the *V. Francigena*, which explains the number of local churches and monasteries, but now the villages are depopulated and the terrain mostly left to wild boar and natural woodland. Ancient stone-paved tracks make marvellous walking country. Siena's APT produces a free leaflet on this region, and a 1:25,000 trail map, *Itinerari nella Montagnola Senese*, is available from Siena's CAI, *V. le Mazzini 95; tel: (0577) 270666.* Leaving Siena on the S73 (Massa Marittima road), turn off after 7 km to **Lecceto** and **San Leonardo al Lago**, where there are two ancient frescoed hermitages. Retrace steps through **Sovicille**, where there is a fine Romanesque church, **Pieve di Ponte alla Spina**. **Rosia** back on the S73 has another good church, and **Torri** to the south boasts a 13th-century Vallombrosan abbey with a striking Moorish-looking, three-storey cloister. There are villas at **Centinale** and **Castelo di Celsa** in the heart of the Montagnola, and more interesting churches further west at **Casole d'Elsa**, **Radicondoli** and **Mensano**. Take a picnic with you; few restaurants exist in this area. A couple of attractive converted farmhouses offer accommodation near Sovicille: **Borgo Pretale**, *Loc. Pretale; tel: (0577) 345401* and **Borgo di Toiano**, *Loc. Toiano; tel: (0577) 314639* and there is a pleasant campsite, **La Montagnola**, *V. Cava del Siciliano; tel: (0577) 314473*, open late Mar–Sept. **⬩**

SIENA–PISA

The landscapes between Siena and Pisa are a mixed bunch. The best bits lie on the earlier stages of the route, where rural, poppy-splashed lanes contrast with the strange, bare hills of the Volterrana. Closer to the bustling, densely trafficked Arno basin, the scenery is less alluring, but even here, an occasional gem like San Miniato sparkles on a hill top. This tour visits two of Tuscany's most distinctive and well-preserved hill towns: many-towered San Gimignano and stern Etruscan Volterra. The lesser towns are often undeservedly bypassed on fast-moving highways. Prepare to be cultivated – this is a trip full of art, history, architecture and literary associations. But there are plenty of places for fresh air, and lots of good living too. Allow a couple of days to enjoy it at leisure. San Gimignano is an obvious place to break your journey, but expensive and often overbooked. There are pleasant alternatives in the Valdelsa or around Volterra.

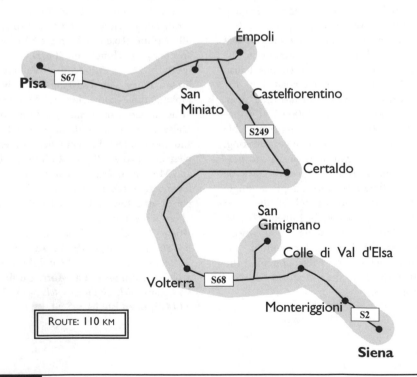

ROUTE

Leave Siena by the north-west on the *V. Cassia* (the old S2 for Florence) and head for **Monteriggioni**. From here, follow signs directly to **Colle di Val d'Elsa** (keep west of the *autostrada* – the busy junction of Poggibonsi has little to recommend it). From Colle, head west along the S68, turning right after 10 km towards **San Gimignano** via San Donato, a pretty rural drive. From San Gimignano, retrace steps to the S68 and continue to **Volterra**, a roller-coaster ride through bald, grandly sculpted hills.

From Volterra, take minor back roads (P15) north-east via Il Castagno, and follow signs to **Certaldo** on the main S429. Continue north-west through **Castelfiorentino** to **Émpoli**, then follow signs from the west end of town to **San Miniato**. This section of the Arno Valley isn't a very enticing place to stay, but from San Miniato, it's an easy *superstrada* run to Pisa or back to Florence; alternatively you can hop over the Arno through Fucecchio and make your way to Lucca via Altopascio (a motorway junction). North of Émpoli lies a very pretty stretch of hilly scenery around **Vinci** (Leonardo's birthplace); which is itself a popular holiday base.

MONTERIGGIONI

This little town above the Elsa valley is a knockout. Intact 13th-century walls form a triumphal crown on its hilltop of terraced vines and olives. A Sienese bastion in the long-running struggle against the Florentines, the 14 fortress towers famously impressed Dante, who compared them to the giants guarding the ninth circle of his *Inferno*.

The **Hotel Monteriggioni**, *V. 1 Maggio (i.e. First of May Street) Maggio 4; tel: (0577) 305009* makes a lovely stay in a beautiful medieval building with a good restaurant next door: **Il Pozzo**, *Pza Roma 2; tel: (0577) 304127* (closed Sun eve and Mon). Buses from Siena stop on the main road; you must walk up the hill. Monteriggioni is a starting-point for some good walks (see the CAI map, *Itinerari nella Montagnola Senese* available in Siena, *V. le Mazzini 95; tel: (0577) 270666*.

You can walk or drive to the **Abbadia dell'Isola**, a Cisterican Romanesque monastery containing a Taddeo di Bartolo fresco (ask at the left-hand house for the key) 3 km west of Monteriggioni, near Strove.

COLLE DI VAL D'ELSA

Tourist Office: *V. Campana 18; (0577) 912111* or *V. Campana 46; tel: (0577) 922791*, open daily 1000–1300 (Apr–Sept).

Like many towns in the region, Colle suffered from the long-running feud between Florence and Siena and was the site of a significant battle in 1269. Colle has been a thriving manufacturing town for centuries. Former industries of wool, paper and ceramics have been superseded by glass crystal; products are on sale locally. The lower town is a messy valley sprawl in a tangle of road junctions, but the handsome upper town, strung along a panoramic ridge, definitely deserves exploration. It is easily reached by bus from Siena or San Gimignano. A large, free car-park at the foot of the walls makes access easy up a stepped path. The long main street connects a surprisingly monumental series of palaces, churches and squares. The main sights are the **Palazzo Campana**, a Mannerist building which now forms one of the town's gateways. The **Duomo**, *Pza del Duomo; tel: (0577) 923125*, contains several fine art-works, including a noteworthy marble

301

Renaissance pulpit. The other main church is **San Francesco**, with a fairy-tale Sano di Pietro altarpiece of miracles, princesses and dragons. Colle's small museums are of passing interest, look out for the **Museo Civico e d'Arte Sacra**, *V. del Castello 31*, open weekends and public holidays 1000–1200 and 1530–1830 (Nov–Mar); Tues–Sun 1000–1200 and 1600–1900 (Apr–Oct); L5000, with cheery hunting frescos as well as devotional art, and the **Museo Archeologico**, *Palazzo Pretorio, Pza del Duomo*, open Tues–Fri 1530–1730, Sat–Sun and public holidays 1000–1200 and 1530–1830 (Oct–Mar); Tues–Fri 1700–1900, Sat–Sun and public holidays 1000–1200 and 1600–1900 (Apr–Sept); L3000, whose *sgraffito* plastered setting is perhaps more interesting than its contents. Colle has several celebrated restaurants. In the upper town, **Arnolfo** (also a comfortable hotel at *V. F. Campana 8; tel: (0577) 922020*), *V. XX Settembre 52; tel: (0577) 920549* (closed Tues), produces august *cucina nuova*; **Antica Trattoria**, *Pza Arnofo 23; tel: (0577) 923747*, is a homelier bet in the lower town (closed Tues off season). If you need an hotel, consider the **Villa Belvedere** (3.5 km south east), *Loc. Belvedere; tel: (0577) 920996*, an 18th-century house with sports facilities. Just south of Poggibonsi, the **Villa San Lucchese**, *Loc. San Lucchese 5; tel: (0577) 937119*, makes a lovely peaceful stay with gorgeous views (excellent restaurant; closed Tues).

SAN GIMIGNANO

Tourist Office: *Pza del Duomo 1; tel: (0577) 940008*, open 0900–1300 and 1400–1800 (Nov–Feb); 0900–1300 and 1500–1900 (Mar–Oct). A lacklustre office for a place of this significance, but several useful handouts are available, including accommodation lists and good museum details.

The up-side of this astonishing town is immediately apparent. Fourteen tall towers loom across the skyline, inviting instant comparisons with Manhattan's skyscrapers and placing San Gimignano firmly on any visitor's list of 'must-see' destinations. This, unfortunately, is its downfall. Of all Tuscan towns, few have such high prices, such blatantly tourist-oriented shops, or such officious cultural guardians. Some sympathy is due. This is a small place, constantly besieged in summer, and tourism is its living. If you can, try to enjoy it off season, or at a quieter time of day before or after the coach parties jam the town centre. At least step off the main drag. It is amazing how few tourists bother to stray from the souvenir-lined spinal route to the quiet and charming alleys beside the walls, where only dashing swifts break the medieval stillness.

Imagine what San Gimignano must have looked like in its heyday, when there were no fewer than 76 towers. They were built during the 12th and 13th centuries by rival *nouveau-riche* merchant families who aspired to nobility. The tower-building craze was not unique to San Gimignano, or even to Italy, but nowhere else have medieval towers survived in such numbers. The aim was initially defensive; it was an age when, if some invading marauder didn't attack you that week, your next-door neighbour would. Increasingly, though, the high towers became merely a status symbol, a literal expression of social climbing.

ARRIVING AND DEPARTING

Large car-parks surround the northern walls. Charges are high, and pressure on space can be intense. A permit must be obtained to take a vehicle to hotels inside the walls; approach through Porta San Jacopo. There is no convenient rail station. Buses from Siena are frequent, less so from Florence, Certaldo, Colle Val d'Elsa and Volterra, but most routes involve changing at Poggibonsi. San Gimignano is a popular coach excursion from many Tuscan tourist centres.

ACCOMMODATION AND FOOD

Attractive hotels and restaurants abound in and around the town, but don't expect too many bargains. In high season (anytime in summer), book ahead. The tourist office supplies lists of accommodation, including guesthouses, private rooms, apartments and *agriturismo*.

A convent, a good youth hostel on *V. della Fonti; tel: (0577) 941991* and a simple campsite, **Il Boschetto** (3km south-east); *tel: (0577) 940352* (Apr–midOct) provide alternative budget choices. The **Cooperativa Siena Hotels Promotion** just outside Porta San Giovanni, *V. San Giovanni 125; tel: (0577) 940809,* open 0930–1230 and 1430–1730, is helpful. Within the walls, best choice is **La Cisterna**, *Pza della Cisterna 24; tel: (0577) 940328,* an elegant place bang on one of the central squares (good restaurant). Close by, **Leon Bianco**, *Pza della Cisterna 13; tel: (0577) 941294,* is an attractive older-style hotel. **L'Antico Pozzo**, *V. San Matteo 87; tel: (0577) 942014,* is smartly up-market. Outside the town, **Casale del Cotone** (2km north), *Loc. Cellole 59; tel: (0577) 943236*; **Le Renaie** (6 km north), *Loc. Pancole; tel: (0577) 955044,* and **Villa San Paolo** (5 km north), *Loc Casini; tel: (0577) 955100* are three of the most charming options.

There are plenty of restaurants, some of them touristy, though it is no hardship to sit at outside tables enjoying one of the main squares. **Il Pino**, *V. San Matteo 102;*

tel: (0577) 942225 (closed Thur), is a well-reputed choice on the main street. **Dorando**, *Vicolo del Oro 2; tel: (0577) 941862* (closed Mon), has some adventurous dishes allegedly based on Etruscan cuisine. Look out for the local wine, Vernaccia di San Gimignano, an acidic white on which opinions vary. The main street is full of attractive delicatessens and cake shops where you can buy picnic fodder or presents (expensive). **La Buca**, *V. San Giovanni 16; tel: (0577) 940407,* has a mouth-watering range of salamis and pâtés, including wild boar specialities. Try **Armando e Marcella**, *V. San Giovanni 88; tel: (0577) 941051* for cakes. The **Gelateria di Piazza**, *Pza della Cisterna,* has some wonderful ice-cream. The little market stalls near the Rocca offer good country cheeses and fruit. Picnic spots lie within easy walking distance of the city gates; a short drive in any direction takes you through idyllic scenery.

EVENTS

Expect more crowds than usual at carnival time (Jan–Feb), and during the annual festivals. A medieval pageant is held in late June, and a popular arts festival of opera, music and theatre in July–August. Details from the tourist office.

Regular guided walking tours are organised through the countryside from March to October.

SIGHTSEEING

The medieval towers must mostly be admired from below; only one, the **Torre Grossa** on the **Palazzo del Popolo,** can be climbed (54 m; beware the noon day bell). This was the maximum height the civic authorities would permit for any of the town's towers. There are plenty of vantage points in San Gimignano, however. The ruined 14th-century **Rocca** on

303

the western walls gives splendid views over olive groves and cypress trees and can be enjoyed free of charge. A wander through the charming streets is also free, as long as you resist the tourist shops proffering ceramics and many other products on all sides. The main itinerary followed by most visitors leads from Porta San Giovanni, through the interlocking main squares, and on down *V. San Matteo* to Porta San Matteo and *Pza San Agostino*. If you do this one way, try to find a different route back along the eastern walls which are far quieter. *En route*, notice the charming well and herring-boned brickwork on *Pza della Cisterna*, and the churches of San Lorenzo in Ponte, San Jacopo and Sant'Agostino (frescos by Gozzoli).

The **Collegiata** church, no longer technically a *duomo* as the town has no bishop, dates from the 12th century. The interior is smothered with fascinating frescos by Florentine and Sienese artists, notably Benozzo Gozzoli (*San Sebastian*), Taddeo di Bartolo (*Last Judgement*) and Bartolo di Fredi (*Testament* and *Creation*). The artists responsible for the New Testament scenes are less certain. It takes some time to admire these delightful and lively works properly; make sure you have plenty of change ready to illuminate them. Famous scenes include *The Creation of Eve, The Drunkenness of Noah, The Kiss of Judas* and the *Resurrection of Lazarus*. The *Last Jusgement* frescos are gruesomely vivid. At the far end of the right aisle, the **Cappella di Santa Fina** is a smaller jewel box of frescos by Domenico Ghirlandaio (1475) depicting the curious tale of the local patron saint. This requires a separate entrance charge, open daily 0930–1230 and 1500–1730; L3000, but see below).

San Gimignano's museums are expensive. If you want to visit more than two, the best way to do it is to purchase a combined ticket, which takes you into four sights: the Museo Civico (including the Torre Grossa), the Museo d'Arte Sacra e Museo Etrusco, the Capella di Santa Fina (see above) and the Museo Ornitologico. In for a penny, in for L16,000! Tickets can be purchased from any of the museums. The **Museo Civico**, *Pza del Duomo; tel: (0577) 940340*, open Tues–Sun 0930–1330 and 1430–1630 (Nov–Feb); 0930–1930 (Mar–Oct); L7000 or L12,000 including the tower, is housed in the **Palazzo del Popolo** (sometimes called the Palazzo del Podestà), – San Gimignano's town hall. It contains a very fine collection of masterpieces, including frescos by Sodoma and Taddeo di Bartolo, *Tondi* by Filippino Lippi, *Madonnas with Saints* by Pinturicchio and Gozzoli, and a *Maestà* by Lippo Memmi, to mention but a few. Most charming, perhaps, are the wedding frescos by Memmo di Filippuccio displayed in a separate room, which unsalaciously depict the honeymooners enjoying a bath together, and climbing into bed. While you're here, don't forget to climb the **Torre Grossa** (same times as museum but a separate entrance charge unless you buy a combined ticket; L8000).

The **Museo d'Arte Sacra e Museo Etrusco**, *Pza Pecori; tel: (0577) 940316*, open Tues–Sun 0930–1330 and 1430–1630 (Nov–Feb); 0930–2000 (Mar–Oct); L7000, houses liturgical and Etruscan artefacts, including some fine devotional sculptures, black and red glazed Volterran pottery and cinerary urns. The **Museo Ornitologico**, *Oratorio di San Francesco, V. Quercecchio; tel: (0577) 940340*, open Tues–Sun 0930–1330 and 1430–1630 (Nov–Feb); open until 1730 (Mar); 0930–1230 and 1500–1800 (Apr–Sept); 0930–1330 and 1430–1630 (Oct); L4000, is a rare collection of 250 different bird species assembled in the late 19th century and displayed in a deconsecrated church. A small privately run diversion, the **Museo della Tortura** (aka **Criminologia medioevale** – instruments of torture), *V. del Castello; tel: (0577) 942243*, open Sat–Sun 1000–1300 and 1400–1900 (Nov–Dec); daily 1000–1300 and 1400–1900 (Feb–Nov); L10,000, may appeal to some tastes.

VOLTERRA

Tourist Office: *V. G. Turazza 2 or Pza dei Priori 20; tel: (0588) 87257*, open daily 0930–1300 and 1400–1930. Excellent tourist literature and good clear maps are available at these helpful offices, which offer a free accommodation service.

Volterra's spectacular location on a high plateau overlooking a curious landscape of eroded cliffs and sallow volcanic hills is only one of its attractions. From a distance, its windswept fortifications make it appear forbidding and austere, but within its walls, it is a delightful and fascinating town; well-preserved without being ossified. All around are alabaster workshops making statues, ornaments and vases from the locally quarried stone.

Volterra was an important Etruscan settlement, one of the 12 great cities of the League. It survived through Roman times as a *municipium* and acquired numerous medieval and Renaissance monuments, despite its destructive overthrow by the Medicis in 1472 for control of its alum mines. Erosion and subsidence affected the town, which is now much smaller than in ancient times, but the numerous landslips have had the beneficial effect of revealing buried archaeological remains.

Summer sees a busy cultural programme, with theatre, art exhibitions, concerts and folklore festivals, including the **Astiludio**, a flag-hurling competition

(Sept) and a crossbow tournament (July–Aug).

ARRIVING AND DEPARTING

Numbered car-parks stud the outer walls; they can get very busy. Best chances are on the north side. Remember which gateway is nearest to your car. Buses arrive on the south side; *tel: (0588) 86150*. You can buy bus tickets at the tourist office. The nearest rail station is 9 km west at Saline di Volterra (Pisa–Rome line, *tel: (0588) 44116)*, connected by bus. Volterra's slightly out-of-the-way location makes it less touristy than some Tuscan towns. Nonetheless, it is popular, so expect parking problems and high prices in summer.

ACCOMMODATION AND FOOD

Volterra hasn't as much hotel accommodation as you might expect, though there are alternatives in the shape of a youth hostel, campsite, villas, apartments and *agriturismo*. Grandest of the central hotels is the **San Lino**, *V. San Lino 26; tel: (0588) 85250*, with parking. The **Etruria**, *V. Matteotti 32; tel: (0588) 87377*, also has a very good restaurant. **Sole**, *V. dei Cappuccini 10; tel: (0588) 84000*; **Villa Nencini**, *Borgo Santo Stefano 55; tel: (0588) 86368*; **Villa Giardino**, *San Girolamo; tel: (0588) 85634* and **Villa Domus Aeoli**, *Borgo San Lazzero; tel: (0588) 86041* make good choices a short distance from the city walls.

There are some good places to eat. Look out for wild boar on local menus. Stuffed heads adorn the town's food shops. In town, try **Da Beppino**, *V. delle Prigioni 15; tel: (0588) 86051* (closed Wed) or **Osteria dei Poeti**, *V. Matteotti 55; tel: (0588) 86029* (closed Thur). **Il Sacco Fiorentino**, *Pza XX Settembre 18; tel: (0588) 88537*, has good Tuscan cuisine (closed Fri). Three km down the S68,

305

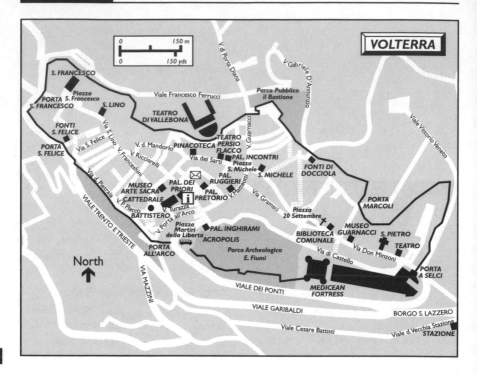

VOLTERRA

Biscondola, *Strada Statale 68; tel: (0588) 85197,* is a good choice (closed Mon).

SIGHTSEEING

As in San Gimignano, Volterra endeavours to ensure its visitors acquire a thoroughly rounded cultural picture by charging a hefty fee for sightseeing. In Volterra, you must purchase a combined ticket costing L12,000 to see any of the museums (no separate entrance fees). This includes the Museo Etrusco Guarnacci, the Pinacoteca e Museo Civico, the Museo di Arte Sacra and the Area Archeologiche (which can in fact be explored free of charge). At current exchange rates, it's not such a bad deal; the museums are compact but of high quality.

Medieval walls and Renaissance palaces grace the town, notably around the monumental **Pza dei Priori**, which is the heart of Volterra. The castellated **Palazzo dei Priori** (now the town hall) dates from the early 13th century. The first floor **Sala del Consiglio Comunale** contains a large *Annunciation* fresco. Notice the carving of a boar on the Torre del Porcellino (Piglet Tower) of the **Palazzo Pretorio** opposite. The **Palazzo Vescovile** was the Bishop's Palace, now housing the Museo di Arte Sacra (see below). The **Duomo** is an understated stripy Tuscan building with a richly furnished interior.

The **Museo Guarnacci**, *V. Don Minzoni 15; tel: (0588) 86347,* open daily 0900–1900 (mid Mar–Oct); 0900–1400 (Nov–mid Mar), is one of the best places in Tuscany to get an idea of Etruscan civilisation. It contains a remarkable collection of over 600 funerary urns, characterised by sculpted reclining figures propped up on their elbows. Two prize exhibits are the terracotta *Married Couple*, an elderly pair with haggard faces, and the *Ombra della Sera*, an elongated bronze votive figure of the 3rd century BC which inspired the modern sculptor Giocometti. The name of the work (Evening Shadow) was suggested by the poet Gabriele d'Annunzio. Its history is remarkable; ploughed up by a farmer in 1879, it was used as a fire poker for several years.

The **Pinacoteca**, *Palazzo Minucci Solaini, V. dei Sarti 1; tel: (0588) 87580*, open daily 0900–1900 (mid Mar–Oct); 0900–1400 (Nov–mid Mar) features Florentine, Sienese and Volterran art from the 14th–17th centuries. Notable works include Guirlandaio's *Christ in Majesty*, and Signorelli's *Madonna and Child* and *Annunciation*, but pride of place goes to Rosso Fiorentino's *Deposition* (1521) a brilliantly composed Mannerist painting full of colour and energy. The **Museo di Arte Sacra**, *V. Roma 1; tel: (0588) 87580*, open daily 0900–1300 and 1500–1800 (mid Mar–Oct); 0900–1300 (Nov–mid Mar) contains sculpture and liturgical art from some local churches, including bells, silver, manuscripts and a Della Robbia terracotta of St Linus, Volterra's patron saint. The archaeological remains consist of the **Teatro Romano** at the foot of the walls dating from the 1st century BC (a clear overview is visible from *V. Lungo le Mura del Mandorlo*), and a few vestigial ruins in a public **Parco Archeologico**, open 1100–1600 except during rain, near the Medicean Fortezza, which is now a top-security prison. The park makes a good picnic site. West of the park is the **Arco Etrusco**, an Etruscan gateway.

CERTALDO

Tourist Information: **Comune**; *tel: (0571) 661211* or *661241*.

Boccaccio's charming rose-red village stands high over the Elsa. Don't miss it. A scenic unsurfaced track through fields from the main S429 gives a fine warm-up to Certaldo Alto, the medieval *borgo*. Don't embarrass yourself by trying to drive round its narrow streets; it is much better enjoyed on foot. The **Casa di Boccaccio**, a renovated house where the *Decameron* author possibly spent his last 13 years, stands at *V. Boccaccio 18*, and is now a literary studies centre; *tel: (0571) 664208*. Boccaccio died here in 1375, much gloomier than he had lived, after repenting his frivolous ways. He is buried in **Santi Jacopo e Filippo** church, alongside Certaldo's patron St Giulia. The 14th-century **Palazzo Vicariale**, open Tues– Sun 1000–1230 and 1630–1930 (summer); 1000–1200 and 1530–1800 (winter); L2500), the governor's residence, is emblazoned with ecclesiastical crests. The arcaded interior contains the old prison and some faded frescos. **Il Castello**, *V. della Rena 6; tel: (0571) 668250* makes a nice old-town base to stay; **Osteria del Vicario**, *V. Rivellino; tel: (0571) 668228*, will feed you well in a lovely monastery with a garden (simple rooms available). A good campsite lies south of town: **Toscana Colliverdi**, *V. Marcialla 108/bis; tel: (0571) 669334*, open late Mar–Sept. Certaldo has a lively programme of events including a Sept festival.

Up the road 9 km, **Castelfiorentino** is a sprawling town, by no means an obligatory stop, but with an extraordinarily helpful tourist office on the main road through the centre; *V. Ridolfi; tel: (0571) 62049*, open Apr–Oct. The old town's **Biblioteca Comunale**, open Tues, Thur, Sat 1600–1900; L3000 displays some talented frescos from local chapels by Benozzo Gozzoli, whose other work you may encounter in Montefalco and San Gimignano.

ÉMPOLI

Tourist Office: *Pza Farinata degli Ubero 9; tel: (0571) 76115*, open daily 0730–1330).

Émpoli is a busy route-hub in the Arno basin between Pisa, Siena and Florence. It is an important market and manufacturing town (glass and clothing), initially charmless, but concealing a tight knot of *centro storico* within its bewildering carapace of road systems. When you find a bit you can't drive into somewhere along its central axis, stop and walk to the **Pza Farinata degli Uberti**, a fine square named after the Ghibelline army commander who defeated the Florentines at Montaperti (1260). At the post-battle conference which decided Florence's fate (held at Émpoli), he played a key role in dissuading the Sienese from taking the city apart – a decision they later regretted, since Florence quickly recovered and exacted awful revenge.

Émpoli's main sights stand on the square, graced by a marble fountain of nymphs and supine lions. Most impressive is its well-balanced green-and-white-striped **Collegiata Sant'Andrea** in Florentine Romanesque style, and next to it the **Museo Collegiata**; *tel: (0571) 55707*, open Tues–Sun 0900–1200 and 1600–1900; L5000, if you plan detailed exploration of the area, a combined ticket at L8000 also covers admission to Montelupo's Museo Archeologico e della Ceramica and the Museo Leonardiano in Vinci. It contains some worthy Tuscan art, including a Lippi *Maestà*. The **Museo di Paleontologia** and the local archives are held in the **Palazzo Ghibellino**, where the famous 13th-century parliamentary meeting was held, open Thur, Sat, Sun 1700–1930; entrance included in Museo Collegiata ticket). A block south, the Augustinian church of **San Stefano** is worth a glance if you find it open; *V. dei Neri* (Masolino frescos). **San Michele** in Pontorme on the eastern outskirts has Mannerist panels by Jacopo Carrucci. Émpoli commemorates its native composer Ferruccio Busoni (1866–1924) with an annual festival of piano music (Oct–Nov) and a small museum in his birthplace in *Pza della Vittoria*. There are good public transport links in all directions from Émpoli, but the town offers little as a touring base.

By way of beefing up Émpoli's meagre attractions, the local tourist authorities now promote it as Le Terre del Rinascimento, along with several quainter villages nearby. **Montelupo** (7 km east) is renowned for ceramics, and its **Museo Archeologico e della Ceramica**, *V. B. Sinibaldi 45; tel: (0571) 51352*, open Tues–Sun 0900–1200 and 1430–1900, contains examples of the local products. **Cerreto Guidi** (8 km north-west) has a Medici villa (see box), *tel: (0571) 55707*, open daily 0900–1900, closed 2nd and 3rd Mon of the month, containing a portrait of the hapless Isabella, daughter of Cosimo I, murdered by her jealous husband in 1576. **Vinci** (12 km north) is of course where Leonardo hailed from, a pretty place amid vineyards and olive groves.

The **Museo Leonardiarno** in the Castello dei Conti Guidi; *tel: (0571) 56055*, open daily 0930–1900 (Mar–Oct); 0930–1800 (Nov–Feb); L5000, contains remarkable models made up by local students from Leonardo's notebook sketches. Some are wildly impractical ideas, but among them are tanks, gearboxes, parachutes, helicopters, looms, diving kit, a bicycle, paddle boat, a machine gun and a mechanical car, all dreamt up by a Renaissance genius several hundred years ahead of his time.

Vinci has a regional tourist office, *V. della Torre 11; tel: (0571) 568012* and several hotels.

SAN MINIATO

Tourist Office: *Pza del Populo; tel: (0571) 42745*, open 0900–1300 and 1530–1930.

Surveying the confluence of the Elsa and Arno valleys, this conspicuous little hill town crowns an enviable defensive site. It is predictably ancient, a former pilgrimage halt on the *V. Francigena*, and a seat of the Holy Roman Empire. In two lesser-known guises, San Miniato acts as a centre of the white truffle trade (a record specimen weighing over 2 kg was discovered here in 1954), and a venue for Italy's national kite-flying championships (Sunday after Easter). You will discover why this hilltop town is so suitable for kite-flying as you climb the steep road that winds up to San Miniato Alto, the breezy old quarter that seems to stand higher than any other hill around. If you arrive in the lower town by train, an orange minibus runs up the hill about every ½ hr. You can park just below the walls in *Pzle Dante*

Alighieri. The most prominent monument is the toothy red-brick **Rocca** constructed by Frederick II. From here the emperor's treasurer, Pier della Vigna, falsely accused of treason and blinded, leapt to his death, perhaps partly in desperation at being denied these awesome views. The nearby **Duomo**, also in glowing red brick, has a Baroque interior. A small diocesan museum stands next door.

From these grand buildings, the main streets meander down the hillside past a stately clutch of churches, convents and palaces; **San Domenico** and **San Francesco** contain Florentine works of art. San Miniato is a popular excursion destination and has a full diary of concerts and events. It hosts a regular antiques market (first Sunday of each month). The hotel **Miravalle**, *Pza del Castello 3; tel: (0571) 418075,* occupies a prime location at the top of the town. **Da Canapone**, *Pza Buonaparte; tel: (0571) 418121* (closed Mon), is a reliable central restaurant. **Il Convio–San Maiano**, *V. San Maiano 2; tel: (0571) 48114* (closed Wed), combines good cooking with terrace views.

309

LUCCA–FLORENCE

Three major historic towns and one of Italy's most upbeat spas form the backbone of this route. Churches in classic Pisan Romanesque style banded with white and racing green marble are among the most memorable features of the region. Lucca may well prove your favourite port of call. Everyone loves Lucca, including its sophisticated and affluent citizens, who are justly proud of their town. Prato and Pistóia, ensnared in grimy traffic-ridden outskirts, are harder to like until you abandon your car and penetrate their calm centres on foot. Driving in this busy trench between Florence and Pisa affords little pleasure, and rush-hour delays can be tedious. The A11 autostrada offers an efficient way of travelling between the main centres, though you will be charged for its use. Keep plenty of change ready for the toll gates, choose a handy place to stow your ticket for rapid recovery, and avoid the automatic (unmanned) toll gates unless you have previously purchased a motorway pass.

Montecatini, Pistóia and Prato can easily be reached by public transport from Florence or Lucca, though this may preclude exploring the surrounding countryside. The A11 route is mainly urban through a densely populated and industrialised zone, but surprising respites lurk off-track in the shape of huge, neat horticultural plots, a strange wetland region of rare birds, and several exquisite if faded villas – relics of a more gracious age. The hills north and south of the motorway conceal idyllic holiday retreats which may be preferable to a city-centre stay. Abetone, to the north, offers challenging winter skiing.

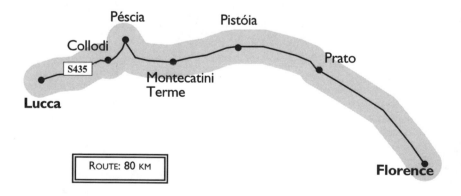

ROUTE

From Lucca, follow the back route (S435) eastwards via **Péscia** and **Montecatini Terme** to Florence. This gives a chance to explore several villas en route, and Pinocchio's town of **Collodi**. From Montecatini Terme, the older villages of Montecatini Alto and Monsummano are a stone's throw away. Bird-watchers may like to investigate the wooded marshlands of the **Padule de Fucecchio**, to the south – a haunt of heron and bittern. **Pistóia** and **Prato** can conveniently be approached from the motorway, as the back roads are often clogged with traffic.

Prato makes a good springboard for more villas at **Póggio a Caiano** (8 km south) or near **Sesto Fiorentino,** just north of Florence.

LUCCA

Tourist Office: *Pzle Verdi; tel: (0573) 419689,* open 0900–1900 (Apr–Oct); 0900–1330 (Nov–Mar). This helpful office by the city gate of San Donato has lots of information on accommodation, transport and local sights, and exchanges currency.

GETTING AROUND

Lucca is at the centre of a major transport network, and has good connections with the surrounding region. **CLAP buses** serve local villages, the Appuan Alps and the coast north of Pisa. **Lazzi buses** run to major centres such as Florence, Siena, Pisa and Livorno, plus intervening centres like Pistóia, Prato, Montecatini and Empoli. The **main bus terminal** is on *Pza Verdi* (near the tourist office); *tel: (0583) 587897*. **Trains** (less frequent than buses) serve destinations on the Florence–Viareggio line. The **rail station** is south of the city walls near Porta San Pietro; *tel: (0583) 47013.*

Central Lucca is restricted to traffic; free parking is available all around the walls. There are some pay car-parks near *Pza Napoleone*. A bike hire office stands next door to the tourist office (L12,000 per day). Lucca's flat terrain makes cycling a popular method of transport in and around the city, a peaceful contrast to the ubiquitous waspish whine of the motorscooter in Florence and other cities.

ACCOMMODATION AND FOOD

There are no very interesting central hotels, and accommodation soon gets booked up. **La Luna**, *V. Fillungo–Corte Compani 12; tel: (0583) 493634,* is inexpensive and pleasantly located just off the main shopping street (garage facilities). Outside the city lie several expensive luxury palaces, such as the **Villa La Principessa** (4 km south), *Loc. Massa Pisana, V. Nuova per Pisa; tel: (0583) 370037,* open Apr–Oct. HI: **Ostello Il Serchio** (3 km north), *V. del Brennero; tel: (0583) 341811* (Mar–Nov), offers a modern budget option.

Lucca is a well-heeled and sophisticated city, with restaurants to match. You can try a great range of dishes: fish and game, hearty dishes of maize and chestnut flour, and roast mountain goat (*capretto*). Look out for locally grown asparagus (from Péscia) and Montecarlo wine. The **Buca di Sant'Antonio**, *V. della Cervia 1/5; tel: (0583) 55881* (closed Sun eve, Mon) is one of the most prestigious restaurants, offering Garfagnana specialities. **Giulio in Pelleria**, *V. delle Conce 45; tel: (0583) 55948* (closed Sun, Mon and during Aug), is a bustling and popular trattoria.

SHOPPING

V. Fillalungo is Lucca's main shopping street, an attractive place for gazing in the windows, though prices can be high in its fashion boutiques and art galleries. A flea

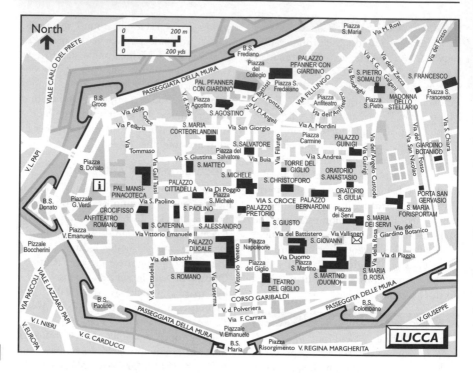

North ↑

0 ___ 200 m
0 ___ 200 yds

LUCCA

market offers cheaper deals. One of Lucca's products is high-quality olive oil.

SIGHTSEEING

Lucca is high on culture. The **Estate Musicale Lucchese** is a classical music festival from July–September, followed by an opera season (based on local hero Puccini) and the **Settembre Lucchese** (a general arts festival) in Sept. On 13 September the Volto Santo is carried through the streets in a religious procession from San Frediano church to the Duomo. Open-air cinema takes place in *Pza Guidiccioni*, and an antiques market is held every month (3rd Sunday) in *Pza San Martino*.

One of the best ways to get the measure of the city is to take a circular walk around the shady tree-lined ramparts overlooking red-brick buildings, tidy Italianate gardens

and the surrounding alluvial plain. A favourite even in Roman times, Caesar, Pompey and Crassus met here in 56BC to organise their triumvirate. Oddly, considering its attractions, Lucca never seems crowded with tourists. It is a connoisseur's city, a place to wander quietly absorbing the atmosphere.

The main monuments can easily be found on its grid-like streets, chief among them being **San Martino**, Lucca's Duomo on its eponymous *piazza*, open 0700–1900 (summer); 0700–1700 (winter); free except the tomb of Ilario del Carretto, L3000. Built in Romanesque style, the asymmetrical façade (1204) is lavishly adorned with three tiers of individually carved colonnades incorporating hunting scenes, *Labours of the Months* reliefs showing seasonal tasks, and St Martin dividing his cloak with a beggar. The tall *campanile* on one side dates from 1060. Inside, the cathedral is full of interest. Major monuments include the beautiful marble tomb of Ilaria del Carretto, wife of Paolo Guinigi, Lucca's 15th-century ruler, carved by Jacopo della Quercia (1405–6). To the left of the nave, a strange birdcage-like structure called the Tempietto holds a revered 13th-century wooden crucifixion statue called the **Volto Santo**. The altar painting in the Sacristy is a *Madonna and Saints* by Ghirlandaio. There are entrance charges to the adjacent **Museo della Cattedrale**; *tel: (0583) 490530*, open daily 0930–1800 (May–Oct); 1000–1800 (Nov–Apr); L7000, includes access to excavations in the 12th-century church of San Giovanni and the tomb of Ilaria del Carretto. Lucca has several other striking churches. **San Michele in Foro** on *Pza San Michele* (the old Roman forum) displays another virtuoso façade of astonishing complexity, with four tiers of loggias, marble inlaid wild beasts and barley-sugar columns. The winged figure of St Michael guards the pediment. **San Frediano**, near the northern walls, is decorated with bright 13th-century mosaics. Inside is a huge Romanesque font and a Gothic altarpiece.

Close to San Frediano is the **Palazzo Pfanner**, *V. degli Asili 33; tel: (0583) 48524*, open daily 1000–1800 (Mar–Oct); off season by appointment; L2000, an imposing mansion dating from 1667, housing a costume museum and some of the silk textiles that made Lucca wealthy. Behind the palace is a lovely Italianate garden of statuary and citrus trees in terracotta pots, which is visible from the ramparts. Don't miss the elliptical medieval enclosure of **Pza del Mercato**, the former Roman amphitheatre. A couple of blocks south-east of the square on *V. Sant'Andrea*, the unmistakable **Torre dei Guinigi**; *tel:*

(0583) 48324, looms over the city, crowned with a surreal grove of holm-oak trees. It can be climbed, 0900–1930 (Mar–Sept); 1000–1800 (Oct); 1000–1630 (Nov–Feb); L 4500, for a marvellous view of Lucca.

Towards the eastern walls is an even larger Guinigi palace housing the **Museo Nazionale di Villa Guinigi**, *V. della Quarquonia; tel: (0583) 496033*, open Tues–Sun 0900–1400; L4000, with a collection of archaeological finds and paintings.

On the other side of town, the **Palazzo Mansi**, *V. G. Tassi; tel: (0583) 55570*, open Tues–Sat 0900–1400, Sun 0900–1400; L8000, houses Lucca's Pinacoteca Nazionale. The building of 17th-century Rococo is more interesting than the contents. The **Casa di Puccini**, *Corte San Lorenzo 9; tel: (0583) 584028*, open Tues–Sun 1000–1300 and 1500–1800 (midMar–June and Sept–midNov); 1000–1300 and 1500–1900 (July–Aug); 1000–1300 (midNov–Dec); L5000, birthplace of the composer, is now a museum.

Lucca's secluded corners and architectural details are just as enjoyable as its major sights. Don't miss a wander down *V. Fillalungo*, the main shopping street, full of art nouveau details and enticing boutiques, or the pretty *V. del Fosso* with its central canal. The **Botanic Gardens**, *V. del Giardino Botanico 14; tel: (0583) 442160*, open Tues–Sat 0900–1300, Sun 0900–1300 and 1530–1830 (Apr–Oct); 0900–1300 (Nov–Mar); L5000, can be found at its southern end, a collection of Tuscan species laid out in 1820. Half-way up, past the Porta dei SS Gervasio e Protasio, is the **Villa Bottini**, *V. Elisa; tel: (0583) 442140*, gardens open Mon–Sat 0900–1300; free, a 16th-century building in park-like grounds sometimes used for summer events.

313

SIDE TRACKS FROM LUCCA

Several villas can be explored in the surrounding countryside. These were built by Lucca's wealthy merchants and nobles. Three within a short distance of each other north-east of the city are the **Villa Reale** at Marlia (off the Barga road); *tel: (0583) 30108,* guided tours of gardens Tues–Sun 1000–1100 and 1500–1800 (Mar–Nov); Tues, Thur, Sun (July); L9000, the **Villa Mansi**, at Segromigno; *tel: (0583) 920234 ,* open Tues–Sun 1000–1230 and 1500–1900 (summer); 1000–1230 and 1500–1700 (winter); L9000, and the **Villa Torrigiani** at Camigliano; *tel: (0583) 320 9614,* open Wed–Mon 1000–1300 and 1500–1800 (Mar–Nov); until 1900 in summer; L12,000. **Collodi**, 15 km east of Lucca, celebrates its native classic children's writer Carlo Lorenzini with the **Parco di Pinocchio**, open daily 0830–sunset; L11,000, aged 3–14 L6000, a theme park of tableaux depicting the puppet's adventures, possibly too gentle and static to impress today's Disneyfied youth. Nearby, the gaunt **Villa Garzoni** surveys an imposing formal garden of cascades, topiary and statuary, open daily 0900–sunset; L10,000. Entrance tickets are sold in the adjacent *enoteca* selling local wines and grappa, a popular if rather touristy lunch spot.

MONTECATINI TERME

Tourist Office: *V. le Verdi 66; tel: (0572) 772244,* open Mon–Sat 0900–1230 and 1530–1845, Sun 0900–1200. This efficient, friendly office provides a sackful of well-produced information on Montecatini's delights, including its huge range of accommodation, leisure facilities, and the treatments you can enjoy or endure in

its hot springs. The local region is romantically promoted as the **Valdinievole** (Vale of Mists), and is well served by public transport and organised excursions.

Montecatini Terme is one of Italy's largest and most fashionable spas, and, even for those unconvinced of thermal curative powers, one of the most enjoyable. Even in monsoon conditions it seems a cheerful, elegant place of trim parks and gardens, frothy 1920s' architecture and sedate amusements. Though undoubtedly up-market and well mannered, it is not snobbishly exclusive. Developed by Grand Duke Leopoldo I in the 18th century, the centre of the resort lies around the **V. le Verdi**, where spa-goers promenade sampling ice-cream cocktails in smart cafés, and the **Parco delle Terme**, where nine sulphur springs bubble through separate thermal pleasure-domes. Grandest of these is the magnificent **Terme Tettuccio**, lined with art nouveau tiles and paintings. The **Terme Torretta** specialises in palm-court concerts, and **Terme Leopoldine** (1926) emulates the style of a classical temple. Visitors may buy day tickets to absorb the waters via an alarming range of orifices, try out innumerable beauty treatments, or simply relax in the reading, writing or music rooms. For more information, contact the Direzione delle Terme at *V. le Verdi 41; tel: (0572) 778451.* Most of the spas are open May–Oct; the **Excelsior** stays open all year. If you don't want any treatments, it is possible to obtain a ticket just to look at the more elaborate spa buildings, or visit them on a guided tour. With such a vast range of hotels, you are almost certain to be sure of a room (except in winter when many places close), though Montecatini lacks much zest as a touring base if you don't want to take the waters.

One of Montecatini's most enjoyable

excursions utilises a toytown funicular railway, Apr–Oct every 30 mins from 1000–2400 except 1300–1500 and Mon eve; L3500 single, L6000 return, to the medieval fortified village of **Montecatini Alto** (5 km by road), where visitors can enjoy magnificent views from panoramic terraces, and have lunch or shop in its attractive old *piazza*. Try **La Torre**, *Pza Giusti 8/9; tel: (0572) 70650* (closed Tues) or **Trattoria Albergo L. Etrusco**, *V. Talenti 2; tel: (0572) 79645* (good Tuscan cooking and simple rooms). The **Grotta Maona**, a stalactite cave, can be visited 2 km west, open 0900–1200 and 1430–1830 (Apr–Oct); L7000. South-east of Montecatini Terme is the smaller, older spa of **Monsummano Terme** offering speciality 'steam-cave' treatments in its **Grotta Giusti Terme**, *V. Grotta Giusti 171; tel: (0572) 51008*, open Mar–Oct. The perched village of Monsummano Alto has a ruined castle and a 12th-century church.

Ten km north-west of Montecatini, the little town of **Péscia** straddles its riverbank, strewn with battered churches of minor interest. Péscia is renowned for its horticultural industry, producing millions of lilies, gladioli and carnations for sale in its ultra-modern flower market to the south of the town.

PISTÓIA

Tourist Office: *Pza del Duomo 4; tel: (0573) 21662*, open Mon–Sat 0900–1300 and 1515–1830, also Sun 0900–1300 (July–Aug). The regional tourist office is at *Corso Gramsci 110; tel: (0572) 34326*.

After a maelstrom of confusing approach roads, the historic centre of this thriving provincial capital seems agreeably peaceful, though you may find Pistóia busier than usual during its annual costumed bunfight, the **Giostro dell'Orso**

(the Joust of the Bear) on 25 July. For advance tickets, contact the regional tourist office (see above).

If you prefer not to drive, trains or buses leave you less than 5-mins walk from the city walls. By car, head for the station and park near the southern walls. The main sights focus on the **Pza del Duomo**, a spacious and impressive assembly of medieval architecture dominated by the **Cattedrale di San Zeno**, a flamboyant example of Pisan Romanesque decorated with striped marble, Della Robbia ceramics and tiered arcades. It has a rich interior of funerary sculpture and a silver altarpiece weighing a ton in the **Cappella di San Jacopo**, open Mon–Sat 1000–1200 and 1600–1800, Sun 0930–1030, 1130–1200 and 1600–1800; L2000. The adjacent *campanile* was used as a watchtower in the 12th century; the octagonal Baptistery opposite dates from 1359. The adjoining Palazzo dei Vescovi houses the tourist office and the **Museo della Cattedrale**, tours available Tues, Thur and Fri; L5000; free Saturday pm, with a Ghiberti reliquary of St James and Roman remains. Left of the Duomo is the 14th-century **Palazzo Comunale**, bearing a strange black marble head on its façade, possibly of a defeated Moorish king. The **Museo Civico** is inside, open Tues–Sat 0900–1300 and 1500–1900, Sun 0900–1230; L5000, a collection of medieval and baroque art. A short distance north of the main square stands the **Ospedale del Ceppo**, a medieval orphanage and hospital strikingly decorated with a 16th-century frieze of brightly coloured terracotta by Giovanni Della Robbia. A lively procession of prisoners, pilgrims, sick and poor bestrides the building in Renaissance costume.

Several churches are worth tracking down in central Pistóia: **Sant'Andrea**,

315

V. Stant'Andrea 21 contains a wonderful pulpit by Giovanni Pisano; Romanesque **San Bartolomeo in Pantano**, *Pza San Bartolomeo 6,* has another fine pulpit from 1250, the **Madonna dell'Umiltà** on *V. della Madonna* staggers beneath a massive dome by Vasari. On *V. Cavour,* don't miss the dazzling green-and-white exterior of **San Giovanni Fuorcivitas**. Nearby, the **Cappella del Tau**, *Corso Silvano Fedi 70,* contains some early frescos; its adjacent *palazzo* houses a museum dedicated to the modern Pistóian sculptor Marino Marini, open Tues–Sat 0900–1300 and 1500–1900, Sun 0900–1230; L4000, whose horse-and-rider works embellish many of Italy's public spaces.

Pistóia hasn't a great deal of central accommodation. If the town grows on you, you could do worse than stay at the **Patria**, *V. Crispi 8; tel: (0573) 25187.* There's a good little restaurant opposite: **San Jacopo**, *V. Crispi 15; tel: (0573) 27786* (closed Mon eve and Tues). The modest 3-star hotel **Leon Bianco**, *V. Panciatichi 2; tel: (0573) 26675* has a neighbouring restaurant, the **Leon Rosso**, *V. Panciatichi 4; tel: (0573) 29230,* offering home-produced fare from the family farm with prompt, friendly service (closed Sun). Six km north of town, set high above wooded hills, the **Villa Vannini**, *Loc. Piteccio; tel: (0573) 42031* (follow signs for Abetone from Pistóia, then turn off right), is a delightful old country house with stacks of charm (excellent value).

PRATO

Tourist Office: *V. Cairoli 48; tel: (0574) 24112* or *V. L. Muzzi 38; tel: (0574) 35141,* open Mon–Sat 0900–1300 and 1530–1830, restricted hours in winter.

Prato's walled *centro storico* is a distinctive place to spend an hour or two. It's an easy walk over the river from the railway station; buses take you to the old town.

The **Castello dell'Imperatore**, *Pza delle Carceri; tel: (0574) 38207,* open Mon and Wed–Sat 0830–1230 and 1500–1730, Sun 0830–1230; free, a pale fortress built by the Holy Roman Emperor Frederick II, may well be the first landmark you see if you arrive by rail or car (park on *Pza Mercatale*). It is largely empty except for exhibition space, but there are good views from the ramparts, and concerts in summer. Nearby on the same square stands **Santa Maria delle Carceri**; a classically proportioned and Pisan-striped Renaissance church with Della Robbia *tondi (bas-reliefs)*. **San Francesco**, on the other side of the square, contains the tomb of a local merchant, Francesco di Marco Datini, who became one of Europe's wealthiest men from the cloth trade. His meticulous books of accounts were inscribed 'To God and profit', but he generously left all his profits to charity on his death. Towards the town centre lies the **Palazzo Datini**, *V. Ser Lapo Mazzei 13; tel: (0574) 21391,* home of the 'Merchant of Prato'. A block away stands the medieval **Palazzo Pretorio** housing the **Museo Civico**, *Pza del Comune; tel: (0574) 452302,* open Mon, Wed–Sat 0930–1230 and 1500–1830, Sun 0930–1230; L5000, including entry to the other main museums. Prize exhibits include Bernardo Daddi's *Story of the Holy Girdle* (see below) and paintings by Prato's most renowned painter, Fra Filippo Lippi (*Madonna del Ceppo*) and his son Filippino. The **Duomo** in the main square has a typical stripy façade graced with the unusual exterior **Pulpit of the Sacred Girdle**. Surmounted by a canopy, it is decorated with a frieze of lively dancing cherubs designed by Donatello (a copy). A chapel off the left of the nave holds Prato's

Medici Villas

Foremost among the ruling families of Tuscany during the 16th and 17th centuries were the Medicis. A number of their beautiful houses can be visited. One of the finest is 18 km north-west of Florence in **Póggio a Caiano**, *Pza dei Medici; tel: (055) 877012* (Mon–Sat 0900–1400, Sun 0900–sunset; L4000), accessible by car (Pistóia road) or COPIT bus from *Pza Santa Maria Novella* in Florence. Built around 1480 by Sangallo for Lorenzo the Magnificent, its imposing classical façade was modified in the 18th century. Inside, the splendid Salone di Leone X room is frescoed by Pontormo and Andrea del Sarto in a masterly example of Florentine Mannerism. Also west of Florence, the **Villa dell'Artimino** was built in 1594, originally as a hunting lodge for Ferdinand I. Its roof-line bristles with curious chimney pots (prebooked tours on Tues; *tel: (055) 879 2030*). Finds from local Etruscan tombs are displayed in a small basement museum. An attractive hotel (**Paggeria Medicea**, *Vle Papa Giovanni XXIII, Artimino; tel: (055) 871 8081*) has been converted from the former stable block. On the north-eastern side of Florence, several Medici villas lie close together. **La Petraia**, open daily 0900–1930 (Apr–Sept); 0900–1730 (Mar and Oct); 0900–1630 (Nov–Feb); L4000 including entry to Castello) was a former Brunelleschi castle, grandly converted with Italianate gardens and a frescoed ballroom. Just down the road, the **Villa di Castello** (same hours and admission) is best known for its lovely gardens of mazes, grottoes, parterres and trick fountains.

revered relic, the Virgin's Girdle, a thin sash alleged to have been presented to St Thomas (of the Doubts), which is displayed from the pulpit on just five days a year. Around the high altar are Filippo Lippi's frescos of John the Baptist and St Stephen, scandalously associated with Fra Lippi's mistress Lucrezia Buti (he a monk and she a nun), the mother of his son Filippino and allegedly the model for the winsome dancing Salome. The **Museo dell'Opera del Duomo**, *tel: (0574) 29339,* houses the original Donatello panels from the Holy Girdle pulpit and more works by the Lippis (*père et fils*). On the southern outskirts are some respites from Prato's convoluted girdle legend: the **Museo del Tessuto** (Textile Museum), *Vle della Repubblica 9; tel: (0574) 570352,* documents Prato's major industry from medieval times; and on the same street, the **Centro per l'Arte Contemporanea Luigi Pecci**, *Vle della Repubblica; tel: (0574) 570620,* Wed–Mon

1000–1900; L10,000, exhibition of contemporary art. Prato also has an adventurous programme of theatre and film.

Most of Prato's central hotels are designed for business use; just 4 km north east is the **Villa Rucellai**, *V. di Cannetto 16; tel: (0574) 460392,* a delightful old villa with a garden of lemon trees. Further afield, the **Fattoria di Baccchereto**, *Loc. Baccchereto, V. Fontemorana 179; tel: (055) 871 7191,* is a charming old farmhouse in steep hills near Carmignano (13 km southwest). Prato has several excellent restaurants: most reputable is **Il Pirana**, *V. G. Valentini 110; tel: (0574) 25746*; less expensive are **La Veranda**, *V. dell'Arco 10/12; tel: (0574) 38235*; **Osvaldo Baroncelli**, *V. Fra Bartolomeo 13; tel: (0574) 23810* (all closed Sat lunch, Sun and Aug); and **Baghino**, *V. dell'Accademia 9; tel: (0574) 27920* (closed Mon lunch and Sun eve in winter). Look out for Prato's speciality almond biscuits (*biscottini*) sold in local bakeries.

317

PISA–LUCCA

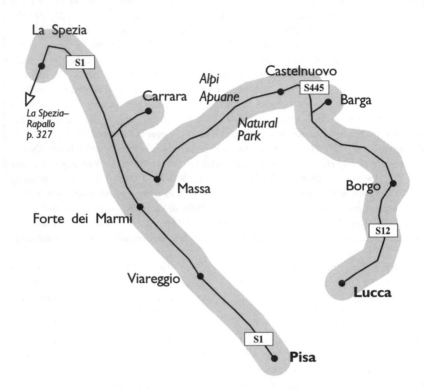

After a longer look at Pisa than is generally allocated, this horseshoe route explores the northern tip of Tuscany, following the Versilia coast northwards via Viareggio, through the unspoilt Alpi Alpuane regional park and an intensely developed zone of merged seaside resorts. Inland, the marble quarry town of Carrara offers a memorable excursion in Michelangelo's footsteps. The green, hilly scenery of the Alpi Apuane and the Garfagnana is effectively crossable by only one road, but the wilder sections of this mountainous region can be explored on good footpaths by keen walkers. Castelnuovo makes an attractive touring base for several rural excursions. A pleasant valley drive follows the Serchio downstream to Lucca – a thoroughly rewarding destination. You could hammer through this drive in a day if you were so minded, or you could spend a week or more sampling the northern Tuscan coast and bumbling round the rural Garfagnana.

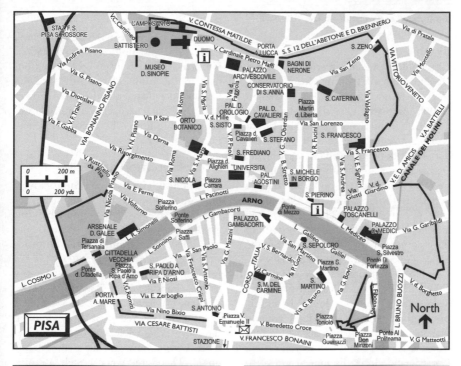

ROUTE

From **Pisa**, take the *V. Aurelia* S1 north-wards. Continue northwards via **Viareggio** and **Forte dei Marmi** along the seafront road, veering inland at **Carrara** for an excursion to the marble quarries. The coastal road continues towards the dramatic wooded promontory of **La Spezia** (see p. 327). Returning south-east to **Massa** (a busy but forget-table administrative town), take the minor road eastwards for **Castelnuovo** across the **Alpi Apuane Natural Park**. Take a pic-nic with you; there aren't many restaurants on the way. From Castelnuovo, several excursions are suggested through the **Garfagnana** region. Then head south fol-lowing the valley route through **Barga**, **Bagni di Lucca** and **Borgo**, crossing the river where necessary. The tour ends in **Lucca** (see p. 311).

PISA

Tourist Office: *Pza Stazione; tel: (050) 42291* or *Pza Duomo; tel: (050) 560464.* These offices are small and not especially well stocked, but valiantly serve hordes of polyglot visitors.

Once one of Italy's great maritime republics, Pisa has dwindled in status to a humdrum provincial capital. It is still vis-ited by millions of visitors in transit through its convenient airport, but often awarded no more than a passing glance at that famous lopsided tower. There is more to see than this, though it doesn't deserve more than a single night's stay, perhaps just before, or after, your flight. There are two main focal points to the town. Visitors to the Leaning Tower in the northernmost corner of the city, do not realise that the heart of the town lies on the Arno, some way south.

ARRIVING AND DEPARTING

By Air

Charter, domestic and international flights serve Pisa, one of Tuscany's main airgates. After a recent face-lift, Pisa's **Galileo Galilei Airport** (3 km south); *tel: (050) 500707,* is a much more agreeable place to wait for a flight than it used to be, but duty-free shopping facilities are limited. Exchange rates are slightly lower than you may find in downtown banks, and the airport tourist information desk has unreliable opening hours. The airport is an inexpensive 5-min train or bus ride from the city centre (you can buy tickets in the airport concourse; L1300–1500). Bus services (no.7) are more frequent, and slightly cheaper. About a dozen car hire firms have desks at the airport, but don't rely on getting a good deal (or any deal!) without prebooking. Driving into the city is not easy; ask for directions before you set off. Coastal and long-distance routes (to Florence, Lucca, etc.) are much more straightforward. If you just want a single night or a few hours to explore the city, consider dumping heavy baggage in the left-luggage office and travelling in by public transport. A vehicle is an embarrassment in the centre of Pisa, though fortunately there are places on the city fringes where you can park.

By Rail

Pisa's **main station** lies south of the Arno (Florence–Viareggio and Genoa–Rome lines); *tel: (050) 41385.* There are good connections with Lucca and Florence; change at Empoli for Siena. Other services run up and down the coast. Pisa has another station, **San Rossore**, north-west of the centre, used by some local services (convenient for the Campo dei Miracoli and the youth hostel).

By Bus

The **main bus terminal** is on *Pza Vittoria Emanuele II,* just north of the rail station. Regular city buses (e.g. no.1) run from here to the banks of the Arno and the Campo dei Miracoli (Leaning Tower area). APT or Lazzi services run to main centres (Volterra, Livorno, Florence, Lucca, La Spezia).

ACCOMMODATION AND FOOD

Most holiday visitors spend comparatively little time in Pisa, so hotels cater mainly for business travellers. A comfortable but expensive base near the Campo dei Miracoli is the **Grand Hotel Duomo**, *Via Santa Maria 94; tel: (050) 56126* (garage). For more character in the city centre, consider the **Royal Victoria**, *Lungarno Pacinotti; tel: (050) 940111,* a charmingly battered *palazzo* overlooking the Arno where Dickens once stayed (a room with a view will have some traffic noise). There are several hostels, a campsite and budget hotels near the city centre, with many other choices on the coast. The station area is cheap but uninteresting; Campo dei Miracoli thronged with tourists; *Pza Dante* attractive but full of students in term-time. Restaurants near the Leaning Tower cater for tourists; for a more authentic ambience and better value, try the university area around *Pza Dante* and *Pza Cavalieri,* or even south of the river. Seafood is the mainstay of this coastal city. The **Osteria dei Cavalieri**, *V. San Frediano 16; tel: (050) 580858* (closed Sat lunch, Sun and Aug) has a pleasant olde-worlde atmosphere. The **Osteria del Porton Rosso**, *V. Porton Rosso 11; tel: (050) 56126* (closed Sun and Aug), specialises in fish. **Da Bruno**, *V. L. Bianchi 12; tel: (050) 560818* (closed Mon eve and Tues), is just outside the walls near the Campo dei Miracoli. For a little history, try Pisa's oldest coffee house, **Antico Caffè dell'Usero**, *Lungarno Pacinotti 27*, dating from 1794 and patronised by many famous Risorgimento writers (Byron, Dickens, Shelley also strolled this way in the 19th century).

SIGHTSEEING

Pisa's great annual celebration is the **Gioco del Ponte** (last Sunday of June), a medieval pageant involving a tug of war (more correctly a push of war) on one of the central bridges. Also in June, the **Luminaria di San Ranieri** is a colourful regatta and lights festival on the waterfront. Every four years, Pisa takes its turn as the venue for the old maritime republics boat race between Pisa, Genoa, Venice and Amalfi (next one 1999).

You will get a more rounded picture of Pisa by leaving the climactic Campo dei Miracoli (Field of Miracles) until last. Start explorations on the banks of the Arno, which carves a broad, coffee-coloured arc through the heart of the old city. The riverscape makes an interesting comparison with Florence, further upstream. In Pisa, as in Florence, the banks are lined with stately *palazzi* in faded, peeling shades of ochre and terracotta and a medley of church towers. Bridges ancient and modern span the Arno, though there is nothing to match the Ponte Vecchio. The south bank, or Mezzogiorno, has a few churches worth a glance. Notice the little oratory of **Santa Maria della Spina** in spiky but elegant Gothic, built to house one of Christ's crowning thorns. Further west stand on the arcaded façade of **San Paolo a Ripa d'Arno** and its quaint neighbouring **Cappella di Sant'Agata** in octagonal Romanesque. On the north bank is the **Museo Nazionale di San Matteo**, *Lungarno Mediceo; tel: (050) 541865*, open Tues–Sat 0900–1900, Sun 0900–1300; L8000 in a medieval convent, containing Pisan painting, sculpture and ceramics. From *Pza Garibaldi*, wander along picturesquely arcaded Borgo Stretto, then bear left to the **Pza dei Cavalieri**, a large open space hemmed by narrow backstreets, on which stand several imposing buildings. The **Palazzo dei Cavalieri**, easily recognised by its striking *sgraffito* decoration, houses one of Pisa University's colleges. It was once the headquarters of a military order, the Knights of St Stephen, whose ornate 16th-century church of **Santo Stefano dei Cavalieri** stands adjacent. A grisly episode took place in the **Palazzo dell'Orologio** opposite; Count Ugolino, a mayor of Pisa suspected of treason, was walled up here in 1288 with all his male descendants and starved to death, an act denounced in Dante's *Inferno*.

Head north again towards *Pza Arcivescovado*. The astonishing spectacle of the Leaning Tower suddenly rearing at maximum tilt over a mundane roofline of huddled houses will make your senses reel. It is, of course, the sight you've been waiting for, one of the most instantly recognisable and hackneyed images of Italy. But for a split second, your brain will simply refuse to process the information your eyes give you.

The Campo dei Miracoli is an amazing assembly of buildings staged in unnatural drama on velvet lawns. The Tower itself, which the Italians call the **Torre Pendente**, would be a beautiful and striking structure even without its inclination. Begun in 1173 on shallow, unstable foundations, it began to tilt even before the third storey was reached (one school of thought maintains that the distortion was deliberate). To rectify the balance, the upper storeys were built more vertically, so the result is gently skewed like a banana.

Six tiers of intricate marble arcades surround an internal staircase and a hollow core. The upper section contains a belfry. At the top, the tower now leans over 5.4 m from the vertical. Accelerated movement caused the closure of the tower to the public in 1990, and since then, engineers have racked their brains to think of ways, not of straightening the tower (a disastrous PR move), but of stabilising the tilt to stop the building collapsing. At present, huge ugly weights counterbalance the base of the tower, and the site is fenced off – just in case. No one will predict if or when the tower can be made safe enough to climb, as Galileo famously did with lead weights to test his theory of constant gravity. Defying the laws of physics, modern visitors endlessly photograph themselves pretending to prop up the tower.

The remaining buildings on the Campo dei Miracoli, all in harmonious Pisan style faced in gleaming Carrara marble, consist of the Duomo, its circular Battistero, and the rectangular Camposanto, which is a cloistered cemetery. You can walk round all the exteriors free of charge. To go inside all of them, buy a combined ticket costing L17,000 (available at any of the sights). Separate entrance charges are quoted below. Queues can be significant in high season; try to time your visit early or late to miss some of the coach parties. For information about any of the Campo dei Miracoli sights, *tel: (050) 560547.*

The **Duomo**, open daily 1000–1940 (summer); 1000–1700 (winter); L2000, is a magnificent and complex building. Outstanding features include Pisano's masterly pulpit, the flamboyant Romanesque façade of sandstone, inlaid marble and majolica, Bonnano's bronze doors

Correcting the Tilt

Engineers tasked with rescuing the Leaning Tower have a problem: how to correct the tilt without bringing the Tower crashing down – nobody wants to suffer the ignominy of being held responsible for destroying one of the world's most famous architectural monuments. Consequently nothing is being done with haste and nobody should complain that it has taken so long for tests to even diagnose the reason for the tilt. Currently, the 18th commission of enquiry is deliberating what to do (the first was established as far back as 1911).

So what are the results of the most recent commission? One is to confirm that the Tower very definitely is on the verge of collapse: computer models say that the Tower's 14,500 tonnes of masonry should come plummeting to earth if the tilt reaches more than 5.44 degrees. The fact that the tilt is now 5.5 degrees means that something spectacular could happen at any moment – hence the hoarding that keeps visitors well clear of the tower. The second finding is that the angle of tilt varies substantially during the day, depending on the effects of sunlight expanding the masonry, and the amount of water in the subsoil – if the Tower does collapse, it will probably be after a rainstorm. The third finding is that the Tower isn't just subsiding sideways, it is actually twisting and rotating its way into the ground.

Understanding the problem is the prelude to fixing a solution. Attempts will now be made to support the tower temporarily using cables, attached around the third storey of the tower and then tensioned using hydraulic pistons. Then drills will be inserted into the ground to extract just sufficient soil from beneath the northern side of the tower to let it settle back to a more stable position. If all this works, visitors will be allowed back into the tower for the millennium. If not, expect the Tower to be closed for decades to come.

with delicate biblical scenes, and the mosaic of Christ Pantocrator in the apse by Cimaue. The adjacent **Battistero**, open daily 0800–2000 (summer); 0900–1700 (winter); L10,000 including the Duomo, ornate outside, is mostly empty apart from another seething Pisano pulpit. The **Camposanto**, open daily 0900–1700 (winter); 0800–2000 (summer); L10,000 including Duomo) is a huge rectangular structure enclosing tombs and astonishing frescos. Some of these were badly damaged during the last war; those that survive give a graphic picture of death and judgement (painted in 1348 during a time of plague, these were understandable preoccupations).

Around the edges of the Campo dei Miracoli you will find, besides a bizarrely entertaining array of tasteless souvenirs, two museums, also accessible on your combined ticket. The **Museo dell'Opera del Duomo**, *Pza Arcivescovado 6*, open daily 0800–2000 (summer); 0900–1700 (winter); L12,000, is housed in the tourist office building south-east of the campo and contains exhibits from the cathedral and baptistery (statues, paintings, archaeological finds, liturgical treasures and some fascinating inlaid panelling – spot the thieving magpie). Spectacular close-ups of the Leaning Tower are visible from the cloister and loggia. The **Museo delle Sinopie**, *Pza Duomo*, open daily 0800–2000 (summer); 0900–1230 and 1500–1700 (winter); L10,000, contains sketches of the Camposanto frescos which distintegrated during the 1944 air raid.

South of the Campo dei Miracoli, wind down with a saunter round Pisa's charming **Orto Botanico** (Botanic Gardens) with its mellow, shell-smothered museum, accessed from *V. Luca Ghini 5*, open Mon–Fri 0800–1300 and 1400–1730, Sat 0800–1300; free, and have a look at Galileo's house on *V. Santa Maria*.

SIDE TRACKS FROM PISA

The Arno has dumped so much silt near its mouth that Pisa is now stranded some way inland. Its seaside resorts are popular summer retreats for local residents. Marina di Pisa retains a few Liberty-style villas, but the water is polluted. Its redeeming feature is the **Parco Naturale di San Rossore** extending in dense pinewoods, marshland and shoreline over much of the coastal hinterland between Viareggio and Livorno, full of varied habitats and much wildlife, including deer, goats and wild boar. Guided tours are arranged: contact the park office at Massaciuccoli; *tel: (050) 525500* for information. At **Gombo**, the drowned poet Shelley washed ashore in 1882 and was cremated on the beach. Lord Trelawny seized his incombustible heart from the flames, burning his hand badly in the process. **San Piero a Grado**, 6 km west of Pisa, is a fine 11th-century church with a Moorish interior and some early frescos. Ten km east of Pisa, **La Certosa di Pisa** is a huge Carthusian monastery in ornate baroque style, open Tues–Sat 0900–1800 (May–Sept); closes earlier in winter; Sun 0900–1200; L8000. ⬆

VIAREGGIO AND THE RIVERA DELLA VERSILIA

Tourist Office: *Vle Carducci 10; tel: (0584) 962233*. A summer-only office operates at the station.

Tuscany's largest seaside resort spreads in a strip of grid-like development along the straight Tyrrhenian coast. It is a smart place and prices are high. The Lungomare, a 3 km promenade of oleander, pine and tamarisk runs along the seafront past light-hearted buildings designed by Galileo

Chini in a particularly exuberant brand of art nouveau known as Liberty style. The **Gran Caffè Margherita** is a typical example. The fishing port at the southern end adds a bit of traditional colour to what is otherwise an artificial community. Viareggio holds a famously flamboyant carnival (Jan–Feb). Most of the gently shelving beaches are privately owned and covered in parasols. There's a non-concessioned section near Torre del Lago, where the composer Puccini spent his last years. His house, the **Villa Puccini**, *Vle Puccini 264; tel: (0584) 341445* can be visited on guided tours, Tues–Sun (Oct–Jun); daily (July–Sept); L5000. Viareggio is easily reached by bus or train from Pisa and Florence; summer weekends are very crowded.

North of Viareggio, nondescript seaside development continues for block after block, more or less unbroken as far as Marina di Carrara, but slithering subtly downmarket beyond Forte dei Marmi, where hotels, villas and beach clubs stand in fenced compounds of screening vegetation. Despite the Walrus and Carpenter beaches of endless soft sand and the picturesque backdrop of the Apuan Alps, it is hard to understand the magnetic attractions of this flat and featureless coastline for so many cultivated Italians.

CARRARA

Tourist Office: *Vle G. Galilei 133, Marina di Carrara, tel: (0585) 632218* or *Vle Potrignano 13, Carrara.*

The rail station (Genoa–Rome line) and out-of-town bus station are at Marina di Carrara, linked by bus to *Pza Matteotti* in the old town. Most accommodation is on the coast, which has few charms as a touring base. There are plenty of eating places in the old town.

The town is in two halves: the scrappy little seaport resort of Marina di Carrara where giant blocks of stone await export on the quayside, and the bustling hill town above the *V. Aurelia*, ever resounding with the noise of drilling, hammering, sawing and chipping. Carrara has been synonymous with the marble industry since Roman times, and given the scale of modern extraction, it is astonishing there is any left. The hills around the town, gashed jagged white by quarrying and strewn with heavy lifting gear, gives a fleeting impression of a ski resort from a distance. Close up, the whiteness hardens into the metamorphic limestone which is the lifeblood of the local economy.

There is something of an old town based on a series of *piazzas* adorned with sculpted marble, but it is scarcely obligatory viewing. The main monuments are an 11th-century **Duomo** with a fine rose-windowed façade, and a fortress now used as the **Accademia delle Belle Arti**. A small **Museo Civico di Marmo**, *Vle XX Settembre; tel: (0585) 845746*, Mon–Fri 1000–1300 and 1600–1900 (Apr–Sept); 1000–1300 and 1400–1700 (winter); L5000, presents an exhibition about the marble industry on the road towards the port.

THE ALPI APUANE AND THE GARFAGNANA

Tourist Office: Castelnuovo: *Loggiata Porta 10; tel: (0583) 644354* or *Pza delle Erbe 1; tel: (0583) 65169* (for information on the Alpi Apuane Regional Park, *tel: (0583) 644242*). These friendly offices in the main regional centre offer a wealth of information and maps on hiking, wildlife and leisure facilities, and help with accommodation. There is a **Club Alpino** office in *V. Vittorio Emanuele* (specialist climbing information).

There are small seasonal offices at

Barga, *Pza Angelio 3*, open daily
1000–1200 and **Bagni di Lucca**, *V. dei
Casino 4; tel: (0583) 87946*, open Mon–
Sat 0900–1400.

Behind the multi-strand road systems
clustered in the narrow coastal plain, the
jagged green hills of the Alpi Apuane rise
steeply, reaching a maximum of 1945m at
Monte Pisanino. The region has been designated a nature park, and attracts many
visitors for walking and other leisure activities. It has special interests for naturalists
and speleologists, with rare plants and birds
and one of the largest karst cave systems in
the world. It is difficult to explore in detail
by car; only one convenient route crosses
it, from Massa to Castelnuovo through the
desolate valley of the Turrite Secca. Half-
way along, an alpine garden of local flora
makes a place to stretch legs: the **Orto
Botanico Pietro Pellegrini**, at Pian della
Fioba, offers free guided tours, 0900–1200
and 1500–1800 or 1900 in summer; wear
rubber-soled shoes; no smoking. A number of mountain roads from the fringes of
the park provide cul-de-sac access to
villages and places of interest. Local
curiosities include the **Marmitte dei
Giganti** (Giant's Cooking Pots), glacial
hollows near Arni, and the **Grotta del
Vento** (Cave of the Wind) – a stalactite
cavern at Fornovolasco.

Castelnuovo, poised between the Alpi
Apuane and the Serchio Valley region
known as the **Garfagnana**, is a quaint if
dispersed village. Its 13th-century Rocca
now functions as the town hall, and with
two helpful tourist offices, it makes an
attractive touring base. There is plenty of
modest accommodation in the area, including campsites, *agriturismo*, simple hotels,
private rooms and mountain refuges.
Good country cooking is not difficult to
find, either try **La Lanterna** (1.5km
north); *Loc. Piano Pieve; tel: (0583) 63364.*

Marble

The Romans first began extracting
marble from the hills near Carrara,
driving soaked wooden wedges
into the hairline faults of the stone and
lowering the blocks down the mountainside with ropes, roller 'sledges' made of
treetrunks, and huge teams of oxen.
Similar methods were used in the 16th
century, when Michelangelo would visit to
choose marble for his statues. Today the
methods are more mechanised, using giant
earth-moving equipment and diamond
wire saws. There are about a hundred
quarries near Carrara scattered over an
area of about 2000 ha. It is an important
source of local employment, and environ-
mental objections to the despoilation of
the landscape have so far been fiercely
resisted. At the present rates of extraction, however, the best sections of Carrara
marble will soon be worked out, and what
is left behind will be a desolate scene. For
the time being, the marble quarries make
an interesting excursion for visitors to the
Versilia coast. Colonnata is one of the
most accessible extraction points. Follow
signs saying *Visita Cave* to see the dazzling
mountainsides being relentlessly dis-
membered in regular chunks. The hazards
and efforts involved, even with modern
machinery, make the pre-mechanised
extraction methods of Michelangelo's day
seem truly awesome. Beware of heavy
trucks on the roads, and pray their brakes
don't fail with those colossal blocks
aboard. Souvenir shops line the approach
road, selling many small, portable artefacts.
Some of these are very attractive, though
by no means all are made of Carrara
marble; many types of stone from all over
the world are worked in the local factories. Bus services run to the quarries
from Carrara town.

325

Castelnuovo is on regular bus and rail routes (Lucca–Aulla line) from Lucca.

Accessible destinations by car include the ancient stone villages of **Vagli di Sotto** and **Vagli di Sopra**, to the north-west, above an artificial lake. Due north, head for the pretty village of **Corfino**, a starting-point for the **Parco dell'Orechiella** and numerous walks. The park visitor centre at Corfino, *tel: (0583) 619098*, open weekends only (May–Sept); daily (July–Aug); by appointment off season, has a fascinating botanic garden, the **Orto Botanico Pania di Corfino**; *tel: (0583) 658990*, open (mid June–mid Sept); by appointment off-season.

If you want to stay in this attractive location, try the **La Baita**, *V. Prato all'Aia; tel: (0583) 68680 or 660084*, a friendly, family-run *albergo* with good food. The north-east route from Castelnuovo leads to the monastery of **San Pellegrino in Alpe**, with marvellous views. It contains an interesting ethnographic museum, the **Museo della Campagna**, *V. del Voltone 14; (0583) 649072*, open Tues–Sun 0930–1300 and 1430–1900 (June–Sept); 0900–1200 and 1400–1700 (Oct–May); L3000, chronicling local life in the Garfagnana.

From Castelnuovo, it's a straight-forward journey down the Serchio Valley to Lucca. Roads run on either side of the river, with bridging points in the major settlements. It's worth having a quick look

at **Barga**, a steep little medieval town with a July opera festival and a fine 11th-century **Duomo**. The exterior shows intricate carvings; inside is an early statue of St Christopher and a massive marble pulpit. At **Borgo a Mozzano** an eye-catching Romanesque bridge forms a perfect circle in the mirror-like water. The **Ponte della Maddalena** is popularly known as the 'Devil's Bridge', after one of those dog legends which are told of many other bridges, as well as this one. Apparently the villagers enlisted the help of the Devil in building the bridge, in return for which he demanded the first soul to cross. The crafty villagers ensured that the first to cross was a dog. **Bagni di Lucca**, 4 km east up a side-valley, is famed for its lime sulphate springs. Once a fashionable spa, it boasted Europe's first licensed casino. The English church and Protestant cemetery indicate its favoured clientele; Shelley, Byron and the Brownings encouraged a minor Anglo-Saxon invasion. Modern visitors may find it too sedate for a long-term stay, but there is plenty of accommodation and several excellent restaurants. Try the **Bridge**, *Pza di Ponte a Serraglio 5; tel: (0583) 805324*, for accommodation or the **Locanda Maiola**, *Loc. Maiola di Sotto; tel: (0583) 86296*, a restaurant with rooms. **Circolo Dei Forestieri**, *Pza Varraud 10; tel; (0583) 86038* (closed Mon and Tues lunch), is highly recommended for food.

LA SPEZIA–RAPALLO

This route covers arguably the most scenic stretch of coastline in Italy. Beginning in the ancient town of Lérici, it takes you in easy stages around the 'Gulf of Poets' – the Gulf of La Spezia – to the city of that name and then through the romantic, near-illusionary world of the Cinque Terre to Lévanto before continuing up the coast to Rapallo.

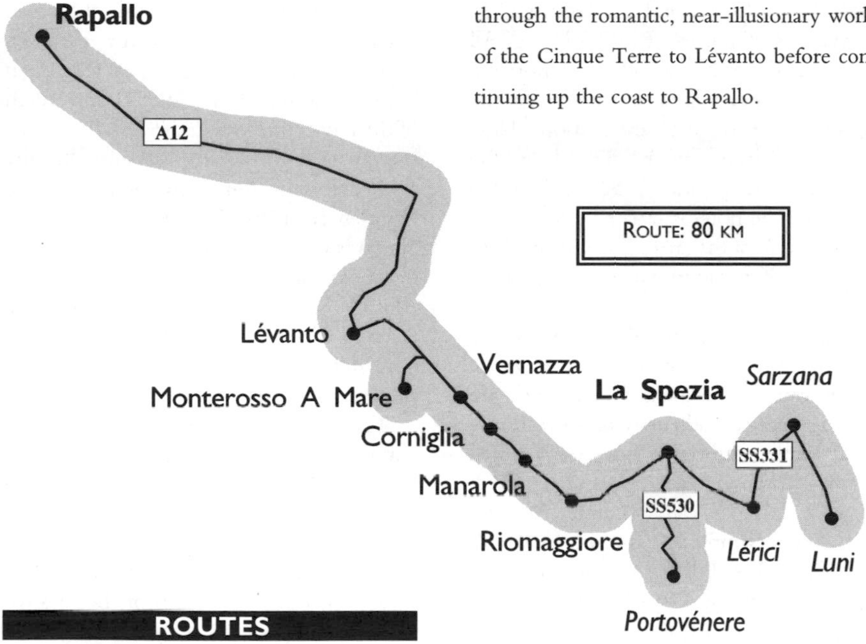

Rapallo

A12

ROUTE: 80 KM

Lévanto

Monterosso A Mare

Corniglia

Manarola

Riomaggiore

Vernazza

La Spezia

Sarzana

SS331

SS530

Lérici

Luni

Portovénere

327

ROUTES

DIRECT ROUTE

The A1 autostrada provides a direct link between La Spezia and Rapallo, via Lévanto,l but in taking this road you will miss much of the spectacular coastal scenery that makes the route worthwhile.

SCENIC ROUTE

From La Spezia, some of Italy's most tortuous local roads will take you north-westwards through the Cinque Terra to Lévanto. From here, the coast road ploughs underground, continuing through tunnels to emerge at Sestri Levante, where you join the N1 for the final leg to Rapallo.

LA SPEZIA

Tourist Office: *V. Mazzini 45; tel: (0187) 770900.* The office, which is on the seafront, is open Mon–Sat 0930–1230 and 1530–1830.

ACCOMMODATION AND FOOD

La Spezia is predominantly a large naval port and business centre, so it shouldn't come as a surprise to learn that much of the accommodation here is at the top end of the price range. With unlimited funds, you could indulge yourself at the immensely comfortable **Jolly el Golfo**, *V. XX Settembre 2; tel: (0187) 739555.* Other highly rated hotels include the **Ghironi**, *V. Tino 62; tel: (0187) 504141,* the **Firenze e Continentale**, *V.Paleocapa 7; tel: (0187) 713210,* and the **Genova**, *V. Fratelli Rosselli 84; tel: (0187) 731766.* All of these three hotels offer comfortable rooms, but none has a restaurant. At the cheaper end of the scale, more basic accommodation can be found at the **Spezia**, *V. F. Cavalotti 31; tel: (0187) 735164.* The hotel is situated close to the water in one of the area's few pretty streets and some of its rooms contain fine antique furniture.

Like many cities in Italy of comparable size, La Spezia offers a wide range of dining-out opportunities, whether you are seeking refined cathedrals of gastronomy or a simple trattoria or cafés for a quick lunch. **Parodi***, Vle Amendola 212; tel: (0187) 715777,* attracts diners from far and wide to sample its exquisite pasta, fish and veal dishes. For less ostentatious dining, both **Antica Osteria Negrao**, *V. Genova 428; tel: (0187) 701564,* and **Da Francesco**, *V. delle Pianazze 35*; *tel: (0187) 980946,* can be recommended. At the latter you can dine out al fresco in summer in an attractive garden. Close to the *V. del Pione* and the Arsenale, there are a number of restaurants offering good value, such as **Da Luciana** at *V.Colombo 27,* while in the heart of the old city, good pizza and pasta dishes are available at **Da Sandro**, *V. del Prione 268. Farinata* – a tasty tart made with chick pea flour – is available at many take-away establishments. If you are buying food for a picnic, go to the daily covered market in *Pza Cavour* for the freshest produce.

SIGHTSEEING

Illustrious writers like Shelley, Byron and D. H. Lawrence may have lingered here and waxed lyrically about the Gulf of Spezia, but first impressions of this important naval base are not particularly appealing. It is a large commercial city and, on the surface, doesn't have much to make you want to delay your push up the coast. There is an explanation for this. Its importance as a naval base attracted Allied bombers during World War II and much of the city centre was destroyed. But while it may lack the charm of some of the smaller towns along this section of the Ligurian coast, its position is stunning. La Spezia is on one of Italy's, if not Europe's, finest natural harbours, and with the Apian Alps in the background, it's a memorable place to while away a day – longer, if you have difficulty finding accommodation in the resorts nearby.

The city is sandwiched between the commercial port to the east and the naval base to the west. The main street – and scene of the evening *passeggiata* – is the *V. Prione*, which runs from the waterfront to the rail station. Old La Spezia lives on in the form of the remains of the massive **Castel San Giorgio**, which was built in the 13th century. And the post-war rebuilding programme has thrown up at least one 20th-century architectural gem – the modern **Duomo** in *V. Chiodo*, its boldly minimalist white tower standing out against the backdrop of the hills behind the city. If you're after something a little more traditional, the **church of Santa Maria** in the **Pza Giulio Beverini**, fits the bill. It was originally built in the 13th century before being enlarged in the 17th century, and today displays black and white stone banding on its façade.

La Spezia is also something of a museum city. The **Naval Museum**, to the left of the entrance to the **Arsenale**, contains relics of battles, figure-heads and armoury dating back to the 16th century. The museum is open Tues, Wed, Thurs, Sat 0900–1200 and 1400–1800 and Mon, Fri 1400–1800. In the **Museo Civico**, *V. Curtatone 9,* can be found some striking examples of faces sculpted on stone during the Bronze and Iron ages, as well archaeological relics from all over eastern Liguria. This museum is open Tues–Sat 0830–1300 and 1400–1900, Sun 0900–1300, closed on Mon.

⮊ SIDE TRACKS FROM LA SPEZIA

LUNI

As a relief from the admittedly splendid scenery of the Ligurian coast, divert inland on the minor road to the ancient towns of Sarzano and Luni. The turning, on the right, is about midway between Lérici and La Spezia. Behind the coast the hills end suddenly, giving way to the flatlands of the *Bocca di Magra* – the estuary of the River Magra – which is an important habitat for birds. The river was once the boundary between Liguria and Etruria – and later a dividing line in the squabbles between the Pisans and the Genoese. Today it is a little-known backwater with the well-fortified village of Ameglia, which is set above the plain, and Sarzano, whose medieval quarter contains a 15th-century citadel. Also worth seeing here is the Romanesque church of Sant'Andrea and the Cattedrale di Santa Maria Assunta, which contains a 12th-century panel painting of the Crucifixion by Maestro Guglielmo, the earliest dated panel painting in Italy. Luni, farther on on the plain, towards the border with Tuscany, was a Roman

Lunigiana

L unigiana, the region that lies between Viareggio, in Tuscany, and La Spezia, in Liguria, is named after Luni, the former Roman colony that flourished as a port until its harbour silted up in the 13th century. Lunigiana's alternative name is the Land of a Thousand Castles, referring to the many fortifications built in the 13th to 16th centuries by the ruling Malaspina family. A good place to start, if you are exploring the region, is Pontremoli, where a fine Malaspina castle, the Castello del Piagnaro, now houses the Museo delle Statue Stele Lunigianesi; *tel: 0187 831439,* open Tues–Sun 1000–1300 and 1500–1700. The *statue stele* exhibited in this museum consist of fascinating carved stone figures, or menhirs, dating from the Bronze Age.

shipbuilding colony, founded in 177 BC. The town took its name from a cult of the moon goddess and was eventually destroyed by war and malaria. In the town museum, which is open Tues–Sun 0900–1200 and 1500–1900 (summer); 0900–1200, 1400–1700 (winter), are finds from villas in the Bocca di Magra.

Retrace your steps back to the main road and continue through the unlovely outskirts to **La Spezia**.

LÉRICI

Tourist Office, *V. Gerini 38; tel: (0187) 967346,* has masses of local information. Open Tues–Sat 0930–1230 and 1530–1800, Sun 0930–1230.

ACCOMMODATION AND FOOD

Lérici is very much an upwardly mobile and fashionable resort and its range of

329

hotels tends to reflect this. The **Doria Park Hotel**, pleasingly set in quite spacious grounds at *V. Privato Doria 2; tel: (0187) 967346*, is generally reckoned to be the town's best and offers good value. Other favourites include the nostalgically and romantically named **Shelley e Delle Palme** at *Lungomare Biaggini 5; tel: (0187) 968205*, and the **Europa**, *V. Carpanini 1; tel: (0187) 967800*, both of which offer good views. Finding good budget accommodation in Lérici is more difficult, although one such establishment is **Hotel del Golfo**, which is situated about 100m from the tourist office at *V. Gerini 37; tel: (0187) 967400*. A stylish resort generally means stylish restaurants and Lérici is no exception. There are any number of good dining places, with **Il Frantoio**, *V. Cavour 21; tel: (0187) 964174*, and **La Barcaccia**, *Pza Garibaldi 8; tel: (0187) 967721*, among the most reliable. Among cheaper places to eat are the **Piccolo**

Oasi at *V. Cavour 60*, and **Il Giogo**, which is on the main road running up from the seafront square at *V. O. Petriccioli 4*. Down on the harbour, the outdoor pizzerias provide an attractive alternative, particularly at sunset.

SIGHTSEEING

Lérici, magnificently situated on the southern side of the Gulf of Spezia, is a place to relax in rather than for sightseeing. But it does have at least one worthy 'must see'– its medieval **Castello**. In a virtually impregnable position on a projecting spit of land, the castle was built in the 12th century by the Pisans to keep out the Genoese, who had already established themselves at Portovénere, just across the water on the opposite side of the gulf. You can walk up to the castle, which is open daily 0930–1230 and 1400–1800 (Sept–June); daily from 0930–1230, 1530–2000 (July–Aug). The building does not offer a great deal to see inside – it is

Northern Italy in Literature

Has any other part of the world inspired so many literary classics as Northern Italy, and Tuscany in particular? Three Tuscans – Dante, born in Florence, Boccaccio, born in Certaldo, and Petrarch (born in Arezzo) – created the classics of Italian vernacular literature that provided the models for such other great writers as Chaucer, Shakespeare and Milton. Later came another clutch of classical works all penned by Florentines – Machiavelli's *The Prince*, the manual for all practitioners of *realpolitik*, Cellini, the Florentine jeweller and sculptor who wrote one of the world's first autobiographies and Vasari, author of the world's first art history, disguised in the form of a series of biographical *Lives of the Artists*. Equally influential in their day were Galileo's scientific *Dialogues*, penned while he was Florentine court mathematician and astronomer, the sonnets and neo-platonic treatises of Politian and Lorenzo de Medici, and even the evangelical hymns of Savonarola.

Of non-Italians, E M Forster, Dickens, the Brownings, Henry James and D H Lawrence all wrote books set in Tuscany. None is as amusing, however, as Mark Twain's deliciously witty invective, contained in his *Innocents Abroad*. Those who have seen the Arno in summer will readily recognise the justice of his description: 'they all call it a river, and they honestly think it is a river, do these dark and bloody Florentines. They even help out the delusion by building bridges over it. I do not see why they are too good to wade'.

Walking routes

North of La Spezia, the Riviera road briefly pushes inland, leaving travel along the coast mostly, but not exclusively, in the hands of walkers. In the 'hidden' villages of the Cinque Terre – the so-called Five Lands – it is as easy to get around on foot as it is by car and all along this beguiling coast is a network of footpaths which makes for a unique holiday experience. Between Riomaggiore, the most southerly of the Cinque Terre villages, and Monterosso, the most northerly, you can explore arguably Italy's most scenic stretch of coast free of exhaust fumes. Every so often, steps leading down to the pellucid sea have been cut into the side of the cliff – and there are rock-hewn seats where you can sit and quietly consume a picnic, washed down, perhaps, by a glass or two of the excellent Cinque Terre wine.

There are paths, in fact, all the way along the Cinque Terre coast and to plan a walk you should buy the map entitled *Carta dei Sentieri delle Cinque Terre*, which is available for a few pence from local news-stands. The stretches between Lévanto, Monterosso, Vernazza and Corniglia are very scenic, the one from Manarola to Riomaggiore less so, despite being known as the *V. d'Amore* – Lover's Way. The longest stretch, and the most difficult, is from Riomaggiore to Portovénere. It takes about six hours. But the climb to Madonna di Montenero, where you can get lunch – and the subsequent descent along the steep mountain side to Portovénere – will stay with you for the rest of your days.

---

used from time to time for exhibitions – but there are splendid views from the top terrace across the gulf to Portovénere and the island of Palmaria. If you want to see Portovénere at closer quarters, there are six regular boat trips across the gulf from Lérici. Details from the tourist office (see above). There is also a pleasant drive south, passing a number of pretty coves with unbelievably clear water, to the village of Tellaro, located on a rocky spur, with terraces down to the sea.

Back in Lérici, take the coast road north towards La Spezia.

PORTOVÉNERE

From La Spezia, take the scenic SS530 which hugs the west side of the Gulf of Spezia to **Portovénere** 15 km away. There are some hair-raising bends along this road, but the views, particularly to the islands of Palmária and Tino, make it worthwhile.

Tourist Office, *Piazza Bastreri 1; tel (0187) 790 691,* open Mon–Sat 0900–1300 and 1600–1800.

ACCOMMODATION AND FOOD

Portovénere is very much on the tourist trail and has hotels to suit most budgets. The **Royal Sporting**, *Loc. Seno dell'Olivio; tel: (0187) 790326,* and the **Grand Hotel Portovénere**, *tel: (0187) 792610,* both offer high standards of comfort and food and good views. Of the smaller hotels, the **Paradiso**; *tel: (0187) 790612,* and **Le Grazie**, *V. Roma 43; tel: (0187) 790017,* represent the pick of the bunch. The town is also well endowed with good restaurants; most, such as the **Taverna del Corsaro**, *Calata Doria 102; tel: (0187) 790622,* and the **Trattoria La Marina–da Antonio**, *Pza Marina 6; tel: (0187) 790686,* offering a good mix between Ligurian and seafood dishes.

SIGHTSEEING

Portovénere is a pretty little place. It is also extremely old, the Romans founded it 2000 years ago as a staging post on the route between Gaul and Spain. Wander through its narrow streets today and the place fairly creaks and groans under the full weight of its history. Some of the colourful houses date back to the 12th century and were once connected to the citadel so that, in times of attack, the villagers could reach the safety of the castle. It's also a poets' place and Byron is supposed to have written *Childe Harold* here. He is remembered in the village today in the grotto at the base of the sea–swept cliffs, from where he swam across the gulf to meet up with his friend Shelley. Just above the grotto, the 13th-century **church of San Pietro** is built on a solid mass of rock, its black and white striped walls visible for miles out to sea. Retrace your steps along the road back towards La Spezia and then bear left on to the road which skirts around the 543 m peak of Monte Santa Croce. This is a narrow back road leading to one of Liguria's greatest tourist attractions – the five 'toy-town' villages of the **Cinque Terra**. Until fairly recently, it was only possible to reach the villages, perched on the top of the cliffs, by boat or by the little train which shuttles down the coast from Genoa to La Spezia. However, a road (of sorts) now exists and you can now reach each of the five fishing villages by road, although you have to leave your car at the entrance, making the rest of the way on foot. The disadvantage, though, is that you enter, so to speak, via the back door, thus denying yourself a glimpse of the village's stage-set beauty, which is available to those who approach the villages from the sea, or along the coastal path. The five villages, from south to north, are detailed below. ⬑

RIOMAGGIORE

Its proximity to La Spezia makes this the easiest village to reach. Riomaggiore gained fame during the last century when the artist Telemaco Signorini came here to paint. But there are sights worth seeing – notably the 14th-century **church of San Giovanni**, for its pulpit with marble reliefs and its fine Renaissance doorway, and, on a hill to the north-west, the remains of a 15th-century castle. Riomaggiore probably offers the best value of the Cinque Terre villages in terms of accommodation and food. The best hotels here are probably the **Due Gemelli**, *Loc. Campi; tel: (0187) 731320,* and the **Villa Argentina**, *tel: (0187) 920213,* although it's often difficult finding rooms in either of these hotels, particularly in season.

Most of Riomaggiore's restaurants are in the *V. Colombo,* which runs through the village from the waterfront. **Veciu Muin**, at *V. Colombo 31,* is an inexpensive restaurant which serves good pizzas. For a more elaborate dining out experience try **La Lanterne** at *V. San Giacomo 10; tel: (0187) 920589.*

MANAROLA

Just along the path from Riomaggiore on the *V. dell'Amore* – Lover's Lane – through olive groves and steep terraces of vineyards – is Manarola. Like the other villages, Manarola fills a crevice along the rocky shore and even if cars were allowed in, few would be able to cope with the gradients or the narrow lanes. This is the place to come if you just want to admire quaintness, while away a few hours over a long lunch, and do nothing much more active than watch the fishermen land their catch or push their boats up the steep street. Hotels include the **Ca'd'Andrean**, *V. Antonio Discovolo; tel: (0187) 920040,* and the **Marina Piccola**, also in the *V. Antonio Discovolo; tel: (0187) 920103.* Both are charming, but because neither has more than 10 rooms it is often difficult securing a booking.

For a dining experience in Manarola, try the *zuppa di datteri* – date-clam soup – at **Aristide**; *tel: (0187) 920000,* one of the many small, unpretentious trattorias to be found in the Cinque Terra.

CORNIGLIA

The village is situated high above the water, perched on the cliff, a small place of tall, thin houses and empty alleyways. The Romans knew it and Corniglia's wine was highly praised and drunk as far south as Pompeii. But there is not much left of the old village, unless you count the 14th-century rose window in the parish church.

Corniglia is almost too small to have any accommodation, unless you count the **Villaggio Marino Europa**; *tel: (0187) 812279,* a row of self-contained bungalows, each sleeping up to six people, on the path to Manarola. The accomodation may be fairly basic, but the views are superb.

VERNAZZA

This is generally reckoned to be the most handsome of the Cinque Terre villages. Down at the water's edge, it comprises a cluster of pastel-coloured houses surrounding a sun-drenched square facing directly on to the water. Above the village is a perfect, round Genoese tower and the parish church is similarly attractive. In this setting, it is perhaps hardly surprising to find good little hotels and restaurants.

Hotels include the Barbara; *tel: (0187) 812201,* the Sorriso; *tel: (0187) 812224,* and the Da Sandro, *V. Roma 62; tel: (0187) 812223.* The Da Sandro's restaurant offers excellent *pasta al gambera* with whole prawns.

Other noteworthy, if more expensive, places to eat in Vernazza include the Vulnetia, *Pza Marconi 29; tel: (0187) 821193,* and Gianni Franzi, *Pza Marconi 5; tel: (0187) 812228,* both of which have wonderful views of the harbour.

MONTEROSSO A MARE

Tourist Office: *V. Fegina; tel: (0187) 817506.* The office, which is open from Easter to Oct, can provide details of the local area and cliff walks.

ACCOMMODATION

As the largest village in the Cinque Terre, Monterosso also has the most hotel rooms and choices of places to eat and drink.

The **Porto Roca**, *Corone 1; tel: (0187) 817502,* has comfortable rooms and excellent views over the sea and down the coast. Other recommended hotels include the **Jolie**, *V.Gioberti 1; tel: (0187) 817539,* and the less expensive **Degli Amici**, *tel: (0187) 8117544,* which occupies a quiet position in the old town and has rooms with private bath, TV and telephone. There are good restaurants here, too, such as the **Miki**, *V. Fegina 104; tel: (0187) 817608,* and **La Cambusa**, *V. Roma 6; tel: (0187) 817546,* both of which serve Ligurian and fish dishes. For those in search of less finesse in the evening, or simply a lunch stop, there are any number of trattorias in Monterosso, offering the usual mixture of fish and pasta dishes. Incidentally, you won't taste better *pesto* – the sauce now available on supermarket shelves around the world – than you will in Monterosso, its place of origin.

333

SIGHTSEEING

Monterosso is, in fact, two villages – one, the new resort and, tucked away behind a promontory, reached through a tunnel, the old quarter of pretty houses and, in the harbour, fishermen leaning on their boats mending nets. And while Monterosso may be the largest, and therefore the most commercialised, of the Cinque Terre villages, it does have one priceless asset – a real beach. Sheltered behind the headland which protects the Cinque Terre from the worst of the weather, this genuine swathe of sand stretches in front of the rail station and is reason enough why you might want to spend more time here than in the other villages. Nevertheless, Monterosso does have a number of interesting buildings: the 14th-century **Loggia del Podestà**, the **church of San Giovanni Battista**, with its distinctive tower, originally built as a watch tower for the Genoese, and the tall, pastel-coloured houses in the old quarter.

From Monterosso, you have to take a winding back road across some of the most rugged terrain in the Cinque Terre to **Lévanto**, an unpretentious resort with one of the best beaches for miles around.

LÉVANTO

Tourist Office: *Pza Cavour 12; tel: (0187) 808125*. The office is open Mon–Sat 0930–1230 and 1530–1930, Sun 0930–1230.

ACCOMMODATION AND FOOD

In many respects it's easier staying here than in the Cinque Terre, since many more rooms are available – a big consideration at the height of the season – and you can reach the five villages in a few minutes from here on the train. The hotels tend to be smallish, family-styled establishments and generally offer better value than those

in the Cinque Terre. The best hotels are probably the **Dora** at *V.Martin della Liberta 27; tel: (0187) 808168*, and the **Nationale**, *V. Jacopo 20; tel: (0187) 808102*, both of which have restaurants serving reasonably priced meals. Budget options include the **Pensione Garden**, *Corso Italia 8; tel: (0187) 808173*, which offers clean, comfortable rooms, but without private bath, on the first floor of a modern apartment block only about 20 m from the beach, and the characterful **Europa** at *V. Dante 41; tel: (0187) 808126*. There are several good restaurants in Lévanto where you can enjoy Ligurian food and fish dishes at prices lower than many other places along the coast. Among the most reliable restaurants are the **Hostaria da Franca** at *V. Privato Olivi 8; tel: (0187) 808647*, and **Araldo**, *V. Jacobi da Lévanto 24; tel: (0187) 807253*, where you eat under a vaulted, painted ceiling. Cheaper options for food include the **Caffé Roma**, which is centrally situated on *Pza Staglieno*, and **Pizzeria Miky**, at *Corso Italia 52*.

SIGHTSEEING

Lévanto is not big on sightseeing, unless you count the huge market held every Wed, which draws people from miles around. It's much more a place for lying on the beach and soaking up the sun. But when you tire of the beach it's well worth the climb up to see the **church of Sant'Andrea**, an impressive black and white striped building, parts of which date back to the 13th century, which feels as old as it is. Lévanto is also a good place in which just to stroll around. Many of the buildings in the town are decorated with clever *trompe-l'œil* paintings, which rather give the impression that someone, somewhere is keeping an eye on what tourists get up to!

RAPALLO–SAN REMO

It would seem that nature has been kind to Liguria, whose majestic coastline curves in an east–west arc from Tuscany to the French border. Liguria, never more than 40 km wide, has a Utopian climate – mild winters and hot summers. The sun shines down on seascapes which throw poets and landscape painters into raptures. But it is the sea which has given the region its character and characters. Every schoolboy knows that Christopher Columbus, the great explorer, was born in Genoa. And it is Genoa, at the centre of the coastal arc, which conveniently separates Liguria's most priceless assets – the tourist beaches of the Riviera di Levante (east) and the Riviera di Ponente (west.)

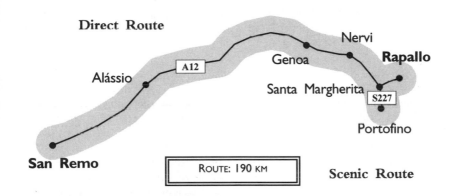

Direct Route

Nervi

Genoa

Rapallo

Alássio

A12

Santa Margherita

S227

Portofino

San Remo

ROUTE: 190 KM

Scenic Route

335

ROUTES

DIRECT ROUTE

➡ The A12 motorway provides a fast and efficient means of traversing the Ligurian coast. From Rapallo, south of Genoa, to the border with France is about 190 km and the journey can be comfortably completed, travelling without a stop, in a little over 2 hrs. The beauty of using the motorway is that it allows easy access, through spur roads, to the coastal resorts, enabling you to choose your stopping points at will.

SCENIC ROUTE

▪▪▪➤ All the way from Rapallo to the border, the coastal road S1 keeps the sea – and the scenery – in its sights. And what scenery! You cannot get lost and the reward is one of the most stunning stretches of coastal road in Italy, with opportunity to explore Camogli and Nervi, San Remo and Bordighera, and of course Genoa, along the way. The drawback is that progress along this road can be slow at any time of the year. The secret is not to be in a hurry. If you get caught in a traffic jam, pull off the road and do what the Italians do in such circumstances – find a cafe and enjoy a long *cappuccino*. Allow at least four days to see this stretch of the coast at leisure.

RAPALLO

Tourist Office: *V. Diaz 9; tel: (0185) 230346*. The office is open throughout the year Mon–Sat 0900–1230 and 1430–1900, Sun 0900–1230 and has helpful staff who will provide information about local attractions and maps of footpaths leading up to Montallegro, in the hills behind the resort.

ACCOMMODATION AND FOOD

Rapallo, virtually unknown at the turn of the century, has been transformed into a chic resort with hotels to match. Find a base, if you can, close to the seafront, whose balmy little harbour is attractive in the evening, when the day visitors have gone. **Grand Hotel Bristol**, *V. Aurelia Orientale 369; tel: (0185) 273313,* has good views of the harbour and a style and elegance which matches the resort. Other hotels here which can be recommended include the **Astoria**, *V. Grasci 4; tel (0185) 273533,* and the **Rosabianca**, *lungomare Vittorio Véneto 42; tel: (0185) 50390.* Pensione Bandoni, *V. Marsala 24; tel: (0185) 50423,* has tastefully furnished rooms in an old *palazzo* and friendly service.

The resort is also well endowed with restaurants, many along the seafront encased in glass, and cheaper eateries. There is distinguished cooking at **Da Monique**, centrally positioned overlooking the harbour at *Lungomare Vittorio Véneto 6; tel: (0185) 50541,* and also at **Hostaria Vecchia Rapallo**, *V. Cairoli 20–24; tel: (0185) 50053.* La Goletta,

V. Magenta 28; tel: (0185) 669261, is a speciality fish restaurant. Other recommended restaurants include **Roccabruna**, *Lungomare Vittorrio Véneto 42; tel: (0185) 261400,* and, for typically Ligurian cuisine, the **Eden**, *V. Diaz 5; tel: (0185) 50553.* For the more budget conscious, there are any number of cheaper trattorias in the alleyways behind the seafront – notably the moderately-priced fish restaurant **Da Mario** at *Pza Garibaldi 23; tel: (0185) 51736,* and, behind the main church, **Al Cuoco d'Oro**, *V. della Vittoria 3; tel: (0185) 50745.*

SIGHTSEEING

The first town at the northern end of the Golfo di Tigullio, Ravenna remained virtually unknown until Ezra Pound, D. H. Lawrence and other prominent writers and artists came to live here. Today the fame lives on, as can be gauged by the myriad of yachts moored in the natural harbour. But after you've seen the **castle**, the single-span **Hannibal Bridge** (the great man is said to have passed through here after crossing the Alps) and wandered around the medieval streets at the back of the town, you might feel inclined to lie on the beach or sip a *cappuccino* at a pavement café, watching the world go by. If you want to be active, there are plenty of good walks in the area, including one to **Montallegro**, 600 m up in the hills behind the town (the less energetic can take the cable car from *V. Castegneto,* L11,000 return), indulge in water sports or go horse-riding. The **Rapallo Riding Club** is at *V. Santa Maria Campo 196; tel: (0185) 50462.*

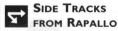

SIDE TRACKS FROM RAPALLO

On the north side of the Gulf of Tigullio, a narrow road snakes its way from Rapallo along the Portofino peninsula to two other prominent holiday destinations on the Ligurian coast – first to **Santa Margherita** (3km) and then to **Portofino** itself. Both make ideal stopovers, although accommodation can be expensive, particularly in Portofino, and difficult to find at the height of the season.

SANTA MARGHERITA

Tourist Office: *V. XXV Aprile 2b; tel: (0185) 287485.*

Santa Margherita is an attractive resort in the Ligurian fashion – palm-laden and laid back, with good hotels across the price range. The grandest of these is the **Imperiale Palace**, *V. Pagana 19; tel: (0185) 288991,* an old world luxury hotel set in an extensive park above the town, which comes complete with rooms furnished with antiques, a private beach and pool – as well as splendid views over the sea. Not far behind is **Grand Hotel Miramare**, *Lungomare Milite Ignoto 30; tel: (0185) 287013,* a turn-of-the-century establishment with light and airy rooms and a lush garden and swimming pool. Other reliable hotels include the **Metropole**, *V. Pagana 2; tel: (0185) 286134,* and the **Lido Palace**, *V. Doria 3; tel: (0185) 285821.* Budget range hotels include the **Nuovo Riviera**, tucked away in a pleasant side street at *V.Belvedere 10; tel: (0185) 287403,* whose room rates include breakfast, and the **Albergo Fasce**, *V. L. Bozzo; tel: (0185) 286435,* which has modern rooms, a roof terrace, and a restaurant which offers excellent value.

A further 5 km along the peninsula road is Portofino, which has become one of the most exclusive resorts in Italy.

PORTOFINO

Tourist Office: *V. Roma 35; tel: (0185) 269024.*

The chances are that the luxury cruisers you will find in the harbour belong to a millionaire businessman or film star, so be prepared here for high prices. Portofino is Italy's answer to St Tropez and the shortage of accomodation in this tiny village – resident population about 600 – has placed further pressure on room rates. **Hotel Splendido**, *Salita Baratta 13; tel: (0185) 269551,* is aptly named, occupying a delightful position high on the hill above the harbour. This one-time 17th-century villa sits in the middle of four acres of lush gardens and a tennis court and large swimmig pool add to the already romantic setting. More modest accommodation can be found at the **Piccolo**, *V. Duca Degli Abruzzi 31; tel: (0185) 269015,* and the **Eden**, *Vico Dritto 20; tel: (0185) 269091.*

RAPALLO TO GENOA

Back on the S1 in Rapallo, the road twists and turns, every so often throwing up the most magnificent sea views, to **Camogli**, an outstandingly pretty village, full of brightly painted houses and steep streets dropping down to the shore. Charles Dickens once described it as 'the saltiest, roughest, most piratical place'. Today it has a sleeping charm and it is here where, on the second Sunday in May, the villagers celebrate the Sagra del Pesce, cooking vast quantities of fish in the streets in giant frying pans for anyone who happens to be passing by.

A few more twists in the S1 – a few more inspiring views from beyond wrought-iron gates or from beneath an umbrella of pine – and you are on the outskirts of Genoa.

NERVI

This is another elegant turn-of-the-century resort, complete with stately villas, parks rich in orange and other exotic trees, and an impressive *passeggiata*, which winds around the headland and through gardens underneath the cliff. The quiet gentility of a former age lives on here.

Nervi's relaxed lifestyle is reflected in hotels such as the **Astor**, set in an attractive garden at *Viale delle Palme 16; tel: (010) 372 8325*. The hotel also has one of Nervi's best restaurants. A little more unusual is the **Villa Pagoda**, *V. Capolungo 15; tel: (010) 3726161*. Built at the turn of the century when things oriental were fashionable, the hotel is shaped like a pagoda, although inside the rooms have modern decoration and furnishings.

From Nervi, it is a slow 10km along the SS1 to Genoa. If possible, avoid travelling in the morning and evening rush hours, when the traffic on the road is particularly heavy.

GENOA (GENOVA)

Tourist Office: there are four principal tourist offices in Genoa: *Palazzina Santa Maria, Porto Antico; tel: (010) 24871; V. Roma 11; tel: (010) 576791; Stazione Pza Principe, Pza Acquaverde; tel: (010) 246 2633;* and *Stazione Marittima, Terminal Crociere, Ponte dei Mille; tel: (010) 2463686.* All have a good supply of pamphlets and maps of the city and the surrounding area.

ACCOMMODATION AND FOOD

Genoa offers a wide range of accommodation, but room rates here tend to be slightly higher than most other Italian cities, perhaps because of the demand for rooms in the city by businessmen. At the top end of the scale, hotels such as the **Starhotel President**, *Corte Lambruschini 4; tel: (010) 5727,* and the **Jolly Hotel Plaza**, *V. Martin Piaggio 11; tel: (010) 8393641,* cater for just that market. The **Bristol**, *V. XX Settembre 35; tel: (010) 592541,* is a *grande dame* of hotels. Built in the last century, it offers large rooms, the style of the hotel is reflected in its service which is both discreet and courteous. **Novotel Genova Ovest**, *V. Cantore 8c; tel: (010) 64841,* also has comfortable rooms, a good restaurant and outdoor pool. **Villa Bonera** is a delightful hotel in a 500-year-old building at *V. Sarfatti 8; tel: (010) 372 6164.* Two other characterful hotels offering good value are the **Agnello d'Oro**, in a central position in Genoa's old quarter at *Vico delle Monachette 6; tel: (010) 262084,* and the **Rio**, near the Ponte Calvi in the old port district at *V. al Ponte Calvi 5; tel: (010) 290551.*

Ligurian cuisine features prominently on Genoese restaurant menus, not least at arguably the city's most famous restaurant, the **Gran Grotto**, *Vle Brigate Bisagno 69; tel: (010) 564344.* This small, elegant restaurant near the Stazione Brignole offers specilities such as *filetti di triglia al rosmarino* (fillet of mullet with rosemary) and excellent deserts. The decor at **Zefferino**, *V. XX Settembre 20; tel: (010) 591990,* is a mixture of styles, but the food, particularly dishes like *passutelli* – ravioli stuffed with ricotta cheese and fruit – is reliable. Other fine dining restaurants include, in the eastern suburb of Baccadasse, **Vittorio al Mare**, *Belvedere Edoardo Firpo 1; tel: (010) 3760141; and **Edilio**, at *Corso De Stefanis 104; tel: (010) 811260.* In addition there are scores of trattorias and cafés offering inexpensive fare. Among the best are **Trattoria Carletto**, an old town restaurant which does excellent seafood, at *Vico del Tempo Bueno 5,* off *V. della Maddalena* in the old town, and **Da Genio**, a long-established restaurant at the top of a steep

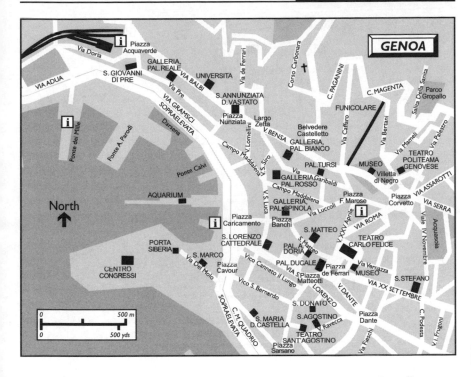

GENOA

North ↑

0   500 m
0   500 yds

hill at *Salita San Leonardo 61; tel: (010) 546463.*

SIGHTSEEING

At first sight Genoa looks a little like Liverpool beside the Mediterranean – a vast sprawling port which, with its multitude of façades with peeling paintwork, seems to have seen better days. But first impressions are deceptive. There is here a wealth of fine buildings, notably churches like the **Cathedrale di San Lorenzo**, whose elaborate inlaid and carved walls have been scrubbed recently. South of *V. San Lorenzo*, on which the cathedral stands, the twin towers of the Porto Soprana mark the entrance to the **old town**. Columbus's father was believed to be the gatekeeper here and nearby, in the *Pza Dante*, stands the ruined, creeper-clad family home. Between here and the

waterfront is an area of small squares, monasteries and convents which are still in the process of being rebuilt after damage caused in World War II. The church of **Santa Maria di Castello**, which dates back to the 12th century, served as a hostel for the Crusaders on their way to the Holy Land and an adjacent museum has paintings by Lodovico Brea, including the richly coloured *Coronation of Our Lady*.

Genoa is a fine museum city, too. Two palaces on *V. Garibaldi*, one of Europe's finest streets, have been turned into art galleries. In the **Palazzo Bianco**, at *V. Garibaldi 10; tel: (010) 291803*, there is an impressive art collection of works by Dutch and Flemish painters. The museum is open Tues–Sat 0900–1900, Sun 0900 –1200. At no. 18, the **Palazzo Rosso**; *tel: (010) 282641*, has paintings by Caravaggio, Titian, Rubens and Van

LIGURIAN RIVIERA

Dyke and is open Tues–Sun 0900–1230. A third museum, the **Palazzo Balbi Durazzo**, *V. Balbi 10; tel: (010) 2470640,* which was once a royal palace, houses a fine collection of paintings, as well as tapestries, sculptures and oriental ceramics. This museum is open daily 0900–1300.

Also worth exploring is the **Porto Antico** – old port – area of the city, which has been revitalised, a place where people can go for a stroll, have a meal, go for a ride on the Grande Bigo, a circular elevator which takes you 60 m above the ground for a bird's-eye view of the harbour, or visit the aquarium (open Tues, Wed, Fri 0930–1900, Thurs, Sat, Sun 0930–2030, closed Mon) which contains sea ceatures from all over the world.

To continue your journey, get on to the overhead highway, known as the *Corsos Aurelio Saffi e Maurizio Quadrio,* which whisks you past the new harbour and the airport to the western suburb of Voltri. From here it is a straight run along the coast. Immediately to the west of Genoa, the resorts are unexciting; they have good beaches and are inexpensive, but in the main they are fairly characterless. It would be far better to journey on along the SS1 to towns such as Alássio and San Remo, which have a great deal to offer.

ALÁSSIO

Tourist Office: *V. Gibb 26; tel: (0182) 640346,* open Mon–Sat 0900–1230, 1500–1830, Sun 0900–1230.

ACCOMMODATION AND FOOD

There are more than 100 hotels and most are geared to the holiday market. Many hotels offer special rates, usually on half board, for three nights or more, making

Christopher Columbus (1451-1506)

Perhaps Genoa's most famous citizen, Christopher Columbus, is celebrated all over the city in statues and paintings – not to mention in the names of buildings and of the local airport – this despite the fact that nobody is quite sure whether he was born in Genoa at all. In fact, when the quincentenary of his first voyage to the Americas was celebrated in 1992, historians found that the more they researched the less than they could actually pin down about this famous navigator.

It seems that he went to sea as a teenager, and it is known that he was regularly sailing to Madeira and the Canary Islands in the 1470s, probably working as a buyer for a group of Lisbon-based sugar merchants. In 1478, while visiting Madeira, he sought out the company of his compatriot Bartolomeu Perestrelo, the Genoa-born governor of the island of Porto Santo. Not long after, he married Dona Filipa Moniz, Perestrelo's daughter. During his stay on Porto Santo, Columbus became convinced by the seeds and vegetation washed up on the island's shores that there must be land beyond the western horizon. Twelve years later he persuaded the Castilian monarchs, Ferdinand and Isabelle, to fund the voyage that proved his hunch to be correct. Even so, few believed his story when he returned to Europe. King Ferdinand of Spain hired another navigator, the Florentine, Amerigo Vespucci, to retrace Columbus' route. Thus it was that the new world got to be called Amerigo, later corrupted to America, rather than Columbo.

this an attractive, and inexpensive, place to make a base for exploring the Riviera del Ponente. The accommodation ranges downwards from **Grand Hotel Diana**, an extremely comfortable hotel with an attractive garden and terrace and indoor swimming pool, *V. Garibaldi 110; tel: (0182) 642701*. The **Lamberti**, standing back slightly from the beach in a good position close to the town centre, *V. Gramsci 57; tel: (0182) 642747,* is a smallish (25 rooms) hotel with a good restaurant. Another charming hotel is the **Eden**, which has a beachfront location in a quiet part of town at *Passeggiata Cadorna 20; tel: (0182) 640281*. For a dining experience, try **Palma**, a small, elegant restaurant at *V. Cavour 5; tel: (0182) 640314*. The restaurant specialises in Ligurian seafood dishes.

SIGHTSEEING

Like many towns along the coast, Alássio

grew out of a small fishing village, with stone houses gathered in narrow streets. The 16th-century church of **Sant'Ambrogio** is topped by a Romanesque bell tower, but sightseeing opportunities are few. Go for the 4 km-long beach, summer water-skiing and windsurfing, and the **Isola Gallinara** nature reserve, where there are remains of a Benedictine monastery.

Back on the SS1, the road hugs the coast virtually all the way to the French border. Where it climbs a headland, progress becomes slow. Along the way are other smallish resorts like **Diano Marina**, and **Imperia**, which Mussolini created as a provincial capital before World War II by joining the towns of Oneglia and Porto Maurizio, although there is little to hold the interest here.

Press on to **San Remo**, **Bordighera** and **Ventimiglia**, with their blend of French and Italian culture.

SAN REMO

Tourist Office: *Corso Nuvoloni 1, San Remo; tel: (0184) 571571;* **Bordighera***; V. Roberto 1; tel: (0184) 262322;* **Ventimiglia***: V.Cavour 59; tel: (0184) 351183.*

ACCOMMODATION

San Remo, a major resort, has lost some of its appeal since the heady days earlier this century when Europe's finest paraded along the *Corso Imperiatrice* – but it still has some fine hotels. The **Royal***, Corso Imperatrice 80; tel: (0184) 270511,* has style and elegance and an attractive garden with outdoor pool.

More modest rooms can be found at hotels like the **Morandi***, Corso Matuzia 51; tel: (0184) 667641,* and the **Villa Maria***, Corso Nuvoloni 30; tel: (0184) 531422.* In nearby Bordighera, accommodation is on a smaller scale, with hotels like the **Villa Elisa***, V. Romana 70; tel: (0184) 61313,* and the **Riviera**, right on the sea at *V. Trento 12; tel: (0184) 261323,* popular places to stay. Just 11 km from the border, Ventimiglia is a busy town but it has one or two charming small hotels like the **Seagull***, V. Marconi 24; tel: (0184) 351726* and, just before the border, the **Baia Beniamin***, Grimaldi Inferiore, Corso Europa 63; tel: (0184) 38002,* which also has an outstanding restaurant.

San Remo used to be a fixture on the European tour circuit of the rich and famous in the 19th century, being particularly popular with members of the Russian imperial family. The onion-shaped domes of the **Russian Orthodox Church** in *Pza Nuvoloni*, dating from 1906, are just one legacy of that period.

One resident of San Remo who left an explosive reputation behind him was Alfred Nobel, the Swedish inventor of dynamite who established the series of

international prizes named after him. The **Nobel Villa** is at *C. Cavalotti 112,* and is open to the public for visits.

Early risers can visit the incredible **Flower Market** that takes place every morning from June to October between 0600 and 0800 in *C. Garibaldi.*

Gardens

Liguria's gentle climate enables flowers of all varieties to thrive here virtually year round, even in February. Small wonder, then, that the province's western arm, the Riviera di Ponente, is also known as the Riviera of Flowers. All along the coast are fields of brightly coloured blooms and almost every town shows off its horticultural skills in formal gardens. None is more impressive than the *Giardino Hanbury* – the Hanbury Gardens, near Ventimiglia, created by Sir Thomas Hanbury, a wealthy tea merchant.

Taking advantage of Liguria's benign climate, Sir Thomas and his brother Daniel, a botanist, planted out more than 5000 species of plants from all over the world in 1867. Five continents are represented and there are many exotic species from Africa and Asia, carefully nurtured and developed to grow alongside the many Mediterranean varieties. Particularly impressive are the many palms and succulents (members of the cacti family). Over the years, many of the original species have been lost, but the gardens still rank as some of the most important in Italy. Pergolas run riot, terraces tumble down the cliff towards the sea and the views are tremendous.

Hanbury Gardens is situated at *Corso Monte Carlo 43*, near the village of Mortola Inferiore, which is about 6 km from Ventimiglia, open Thurs–Tues in winter, daily in summer; *tel: (0184) 229507.*

343

DRIVING DISTANCES AND TIMES

A selection of longer distances between major cities and tourist centres, other than those covered by recommended routes in this book, is given below; journeys follow the fastest roads, i.e. autostrada, wherever possible. Driving times are meant as an average indication only, allowing for the nature of the roads but not for traffic conditions, which can be very variable. They do not include allowance for stops or breaks en route.

Venice to . . .	km	Hours
Padua	38	½
Cortina	161	2¾
Bolzano	214	4
Verona	120	2
Brescia (Lake Garda)	180	3

Milan to . . .	km	Hours
Venice	273	4¾
Bolzano	295	5
Padua	235	4
Brescia (Lake Garda)	97	1½
Como	49	¾
Varese (Lake Maggiore)	57	1
Aosta	181	3

Turin to . . .	km	Hours
Venice	402	6
Bolzano	410	6
Padua	366	5½
Verona	292	5
Brescia (Lake Garda)	228	4
Como	165	3
Varese (Lake Maggiore)	145	2½

Genoa	km	Hours
Turin	170	3
Mantua	239	4
Piacenza	144	2½
Ravenna	371	6
Rome	510	6
Pisa	156	2
Lucca	156	2½
La Spezia	102	1½

Bologna	km	Hours
Piacenza	150	3
Ravenna	76	1¼
Sansepolcro	178	3
Perugia	262	4½
Assisi	292	4½
Rome	383	6
Arezzo	186	3
Florence	106	1¾
Pisa	181	3
Lucca	159	2½

Florence	km	Hours
Perugia	153	2½
Assisi	172	3
Spoleto	202	3½
Terni	227	3
Siena	68	1
Orvieto	166	2½
Rome	278	3
Orbetello	188	3
Pisa	91	1½
La Spezia	146	2¼

Rome	km	Hours
Perugia	192	3
Assisi	164	2½
Spoleto	126	2
Terni	104	1¾
Siena	231	3½
Arezzo	219	3½
Florence	278	4
Pisa	342	5
La Spezia	427	5½

344

HOTEL CODES
AND CENTRAL BOOKING NUMBERS

The following abbreviations have been used throughout the book to show which chains are represented in a particular town. Most chains have a centralised worldwide-reservations system in every country where they have hotels (occasionally these do not cover hotels within the country itself). Most telephone calls are either completely free (usually incorporating *800*) or charged at the rate for a local call (e.g. 0345 in the UK). (Aus=Australia, Can=Canada, Ire=Ireland, NZ=New Zealand, SA =South Africa, UK=United Kingdom, USA=United States of America.)

Accor
This is a group name that encompasses Ibis, Mercure, Novotel and Sofitel, with central reservation nos that cover them all
Aus *(1 800) 642 244*
Can *(1 800) 221 45 42*
UK *(0171) 724 1000*
USA *(1 800) MERCURE*

BW Best Western
Aus *(1 800) 222 422*
Can *(800) 528 1234*
Ire *(1 800) 709 101*
NZ *(0800) 800 567*
SA *(0800) 120 886*
UK *(0800) 393130*
USA *(800) 528 1234*

Ch Choice
Aus *(008) 090 600*
Ire *(1 800) 500 600*
NZ *(0800) 86 86 88*
UK *(0800) 444444*
USA/CAN:
(800) 228 5150 (Comfort)
(800) 228 5151 (Quality)
(800) CLARION (Clarion)
(800) 228 3323 (hearing impaired, TTY phone)
USA *(800) 888 4747*

Ex Excelsior
UK *(0345) 40 40 40*

FE Forte
(Also covers Exclusive and Méridien)
Aus *(800) 622 240*
Can *(800) 225 5843*
Ire *(800) 409040*
NZ *(800) 454040*
SA *(011) 442 9201*
UK *(0345) 404040*
USA *(800) 225 5843*

Fm Forum
See Inter-Continental *(IC)*

GT Golden Tulip
Netherlands *(06) 02 27711*
Aus *(800) 221 176*
Can/USA *(800) 344 1212*
Ire *(01) 872 3300*
NZ *(0800) 656 666*
SA *(021) 419 2965*
UK *(0800) 951 000*

Hd Holiday Inn
Aus *(800) 221 066*
Can *(800) 465 4329*
Ire *(1 800) 553 155*
NZ *(0800) 442 222*
SA *(0800) 11 7711*
UK *(0800) 897121*
USA *(800) 465 4329*

HI Hostelling International
UK *(0171) 248 6547*

Hn Hilton
Aus *(1 800) 222 255*
Can *(800) 445 8667*
NZ *(0800) 448 002*
SA *(011) 880 3108*
UK *(0345) 581595*
USA *(800) 445 8667*

Ib Ibis
See Accor

IC Inter-Continental
(Also covers Forum)
Aus *(008) 221 335*
Can/USA *(800) 327 0200*
NZ *(0800) 654 343*
SA *(011) 331 7422*
UK *(0345) 581237*
USA *(800) 426 3135*

Jolly Jolly Hotels
01923 896272

Ma Marriott
Aus *(1 800) 251 259*
Can *(800) 228 9290*
NZ *(0800) 441 035*
UK *(0800) 221222*
USA *(800) 228 9290*

Nv Novotel
Can *(800) NOVOTEL*
UK *(0181) 748 3433*
USA *(800) NOVOTEL*
(See also Accor)

Pu Pullman Hotels
see Accor

RC Relais & Chateaux
Aus *(02) 9957 4511*
UK *(0171) 287 0987*
USA *(212) 856 0115*

Rd Radisson
Aus *(1 800) 333 333*
Can *(800) 333 3333*
Ire *(1 800) 557 474*
NZ *(0800) 443 333*
UK *(0800) 191991*
USA *(800) 333 3333*

Rm Ramada
Aus *(1 800) 222 431*
Can *(800) 854 7854*
Ire *(1 800) 252 627*
NZ *(0800) 441 111*
UK *(0800) 181 737*
USA *(800) 854 7854*

Rn Renaissance
As Ramada, except:
Can/USA *(1 800) HOTELS 1*

Sh Sheraton
Aus *(800) 07 3535*
Ire *(1 800) 535 353*
NZ *(0800) 443 535*
UK *(0800) 353535*
USA/Can *(800) 325 3535*
or *(800) 325 1717* (hearing impaired)

St Starhotels
UK *(0990) 300 200*
US *(800) 44 UTELL*

345

CONVERSION TABLES

DISTANCES (approx. conversions)
I kilometre (km) = 1000 metres (m)   I metre = 100 centimetres (cm)

Metric	Imperial/US	Metric	Imperial/US		Metric	Imperial/US
I cm	3/8 in	9 m	(10 yd)	29 ft	0.75	½ mile
I m 0 cm	3 ft 3 in	10 m	(11 yd)	33 ft	I km	5/8 mile
2 m 0 cm	6 ft 6 in	20 m	(22 yd)	66 ft	5 km	3 miles
3 m 0 cm		50 m	(54 yd)	164 ft	10 km	6 miles
4 m 0 cm	13 ft 0 in	100 m	(110 yd)	330 ft	20 km	12½ miles
5 m 0 cm	16 ft 6 in	200 m	(220 yd)	660 ft	30 km	18½ miles
6 m 0 cm	19 ft 6 in	250 m	(275 yd)	820 ft	50 km	31 miles
7 m 0 cm	23 ft 0 in	300 m	(330 yd)	984 ft	75 km	46 miles
8 m 0 cm	26 ft 0 in	500 m	(550 yd)	1640 ft	100 km	62 miles

24-HOUR CLOCK
(examples)

0000 = Midnight	1200 = Noon	1800 = 6.00 p.m.
0600 = 6.00 a.m.	1300 = 1.00 p.m.	2000 = 8.00 p.m.
0715 = 7.15 a.m.	1415 = 2.15 p.m.	2110 = 9.10 p.m.
0930 = 9.30 a.m.	1645 = 4.45 p.m.	2345 = 11.45 p.m.

TEMPERATURE
Conversion Formula: $°C × 9 ÷ 5 + 32 = °F$

°C	°F	°C	°F	°C	°F	°C	°F
-20	-4	-5	23	10	50	25	77
-15	5	0	32	15	59	30	86
-10	14	5	41	20	68	35	95

WEIGHT
I kg = 1000 g   100 g = 3½ oz

Kg	Pounds	Kg	Pounds	Kg	Pounds
1	2¼	5	11	25	55
2	4½	10	22	50	110
3	6½	15	33	75	165
4	9	20	45	100	220

FLUID MEASURES
I litre(l) = 0.88 Imperial quarts = 1.06 US quarts

Litres	Imp.gal.	US gal.	Litres	Imp.gal.	US gal.
5	1.1	1.3	30	6.6	7.8
10	2.2	2.6	35	7.7	9.1
15	3.3	3.9	40	8.8	10.4
20	4.4	5.2	45	9.9	11.7

MEN'S CLOTHES

UK	Europe	US
36	46	36
38	48	38
40	50	40
42	52	42
44	54	44
46	56	46

MENS' SHOES

UK	Europe	US
6	40	7
7	41	8
8	42	9
9	43	10
10	44	11
11	45	12

LADIES' CLOTHES

UK	France	Italy	Rest of Europe	US
10	36	38	34	8
12	38	40	36	10
14	40	42	38	12
16	42	44	40	14
18	44	46	42	16
20	46	48	44	18

MEN'S SHIRTS

UK	Europe	US
14	36	14
15	38	15
15½	39	15½
16	41	16
16½	42	16½
17	43	17

LADIES' SHOES

UK	Europe	US
3	36	4½
4	37	5½
5	38	6½
6	39	7½
7	40	8½
8	41	9½

AREAS
I hectare = 2.471 acres

I hectare = 10,000 sq metres

I acre = 0.4 hectares

INDEX

References are to page numbers. **Bold** numbers refer to the grid squares on the planning maps at the end of the book.

349

READER SURVEY

If you enjoyed using this book, or even if you didn't, please help us improve future editions by taking part in our reader survey. Every returned form will be acknowledged, and to show our appreciation we will give you £1 off your next purchase of a Thomas Cook guidebook. Just take a few minutes to complete and return this form to us.

When did you buy this book?

Where did you buy it? (Please give town/city and if possible name of retailer)

When did you/do you intend to travel around Italy?

For how long (approx.)?
How many people in your party?

Which towns, cities, regions and other locations did you/do you intend mainly to visit?

351

Did you/will you:
☐ Make all your travel arrangements independently?
☐ Travel on a fly-drive package?
Please give brief details:

Did you/do you intend to use this book:
☐ For planning your trip?
☐ During the trip itself?
☐ Both?

Did you/do you intend also to purchase any of the following travel publications for your trip?
Thomas Cook Travellers: *Rome/Venice/Florence and Tuscany*
A road map/Atlas (please specify)
Other guidebooks (please specify)

Have you used any other Thomas Cook guidebooks in the past? If so, which?

Please rate the following features of On the Road around Northern Italy for their value to you (Circle VU for 'very useful', U for 'useful', NU for 'little or no use'):

The 'Travel Essentials' section on pages 15–27	VU	U	NU
The 'Driving in Italy' section on pages 28–33	VU	U	NU
The 'Touring Itineraries' on pages 40–42	VU	U	NU
The recommended driving routes throughout the book	VU	U	NU
Information on towns and cities, etc	VU	U	NU
The maps of towns, cities, etc	VU	U	NU
The colour planning map	VU	U	NU

Please use this space to tell us about any features that in your opinion could be changed, improved, or added in future editions of the book, or any other comments you would like to make concerning the book:

352

Your age category: ☐ 21-30   ☐ 31-40   ☐ 41–50   ☐ over 50

Your name: Mr/Mrs/Miss/Ms
(First name or initials)
(Last name)

Your full address: (Please include postal or zip code)

Your daytime telephone number: _____

Please detach this page and send it to: The Project Editor, On the Road around Northern Italy, Thomas Cook Publishing, PO Box 227, Peterborough PE3 6PU, United Kingdom.

We will be pleased to send you details of how to claim your discount upon receipt of this questionnaire.

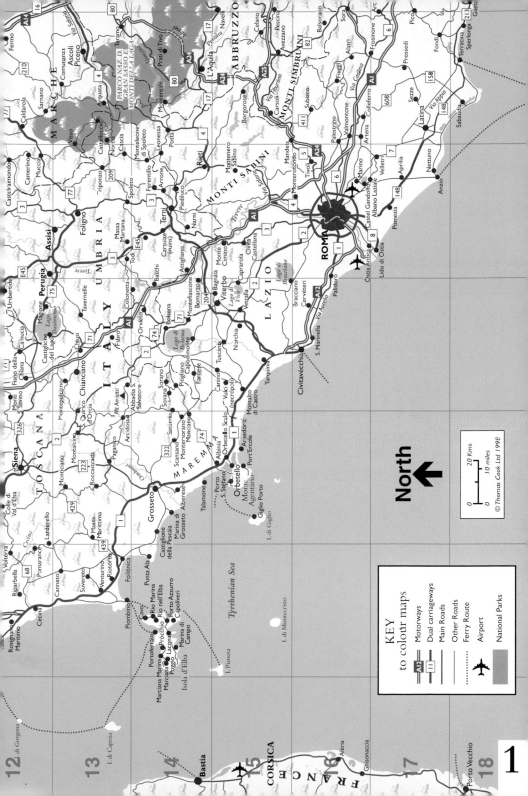